CIGARETTE CA

1999 Catalogue of
other Trade

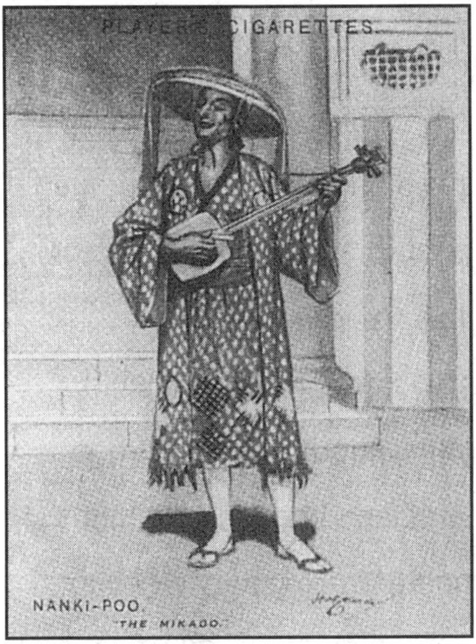

"My catalogue is long, through every passion ranging"
W. S. Gilbert (The Mikado)

Compiled and published by

MURRAY CARDS (INTERNATIONAL) LIMITED
51 Watford Way, Hendon Central, London NW4 3JH
Tel: (0181) 202-5688
Fax: (0181) 203-7878
E-mail: murraycards@ukbusiness.com
Web site: http://www.murraycards.com/
For International Calls dial (011) 44181 202 5688

Opening hours — 9am-5pm, Monday-Friday

Watford Way is the A41 road into London, and is one mile from the end of the M1 Motorway. It can be reached via Hendon Central Underground Station (Northern Line), which is 100 yards away, and is also served by a number of bus routes and Green Line.

ISBN 0-946942-20-X

HEAD OFFICE AND MAIN RETAIL SHOWROOM

When in London, why not pay us a visit?

* Fast, courteous service.
* Odds lists filled while you wait.
* Sample albums of cards arranged thematically.
* New Issues and additions to stock.
* Monthly Special Offers.
* Unlisted lines always available.
* Albums without postal charges.
* Second hand books and albums.
* Complete framing service.
* Packets, playing cards and other ephemera.
* Spot cash for purchases.

Murray Cards (International) Limited

51 Watford Way, Hendon Central, London NW4 3JH

Opening hours 9.00 a.m. to 5.00 p.m., Monday-Friday

Watford Way is the A41 road into London, and is one mile from the end of the M1 Motorway. It is 100 yards from Hendon Central Underground Station (Northern Line), and is also served by a number of bus routes and Green Line. Private parking bay available for customers.

Introduction

Since last year, when we announced our own web site, the use of electronic communication has increased dramatically. It is already the norm in the U.S.A., but this year more and more people in Great Britain are investing in Personal Computers and modems, so that they can "surf the net". Our own web site is updated regularly, at least monthly, and contains details of new issues and current news, as well as highlights from the next auction. With many excellent coloured illustrations it is well worth a visit, at "http://www.murraycards.com/"

This year has as usual seen a number of new issues, many of which are on the commercial front. The American trading cards continue to find their way to Britain, and there are now several issuers, such as Merlin and Futera, which are copying the American style but with perhaps more domestic subjects, particularly football. There also continues to be a seemingly never-ending supply of new sets from other commercial enterprises, notable Golden Era. The customary annual new set has been launched with Castella Cigars. And at last Brooke Bond has moved away from its chimpanzee friends with the issue of a set of footballers, in a much larger size than its traditional issues. The World Cup fever resulted in yet another soccer series, by BP Petrol, and the Nostalgia range of reprints of Taddy Prominent Footballers has seen the arrival of six further complete teams. Perhaps most important of all, the Liebig Company has recommenced the issue of cards in Italy, with the launch last May of three exciting new sets of cards.

Soccer has certainly become the number one subject for thematic collectors. With the large amounts of money being spent on season tickets and replica kit, the addition of a few sets of cards on one's home team is comparatively modest in cost – and will not become obsolete at the end of the season! There is also a more noticeable increase in the proportion of thematic collectors, with sport, transport, poultry and scouts being very popular.

After a fairly long period of holding our fair and auction at the Royal National Hotel, we have now decided that the time has come to move on. We are very pleased to say however that we have managed to secure an excellent new location at the University of London Students Union building in Malet Street, which is only 200 yards from the previous site. When in London, do try and pay it a visit, on the third Sunday of EVERY month. You may be surprised at the selection of cards available there.

Our new Catalogue once more presents our assessments of the current values of cigarette, trade and trading cards, each one based on an individual evaluation. Some prices have increased since last year, reflecting our changing stocks and the demand, but there are still very many inexpensive sets throughout the book, and quite a few real bargains to be found.

Finally, may we point out that we have also published a new edition of our popular Liebig catalogue, which includes the new sets, and lists every set in English, with realistic values for each.

HOW TO USE THE CATALOGUE

The Catalogue is in three parts.

Part I contains all known issues by British-based tobacco companies. Thus all cards by the firm W. D. & H. O. Wills, which was located in Bristol, are shown, even though they may have been issued in a Wills brand abroad. Issues from the Channel Islands and the Republic of Ireland are included in this part. Excluded are most post cards and larger non-insert items.

Part II contains tobacco issues by most of the major manufacturers in the English-speaking world, and a selection of other series, including all the sets readily available to collectors.

Part III comprises series issued with commodities other than tobacco (commonly known as "trade cards"). Although mainly British issues, there are a number of overseas sets included. Each issuer's name is followed by the commodity with which the cards were issued; where the set was not given away free, but produced in order to be sold, the issuer is described as "commercial".

Parts I and III commence with an index of brand names, and the issuer's name under which that item appears. Series are listed in alphabetical order of series title under the issuing firm, regardless of country of origin. Where the issuer was not normally located in the United Kingdom the country of origin is given. In the case of certain larger issuers series have been listed in logical groups so that they may be more readily found.

For each set the following information is given:–

(1) **Size information.** Cards are assumed to be standard size unless otherwise stated. Sizes used generally correspond to the page sizes used for our plastic albums (see separate notice) i.e. when a letter is used it may be assumed that at least one dimension is greater than the size shown by the previous letter. Abbreviations used are:–

K	smaller than standard.	51 x 41 mm.
M	medium size.	80 x 52 mm.
L	large size.	80 x 71 mm.
T	Typhoo/Doncella size.	106 x 52 mm.
X	extra large size.	80 x 113 mm.
P	postcard size.	165 x 110 mm.
G	cabinet size.	228 x 165 mm.
E	too large for albums.	
D	dual (more than one) size.	
S	stereoscopic series.	
F	photographic production.	

(2) **Number of cards in set.** When there are several rare numbers in a set the quantity normally available is shown. Thus 35/37 means that the series consists of 37 cards, but that only 35 are usually obtainable.

(3) **Series title.** Where the set has no name, then the title accepted by common usage is given. Sect. = sectional series. Silk = silk, satin or canvas. P/C = playing card. When a dimension is shown this may be compared on the ruler printed on page 304.

(4) **Year of issue.** This is approximate only, and should in no way be considered to be binding. Particularly in the case of overseas and pre-1900 issues the date should be treated as merely an indication of the era in which the set was produced.

(5) **Price of odd cards.** Because of high labour costs and overheads it is not an economic proposition to offer odd cards from many post-1945 series. Where

shown the price is that of normal cards in the set. End numbers (e.g. numbers 1 and 50 from a set of 50 cards) are DOUBLE the price shown. Known scarce subjects from a series, and also thematic subjects from general series (e.g. cricketers from general interest series) would be more expensive than the price shown here.

Where no cards from a series were actually in stock at the time of compilation the price is shown in *italics.* It must be borne in mind that many of these prices are only approximate, since the discovery of just a few cards from a scarcer series could greatly affect the price.

(6) **Price of complete sets.** Prices shown are for sets in clean, undamaged condition. Where mint sets are required (and available) there will be a premium of 50% extra for sets 1920-1940, and 100% for pre 1920 sets. Where no set price is quoted we had no complete sets in stock at the time of compilation; however, when available these will be sold at prices based on the odds figure. *With each pre 1940 set the appropriate Nostalgia album pages are presented FREE!*

UNLISTED SERIES

Because our stocks are constantly changing we always have in stock a large number of series which are unlisted. In particular we can presently offer an excellent selection of German sets, loose or in their special albums and also a good choice of Australian trade issues. If you require a specific item please send us a stamped addressed envelope for an immediate quotation.

ALIKE SERIES

There are many instances where affiliated companies, or indeed completely independent groups issued identical series, where the pictures are the same, and only the issuer's name is altered. Examples are Fish & Bait issued by Churchman, I.T.C. (Canada) and Wills; British Cavalry Uniforms of the Nineteenth Century issued by Badshah, Browne, Empson, Rington and Wilcocks & Wilcocks; or even Interesting Animals by Hignett or Church & Dwight. If wishing to avoid duplication of pictures, please state when ordering which series you already **have.**

SNAP-IT CARD HOLDERS

We are the appointed U.K. Distributors for this useful American product. Individual cards are held in perfect safety between two sheets of perspex, which snap together securely. Available in two sizes — to hold standard A size cards and American trading card size — these holders enable scarcer cards to be transported in your pocket with no fear of damage occurring. Simple stands are also available, enabling cards to be displayed on your desk or mantlepiece.

Snap-it holders cost just 90p each, with the stands available for 9p each. In stock now at both our shops, at Fairs and from approved dealers. When ordering <u>stands</u> by post the minimum order is 10.

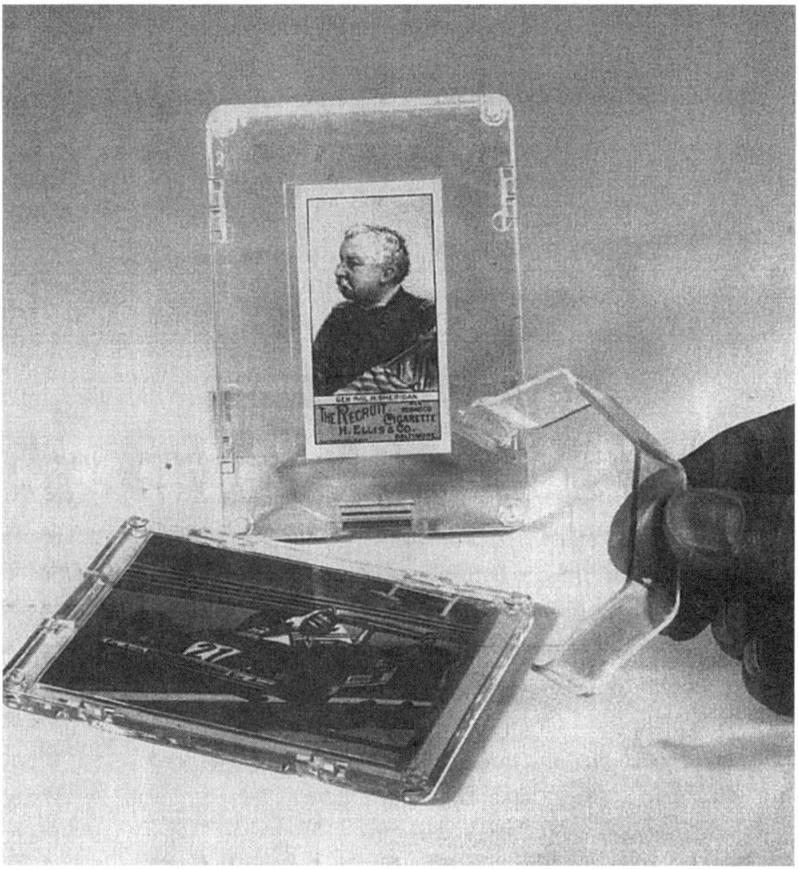

CENTRAL LONDON BRANCH

For the convenience of our customers why not visit our branch in Central London? Less than 100 yards from Trafalgar Square, it is in an ideal location for visitors to London. It is three minutes walk from Charing Cross Main Line Station, and just around the corner from Charing Cross and Leicester Square underground stations (Bakerloo, Jubilee, Northern and Victoria Lines).

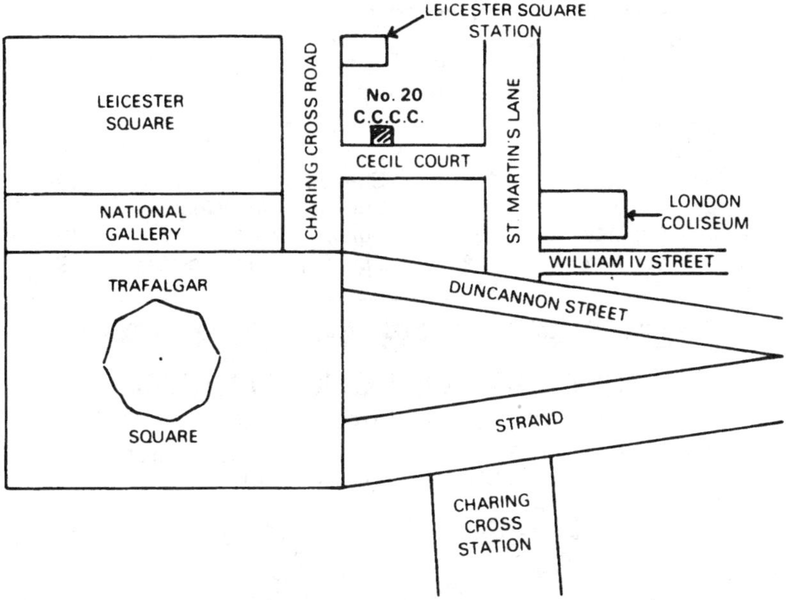

Cecil Court Collectors Centre is open from 10.30 a.m. to 5.30 p.m. Monday to Saturday. As well as cigarette cards you may purchase banknotes, coins, share certificates, telephone cards and stamps all under one roof.

Since we cannot split our stocks of the scarcer and more elusive cards the items available at Cecil Court will be restricted to those shown below. We can however arrange for any specific items not covered by this list to be made available for collection at the Collectors Centre provided that we have at least 72 hours warning. All correspondence and telephone calls should still be made to our Head Office at 51 Watford Way, Hendon Central (0181 202-5688).

Available at Cecil Court Collectors Centre

* A large selection of complete sets only.
* Liebig sets, albums and frames.
* Framed sets and framing kits.
* Nostalgia and Hendon albums without postal charges.
* Catalogues, books and other accessories.
* New issues hot off the press, including American Trading cards.

CECIL COURT COLLECTORS CENTRE
20 Cecil Court, Charing Cross Road, London WC2

CIGARETTE CARD FAIRS & AUCTIONS

* Regular monthly meetings — the third Sunday of every month (except March 1999**)
* Many leading dealers' tables, all heavily laden with cards
* The world's leading auctions — 465 lots each month
* Easy access, ample street parking
* Licensed bar, snacks, meals
* Admission FREE

1999 DATES

Sunday, 17th January	1999	Sunday, 18th July	1999
Sunday, 21st February	1999	Sunday, 15th August	1999
Sunday, 28th March**	1999	Sunday, 19th September	1999
Sunday, 18th April	1999	Sunday, 17th October	1999
Sunday, 16th May	1999	Sunday, 21st November	1999
Sunday, 20th June	1999	Sunday, 19th December	1999

NEW VENUE FOR 1999

UNIVERSITY OF LONDON UNION

Malet Street, London WC1

Fair open 10.30 a.m. to 4.30 p.m. Auction at 2.00 p.m.

All enquiries to: Murray Cards (International) Ltd.

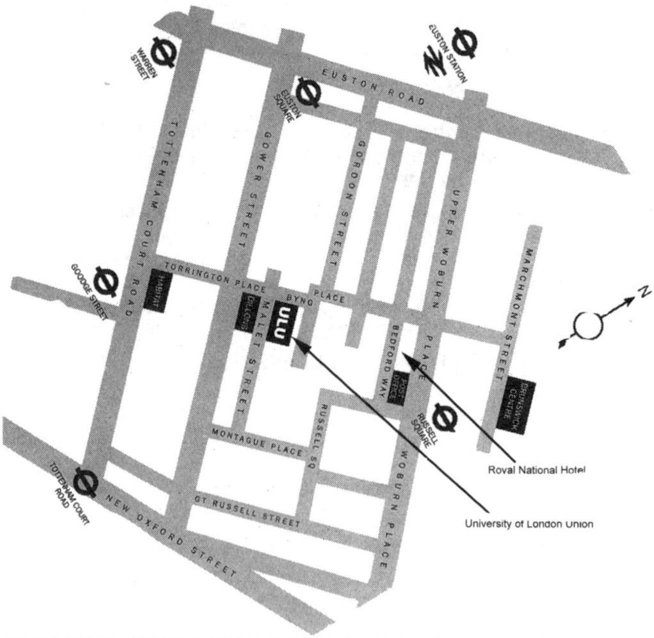

CIGARETTE CARD AUCTIONS

Our auctions are the largest and most successful in the world!

Every month over 465 interesting lots are sold. These include rare sets and type cards, cheaper sets and mixtures, sets in excellent to mint condition, literature, overseas and trade cards not recorded in our Catalogue and highly specialised collections such as Guinea Golds and silks. Lots are submitted to us from other dealers, collectors disposing of their unwanted cards, estates, overseas sources and antique dealers.

Highlights of recent years have included:–

Sets: Taddy Clowns & Circus Artistes, Actresses with Flowers, V.C. Heroes (125).
Wills Waterloo, Soldiers & Sailors, Cricketers 1896.
Players Military Series, Old England's Defenders.
Smith Races of Mankind, Boer War Series.
Ogden Guinea Golds 1-1148 complete.
Fairweather Historic Buildings of Scotland.
Cope Golfers.

Odds: Players, Wills, Smith Advertisement Cards, Clarke Tobacco Leaf Girls, Kinnear Cricketers, Edwards Ringer & Bigg Eastern Manoeuvres, Taddy Wrestlers, etc.

But there is something for everyone each time, from beginner to advanced collector, as the more than 200 participants every month will attest.

You do not have to attend in order to bid. Most of our clients bid by post, knowing that their instructions will be dealt with fairly and in confidence.

How do you bid? Just assess each lot that interests you. Then tell us the maximum amount that you are prepared to pay for it. We will then obtain it (if there are no higher bids) for the cheapest price possible — if for example your bid is £30 and the next highest received is £20 then you will obtain the lot for just £21. If you wish to put a ceiling on your total spending in any auction we can accommodate this too.

How do you obtain Auction Catalogues? Send £1.50 (£2.00 Overseas) for a sample, or else £15.00 (£20.00 Overseas) will cover the cost of all 12 Catalogues for 1999 including Prices Realised Lists. £1.00 is refundable to each successful bidder, each month. Auctions are held on the third Sunday of every month and Catalogues are sent out at least three weeks before sale date.

TERMS OF BUSINESS

All previous lists are cancelled.

Cash with order. Any unsatisfactory items may be returned for credit or refund within seven days of receipt.

Overseas payments can only be accepted by sterling cheque drawn on a British bank, or by Credit Card.

Credit Cards. We can accept payment by American Express, Access, Eurocard, Mastercard and Visa at no extra charge. Just quote your card number and expiry date, and we will complete the amount of items actually sent. This is particularly useful for overseas customers, saving bank and currency conversion problems. Minimum credit card order — £5.00.

Condition. All prices are based on cards in clean, undamaged condition. Where available mint sets 1920-1940 will be at a premium of 50% above the normal price, and mint sets pre 1920 and all mint odd cards will be an extra 100%.

Minimum Order. We are unable to accept orders totalling less than £2.00. For payments of less than £2, in conjunction with credit notes, we can only accept stamps and postal orders, not cheques.

Postage. Inland second class or parcel post, which is now a guaranteed 2 working day delivery, is included in all prices quoted. Overseas letter post is sent free by surface mail. Overseas parcels and air mail are charged at cost. Overseas orders will be sent by air unless otherwise specified. For overseas orders outside Europe an Express service via Federal Express is available at competitive rates, please enquire for details.

Value Added Tax at the rate current on publication is included. Customers outside the E.E.C. should deduct 7/47 (approx 15%) from everything except books.

When ordering cards please quote the issuer's name, the name of the set, the date of issue, and the price. This will enable us to identify the precise series.

Odd Lists must be submitted on a separate sheet of paper with the name and address clearly shown; this will be returned with the cards for checking if sent in duplicate. Remember that end cards are double the normal price. Please write all the numbers required, e.g. NOT "17-20" but 17, 18, 19, 20. If the cards are required to complete an unnumbered set, and you do not know the missing titles, we can supply them provided that you list all the cards that you HAVE in alphabetical order. Please note we cannot accept telephone orders for odd cards.

Alternatives. Although this catalogue is based upon current stocks, these are bound to fluctuate. Therefore, whenever possible give alternatives.

Credit Notes. When items are out of stock a credit note is normally sent. This may be utilised or encashed at any time, but MUST be returned when so doing.

Unlisted series. We are always pleased to quote for series unlisted, or unpriced.

Purchasing. We are always pleased to purchase or exchange collectors' unwanted cards. Please write with full details before sending cards.

Enquiries. We are always pleased to offer our advice on all collectors' queries. Please enclose a stamped addressed envelope with all enquiries.

Callers. Our shop is open from 9.00 a.m. to 5.00 p.m. each Monday to Friday, and collectors are always welcome to select from our complete range of cards and accessories. Watford Way is at Hendon Central (Underground, Northern Line), and is served by a number of buses, including Green Line. Private parking bay available for customers.

Fax Machine/E-mail/Web site. Our machines are always on. They can be used to place orders (including odd cards) when a credit card number and expiry date are quoted, and also for Auction bids. The Fax number is 0181-203-7878 (International 011-44181-203-7878) E-mail is murraycards@ukbusiness.com Web site: www.murraycards.com

Answering machine. For the convenience of customers an answering machine is in operation whenever the shop is closed. Just leave your message, or order with Credit Card number and expiry date, and it will be dealt with as soon as we re-open. Please note we cannot accept telephone orders for odd cards.

No Hidden Extras. Remember that all prices shown include postage, packing, insurance and (where applicable) V.A.T. And that with every pre-1940 set we include Nostalgia pages *absolutely free!*

CARTOPHILIC SOCIETY REFERENCE BOOKS

A number of the earlier Reference Books have been unavailable for some years. However we are now pleased to be able to offer the following paper backed reprints at exceptionally low cost.

No. 1 Faulkner.
No. 2 Hill.
No. 4 Gallaher.
No. 5 Abdulla, Adkin & Anstie.
No. 6 Ardath.
No. 7 Directory of British Cigarette Card Issuers (16 cards illustrated).
No. 8 Glossary of Cartophilic Terms (27 cards illustrated).
No. 9 Lambert & Butler (25 cards illustrated).
No. 10 Churchman (29 cards illustrated).
No. 12 Taddy (30 cards illustrated).
No. 13 Phillips (225 cards illustrated).
No. 17 Player (26 cards illustrated).

ONLY £3.50 Per Booklet!

The following reprints have been combined in hard cover. The information contained cannot be found elsewhere, and each book represents excellent value. Each contains lists of unnumbered series, illustrations of untitled cards, and background information to most sets.

The Ogden Reference Book (including Guinea Golds). 244 pages, 536 cards illustrated. **PRICE £12.50**

The Cigarette Card Issues of Wills and The B.A.T. Book. New combined volume. Over 500 pages, 2518 cards illustrated. **PRICE £20.00**

A MUST FOR ALL COLLECTORS THE WORLD TOBACCO ISSUES INDEX

Published by the Cartophilic Society of G.B. Ltd., this work is now in five volumes, which between them list every card issued by tobacco manufacturers that was known at the end of 1990.

Part 1. World Index and Handbook reprinted as one volume. 701 pages, 1977 cards illustrated. This is the basic reference work for all serious collectors, including details of nearly every British cigarette card series. First published in 1956. **PRICE £23.50**

Part II. 452 pages, with 3,600 cards illustrated. This volume covers additions to Part 1, which are mainly overseas cards. In particular it includes most of the information from the American Book of Checklists. **PRICE £15.50**

Part III. 504 pages, 666 cards illustrated. Published in 1978, this work updates the information in Parts I and II, and also repeats the lists (amended) which were previously in the Churchman, Lambert & Butler, Taddy, Phillips and Australasian Booklets. Also featured are American non-insert cards, blankets and pins. **PRICE £25.00**

Part IV. 688 pages. Lists of U.S. Baseball, photographic, Maltese etc. as well as additions to three previous parts. **PRICE £18.50**

Part V. 552 pages, 1,329 cards illustrated. Additions to previous four parts and cross-referencing to previous parts and Continental Catalogue. (Published 1991). **PRICE £18.50**

OTHER LITERATURE

GENERAL WORKS

The Story of Cigarette Cards by Martin Murray, Hardback, 128 pages, including 32 in colour. **£7.25**
Collecting Cigarette Cards by Dorothy Bagnall, 112 pages, illustrated. **£5.00**

Operation Red Poppy by Jack Nickle Smith. A spy thriller featuring a cartophilist. Hard cover. 158 pages. **Now Only £5.00**
Figurine Pubblicita, arte, collezionismo e industria 1867-1985. Italian text. A history of cards 1867-1985. Many pages of colour and black and white illustrations. **£15.00**
Collecting Cigarette & Trade Cards by Gordon Howsden. 152 large pages. An excellent work with 750 cards illustrated in colour. **£14.25**

REFERENCE BOOKS

Handbook Part I. Published by L.C.C.C. Lists and illustrations of pre-1918 unnumbered and alike series (tobacco only). Essential reference. **£12.00**
Handbook Part II. Published by L.C.C.C. Lists of post-1918 series and all silks, with additions to Part 1. **£12.00**
Smith Cigarette Cards. 36 pages with illustrations. Lists all known series, including back varieties. **£3.50**
British Trade Index, Part I. Series up to 1940. 216 pages, many illustrations. **£10.00**
British Trade Index, Part II. 232 pages. Additions to Part 1 and also issues 1945-1968 **£10.00**
British Trade Index, Part III. 400 pages, many illustrations. Additions to Parts I and II, with new issues to the end of 1985. **£12.50**
British Trade Index, Part IV. 411 pages, many illustrations. Additions to Parts I, II and III with new issues to the end of 1994. This well printed book includes an Index to the three previous volumes. **£20.00**
Typhoo Tea Cards. 36 pages with illustrations. Lists of back varieties. **£3.50**
A. & B.C. Gum Cards. Revised Edition. 42 pages with illustrations. Many lists. **£3.50**
British Silk Issues by Dorothy Sawyer. New Edition, amended, many illustrations, 64 pages with details of all known British Tobacco and Trade silk issues. Essential reading for silk collectors. **£5.00**
Lawn Tennis Cards by Derek Hurst. 90 pages, including 4 pages of illustrations. Combined listing of Tobacco and Trade Cards. **£8.45**
Half Time (Football and the cigarette card 1890-1940) by David Thompson. 104 pages, listing every tobacco issue. **£9.50**
Errors & Varieties, British Cigarette Cards by W. B. Neilson. Lists of all known varieties, corrected or uncorrected. **£7.50**
Errors & Varieties, British Cigarette Cards, Part 2 by W. B. Neilson. 37 pages. Additions to Part 1, plus Guinea Golds, Tabs. **£3.00**
Errors & Varieties, British Trade Cards by W. B. Neilson. 36 pages, with illustrations. Include pre & post-1945. **£3.00**
Huntley & Palmers Catalogue of Cards by E. Vansevenant. 63 pages, paper back, many cards illustrated. **£10.00**
Peak Frean Catalogue of Cards. 76 pages, many illustrations. **£13.50**
Cricket Cigarette & Trade Cards by Derek Deadman. The definitive work. 254 pages, 16 pages of illustrations. Comprehensive list of all titles known until the end of 1984. 'Monumental'. **£10.95**
Cricket Cigarette & Trade Cards. A further listing by Alan Harris and Geoff Seymour. 143 pages, 16 pages of illustrations. Lists all cards issued since the Deadman book and updated information. **£7.50**
A Century of Golf Cards by Bruce Berdock and Michael Baier. 126 pages, 18 pages of mostly coloured illustrations. List all known golf cards — an essential reference book. **£19.50**
Seconds Out, Round One by Evan Jones. 172 pages, over 700 illustrations. Lists all known English language boxing cards (except recent commercial issues). A well researched book with interesting biographical information. **£14.50**
Brooke Bond Picture Cards 'The First Forty Years' by A. L. Waterhouse. A reference book of all Issues in Great Britain and Overseas. 72 pages with many illustrations. **£7.25**
The Price Guide to Golf Cards Part 1: Tobacco Cards by Philip Smedley & Bruce Berdock. 108 pages. All cards individually priced, illustrations from each series, including singles. **£9.00**
Anonymous Football Cards by Paul Clarkson. 52 pages. Over 200 anonymous Tobacco and Trade Soccer cards illustrated and identified. **£3.00**

FOREIGN CARDS

Australian & New Zealand Index. Published by Cartophilic Society. Over 300 pages — 600 cards illustrated. Lists all tobacco and trade cards. Published 1983. **£10.50**

Cigarette Cards Australian Issues & Values by Dion H. Skinner. A truly magnificent work. 245 pages, with coloured illustrations of at least one sample front and back(s) of each series. Lists of every card in each series (or illustrations of untitled sets). **£25.00**

Baseball Card Price Guide. 1st Edition 1987. Published by Sports Collectors Digest. 65,000 cards listed and individually priced. Many illustrations. Reduced. **£3.50**

Index of Suchard Issues (based on Wieser's Catalogue). Published by The Cartophilic Society. 104 Pages. Lots of Diverse issues illustrated including sets, menus, etc. **£12.00**

LIEBIG CARDS

Liebig Catalogue in English. Eighth Edition. See page 248 for full details. **£4.95**

Sanguinetti Liebig Catalogue. 1991 Edition. 431 pages, listing all titles from 1,974 sets and menus, Italian text, illustrations of 1,308 series. Indices in various languages. **£20.00**

Liebig Menu and Table Cards by L. De. Magistris. 118 page listing of all known Table and Menu cards, plus printing varieties. Colour illustrations of each series. **£20.00**

Unificato Liebig Catalogue, 1998. Hardback Ring Binder with over 400 pages. Published by CIF Italy. Complete listing of Chromos, Menus and Table cards in Fada sequence. Two coloured illustrations from each chromo series and one from other series. Prices in lira and details of different languages. A magnificent achievement. **£35.00**

MISCELLANEOUS

Picture Postcard Values, 1999. Previously known as the I.P.M. Postcard catalogue. Many illustrations. 192 pages. **£9.95**

Postcard Collecting, a beginner's guide to old and modern picture postcards. **£1.75**

Golf on Old Picture Postcards by Tom Serpell. 64 pages heavily illustrated in both black and white and colour. **£5.50**

Jacobs Famous Picture Cards from History. 32 colour reproductions from 32 sets dealing with Transport & Natural History, together with an album including details of each card and a general introduction to card collecting. **£2.00**

Sweet Cigarette Packets by Paul Hart. 50 pages including 5 pages of illustrations. A long awaited book for sweet cigarette packet collectors. **£6.50**

FRAMING SERVICE

The last few years have seen a big upsurge in the framing of cigarette cards, both originals and reprints. We can offer an individual framing service for a favourite set or a specific interest.

Standard sets can be accommodated in the kits detailed on page 14, but if you have a Gallaher set, a non-standard set or require a special frame with a larger centrepiece please enquire.

FRAMING KITS

Best materials — Competitive prices
Easy to do-it-yourself — Cards positioned without damage
— Backs can be read —

MOUNTING BOARDS

(Can be used horizontally or vertically)
(Most available in Black, Brown, Green and Maroon)

					Size
	A	To hold	25	Standard sized cards.	259 x 421 mm
**	B	To hold	50	Carreras Black Cat cards.	470 x 421 mm
	C	To hold	24	Large cards.	383 x 469 mm
	D	To hold	10	Large cards.	259 x 421 mm
	E	To hold	25	Large cards.	383 x 469 mm
	F	To hold	50	Standard sized cards.	470 x 421 mm
	G	To hold	12	Large sized cards.	259 x 421 mm
**	H	To hold	15	Standard sized cards.	278 x 289 mm
**	J	To hold	20	Large sized cards.	348 x 502 mm
	K	To hold	10	Standard sized cards.	251 x 202 mm
	L	To hold	6	Liebig cards.	278 x 289 mm
	M	To hold	10	Extra large cards.	315 x 310 mm
**	R	To hold	15	Large cards.	300 x 526 mm
	S	To hold	7	Large cards.	278 x 289 mm
	T	To hold	3	Standard sized cards.	127 x 174 mm
	W	To hold	6	Large sized cards.	251 x 223 mm
**	X	To hold	12	American Gum sized cards	259 x 421 mm

** = Available in Black only

PRICES (Rate applied to total quantity ordered).

		1-6	**7+**
Boards	A, D, G, M, X	£3.50	£2.00
Boards	B, C, E, F, J	£5.00	£3.50
Boards	H, L, S	£2.00	£1.35
Boards	K, W	£1.50	£1.00
Board	R	£4.00	£2.70
Board	T	£0.75	£0.50

COMPLETE KITS

Comprising frame, glass, mounting board, spring clips, rings and screws.

PRICES (Now Post Free!)

A, G, X	£22.00	each
B, C, E, F, J	£35.00	each
H, L	£16.50	each
K, W	£14.00	each

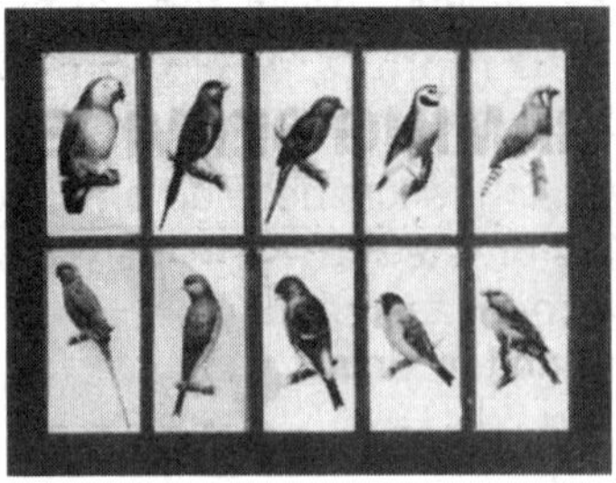

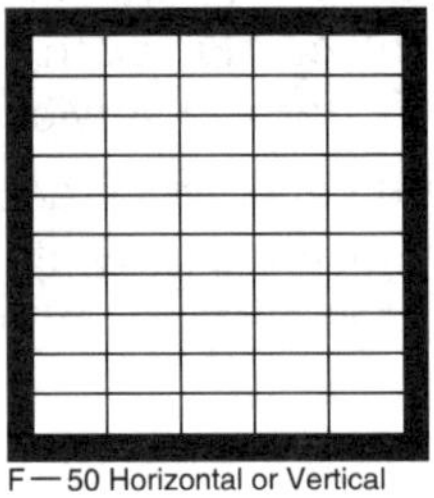

F — 50 Horizontal or Vertical

"NOSTALGIA" REPRINTS

An exciting concept for collectors. Reproductions of Classic card sets, all of which are almost impossible to obtain, at a price that everyone can afford.

These cards are of the highest quality, and the latest technology has been used to recreate as closely as possible the beauty of the originals. They have received universal acclaim in the cigarette card world, and are indeed becoming collector's items in their own right.

Because of the difficulty of distinguishing our reproductions from the originals each reprint has 'A Nostalgia Reprint' printed on the back of the card.

TITLES CURRENTLY AVAILABLE

Taddy County Cricketers

15 Derbyshire
15 Essex
16 Gloucestershire
15 Hampshire
15 Kent
15 Lancashire
14 Leicestershire
15 Middlesex
15 Northamptonshire
14 Nottinghamshire
15 Somersetshire (sic)
15 Surrey
15 Sussex
15 Warwickshire
14 Worcestershire
15 Yorkshire

ONLY £2.00 per County, or all 238 cards for £27.50

Taddy Prominent Footballers

15 Aston Villa
15 Chelsea
15 Everton
15 Leeds City
15 Liverpool
15 Manchester United
15 Middlesborough
15 Newcastle
15 Queen's Park Rangers
15 Sunderland
15 Tottenham Hotspur
15 West HamUnited
15 Woolwich Arsenal

ONLY £2.00 per Club

Allen & Ginter	50	American Indian Chiefs	**£7.50**
Allen & Ginter	50	Fruits	**£7.50**
Berlyn	25	Humorous Golfing Series	**£6.00**
Cope	50	Cope's Golfers	**£7.50**
Cope	50	Dickens Gallery	**£7.50**
Cope	50	Shakespeare Gallery	**£7.50**
Ellis	25	Generals of the Late Civil War	**£6.00**
Gabriel	20	Cricketers Series	**£3.50**
Jones Bros.	18	Spurs Footballers	**£2.00**
Kinney	25	Leaders	**£6.00**
Player	50	Military Series	**£7.50**
Taddy	20	Clowns and Circus Artistes	**£6.00**
Thomson	24	Motor Bike Cards	**£6.00**
Thomson	20	Motor Cycles	**£6.00**
U.S. Tobacco	28	Baseball Greats of the 1890's	**£6.00**
Wills	50	Cricketers 1896	**£7.50**
Wills	50	Cricketers Series 1901	**£15.00**

A specially designed frame, is available for Taddy Clowns priced at £30 (to include special mounting board, glass and set).

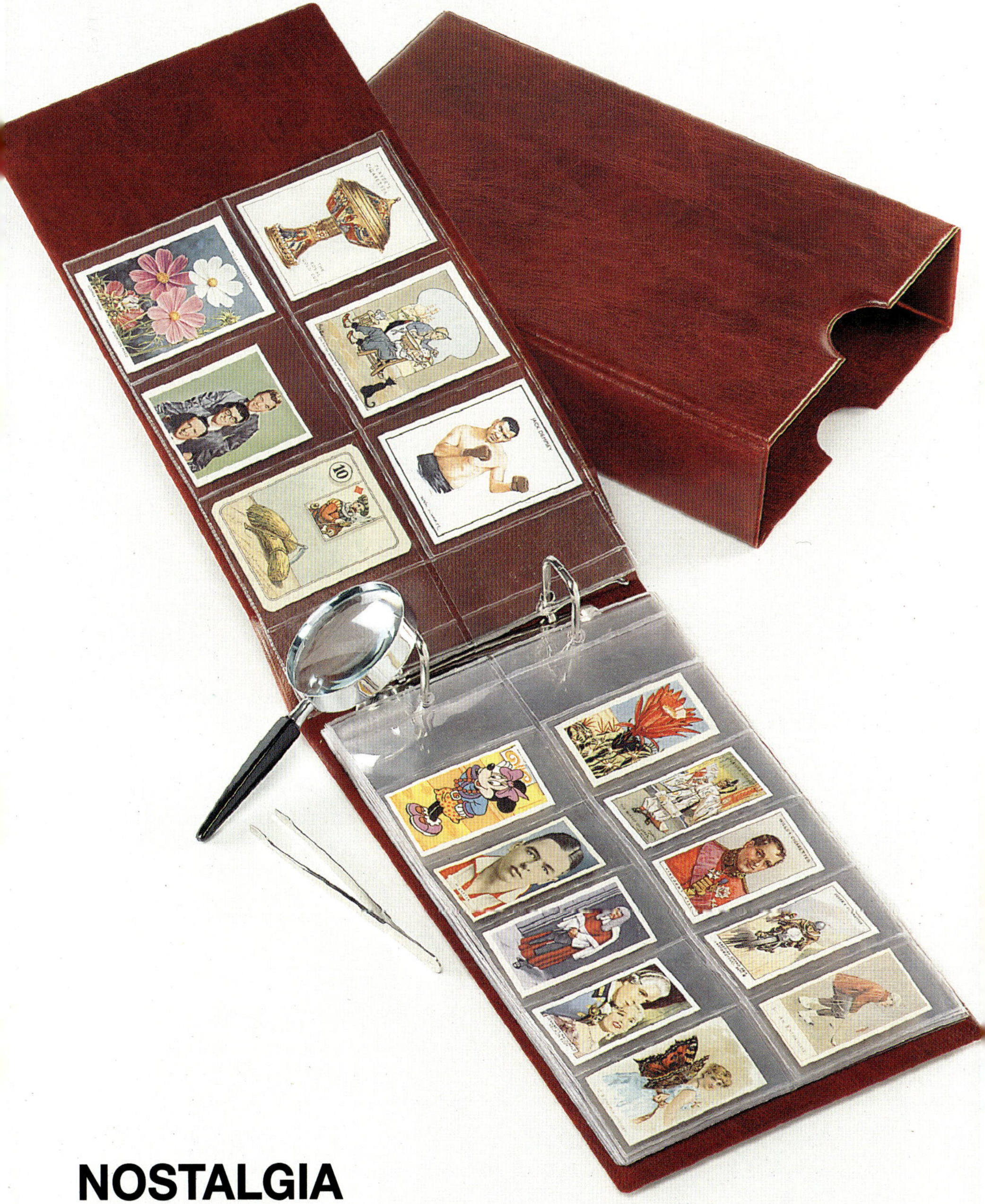

NOSTALGIA ALBUMS

Preserve the best of the past in the best of the present. See opposite page for details.

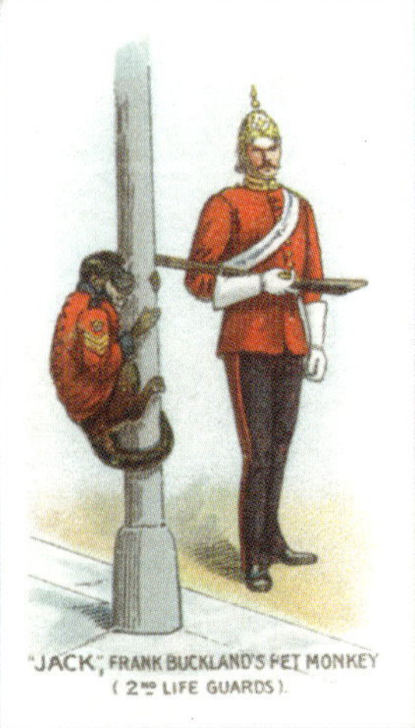

Regimental Pets
B.A.T., Wills (Scissors)

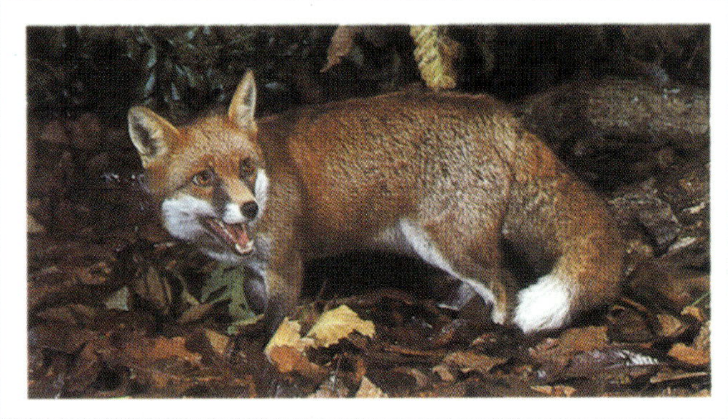

Britain's Nocturnal Wildlife
Grandee

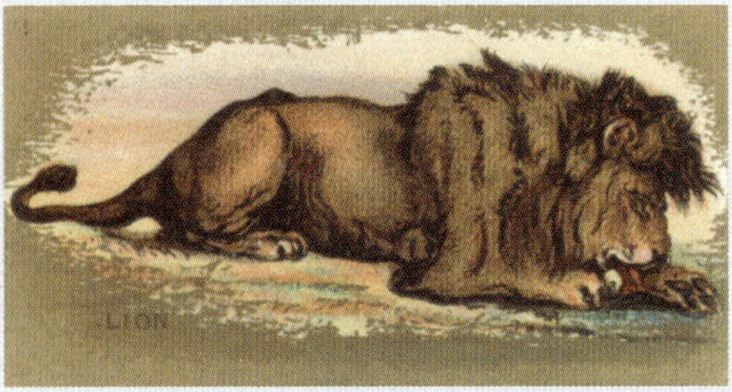

Animals
Kinney

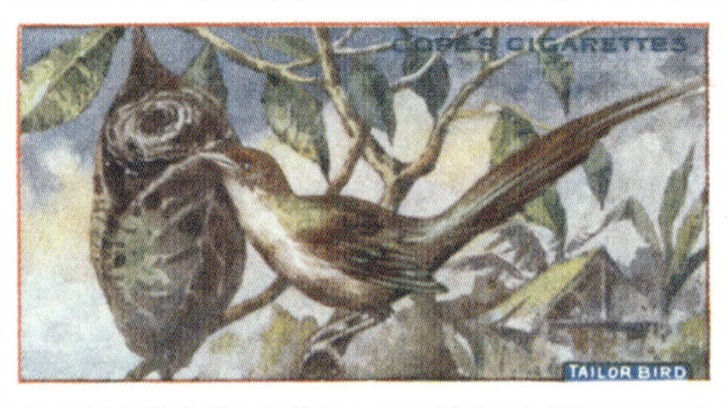

Wild Animals & Birds
Cope

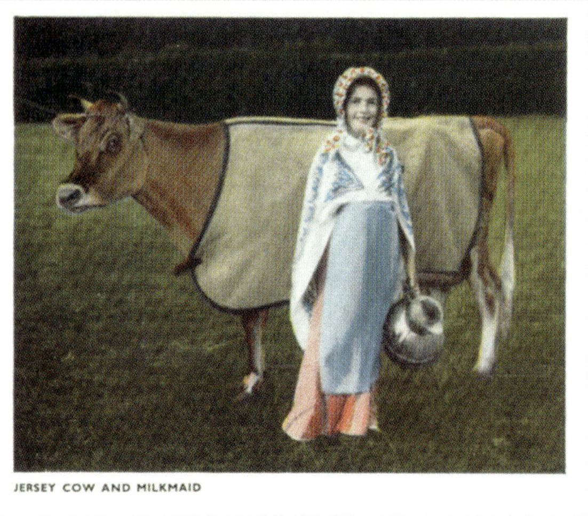

Around & About in Jersey
Ching

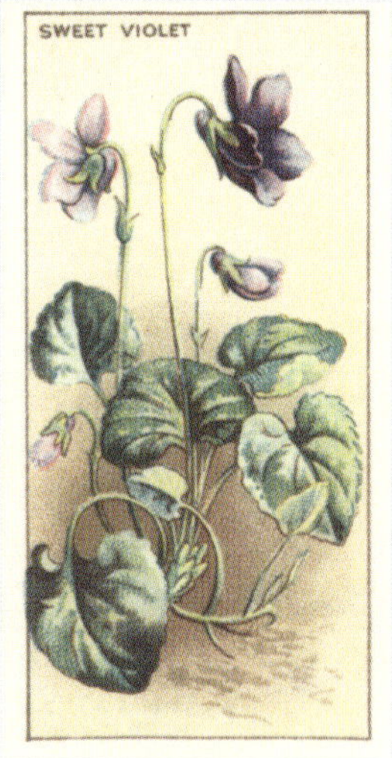

Wayside Flowers
C.W.S.

THE "HENDON" ALBUM

For Postcards, trade cards, and all printed ephemera.

* Page in crystal clear material, free of plasticiser.
* 7 different page formats.
* Handsome loose leaf binders, in choice of blue, brown, green or red.
* Matching slip cases.
* Big enough for BIG cards, small enough for small muscles.

Pages available

1. Pocket.	Cards size	294 x 214mm.	
2. Pockets.	Cards size	143 x 214mm.	Ideal for banknotes.
3. Pockets.	Cards size	93 x 214mm.	Ideal for banknotes.
4. Pockets.	Cards size	143 x 105mm.	Especially for postcards.
6. Pockets.	Cards size	92 x 105mm.	
8. Pockets.	Cards size	67 x 105mm.	Ideal for Gum cards, XL cigarette cards and phone cards.
9. Pockets.	Cards size	94 x 68mm.	Suitable for playing cards.

Binder with 25 pages	**£13.50**	(including postage).
Extra pages	**33p**	each.
Matching slip case	**£3.25**	(must be ordered with binder).
Black interleaving, full page size	**£1.50**	per 25.
Black inserts for postcard pages	**£1.50**	per 100.

COLLECTORS' AIDS

Cleartex strips, for wrapping standard size sets	**200 for £2.80**
large size sets	**200 for £3.20**
extra large sets	**200 for £3.50**
Tweezers, fine quality, with plastic sheath	**£1.50**
Magnifying Glasses, 2½" diameter	**£4.00**
4" diameter	**£7.00**
Printed wants lists, numbered 1-50 on thin card	**30 for 75p**
Plastic Wallet. Pocket size with 10 postcard size pages. Ideal for carrying odds (and ends)	**£1.75**
Postcard pockets, thin PVC	**100 for £3.50**

INDEX OF BRANDS (Tobacco)

These appear on cards without the Manufacturer's name (see also Information opposite Page 129)

HAVELOCK CIGARETTES — See Willis (Part 1)
HAWSER Etc. — See Wholesale Tobacco Co. (Part 1)
HEARTS DELIGHT CIGARETTES — See Pritchard & Burton (Part 1)
HERBERT TAREYTON CIGARETTES — See American Tobacco Co. (Part 2)
HOFFMAN HOUSE MAGNUMS — See American Tobacco Co. (Part 2)
HONEST LONG CUT — See Duke or American Tobacco Co. (Part 2)
HUDAVEND CIGARETTES — See Teofani (Part 1)
HUSTLER LITTLE CIGARS — See American Tobacco Co. (Part 2)

ISLANDER, FAGS, SPECIALS, CLUBS — See Bucktrout (Part 1)

JACK ROSE LITTLE CIGARS — See American Tobacco Co. (Part 2)
JERSEY LILY CIGARETTES — See Bradford (Part 1)
JUNIOR MEMBER CIGARETTES — See Pattreiouex (Part 1)

KENSITAS CIGARETTES — See J. Wix (Part 1)

LENOX CIGARETTES — See American Tobacco Co. (Part 2)
LE ROY CIGARS — See Miller (Part 2)
LEVANT FAVOURITES — See B. Morris (Part 1)
LIFEBOAT CIGARETTES — See United Tobacco Co. (Part 2)
LIFE RAY CIGARETTES — See Ray (Part 1)
LITTLE RHODY CUT PLUG — See Geo. F. Young (Part 2)
LOTUS CIGARETTES — See United Tobacco Co. (Part 2)
LUCANA CIGARETTES — See Sandorides (Part 1)
LUCKY STRIKE CIGARETTES — See American Tobacco Co. (Part 2)
LUXURY CIGARETTES — See American Tobacco Co. (Part 2)

MAGPIE CIGARETTES — See Schuh (Part 2)
MANIKIN CIGARS — See Freeman (Part 1)
MATTOSSIANS IMPORTED EGYPTIAN CIGARETTES — See Henly & Watkins (Part 1)
MAX CIGARETTES — See A. & M. Wix (Part 1)
MAYBLOSSOM CIGARETTES — See Lambert & Butler (Part 1)
MECCA CIGARETTES — See American Tobacco Co. (Part 2)
MILLBANK CIGARETTES — See Imperial Tobacco Co. (Canada) (Part 2)
MILLS CIGARETTES — See Amalgamated Tobacco Corporation (Part 1)
MILO CIGARETTES — See Sniders & Abrahams (Part 2)
MINERS EXTRA SMOKING TOBACCO — See American Tobacco Co. (Part 2)
MOGUL CIGARETTES — See American Tobacco Co. (Part 2)
MURAD CIGARETTES — See American Tobacco Co. (Part 2)

NASSA CIGARETTES — See Policansky Bros. (Part 2)
NEBO CIGARETTES — See American Tobacco Co. (Part 2)

OK CIGARETTES — See Hartleys T.C. (Part 2)
OBAK CIGARETTES — See American Tobacco Co. (Part 2)
OFFICERS MESS CIGARETTES — See African Tobacco Mfrs. (Part 2)
OLD GOLD CIGARETTES — See American Tobacco Co. (Part 2)
OLD JUDGE CIGARETTES — See B.A.T. or Goodwin (Part 2)
ONE OF THE FINEST — See Buchner (Part 2)
ORACLE CIGARETTES — See Tetley (Part 1)
OUR LITTLE BEAUTIES — See Allen & Ginter (Part 2)
OXFORD CIGARETTES — See American Tobacco Co. (Part 2)

PALACE CIGARETTES — See Teofani (Part 1)
PAN HANDLE SCRAP — See American Tobacco Co. (Part 2)
PETER PAN CIGARETTES — See Sniders & Abrahams (Part 2)
PHAROAH'S DREAM CIGARETTES — See Teofani (Part 1)
PIBROCH VIRGINIA — See Fryer (Part 1)
PICCADILLY LITTLE CIGARS — See American Tobacco Co. (Part 2)
PICK-ME-UP CIGARETTES — See Drapkin & Millhoff (Part 1)
PIEDMONT CIGARETTES — See American Tobacco Co. (Part 2)
PINHEAD CIGARETTES — See British American Tobacco Co. (Part 2)
PINNACE — See G. Phillips (Part 1)
PIONEER CIGARETTES — See Richmond Cavendish (Part 1)
PIRATE CIGARETTES — See Wills (Part 1)
POLO MILD CIGARETTES — See Murray (Part 1)
PURITAN LITTLE CIGARS — See American Tobacco Co. (Part 2)
PURPLE MOUNTAIN CIGARETTES — See Wills (Part 1)

R. S. — See R. Sinclair (Part 1)
RECRUIT LITTLE CIGARS — See American Tobacco Co. (Part 2)
RED CROSS — See Lorillard or American Tobacco Co. (Part 2)
REINA REGENTA CIGARS — See B. Morris (Part 1)
RICHMOND GEM CIGARETTES — See Allen & Ginter (Part 2)
RICHMOND STRAIGHT CUT CIGARETTES — See American Tobacco Co. (Part 2)
ROSELAND CIGARETTES — See Glass (Part 1)
ROYAL BENGALS LITTLE CIGARS — See American Tobacco Co. (Part 2)
RUGGER CIGARETTES — See United Tobacco Companies (Part 2)

ST. DUNSTANS CIGARETTES — See Carreras (Part 1)
ST. LEGER LITTLE CIGARS — See American Tobacco Co. (Part 2)
SCOTS CIGARETTES — See African Tobacco Mfrs. (Part 2)
SCRAP IRON SCRAP — See American Tobacco Co. (Part 2)
SEAL OF NORTH CAROLINA PLUG CUT TOBACCO — See Marburg Bros. (Part 2)
SENATOR CIGARETTES — See Scerri (Part 2)
SENIOR SERVICE CIGARETTES — See Pattreiouex (Part 1)
SENSATION CUT PLUG — See Lorillard (Part 2)
SHANTUNG CIGARETTES — See British American Tobacco Co. (Part 2)
SILKO CIGARETTES — See American Tobacco Co. (Part 2)
SMILE AWAY TOBACCO — See Carreras (Part 1)
SOVEREIGN CIGARETTES — See American Tobacco Co. (Part 2)
SPANISH FOUR — See W. R. Gresh (Part 2)
SPANISH PUFFS — See Mandelbaum (Part 2)
SPINET CIGARETTES — See Hill (Part 1)
SPOTLIGHT TOBACCOS — See Hill (Part 1)
SPRINGBOK CIGARETTES — See United Tobacco Co. (Part 2)
STAG TOBACCO — See American Tobacco Co. (Part 2)
STANDARD CIGARETTES — See Carreras (Part 1) or Sniders & Abrahams (Part 2)
STATE EXPRESS CIGARETTES — See Ardath (Part 1)
SUB ROSA CIGARROS — See American Tobacco Co. (Part 2)
SUMMIT — See International Tobacco Co. (Part 1)
SUNRIPE CIGARETTES — See Hill (Part 1)
SUNSPOT CIGARETTES — See Theman (Part 1)
SWEET CAPORAL — See Kinney or American Tobacco Co. (Part 2)
SWEET LAVENDER — See Kimball (Part 2)

TATLEY CIGARETTES — See Walkers (Part 1)
TEAL CIGARETTES — See British American Tobacco Co. (Part 2)
THREE BELLS CIGARETTES — See Bell (Part 1)
THREE CASTLES CIGARETTES — See Wills (Part 1)
THREE DOGS CIGARETTES — See Sandorides (Part 1)
THREE STAR CIGARETTES — See Teofani (Part 1)
TIGER CIGARETTES — See British American Tobacco Co. (Part 1)
TIPSY LOO CIGARETTES — See H. C. Lloyd (Part 1)
TOKIO CIGARETTES — See American Tobacco Co. (Part 2)
TRAWLER CIGARETTES — See Pattreiouex (Part 1)
TRUMPS LONG CUT — See Moore & Calvi (Part 2)
TURF CIGARETTES — See Carreras (Part 1)
TURKEY RED CIGARETTES — See American Tobacco Co. (Part 2)
TURKISH TROPHY CIGARETTES — See American Tobacco Co. (Part 2)
TWELFTH NIGHT CIGARETTES — See American Tobacco Co. (Part 2)

U.S. MARINE — See American Tobacco Co. (Part 2)
UZIT CIGARETTES — See American Tobacco Co. (Part 2)

VANITY FAIR CIGARETTES — See Kimball (Part 2)
VICE REGAL CIGARETTES — See Wills (Part 1)
VICTORY TOBACCO — See Buchner (Part 2)
VIRGINIA BRIGHTS CIGARETTES — See Allen & Ginter (Part 2)

WEST END CIGARETTES — See Teofani (Part 1)
WINGS CIGARETTES — See Brown & Williamson (Part 2)

YANKEE DOODLE — See British Australasian Tobacco Co. (Part 2)

ZIRA CIGARETTES — See American Tobacco Co. (Part 2)

Part 1

BRITISH TOBACCO MANUFACTURERS

(Including Channel Islands, Eire, and Overseas Issues by British-based firms)

ABDULLA & CO. LTD.

24 Page Reference Book (with Anstie & Adkin) — £3.50

Qty		*Date*	*Odds*	*Sets*
50	Beauties of To-Day	1938	£3.25	—
L1	Bridge Rule Cards (Several Printings)	1936	—	£12.00
25	British Butterflies	1935	£1.00	£25.00
F52	Cinema Stars	1932	£3.25	—
30	Cinema Stars (Brown Back)	1932	£4.25	—
30	Cinema Stars (Black Back)	1933	£3.25	—
32	Cinema Stars (Brown Glossy Front)	1933	£2.20	£70.00
32	Cinema Stars (Hand Coloured)	1934	£2.00	£64.00
30	Cinema Stars (Hand Coloured)	1934	£2.60	£78.00
P2	Commanders of the Allies	1914	£62.50	—
25	Feathered Friends	1935	90p	£22.50
50	Film Favourites	1934	£3.50	—
50	Film Stars	1934	£5.50	—
P24	Film Stars (Series of Cards)	1934	£6.50	—
P24	Film Stars (Series of 24 Cards)	1934	*£7.00*	—
P24	Film Stars, 2nd (25-48)	1934	£6.50	—
M3	Great War Gift Packing Cards	1916	£55.00	£165.00
18	Message Cards (Blue Printing)	1936	£10.00	—
18	(Green Printing)	1936	*£11.00*	—
18	(Red Printing)	1936	*£11.00*	—
K18	Message Cards(Two Wordings)	1936	*£10.00*	—
25	Old Favourites	1936	80p	£20.00
L1	Princess Mary Gift Card	1914	—	£16.50
40	Screen Stars (No "Successors"Clause)	1939	£1.20	£48.00
40	(With Successors Clause)	1939	£1.80	£72.00
50	Stage and Cinema Beauties	1935	£3.00	—
30	Stars of the Stage and Screen	1934	£3.40	—

GERMAN ISSUES

M150	Autobilder Serie I	1931	£1.00	£150.00
M150	Autobilder Serie II	1932	£1.00	£150.00
M160	Im Auto Mit Abdulla Durch Die Welt	1930	80p	£128.00
M110	Landerwappen-Sammlung	1932	80p	—
M110	Landerwappen-Sammlung Serie II	1932	80p	—
M150	Landerwappen-Sammlung Serie III	1932	80p	£120.00
M200	Nationale und Internationale Sport Rekorde	1931	£1.75	—
M50	Soldatenbilder Europaischer Armeen	1928	£1.75	—
X80	Wappenkarten	1928	65p	£52.00

ADCOCK & SON

11/12	Ancient Norwich	1928	£3.20	£35.00

ADKIN & SONS

24 Page Reference Book (with Anstie & Abdulla) — £3.50

25	Actresses-French	1898	*£150.00*	—
12	A Living Picture (Adkin & Sons Back)	1900	£6.00	£72.00
12	(These Cards Back)	1900	£6.50	£78.00
P12	A Living Picture	1900	*£85.00*	—
12	A Royal Favourite	1900	£11.00	£130.00
15	Beauties "PAC" (7 Brands)	1898	*£200.00*	—
50	Butterflies & Moths	1924	£1.80	£90.00

ADKIN & SONS — cont.

Qty		Date	Odds	Sets
12	Character Sketches (Black Back)	1901	£6.50	£78.00
12	(Green Back)	1900	£6.50	£78.00
P12	Character Sketches	1900	£80.00	—
P4	Games by Tom Browne	1900	*£175.00*	—
25	Notabilities	1915	£4.20	£105.00
12	Pretty Girl Series (Actresses)	1897	£45.00	£540.00
12	Pretty Girl Series (12 Calendar Backs)	1900	£45.00	—
12	(6 Verse Backs)	1900	£32.00	—
12	(32 Other Backs)	1900	£25.00	—
	Soldiers of the Queen			
25	("Series of 50, Issued Exclusively with")	1899	£20.00	—
50	("Series of 50")	1900	£4.25	—
59	("Series of 60")	1900	£4.25	£255.00
31	Soldiers of the Queen & Portraits	1901	£5.00	£150.00
30	Sporting Cups & Trophies	1914	£16.00	£480.00
25	War Trophies	1917	£4.00	£100.00
50	Wild Animals of the World	1923	£1.50	£75.00

AIKMAN'S

Qty		Date	Odds	Sets
30	Army Pictures, Cartoons, etc	1916	*£85.00*	—

H. J. AINSWORTH

Qty		Date	Odds	Sets
30	Army Pictures, Cartoons, etc	1916	*£85.00*	—

ALBERGE & BROMET

Qty		Date	Odds	Sets
25	Boer War & General Interest			
	(Brown Bridal Bouquet)	1900	*£85.00*	—
	(Green Bridal Bouquet)	1900	*£85.00*	—
	(Green La Optima)	1900	*£85.00*	—
40	Naval & Military Phrases (Bridal Bouquet)	1904	£80.00	—
40	(La Optima)	1904	*£80.00*	—
30	Proverbs	1903	*£80.00*	—

PHILLIP ALLMAN & CO. LTD.

Qty		Date	Odds	Sets
50	Coronation Series	1953	50p	£25.00
12	Pin Up Girls, 1st Series			
	(Numbered)	1953	£3.50	£42.00
	(Unnumbered, "Ask For Allman-Always")	1953	£2.50	£30.00
	(Unnumbered, "For Men Only")	1953	£2.50	£30.00
L12	Pin Up Girls, 1st Series	1953	£3.25	£39.00
12	Pin Up Girls, 2nd Series	1953	£3.50	£42.00
L12	Pin Up Girls, 2nd Series	1953	£3.25	£39.00
24	Pin Up Girls, Combined Series			
	(Numbered "First Series of 24")	1953	*£6.00*	—

AMALGAMATED TOBACCO CORPORATION LTD. (Mills)

Qty		Date	Odds	Sets
25	Aircraft of the World	1958	—	£7.50
25	A Nature Series	1958	—	£2.50

AMALGAMATED TOBACCO CORPORATION LTD. (Mills) — cont.

Qty		Date	Odds	Sets
25	Animals of the Countryside	1958	—	£3.00
25	Aquarium Fish	1961	—	£2.50
25	Army Badges-Past and Present	1961	—	£15.00
25	British Coins and Costumes	1958	—	£5.00
25	British Locomotives	1961	—	£6.50
25	British Uniforms of the 19th Century	1957	—	£16.00
25	Butterflies and Moths	1957	—	£2.50
25	Cacti	1961	—	£8.00
25	Castles of Britain	1961	—	£22.50
25	Coins of the World	1961	—	£3.00
25	Communications	1961	—	£17.50
25	Dogs	1958	—	£16.00
25	Evolution of the Royal Navy	1957	—	£15.00
M25	Famous British Ships, Series No.1	1952	—	£3.00
M25	Famous British Ships, Series No.2	1952	—	£3.00
25	Football Clubs and Badges	1961	—	£25.00
25	Freshwater Fish	1958	—	£6.00
25	Guerriers a Travers Les Ages (French)	1961	—	£15.00
25	Histoire De L'Aviation, Première Série	1961	—	£3.00
25	Histoire De L'Aviation, Seconde Série	1962	—	£20.00
25	Historical Buildings	1959	—	£17.50
M25/50	History of Aviation	1952	—	£4.00
M50	History of Aviation	1952	—	£40.00
25	Holiday Resorts	1957	—	£2.50
25	Interesting Hobbies	1959	—	£7.50
25	Into Space	1959	—	£6.00
25	Kings of England	1954	£1.30	£32.50
25	Les Autos Modernes (French Text)	1961	—	£8.50
25	Medals of the World	1959	—	£5.00
25	Merchant Ships of the World	1961	—	£10.00
25	Merveilles Modernes (French Text)	1961	—	£7.50
25	Miniature Cars & Scooters	1958	—	£22.50
25	Naval Battles	1959	—	£7.00
25	Ports of the World	1959	—	£2.50
25	Propelled Weapons	1953	—	£3.00
25	Ships of the Royal Navy	1961	—	£7.50
25	Sports and Games	1958	—	£24.00
25	The Wild West	1960	—	£20.00
25	Tropical Birds	1958	—	£20.00
25	Weapons of Defence	1961	—	£15.00
25	Wild Animals	1958	—	£5.00
25	World Locomotives	1959	—	£13.50

THE ANGLO-AMERICAN CIGARETTE MAKING CO. LTD.

20	Russo-Japanese War Series	1904	*£200.00*	—

ANGLO CIGARETTE MANUFACTURING CO. LTD.

36	Tariff Reform Series	1909	£24.00	—

ANONYMOUS ISSUES — TOBACCO

PRINTED BACKS

40	Beauties "KEWA" ("England Expects"Back)	1899	*£90.00*	—
41	V.C. Heroes	1916	£6.50	£265.00
50	War Portraits	1915	£20.00	—

ANONYMOUS ISSUES — TOBACCO — cont.

Qty		*Date*	*Odds*	*Sets*
PLAIN BACKS				
25	Actors & Actresses "FROGA"-C	1900	£8.50	—
?25	Actresses "ANGLO"	1896	*£50.00*	—
?20	Actresses "ANGOOD" (Brown Front)	1898	£30.00	—
?20	(Grey Front)	1898	£18.00	—
20	Actresses "BLARM"	1900	£7.50	£150.00
?50	Actresses "DAVAN"	1902	*£25.00*	—
26	Actresses "FROGA A" (Brown)	1900	£8.00	£200.00
26	(Coloured)	1900	£8.50	—
?25	Actresses "HAGG"	1900	£7.50	—
25	Beauties "BOCCA"	1900	£12.00	—
50	Beauties "CHOAB" (Brown)	1902	£8.00	—
50	(Coloured)	1902	£8.50	—
50	Beauties "FECKSA"	1903	£7.50	—
20	Beauties "FENA"	1899	£40.00	—
25	Beauties "GRACC"	1898	£12.00	£300.00
26	Beauties "HOL"	1900	£8.50	—
20	Beauties "PLUMS"	1898	£35.00	—
25	Boer War & General Interest	1901	£20.00	—
20	Boer War Cartoons	1900	£11.50	—
20	Boer War Generals "CLAM"	1901	£10.00	—
12	Boer War Generals "FLAC"	1901	£11.50	—
25	Boxer Rebellion-Sketches	1904	£8.50	—
M108	British Naval Crests	1916	£3.00	—
16	British Royal Family	1902	£7.50	—
F?12	Celebrities of the Great War	1915	£14.00	—
50	Colonial Troops	1902	£6.50	—
M108	Crests & Badges of the British Army	1916	£2.50	—
20	Cricketers Series	1902	*£200.00*	—
50	Dogs (as Taddy)	1900	*£22.50*	—
30	Flags & Flags with Soldiers (Draped)	1902	£5.50	£165.00
15	Flags & Flags with Soldiers (Undraped)	1902	£6.50	—
24	Flags Arms & Types of Nations	1904	£5.00	£120.00
40	Home & Colonial Regiments	1900	£6.50	—
2	King Edward & Queen Alexandra	1902	£16.50	£33.00
1	Lord Kitchener	1915	—	£16.00
40	Naval & Military Phrases	1904	£7.00	—
F30	Photographs (Animal Studies)	1935	£1.50	—
?50	Pretty Girl Series "BAGG"	1898	£13.50	—
12	Pretty Girl Series "RASH"	1899	£11.50	—
30	Proverbs	1901	£8.50	—
19	Russo Japanese Series	1904	£13.50	—
20	Russo Japanese War Series	1904	£17.00	—
25	Star Girls	1900	£7.50	—
20	The European War Series	1915	£5.50	£110.00
25	Types of British & Colonial Troops	1900	£16.50	—
25	Types of British Soldiers	1914	£6.50	£162.50

E. & W. ANSTIE

24 Page Reference Book (with Abdulla & Adkin) — £3.50

25	Aesop's Fables	1934	£2.00	£50.00
16	British Empire Series	1904	£9.00	£144.00
10	Clifton Suspension Bridge (Sect.)	1938	£2.50	£25.00

E. & W. ANSTIE — cont.

Qty		*Date*	*Odds*	*Sets*
M40	Flags (Silk)	1915	£1.30	—
X10	Flags (Silk)	1915	£10.00	—
40	Nature Notes	1939	£6.00	—
50	People of Africa	1926	£2.70	£135.00
50	People of Asia	1926	£2.70	£135.00
50	People of Europe	1925	£2.60	£130.00
40	Places of Interest (Matt Front)	1939	£2.00	—
40	(Varnished Front)	1939	80p	£32.00
8	Puzzle Series	1900	£120.00	—
25	Racing Series (1-25)	1922	£3.30	£82.50
25	Racing Series (26-50)	1922	£5.20	£130.00
60/86	Regimental Badges (Silk)	1915	£1.25	—
M5	Royal Mail Series	1900	*£220.00*	—
X5	Royal Standard & Portraits (Silk)	1915	£13.50	—
2	Royal Portraits (Silk)	1915	£40.00	—
50	Scout Series	1923	£2.40	£120.00
10	Stonehenge (Sect.)	1936	£2.50	£25.00
10	The Victory (Sect.)	1936	£2.50	£25.00
50	The World's Wonders	1924	£1.30	£65.00
20	Wells Cathedral (Sect.)	1935	£1.80	£36.00
40	Wessex	1938	£1.25	£50.00
20	Wiltshire Downs (Sect.)	1935	£1.80	£36.00
10	Windsor Castle (Sect.)	1937	£2.50	£25.00

HENRY ARCHER & CO.

51	Actresses "FROGA" (Golden Returns Back)	1900	*£55.00*	—
51	(M.F.H. Back)	1900	£50.00	—
50	Beauties "CHOAB" (Brown)	1900	£25.00	£1250.00
25	Beauties "CHOAB" (Coloured, Golden Returns)	1900	*£65.00*	—
25	(Coloured, M.F.H.)	1900	*£65.00*	—
20	Prince of Wales Series	1912	£24.00	—

ARDATH TOBACCO CO. LTD.

28 Page Reference Book — £3.50

50	Animals at the Zoo (Descriptive Back)	1924	£2.00	—
50	(Double Ace Back)	1924	£12.50	—
F54	Beautiful English Women	1930	£2.75	—
25	Big Game Hunting (Descriptive Back)	1930	£3.00	—
25	(Double Ace Back)	1930	*£11.00*	—
L30	Boucher Series	1915	£2.50	£75.00
50	Britain's Defenders	1936	65p	£32.50
50	British Born Film Stars	1934	£1.30	£65.00
M50	British Born Film Stars	1934	£2.40	—
X1	Calendar 1942	1941	—	£2.50
X1	Calendar 1942-3	1942	—	£2.50
X1	Calendar 1943	1942	—	*£7.50*
X1	Calendar 1943-4	1943	—	£1.75
X1	Calendar 1944	1943	—	£1.75
MF36	Camera Studies	1939	£1.00	£36.00
LF45	Camera Studies	1939	80p	£36.00
L8	Christmas Greeting Cards (Folders)	1943	£2.00	£16.00
X25	Champion Dogs	1934	£1.20	£30.00
X100	Contract Bridge Contest Hands	1930	*£16.50*	—

Qty		Date	Odds	Sets
50	Cricket, Tennis & Golf Celebrities (Brown, N.Z. Issue)	1935	£2.00	£100.00
50	(Grey, G.B. Issue)...	1935	£1.25	£62.50
X25	Dog Studies (State Express etc.)	1938	£3.50	£87.50
X25	(Firm's Name Only, N.Z.)	1938	*£9.00*	—
25	Eastern Proverbs	1932	£1.40	£35.00
48	Empire Flying-Boat (Sect.)	1938	£1.50	£72.00
50	Empire Personalities	1937	60p	£30.00
50	Famous Film Stars	1934	75p	£37.50
50	Famous Footballers	1934	£1.25	£62.50
25	Famous Scots	1935	£1.00	£25.00
X25	Fighting & Civil Aircraft	1936	£1.80	£45.00
50	Figures of Speech	1936	65p	£32.50
50	Film, Stage and Radio Stars	1935	90p	£45.00
X25	Film, Stage & Radio Stars (Different)	1935	£1.00	£25.00
PF?	Film Stars (State Express)	1938	*£25.00*	—
PF?	Film Stars (Straight Cut)	1938	*£25.00*	—
M50	Flags 4th Series (Silk)	1914	*£37.50*	—
M50	Flags 5th Series (Silk)	1914	*£37.50*	—
M25	Flags 6th Series (Silk)	1914	*£45.00*	—
L40	Franz Hals Series (No Overprint)	1916	£12.50	£500.00
L40	(2.5 Cents Overprint)	1916	*£15.00*	—
X50	From Screen and Stage	1936	80p	£40.00
L30	Gainsborough Series (Multi-Backed)	1915	£2.50	£75.00
L30	Girls of All Nations	1916	£15.00	—
50	Great War Series	1916	£4.50	—
50	Great War Series "B"	1916	£5.00	—
50	Great War Series "C"	1916	£5.50	—
35	Hand Shadows	1930	*£20.00*	—
X25	Historic Grand Slams	1936	*£22.50*	—
L25	Hollandsche Oude Meesters (4 Backs)	1916	£13.00	—
L25	Hollandsche Oude Meesters (26-50)	1916	£13.00	—
X48	How to Recognise the Service Ranks	1940	£3.50	—
X2	Industrial Propaganda Cards (Black)	1943	£4.00	—
X4	Industrial Propaganda Cards (Coloured)	1943	£5.00	—
X11	Industrial Propaganda Cards (White)	1943	£4.00	—
X150	Information Slips	1940	£2.25	—
L24/25	It all depends on ME	1940	£1.25	£30.00
50	Life in the Services (Adhesive)	1938	70p	£35.00
50	(Non-adhesive N.Z.)	1938	£1.20	£60.00
96	Modern School Atlas	1936	£1.25	£120.00
50	National Fitness (Adhesive)	1938	50p	£25.00
50	(Non-adhesive N.Z.)	1938	80p	£40.00
50	New Zealand Views	1928	£2.00	£100.00
L1	On the Kitchen Front	1942	—	£2.25
50	Our Empire	1937	£1.20	£60.00
LF110	Photocards "A" (Lancs. Football Teams)	1936	£1.20	£132.00
LF110	Photocards "B" (N.E. Football Teams)	1936	£1.20	£132.00
LF110	Photocards "C" (Yorks. Football Teams)	1936	£1.10	£121.00
LF165	Photocards "D" (Scots. Football Teams)	1936	90p	£150.00
LF110	Photocards "E" (Midland Football Teams)	1936	£1.20	£132.00
LF110	Photocards "F" (Southern Football Teams)	1936	90p	£99.00
LF99	Photocards "Z" (Sport & General Interest)	1936	50p	£50.00
LF11	Photocards "Supplementary"	1936	£3.20	£35.00
LF22	Photocards Group "A" (Sports)	1937	75p	£16.50
LF21/22	Photocards Group "B" (Coronation, Sports)	1937	60p	£12.50

ARDATH TOBACCO CO. LTD. — cont.

Qty		Date	Odds	Sets
LF21/22	Photocards Group "C" (Lancs. Celebrities)	1937	90p	£19.00
LF22	Photocards Group "D" (Irish Celebrities)	1937	£1.00	£22.00
LF22	Photocards Group "E" (Films, Sports)	1938	80p	£18.00
LF22	Photocards Group "F" (Films, Sports)	1938	80p	£18.00
LF11	Photocards Group "G" (Cricketers)	1938	£16.50	—
LF66	Photocards Group "GS" (Various)	1938	£2.25	—
LF22	Photocards Group "H" (Films, Sports)	1938	80p	£18.00
LF22	Photocards Group "I" (Films, Various)	1938	£1.00	£22.00
LF22	Photocards Group "J" (Films, Various)	1939	75p	£16.50
LF22	Photocards Group "K" ("KINGS" Clause)	1939	80p	£18.00
LF22	(No Clause)	1939	£1.25	—
LF44	Photocards Group "L" (Various)	1939	50p	£22.00
F45	Photocards Group "M" (Films, Various)	1939	80p	£36.00
LF45	Photocards Group "M" ("KINGS" Clause)	1939	80p	£36.00
LF45	(No Clause)	1939	70p	£31.50
F45	Photocards Group "N" (Films)	1939	80p	£36.00
LF45	Photocards Group "N" (Films)	1939	60p	£27.00
LF66	Photocards Views of the World	1938	80p	£55.00
25	Proverbs (1-25)	1936	80p	£20.00
25	Proverbs (26-50)	1936	£2.00	—
L30	Raphael Series	1916	£2.60	£78.00
LF45	Real Photographs Group "O" (Films)	1939	50p	£22.50
F45	Real Photographs 1st Series	1939	90p	£40.00
XF18	Real Photographs 1st Series (Views)	1937	£2.25	£40.50
F54	Real Photographs 2nd Series	1939	90p	£48.00
XF18	Real Photographs 2nd Series	1937	£2.25	£40.50
XF18	Real Photographs 3rd Series (Views)	1937	£2.25	£40.50
XF18	Real Photographs 4th Series	1938	£2.25	£40.50
XF18	Real Photographs 5th Series (Views)	1938	£2.25	£40.50
XF18	Real Photographs 6th Series	1938	£2.25	£40.50
LF44	Real Photographs Series 1-GP1	1939	80p	£35.00
LF44	Real Photographs Series 2-GP2	1939	30p	£13.50
LF44	Real Photographs Series 3-GP3	1939	£2.50	—
LF44	Real Photographs Series 3-CV3 (Views)	1939	70p	£30.00
LF44	Real Photographs Series 4-CV4 (Views)	1939	30p	£13.50
XF36	Real Photographs Series 7	1938	65p	£22.50
XF54	Real Photographs Series 8	1938	50p	£27.00
LF54	Real Photographs Series 9	1938	50p	£27.00
XF54	Real Photographs Series 9	1938	50p	£27.00
LF54	Real Photographs Series 10	1939	50p	£27.00
XF54	Real Photographs Series 10	1939	50p	£27.00
LF54	Real Photographs Series 11	1939	50p	£27.00
XF54	Real Photographs Series 11	1939	75p	£40.50
LF54	Real Photographs Series 12	1939	50p	£27.00
LF54	Real Photographs Series 13	1939	50p	£27.00
LF36	Real Photographs of Famous Landmarks	1939	£2.75	—
XF36	Real Photographs of Famous Landmarks	1939	£1.25	£45.00
LF36	Real Photographs of Modern Aircraft	1939	£3.50	—
XF36	Real Photographs of Modern Aircraft	1939	£2.50	£90.00
L30	Rembrandt Series	1914	£3.00	£90.00
L40	Ditto (Splendo Cigarettes)	1914	£15.00	£600.00
X30	Rembrandt Series	1914	£5.00	£150.00
L30	Rubens Series	1916	£2.60	£78.00
L30	Ditto ("N.Z." at Base)	1916	*£12.50*	—
L30	(Splendo Cigarettes)	1916	*£12.50*	—
L30	(Winfred Cigarettes)	1916	*£12.50*	—

ARDATH TOBACCO CO. LTD. — cont.

Qty		Date	Odds	Sets
100	Scenes from Big Films	1935	£1.60	—
M100	Scenes from Big Films	1935	£3.50	—
X20	Ships of the Royal Navy (Package)	1953	*£10.00*	—
50	Silver Jubilee	1935	65p	£32.50
50	Speed Land Sea & Air (State Express)	1935	£1.20	£60.00
50	("Ardath"-N.Z.)	1935	£1.60	£80.00
X25	Speed Land Sea & Air (Different)	1938	£1.00	£25.00
50	Sports Champions (Title In 1 Line)	1935	90p	£45.00
50	(Title In 2 Lines-N.Z.)	1935	£1.60	£80.00
6	Sportsmen (Double Ace)	1953	*£4.00*	—
50	Stamps Rare & Interesting	1939	£1.25	£62.50
50	Swimming Diving and Life-Saving	1937	£1.25	£62.50
50	Tennis	1938	£1.60	£80.00
L?	The Beauty of State Express (Circular)	1928	*£65.00*	—
9	The Office of Chief Whip	1955	£2.40	—
48	Trooping the Colour (Sect.)	1939	£1.75	£84.00
L?	Types of English Manhood (Circular)	1935	*£25.00*	—
M1	Union Jack Folder	1943	—	£5.00
L30	Velasquez Series	1916	£3.50	£105.00
X30	Velasquez Series	1916	£5.00	—
50	Who is this? (Film Stars)	1936	£1.80	£90.00
X?	Wonderful Handcraft	1935	*£20.00*	—
X24/25	World Views (2 Printings)	1937	30p	£7.50
50	Your Birthday Tells Your Fortune	1937	60p	£30.00

ASSOCIATED TOBACCO MANUFACTURERS

Qty		Date	Odds	Sets
25	Cinema Stars (5 Brands)	1926	*£20.00*	—

ATKINSON

Qty		Date	Odds	Sets
30	Army Pictures, Cartoons, etc	1916	*£85.00*	—

AVISS BROS. LTD.

Qty		Date	Odds	Sets
40	Naval & Military Phrases	1904	*£85.00*	—

J. A. BAILEY

Qty		Date	Odds	Sets
40	Naval & Military Phrases	1904	*£135.00*	—

A. BAKER & CO. LTD.

Qty		Date	Odds	Sets
25	Actresses, 3 Sizes	1901	£24.00	£600.00
L25	Actresses, 3 Sizes (Different)	1901	£37.50	—
P?25	Actresses, 3 Sizes (Different)	1901	*£175.00*	—
20	Actresses "BLARM" (Back Design 58mm Long)	1900	£25.00	—
20	(Back Design 64mm Long)	1900	£25.00	—
10	Actresses "HAGG"	1900	£24.00	£240.00

A. BAKER & CO. LTD. — cont.

Qty		Date	Odds	Sets
41	Baker's Tobacconists Shops			
	(Cigar etc. Manufacturers)	1901	£105.00	—
	(Try Our 3½d Tobaccos)	1901	*£160.00*	—
25	Beauties of All Nations (Albert Baker)	1898	£15.00	£375.00
25	(A. Baker)	1899	£10.00	£250.00
16	British Royal Family	1902	£45.00	—
20	Cricketers Series	1902	*£250.00*	—
25	Star Girls	1898	*£135.00*	—

BAYLEY AND HOLDSWORTH

Qty		Date	Odds	Sets
26	Flag Signalling Code Series	1912	£150.00	—

THOMAS BEAR & SONS LTD.

Qty		Date	Odds	Sets
50	Aeroplanes	1926	£3.50	—
50	Cinema Artistes, Set 2	1936	*£2.50*	—
50	Cinema Artistes, Set 4	1937	*£3.00*	—
50	Cinema Stars "BAMT" (2 printings)	1928	£1.75	—
50	Do You Know?	1923	£1.50	£75.00
270	Javanese Series (Blue)	1925	£1.10	£300.00
100	Javanese Series (Yellow)	1925	*£6.50*	—
50	Stage and Film Stars	1926	£3.25	—

E.C. BEESTON

Qty		Date	Odds	Sets
30	Army Pictures, Cartoons, etc	1916	*£100.00*	—

BELFAST SHIP STORES CO. LTD.

Qty		Date	Odds	Sets
?10	Dickens Characters Burlesqued	1893	*£225.00*	—

J. & F. BELL LTD

Qty		Date	Odds	Sets
10	Actresses "HAGG"	1900	£65.00	—
25	Beauties (Scotia Back)	1897	£90.00	—
25	(Three Bells Back)	1897	£90.00	—
25	Colonial Series	1901	£30.00	—
30	Footballers	1902	£47.50	—
60	Rigsvaabner	1925	£27.50	—
25	Scottish Clan Series	1903	£11.00	£300.00
60	Women of All Nations	1925	£27.50	—

R. BELLWOOD

Qty		Date	Odds	Sets
18	Motor Cycle Series	1913	*£85.00*	—

RICHARD BENSON LTD.

Qty		Date	Odds	Sets
L23/24	Old Bristol Series	1925	£2.50	£60.00
X24	Old Bristol Series (Re-Issue)	1946	£2.00	£48.00

BENSON & HEDGES LTD.

Qty		*Date*	*Odds*	*Sets*
1	Advertisement Card, Original Shop	1973	—	£2.00
48	Ancient & Modern Fire Fighting Equipment	1947	£5.00	£240.00
L10	B.E.A. Aircraft	1958	£7.50	—
X?25	"Oxford" University Series	1912	*£25.00*	—

FELIX S. BERLYN

25	Burline Mixture (Golfers Blend) Series	1910	*£300.00*	—
P25	Burline Mixture (Golfers Blend) Series	1910	*£400.00*	—

BERRY'S

20	London Views	1904	*£150.00*	—

BEWLAY & CO.

6	Comic Advertisement Cards (7 Backs)	1909	£175.00	—
P6	Comic Advertisement Cards	1909	£85.00	—
12	War Series (Portraits, Multi-Backed)	1915	£10.00	£120.00
12	(Portraits, Plain Backed)	1915	£10.00	—
25	War Series (Scenes, Multi-Backed)	1915	£11.00	£275.00

W. O. BIGG & CO.

37	Flags of All Nations (Horizontal Back)	1904	£7.00	—
37	(Vertical Back)	1904	£7.00	—
50	Life on Board a Man of War	1905	£9.00	£450.00

JAS BIGGS & SON

26	Actresses "FROGA A" (Brand In Black)	1900	*£50.00*	—
26	(Brand In White)	1900	£32.50	—
26	Actresses "FROGA B"	1900	£50.00	—
25	Beauties "BOCCA" (Black Back)	1900	£62.50	—
25	(Blue Back)	1900	*£65.00*	—
25	Beauties "CHOAB" (Blue Back)	1902	*£65.00*	—
50	(Black Overprint)	1902	*£60.00*	—
30	Colonial Troops	1901	£28.00	—
30	Flags & Flags with Soldiers	1903	£25.00	—
25	Star Girls	1900	*£140.00*	—

J. S. BILLINGHAM

30	Army Pictures, Cartoons, etc	1916	*£90.00*	—

R. BINNS

?15	Halifax Town Footballers	1924	£120.00	—

BLANKS CIGARETTES

50	Keystrokes in Break-building	1910	*£160.00*	—

BOCNAL TOBACCO CO.

Qty		Date	Odds	Sets
25	Luminous Silhouettes of Beauty & Charm	1938	£2.20	£55.00
25	Proverbs Up-to-Date	1938	£2.00	£50.00

ALEXANDER BOGUSLAVSKY LTD.

Qty		Date	Odds	Sets
P12	Big Events on the Turf	1924	£35.00	—
25	Conan Doyle Characters (Black Back)	1923	£6.50	£162.50
25	(Green Back)	1923	£6.00	£150.00
25	Mythological Gods and Goddesses	1924	£2.00	£50.00
25	Sports Records (1-25)	1925	£1.20	£30.00
25	Sports Records, 2nd Series (26-50)	1925	£1.20	£30.00
25	Winners on the Turf (Name no Serifs)	1925	£3.00	£75.00
25	(Name with Serifs)	1925	£4.50	—
L25	Winners on the Turf	1925	£5.00	£125.00

R. & E. BOYD LTD.

Qty		Date	Odds	Sets
25	Places of Interest	1938	*£40.00*	—
M25	Places of Interest	1938	*£40.00*	—
L25	Wild Birds at Home	1938	*£40.00*	—

WM. BRADFORD

Qty		Date	Odds	Sets
50	Beauties "CHOAB"	1902	£26.00	—
?25	Beauties, Jersey Lily	1900	*£200.00*	—
20	Boer War Cartoons	1901	*£90.00*	—

THOS. BRANKSTON & CO. LTD.

Qty		Date	Odds	Sets
30	Colonial Troops (Golf Club Mixture)	1901	£28.50	—
30	(Red Virginia)	1901	£27.50	—
30	(Sweet as the Rose)	1901	£27.50	—
12	Pretty Girl Series "RASH"	1900	*£160.00*	—

BRIGHAM & CO.

Qty		Date	Odds	Sets
L16	Down the Thames from Henley to Windsor	1912	£90.00	—
16	Reading Football Players	1912	*£140.00*	—
X3	Tobacco Growing in Hampshire, England	1928	£15.00	£45.00

BRITANNIA ANONYMOUS SOCIETY

Qty		Date	Odds	Sets
?29	Beauties & Couples	1914	*£70.00*	—

BRITISH & COLONIAL TOBACCO CO.

Qty		Date	Odds	Sets
25	Armies of the World	1900	*£115.00*	—

BRITISH FASCISTS CIGARETTES

Qty		Date	Odds	Sets
?3	Recruiting Cards	1935	*£50.00*	—

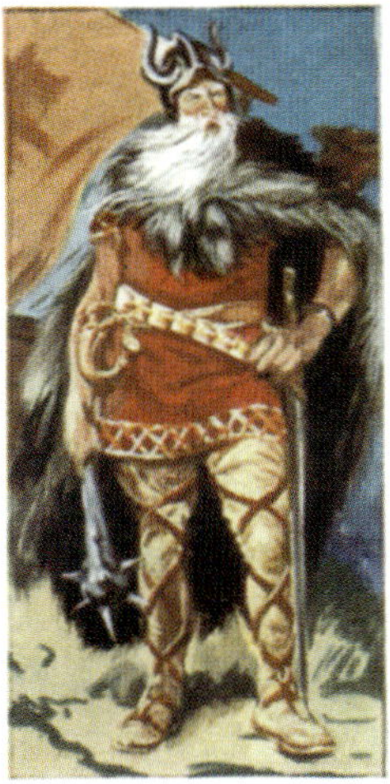

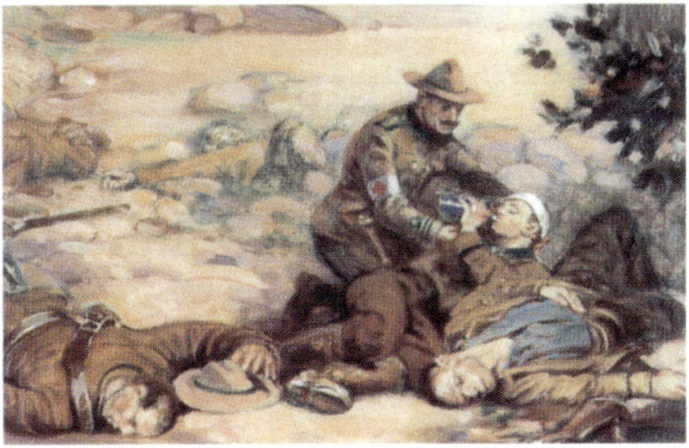

Centenary Year RAMC Victoria Crosses
RAMC Historical Museum

Warriors of the World
Reddings Tea

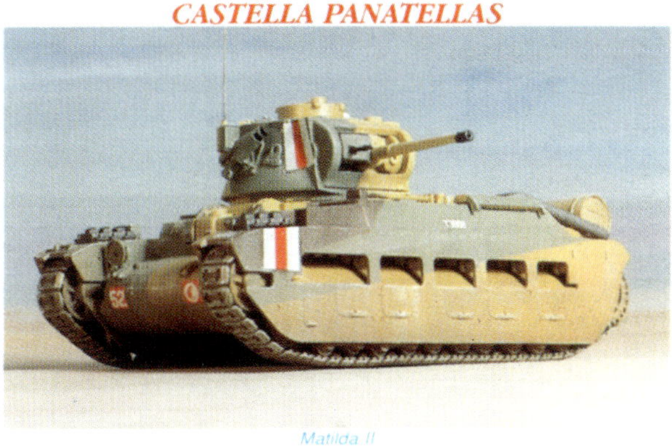

The Tank Story
Wills – Castella

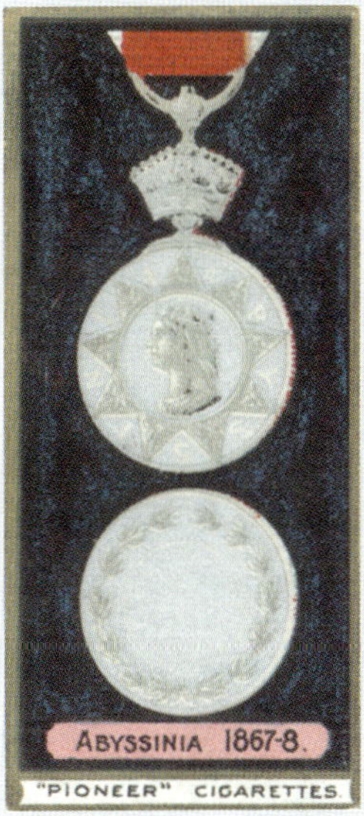

Medals
Richmond Cavendish
Also Hignett

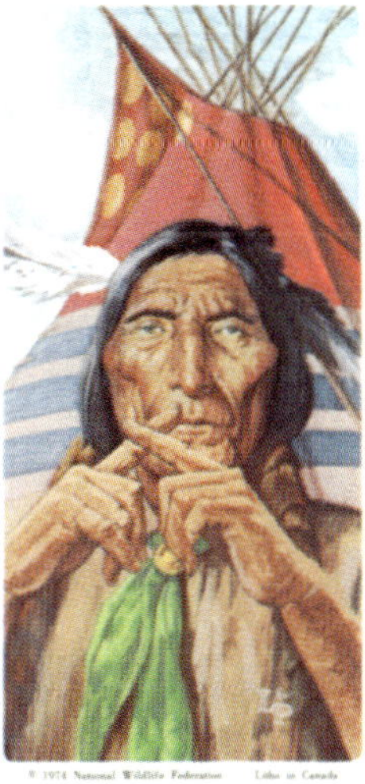

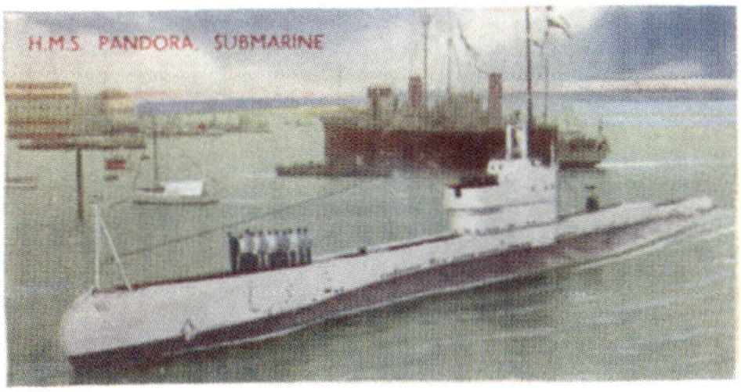

Our Navy
Carreras

Indians of Canada
Brooke Bond

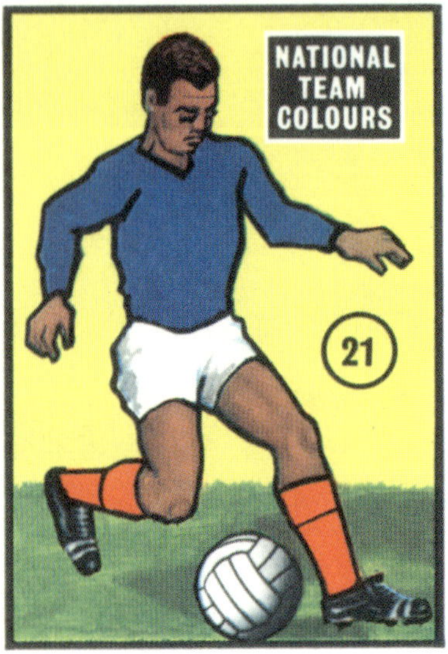

National Team Colours
Anglo Confectionery

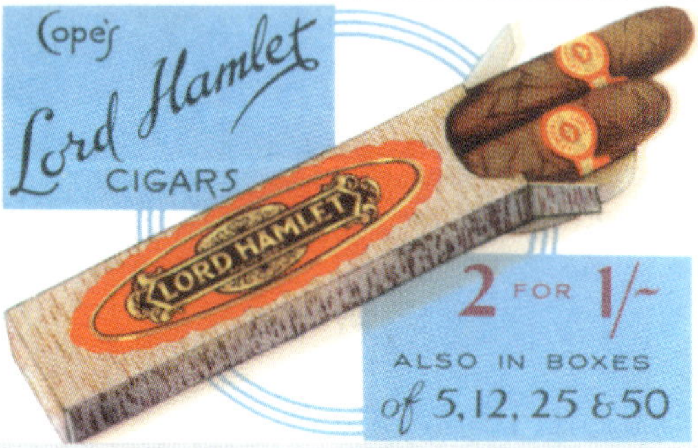

General Knowledge – Cope

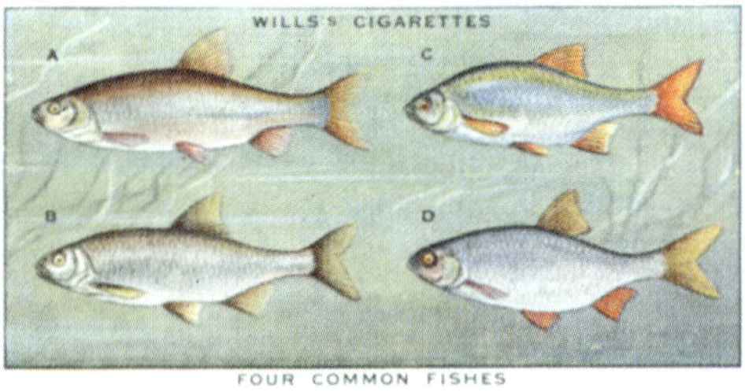

Pond & Aquarium
Wills

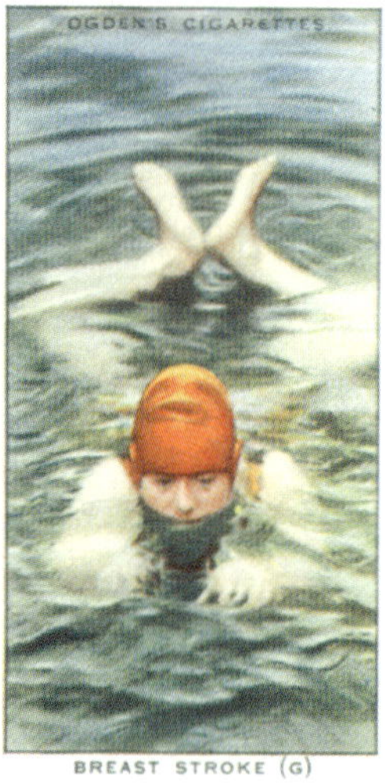

Swimming, Diving and Life-Saving
Ogdens. Also Ardath

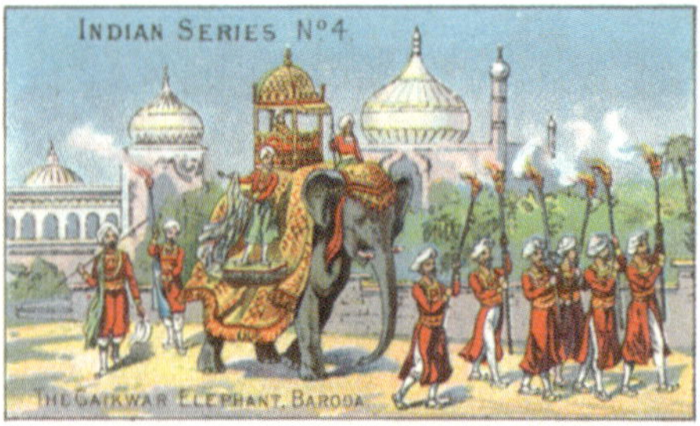

Indian Series
Godfrey Phillips

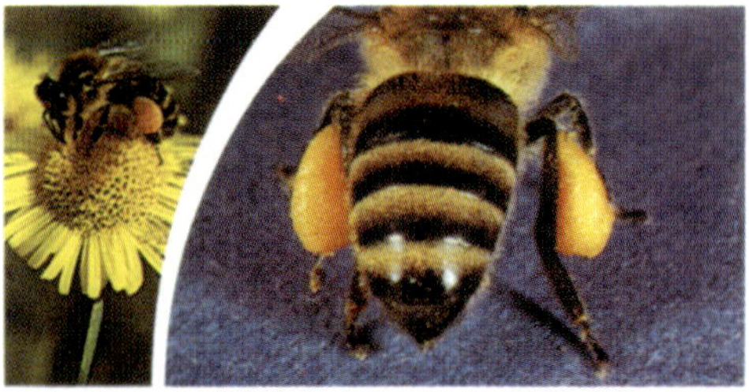

Small Wonders
Brooke Bond

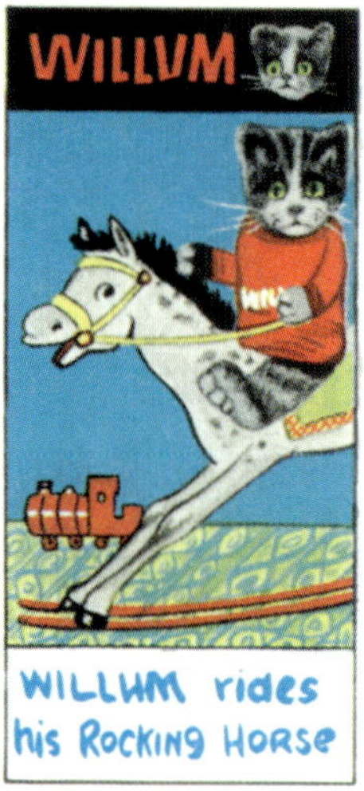

Willum – Barratt

J. M. BROWN

Qty		Date	Odds	Sets
30	Army Pictures, Cartoons, etc	1916	£75.00	—

JOHN BRUMFIT

Qty		Date	Odds	Sets
50	The Public Schools Ties Series	1925	£3.20	£160.00

BUCKTROUT & CO. LTD. (Channel Isles)

Qty		Date	Odds	Sets
M416	Around The World/Places of Interest	1924	50p	£210.00
24	Birds of England	1924	£2.75	£66.00
50	Cinema Stars, 1st	1926	£1.60	£80.00
50	Cinema Stars, Second Series	1927	£2.00	£100.00
M50	Football Teams	1928	£2.40	£120.00
L22	Football Teams of the Bailiwick	1927	75p	£16.50
123	Guernsey Footballers (Multi-Backed)	1923	£2.20	—
20	Inventors Series	1924	£1.00	£20.00
25	Marvels of the Universe Series	1919	£2.40	£60.00
M54	Playing Cards	1930	70p	£37.50
25	Sports & Pastimes	1926	£3.50	£100.00

G. A. BULLOGH

Qty		Date	Odds	Sets
30	Army Pictures, Cartoons, etc	1916	*£80.00*	—

BURSTEIN ISAACS & CO. LTD.

Qty		Date	Odds	Sets
50	Famous Prize Fighters (Names in Capitals)	1923	£5.00	—
50	(Mixed Lettering)	1923	£4.00	£225.00
F27/28	London View Series	1922	£3.25	£88.00

BYRT WOOD & CO.

Qty		Date	Odds	Sets
25	Pretty Girl Series "BAGG"	1900	£110.00	—

CABANA CIGAR CO.

Qty		Date	Odds	Sets
M1	Little Manturios Advertisement Card (2 Types)	1904	—	*£175.00*

PERCY E. CADLE & CO.

Qty		Date	Odds	Sets
20	Actresses "BLARM"	1900	£30.00	—
26	Actresses "FROGA" (Brown, Printed Back)	1900	£35.00	—
26	(Brown, Stamped Back)	1900	*£125.00*	—
26	Actresses "FROGA" (Coloured)	1900	*£45.00*	—
12	Boer War & Boxer Rebellion Sketches	1901	£42.00	—
10	Boer War Generals	1901	£62.50	—
20	Footballers	1904	£40.00	£800.00

CARRERAS LTD.

Qty		Date	Odds	Sets
F24	Actresses and their Pets (2 Printings)	1926	£4.00	£96.00
50	A Kodak at the Zoo, A Series	1924	55p	£27.50

CARRERAS LTD. — cont.

Qty		Date	Odds	Sets
50	A Kodak at the Zoo, 2nd Series	1925	55p	£27.50
48	Alice in Wonderland (Round Corners)	1930	£1.40	£67.50
48	(Square Corners)	1930	£2.75	£132.00
L48	Alice in Wonderland	1930	£1.75	£84.00
X1	Alice in Wonderland (Instructions)	1930	—	*£11.00*
50	Amusing Tricks & How To Do Them	1937	70p	£35.00
22	Battle of Waterloo	1934	£1.25	—
L15	Battle of Waterloo	1934	£2.25	—
M1	Battle of Waterloo (Instructions)	1934	—	*£10.00*
M50	Believe It Or Not	1934	50p	£25.00
50	Birds of the Countryside	1939	80p	£40.00
200	Black Cat Library	1913	£10.00	—
50	Britain's Defences	1938	60p	£30.00
25	British Costumes	1927	£1.10	£27.50
L25	British Costumes	1927	£1.20	£30.00
F27	British Prime Ministers	1928	£1.40	£38.00
1	Calendar	1934	—	£20.00
50	Celebrities of British History	1935	90p	£45.00
25	Christie Comedy Girls	1928	£1.60	£40.00
30	Cricketers	1934	£3.00	£90.00
50	Cricketers (A Series of 50, Brown)	1934	£3.00	£150.00
50	(A Series of 50, Black)	1934	*£34.00*	—
F50	Dogs & Friend	1936	25p	£12.50
50	Do You Know?	1939	20p	£10.00
50	Famous Airmen & Airwomen	1936	£1.40	£70.00
25	Famous Escapes	1926	£1.20	£30.00
L25	Famous Escapes	1926	£1.20	£30.00
P10	Famous Escapes	1926	£2.25	£22.50
96	Famous Film Stars	1935	£1.20	£116.00
48	Famous Footballers	1935	£1.20	£58.00
24	Ditto (25-48 Redrawn)	1935	£1.50	£36.00
25	Famous Men	1927	£1.20	£30.00
LF24	Famous Naval Men	1929	£1.10	£26.50
X6	Famous Posters (St. Dunstans)	1923	£20.00	—
LF12	Famous Soldiers	1928	£5.00	£60.00
F27	Famous Women	1929	£1.00	£27.00
25	Figures Of Fiction	1924	£1.60	£40.00
F54	Film & Stage Beauties	1939	40p	£21.50
LF54	Film and Stage Beauties (2 Printings)	1939	50p	£27.00
LF36	Film and Stage Beauties (2 Printings)	1939	80p	£28.50
XF36	Film and Stage Beauties	1939	£1.00	£36.00
50	Film Favourites	1938	£1.10	£55.00
F54	Film Stars, A Series	1937	75p	£40.00
F54	Film Stars, 2nd Series	1938	45p	£24.50
LF54	Film Stars (as 2nd Series)	1938	85p	£45.00
XF36	Film Stars (Different)	1936	£2.50	£90.00
XF36	Film Stars, Second Series (Different)	1936	£2.50	£90.00
XF36	Film Stars, Third Series	1937	£2.25	£81.00
XF36	Film Stars, Fourth Series	1938	£2.50	£90.00
50	Film Stars (by Desmond)	1936	80p	£40.00
72	Film Stars (Oval, Half-Tone)	1934	£1.25	£90.00
F72	(Oval, "Real Photos")	1934	£2.00	—
60	Flags of all Nations	Unissued	—	£27.50
28	Flag Dominoes (Unissued)	1926	£8.00	£225.00
K6	Flags & Arms (Circular)	1915	£50.00	—

Qty		Date	Odds	Sets
K7	Flags of the Allies (Shaped)	1915	£40.00	—
K?6	Flags of the Allies (Pin as Mast)	1915	£95.00	—
50	Flowers	1936	50p	£25.00
75	Footballers (Large Titles)	1934	£1.50	£112.50
75	(Small Titles)	1934	£1.50	£112.50
36	Fortune Telling (Card Inset)	1926	25p	£9.00
36	(Head Inset, Black No.)	1926	25p	£9.00
36	(Head Inset, Brown No.)	1926	70p	—
L36	Fortune Telling (Card Inset)	1926	25p	£9.00
L36	(Head Inset)	1926	30p	£10.50
X1	Fortune Telling (Instructions)	1926	—	£10.00
F54	Glamour Girls of Stage and Films	1939	50p	£27.00
LF54	Glamour Girls of Stage and Films	1939	50p	£27.00
LF36	Glamour Girls of Stage and Films	1939	£1.10	£40.00
XF36	Glamour Girls of Stage and Films	1939	£1.25	£45.00
M50	Gran-Pop	1934	40p	£20.00
L50	Gran-Pop	1934	30p	£15.00
M16	Guards Series (Sectional)	1970	50p	£8.00
M8	Guards Series (Full Length)	1970	65p	£5.00
M4	Guards Series (Mugs)	1971	75p	£3.00
48	Happy Family	1925	25p	£12.00
L48	Happy Family	1925	25p	£12.00
25	Highwaymen	1924	£2.00	£50.00
50	History of Army Uniforms	1937	£1.00	£50.00
50	History of Naval Uniforms	1937	90p	£45.00
25	Horses and Hounds	1926	£1.60	£40.00
L20	Horses and Hounds	1926	£1.70	£34.00
P10	Horses and Hounds	1926	£3.20	£32.00
50	Kings & Queens of England	1935	£1.40	£70.00
L50	Kings & Queens of England	1935	£2.20	£110.00
L?84	Lace Motifs	1915	£6.25	—
P?12	Lace Motifs (Double Size)	1915	£30.00	—
G?6	Lace Motifs (Quadruple Size)	1915	*£50.00*	—
F27	Malayan Industries	1929	75p	£20.00
F24	Malayan Scenes	1928	£2.00	—
LF24	Malayan Scenes	1928	65p	£15.00
7	Millionaire Competition	1971	£1.60	—
K53	Miniature Playing Cards	1934	20p	£8.50
50	Notable M.P.s	1929	90p	£45.00
L50	Notable M.P.s	1929	45p	£25.00
F25	Notable Ships Past & Present	1929	£1.10	£27.50
24	Old Staffordshire Figures	1926	£1.00	£24.00
P12	Old Staffordshire Figures	1926	£2.25	£27.00
L24	Old Staffordshire Figures (Different)	1926	£1.25	£30.00
24	Orchids	1925	£1.25	£30.00
L24	Orchids	1925	£1.10	£26.50
P24	Orchids	1925	£3.00	£72.00
50	Our Navy	1937	90p	£45.00
50	Palmistry	1933	35p	£17.50
F27	Paramount Stars	1929	£1.20	£32.50
25	Picture Puzzle Series	1923	£1.20	£30.00
52	Playing Cards	1926	£1.10	—
52	Playing Cards & Dominoes (Numbered)	1929	20p	£7.50
52	(Unnumbered)	1929	20p	£9.50

CARRERAS LTD. — cont.

Qty		Date	Odds	Sets
L26	Playing Cards & Dominoes (Numbered)	1929	25p	£6.50
L26	(Unnumbered)	1929	30p	£8.00
48	Popular Footballers	1936	£1.00	£48.00
72	Popular Personalities (Oval)	1935	75p	£54.00
10	Irish Subjects (1-10)	1935	£16.00	—
E12	Premium Silks (Assorted Subjects)	1914	£160.00	—
25	Races-Historic & Modern	1927	£2.00	£50.00
L25	Races-Historic & Modern	1927	£2.00	£50.00
P12	Races-Historic & Modern	1927	£4.00	£48.00
50	Radio & T.V. Favourites	Unissued	£7.50	£375.00
140	Raemaekers War Cartoons (Black Cat)	1916	85p	£120.00
140	(Carreras)	1916	£3.50	—
25	Regalia Series	1925	40p	£10.00
L20	Regalia Series	1925	50p	£10.00
P10	Regalia Series	1925	£1.75	£17.50
L50	Round the World Scenic Models	1925	65p	£32.50
50	School Emblems	1929	80p	£40.00
L40	School Emblems	1929	70p	£28.00
P20	School Emblems	1929	£2.00	£40.00
L216	Sportsman's Guide-Fly Fishing (Canada)	1950	90p	—
48	Tapestry Reproductions of Paintings (Sect.)	1938	50p	£24.00
52	The Greyhound Racing Game	1926	20p	£10.00
L52	The Greyhound Racing Game	1926	20p	£10.00
X1	The Greyhound Racing Game (Instructions)	1926	—	£10.00
M5	The Handy English-French Dictionary	1915	£18.00	—
50	The Nose Game	1927	30p	£15.00
L50	The Nose Game	1927	30p	£15.00
X1	The Nose Game (Instructions)	1927	—	£11.00
50	The Science of Boxing (Black Cat)	1914	£2.20	£110.00
50	(Carreras)	1914	£3.25	—
50	Tools and How to use Them	1935	80p	£40.00
80	Types of London	1919	£1.20	£96.00
F27	Views of London	1929	30p	£8.00
F27	Views of the World	1927	65p	£17.50
M15/20	Wild Animals (Canada)	1985	30p	£4.50
25	Wild Flower Art Series	1923	£1.00	£25.00
50	Women on War Work	1916	£5.50	£275.00

TURF SLIDES (Cut to Size)

Qty		Date	Odds	Sets
50	British Aircraft	1953	45p	£22.50
50	British Fish	1954	20p	£10.00
50	British Railway Locomotives	1952	60p	£30.00
50	Celebrities of British History	1951	60p	£30.00
50	Famous British Fliers	1956	£1.50	£75.00
50	Famous Cricketers	1950	£2.20	£110.00
50	Famous Dog Breeds	1952	75p	£37.50
50	Famous Film Stars	1949	£1.00	£50.00
50	Famous Footballers	1951	£1.50	£75.00
50	Film Favourites	1948	£1.50	£75.00
50	Film Stars	1947	£1.00	£50.00
50	Footballers	1948	£1.60	£80.00
50	Olympics 1948	1948	£1.60	£80.00
50	Radio Celebrities	1950	55p	£27.50
50	Sports	1949	£1.10	£55.00
50	Zoo Animals	1954	20p	£10.00

CARRERAS LTD. — cont.

Qty		Date	Odds	Sets
"BLACK CAT" MODERN ISSUES				
50	British Birds	1976	15p	£4.00
50	Flowers all the Year Round	1977	20p	£10.00
50	Kings & Queens of England	1977	20p	£10.00
50	Military Uniforms	1976	15p	£4.50
50	Palmistry	1979	£1.00	£50.00
50	Sport Fish	1978	15p	£4.00
50	Vintage Cars (With "Filter")	1976	15p	£6.00
50	(Without "Filter")	1976	15p	£4.50
AUSTRALIAN ISSUES				
72	Film Stars Series (Smile Away)	1933	£2.20	—
72	(Standard)	1933	£1.10	£80.00
72	Football Series	1933	£1.10	£80.00
24	Personality Series	1933	£1.40	£33.50
72	Personality Series, Film Stars	1933	£1.00	£72.00
72	Personality Series, Footballers	1933	£1.10	£80.00

CARRERAS & MARCIANUS

Qty		Date	Odds	Sets
1	Photo Miniatures Folder (3 Printings)	1909	—	*£75.00*
100	War Series	1915	£60.00	—

CARRICK

Qty		Date	Odds	Sets
12	Military Terms	1900	£55.00	£660.00

P. J. CARROLL & CO.

Qty		Date	Odds	Sets
25	Birds	1939	70p	£17.50
25	British Naval Series	1915	£36.00	—
25	Derby Winners (Black Back)	1914	*£75.00*	—
25	(Green Back)	1914	*£80.00*	—
K26	Grand Slam Spelling Bee Cards	1936	*£8.00*	—
24	Jig Saw Puzzles	1935	£17.50	—
20	Louth All-Ireland Champions	1912	£24.00	—
25	Ship Series	1934	£6.00	£150.00

THE CASKET TOBACCO & CIGARETTE CO. LTD.

Qty		Date	Odds	Sets
?	Cricket Fixture Cards	1905	*£250.00*	—
1	Cyclists Lighting Up Table	1909	—	*£200.00*
?	Football Fixture Cards	1909	*£200.00*	—
?	Road Maps	1909	*£200.00*	—

S. CAVANDER & CO.

Qty		Date	Odds	Sets
?25	Beauties "PLUMS"	1898	*£200.00*	—

CAVANDERS LTD.

Qty		Date	Odds	Sets
25	Ancient Chinese	1926	£1.00	£25.00
25	Ancient Egypt	1928	£1.20	£30.00

CAVANDERS LTD. — cont.

Qty		Date	Odds	Sets
L25	Ancient Egypt (Different)	1928	£1.20	£30.00
F36	Animal Studies	1936	30p	£11.00
F50	Beauty Spots of Great Britain	1927	20p	£10.00
MF50	Beauty Spots of Great Britain	1927	20p	£10.00
F54	Camera Studies	1926	20p	£7.50
MF56	Camera Studies	1926	20p	£10.00
30	Cinema Stars	1934	£1.10	£33.00
MS50	Coloured Stereoscopic	1931	45p	£22.50
25	Feathered Friends	1926	£2.00	£50.00
25	Foreign Birds (Same Subjects As Above)	1926	£1.20	£30.00
MS50	Glorious Britain	1930	40p	£20.00
25	Little Friends	1924	90p	£22.50
FS72	Peeps into Many Lands, A Series	1927	30p	£22.00
MFS72	Peeps into Many Lands, A Series	1927	65p	£46.50
XFS36	Peeps into Many Lands, A Series	1927	£1.80	£65.00
FS72	Peeps into Many Lands, 2nd Series	1928	60p	£43.00
MFS72	Peeps into Many Lands, 2nd Series	1928	65p	£46.50
FS48	Peeps into Many Lands, 3rd Series	1929	30p	£14.50
MFS48	Peeps into Many Lands, 3rd Series	1929	90p	£45.00
MFS48	Ditto (Reprinted)	1929	£1.10	£52.50
FS48	Peeps into Prehistoric Times, 4th Series	1930	40p	£20.00
MFS48	Peeps into Prehistoric Times, 4th Series	1930	80p	£40.00
F33	Photographs	1935	£1.40	—
L48	Regimental Standards	1923	£10.00	—
25	Reproductions of Celebrated Oil Paintings	1925	80p	£20.00
F108	River Valleys	1926	25p	£25.00
MF108	River Valleys	1926	30p	£31.50
25	School Badges (Dark Blue Back)	1928	£1.00	£25.00
25	(Light Blue Back)	1928	£1.00	£25.00
MF30	The Colonial Series (Large Captions)	1925	40p	£12.00
MF30	(Small Captions)	1925	30p	£9.00
F54	The Homeland Series (Black Back)	1924	20p	£12.50
F50	(Blue Back)	1924	85p	£42.50
MF50	The Homeland Series "Hand Coloured"	1924	20p	£8.50
MF56	"Real Photos"	1924	30p	£17.00
MF56	Uncoloured	1924	30p	£17.00
MF56	"Reprinted"	1925	30p	£17.50
M25	The Nation's Treasures	1925	40p	£10.00
MF30	Wordsworth's Country	1926	60p	£18.00

R. S. CHALLIS & CO. LTD.

Qty		Date	Odds	Sets
50	Comic Animals	1936	60p	£30.00
?42	Flickits (Fresher Cigarettes)	1936	£32.50	—
36	Wild Birds at Home (Baldric Cigarettes)	1935	60p	£22.00
36	(Baldric Deleted)	1935	£1.25	—

H. CHAPMAN & CO.

Qty		Date	Odds	Sets
30	Army Pictures, Cartoons, etc	1916	*£175.00*	—

CHARLESWORTH & AUSTIN

Qty		Date	Odds	Sets
50	Beauties "BOCCA"	1900	£25.00	£1250.00
16	British Royal Family	1902	£40.00	—

CHARLESWORTH & AUSTIN — cont.

Qty		Date	Odds	Sets
50	Colonial Troops (Black Back)	1901	£30.00	—
30	(Brown Back)	1901	£27.50	—
20	Cricketers Series	1902	£250.00	—
30	Flags & Flags with Soldiers	1903	£27.50	—

CHESTERFIELD CIGARETTES

M6	Chesterfield Cocktails	1980	40p	£2.50

A. CHEW & CO.

30	Army Pictures, Cartoons, etc	1916	*£100.00*	—

CHING & CO. (Channel Isles)

L24	Around & About in Jersey, 1st Series	1963	30p	£7.50
L24	Around & About in Jersey, 2nd Series	1964	55p	£13.50
25	Do You Know?	1962	—	£2.25
M48	Flowers	1962	80p	£38.50
L24	Jersey Past & Present, A Series	1960	—	£5.00
L24	Jersey Past & Present, Second Series	1962	—	£9.00
L24	Jersey Past & Present, Third Series	1963	—	£5.00
25	Ships and their Workings	1961	—	£2.25
50	Veteran and Vintage Cars	1960	35p	£17.50

W. A. & A. C. CHURCHMAN

36 Page Reference Book — £3.50

24	Actresses, Unicoloured (Blue Printing)	1897	£60.00	—
24	(Brown Printing)	1897	£60.00	—
26	Actresses, "FROGA A"	1900	£27.50	—
26	Actresses, "FROGA B"	1900	£36.50	—
M48	Air-Raid Precautions	1938	25p	£12.00
25	Army Badges of Rank	1916	£4.00	£100.00
50	Association Footballers, A Series	1938	70p	£35.00
50	Association Footballers, 2nd Series	1939	90p	£45.00
50	A Tour Round the World	1911	£5.50	£275.00
12	Beauties "CERF"	1899	£50.00	£600.00
25	Beauties "CHOAB"	1900	£100.00	—
M?25	Beauties "CHOAB" (Circular)	1900	*£350.00*	—
25	Beauties "FECKSA"	1903	£75.00	—
25	Beauties "GRACC"	1898	£75.00	—
50	Birds & Eggs	1906	£5.50	£275.00
20	Boer War Cartoons	1901	£90.00	—
41	Boer War Celebrities & Actresses	1901	£16.00	£650.00
20	Boer War Generals "CLAM" (Black)	1901	£34.00	—
20	(Brown)	1901	£32.50	£650.00
25	Boxing	1922	£4.50	£112.50
50	Boxing Personalities	1938	£1.60	£100.00
50	Boy Scouts, A Series	1916	£6.00	£300.00
50	Boy Scouts, 2nd Series	1916	£6.00	£300.00
50	Boy Scouts, 3rd Series (Blue Back)	1916	£9.00	—
50	(Brown Back)	1916	£6.00	£300.00

Qty		Date	Odds	Sets
25	British Film Stars	1934	£1.60	£40.00
54/55	Can You Beat Bogey at St. Andrews?	1934	£2.00	£180.00
54/55	Ditto (Red Overprint)	1934	£2.20	£200.00
25	Cathedrals & Churches	1924	£1.70	£42.50
X12	Cathedrals & Churches	1924	£9.00	£108.00
50	Celebrated Gateways	1925	£1.80	£90.00
M1	Christmas Greeting Card	1938	—	£1.40
25	Civic Insignia and Plate	1926	£1.70	£42.50
50	Contract Bridge	1935	50p	£25.00
50	Cricketers	1936	£3.00	£150.00
25	Curious Dwellings	1926	£1.60	£40.00
L12	Curious Dwellings	1926	£4.00	£48.00
25	Curious Signs	1925	£1.80	£45.00
38	Dogs and Fowls	1908	£6.00	£228.00
25	Eastern Proverbs, A Series	1931	60p	£15.00
L12	Eastern Proverbs, A Series	1931	£3.25	£39.00
25	Eastern Proverbs, 2nd Series	1932	70p	£17.50
L12	Eastern Proverbs, 2nd Series	1932	£1.75	£21.00
L12	Eastern Proverbs, 3rd Series	1933	£1.40	£17.00
L12	Eastern Proverbs, 4th Series	1934	£1.25	£15.00
50	East Suffolk Churches (Black Front)	1912	£1.60	£80.00
50	(Sepia Front)	1917	£1.50	£75.00
50	Empire Railways	1931	£2.00	£100.00
25	Famous Cricket Colours	1928	£3.40	£85.00
50	Famous Golfers	1927	£8.50	£625.00
L12	Famous Golfers, A Series	1927	£20.00	—
L12	Famous Golfers, 2nd Series	1928	£20.00	—
25	Famous Railway Trains	1929	£2.40	£60.00
L12	Famous Railway Trains, A Series	1929	£4.25	£51.00
L12	Famous Railway Trains, 2nd Series	1929	£4.25	£51.00
50	Fish & Bait	1914	£5.00	£250.00
50	Fishes of the World	1912	—	£250.00
30/50	Fishes of the World	1924	£1.50	£45.00
50	Flags & Funnels of Leading Steamship Lines	1912	£5.50	£275.00
50	Football Club Colours	1909	£8.00	£400.00
50	Footballers (Brown)	1914	£22.50	£1125.00
50	Footballers (Coloured)	1914	£12.00	£600.00
52	Frisky	1935	£3.50	£182.00
1	Frisky (Instructions)	1935	—	£10.00
50	History & Development of the British Empire	1934	£1.30	£65.00
M48	Holidays in Britain (Views & Maps)	1937	20p	£8.00
M48	Holidays in Britain (Views Only)	1938	20p	£9.00
40	Home & Colonial Regiments	1902	£40.00	—
40	Howlers	1937	20p	£8.00
L16	Howlers	1937	50p	£8.00
50	Interesting Buildings	1905	£5.50	£275.00
25	Interesting Door-Knockers	1928	£2.20	£55.00
25	Interesting Experiments	1929	£1.20	£30.00
50	In Town To-Night	1938	25p	£12.50
L12	Italian Art Exhibition, 1930, 1st Series	1930	£1.00	£12.00
L12	Italian Art Exhibition, 1930, 2nd Series	1931	£1.00	£12.00
50	Kings of Speed	1939	60p	£30.00
50	Landmarks in Railway Progress	1931	£2.50	£125.00
L12	Landmarks in Railway Progress, 1st Series	1932	£4.25	£51.00
L12	Landmarks in Railway Progress, 2nd Series	1932	£4.25	£51.00

Qty		*Date*	*Odds*	*Sets*
50	Lawn Tennis	1928	£2.50	£125.00
L12	Lawn Tennis	1928	£8.50	—
50	Legends of Britain	1936	80p	£40.00
L12	Legends of Britain	1936	£1.50	£18.00
25	Life in a Liner	1930	£1.40	£35.00
L12	Life in a Liner	1930	£2.40	£29.00
50	Medals	1910	£6.00	£300.00
50	Men of the Moment in Sport	1928	£2.25	£240.00
L12	Men of the Moment in Sport, 1st Series	1928	£6.50	£225.00
L12	Men of the Moment in Sport, 2nd Series	1928	£6.50	—
M48	Modern Wonders	1938	25p	£12.50
25	Musical Instruments	1924	£2.80	£70.00
25	Nature's Architects	1930	£1.20	£30.00
L12	Nature's Architects	1930	£2.00	£24.00
D55	Olympic Winners Through the Years	1960	£1.25	—
50	Phil May Sketches (Gold Flake)	1912	£5.00	£250.00
50	(No Brand)	1912	£7.00	—
25	Pipes of the World	1927	£2.40	£60.00
50	Prominent Golfers	1931	£8.00	£500.00
L12	Prominent Golfers	1931	£20.00	£350.00
50	Racing Greyhounds	1934	£2.40	£120.00
25	Railway Working, A Series	1926	£3.00	£75.00
L12	Railway Working, A Series	1926	£7.50	—
25	Railway Working, 2nd Series	1927	£2.20	£55.00
L13	Railway Working, 2nd Series	1926	£7.50	£97.50
L12	Railway Working, 3rd Series	1927	£7.50	£90.00
50	Regimental Colours & Cap Badges	1912	£5.50	£275.00
50	Rivers & Broads	1921	£5.00	£250.00
50	Rivers & Broads of Norfolk & Suffolk	1922	£4.00	£200.00
50	Rugby Internationals	1935	£1.50	£75.00
50	Sectional Cycling Map	1913	£5.00	£250.00
50	Silhouettes of Warships	1915	£7.00	£350.00
50	Sporting Celebrities	1931	£2.00	£120.00
25	Sporting Trophies	1927	£2.20	£55.00
L12	Sporting Trophies	1927	£4.50	£54.00
25	Sports & Games in Many Lands	1929	£2.20	£80.00
25	The Houses of Parliament & Their Story	1931	£1.60	£40.00
25	The Inns of Court	1922	£2.40	£60.00
50	The King's Coronation	1937	20p	£10.00
L15	The King's Coronation	1937	80p	£12.00
M48	The Navy at Work	1937	25p	£12.00
50	The Queen Mary	1936	£1.25	£62.50
L16	The Queen Mary	1936	£2.25	£36.00
M48	The R.A.F. at Work	1937	80p	£38.50
50	The Story of London	1934	£1.20	£60.00
L12	The Story of London	1934	£2.50	£30.00
50	The Story of Navigation	1937	20p	£10.00
L12	The Story of Navigation	1937	£1.25	£15.00
D40	The World of Sport	1961	£1.30	—
36	3 Jovial Golfers	1934	£3.25	£117.00
73	3 Jovial Golfers (Irish Issue)	1934	£6.50	—
50	Treasure Trove	1937	20p	£8.00
L12	Treasure Trove	1937	£1.25	£15.00
25	Types of British & Colonial Troops	1899	£40.00	—
25	Warriors of All Nations	1929	£2.40	£60.00

W. A. & A. C. CHURCHMAN — cont.

Qty		Date	Odds	Sets
L12	Warriors of All Nations, A Series	1929	£3.75	£45.00
L12	Warriors of All Nations, 2nd Series	1931	£3.75	£45.00
50	Well-Known Ties, A Series	1934	75p	£37.50
L12	Well-Known Ties, A Series	1934	£1.60	£19.50
50	Well-Known Ties, Second Series	1935	65p	£32.50
L12	Well-Known Ties, 2nd Series	1935	£1.60	£19.50
25	Wembley Exhibition (2 Printings)	1924	£2.00	£50.00
50	West Suffolk Churches	1919	£1.30	£65.00
50	Wild Animals of the World	1907	£5.50	£275.00
M48	Wings Over the Empire	1939	30p	£14.50
50	Wonderful Railway Travel	1937	25p	£12.50
L12	Wonderful Railway Travel	1937	£1.25	£15.00
50	World Wonders Old and New	Unissued	—	£16.00

OVERSEAS ISSUES (No I.T.C. Clause)

Qty		Date	Odds	Sets
M48	Air-Raid Precautions	1938	£1.50	—
M48	Holidays In Britain (Views & Maps)	1937	£1.50	—
M48	Holidays In Britain (Views Only)	1938	£1.50	£72.00
M48	Modern Wonders (Plain Base)	1938	£1.50	—
M48	(Silver Line at Base)	1938	£5.00	—
M48	The Navy at Work	1937	£1.75	£84.00
M48	The R.A.F. at Work	1937	£1.60	—
25	Warriors of All Nations (No Name on front)	1929	*£7.00*	—
M48	Wings Over the Empire	1939	£1.50	—

CIGARETTE COMPANY (Channel Isles)

Qty		Date	Odds	Sets
72	Jersey Footballers (Blue Background)	1910	£5.00	—
50	Jersey Footballers (Grey Background)	1910	£5.00	—
?54	Jersey Footballers (No Frame for Name)	1910	£12.50	—

WM. CLARKE & SON

Qty		Date	Odds	Sets
25	Army Life	1915	£10.00	£250.00
16	Boer War Celebrities	1901	£23.00	£365.00
50	Butterflies & Moths	1912	£7.00	£350.00
30	Cricketer Series	1901	£125.00	—
66	Football Series	1902	£17.50	—
25	Marine Series	1907	£12.00	£300.00
50	Royal Mail	1914	£9.00	£450.00
50	Sporting Terms (Multi-backed)	1900	£36.00	—
20	Tobacco Leaf Girls	1898	£375.00	—
25	Well-Known Sayings	1900	£20.00	£500.00

J. H. CLURE & SON

Qty		Date	Odds	Sets
30	Army Pictures, Cartoons, etc. (No Brands)	1916	*£90.00*	—
30	(Havana Mixture)	1916	*£90.00*	—
50	War Portraits	1916	*£70.00*	—

J. LOMAX COCKAYNE

Qty		Date	Odds	Sets
50	War Portraits	1916	*£65.00*	—

COHEN WEENEN & CO.

Qty		Date	Odds	Sets
F40	Actresses, Footballers & Jockeys	1901	£40.00	—
26	Actresses "FROGA"	1900	*£55.00*	—
25	Beauties "BOCCA"	1899	£65.00	—
25	Beauties "GRACC"	1899	*£80.00*	—
65	Celebrities, Black & White ("250" Back)	1900	£4.00	—
25	("500" Back)	1900	£9.00	—
45	Celebrities, Coloured ("100" Back)	1901	£4.00	£180.00
45	("250" Back)	1901	£8.00	—
76	Celebrities, Coloured ("250", Different)	1901	£4.00	£300.00
30	Celebrities, Gainsborough ("400" Back)	1902	£10.00	£300.00
M39	("250" Back)	1902	£35.00	—
M39	(Gold Border)	1902	£35.00	—
M40	(Metal Frame)	1902	*£50.00*	—
MF?150	Celebrities, Gainsborough (No Frame)	1901	£4.00	—
MF?150	(Metal Frame)	1901	£13.50	—
25	Cricketers	1926	£12.00	£300.00
20	Cricketers, Footballers & Jockeys	1900	£16.00	£320.00
25	Famous Boxers (Black Back)	1912	£12.00	—
25	(Green Back)	1912	£9.00	£335.00
25	(Anonymous)	1912	£15.00	—
40	Fiscal Phrases (Copyright Registered)	1902	£10.00	£400.00
40	Fiscal Phrases (No Copyright Clause)	1902	£10.00	£400.00
60	Football Captains 1907-8	1908	£11.00	£660.00
100	Heroes of Sport	1897	£65.00	—
40	Home & Colonial Regiments ("100" Back)	1901	£7.50	£300.00
40	("250" Back)	1901	£11.00	—
40	(Gold Border)	1901	*£100.00*	—
20	Interesting Buildings & Views (Plain)	1902	£8.50	£170.00
20	(Gold Surround)	1902	*£85.00*	—
K52	Miniature Playing Cards (Bandmaster)	1910	£3.75	—
20	Nations (Non Descriptive)	1902	£11.50	£230.00
20	(Descriptive)	1923	£4.25	£85.00
40	Naval & Military Phrases (Blue Back)	1904	£25.00	—
40	(Red Back)	1906	£15.00	£600.00
40	(Gold Border)	1906	*£85.00*	—
50	Owners, Jockeys, Footballers, Cricketers Series 2	1906	£11.00	£550.00
20	Owners, Jockeys, Footballers, Cricketers Series 3	1907	£12.00	£240.00
30	Proverbs	1903	£13.50	£400.00
20	Russo Japanese War Series	1904	£15.00	£300.00
25	Silhouettes of Celebrities	1903	£11.00	£300.00
50	Star Artistes	1907	£9.00	£450.00
L16	Victoria Cross Heroes (Silk)	1915	£36.50	—
50	Victoria Cross Heroes (51-100)	1916	£8.00	£400.00
25	(51-75, Anonymous)	1916	£11.50	—
50	War Series	1916	£7.50	£375.00
25	Ditto (26-50, Anonymous)	1916	£11.00	—
30	Wonders of the World (Green Back)	1908	£7.00	£210.00
30	Wonders of the World (Grey Back)	1923	£2.50	£75.00

T. H. COLLINS

Qty		Date	Odds	Sets
25	Homes of England (Black Front)	1924	*£11.50*	—
25	(Mauve Front)	1924	£5.00	£125.00
25	Sports & Pastimes	1923	£6.00	£170.00

F. COLTON JR.

Qty		Date	Odds	Sets
30	Army Pictures, Cartoons, etc. ("Best Brands")	1916	*£100.00*	—
30	("Trade Supplied")	1916	*£100.00*	—
50	War Portraits	1916	*£70.00*	—

T. W. CONQUEST

Qty		Date	Odds	Sets
30	Army Pictures, Cartoons, etc	1916	*£90.00*	—

CONTINENTAL CIGARETTE FACTORY

Qty		Date	Odds	Sets
25	Charming Portraits (Firm's Name)	1920	£5.00	£125.00
25	(Club Mixture, Blue)	1920	£6.50	—
25	(Club Mixture, Brown)	1920	*£7.50*	—
25	(Plain Back)	1920	£3.50	—

COOPER & CO.

Qty		Date	Odds	Sets
25	Boer War Celebrities "STEW" (Alpha)	1901	*£110.00*	—
25	(Gladys)	1901	*£110.00*	—

CO-OPERATIVE WHOLESALE SOCIETY (C.W.S.)

Qty		Date	Odds	Sets
6	Advertisement Cards	1915	£225.00	—
24	African Types	1936	50p	£12.00
M50	Beauty Spots of Britain	1936	20p	£10.00
50	Boy Scout Badges	1939	90p	£45.00
25	Boy Scout Series	1912	£26.50	—
48	British and Foreign Birds	1938	60p	£29.00
50	British Sport Series (Multi-Backed)	1904	£25.00	—
25	Cooking Recipes	1923	£2.20	£55.00
28	Co-operative Buildings & Works	1916	£12.00	£335.00
24	English Roses	1924	£3.50	£84.00
50	Famous Bridges	1937	75p	£37.50
48	Famous Buildings	1935	60p	£29.00
25	How To Do It (Mixed Backs)	1924	—	£55.00
25	(Anglian Mixture)	1924	£2.40	—
25	(Equity Tobacco)	1924	£2.40	—
25	(Jaycee Brown Flake)	1924	£2.40	—
25	(Raydex Gold Leaf)	1924	£2.40	—
48	Musical Instruments	1934	£3.40	£164.00
25	Parrot Series	1910	£30.00	—
48	Poultry	1927	£6.00	£288.00
48	Railway Engines	1936	£2.80	£135.00
24	Sailing Craft	1935	£1.25	£30.00
18	War Series	1914	£24.00	—
48	Wayside Flowers (Brown Back)	1923	£1.75	£84.00
48	Wayside Flowers (Green Back, Different)	1928	75p	£36.00
48	Wayside Woodland Trees	1924	£2.40	£115.00
24	Western Stars	1957	—	£12.00

COPE BROS. & CO. LTD.

Qty		Date	Odds	Sets
KF?50	Actors & Actresses	1900	£23.00	—

COPE BROS. & CO. LTD. — cont.

Qty		Date	Odds	Sets
20	Actresses "BLARM" (Plain Back)	1902	£34.00	—
20	(Printed Back, 63mm Long)	1902	£34.00	—
20	(Printed Back, 70mm Long)	1902	£32.50	£650.00
6	Actresses "COPEIS"	1898	£130.00	—
26	Actresses "FROGA"	1900	£85.00	—
F50	Actresses & Beauties	1900	£11.00	£550.00
P?6	Advertisement Cards (Humorous)	1885	*£200.00*	—
P6	Advertising Postcards	1924	£60.00	—
52	Beauties, Playing Card Inset	1899	£42.50	—
15	Beauties "PAC"	1898	£70.00	—
50	Boats of the World	1912	£11.00	£550.00
25	Boxers (1-25)	1915	£14.00	£350.00
25	Boxers (26-50)	1915	£11.00	£275.00
25	Boxers (51-75)	1915	£12.00	£300.00
25	Boxers (76-100)	1915	£16.00	£400.00
25	Boxers (101-125)	1915	£11.00	£275.00
1	Boxers (New World's Champion)	1915	—	£32.50
25	Boxing Lessons	1935	£3.75	—
35	Boy Scouts & Girl Guides (English)	1910	£10.00	£350.00
35	(Scandinavian)	1910	£30.00	—
X25	Bridge Problems	1924	*£22.00*	—
25	British Admirals	1915	£11.00	£275.00
50	British Warriors (Black Printing)	1912	£6.25	£312.50
50	(Grey Printing)	1912	£8.50	£425.00
25	Castles	1939	£1.20	£30.00
25	Cathedrals	1939	£1.30	£32.50
50	Characters from Scott	1900	£11.00	£550.00
20	Chinese Series (1-20)	1903	£10.00	£200.00
20	Chinese Series (21-40, Bond of Union)	1903	£10.00	—
20	(21-40, Cope's Courts)	1903	£10.00	—
20	(21-40, Golden Cloud)	1903	£10.00	—
20	(21-40, Golden Magnet)	1903	£10.00	—
20	(21-40, Solace)	1903	£10.00	—
25	Chinese Series (41-65, 2 Printings)	1903	£10.00	—
50	Chinese Series (66-115, Multi-Backed)	1903	£11.00	—
50	Cope's Golfers	1900	£75.00	—
L25	Dickens Character Series	1939	90p	£22.50
50	Dickens Gallery (Back-Listed)	1900	£9.00	£450.00
50	(Solace Back)	1900	£85.00	—
E1	Dickens Gallery Album	1900	—	£130.00
50	Dogs of the World (English)	1912	£10.00	£500.00
50	(Scandinavian)	1912	£30.00	—
25	Eminent British Regiments Officers Uniforms			
	(English)	1908	£11.00	£275.00
	(Scandinavian)	1908	£25.00	—
24	Flags, Arms & Types of All Nations (Numbered)	1904	£6.50	£156.00
24	(Unnumbered)	1904	*£45.00*	—
30	Flags of Nations (Black Back)	1903	£10.00	£300.00
30	(Indian, Blue Back)	1903	£50.00	—
30	(Plain Back)	1903	£8.00	£240.00
M50	General Knowledge	1925	£3.50	—
M32	Golf Strokes	1923	£12.50	—
60	Happy Families	1937	£1.25	£75.00
M50	Household Hints	1925	£1.30	£65.00
X6	Hunting Scenes	1885	*£175.00*	—
X20	Kenilworth Phrases	1910	*£160.00*	—

COPE BROS. & CO. LTD. — cont.

Qty		Date	Odds	Sets
25	Lawn Tennis Strokes	1924	£5.00	£125.00
5	Lawn Tennis Strokes (26-30)	1925	£16.00	—
L50	Modern Dancing	1926	£12.50	—
50	Music Hall Artistes ("Series of 50")	1913	£32.50	£1625.00
50	(No Quantity)	1913	£8.50	£425.00
120	Noted Footballers (Clips, 120 Subjects)	1910	£10.00	—
162	Noted Footballers (Clips, 282 Subjects)	1910	£9.00	—
471	Noted Footballers (Clips, 500 Subjects)	1910	£9.00	—
1	Noted Footballers (Clips, Unnumbered)	1910	—	£40.00
195	Noted Footballers (Solace Cigarettes)	1910	£10.00	—
24	Occupations for Women	1897	£80.00	—
X6	Phases of the Moon	1885	*£175.00*	—
T12	Photo Albums for the Million (Buff)	1902	£13.50	£160.00
T12	Photo Albums for the Million (Green)	1902	£12.50	£150.00
25	Pigeons	1926	£7.00	£175.00
52	Playing Cards (Rounded Corners)	1902	£10.00	—
52	(Squarer Corners)	1902	£10.00	—
30	Scandinavian Actors & Actresses	1910	£40.00	£1200.00
50	Shakespeare Gallery	1900	£11.00	£550.00
G14	Smoke Room Booklets	1890	£18.00	—
25	Song Birds	1926	£6.50	£162.50
25	Sports & Pastimes	1925	£4.00	£100.00
L25	The Game of Poker	1936	40p	£10.00
X7	The Seven Ages of Man	1885	*£175.00*	—
25	The World's Police	1937	£4.00	£100.00
L25	Toy Models – The Country Fair	1925	40p	£10.00
25	Uniforms (Circular Medallion Back)	1898	£25.00	£625.00
25	(Square Medallion Back, Narrow)	1898	£20.00	£500.00
25	(Square Medallion Back, Wide)	1898	£50.00	—
50	V.C & D.S.O. Naval & Flying Heroes (Unnumbered)	1916	£5.50	£375.00
25	V.C & D.S.O. Naval & Flying Heroes (Numbered 51-75)	1916	£7.00	£175.00
20	War Pictures	1915	£9.00	£180.00
25	War Series	1915	£10.00	—
25	Wild Animals & Birds (English)	1907	£16.00	£400.00
25	(Scandinavian)	1907	£35.00	—

E. CORONEL

25	Types of British & Colonial Troops	1900	£60.00	—

DAVID CORRE & CO.

1	Advertisement Card	1903	*£275.00*	—
40	Naval & Military Phrases (With Border)	1904	£62.50	—
40	(No Border)	1904	£62.50	—

JOHN COTTON LTD.

L50	Bridge Hands	1934	£8.00	—
50	Golf Strokes A/B	1936	£7.50	£375.00
50	Golf Strokes C/D	1937	£8.50	£425.00
50	Golf Strokes E/F	1938	£12.50	—
50	Golf Strokes G/H	1939	*£400.00*	—
50	Golf Strokes I/J	1939	*£400.00*	—

A. & J. COUDENS LTD.

Qty		*Date*	*Odds*	*Sets*
F60	British Beauty Spots (Numbered)	1923	£1.20	£72.00
F60	(Unnumbered)	1923	£2.20	—
F60	(Rubber Stamped)	1923	£4.00	—
F60	(Plain Back Anonymous)	1923	£3.80	—
F60	Holiday Resorts in East Anglia	1924	£1.00	£60.00
25	Sports Alphabet	1924	£7.00	£175.00

THE CRAIGMILLAR CREAMERY CO.

M?	Scottish Views	1901	*£250.00*	—

W. R. DANIEL

30	Colonial Troops (Black Back)	1902	*£75.00*	—
30	(Brown Back)	1902	£75.00	—
25	National Flags & Flowers-Girls	1901	*£120.00*	—

W. T. DAVIES & SONS

?50	Actresses	1902	£75.00	—
30	Aristocrats of the Turf, A Series (1-30)	1924	£5.00	£150.00
12	Aristocrats of the Turf (31-42)	1924	£15.00	—
36	Aristocrats of the Turf, Second Series	1924	£4.00	£144.00
25	Army Life	1915	£10.00	£250.00
12	Beauties	1903	£37.50	—
25	Boxing	1924	£4.00	£100.00
50	Flags & Funnels of Leading Steamship Lines	1913	£10.00	—
?15	Newport Football Club	1904	£135.00	—
?5	Royal Welsh Fusiliers	1904	*£160.00*	—

S. H. DAWES

30	Army Pictures, Cartoons, etc	1916	*£120.00*	—

J. W. DEWHURST

30	Army Pictures, Cartoons, etc	1916	*£90.00*	—

R. I. DEXTER

30	Borough Arms	1900	£1.00	£30.00

DIANELLOS & VERGOPOULOS

XF?	Views of Cyprus	1926	*£30.00*	—

GEORGE DOBIE & SON LTD.

M?28	Bridge Problems	1933	*£25.00*	—
M32	Four Square Books (1-32)	1959	£1.50	—
M32	Four Square Books (33-64)	1960	£1.50	—

GEORGE DOBIE & SON LTD. — cont.

Qty		*Date*	*Odds*	*Sets*
M32	Four Square Books (65-96)	1960	£1.50	—
25	Weapons of All Ages	1924	£6.00	£150.00

DOBSON & CO. LTD.

Qty		Date	Odds	Sets
8	The European War Series	1917	£37.50	—

DOMINION TOBACCO CO. (1929) LTD.

Qty		Date	Odds	Sets
25	Old Ships, 1st Series	1934	£1.60	£40.00
25	Old Ships, 2nd Series	1935	80p	£20.00
25	Old Ships, 3rd Series	1936	80p	£20.00
25	Old Ships, 4th Series	1936	£1.00	£25.00

JOSEPH W. DOYLE LTD.

Qty		Date	Odds	Sets
F12	Beauties (Series CC.D)	1928	£26.00	—
F12	Beauties (Series CC.E)	1928	*£26.00*	—
F12	British Views (Series CC.B)	1928	£26.00	—
F12	Castles (Series CC.C)	1928	£26.00	—
XF18	Children	1928	£12.00	—
F12	Dirt Track Riders (Series CC.A)	1928	*£50.00*	—

DOYLE'S (READING)

Qty		Date	Odds	Sets
?	Merry Miniatures (Booklets)	1924	£100.00	—

MAJOR DRAPKIN & CO.

Qty		Date	Odds	Sets
12	Actresses	1910	£6.00	£72.00
8	Advertisement Cards	1926	£6.50	£52.00
M1	Army Insignia	1915	*£150.00*	—
50	Around Britain	1929	£1.20	£60.00
L50	Around Britain	1929	£2.50	—
50	Around the Mediterranean	1926	£1.25	£62.50
L50	Around the Mediterranean	1926	£2.25	—
F40	Australian & English Test Cricketers	1928	£1.65	£66.00
?120	Bandmaster Conundrums	1907	£8.00	—
25	British Beauties	1930	£2.40	£60.00
F36	Celebrities of the Great War (Printed Back)	1916	65p	£23.50
F34	(Plain Back)	1916	60p	£20.50
M96	Cinematograph Actors	1913	£9.00	—
15	Dogs and their Treatment	1924	£5.00	£75.00
L15	Dogs and their Treatment	1924	£6.00	£90.00
50	Girls of Many Lands	1929	£3.00	—
M50	Girls of Many Lands	1929	30p	£15.00
25	How To Keep Fit (Crayol Cigarettes)	1912	£12.00	£300.00
25	How To Keep Fit (Drapkin's Cigarettes)	1912	£12.00	£300.00
54	Life at Whipsnade Zoo	1934	50p	£27.00
50	Limericks	1929	£1.00	£50.00
F36	National Types of Beauty	1928	60p	£22.00

CODE NAMES

When cigarette cards first became popular in this country the most prolific subjects were actresses and militaria—since virtually all cigarette smokers were men! In the golden age around the turn of the century many manufacturers including many of the largest issued some of the same sets as their competitors. In order to distinguish the many similar series a coding system has been developed for series of Actresses and Boer War subjects that in general do not have a series title of their own. This is based on the first letter (or letters) of the names of some of the leading issuers of the particular set.

Thus Beauties PAC were issued by Pritchard & Burton, Adkin and Cope, and Beauties HOL by Harris, Ogden & Lambert & Butler. Actresses HAGG were issued by Hill, Anonymous, Gabriel and Glass (as well as Baker and Bell), while Boer War Celebrities CLAM, is taken from Churchman, Lambert & Butler, Anonymous and Muratti. The most popular of this set must surely have been Actresses FROGA which includes four sets all similar in appearance and was issued by more than 25 different companies, including Dunn's Hats in Britain, and tobacco issuers in Canada and India.

It is fortunate that so many of the series had an anonymous version, allowing the frequent use of the letter 'A', and hence some sort of pronounceable acronyms.

As a general rule in British issues Actress series are those in which the subject's name is printed, while the unidentified ladies are known as Beauties.

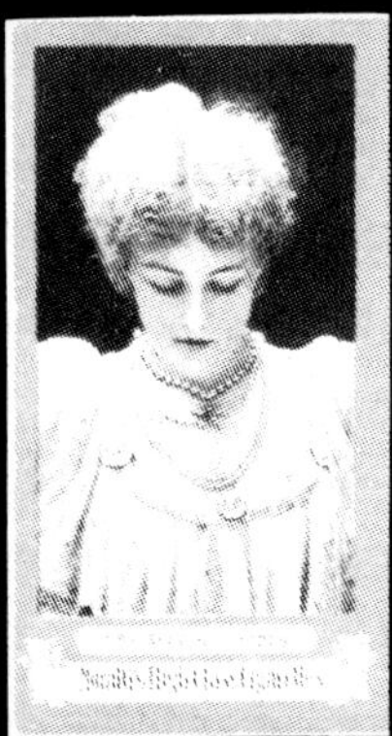

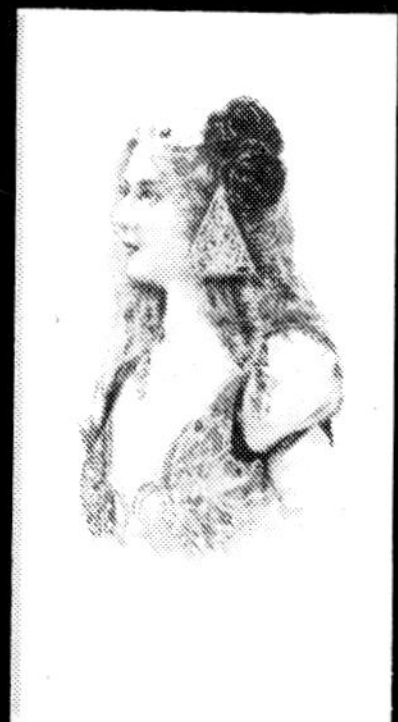

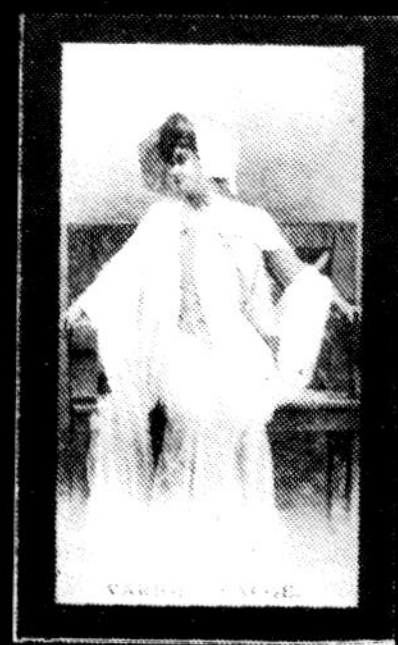

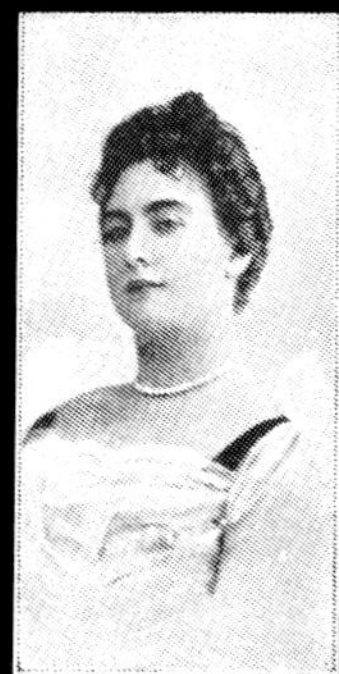

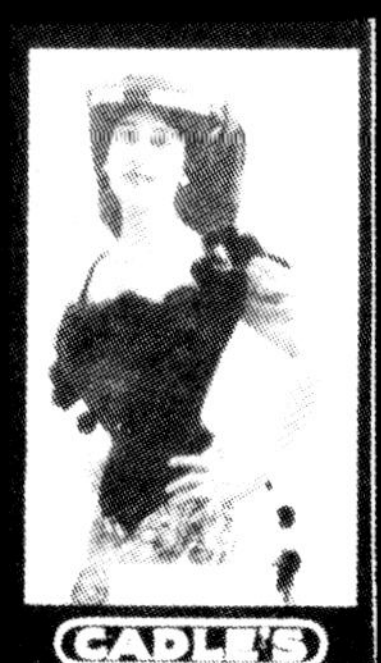

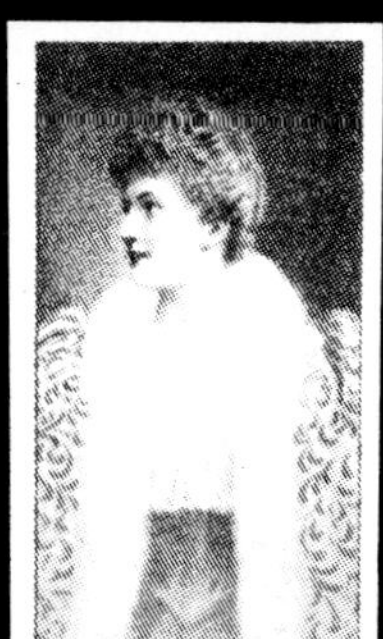

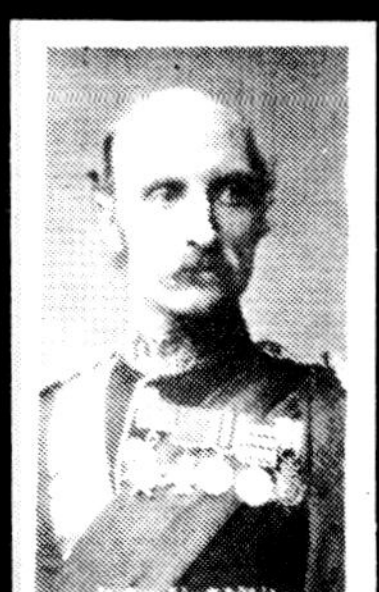

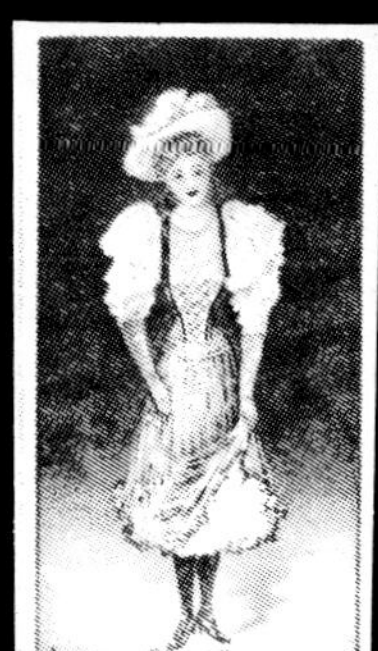

TYPE COLLECTING

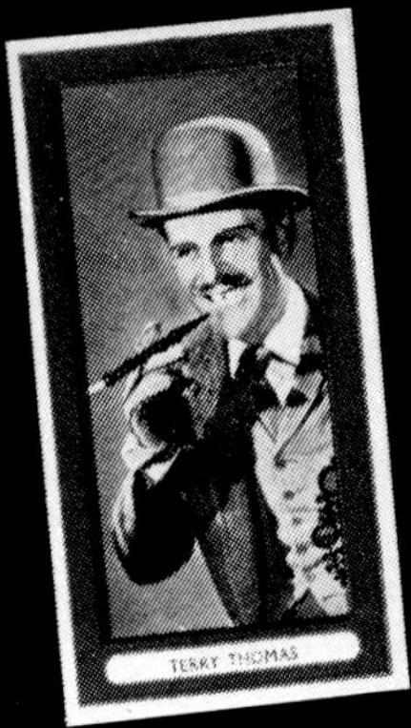

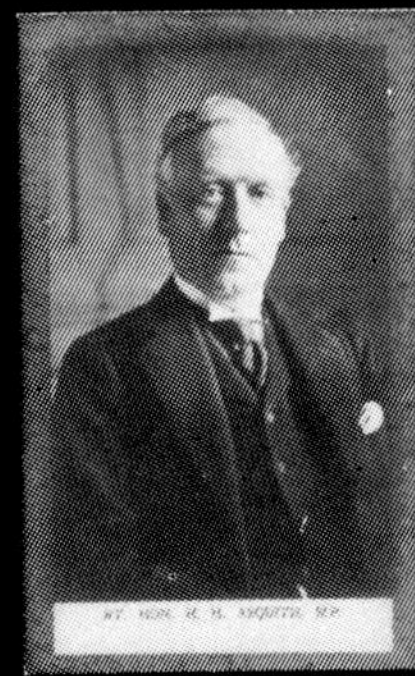

There are now many collectors who concentrate on types either exclusively or in addition to their main collections. This involves keeping one or two cards from every series issued. Limitations of space and money make this a good compromise for many people, since they can have a limited goal, yet still providing a sufficient challenge to maintain their interest.

The advent of modern albums has eased one problem for type collectors, since they can now limit themselves to just one card per series, and still be able to see both front and back of that type. Further limitations may also be self-imposed by collecting the issues of just one country, or commodity. One collector 'only' collects one card from each manufacturer, while a lifetime could be spent just in trying to collect the different types issued by the tobacco firm of Wills!

The general collector can also acquire types as a method of identifying those series of which he wishes to obtain complete sets—and those that he wishes to avoid. It is also a useful idea to obtain type cards of all the varieties of one series, so that one can have a complete set of all the pictures and also a specimen of all the different backs that could be found with that front.

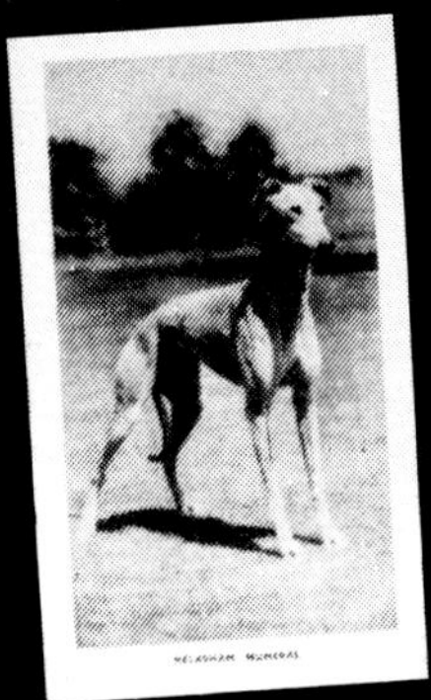

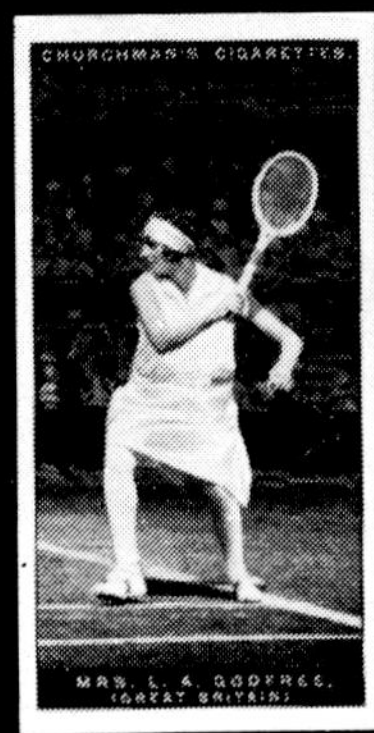

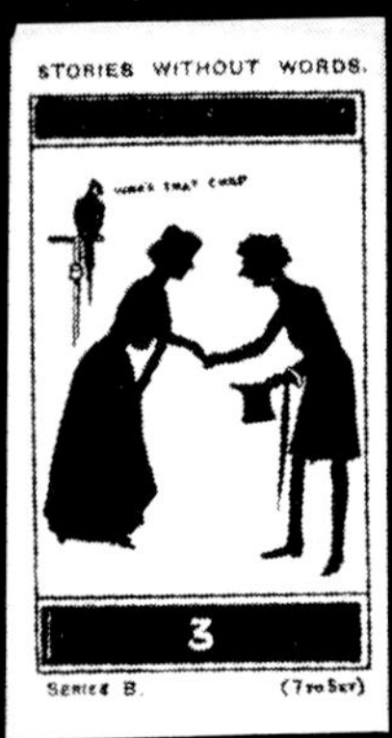

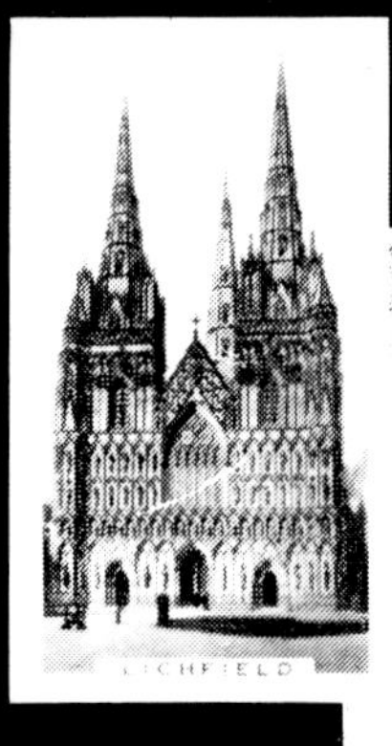

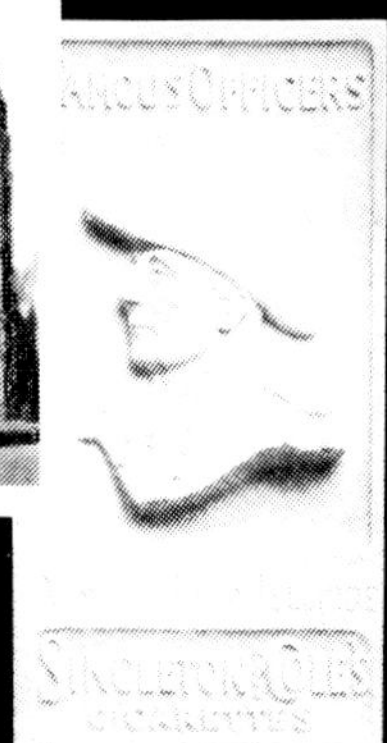

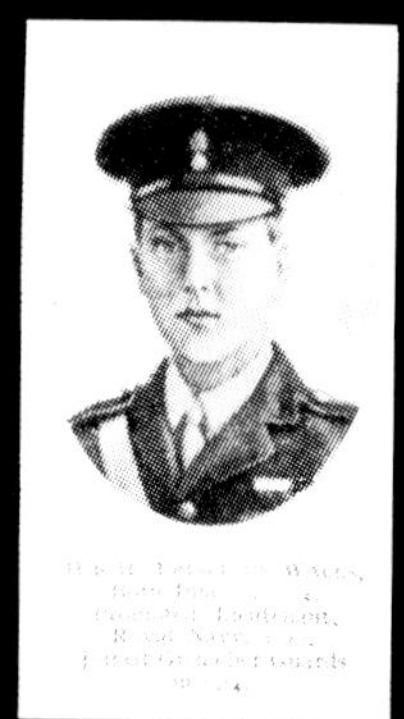

MAJOR DRAPKIN & CO. — cont.

Qty		*Date*	*Odds*	*Sets*
25	Optical Illusions (Panel 23 x 7mm)	1926	£2.60	£65.00
25	(Panel 26 x 9mm)	1926	£2.60	£65.00
L25	Optical Illusions	1926	£3.20	£80.00
25	Palmistry	1927	£2.60	£65.00
L25	Palmistry	1927	£2.50	£62.50
48	Photogravure Masterpieces	1915	£8.50	—
25	Puzzle Pictures	1926	£3.00	£75.00
L25	Puzzle Pictures	1926	£3.50	£87.50
M40	Regimental Colours & Badges of the Indian Army			
	(Silk, "Buffs")	1915	£3.50	—
	(Silk, No Brand)	1915	*£25.00*	—
?26	Shots from the Films (Package Issue)	1934	*£5.00*	—
T25	Soldiers & their Uniforms (Die-Cut)	1914	—	£74.00
T25	(Crayol)	1914	90p	—
T25	(Drapkin)	1914	90p	—
T22/25	Soldiers & their Uniforms (Die-Cut)	1914	—	£20.00
F35/36	Sporting Celebrities in Action	1930	£2.25	£180.00
40	The Game of Sporting Snap	1928	£3.25	£130.00
1	The Greys Advertisement Card	1935	—	£6.00
12	Views of the World	1910	£4.50	—
6/8	Warships	1912	£9.00	£54.00

DRAPKIN & MILLHOFF

?40	Beauties "KEWA" (Eldona Cigarettes)	1899	*£115.00*	—
?40	(Explorer Cigarettes)	1899	*£115.00*	—
25	Boer War Celebrities "PAM" (Multi-Backed)	1901	£26.00	—
30	Colonial Troops (Multi-Backed)	1902	£42.50	—
X?	Pick-Me-Up Paper Inserts	1900	*£90.00*	—
?25	Pretty Girl Series "BAGG"	1898	*£120.00*	—

DU MAURIER CIGARETTES

X?50	Advertising Inserts	1931	£5.25	—

J. DUNCAN & CO. LTD.

47/50	Evolution of the Steamship	1925	65p	£30.00
48	Flags, Arms & Types of Nations (Blue)	1911	£25.00	—
48	(Green)	1911	*£40.00*	—
20	Inventors & their Inventions	1915	*£50.00*	—
30	Scottish Clans, Arms of Chiefs (Black)	1912	*£90.00*	—
30	(Green)	1912	£16.00	£480.00
L72	Scottish Gems (Coloured)	1912	£12.00	—
L50	Scottish Gems, 2nd Series	1913	£13.00	—
L50	Scottish Gems, 3rd Series	1914	£10.00	£500.00
L50	Scottish Gems (Reprint, Black & White)	1925	50p	£25.00
25	Types of British Soldiers	1910	£40.00	—

GEO. DUNCOMBE

30	Army Pictures, Cartoons, etc.	1916	*£90.00*	—

ALFRED DUNHILL LTD.

Qty		Date	Odds	Sets
M25	Dunhill King Size Ransom	1985	£1.40	—

EDWARD VII CIGARETTES

Qty		Date	Odds	Sets
40	Home & Colonial Regiments	1901	*£200.00*	—

EDWARDS, RINGER & CO.

Qty		Date	Odds	Sets
X50	How to Count Cribbage Hands	1908	*£65.00*	—

EDWARDS, RINGER & BIGG

Qty		Date	Odds	Sets
25	Abbeys & Castles (Exmoor Hunt Back)	1912	£7.00	£175.00
25	(New York Back)	1912	£7.00	£175.00
25	Abbeys and Castles (Type Set Back)	1912	£8.00	£200.00
25	Alpine Views (Exmoor Hunt Back)	1912	£7.00	£175.00
25	(New York Back)	1912	£7.00	£175.00
50	A Tour Round the World	1909	£8.50	£425.00
12	Beauties "CERF"	1905	£55.00	£660.00
25	Beauties "FECKSA"	1900	£34.00	—
50	Birds & Eggs	1906	£11.00	—
?25	Boer War Sketches	1901	*£100.00*	—
25	Boer War Celebrities "STEW"	1901	£40.00	—
25	British Trees & their Uses	1933	£2.20	£55.00
1	Calendar & Lighting up Table	1899	—	*£250.00*
1	Calendar	1905	—	*£225.00*
1	Calendar (Empire Back)	1910	—	*£250.00*
1	(New York Back)	1910	—	*£250.00*
50	Celebrated Bridges	1924	£2.20	£110.00
50	Cinema Stars	1923	£1.25	£62.50
L25	Cinema Stars	1923	£1.70	£42.50
25	Coast and Country (Exmoor Hunt Back)	1911	£7.00	£175.00
25	(New York Back)	1911	£7.00	£175.00
23	Dogs Series (Exmoor Hunt Back)	1908	£8.50	—
23	(Klondyke Back)	1908	£3.40	£79.00
3	Easter Manoeuvres of our Volunteers	1897	£250.00	£750.00
25	Flags of All Nations (1st Series)	1907	£5.60	£140.00
12	Flags of All Nations (2nd Series)	1907	£5.60	£67.50
37	(Exmoor Hunt)	1907	£5.75	£212.50
37	(Globe & Flags)	1907	£5.75	£212.50
37	(Stag Design)	1907	£5.75	£212.50
37	(Vertical Back)	1907	£6.00	—
25	Garden Life	1934	£3.20	£80.00
25	How to Tell Fortunes	1929	£3.50	£87.50
50	Life on Board a Man of War	1905	£9.00	£450.00
1	Miners Bound for Klondyke	1897	—	*£375.00*
50	Mining	1925	£2.20	£110.00
25	Musical Instruments	1924	£3.20	£80.00
25	Optical Illusions	1936	£2.50	£62.50
25	Our Pets, A Series	1926	£2.20	£55.00
25	Our Pets, 2nd Series	1926	£2.00	£50.00
25	Past & Present	1928	£3.20	£80.00
10	Portraits of His Majesty the King	1902	£36.00	£360.00

EDWARDS, RINGER & BIGG — cont.

Qty		Date	Odds	Sets
25	Prehistoric Animals	1924	£4.00	£100.00
25	Sports & Games in Many Lands	1935	£3.20	£110.00
56	War Map, Western Front	1916	£8.50	£475.00
54	War Map of the Western Front, Series 2			
	(Exmoor Hunt Back)	1917	£9.00	—
	(New York Back)	1917	£8.50	£460.00

S. EISISKI

Qty		Date	Odds	Sets
?20	Actresses "ANGOOD"	1900	*£135.00*	—
6	Actresses "COPEIS"	1899	*£135.00*	—
?20	Beauties "FENA" (Printed Back)	1899	*£135.00*	—
?20	(Rubber Stamped Back)	1899	*£135.00*	—
?40	Beauties "KEWA" (Birds Eye Back)	1900	*£135.00*	—
?40	(New Gold Back)	1900	*£135.00*	—
?40	(Rubber Stamped Back)	1900	*£135.00*	—

R. J. ELLIOTT & CO. LTD.

Qty		Date	Odds	Sets
1	Bulldog Advertisement Card (2 Types)	1910	—	£140.00

EMPIRE TOBACCO CO.

Qty		Date	Odds	Sets
6	Franco British Exhibition	1907	*£165.00*	—

ENCHANTERESSE EGYPTIAN CIGARETTE CO.

Qty		Date	Odds	Sets
20	Actresses "ANGOOD"	1898	*£130.00*	—
K52	Miniature Playing Cards	1931	*£5.00*	—

THE EXPRESS TOBACCO CO. LTD.

Qty		Date	Odds	Sets
M50	How It Is Made (Motor Cars)	1939	£2.60	£150.00

L. & J. FABIAN

Qty		Date	Odds	Sets
F24	The Elite Series (Numbered LLF1-24)	1932	*£32.50*	—
F?48	The Elite Series (Plain Numerals)	1932	*£32.50*	—

FAIRWEATHER & SONS

Qty		Date	Odds	Sets
50	Historic Buildings of Scotland	1914	£40.00	£2000.00

W. & F. FAULKNER

12 Page Reference Book — £3.50

Qty		Date	Odds	Sets
26	Actresses "FROGA"	1900	£42.50	—
25	Angling	1929	£6.00	£150.00
12	'Ation Series	1901	£20.00	£240.00
25	Beauties (Coloured)	1898	£55.00	—

W. & F. FAULKNER — cont.

Qty		Date	Odds	Sets
49	Beauties "FECKSA"	1901	£17.00	£830.00
16	British Royal Family	1901	£32.00	£510.00
50	Celebrated Bridges	1925	£2.20	£110.00
12	Coster Series	1900	£22.00	£264.00
20	Cricketers Series	1902	£225.00	—
12	Cricket Terms	1899	£60.00	—
12	Football Terms, 1st Series	1900	£22.50	£270.00
12	Football Terms, 2nd Series	1900	£22.50	£270.00
12	Golf Terms	1901	£80.00	—
12	Grenadier Guards	1899	£20.00	£240.00
40	Kings & Queens	1902	£20.00	—
12	Kipling Series	1900	£20.00	£240.00
12	Military Terms, 1st Series	1899	£18.00	£215.00
12	Military Terms, 2nd Series	1899	£20.00	—
12	Nautical Terms, 1st Series (2 Printings)	1900	£17.50	£210.00
12	Nautical Terms, 2nd Series (Grenadier)	1900	£17.50	£210.00
12	(Union Jack)	1900	£18.00	£215.00
25	Old Sporting Prints	1930	£3.20	£80.00
25	Optical Illusions	1935	£2.40	£60.00
90	Our Colonial Troops (Grenadier)	1900	£11.00	£1000.00
30	(Grenadier, with "Copyright", 1-30)	1900	£24.00	—
60	(Union Jack, 31-90)	1900	£14.00	—
20	Our Gallant Grenadiers (No I.T.C. Clause)	1902	£14.00	£280.00
20	(I.T.C. Clause)	1903	£26.50	£530.00
20	Our Gallant Grenadiers (Numbered 21-40)	1902	£21.50	£430.00
25	Our Pets, A Series	1926	£3.00	£75.00
25	Our Pets, 2nd Series	1926	£2.50	£62.50
12	Policemen of the World (Grenadier)	1899	*£125.00*	—
12	(Nosegay)	1899	£27.50	£330.00
12	Police Terms	1899	£22.50	£270.00
25	Prominent Racehorses of the Present Day	1923	£2.75	£70.00
25	Prominent Racehorses of the Present Day, 2nd Series	1924	£4.50	£112.50
12	Puzzle Series (Grenadier)	1898	*£125.00*	—
12	(Nosegay)	1898	£50.00	—
25	South African War Series	1901	£12.00	£300.00
12	Sporting Terms	1900	£26.50	£320.00
12	Street Cries	1902	£20.00	£240.00
12	The Language of Flowers (Grenadier)	1900	£27.50	£330.00
12	(Nosegay)	1900	£27.50	£330.00

FIELD FAVORITES CIGARETTES

F?	Footballers	1893	*£300.00*	—

THE FIGARO CIGARETTE

X?12	Caricatures	1880	*£300.00*	—

FINLAY & CO. LTD.

?27	Our Girls	1910	£125.00	—
30	World's Aircraft	1912	£55.00	—

FLYNN

Qty		*Date*	*Odds*	*Sets*
26	Beauties "HOL"	1899	*£200.00*	—

C. D. FOTHERGILL

Qty		*Date*	*Odds*	*Sets*
?	Football Shields	1900	*£125.00*	—

FRAENKEL BROS.

Qty		*Date*	*Odds*	*Sets*
?20	Beauties — Don Jorge (2 Printings)	1897	*£200.00*	—
?20	Beauties — "FENA"	1899	£90.00	—
25	Beauties — "GRACC"	1898	*£120.00*	—
24	Beauties — "HUMPS"	1899	*£100.00*	—
26	Music Hall Artistes (Pink Card)	1900	£85.00	—
26	(White Card)	1900	£85.00	—
25	Types of British & Colonial Troops	1900	£62.50	—

FRANKLYN DAVEY & CO.

Qty		*Date*	*Odds*	*Sets*
12	Beauties "CERF"	1905	£55.00	£660.00
50	Birds	1896	£45.00	—
10	Boer War Generals	1901	£80.00	—
25	Boxing	1924	£3.00	£75.00
25	Ceremonial and Court Dress	1915	£8.00	£200.00
50	Children of All Nations	1934	70p	£35.00
1	Comic Dog Folder	1898	—	*£250.00*
50	Football Club Colours	1909	£11.50	—
50	Historic Events	1924	£2.40	£120.00
25	Hunting	1925	£1.00	£25.00
50	Modern Dance Steps, A Series	1930	£3.70	£185.00
50	Modern Dance Steps, 2nd Series	1931	70p	£35.00
50	Naval Dress & Badges	1916	£9.00	—
50	Overseas Dominions (Australia)	1923	£3.75	—
25	Star Girls	1901	*£135.00*	—
10	Types of Smokers	1898	£47.50	£475.00
50	Wild Animals of the World	1902	£10.00	—

A. H. FRANKS & SONS

Qty		*Date*	*Odds*	*Sets*
56	Beauties	1901	£60.00	—
24	Nautical Expressions	1902	*£75.00*	—
25	Types of British & Colonial Troops	1900	£50.00	—

J. J. FREEMAN & CO.

Qty		*Date*	*Odds*	*Sets*
12	Actresses "FRAN"	1915	£37.50	—
12	Views of the World	1910	£37.50	—

J. R. FREEMAN

Qty		*Date*	*Odds*	*Sets*
33	Football Challenge (3 Printings)	1969	£3.50	£115.00
M12	Manikin Cards	1915	*£60.00*	—

C. FRYER & SONS LTD.

Qty		Date	Odds	Sets
25	Boer War & General Interest (3 Backs)	1900	£100.00	—
X50	Clan Sketches	1930	£9.00	£450.00
40	Naval & Military Phrases	1904	£50.00	—
?25	Vita Berlin Series	1901	*£135.00*	—

FRYER & COULTMAN

X12	Almanack	1893	*£200.00*	—

J. GABRIEL

10	Actresses "HAGG"	1900	£65.00	—
25	Beauties "GRACC"	1898	*£115.00*	—
20	Cricketers Series	1902	*£325.00*	—
40	Home & Colonial Regiments	1902	*£80.00*	—
55	Pretty Girl Series "BAGG"	1898	£65.00	—
25	Types of British & Colonial Troops	1899	£62.50	—

GALA CIGARETTES

1	Stamp Cards	1910	—	£110.00

GALLAHER LTD.

40 Page Reference Book — £3.50

F110	Actors & Actresses	1901	£4.50	—
P3	Advertising Postcards	1923	£60.00	—
48	Aeroplanes	1939	85p	£40.00
25	Aesop's Fables ("Series of 25")	1931	£1.20	£30.00
25	("Series of 50")	1931	£1.20	£30.00
100	Animals & Birds of Commercial Value	1921	55p	£55.00
48	Army Badges	1939	65p	£31.50
L24	Art Treasures of the World	1930	50p	£12.00
100	Association Football Club Colours	1910	£6.00	£600.00
52	Beauties (Playing Card Inset)	1905	£10.00	£500.00
52	(No Inset)	1905	£11.00	£570.00
MF48	Beautiful Scotland	1939	90p	£45.00
50	Birds & Eggs ("Gallaher Ltd" Only Label)	1905	*£35.00*	—
50	("Manufactured By" Label)	1905	£6.75	—
100	Birds, Nests & Eggs	1919	£1.25	£125.00
100	Boy Scout Series (Green, Belfast & London)	1911	£1.60	£160.00
86	(Green, London & Belfast)	1911	£2.00	—
100	Boy Scout Series (Brown Back, Redrawn)	1922	£1.40	£140.00
48	British Birds	1937	35p	£17.00
100	British Birds by George Rankin	1923	£1.10	£110.00
100	by Rankin	1923	£10.00	—
75	British Champions of 1923	1924	£1.40	£105.00
50	British Naval Series	1914	£3.80	£190.00
48	Butterflies & Moths	1938	35p	£17.00
25	Champion Animals & Birds of 1923	1924	£1.30	£32.50
48	Champions, A Series (No Captions on Front)	1934	40p	£20.00
48	(Captions on Front)	1934	40p	£20.00
48	Champions, 2nd Series	1935	50p	£24.00

Qty		Date	Odds	Sets
48	Champions of Screen & Stage			
	(Red Back)	1934	50p	£24.00
	(Blue Back, Gallaher's Cigarettes)	1934	90p	£45.00
	(Blue Back, Gallaher Ltd.)	1934	90p	£45.00
100	Cinema Stars	1926	£1.30	£130.00
MF48	Coastwise	1938	85p	—
24	Dogs (Caption in Block)	1934	£1.00	£24.00
24	(Caption in Script)	1934	£2.00	£48.00
L24	Dogs (Caption in Block)	1934	£1.25	£30.00
L24	(Caption in Script)	1934	£2.00	£48.00
48	Dogs, A Series	1936	50p	£24.00
48	Dogs, 2nd Series	1938	40p	£20.00
F100	English & Scotch Views	1910	£2.50	£250.00
100	Fables & their Morals (No. by Caption)	1912	£1.40	£140.00
100	(Thick Numerals)	1922	60p	£60.00
100	(Thin Numerals)	1922	70p	£70.00
100	Famous Cricketers	1926	£2.40	£240.00
48	Famous Film Scenes	1935	60p	£29.00
50	Famous Footballers (Brown Back)	1926	£1.80	£90.00
100	Famous Footballers (Green Back)	1925	£1.40	£140.00
48	Famous Jockeys (Blue Printing)	1936	£1.25	£60.00
48	(Mauve Printing)	1936	£2.25	—
48	Film Episodes	1936	60p	£29.00
48	Film Partners	1935	85p	£41.00
M24/25	Flags (Silk)	1915	£7.00	—
MF48	Flying	1938	£1.00	—
50	Footballers (1-50)	1928	£1.80	£90.00
50	Footballers (51-100)	1928	£2.00	£100.00
50	Footballers in Action	1927	£1.80	£90.00
48	Garden Flowers	1938	20p	£8.50
100	How to do it	1916	£2.75	£275.00
F100	Interesting Views (Black & White)	1923	£1.25	£125.00
F100	(Coloured)	1923	£2.00	£200.00
400	Irish View Scenery (Numbered on Back)	1908	£1.50	—
400	Irish View Scenery ("Ltd" in Block Letters)	1908	75p	£300.00
F400	(Chocolate Front)	1910	£2.50	—
F400	(Plain Back)	1910	£3.00	—
F400	("Ltd" in Script)	1910	75p	—
F200	Irish View Scenery (401-600)	1910	£1.75	—
LF48	Island Sporting Celebrities	1938	£1.60	—
100	Kute Kiddies Series	1916	£3.30	£330.00
F50	Latest Actresses (Black & White)	1909	£11.00	£550.00
F50	(Chocolate Front)	1909	£16.00	—
50	Lawn Tennis Celebrities	1928	£3.50	£175.00
24	Motor Cars	1934	£4.00	£96.00
48	My Favourite Part	1939	60p	£29.00
MF48	Our Countryside	1938	80p	—
100	Plants of Commercial Value	1917	65p	£65.00
48	Portraits of Famous Stars	1935	£1.00	£48.00
48	Racing Scenes	1938	75p	£36.00
50	Regimental Colours & Standards	1899	£5.50	£275.00
100	Robinson Crusoe	1928	£1.40	£140.00
50	Royalty Series	1902	£5.00	£250.00
LF48	Scenes from the Empire	1939	25p	£12.00

GALLAHER LTD. — cont.

Qty		Date	Odds	Sets
48	Shots from Famous Films	1935	60p	£29.00
MF24	Shots from the Films	1936	£3.00	—
48	Signed Portraits of Famous Stars	1935	£1.75	£84.00
M20	Silk Cut Advertisement Cards	1993	—	£6.00
48	Sporting Personalities	1936	40p	£20.00
100	Sports Series	1912	£5.00	£600.00
100	Stage & Variety Celebrities (Multi-Backed)	1899	£62.50	—
48	Stars of Screen & Stage (Brown Back)	1935	£1.50	£72.00
48	(Green Back)	1935	60p	£29.00
25	The Allies Flags	1914	£4.00	£100.00
100	The Great War Series	1915	£2.00	£200.00
100	The Great War Second Series	1915	£2.20	£220.00
25	The Great War V.C. Heroes, 1st Series	1915	£3.80	£95.00
25	The Great War V.C. Heroes, 2nd Series	1915	£3.80	£95.00
25	The Great War V.C. Heroes, 3rd Series	1915	£3.80	£95.00
25	The Great War V.C. Heroes, 4th Series	1916	£3.80	£95.00
25	The Great War V.C. Heroes, 5th Series	1916	£3.80	£95.00
25	The Great War V.C. Heroes, 6th Series	1917	£3.80	£95.00
25	The Great War V.C. Heroes, 7th Series	1917	£3.80	£95.00
25	The Great War V.C. Heroes, 8th Series	1918	£3.80	£95.00
48	The Navy (Gallaher)	1937	£1.00	£48.00
48	(Park Drive)	1937	60p	£29.00
100	The Reason Why	1924	55p	£55.00
111	The South African Series	1901	£4.50	£500.00
100	The Zoo Aquarium	1924	80p	£80.00
48	Trains of the World	1937	80p	£38.50
100	Tricks & Puzzles Series (Green Back)	1913	£4.00	£400.00
100	Tricks & Puzzles Series (Black Back)	1933	£1.00	£100.00
50	Types of the British Army			
	(Battle Honours Back)	1897	£8.50	£425.00
	(Green Back)	1898	£7.50	£375.00
	(1-50, "Three Pipe Tobaccos " in Brown)	1898	£7.00	£350.00
	(1-50, "Now in Three Strengths")	1898	£7.00	£350.00
50	Types of the British Army (51-100)			
	"Three Pipe Tobaccos"(2 Printings)	1898	£7.00	£350.00
	"Now In Three Strengths"	1898	£7.00	£350.00
100	Useful Hints Series	1915	£2.50	£250.00
25	Views in North of Ireland	1912	£40.00	£1000.00
50	Votaries of the Weed	1916	£5.00	£250.00
100	Why Is It? (Brown Back)	1915	£2.80	£280.00
100	(Green Back)	1915	£2.60	£260.00
48	Wild Animals	1937	25p	£12.00
48	Wild Flowers	1939	40p	£20.00
100	Woodland Trees Series	1912	£4.25	£425.00
50	Zoo Tropical Birds, 1st Series	1928	£1.25	£62.50
50	Zoo Tropical Birds, 2nd Series	1929	£1.25	£62.50

GASPA

Qty		Date	Odds	Sets
?20	Our Great Novelists	1930	*£50.00*	—

SAMUEL GAWITH

Qty		Date	Odds	Sets
X25	The English Lakeland	1926	£16.50	£412.50

F. GENNARI

Qty		Date	Odds	Sets
50	War Portraits	1916	*£80.00*	—

LOUIS GERARD LTD.

Qty		Date	Odds	Sets
50	Modern Armaments (Numbered)	1938	£1.00	£50.00
50	(Unnumbered)	1938	£1.00	£50.00
24	Screen Favourites (Gerard & Co)	1937	£3.00	—
24	(Gerard Ltd)	1937	£3.00	—
48	Screen Favourites & Dancers (Matt)	1937	£2.25	£108.00
48	(Varnished)	1937	£2.50	—

GLASS & CO. LTD.

Qty		Date	Odds	Sets
20	Actresses "BLARM"	1900	£62.50	—
10	Actresses "HAGG"	1900	£65.00	—
25	Beauties "FECKSA"	1903	*£80.00*	—
20	Boer War Cartoons	1901	*£85.00*	—
25	Boer War Celebrities "STEW"	1901	£70.00	—
16	British Royal Family	1901	£62.50	—
20	Cricketers Series	1902	*£325.00*	—
40	Naval & Military Phrases	1902	*£90.00*	—
19	Russo Japanese Series	1904	£55.00	—

R. P. GLOAG & CO.

Qty		Date	Odds	Sets
?25	Actresses "ANGLO" (The Challenge Flat)	1896	*£200.00*	—
?25	(Citamora)	1896	*£200.00*	—
?50	Beauties "PLUMS" (Black & White, Citamora)	1896	£85.00	—
?50	(Black & White, Challenge Flat)	1896	£80.00	—
?50	(Brown, Plain Back)	1896	*£135.00*	—
?50	(Brown, Printed Back)	1896	*£135.00*	—
40	Home & Colonial Regiments	1900	£40.00	—
30	Proverbs	1901	£80.00	—
25	Types of British & Colonial Troops	1900	£50.00	—

THE GLOBE CIGARETTE CO.

Qty		Date	Odds	Sets
25	Actresses – French	1898	£175.00	—

GOLDS LTD.

Qty		Date	Odds	Sets
1	Advertisement Card	1905	*£250.00*	—
18	Motor Cycle Series (Blue Back)	1914	£42.50	—
18	(Grey Back Numbered)	1914	£50.00	—
18	(Grey Back Unnumbered)	1914	£55.00	—
L?20	Prints from Noted Pictures (3 Brands)	1908	*£110.00*	—
L?20	(5 Brands)	1908	*£110.00*	—

T. P. & R. GOODBODY

Qty		Date	Odds	Sets
20	Actresses "ANGOOD"	1898	*£150.00*	—
?50	Beauties "KEWA" (Mauve Back)	1898	*£115.00*	—
?50	(Red Back)	1898	*£115.00*	—
25	Boer War Celebrities (Multi-Backed)	1901	£30.00	—
16	Boer War Celebrities (Different)			
	(Complete Frame, Multi-Backed)	1900	£30.00	—
	(No Vertical Lines, Multi-Backed)	1900	£35.00	—
	(2 Horizontal Lines, Multi-Backed)	1900	£35.00	—
50	Colonial Forces (Black Back)	1900	£60.00	—
50	(Brown Back)	1900	*£65.00*	—
M50	Colonial Forces	1900	*£125.00*	—
67	Dogs (Multi-Backed)	1898	£70.00	—
26	Eminent Actresses (Name At Bottom)	1900	£40.00	£1000.00
26	(Name At Top)	1900	*£100.00*	—
20	Irish Scenery (Donore Castle Cigarettes)	1905	£40.00	—
20	(Furze Blossom Cigarettes)	1905	£40.00	—
20	(Primrose Cigarettes)	1905	£40.00	—
20	(Royal Wave Cigarettes)	1905	£40.00	—
20	(Straight Cut Cigarettes)	1905	£40.00	—
?25	Pretty Girl Series "BAGG" (Grey Back)	1898	*£115.00*	—
?25	"BAGG" (Mauve Back)	1898	*£115.00*	—
?25	"BAGG" (Red Back)	1898	*£115.00*	—
?25	"BAGG" (No Brands)	1898	*£115.00*	—
50	Questions & Answers in Natural History	1924	£2.20	£110.00
25	Sports & Pastimes	1925	£6.00	£175.00
25	Types of Soldiers	1914	£55.00	—
20	War Pictures	1915	£25.00	£500.00
12	With the Flag to Pretoria	1901	£95.00	—

GORDON'S

Qty		Date	Odds	Sets
?4	Billiards	1912	*£200.00*	—

GRAVESON

Qty		Date	Odds	Sets
30	Army Pictures, Cartoons, etc. (3 Backs)	1916	*£125.00*	—

FRED GRAY

Qty		Date	Odds	Sets
25	Types of British Soldiers	1914	*£95.00*	—

GRIFFITHS BROS.

Qty		Date	Odds	Sets
XF18	Children	1928	*£75.00*	—

GUERNSEY TOBACCO CO. (Channel Isles)

Qty		Date	Odds	Sets
49	And When Did You Last See Your Father? (Sect.)	1936	£1.50	£75.00
K52	Miniature Playing Cards	1933	80p	—
48	The Laughing Cavalier (Sect.)	1935	£1.50	£75.00
48	The Toast (Sect., Black Back)	1936	£1.50	£75.00
48	(Sect., Green Back)	1936	*£6.25*	—

HARRIS & SONS

Qty		Date	Odds	Sets
26	Beauties "HOL"	1900	£27.50	—
30	Colonial Troops	1901	*£75.00*	—
25	Star Girls	1899	£175.00	—

JAS. H. HARRISON

Qty		Date	Odds	Sets
18	Motor Cycle Series	1914	*£65.00*	—

HARVEY & DAVY

Qty		Date	Odds	Sets
50	Birds & Eggs	1905	£4.00	£200.00
35	Chinese & South African Series	1901	*£115.00*	—
30	Colonial Troops	1902	£65.00	—
25	Types of British & Colonial Troops	1901	*£75.00*	—

W. HEATON

Qty		Date	Odds	Sets
?6	Birkby Views	1912	*£150.00*	—

HENLY & WATKINS LTD.

Qty		Date	Odds	Sets
25	Ancient Egyptian Gods (Plain Back)	1924	£6.00	£150.00
25	(Printed Back)	1924	£5.50	—

HIGNETT BROS. & CO.

Qty		Date	Odds	Sets
50	Actors Natural & Character Studies	1938	£1.50	£75.00
26	Actresses, "FROGA"	1900	£50.00	—
25	Actresses, Photogravure	1900	£24.00	—
28	Actresses, "PILPI" I	1901	£16.00	£450.00
F50	Actresses, "PILPI" II	1901	£11.00	£550.00
P1	Advertisement Card, Calendar Back	1884	—	*£325.00*
P8	Advertisement Cards (6 Brands)	1890	*£250.00*	—
50	A.F.C. Nicknames	1933	£5.00	£250.00
50	Air-Raid Precautions	1939	70p	£35.00
60	Animal Pictures	1899	£27.00	—
50	Arms & Armour	1924	£2.60	£130.00
25	Beauties "CHOAB"	1900	*£125.00*	—
50	Beauties, Gravure (Cavalier)	1898	£67.50	—
50	(Golden Butterfly)	1898	£67.50	—
MF50	Beauties (Chess Cigarettes) (Set 1)	1927	£1.20	£60.00
MF50	(No Brand) (Set 1)	1927	£1.50	—
MF50	Beauties (Chess Cigarettes) (Set 2)	1927	£1.20	£60.00
50	British Birds & Their Eggs	1938	£2.40	—
50	Broadcasting	1935	£2.00	—
20	Cabinet 1900	1900	£75.00	—
25	Cathedrals & Churches	1909	£3.25	£82.50
50	Celebrated Old Inns	1925	£2.60	£130.00
50	Champions of 1936	1936	£2.50	—
25	Common Objects of the Sea-Shore	1924	£2.20	£55.00
25	Company Drill	1915	£3.20	£80.00
50	Coronation Procession	1937	£2.00	—

HIGNETT BROS. & CO. — cont.

Qty		Date	Odds	Sets
50	Dogs	1936	£2.00	£100.00
50	Football Caricatures	1935	£2.75	£137.50
50	Football Club Captains	1936	£2.60	£130.00
25	Greetings of the World	1907	£2.40	£60.00
25	Historical London	1926	£2.20	£40.00
50	How to Swim	1935	£1.00	—
50	Interesting Buildings	1905	£5.00	£250.00
25	International Caps and Badges	1924	£3.40	£85.00
25	Life in Pond & Stream	1925	£2.60	£65.00
40	Medals	1900	£22.50	—
25	Military Portraits	1914	£4.20	£105.00
50	Modern Railways	1936	£2.50	—
25	Modern Statesmen (Butterfly Cigarettes)	1906	£4.50	£112.50
25	(Pioneer Cigarettes)	1906	£4.50	£112.50
20	Music Hall Artistes	1898	£50.00	£1000.00
50	Ocean Greyhounds	1938	£1.40	£70.00
M1	Oracle Butterfly (Several Printings)	1898	—	£80.00
25	Panama Canal	1914	£6.00	£150.00
12	Pretty Girl Series "RASH"	1900	£50.00	£600.00
50	Prominent Cricketers of 1938	1938	£2.75	£137.50
50	Prominent Racehorses of 1933	1933	£2.40	£120.00
G1	Riddle Folder	1893	—	*£225.00*
50	Sea Adventure	1939	50p	£25.00
25	Ships, Flags & Cap Badges, A Series	1926	£3.50	£87.50
25	Ships, Flags & Cap Badges, 2nd Series	1927	£3.60	£90.00
50	Shots from the Films	1936	£3.00	£150.00
25	The Prince of Wales Empire Tour	1924	£2.00	£50.00
50	Trick Billiards	1934	£3.50	—
25	Turnpikes	1927	£2.40	£60.00
P?	Uniforms & Armies of Countries	1899	*£250.00*	—
25	V.C. Heroes	1901	£45.00	£1125.00
20	Yachts (Black Back)	1898	£60.00	—
20	(White Back)	1898	£65.00	—
50	Zoo Studies	1937	80p	£40.00

R. & J. HILL LTD.

28 Page Reference Book — £3.50

Qty		Date	Odds	Sets
25	Actresses-Belle of New York (39mm Wide)	1899	£20.00	£500.00
25	Actresses-Belle of New York (41mm Wide)	1899	£20.00	£500.00
20	Actresses-Chocolate (Hill Cigarettes)	1917	£16.50	—
20	(Hill Tobaccos)	1917	£16.50	—
20	(Plain Back)	1917	£16.50	—
30	Actresses-Continental (Whisky Back)	1906	£16.00	—
30	(Seven Wonders)	1906	£14.00	£420.00
30	(Plain Back)	1906	£16.00	—
26	Actresses "FROGA"	1900	£50.00	—
?16	Actresses "HAGG" (High Class Cigarettes)	1900	£32.50	—
?16	(Stockrider)	1900	£32.50	—
20	Animal Series (Crowfoot Cigarettes)	1909	£22.50	—
20	(Hill's)	1909	£25.00	—
20	(Anonymous, Cigarettes Back)	1909	*£27.50*	—
20	(Anonymous, Space at Base)	1909	£20.00	—
20	(Anonymous, Plain Back)	1909	£22.50	—

R. & J. HILL LTD. — cont.

Qty		Date	Odds	Sets
F25	Artistas Teatrais Portuguesos	1924	*£35.00*	—
25	Aviation Series (Hill Name)	1934	£2.60	£65.00
25	(Gold Flake Honeydew)	1934	£3.00	—
?15	Battleships (Printed Back)	1914	*£135.00*	—
?15	(Plain Back)	1914	£42.50	—
25	Battleships & Crests	1901	£16.00	£400.00
12	Boer War Generals	1901	£30.00	£360.00
20	Breeds of Dogs (Archer's M.F.H.)	1914	£17.50	—
20	(Badminton)	1914	£17.50	—
20	(Spinet Tobacco)	1914	£17.50	—
20	(Verbena Mixture)	1914	£17.50	—
L30	Britain's Stately Homes (Silk)	1917	£3.50	£105.00
?50	British Navy Series	1902	£24.00	—
L40	Canvas Masterpieces Series 1 (Badminton)	1916	£1.25	£50.00
L40	(Spinet)	1916	£2.00	£80.00
L40	Canvas Masterpieces Series 2 (Silk)	1916	£2.25	£90.00
X10	Canvas Masterpieces Series 2 (Silk)	1916	£2.00	—
50	Caricatures of Famous Cricketers	1926	£2.60	£130.00
L50	Caricatures of Famous Cricketers	1926	£1.60	£80.00
?	Celebrated Pictures	1905	*£150.00*	—
50	Celebrities of Sport (Hill Name)	1939	£1.80	£90.00
50	(Gold Flake)	1939	£3.25	—
P4/5	Chinese Pottery & Porcelain (Silk)	1915	50p	£2.00
X11	Chinese Pottery & Porcelain 2 (Silk)	1915	£5.00	—
10	Chinese Series	1912	£65.00	—
35	Cinema Celebrities (Spinet House)	1936	80p	£28.00
35	(Anonymous)	1936	80p	£28.00
30	Colonial Troops (Leading Lines)	1901	£21.00	£630.00
30	(Perfection Vide Dress)	1901	£21.00	£630.00
50	(Sweet American)	1901	£20.00	£1000.00
40	Crystal Palace Souvenir Cards (Matt)	1937	£1.75	£70.00
40	(Varnished)	1937	£1.40	£56.00
48	Decorations and Medals (Hill Back)	1940	£1.40	£70.00
48	(Gold Flake)	1940	£3.00	—
F48	Famous Cinema Celebrities (Spinet)	1931	£4.00	—
F48	(No Brand)	1931	£3.75	£180.00
LF48	Famous Cinema Celebrities, Series A (Kadi)	1931	*£4.00*	—
LF48	(No Brand)	1931	£4.00	—
F50	Famous Cinema Celebrities, Series C (Devon)	1932	*£6.25*	—
F50	(Toucan)	1932	£6.25	—
F50	(No Brand)	1932	£3.50	—
LF50	Famous Cinema Celebrities, Series D (Kadi)	1932	£3.25	—
LF50	(No Brand)	1932	£4.25	—
28	Famous Cricketers Series (Blue Back)	1912	£60.00	—
28	(Red Back)	1912	£60.00	—
40	Famous Cricketers	1923	£4.50	£180.00
50	Famous Cricketers, including the S. African Team	1925	£4.00	£200.00
L50	Famous Cricketers, including the S. African Team	1925	£4.25	£212.50
50	Famous Dog Breeds	1952	£7.50	—
L30	Famous Engravings, Series XI	1910	£4.00	£120.00
40	Famous Film Stars (English Text)	1938	£1.00	£40.00
40	(Arabic Text)	1938	90p	£36.00

R. & J. HILL LTD. — cont.

Qty		Date	Odds	Sets
20	Famous Footballers Series	1912	£17.50	£350.00
50	Famous Footballers (Brown)	1923	£2.60	£130.00
50	Famous Footballers (Coloured, Archer)	1939	£1.80	£90.00
50	(Coloured, With Address)	1939	£1.70	£85.00
25	Famous Footballers, Additional (51-75)	1939	£2.50	£62.50
25	Famous Pictures (Fine Art Cigarettes)	1913	£3.40	£85.00
25	(Cigarette Series)	1913	£3.40	£85.00
50	Famous Ships (Matt)	1940	£1.20	£60.00
50	(Varnished)	1940	£1.00	£50.00
48	Film Stars and Celebrity Dancers	1935	£1.40	£67.00
30	Flags & Flags with Soldiers	1901	£22.50	—
24	Flags, Arms & Types of Nations	1910	£9.00	£216.00
20	Football Captain Series (Large Print)	1906	£35.00	—
20	(Small Print)	1906	£27.50	—
20	Fragments from France (Coloured)	1916	£20.00	£400.00
10	(Buff)	1916	£24.00	£240.00
10	(Black & White)	1916	£75.00	—
L23	Great War Leaders, Series 10 (Silk)	1917	£5.00	£115.00
50	Historic Places from Dickens' Classics	1926	50p	£25.00
L50	Historic Places from Dickens' Classics	1926	50p	£25.00
50	Holiday Resorts (Brown Back)	1925	£1.25	—
50	(Green Back)	1925	60p	£30.00
L50	Holiday Resorts (Brown Back)	1925	£1.25	—
L50	(Green Back)	1925	80p	£40.00
20	Inventors & Their Inventions (1-20)	1907	£4.00	£80.00
20	(Plain Back)	1934	£1.35	£27.00
20	Inventors & Their Inventions (21-40)	1908	£6.50	£130.00
15	Japanese Series (Black & White)	1904	£40.00	£600.00
15	(Black & White, Lind Back)	1904	*£125.00*	—
15	(Coloured, Blue Panel)	1904	*£125.00*	—
15	(Coloured, Red Panel)	1904	£60.00	—
20	Lighthouse Series (No Frame Line)	1903	£32.50	£650.00
30	(With Frame Line)	1903	£30.00	£900.00
50	Magical Puzzles	1938	£1.60	£80.00
50	Modern Beauties	1939	90p	£45.00
30	Music Hall Celebrities – Past & Present	1930	£2.00	£60.00
L30	Music Hall Celebrities – Past & Present	1930	£2.00	£60.00
20	National Flag Series (Printed Back)	1914	£7.00	£140.00
20	(Plain Back)	1914	£6.50	£130.00
30	Nature Pictures	1930	£1.00	£30.00
30	Nautical Songs	1937	80p	£24.00
M25	Naval Series (Unnumbered)	1901	£45.00	—
20	Naval Series (Numbered 21-40)	1911	£11.00	£220.00
10	Naval Series (Numbered 41-50)	1911	£50.00	—
30	Our Empire Series	1929	35p	£10.50
L30	Our Empire Series	1929	30p	£9.00
M30	Popular Footballers, Series A	1935	£2.40	£72.00
M20	Popular Footballers, Series B	1935	£3.00	£60.00
20	Prince of Wales Series	1911	£10.00	£200.00
L?20	Prints from Noted Pictures	1908	£100.00	—
50	Public Schools and Colleges	1923	60p	£30.00
L50	Public Schools and Colleges	1923	60p	£30.00
75	Public Schools and Colleges	1923	80p	£60.00
L75	Public Schools and Colleges	1923	90p	£67.50

Qty		Date	Odds	Sets
50	Puzzle Series	1937	£1.20	£60.00
42	Real Photographs Set 1 (Space at Back)	1930	£2.50	—
F42	(Space at Back)	1930	£2.50	—
42	(London Idol)	1930	£2.20	£92.50
F42	(London Idol)	1930	£2.40	—
F42	Real Photographs Set 2	1930	£3.00	—
20	Rhymes	1904	£24.00	£480.00
F50	Scenes from the Films	1934	£2.50	£125.00
40	Scenes from the Films	1938	80p	£32.00
35	Scientific Inventions and Discoveries (Black/White)	1929	90p	£32.00
35	(Coloured)	1929	£1.00	£35.00
L35	Scientific Inventions and Discoveries (Coloured)	1929	£1.00	£35.00
F50	Sports	1934	£4.00	—
F50	Sports Series (as above)	1934	*£10.00*	—
F50	Sports Series (as above, no title)	1934	*£10.00*	—
30	Statuary Set 1 (Matt Front)	1898	£25.00	—
30	(Varnished)	1898	£10.00	—
30	(Brown Front)	1898	*£70.00*	—
30	Statuary Set 2	1899	£7.50	£225.00
26	Statuary Set 3 (Black Panel)	1898	£22.50	—
26	(Grey Panel)	1898	*£50.00*	—
26	(White Panel)	1898	£22.50	—
30	The All Blacks	1924	£4.50	£135.00
50	The Railway Centenary, A Series	1925	£1.20	£60.00
L50	The Railway Centenary, A Series (Brown Back)	1925	£1.20	£60.00
L50	(Grey Back)	1925	£3.00	—
25	The Railway Centenary, 2nd Series	1925	£1.60	£40.00
L25	The Railway Centenary, 2nd Series	1925	£1.80	£45.00
25	The River Thames (1-25)	1924	£1.50	£37.50
25	The River Thames (26-50)	1924	£1.25	£31.25
L50	The River Thames (Green Back)	1924	£1.25	£62.50
100	Transfers	1935	£5.00	—
20	Types of the British Army (Badminton)	1914	£25.00	—
20	(Verbena)	1914	£25.00	—
LF48	Views of Interest, 1st Series (Spinet)	1938	25p	£12.00
LF48	(Sunripe)	1938	25p	£12.00
LF48	Views of Interest, 2nd Series	1938	25p	£12.00
LF48	Views of Interest, 3rd Series	1939	25p	£12.00
LF48	Views of Interest, 4th Series	1939	35p	£17.00
LF48	Views of Interest, 5th Series	1939	35p	£17.00
LF48	Views of Interest – Canada	1940	25p	£12.00
LF48	Views of Interest – India	1940	£2.50	£120.00
50	Views of London	1925	75p	£37.50
L50	Views of London	1925	80p	£40.00
L50	Views of The River Thames (Green & Black)	1924	£1.20	£60.00
25	War Series	1915	£11.00	£275.00
50	Who's Who in British Films	1927	£1.60	£80.00
L50	Who's Who in British Films	1927	£1.60	£80.00
84	Wireless Telephony	1923	£1.20	£100.00
L20	Wireless Telephony – Broadcasting Series	1923	£2.40	£48.00
25	World's Masterpieces, Second Series	1914	£2.00	£50.00
50	Zoological Series	1924	80p	£40.00
L50	Zoological Series	1924	90p	£45.00

L. HIRST & SON

Qty		Date	Odds	Sets
T25	Soldiers & Their Uniforms (Cut-outs)	1914	*£125.00*	—

J. W. HOBSON

Qty		Date	Odds	Sets
18	Motor Cycle Series	1914	£80.00	—

HOCKINGS BAZAAR, PORTHCAWL

Qty		Date	Odds	Sets
30	Army Pictures, Cartoons, etc	1916	*£90.00*	—

J. & T. HODGE

Qty		Date	Odds	Sets
?5	Britain's Naval Crests	1896	*£200.00*	—
16	British Royal Family	1901	*£135.00*	—
?20	Scottish Views (Size 74 x 39mm)	1898	*£105.00*	—
?20	(Size 80 x 45mm)	1898	*£115.00*	—

HOOK OF HOLLAND CIGARETTES

Qty		Date	Odds	Sets
?15	Footballers	1900	*£175.00*	—

HUDDEN & CO.

Qty		Date	Odds	Sets
26	Actresses "FROGA"	1900	£55.00	—
25	Beauties "CHOAB"	1901	£50.00	—
20	Beauties, Crown Seal	1898	£115.00	—
24	Beauties "HUMPS" (Blue Back)	1899	£65.00	—
24	(Orange Back)	1899	£35.00	—
24	(Type Set Back)	1899	*£200.00*	—
12	Comic Phrases	1900	£100.00	—
25	Famous Boxers	1927	*£30.00*	—
25	Flags of all Nations	1904	£18.00	£450.00
48	Japanese Playing Cards (Dandy Dot)	1900	*£110.00*	—
48	(Hudden Cigarettes)	1900	£80.00	—
18	Pretty Girl Series "RASH"	1900	£75.00	—
50	Public Schools and Colleges	1924	£2.00	£100.00
25	Soldiers of the Century	1903	£40.00	£1000.00
25	Sports and Pastimes	1926	£55.00	—
25	Star Girls	1900	£85.00	—
25	Types of Smokers	1903	£40.00	—

HUDSON'S

Qty		Date	Odds	Sets
20	Actresses "ANGOOD"	1898	*£200.00*	—
25	Beauties "BOCCA"	1900	*£200.00*	—

HUNTER

Qty		Date	Odds	Sets
?12	Footballers	1910	*£300.00*	—

STORAGE

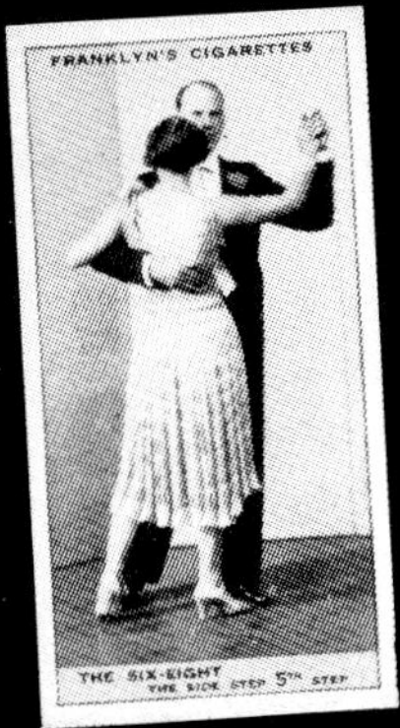

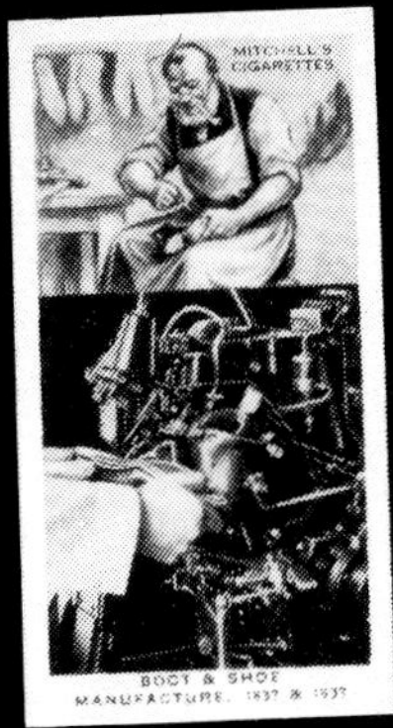

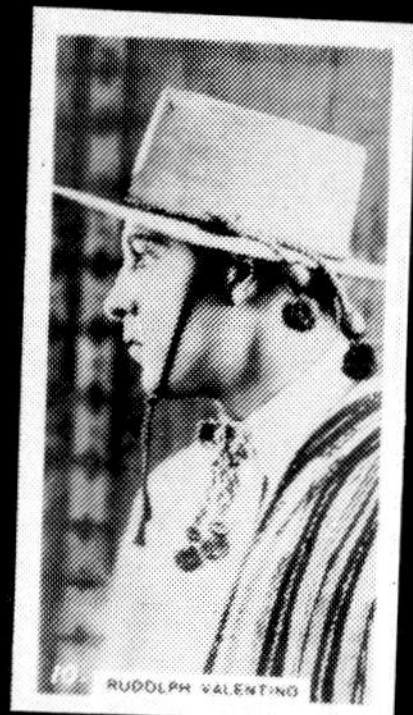

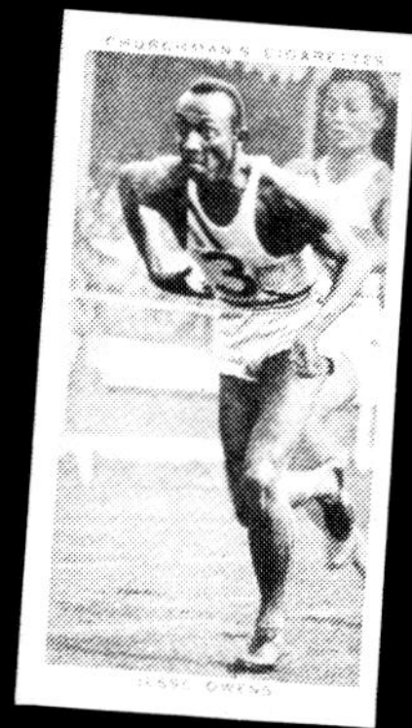

The main problem regarding the storage of cigarette cards lies in the effort to strike a balance between being able to maintain them in as good condition as possible and yet being able to examine them. If the reader is simply an investor there is no problem—he can wrap each set carefully in paper, put it into a box, and thence into a bank vault. But the only way to enjoy cigarette cards is to look at them. The modern method is to house cards in transparent pages, which can accommodate most sizes of cards and can be stored in loose leaf binders. The entire card may be viewed, both back and front, yet will not deteriorate through sticky fingers or spilt coffee. Care should be taken to use a page made from a suitable material—there are on the market now many apparently cheap pages which contain large amounts of plasticiser, a substance which could adversely affect certain cards. Full details of our own Nostalgia and Hendon albums are given on pages 16 and 17 of this book.

Another method of storage which is becoming more popular is to mount cards in frames, which can then be hung on a suitable wall. Several framing systems are now available which hold the cards in position without harming them, and enable the backs to be examined, as well as accommodating complete sets of 50 cards.

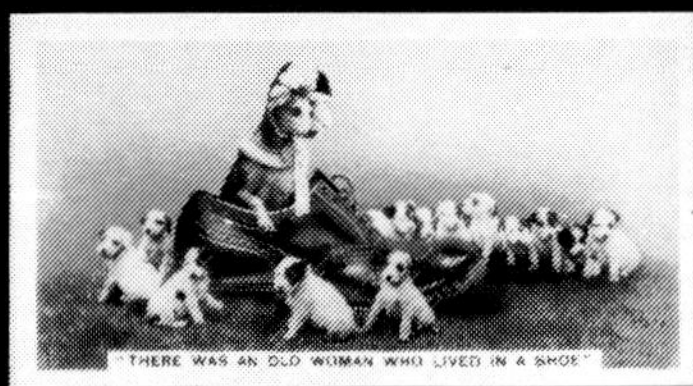

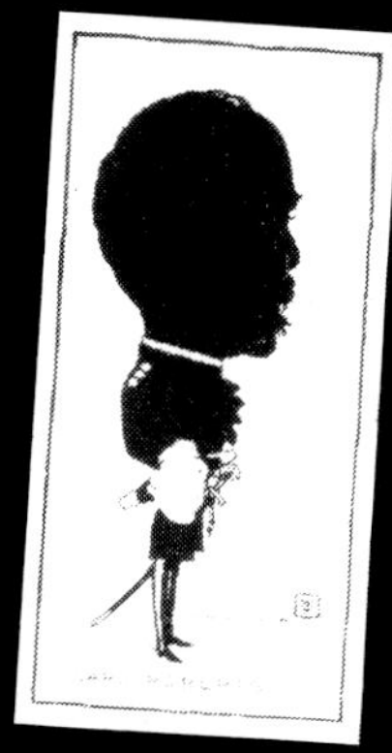

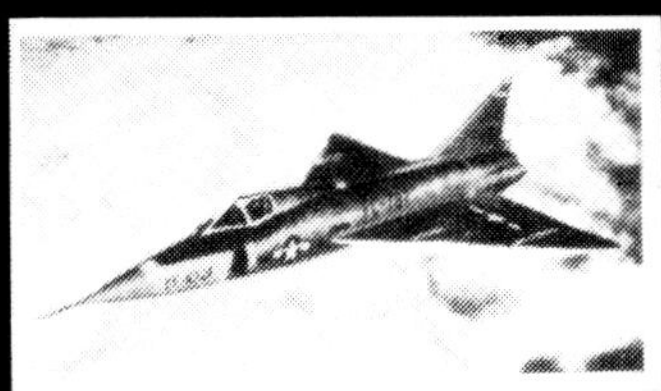

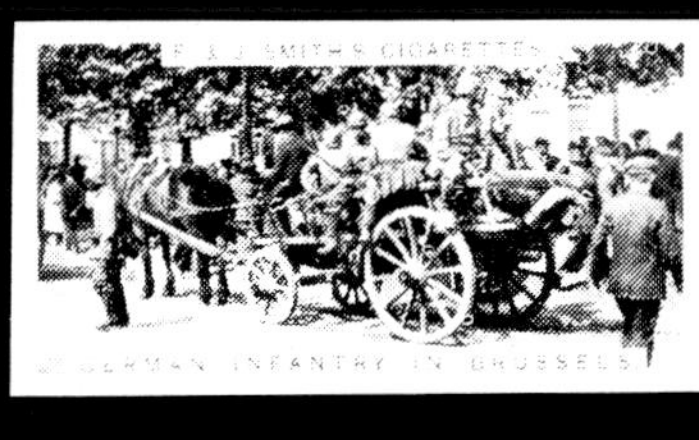

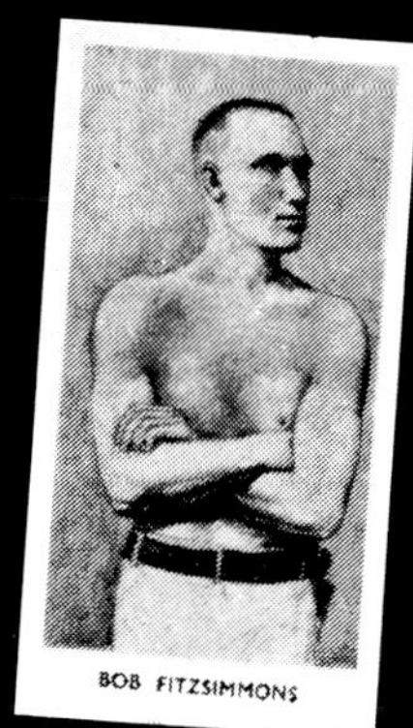

DISSIMILAR SERIES

When a firm decides to issue a new set of cards it may have undertaken some market research, but it will never be certain how successful it may become. If the response is positive it may then produce an extra set, which would normally be distinguished as 2nd or continuation series. In the case of Lea's Pottery or Ogden Boy Scouts this extended to five series. Sometimes when a subject appeared popular, different aspects would be covered by sets with different titles, as in the case of Player with their aircraft sets and Ogden with its racing series.

Sometimes a popular series was extended by producing it in different sizes. Apart from the better known multi sized sets such as those of International T.C. and Jackson, there are examples where the small and large cards depict different subjects. These include Wills English Period Costumes, Baker Actresses and Carreras Old Staffordshire Figures.

Another quite complicated situation can occur when a Company decides to issue a completely new series under the same title as an earlier set. Wills were very fond of this, with two or more series titled Wild Flowers, Association Footballers, Garden Flowers and Speed. Ogden too issued a later set of Boy Scouts some years after its first five, but its newer series of Bird's Eggs and British Birds were easily distinguishable by being cut-outs!

Finally, there is a group of series which are not quite the same. There are series where the pictures have been re-drawn, and show minor differences. These include two sets by Gallaher—Boy Scouts and the first series of Champions; also half the set of Carreras Famous Footballers and Huntley & Palmer's Sports.

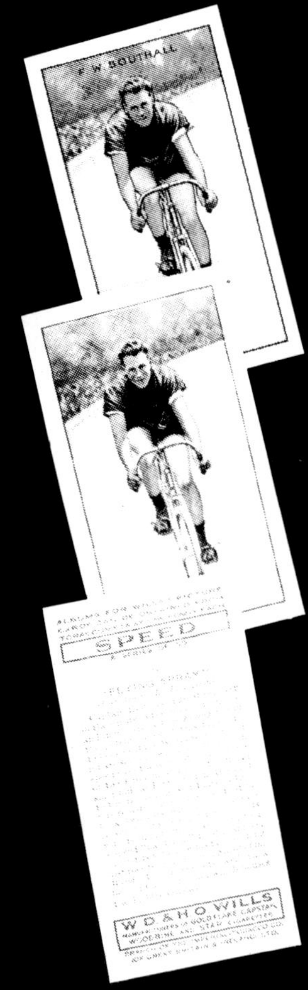

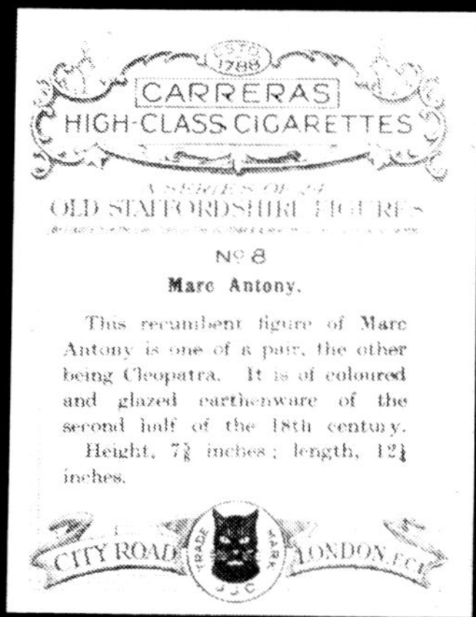

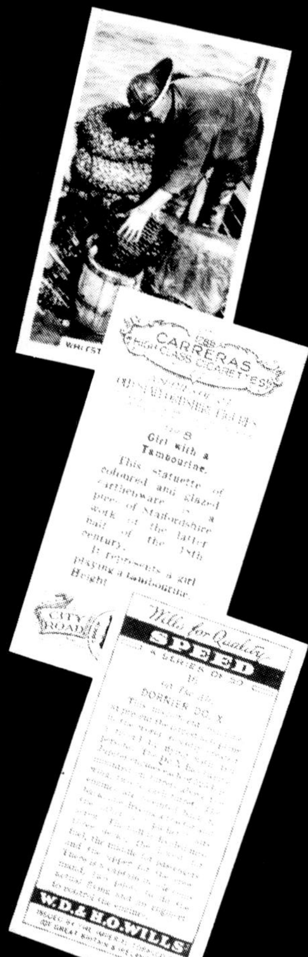

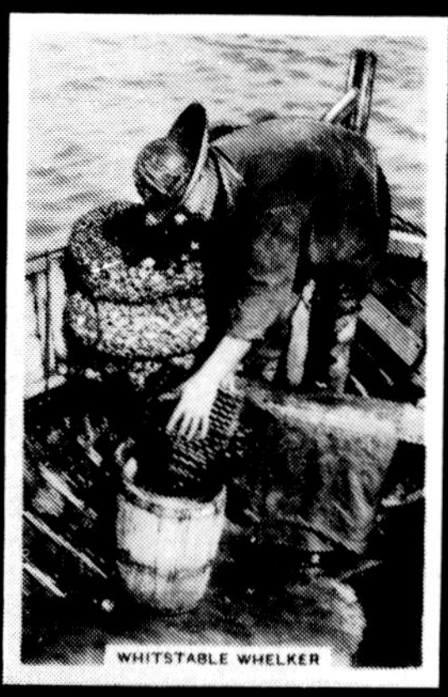

JAMES ILLINGWORTH LTD.

Qty		Date	Odds	Sets
MF48	Beautiful Scotland	1939	£1.50	—
M25	Cavalry	1924	£5.00	£125.00
MF48	Coastwise	1938	£1.00	£48.00
25	'Comicartoons' of Sport	1927	£5.50	£137.50
MF48	Flying	1938	£1.25	—
25	Motor Car Bonnets	1925	£7.00	£175.00
25	Old Hostels	1926	£5.50	£137.50
MF48	Our Countryside	1938	£1.50	—
MF24	Shots from the Films	1937	£4.00	—
?22	Views from the English Lakes	1894	£135.00	—

IMPERIAL TOBACCO CO. LTD.

Qty		Date	Odds	Sets
50	British Birds	1909	£4.00	£200.00
X1	Coronation Folder	1902	—	£80.00

IMPERIAL TOBACCO LTD.

Qty		Date	Odds	Sets
M12	Russ Abbot Advertising Cards	1993	—	£12.00

INGRAMS (Eastleigh)

Qty		Date	Odds	Sets
30	Army Pictures, Cartoons, etc	1916	*£90.00*	—

INTERNATIONAL TOBACCO CO. LTD.

Qty		Date	Odds	Sets
28	Domino Cards	1938	20p	£5.50
D50	Famous Buildings & Monuments, Series A			
	(International Tobacco Co. Ltd.)	1934	80p	£40.00
	(International Tobacco (Overseas) Ltd.)	1934	£1.20	—
D50	Famous Buildings & Monuments, Series B	1934	£1.50	—
100	Film Favourites (Black Back)	1937	£1.75	
100	(Brown Back)	1937	£1.75	—
D100	Gentlemen! The King! (Black Back)	1938	20p	£20.00
D100	(Blue Back)	1938	50p	—
50	International Code of Signals	1934	70p	£35.00
48	Screen Lovers (Summit)	Unissued	£2.75	£132.00

PETER JACKSON

Qty		Date	Odds	Sets
F28	Beautiful Scotland	1939	£1.25	£35.00
MF48	Beautiful Scotland	1939	£1.00	£48.00
F28	Coastwise	1938	£1.25	£35.00
MF48	Coastwise	1938	£1.25	£60.00
F28	Famous Film Stars	1935	£3.25	£91.00
F27	Famous Films	1934	£3.25	£88.00
F28	Film Scenes	1936	£3.25	£91.00
LF28	Film Scenes (Different)	1936	£4.50	£126.00
F28	Flying	1938	£3.00	£84.00
MF48	Flying	1938	£3.00	—

PETER JACKSON — cont.

Qty		Date	Odds	Sets
D100	Gentlemen! The King!			
	(Overprinted on Black International)	1938	£1.00	—
	(Overprinted on Blue International)	1938	£1.00	—
	(Reprinted Black with Jackson Name)	1938	80p	—
	(Reprinted Blue with Jackson Name)	1938	*£2.00*	—
F28	Life in the Navy	1937	£1.60	£45.00
LF28	Life in the Navy (Different)	1937	£2.25	£63.00
F28	Our Countryside	1938	£1.00	£28.00
MF48	Our Countryside	1938	£1.25	—
F28	Shots from the Films	1937	£2.75	£77.00
MF24	Shots from the Films	1937	£3.25	£78.00
D250	Speed through the Ages (Mixed Sizes)	1937	25p	£62.50
F28	Stars in Famous Films	1934	£3.50	£98.00
D150	The Pageant of Kingship (P. Jackson Ltd.)	1937	50p	—
D150	(P. Jackson Overseas Ltd.)	1937	30p	£45.00

JACOBI BROS. & CO. LTD.

Qty		Date	Odds	Sets
?50	Boer War Celebrities "JASAS"	1901	*£115.00*	—

JAMES & CO. (B'HAM) LTD.

Qty		Date	Odds	Sets
M20	Arms of Countries	1915	£115.00	—

JAMES'S

Qty		Date	Odds	Sets
?50	Pretty Girl Series "BAGG"	1898	*£175.00*	—

JERSEY TOBACCO CO. LTD. (Channel Isles)

Qty		Date	Odds	Sets
K53	Miniature Playing Cards	1933	80p	—

SOCIETE JOB

Qty		Date	Odds	Sets
25	British Lighthouses	1925	£5.50	£137.50
M48	Cinema Stars (Numbered)	1926	*£6.50*	—
M48	Cinema Stars (Unnumbered)	1926	85p	£65.00
48	Cinema Stars (Numbered)	1926	£3.00	—
48	Cinema Stars (Unnumbered)	1926	£3.00	—
25	Dogs	1911	£18.00	£450.00
25	Liners	1912	£27.50	—
53	Miniature Playing Cards	1926	*£6.50*	—
25	Orders of Chivalry	1924	£3.00	£75.00
25	Orders of Chivalry, 2nd Series	1927	£3.00	£75.00
3	Orders of Chivalry (Unnumbered)	1927	£8.00	£24.00
25	Racehorses	1909	£18.00	£450.00

GERMAN ISSUES

Qty		Date	Odds	Sets
X70	Sport in Zehn Bildern	1930	*£2.50*	—

J. B. JOHNSON & CO.

Qty		Date	Odds	Sets
25	National Flags, Flowers & Girls	1901	*£135.00*	—

JOHNSTON'S

Qty		Date	Odds	Sets
?	Views	1910	*£150.00*	—

JONES BROS.

Qty		Date	Odds	Sets
14/18	Spurs Footballers	1912	£8.00	£112.00

A. I. JONES & CO. LTD.

Qty		Date	Odds	Sets
M1	Advertisement Card	1901	—	*£325.00*
12	Nautical Terms	1905	£40.00	£480.00

ALEX JONES & CO.

Qty		Date	Odds	Sets
20	Actresses "ANGOOD" (Brown Front)	1898	*£130.00*	—
20	(Green Front)	1898	*£150.00*	—
1	Diamond Jubilee 1897	1897	—	£130.00

A. S. JONES

Qty		Date	Odds	Sets
30	Army Pictures, Cartoons, etc	1916	*£90.00*	—

T. E. JONES & CO.

Qty		Date	Odds	Sets
12	Conundrums	1900	*£135.00*	—
50	Flags of All Nations	1899	*£80.00*	—
?50	Footballers	1900	*£115.00*	—
16	Well-known Proverbs	1900	*£140.00*	—

C. H. JORDEN LTD.

Qty		Date	Odds	Sets
F12	Celebrities of the Great War	1915	£70.00	—

J. & E. KENNEDY

Qty		Date	Odds	Sets
25	Beauties "FECKSA"	1902	£45.00	—

RICHARD KENNEDY

Qty		Date	Odds	Sets
P?25	Army & Navy Cartoons	1906	*£135.00*	—
50	War Portraits	1916	*£75.00*	—

KINNEAR LTD.

Qty		Date	Odds	Sets
13	Actresses	1899	£100.00	—
M1	A Gentleman in Kharki	1900	—	£65.00
15	Australian Cricket Team	1897	£200.00	—

KINNEAR LTD. — cont.

Qty		Date	Odds	Sets
?25	Cricketers	1898	*£350.00*	—
X1	Cricket Fixture Folder	1903	—	*£500.00*
25	Footballers & Club Colours	1898	£130.00	—
12	Jockeys, Set 1	1898	£45.00	£540.00
1	Jockeys, Tod Sloane	1898	—	£80.00
25	Jockeys (Different), (Large Caption)	1898	£90.00	—
25	(Small Caption)	1898	£85.00	—
2	Prominent Personages	1902	*£225.00*	—
13	Royalty	1897	£40.00	£520.00
L1	The Four Generations	1900	—	*£175.00*
K?25	Views	1898	*£225.00*	—

KINNEAR, WHITWHAM & CO. LTD.

Qty		Date	Odds	Sets
18	Motor Cycle Series	1914	*£100.00*	—

B. KRIEGSFELD & CO.

Qty		Date	Odds	Sets
1	Advertisement Card	1900	—	*£350.00*
50	Beauties "KEWA" (Matt Front)	1898	£75.00	—
50	(Semi Glossy Front)	1898	*£135.00*	—
?10	Celebrities (Horizontal Back)	1901	*£135.00*	—
?10	(Vertical Back)	1901	£135.00	—
50	Flags of All Nations	1899	£60.00	—
50	Phrases & Advertisements	1900	£75.00	—

A. KUIT LTD.

Qty		Date	Odds	Sets
K?12	Arms of Cambridge Colleges	1914	*£75.00*	—
K?12	Arms of Companies	1914	*£75.00*	—
F30	British Beauties (Oval)	1914	£50.00	—
F?50	Crosmedo Bijou Cards	1915	*£100.00*	—
25	Principal Streets of British Cities & Towns	1915	£100.00	—
F50	Types of Beauty	1914	£100.00	—

L. & Y. TOBACCO MFG. CO.

Qty		Date	Odds	Sets
26	Actresses "FROGA"	1900	*£200.00*	—

LAMBERT & BUTLER

32 Page Reference Book — £3.50

Qty		Date	Odds	Sets
10	Actresses & Their Autographs (Narrow)	1898	£115.00	—
10	(Wide)	1898	£135.00	—
20	Actresses "BLARM"	1900	£24.00	—
50	Admirals (Mixed Backs)	1900	—	£750.00
50	(Bird's Eye)	1900	£16.00	—
50	(Flaked Gold Leaf Honeydew)	1900	£16.00	—
50	(May Blossom)	1900	£16.00	—
50	(Viking)	1900	£16.00	—
1	Advertisement Card	1898	—	£325.00
50	Aeroplane Markings	1937	£1.60	£80.00
25	A History of Aviation (Brown Front)	1933	£2.60	£65.00
25	A History of Aviation (Green Front)	1932	£2.00	£50.00
40	Arms of Kings & Queens of England	1906	£4.00	£160.00
25	Aviation	1915	£3.00	£75.00

LAMBERT & BUTLER — cont.

Qty		Date	Odds	Sets
26	Beauties "HOL" (Mixed Backs)	1899	—	£780.00
26	(Flaked Gold Leaf)	1899	£30.00	—
26	(Log Cabin)	1899	£30.00	—
26	(May Blossom)	1899	£30.00	—
26	(Viking Navy Cut)	1899	£30.00	—
50	Birds & Eggs	1906	£2.75	£137.50
25	Boer War & Boxer Rebellion – Sketches	1901	£26.50	—
20	Boer War Generals "CLAM" (Black Back)	1901	£27.50	—
20	(Brown Back)	1901	£27.50	—
10	Boer War Generals "FLAC"	1901	£32.50	—
25	British Trees & Their Uses	1927	£1.60	£40.00
1	Colonel Baden-Powell, King of Scouts	1901	—	*£325.00*
25	Common Fallacies	1928	£2.00	£50.00
50	Conundrums (Blue Back)	1901	£18.00	—
50	(Green Back)	1901	£13.00	£650.00
12	Coronation Robes	1902	£17.50	£210.00
25	Dance Band Leaders	1936	£4.00	£100.00
28	Dominoes (Packets)	1955	£2.50	—
50	Empire Air Routes	1936	£1.60	£80.00
25	Famous British Airmen & Airwomen	1935	£1.50	£37.50
25	Fauna of Rhodesia	1929	90p	£22.50
50	Find Your Way! (Drury Lane In Address)	1932	£1.40	£70.00
50	(Without Drury Lane)	1932	£1.40	£70.00
50	(Red Overprint)	1932	£1.50	£75.00
1	Find Your Way Joker Card	1932	—	£11.50
50	Footballers 1930-1	1931	£3.30	£165.00
25	Garden Life	1930	80p	£20.00
25	Hints & Tips for Motorists	1929	£3.50	£87.50
50	Horsemanship	1938	£2.20	£110.00
25	How Motor Cars Work	1931	£2.20	£55.00
50	Interesting Customs & Traditions of the Navy, Army & Air Force	1939	£1.00	£50.00
25	Interesting Musical Instruments	1929	£2.60	£65.00
50	Interesting Sidelights on the Work of the G.P.O.	1939	£1.00	£50.00
20	International Yachts	1902	£55.00	—
25	Japanese Series	1904	£6.00	£150.00
4	Jockeys (No Frame)	1902	£42.50	£170.00
10	Jockeys (With Frame, Different)	1902	£40.00	—
50	Keep Fit	1937	80p	£40.00
25	London Characters	1934	£1.80	£45.00
25	Motor Car Radiators	1928	£5.50	£137.50
25	Motor Cars, A Series (Green Back)	1922	£2.20	£55.00
25	Motor Cars, 2nd Series (26-50)	1923	£2.20	£55.00
50	Motor Cars, 3rd Series	1926	£3.60	£180.00
25	Motor Cars (Grey Back)	1934	£3.20	£80.00
50	Motor Cycles	1923	£3.30	£165.00
50	Motor Index Marks	1926	£2.40	£120.00
25	Motors	1908	£25.00	£625.00
25	Naval Portraits (Series of 25)	1914	£3.20	£80.00
50	(Series of 50)	1915	£3.20	£160.00
25	Pirates & Highwaymen	1926	£1.20	£30.00
25	Rhodesian Series	1928	£1.00	£25.00
50	The Thames from Lechlade to London			
	(Large Numerals)	1907	£5.50	—
	(Small Numerals)	1907	£5.00	£250.00
25	Third Rhodesian Series	1930	50p	£12.50

LAMBERT & BUTLER — cont.

Qty		Date	Odds	Sets
4	Types of the British Army & Navy			
	(Black Specialities Back)	1897	£62.50	—
	(Brown Specialities Back)	1897	£60.00	£240.00
	(Viking Cigarettes)	1897	£65.00	—
PF?	Warships	1910	*£30.00*	—
25	Waverley Series	1904	£10.00	£250.00
25	Winter Sports	1914	£3.20	£80.00
25	Wireless Telegraphy	1909	£4.40	£110.00
25	Wonders of Nature	1924	50p	£12.50
25	World's Locomotives (Series of 25)	1912	£3.50	£87.50
50	(Series of 50)	1912	£4.00	£200.00
25	World's Locomotives (Additional)	1913	£4.00	£100.00

OVERSEAS ISSUES

Qty		Date	Odds	Sets
50	Actors & Actresses "WALP"	1908	£2.75	—
250	Actresses "ALWICS" (With Firm's Name)	1905	£2.75	—
250	(Scout Cigarettes)	1905	£3.00	—
250	(Black Front)	1905	£6.50	—
250	(Mauve Front, 3 Backs)	1905	*£12.50*	—
250	(Red Portrait)	1905	*£12.50*	—
50	Beauties "LAWHA" (Scout Cigarettes)	1908	£3.00	—
50	(No Brand, Black Front)	1908	£2.75	—
50	(No Brand, Unicoloured)	1908	*£12.50*	—
83	Danske Byvaabner	1926	£15.00	—
26	Etchings (Dogs)	1928	*£20.00*	—
L26	Etchings (Dogs)	1928	*£25.00*	—
25	Flag Girls of All Nations	1910	£11.00	£275.00
F50	Homeland Events	1928	£1.20	£80.00
?1	Indian Women (Blue Front)	1910	*£40.00*	—
?1	(Red Front)	1910	*£40.00*	—
25	London Characters	1934	*£12.50*	—
F50	London Zoo	1927	£1.00	£50.00
50	Merchant Ships of the World	1924	£2.25	£112.50
30	Music Hall Celebrities	1906	£4.00	—
F50	Popular Film Stars (Title in 1 Line)	1925	£1.20	£60.00
F50	(Title in 2 Lines)	1925	£1.10	£55.00
F50	(Varsity Cigarettes)	1926	£2.00	£100.00
100	Royalty Notabilities & Events 1900-2	1902	£12.50	—
100	Russo Japanese Series	1905	£4.50	£450.00
F50	The Royal Family at Home and Abroad	1927	£1.20	£60.00
F50	The World of Sport	1927	£1.60	£80.00
F50	Types of Modern Beauty	1927	90p	£45.00
F50	Who's Who in Sport (1926)	1926	£1.50	£175.00
50	Zoological Studies	1928	*£4.00*	—

LAMBKIN BROS.

Qty		Date	Odds	Sets
36	Country Scenes (Series 1-6)	1924	£5.00	—
L36	Country Scenes (Series 7-12)	1926	£5.50	—
L?9	Irish Views (Plain Back)	1925	£27.50	—
L?6	Lily of Killarney Views	1925	£85.00	—

ED. LAURENS LTD.

Qty		Date	Odds	Sets
M55	British Cavalry Uniforms (P/C Inset)	1975	—	£60.00

C. & J. LAW

Qty		Date	Odds	Sets
25	Types of British Soldiers	1914	£24.00	£600.00
50	War Portraits	1915	*£80.00*	—

R. J. LEA LTD.

Qty		Date	Odds	Sets
2	Advertisement Cards	1913	*£225.00*	—
M12	Butterflies & Moths (Silk)	1924	£4.50	£54.00
L12	Butterflies & Moths (Silk, Different)	1924	£4.50	£54.00
P6	Butterflies & Moths (Silk, Different)	1924	£5.00	£30.00
12	Chairman Puzzles	1910	*£150.00*	—
70	Cigarette Transfers (Locomotives)	1916	£6.50	£450.00
25	Civilians of Countries Fighting with the Allies	1914	£10.00	£250.00
F48	Coronation Souvenir (Glossy, Lea Back)	1937	50p	£24.00
F48	(Glossy, Successors)	1937	40p	£20.00
48	(Matt, Lea Back)	1937	60p	£30.00
48	(Matt, Successors)	1937	50p	£24.00
MF48	Coronation Souvenir	1937	60p	£30.00
25	Dogs (1-25)	1923	£3.60	£90.00
25	Dogs (26-50)	1923	£5.20	£130.00
25	English Birds (Glossy)	1922	£2.50	£62.50
25	(Matt)	1922	£4.25	—
F54	Famous Film Stars	1939	£1.25	£67.50
F48	Famous Racehorses of 1926	1927	£2.20	£105.00
MF48	Famous Racehorses of 1926	1927	£2.60	£125.00
F48	Famous Views (Glossy)	1936	25p	£12.00
48	(Matt)	1936	50p	£24.00
MF48	Famous Views	1936	50p	£24.00
F36	Film Stars, 1st Series	1934	£2.50	£90.00
F36	Film Stars, 2nd Series	1934	£2.25	£81.00
25	Fish	1926	£1.80	£45.00
50	Flowers to Grow – The Best Perennials	1913	£3.20	£160.00
F48	Girls from the Shows (Glossy)	1935	£2.00	£96.00
48	(Matt)	1935	£2.25	£108.00
50	Miniatures (No Border)	1912	£2.50	£125.00
50	Miniatures (Gold Border)	1912	£2.50	£125.00
50	Miniatures (51-100)	1912	£2.40	£120.00
46/50	Modern Miniatures	1913	£1.10	£51.00
12	More Lea's Smokers (Green Border)	1906	£65.00	—
12	(Red Frame)	1906	£90.00	—
P24	Old English Pottery & Porcelain	1908	£5.00	£120.00
50	Old English Pottery & Porcelain	1912	£1.60	£80.00
50	Old Pottery & Porcelain, 2nd (Chairman)	1912	£1.40	£70.00
50	2nd (Recorder)	1912	£5.00	—
50	Old Pottery & Porcelain, 3rd (Chairman)	1912	£1.30	£65.00
50	3rd (Recorder)	1912	£5.00	—
50	Old Pottery & Porcelain, 4th Series	1913	£1.30	£65.00
50	Old Pottery & Porcelain, 5th Series	1913	£1.30	£65.00
54	Old Pottery (Silk)	1914	80p	£65.00
72	Old Pottery (Silk, Different)	1914	80p	£62.50
F54	Radio Stars (Glossy)	1935	£2.00	£108.00
54	(Matt)	1935	£2.25	£121.50
100	Regimental Crests & Badges (Silk)	1923	£1.20	£120.00
50	Roses	1924	£1.40	£70.00
50	Ships of the World	1925	£1.80	£90.00
25	The Evolution of the Royal Navy	1925	£1.80	£45.00

R. J. LEA LTD. — cont.

Qty		Date	Odds	Sets
25	War Pictures	1915	£3.50	£87.50
25	War Portraits	1915	£4.50	£112.50
F48	Wonders of the World (Glossy)	1938	50p	£24.00
48	(Matt)	1938	75p	£36.00
MF48	Wonders of the World	1938	60p	£29.00

ALFRED L. LEAVER

M12	Manikin Cards	1915	*£70.00*	—

J. LEES

20	Northampton Town Football Club	1912	£90.00	—

LEON DE CUBA CIGARS

30	Colonial Troops	1902	*£100.00*	—

A. LEWIS & CO. (WESTMINSTER) LTD.

52	Horoscopes	1938	80p	£42.50

H. C. LLOYD & SON LTD.

28	Academy Gems (Green Front, Multi-Backs)	1902	£45.00	—
28	(Mauve Front, Multi-Backs)	1902	£45.00	—
28	(Orange Front, Multi-Backs)	1902	£45.00	—
26	Actresses & Boer War Celebrities	1901	£37.50	—
M18	Devon Footballers (With Frame Line)	1902	*£100.00*	—
M42	Devon Footballers & Boer War Celebrities	1902	£40.00	—
25	Star Girls (Different Printings)	1899	*£175.00*	—
L36	War Pictures	1914	*£125.00*	—

RICHARD LLOYD & SONS

?21	Actresses, Celebrities & Yachts	1900	£85.00	—
25	Atlantic Records	1936	£2.50	£62.50
25	Boer War Celebrities	1899	£32.50	—
F27	Cinema Stars (1-27)	1935	£6.50	—
F27	Cinema Stars (28-54)	1935	£1.50	£40.50
F27	Cinema Stars, 3rd Series (55-81)	1936	£6.00	£162.00
25	Cinema Stars (Matt)	1937	£1.40	£35.00
25	Famous Cricketers Puzzle Series	1930	£6.00	£150.00
96	National Types, Costumes & Flags	1900	£30.00	—
25	Old English Inns	1923	£1.50	£37.50
25	Old Inns, Series 2	1924	£2.60	£65.00
50	Old Inns	1924	£1.30	£65.00
10	Scenes from San Toy	1905	£8.50	£85.00
7	Seven Ages of Man	1900	*£250.00*	—
25	Tricks & Puzzles	1935	£1.00	£25.00
25	Types of Horses	1926	£3.40	£85.00
25	Zoo Series	1926	90p	£22.50

A. LOWNIE

30	Army Pictures, Cartoons etc	1916	*£110.00*	—

LUSBY LTD.

Qty		*Date*	*Odds*	*Sets*
25	Scenes from Circus Life	1902	£110.00	—

HUGH McCALL

Qty		Date	Odds	Sets
1	RAF Recruiting Card	1924	*£125.00*	—

D. & J. MACDONALD

Qty		Date	Odds	Sets
10	Actresses "MUTA"	1901	£100.00	—
L?	Cricket & Football Teams (Tontine)	1902	*£240.00*	—
L?	(Winning Team)	1902	*£225.00*	—
25	Cricketers	1902	£325.00	—
L1	Yorkshire County Team	1900	—	*£500.00*

MACKENZIE & CO.

Qty		Date	Odds	Sets
F50	Music Hall Artistes	1902	£16.50	£825.00
50	The Zoo	1910	£24.00	—
50	Victorian Art Pictures	1910	£20.00	—

WM. McKINNELL

Qty		Date	Odds	Sets
20	The European War Series	1915	£50.00	—
50	War Portraits	1916	*£75.00*	—

MACNAUGHTON JENKINS & CO. LTD.

Qty		Date	Odds	Sets
M50	Castles of Ireland – Ancient & Modern	1924	£2.75	£137.50
50	Various Uses of Rubber	1924	£2.00	£120.00

A. McTAVISH

Qty		Date	Odds	Sets
30	Army Pictures, Cartoons, etc	1916	*£85.00*	—

McWATTIE & SONS

Qty		Date	Odds	Sets
30	Army Pictures, Cartoons, etc	1916	*£85.00*	—

THE MANXLAND TOBACCO CO.

Qty		Date	Odds	Sets
?	Views of the Isle of Man (Matt)	1900	*£200.00*	—
?	(Varnished)	1900	*£200.00*	—

MARCOVITCH & CO.

Qty		Date	Odds	Sets
F18	Beauties (Plain Back)	1932	£1.00	£18.00
6	The Story in Red and White	1955	£2.50	—
L7	The Story in Red and White	1955	£2.25	£16.00

MARCUS'S

Qty		Date	Odds	Sets
?25	Cricketers	1897	*£350.00*	—
25	Footballers & Club Colours	1898	£130.00	—
L1	The Four Generations	1900	—	*£200.00*

MARKHAM

Qty		Date	Odds	Sets
M?25	Views of Bridgwater	1906	£100.00	—

MARSUMA CO.

50	Famous Golfers & Their Strokes	1914	£38.00	£1900.00

C. MARTIN

30	Army Pictures, Cartoons, etc.	1916	*£90.00*	—

MARTINS LTD.

1	Arf A Mo Kaiser!	1915	—	£60.00
D?12	Carlyle Series (Different Printings)	1923	*£85.00*	—
P775	Leading Artistes	1916	£5.50	—
25	V.C. Heroes	1916	£22.00	£550.00

MASCOT CIGARETTES

?20	British Views	1925	*£50.00*	—

R. MASON & CO.

30	Colonial Troops	1902	£50.00	—
40	Naval & Military Phrases (No Border)	1904	£45.00	—
40	(White Border)	1904	£45.00	—

JUSTUS VAN MAURIK

X12	Views of Holland	1915	£100.00	—

MAY QUEEN VIRGINIA CIGARETTES

M10/12	Interesting Pictures	—	50p	£5.00

MENTORS LTD.

32	Views of Ireland	1912	£9.00	£285.00

J. MILLHOFF & CO. LTD.

F54	Antique Pottery	1927	80p	£43.00
MF56	Antique Pottery	1927	75p	£42.00
30	Art Treasures	1927	80p	£24.00
L50	Art Treasures	1926	50p	£25.00
L25	Art Treasures, 2nd Series (51-75)	1928	80p	£20.00
25	British Orders of Chivalry & Valour	1939	£1.50	£37.50
M20	De Reszke Rilette Pictures	1925	£2.50	—
M25	De Reszke Rilette Pictures	1925	£2.50	—
M30	De Reszke Rilette Pictures	1925	£2.50	—
M42	De Reszke Rilette Pictures	1925	£2.25	£95.00
M43	De Reszke Rilette Pictures	1925	£3.00	—
M56	De Reszke Rilette Pictures	1925	*£3.00*	—
M74	De Reszke Rilette Pictures	1925	£2.50	—

J. MILLHOFF & CO. LTD. — cont.

Qty		Date	Odds	Sets
L25	England Historic & Picturesque (1-25)	1928	80p	£20.00
L25	England Historic & Picturesque, 2nd Series	1928	80p	£20.00
F27	Famous Golfers	1928	£12.00	£425.00
F27	Famous Test Cricketers	1928	£4.50	£120.00
MF27	Famous Test Cricketers	1928	£4.00	£108.00
P24	Film Stars	1934	*£6.50*	—
M25	Gallery Pictures	1929	£1.00	£25.00
50	Geographia Map Series (Sect.)	1931	£1.70	£85.00
F36	In the Public Eye	1930	£1.20	£42.50
1	Jigsaw Advertisement Card (4 Types)	1933	—	£11.50
25	Men of Genius	1924	£3.80	£95.00
L25	Picturesque Old England	1931	£1.00	£25.00
F27	Real Photographs, A Series (Glossy)	1931	35p	£9.50
F27	(Matt)	1931	70p	£19.00
F27	Real Photographs, 2nd Series	1931	75p	£20.00
F27	Real Photographs, 3rd Series	1932	35p	£9.50
F27	Real Photographs, 4th Series	1932	60p	£16.50
F27	Real Photographs, 5th Series	1933	£1.00	£27.00
F27	Real Photographs, 6th Series	1933	£1.00	£27.00
25	Reproductions of Celebrated Oil Paintings	1928	£1.20	£30.00
L25	Roses	1927	£2.50	£62.50
MF?9	Theatre Advertisement Cards (Multi-Backed)	1905	*£75.00*	—
XF?9	Theatre Advertisement Cards (Multi-Backed)	1905	*£100.00*	—
F54	The Homeland Series	1933	25p	£13.50
MF56	The Homeland Series	1933	25p	£14.00
50	Things to Make	1935	65p	£32.50
50	What the Stars Say	1934	50p	£25.00
F36	Zoological Studies	1929	20p	£7.25

DUTCH ISSUES

Qty		Date	Odds	Sets
L40	Film Series 1	1932	*£6.25*	—
L60	Film Series 1 (2 Printings)	1932	£6.25	—
L60	Film Series 2 (Coloured, 2 Addresses)	1935	£6.25	—
L25	Film Series 3 (Red-Brown)	1930	*£6.25*	—
MF105	Film Series 4	1933	£5.00	—
MF?249	Film Series 4 (Inscribed Series of 206)	1934	£5.00	—
MF105	Film Series "SERIE 6"	1936	£5.00	—
F?70	Sports Series	1929	*£15.00*	—

MIRANDA LTD.

Qty		Date	Odds	Sets
20	Dogs	1925	£7.00	—
25	Sports and Pastimes	1925	£4.50	£140.00

STEPHEN MITCHELL & SON

Qty		Date	Odds	Sets
51	Actors & Actresses "FROGA" (Coloured)	1899	£18.00	—
26	Actors & Actresses "FROGA B" (Brown)	1899	£18.00	—
26	Actors & Actresses "FROGA C" (Brown)	1899	£18.00	—
50	Actors & Actresses "FROGA D" (Brown)	1899	£18.00	£900.00
1	Advertisement Card (Maid of Honour)	1900	—	*£325.00*
50	A Gallery of 1934	1935	£1.90	£95.00
50	A Gallery of 1935	1936	£2.00	£100.00
50	Air-Raid Precautions	1938	90p	£45.00
30	A Model Army	1932	£1.10	£33.00

STEPHEN MITCHELL & SON — cont.

Qty		Date	Odds	Sets
25	Angling	1928	£4.40	£110.00
50	Arms & Armour	1916	£3.50	£175.00
25	Army Ribbons & Buttons	1916	£3.60	£90.00
50	A Road Map of Scotland (Small Numeral)	1933	£2.00	£100.00
50	(Large Numeral)	1933	£2.00	£100.00
50	(Red Overprint)	1933	£2.75	—
1	A Road Map of Scotland (Substitute)	1933	—	£15.00
25	Boxer Rebellion – Sketches	1901	£23.50	—
25	British Warships (1-25)	1915	£6.00	£150.00
25	British Warships, 2nd Series (26-50)	1915	£6.00	£150.00
50	Clan Tartans, A Series	1927	£1.60	£80.00
25	Clan Tartans, 2nd Series	1927	80p	£20.00
25	Empire Exhibition, Scotland 1938	1938	70p	£17.50
25	Famous Crosses	1923	60p	£15.00
50	Famous Scots	1933	75p	£37.50
50	First Aid	1938	£1.00	£50.00
P3	Glasgow International Exhibition 1901	1901	£70.00	—
50	Humorous Drawings	1924	£2.30	£115.00
50	Interesting Buildings	1905	£6.00	—
40	London Ceremonials	1928	£1.20	£48.00
25	Medals	1916	£4.40	£110.00
25	Money	1913	£4.20	£105.00
25	Old Sporting Prints	1930	£1.40	£35.00
50	Our Empire	1937	45p	£22.50
25	Regimental Crests & Collar Badges	1900	£11.00	£275.00
70	River & Coastal Steamers	1925	£2.60	£182.00
50	Scotland's Story	1929	£1.80	£90.00
25	Scottish Clan Series	1903	£11.00	£300.00
50	Scottish Footballers	1934	£2.00	£100.00
50	Scottish Football Snaps	1935	£2.00	£100.00
25	Seals	1911	£4.40	£110.00
25	Sports	1907	£11.00	£300.00
25	Stars of Screen & History	1939	£2.00	£50.00
25	Statues & Monuments	1914	£4.00	£100.00
50	The World of Tomorrow	1936	90p	£45.00
25	Village Models	1925	£2.00	£50.00
L25	Village Models	1925	£4.00	£100.00
25	Village Models, 2nd Series	1925	£2.20	£55.00
25	2nd (Not Inscribed 2nd)	1925	£4.00	—
L25	Village Models, 2nd Series	1925	£4.00	£100.00
50	Wonderful Century	1937	55p	£27.50

MOORGATE TOBACCO CO. LTD.

Qty		Date	Odds	Sets
D30	The New Elizabethan Age (Matt)	1953	£2.75	—
D30	(Varnished)	1953	£1.75	£52.50

B. MORRIS & SONS LTD.

Qty		Date	Odds	Sets
30	Actresses (Black & White)	1898	£1.60	£68.00
26	Actresses "FROGA A" (Borneo Queen)	1899	£27.50	—
26	(Gold Seals)	1899	£27.50	—
26	(Morris's Cigarettes)	1899	£27.50	—
26	(Tommy Atkins)	1899	£75.00	—

B. MORRIS & SONS LTD. — cont.

Qty		Date	Odds	Sets
L26	Actresses "FROGA B"	1899	*£250.00*	—
1	Advertisement Card	1900	—	*£300.00*
6	Agriculture in the Orient	1910	£6.25	£37.50
50	Animals at the Zoo (Blue Back)	1924	65p	£32.50
50	(Grey Back)	1924	75p	£37.50
6	Architectural Monuments	1910	£6.25	£37.50
35	At the London Zoo Aquarium	1928	40p	£14.00
25	Australian Cricketers	1925	£2.80	£70.00
M24	Battleship Crests (Silk)	1915	£30.00	—
50	Beauties "CHOAB" (Gold Flake Honeydew)	1900	£37.50	—
50	(Golden Virginia)	1900	£37.50	—
50	(Levant Favorites)	1900	£36.50	—
50	(Reina Regenta)	1900	£36.50	—
50	Beauties Collotype (Multi-Backed)	1897	*£120.00*	—
21	Beauties "MOM" (Borneo Queen)	1899	£27.50	—
21	(Gold Seals)	1899	£27.50	—
21	(Morris Cigarettes)	1899	£27.50	—
21	(Tommy Atkins)	1899	£75.00	—
20	Boer War 1900	1900	£32.50	£650.00
25	Boer War Celebrities "PAM"	1901	£26.50	—
25	Captain Blood	1937	£1.00	£25.00
L25	English & Foreign Birds (Silk)	1915	£4.00	£100.00
L25	English Flowers (Silk, Panel Cigarettes)	1915	£3.40	£85.00
L25	("Cruel" Silk)	1915	£6.00	—
L25	(Silk, No Brand)	1915	£5.00	—
L50	English Flowers (Silk)	1915	£4.00	£200.00
50	Film Star Series	1923	£2.80	£140.00
25	Golf Strokes Series	1923	£6.00	£150.00
12	Horoscopes	1936	50p	£6.00
25	How Films are Made	1934	£1.40	£35.00
50	How to Sketch	1929	90p	£45.00
20	London Views (American Gold)	1904	£30.00	—
20	(Borneo Queen)	1904	£30.00	—
20	(Gold Flake)	1904	£30.00	—
20	(Reina Regenta)	1904	£30.00	—
25	Marvels of the Universe Series	1912	£3.40	£85.00
25	Measurement of Time	1924	£1.30	£32.50
25	Motor Series	1922	£4.00	£100.00
50	National & Colonial Arms	1917	£5.40	£270.00
25	Racing Greyhounds	1939	£1.80	£45.00
L25	Regimental Colours (Silk)	1916	£2.75	—
G4	Regimental Colours (Silk)	1916	*£55.00*	—
6	Schools in Foreign Countries	1910	£6.25	£37.50
24	Shadowgraphs	1925	£2.50	£60.00
6	Strange Vessels	1910	£6.25	£37.50
6	The Ice Breaker	1910	£6.25	£37.50
25	The Queen's Dolls House	1925	£2.60	£65.00
13	Treasure Island	1924	£1.20	£16.00
50	Victory Signs Series	1928	60p	£30.00
25	War Celebrities	1916	£5.00	£125.00
25	War Pictures	1916	£7.00	£175.00
25	Wax Art Series	1931	50p	£12.50
25	Whipsnade Zoo	1932	60p	£15.00
25	Wireless Series	1923	£3.60	£90.00

PHILIP MORRIS & CO. LTD.

Qty		Date	Odds	Sets
50	British Views	1924	£2.20	£110.00
L50	British Views	1924	£2.60	—
T108	Classic Collection	1985	£1.25	—
M72	Motormania	1986	£1.25	—

P. MOUAT & CO.

30	Colonial Troops	1902	*£120.00*	—

MOUSTAFA LTD.

F50	Camera Studies (Printed Back)	1923	£2.75	—
F50	(Plain Back)	1923	£2.50	—
25	Cinema Stars	1924	£4.00	—
40	Leo Chambers Dogs Heads	1924	£2.75	£110.00
25	Pictures of World Interest	1923	£2.80	£70.00
F25	Real Photos	1925	50p	£12.50

MUNRO

30	Colonial Troops	1902	*£125.00*	—

B. MURATTI SONS & CO. LTD.

P?25	Actresses, Collotype	1899	£100.00	—
26	Actresses "FROGA" (Cigarette Connoisseur)	1899	£22.00	£570.00
26	(Zinnia)	1899	£26.00	—
P?50	Actresses & Beauties (Horizontal Back)	1899	*£135.00*	—
P?50	(Vertical Back)	1899	£135.00	—
P?50	(Stamped Back)	1899	*£135.00*	—
P?50	(Plain Back)	1899	£130.00	—
X?35	Advertisement Cards	1900	*£250.00*	—
F24	Australian Racehorses	1931	80p	£20.00
50	Beauties "CHOAB" (Black Back)	1900	£40.00	—
50	(Green Back)	1900	*£45.00*	—
M54	Beautiful Women	1900	£85.00	—
20	Boer War Generals "CLAM"	1900	£30.00	—
X?	Book Postcard Series	1902	*£75.00*	—
M15	Caricatures (4 Brands)	1903	£24.00	£360.00
M15	(Vassos)	1903	*£65.00*	—
M15	(Vassos Blanked Out)	1903	£45.00	—
M15	(Zinnia, Black)	1903	£25.00	£375.00
M15	(Zinnia, Brown)	1903	£30.00	—
M35	Crowned Heads	1912	£12.50	£500.00
53	Japanese Series (Printed Back)	1904	£13.50	£715.00
53	(Plain Back)	1904	£12.50	—
XF?	Midget Post Card Series (Glossy)	1902	£7.00	—
X?	(Matt)	1902	£7.00	—
X?	Queens Postcard Series	1902	£10.00	—
19	Russo Japanese Series	1904	£12.00	£230.00
25	Star Girls	1899	*£135.00*	—
50	Views of Jersey (Printed Back)	1913	£17.50	—
50	(Plain Back)	1913	£14.00	—

B. MURATTI SONS & CO. LTD. — cont.

Qty		*Date*	*Odds*	*Sets*
25	War Series I	1916	£20.00	—
25	War Series II	1917	£12.00	£300.00
SILK ISSUES				
L40	Canvas Masterpieces, Series M (Large Globe)	1916	£5.25	—
L40	(Small Globe)	1916	£2.25	£90.00
P16	Canvas Masterpieces, Series P	1916	£11.00	—
M24	Flags, Series A (26-49)	1914	£3.25	£78.00
P3	Flags, Series A (1-3)	1914	£8.50	—
L1	Flags, Series B (No.19)	1914	—	£10.00
M25	Flags, Series C (20-44)	1914	£3.20	£80.00
P18	Flags, Series C (1-18)	1914	£8.50	—
P3	Flags, Series D (45-47)	1914	£8.25	—
M24/25	Flags, Series E (48-72, Green Back)	1914	£3.20	£80.00
M24/25	(48-72, Grey Back)	1914	£3.20	£80.00
P6	Flags, Series F (73-78)	1914	£7.00	—
P18	Great War Leaders, Series P	1916	£12.00	—
M25	Regimental Badges, Series A	1915	£4.00	£100.00
L48	Regimental Badges, Series B	1915	£5.50	—
L15	Regimental Badges, Series B (Different, 4-18)	1915	£5.50	—
L16	Regimental Badges, Series G (79-94)	1915	£7.50	—
L25	Regimental Colours, Series CB	1915	£9.00	—
M72	Regimental Colours, Series RB	1915	£5.00	—
GERMAN ISSUES				
X216	Brennpunkte des Deutschen Sports 1	1935	75p	£162.00
X288	Brennpunkte des Deutschen Sports 2	1936	£1.00	—
X216	Brennpunkte des Deutschen Sports 3	1936	75p	£162.00
?30	Cinema Stars Serie No. 1	1932	*£4.00*	—
?30	Cinema Stars Serie No. 2	1932	*£4.00*	—

MURRAY, SONS & CO.

20	Actresses "BLARM" (Pineapple Cigarettes)	1902	£85.00	—
20	(Special Crown Cigarettes)	1902	*£85.00*	—
F22	Bathing Beauties	1929	£5.00	—
40	Bathing Belles	1939	30p	£12.00
15	Chess and Draughts Problems	1910	£55.00	—
F22	Cinema Scenes	1929	£6.00	—
20	Cricketers (Series H, Black Front)	1912	£65.00	—
20	(Series H, Brown Front)	1912	*£130.00*	—
25	Crossword Puzzles	1923	*£65.00*	—
F26	Dancers	1929	£5.00	£130.00
F25	Dancing Girls (Belfast, Ireland)	1929	£3.00	£75.00
F25	(London & Belfast)	1929	£2.50	£62.50
F26	("Series of 26")	1930	£3.00	£78.00
25	Famous Works of Art	1910	£18.00	—
M16	Flags (Silk)	1910	£20.00	—
X3	Flags & Arms (Silk)	1910	£65.00	—
34	Footballers, Series H	1912	£30.00	—
104	Footballers, Series J	1913	£30.00	—
?29	Football Colours (Shaped, Maple Cigarettes)	1905	*£65.00*	—
?29	(Shaped, Murray Cigarettes)	1905	*£65.00*	—
25	Football Rules	1911	£26.00	£650.00
25	High Class Works of Art	1909	£20.00	—
20	Holidays by the L.M.S.	1927	£10.00	£200.00
20	Inventors Series	1924	£4.00	£80.00

MURRAY, SONS & CO. — cont.

Qty		*Date*	*Odds*	*Sets*
25	Irish Scenery (Hall Mark Cigarettes)	1905	£20.00	—
25	(Pine Apple Cigarettes)	1905	£20.00	—
25	(Special Crown Cigarettes)	1905	£20.00	—
25	(Straight Cut Cigarettes)	1905	£20.00	—
25	(Yachtsman Cigarettes)	1905	£20.00	—
31	Orders of Chivalry (Silk)	1925	£16.50	—
25	Polo Pictures	1910	£22.00	£550.00
M50	Prominent Politicians (With "In two strengths")	1909	£2.30	£115.00
M50	(Without "In two strengths").	1909	£16.00	—
50	Puzzle Series	1929	£6.00	—
M25	Regimental Badges (Silk)	1910	£16.00	—
50	Stage and Film Stars	1926	£2.50	£125.00
25	Steam Ships	1939	£1.20	£30.00
50	The Story of Ships	1940	40p	£20.00
25	Types of Aeroplanes	1929	£1.50	£37.50
20	Types of Dogs	1924	£5.50	£110.00
35	War Series K	1915	£22.00	£770.00
25	War Series L	1916	£2.00	£70.00

H. J. NATHAN

40	Comical Military & Naval Pictures (No Border)	1904	£50.00	—
40	(White Border)...	1904	£50.00	—

JAMES NELSON

?20	Beauties "FENA"	1899	*£200.00*	—

NETTLETON AND MITCHELL

30	Army Pictures, Cartoons, etc	1916	*£150.00*	—

EDWD. J. NEWBEGIN

F50	Actors & Actresses	1901	£45.00	—
10	Actresses "HAGG"	1900	*£130.00*	—
20	Cricketers Series	1902	*£325.00*	—
1	Mabel Love Advert Card (3 Colours)	1900	—	*£350.00*
19	Russo Japanese Series	1904	*£120.00*	—
16	Well-known Proverbs	1900	*£120.00*	—
24	Well-known-Songs	1900	£110.00	—

W. H. NEWMAN LTD.

18	Motor Cycle Series	1914	£75.00	—

THE NEW MOSLEM CIGARETTE CO. LTD.

30	Proverbs	1903	£80.00	—

THOS. NICHOLLS & CO.

50	Orders of Chivalry	1916	£6.00	£300.00

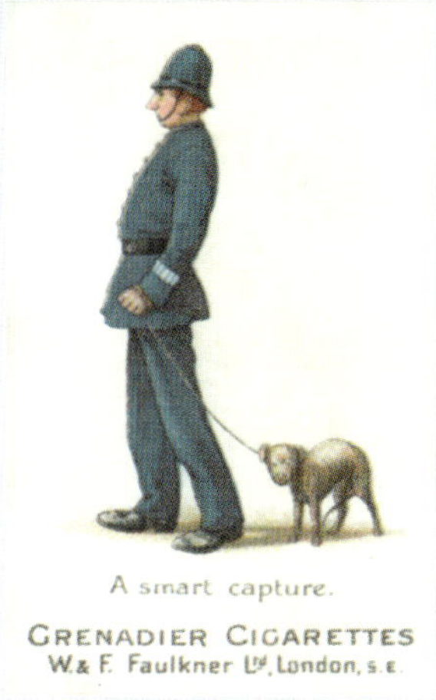

Police Terms
Faulkner

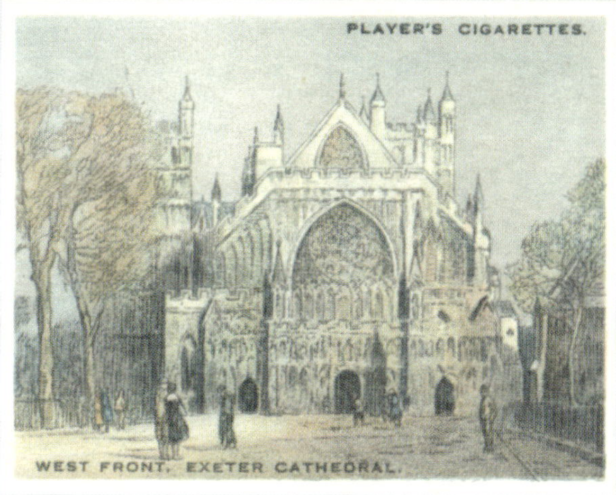

Architectural Beauties
Player

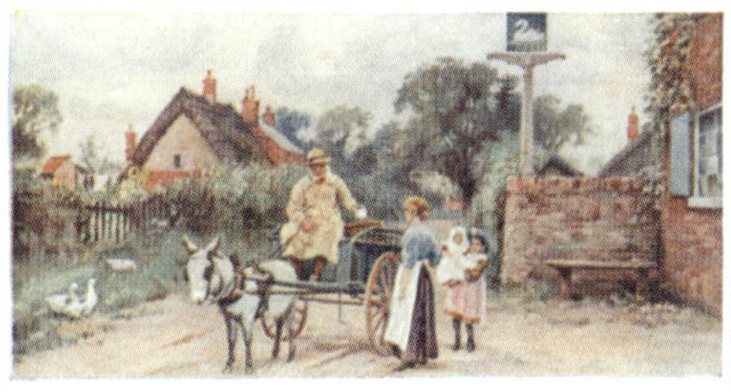

Picture Series
Redford, Simonets, Teofani

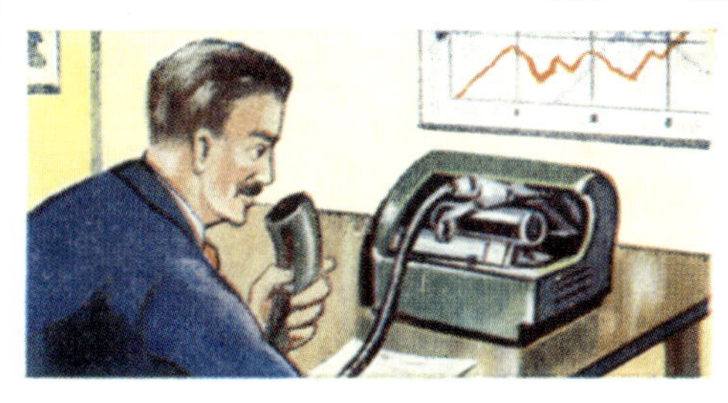

Communications
Amalgamated Tobacco

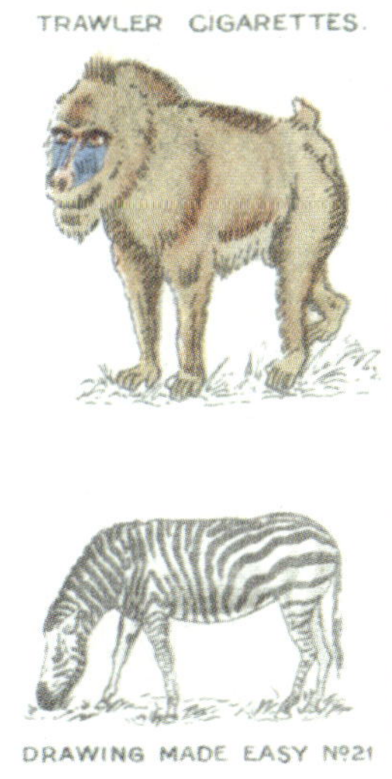

Drawing Made Easy
Pattreiouex

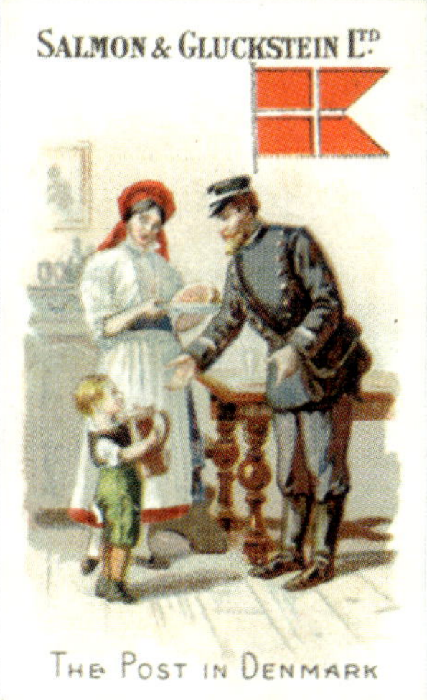

The Post in Various Countries
Salmon & Gluckstein

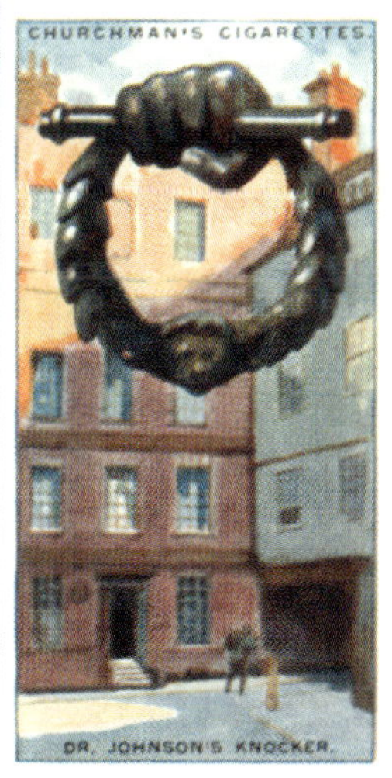

Interesting Door-Knockers
Churchman

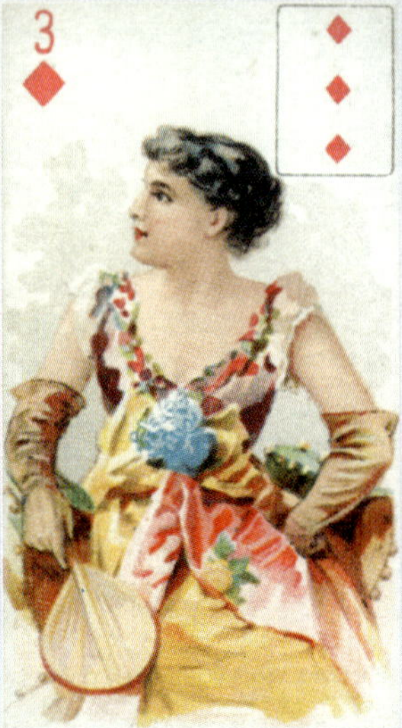

Beauties, P/C Inset
A.T.C., Kimball

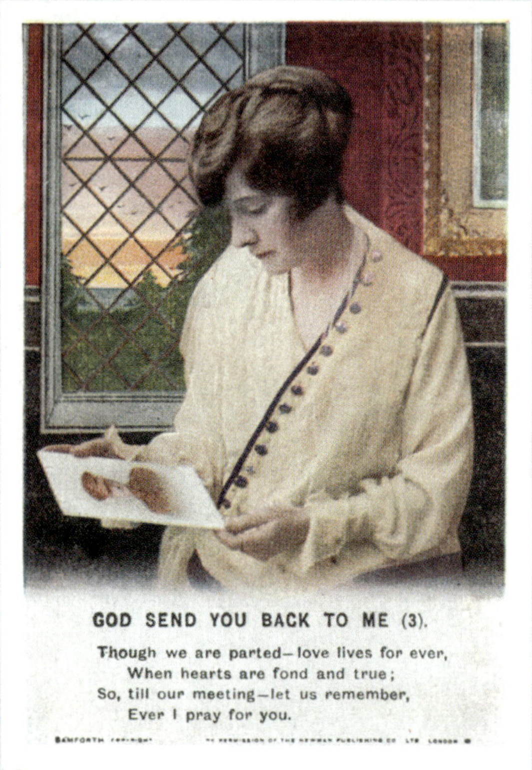

Illustrated Songs
Leng Papers

Beautiful Bathers
Kimball

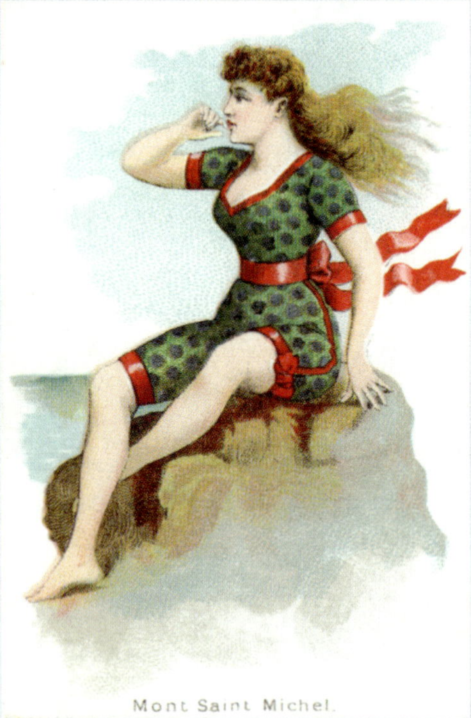

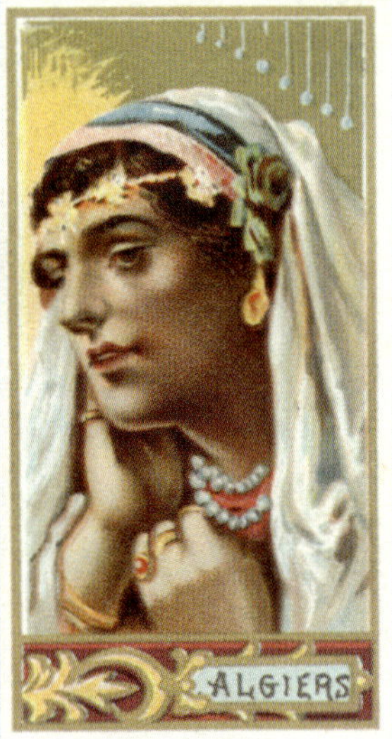

Types of All Nations
Allen & Ginter

THE NILMA TOBACCO COY.

Qty		Date	Odds	Sets
40	Home & Colonial Regiments	1903	*£75.00*	—
30	Proverbs	1903	*£75.00*	—

M. E. NOTARAS LTD.

Qty		Date	Odds	Sets
M24	Chinese Scenes	1925	75p	£18.00
F36	National Types of Beauty	1925	75p	£27.00

A. NOTON

Qty		Date	Odds	Sets
M12	Manikin Cards	1915	*£75.00*	—

OGDENS LTD.

244 Page Illustrated Reference Book (With Guinea Gold) — £12.50

Qty		Date	Odds	Sets
25	A.B.C. of Sport	1927	£2.60	£65.00
50	Actors, Natural & Character Studies	1938	£1.00	£50.00
25	Actresses ("No Glycerine", Black Front)	1895	£80.00	—
25	("No Glycerine", Brown Front)	1895	£80.00	—
?100	Actresses, Collotype (Mauve Stamped Back)	1894	£45.00	—
?100	(Red Stamped Back)	1894	*£70.00*	—
?100	Actresses, Collotype (Printed Back)	1894	£45.00	—
50	Actresses, Green Gravure	1898	£9.00	£450.00
?1	Actresses, Green, Green Border	1898	*£200.00*	—
50	Actresses, Tabs Type, Red Tint	1902	£30.00	—
?210	Actresses, Woodburytype	1894	£32.50	—
F?583	Actresses, Guinea Gold Type	1900	£2.40	—
50	A.F.C. Nicknames	1933	£3.75	£187.50
50	Air-Raid Precautions	1938	70p	£35.00
50	Applied Electricity	1928	£1.00	£50.00
192	Army Crests and Mottoes	1902	£4.00	£770.00
36	Australian Test Cricketers	1928	£3.25	£117.00
28	Beauties "BOCCA"	1899	£22.50	£630.00
50	Beauties "CHOAB"	1899	£25.00	—
26	Beauties "HOL" (Blue Printed Back)	1899	£16.50	£430.00
26	(Rubber Stamped Back)	1899	*£110.00*	—
66	Beauties,Green Net Back (Black & White)	1901	£12.00	£800.00
100	(Coloured)	1901	£22.00	—
52	Beauties, P/C Inset	1899	£25.00	£1300.00
26	Beauties (No Insets, Subjects as Above)	1899	£35.00	—
52	Beauties & Military, P/C Inset	1898	£25.00	£1300.00
F50	Beauty Series (Unnumbered)	1900	£65.00	—
F50	Beauty Series (Numbered)	1900	£2.30	£115.00
50	Billiards by Tom Newman	1928	£1.50	£75.00
50	Birds' Eggs	1908	£1.50	£75.00
50	Bird's Eggs (Cut-outs)	1923	85p	£42.50
F?141	Boer War & General Interest	1901	£2.60	—
LF?52	Boer War & General Interest	1901	*£35.00*	—
50	Boxers	1915	£6.00	£300.00
25	Boxing	1914	£5.00	£125.00
50	Boy Scouts (Blue Back)	1911	£2.40	£120.00
50	(Green Back)	1911	£3.50	£175.00
50	Boy Scouts, 2nd Series (Blue Back)	1912	£2.40	£120.00
50	(Green Back)	1912	£3.60	£180.00
50	Boy Scouts, 3rd Series (Blue Back)	1912	£2.50	£125.00
50	(Green Back)	1912	£3.60	£180.00

Qty		*Date*	*Odds*	*Sets*
50	Boy Scouts, 4th Series	1913	£2.50	£125.00
25	Boy Scouts, 5th Series	1914	£2.50	£62.50
50	Boy Scouts (Different)	1929	£1.50	£75.00
50	British Birds	1905	£1.50	£75.00
50	British Birds, Second Series	1909	£1.80	£90.00
50	British Birds (Cut-outs)	1923	80p	£40.00
50	British Birds & Their Eggs	1939	£2.40	£120.00
50	British Costumes from 100 B.C. to 1904	1905	£5.50	£275.00
50	Broadcasting	1935	£1.20	£60.00
50	By the Roadside	1932	90p	£45.00
44	Captains of Association Football Clubs & Colours.	1926	£2.75	£120.00
50	Cathedrals & Abbeys	1936	90p	£45.00
50	Champions of 1936	1937	£1.60	£80.00
50	Children of All Nations	1924	80p	£40.00
50	Club Badges	1915	£4.50	£225.00
50	Colour In Nature	1932	75p	£37.50
?29	Comic Pictures	1897	£260.00	—
50	Construction of Railway Trains	1930	£2.20	£110.00
50	Coronation Procession (Sect.)	1937	£1.40	£70.00
12	Cricket & Football-Women (Gold Medal)	1896	*£250.00*	—
12	(Cox Back)	1896	*£300.00*	—
12	(Otto De Rose)	1896	*£325.00*	—
50	Cricketers & Sportsmen	1898	£65.00	—
50	Cricket 1926	1926	£2.40	£120.00
25	Derby Entrants 1926	1926	£2.20	£55.00
50	Derby Entrants 1928	1928	£1.70	£85.00
50	Derby Entrants 1929	1929	£2.20	£110.00
50	Dogs	1936	£1.80	£90.00
55	Dominoes	1909	£1.30	£71.50
112	Dominoes – Actress & Beauty Backs			
28	Actresses, Corners Mitred	1900	£24.00	—
28	Actresses, Corners Not Mitred	1900	£22.00	£615.00
56	Beauties, Corners Not Mitred	1900	£24.00	—
25	Famous Dirt-Track Riders	1929	£3.60	£90.00
50	Famous Footballers	1908	£3.40	£170.00
50	Famous Rugby Players	1926	£2.00	£100.00
50	Flags & Funnels of Leading Steamship Lines	1906	£3.60	£180.00
50	Football Caricatures	1935	£2.50	£125.00
43	Football Club Badges (Shaped)	1910	£5.50	—
50	Football Club Captains	1936	£1.70	£85.00
51	Football Club Colours	1906	£3.20	£163.00
50	Foreign Birds	1924	80p	£40.00
50	Fowls Pigeons & Dogs	1904	£2.60	£130.00
25	Greyhound Racing, 1st Series	1927	£3.50	£87.50
25	Greyhound Racing, 2nd Series	1928	£3.50	£87.50
1	History of the Union Jack (Folder)	1900	—	£180.00
50	How to Swim	1935	80p	£40.00
50	Infantry Training	1915	£2.00	£100.00
50	Jockeys, and Owners' Colours	1927	£2.30	£115.00
50	Jockeys, 1930	1930	£2.20	£110.00
50	Leaders Of Men	1924	£1.60	£80.00
MF3	Liners (Guinea Gold Type)	1901	£135.00	—
P6	Liners (6 Brands)	1902	£100.00	—
25	Marvels of Motion	1928	£1.60	£40.00
K52	Miniature Playing Cards (Actresses)	1900	£3.25	—

OGDENS LTD. — cont.

Qty		Date	Odds	Sets
K102	Miniature Playing Cards (Beauty Backs)	1900	£3.50	—
K52	Miniature Playing Cards (Coolie) (No Border)	1904	£2.25	£117.00
	(White Border)	1904	£3.75	—
K52	Miniature Playing Cards (Tabs)	1909	£2.50	£130.00
50	Modern British Pottery	1925	85p	£42.50
50	Modern Railways	1936	£1.90	£95.00
50	Modern War Weapons	1915	£2.60	£130.00
25	Modes of Conveyance	1927	£2.20	£55.00
50	Motor Races 1931	1931	£2.40	£120.00
50	Ocean Greyhounds	1938	90p	£45.00
25	Optical Illusions	1923	£2.50	£62.50
50	Orders of Chivalry	1907	£2.60	£130.00
25	Owners, Racing Colours & Jockeys (Green Back)	1914	£3.50	£87.50
50	Owners, Racing Colours & Jockeys (Blue Back)	1906	£2.70	£135.00
25	Picturesque People of the Empire	1927	£1.20	£30.00
50	Picturesque Villages	1936	90p	£45.00
25	Poultry (1-25) (Ogdens on Front)	1915	£4.00	£100.00
25	(1-25) (No Ogdens on Front)	1915	£4.20	£105.00
25	Poultry, 2nd Series (26-50)	1916	£4.20	£105.00
25	Poultry Alphabet	1924	£3.20	£80.00
25	Poultry Rearing & Management, 1st Series	1922	£2.40	£60.00
25	Poultry Rearing & Management, 2nd Series	1923	£2.40	£60.00
50	Prominent Cricketers of 1938	1938	£1.60	£80.00
50	Prominent Racehorses of 1933	1934	£1.70	£85.00
50	Pugilists & Wrestlers, A Series (1-50)	1908	£3.80	£190.00
25	Pugilists & Wrestlers, Second Series (51-75)	1909	£4.20	£105.00
50	Pugilists in Action	1928	£3.20	£160.00
50	Racehorses	1907	£3.00	£150.00
50	Racing Pigeons	1931	£2.80	£140.00
25	Records of the World	1908	£2.20	£55.00
50	Royal Mail	1909	£3.50	£175.00
50	Sea Adventure	1939	50p	£25.00
50	Sectional Cycling Map	1910	£2.50	£125.00
50	Shakespeare Series (Numbered)	1905	£10.00	£500.00
50	(Unnumbered)	1905	£9.50	£475.00
50	Shots from the Films	1936	£1.80	£90.00
25	Sights of London	1923	£1.30	£32.50
50	Smugglers and Smuggling	1932	£1.80	£90.00
50	Soldiers of the King (Grey Caption)	1909	£4.40	£220.00
25	(Brown Caption)	1909	£5.40	£135.00
P36	Sporting & Other Girls	1898	£350.00	—
50	Steeplechase Celebrities	1931	£1.80	£90.00
50	Steeplechase Trainers & Owners Colours	1927	£1.80	£90.00
50	Swimming, Diving and Life-Saving	1931	£1.00	£50.00
25	Swiss Views (1-25)	1910	£2.50	£62.50
25	Swiss Views (26-50)	1910	£4.50	£112.50
50	The Blue Riband of the Atlantic	1929	£2.30	£115.00
50	The Story of Sand	1935	80p	£40.00
25	Trainers and Owners Colours, 1st Series	1925	£2.00	£50.00
25	Trainers and Owners Colours, 2nd Series	1926	£2.40	£60.00
50	Trick Billiards	1934	£1.40	£70.00
50	Turf Personalities	1929	£2.20	£110.00
48	Victoria Cross Heroes	1901	£12.00	£575.00
25	Whaling	1927	£2.50	£62.50
50	Yachts & Motor Boats	1930	£2.00	£100.00
50	Zoo Studies	1937	50p	£25.00

Qty		Date	Odds	Sets
GUINEA GOLD PHOTOGRAPHIC ISSUES				
LF1	Actresses Base C	1899	—	£40.00
F375	Actresses Base D	1900	£1.10	—
MF55	Actresses Base D (Medium Size)	1900	£11.00	—
LF270	Actresses Base D	1900	£1.25	—
F40	Actresses Base E	1900	£3.00	£120.00
F638	Actresses Base I	1899	£1.00	—
F24	Actresses Base I (¾ White Frame)	1899	£3.50	—
LF21	Actresses Base I	1899	£40.00	—
F30	Actresses Base J	1899	£3.50	£105.00
F239	Actresses Base K	1899	£2.40	—
F216	Actresses Base L	1899	£2.00	—
F60	Actresses, Base M, (¾ White Frame)	1900	£1.80	£108.00
F113	Actresses & Miscellaneous Base I	1900	£1.00	£113.00
F2914	Actresses & Miscellaneous Base M	1900	90p	—
LF403	Actresses & Miscellaneous Base M	1900	£1.25	—
F58	Boer War & Actresses Base F	1901	80p	£45.00
F186	Boer War & Miscellaneous Base D	1901	65p	—
LF153	Boer War & Miscellaneous Base D	1900	£1.00	—
F321	Continental Actresses Base B	1899	£2.50	—
LF71	Continental Actresses Base B	1899	£15.00	—
F11	Cricketers Base I	1901	£12.00	£132.00
F50	Cricketers Base M (Set 1)	1899	£16.00	—
F27	Cricketers Base M (Set 2)	1899	£25.00	—
F57	Cyclists Base M	1899	£5.00	£285.00
F58	Denumbered Group Base D	1900	£2.00	£116.00
LF50	Denumbered Group Base D	1900	£3.00	£150.00
F176	Footballers Base M	1899	£11.00	—
F320	General Interest (White Panel) Base D/I	1900	85p	£275.00
F200	General Interest Numbered 1-200	1899	35p	£70.00
F300	General Interest Numbered 201-500	1900	£1.00	£300.00
F396/398	General Interest Numbered 501-898	1900	85p	£340.00
F180/200	General Interest Numbered 899-1098	1901	£1.50	£270.00
F50	General Interest Numbered 1099-1148	1901	£1.20	£60.00
F18	Golf Base I	1901	£20.00	—
F14	London Street Scenes Base I	1901	£3.00	£42.00
F400	New Series 1	1902	90p	£360.00
F400	New Series B	1902	£1.00	£400.00
F300	New Series C	1902	80p	£240.00
F46	Pantomime & Theatre Artistes Base D	1899	£3.60	£165.00
LF45	Pantomime & Theatre Artistes Base D	1899	£5.25	£236.00
F50	Pantomime & Theatre Artistes Base M	1899	£6.00	—
F60/62	Politicians, Base D	1900	£1.00	£60.00
F3	Royalty Base M	1899	£2.75	£8.25
F32	Turner Paintings Base I	1901	£1.50	£48.00
F10	Views & Scenes Abroad Base I	1901	£1.60	£16.00
TABS TYPE ISSUES				
75	Actresses (Numbered 126-200)	1900	£11.50	—
200	Actresses (Plain Back)	1900	£2.50	—
200	Actresses & Foreign Views	1900	£1.80	—
1	General De Wet	1901	—	£3.75
1	General Interest (Unnumbered)	1901	—	£6.00
?36	General Interest (No Labour Clause)	1900	£25.00	—

OGDENS LTD. — cont.

Qty		Date	Odds	Sets
150	General Interest, A Series	1901	50p	£137.50
200	General Interest, B Series	1901	50p	£162.50
200	General Interest, C Series (1-200)	1902	60p	£120.00
100	General Interest, C Series (201-300)	1902	£2.00	—
50	General Interest, C Series (301-350)	1902	80p	£40.00
200	General Interest, D Series	1902	55p	£110.00
120	General Interest, E Series	1902	85p	£100.00
320	General Interest, F Series (1-320)	1902	80p	£250.00
99	General Interest, F Series (321-420)	1902	£2.50	—
120	General Interest (1-120)	1902	90p	£108.00
196	General Interest (Item 95)	1902	70p	£140.00
100	General Interest (Item 96)	1902	70p	£70.00
100	General Interest (Item 97-1)	1902	£1.20	£120.00
21	General Interest (Item 97-2, Cricket)	1902	£6.00	£125.00
25	General Interest (Item 97-2, Football)	1902	£3.00	£75.00
15	General Interest (Item 97-2, Golf)	1902	£16.50	£250.00
139	General Interest (Item 97-2, Various)	1902	75p	£105.00
?110	General Interest (Oblong Back)	1902	£13.50	—
17	Heroes of the Ring	1901	£5.00	—
1	H.M. The Queen	1901	—	£5.00
2	H.R.H. The Prince of Wales	1901	£3.50	£7.00
14	Imperial Interest	1901	80p	£11.50
106	Imperial or International Interest	1901	70p	£75.00
3	International Interest	1901	£1.65	£5.00
14	International Interest or a Prominent British Officer	1901	70p	£9.50
71	Leading Artistes of the Day			
	(Name in Black)	1901	£1.00	£71.00
	(Name in Black, No Labour Clause)	1901	£20.00	—
25	Leading Artistes of the Day			
	(Name in White, Printed Back)	1901	£13.00	—
	(Name in White, Plain Back)	1901	£13.00	—
	(No Name)	1901	£13.00	—
?75	Leading Artistes of the Day			
	(Non Descriptive, Printed Back)	1901	£11.00	—
	(Non Descriptive, Plain Back)	1901	£11.00	—
22	Leading Athletes	1901	£2.25	£50.00
15	Leading Favourites of the Turf	1901	£3.60	£54.00
54	Leading Generals at the War	1901	90p	—
25	Leading Generals at the War (Different)	1901	90p	—
25	(No"Tabs")	1901	£1.75	—
47	Leading Generals at the War (Non Descriptive)	1901	90p	—
25	Leading Generals at the War			
	(Lucky Star)	1901	£4.50	—
	("Guinea Gold" Rubber Stamped)	1901	£8.00	—
2	Members of Parliament	1901	£3.00	£6.00
11	Notable Coursing Dogs	1901	£6.00	—
12	Our Leading Cricketers	1901	£12.50	£150.00
17	Our Leading Footballers	1901	£5.00	—
37	Prominent British Officers	1901	80p	£30.00
50	Stage Artistes & Celebrities	1900	£2.20	£110.00
1	The Yacht "Columbia"	1901	—	£6.00
1	The Yacht "Shamrock"	1901	—	£6.00
AUSTRALIAN ISSUES TABS TYPE				
1	Christian De Wet	1901	—	£10.00
1	Corporal G.E. Nurse, V.C	1901	—	*£10.00*

OGDENS LTD. — cont.

Qty		Date	Odds	Sets
14	English Cricketer Series	1901	£45.00	£630.00
400	General Interest (Numbered)	1901	£2.50	—
100	General Interest (Unnumbered)	1901	£4.50	—
1	Imperial Interest	1901	—	*£10.00*
27	Imperial or International Interest	1901	£6.50	—
64	International Interest	1901	£6.50	—
1	Lady Sarah Wilson	1901	—	*£10.00*
39	Leading Generals at the War	1901	£6.50	—
13	Prominent British Officers	1901	£7.00	—

OTHER OVERSEAS ISSUES

Qty		Date	Odds	Sets
51	Actresses, Black & White (Polo)	1906	£3.00	—
?10	Actresses, Black & White (Polo, Small Pictures, Numbered)	1906	*£12.50*	—
?10	Actresses, Black & White (Polo,Small Pictures, Unnumbered)	1906	*£12.50*	—
30	Actresses, Brown (Polo, 3 Printings)	1908	£2.50	£75.00
17	Animals (Polo)	1916	£11.00	—
60	Animals (Ruler)	1912	£2.75	£165.00
60	(Tabs, With Captions)	1912	£2.75	£165.00
50	(Tabs, No Captions)	1912	£3.00	£150.00
50	Aviation Series (Tabs, Ogden at Base)	1912	£5.50	—
50	(Tabs, Ogden England)	1912	£6.50	—
45	Beauties – Picture Hats (Polo)	1911	£5.00	—
50	Best Dogs of their Breed (Polo, Blue)			
	(With Eastern Characters)	1916	£7.00	—
	(Without Eastern Characters)	1916	£7.00	—
50	(Polo, Pink)	1916	£7.50	—
52	Birds of Brilliant Plumage			
	(With Frame Line, 2 Printings)	1914	£2.60	£135.00
	(No Frame Line)	1914	£2.60	£135.00
25	British Trees & Their Uses (Guinea Gold)	1927	£1.60	£40.00
25	China's Ancient Warriors (Ruler)	1913	£4.75	—
25	Famous Railway Trains (Guinea Gold)	1928	£2.40	£60.00
20	Flowers (Polo Packet 49mm Long)			
	(No Eastern Characters)	1915	£5.00	—
	(With Eastern Characters)	1915	£5.00	—
20	(Polo Packet 46 mm Long)	1915	£5.00	—
25	Indian Women (Polo, Apple Green Border)	1919	£4.50	£112.50
25	(Polo, Emerald Green)	1919	£4.50	£112.50
30	Music Hall Celebrities (Polo)	1911	£5.00	£150.00
50	(Tabs)	1911	£5.00	—
52	Playing Cards (Polo)	1922	£12.00	—
50	Riders of the World (Polo, Reg. No.1294)	1911	£3.50	£175.00
50	(Polo, No "Reg. No.")	1911	£3.50	£175.00
50	(Polo, Cigarettes Uneven)	1911	£3.50	£175.00
50	Russo Japanese Series	1904	£20.00	—
36	Ships & Their Pennants (Polo)	1911	£5.00	—
32	Transport of the World (Polo)	1917	£5.00	—

THE ORLANDO CIGARETTE & CIGAR CO.

Qty		Date	Odds	Sets
40	Home & Colonial Regiments	1901	*£200.00*	—

W. T. OSBORNE & CO.

Qty		Date	Odds	Sets
40	Naval & Military Phrases (No Border)	1904	£37.50	—
40	(White Border)	1904	£37.50	—

OSBORNE TOBACCO CO. LTD.

Qty		Date	Odds	Sets
50	Modern Aircraft (Blue Front)	1952	50p	£25.00
50	(Brown Front)	1952	80p	£40.00

PALMER & CO.

Qty		Date	Odds	Sets
M12	Manikin Cards	1915	*£80.00*	—

J. A. PATTREIOUEX LTD.

EARLY PHOTOGRAPHIC ISSUES

Qty		Date	Odds	Sets
F96	Animals (CA1-96)	1926	90p	—
LF50	Animals & Scenes (Unnumbered)	1924	£1.00	—
LF50	Animals & Scenes (1-50)	1925	£1.00	—
F192	Animals & Scenes (250-441, Titled)	1925	90p	—
F192	(250-441, Junior Member)	1925	90p	—
F96	(346-441, 3 Brands)	1925	90p	—
F96	Animals & Scenes (CC1-96)	1926	90p	—
LF50	Animals & Scenes (I1-50)	1927	£1.00	—
F96	Animals & Scenes (JS1-96A)	1928	90p	—
LF96	Animal Studies (A42-137)	1925	90p	—
LF50	Animal Studies (A151-200)	1925	90p	—
LF30	Beauties (JM1-30)	1928	£2.50	—
LF50	British & Egyptian Scenes (CM1-50A)	1927	£1.00	—
LF50	British Empire Exhibition (JM1-50B)	1928	£1.70	£85.00
XF100	Cathedrals, Abbeys & Castles (SJ1-100)	1928	£2.40	—
LF30	Child Studies (JM No.1-30)	1928	£3.50	—
F96	Famous Cricketers (C1-96, Plain Back)	1926	£40.00	—
F96	(C1-96, Printed Back)	1926	£40.00	—
F191	Famous Footballers (F1-191)	1922	£7.50	—
LF50	Famous Statues (JCM1-50C)	1928	£1.60	£80.00
F96	Footballers (FA1-96)	1922	£5.50	—
F96	Footballers (FB1-96)	1923	£5.50	—
F96	Footballers (FC1-96)	1923	£5.50	—
LF50	Football Teams (F192-241)	1922	£22.50	—
F96	Natives & Scenes (1-96B)	1926	90p	£85.00
F36	(1-36B) (As Above)	1926	£1.25	—
F96	Natives & Scenes (Numbered CB1-CB96)	1926	£1.00	—
F96	(Numbered 1-96)	1926	90p	—
F96	(JS1-96) (As Above)	1926	90p	£85.00
F96	Overseas Scenes (1-96C)	1926	90p	£85.00
LF50	Overseas Scenes (CM1-50B)	1926	£1.00	—
LF50	(JM1-50) (As Above)	1928	£1.00	£50.00
LF50	Overseas Scenes (CM101-150S)	1927	£1.00	£50.00
LF50	(S101-150) (As Above)	1929	£1.00	£50.00
F96	Overseas Scenes (1-96D)	1927	£1.40	—
LF50	Overseas Scenes (1-50E)	1928	£1.00	£50.00
LF50	Overseas Scenes (1-50F)	1928	£1.00	£50.00
LF50	Overseas Scenes (JM1-50A)	1928	£1.00	£50.00
LF50	Scenes (201-250)	1925	£1.00	£50.00
LF50	Scenes (G1-50)	1927	£1.40	£70.00

Qty		Date	Odds	Sets
LF50	Scenes (1-50H, Grey Back)	1927	£1.00	£50.00
LF50	(1-50H, Brown Back)	1927	£1.10	—
LF50	Scenes (JCM1-50D, With Firm's Name)	1927	£1.00	£50.00
LF50	(JCM1-50D, Junior Member No.10, 2 Sizes)	1927	£1.00	—
LF100	Scenes (S1-100)	1928	£1.00	—
LF4	Scenes (V1-4)	1928	£4.00	—

OTHER ISSUES

Qty		Date	Odds	Sets
F28	Beautiful Scotland	1939	£1.10	£30.00
MF48	Beautiful Scotland	1939	25p	£12.00
MF48	Britain from the Air	1939	25p	£12.00
50	British Empire Exhibition Series	1929	£2.20	£110.00
MF48	British Railways	1938	75p	£36.00
50	Builders of the British Empire	1929	£2.70	£135.00
50	Celebrities in Sport	1930	£3.00	£250.00
F28	Coastwise	1939	£1.10	£30.00
MF48	Coastwise	1939	25p	£12.00
75	Cricketers Series	1928	£8.00	£600.00
50	Dirt Track Riders	1929	£7.50	£375.00
F54	Dirt Track Riders (Descriptive)	1930	£9.50	£515.00
F54	(Non Descriptive)	1930	*£20.00*	—
PF54	Dirt Track Riders (Premium Issue)	1930	£125.00	—
MF48	Dogs	1939	50p	£24.00
30	Drawing Made Easy	1930	£2.00	£60.00
F28	Flying	1938	£1.40	£39.50
MF48	Flying	1938	40p	£19.50
F78	Footballers in Action	1934	£2.75	£215.00
100	Footballers Series (Brown Caption)	1927	£5.50	—
50	(Blue Caption)	1927	£6.50	£325.00
MF48	Holiday Haunts by the Sea	1938	25p	£12.00
X24	Jackpot Jigsaws	1969	75p	—
25	King Lud Problems	1936	£12.50	—
26	Maritime Flags	1931	£8.50	£220.00
F28	Our Countryside	1938	£1.25	£35.00
MF48	Our Countryside	1938	25p	£12.00
25	Photo's of Football Stars	1929	£25.00	—
50	Railway Posters by Famous Artists	1930	£7.00	£350.00
F54	Real Photographs of London	1936	£1.80	£97.50
F28	Shots from the Films	1938	£2.00	£56.00
MF48	Sights of Britain	1936	25p	£12.00
MF48	Sights of Britain, 2nd Series (2 Printings)	1936	25p	£12.00
MF48	Sights of Britain, 3rd Series	1937	25p	£12.00
MF48	Sights of London, First Series	1935	50p	£24.00
MF12	Sights of London – Supplementary Series	1935	75p	£9.00
F54	Sporting Celebrities	1935	£2.50	£135.00
MF96	Sporting Events and Stars	1935	£1.00	£200.00
50	Sports Trophies	1931	£2.40	£120.00
MF48	The Bridges of Britain	1938	25p	£12.00
52	The English & Welsh Counties	1928	£1.75	£91.00
MF48	The Navy (2 Printings)	1937	50p	£24.00
M24	Treasure Isle	1968	*£1.25*	—
F51	Views	1933	£1.10	£56.00
F54	Views of Britain	1937	£1.50	£81.00
MF48	Winter Scenes	1937	35p	£17.00

W. PEPPERDY

Qty		Date	Odds	Sets
30	Army Pictures, Cartoons, etc.	1916	*£85.00*	—

M. PEZARO & SON

Qty		Date	Odds	Sets
25	Armies of the World (Cake Walk)	1900	*£110.00*	—
25	(Nestor)	1900	£110.00	—
?25	Song Titles Illustrated	1900	£140.00	—

GODFREY PHILLIPS LTD.

40 Page Reference Book — £3.50

Qty		Date	Odds	Sets
50	Actresses (Oval)	1916	£6.00	£300.00
50	(Oval, Anonymous)	1916	£5.00	£250.00
25	Actresses, C Series (Ball of Beauty)	1900	£80.00	—
25	(Carriage)	1900	£27.50	£687.50
25	(Derby)	1900	£75.00	—
25	(Horseshoe)	1900	£27.50	—
25	(Teapot)	1900	£80.00	—
25	(Volunteer)	1900	£75.00	—
2	Advertisement Cards	1934	£12.00	£24.00
50	Aircraft	1938	£1.20	£60.00
54	Aircraft Series No.1 (Matt)	1938	40p	£21.50
54	(Varnished)	1938	£2.25	£121.50
54	(Millhoff Back)	1938	£2.75	£148.50
40	Animal Series	1903	£5.50	£220.00
M30	Animal Studies	1936	25p	£7.50
50	Annuals	1939	20p	£10.00
L25	Arms of the English Sees	1924	£4.20	£105.00
48	A Selection of BDV Wonderful Gifts	1930	£1.10	£53.00
48	A Selection of BDV Wonderful Gifts	1931	£1.00	£48.00
48	A Selection of BDV Wonderful Gifts	1932	£1.00	£48.00
24	Beauties "HUMPS " (Phillips Front)	1898	£70.00	—
24	(Plums Front)	1898	*£200.00*	—
30	Beauties, Nymphs	1896	£70.00	—
?50	Beauties, Plums (Black & White Front)	1897	*£130.00*	—
50	(Green Front)	1897	£55.00	—
50	(Plum Front)	1897	£55.00	—
25	Beauties (Numbered B801-B825)	1902	£11.00	£275.00
30	Beauties, Oval (Plain Back)	1914	£2.25	£67.50
44	Beauties of To-Day	1937	£1.30	£57.50
50	Beauties of To-Day	1938	80p	£40.00
36	Beauties of To-Day, 2nd Series	1940	£1.00	£36.00
F54	Beauties of To-Day	1939	£1.30	£70.00
LF36	Beauties of To-Day	1938	£2.50	£90.00
LF36	Beauties of To-Day (Different Subjects)	1938	£4.50	—
XF36	Beauties of To-Day (Unnumbered)	1937	£1.50	£54.00
XF36	Beauties of To-Day, 2nd Series	1938	£1.25	£45.00
XF36	Beauties of To-Day, 3rd Series	1938	£1.00	£36.00
XF36	Beauties of To-Day, 4th Series	1938	90p	£32.50
XF36	Beauties of To-Day, 5th Series	1938	£1.00	£36.00
XF36	Beauties of To-Day, 6th Series	1939	£1.00	£36.00
XF36	Beauties of To-Day, 7th Series	1939	£1.00	£36.00
XF36	Ditto (B.D.V. Back)	1939	30p	£11.00
36	Beauties of the World	1931	£1.50	£54.00

GODFREY PHILLIPS LTD. — cont.

Qty		Date	Odds	Sets
36	Beauties of the World Series No. 2	1933	£1.50	£54.00
50	Beautiful Women (I.F. Series)	1908	£9.00	£450.00
50	(W.I. Series)	1908	£10.00	£500.00
L50	Beautiful Women	1908	£17.50	—
P30	Beauty Spots of the Homeland	1938	30p	£9.00
50	Bird Painting	1938	60p	£30.00
25	Boxer Rebellion	1904	£25.00	£625.00
50	British Beauties (Photogravure)	1916	£6.00	£300.00
K76	British Beauties	1916	£2.60	£200.00
F54	British Beauties, 1-54	1914	£2.20	£120.00
F54	(Plain Back, Glossy)	1914	*£3.50*	—
54	(Plain Back, Brown)	1914	£3.40	—
F54	British Beauties, 55-108 (Glossy)	1915	£2.20	£120.00
54	(Matt)	1915	£2.20	—
54	(Plain Back, Sepia)	1915	£3.20	—
50	British Birds and Their Eggs	1936	80p	£40.00
30	British Butterflies, No.1 Issue	1911	£4.25	£127.50
25	British Butterflies	1927	80p	£20.00
25	Ditto (Transfers)	1936	80p	£20.00
25	British Orders of Chivalry & Valour	1939	£1.60	£40.00
25	British Warships	1915	£6.00	£150.00
L25	British Warships	1915	£32.50	—
F80	British Warships	1916	£12.00	—
50	Busts of Famous People (Brown Back)	1907	*£30.00*	—
50	(Green Back)	1907	£5.50	£275.00
50	(Pale Green)	1907	*£20.00*	—
M36	Characters Come to Life	1938	£1.00	£36.00
?25	Children's Stories (Booklets)	1924	*£30.00*	—
25	Chinese Series (English Text)	1910	£5.00	£125.00
25	(Volunteer Cigarettes)	1910	£7.00	£175.00
G?6	Chinese Series	1910	*£65.00*	—
M25	Cinema Stars (Circular)	1924	£2.80	£70.00
F52	Cinema Stars	1923	£2.50	£130.00
30	Cinema Stars (Brown)	1924	£2.30	£69.00
30	Cinema Stars (Black & White)	1925	£1.50	£45.00
32	Cinema Stars (Black & White)	1930	£1.50	£48.00
32	Cinema Stars (Brown, Hand Coloured)	1934	£1.25	£40.00
30	Cinema Stars (Plain Back)	1935	70p	£21.00
50	Colonial Troops	1902	£23.00	—
50	Coronation of Their Majesties	1937	25p	£12.50
M36	Coronation of Their Majesties	1937	25p	£8.00
P24	Coronation of Their Majesties (Postcard)	1937	£1.25	£30.00
P24	(Non-Postcard)	1937	£4.25	—
KF198	Cricketers (Pinnace)	1924	£7.00	—
F192	Cricketers (Brown Back)	1924	£7.50	—
LF25	Cricketers (Brown Back)	1924	£20.00	£500.00
LF?100	(Pinnace)	1924	£35.00	—
PF?223	Cricketers (Premium Issue)	1924	£32.50	—
1	Cricket Fixture Card	1936	—	£6.00
25	Derby Winners & Jockeys	1923	£3.40	£85.00
30	Eggs, Nests & Birds (Numbered)	1912	£4.50	£135.00
30	(Unnumbered)	1912	£5.00	£150.00
25	Empire Industries	1927	90p	£22.50
49/50	Evolution of the British Navy	1930	£1.00	£49.00
25	Famous Boys	1924	£2.20	£55.00

Qty		*Date*	*Odds*	*Sets*
32	Famous Cricketers	1926	£4.50	£144.00
25	Famous Crowns	1938	30p	£7.50
50	Famous Footballers	1936	£1.50	£75.00
M36	Famous Love Scenes	1939	70p	£25.00
50	Famous Minors	1936	25p	£12.50
P26	Famous Paintings	1936	£1.30	£34.00
25	Feathered Friends	1928	£1.20	£30.00
50	Film Favourites	1934	55p	£27.50
50	Film Stars	1934	60p	£30.00
P24	Film Stars (Series of Cards, Postcard)	1934	£1.10	£26.50
P24	("Series of Cards", Non-Postcard)	1934	£2.75	£66.00
P24	Film Stars (Series of 24 Cards, Postcard)	1934	£2.75	£66.00
P24	("Series of 24 Cards", Non-Postcard)	1934	£4.00	—
P24	Film Stars, 2nd (25-48, Postcard Backs)	1934	£2.75	£66.00
P24	(25-48, Non-Postcard)	1934	£5.00	—
50	First Aid	1923	£1.30	£65.00
25	First Aid Series	1914	£6.00	£150.00
25	Fish	1924	£2.30	£57.50
M30	Flower Studies	1937	20p	£6.00
P30	Flower Studies	1937	50p	£15.00
KF112	Footballers (Brown Oval Back)	1920	£3.25	—
KF400	(Black Oval Back)	1920	£1.40	—
KF?517	(Double Frame Line Back)	1921	£1.40	—
KF940	(1-940, Address "Photo")	1921	90p	—
KF?179	(941-1109, Address "Photo")	1922	£1.70	—
KF940	(1-940, Address "Pinnace")	1922	90p	—
KF1522	(941-2462, Address "Pinnace")	1923	£1.70	—
LF?400	Footballers (Oval Design Back)	1920	£3.00	—
LF?1100	(Oblong Frame "Photo" Back)	1921	£3.00	—
LF?2462	("Pinnace" Back)	1922	£3.00	—
PF2462	Footballers (Premium Issue)	1921	£8.50	—
GF?	Football Teams (Premium Issue)	1923	*£100.00*	—
P1	Franco British Exhibition	1908	—	£20.00
P30	Garden Studies	1938	25p	£7.50
13	General Interest	1896	£37.50	£500.00
90	Guinea Gold Series (Numbered, Glossy)	1902	£3.60	£324.00
90	(Numbered, Matt)	1902	£3.60	£324.00
100	Guinea Gold Series	1902	£4.75	£475.00
161	Guinea Gold Series (Different)	1902	£3.60	£580.00
100	(Brown)	1902	£8.50	—
25	Home Pets	1924	£2.00	£50.00
25	How To Build a Two Valve Set	1929	£2.40	£60.00
25	How To Do It Series	1913	£6.80	£170.00
25	How To Make a Valve Amplifier	1924	£2.60	£65.00
25	How To Make Your Own Wireless Set	1923	£1.80	£45.00
25	Indian Series	1908	£12.50	£312.50
54	In The Public Eye	1935	35p	£19.00
50	International Caps	1936	£1.50	£75.00
35/37	Kings & Queens of England	1925	£1.60	£56.00
25	Lawn Tennis	1930	£2.60	£65.00
K52	Miniature Playing Cards (Red Back)	1906	*£100.00*	—
K53	Miniature Playing Cards (Blue Design)	1934	50p	£26.50
K53	(Buff, 3 Types)	1932	50p	£26.50
K53	(White)	1933	60p	—
K53	(Yellow)	1933	60p	—
25	Model Railways	1927	£2.50	£62.50

GODFREY PHILLIPS LTD. — cont.

Qty		Date	Odds	Sets
30	Morse Signalling	1916	£7.50	£225.00
50	Motor Cars at a Glance	1924	£3.40	£170.00
20	Novelty Series	1924	£9.00	£180.00
25	Old Favourites	1924	£1.40	£35.00
M36	Old Masters	1939	25p	£9.00
36	Olympic Champions, Amsterdam 1928	1928	£2.00	£72.00
25	Optical Illusions	1927	£2.00	£50.00
36	Our Dogs	1939	£1.40	£50.00
M30	Our Dogs	1939	60p	£18.00
P30	Our Dogs	1939	£3.20	£96.00
M48	Our Favourites	1935	25p	£12.00
P30	Our Glorious Empire	1939	50p	£15.00
M30	Our Puppies	1936	£1.20	£36.00
P30	Our Puppies	1936	£1.60	£48.00
25	Personalities of To-Day	1932	£1.50	£37.50
25	Popular Superstitions	1930	£1.40	£35.00
25	Prizes for Needlework	1925	£2.00	£50.00
25	Railway Engines	1934	£2.60	£65.00
KF27	Real Photo Series (War Leaders)	1916	£6.25	£170.00
1	Real Stamp Card	1928	—	£1.20
25	Red Indians	1927	£2.50	£62.50
20	Russo Japanese War Series	1905	*£130.00*	—
25	School Badges	1927	£1.00	£25.00
48	Screen Stars A (Embossed)	1936	85p	£40.00
48	(Not Embossed)	1936	£1.30	£62.50
48	Screen Stars B (Different)	1936	85p	£40.00
30	Semaphore Signalling	1916	£7.50	£225.00
25	Ships and their Flags	1924	£2.60	£65.00
M36	Ships that have Made History	1938	50p	£28.00
M48	Shots from the Films	1934	75p	£36.00
50	Soccer Stars	1936	£1.50	£75.00
36	Soldiers of the King (Adhesive)	1939	£1.40	—
36	(Non-Adhesive)	1939	60p	£21.50
P12	Special Jubilee Series	1935	£1.75	£21.00
M20	Special Jubilee Year Series	1935	20p	£4.00
30	Speed Champions	1930	£1.70	£51.00
36	Sporting Champions	1929	£1.70	£61.00
25	Sporting Series	1910	£16.00	—
25	Sports	1923	£3.20	£80.00
50	Sportsmen – Spot the Winner (Normal)	1937	£1.20	£60.00
50	(Back Inverted)	1937	90p	£45.00
35	Stage and Cinema Beauties A	1933	£1.10	£38.50
35	Stage and Cinema Beauties B (Different)	1933	£1.00	£35.00
50	Stage and Cinema Beauties (Different)	1935	£1.10	£55.00
54	Stars of the Screen	1934	£1.10	£59.50
48	Stars of the Screen (Embossed)	1936	90p	£43.50
48	(Not Embossed)	1936	80p	£38.50
X16	Stars of the Screen (Strips of 3)	1936	£2.00	£32.00
25	Statues & Monuments (Brown Back)	1907	*£40.00*	—
25	(Green, Patent)	1907	£7.50	£187.50
25	(Green, Provisional Patent)	1907	£7.50	£187.50
25	Territorial Series (Motors Back)	1908	£20.00	£500.00
25	The 1924 Cabinet	1924	£1.60	£40.00
48	The "Old Country"	1935	50p	£24.00
50	This Mechanized Age First Series (Adhesive)	1936	25p	£12.50
50	(Non-Adhesive)	1936	30p	£15.00
50	This Mechanized Age Second Series	1937	25p	£12.50

Qty		Date	Odds	Sets
25	Types of British & Colonial Troops	1899	£40.00	—
25	Types of British Soldiers (M651-M675)	1900	£17.00	£425.00
F63	War Photos	1916	£7.50	£472.50
X20	Wrestling Holds	1930	£30.00	—
XS30	Zoo Studies – Come to Life Series	1939	£1.20	£36.00
X1	Zoo Studies Viewer	1939	—	£7.50
BDV PACKAGE ISSUES				
17	Boxers	1932	£5.50	—
54	Cricketers	1932	£6.50	—
67	Film Stars	1932	£2.00	—
132	Footballers	1932	£3.50	—
19	Jockeys	1932	£3.00	—
21	Speedway Riders	1932	£7.00	—
27	Sportsmen	1932	£3.00	—
"SPORTS" PACKAGE ISSUES				
50	All Sports 1st	1948	£3.75	—
25	All Sports 2nd	1949	£3.75	—
25	All Sports 3rd	1953	£3.75	—
25	All Sports 4th	1954	£3.75	—
25	Cricketers 1st	1948	£7.50	—
25	Cricketers 2nd	1951	£7.50	—
25	Footballers 1st	1948	£5.00	—
50	Footballers 2nd	1950	£5.00	—
25	Footballers 3rd	1951	£5.00	—
25	Jockeys	1952	£3.50	—
25	Radio Stars	1949	£2.50	—
25	Rugby & Association Footballers	1952	£4.50	—
OVERSEAS ISSUES				
50	Animal Studies	1930	£1.25	£62.50
50	Annuals	1939	£1.20	£60.00
X32	Australian Birds (Cartons)	1968	—	*£10.00*
X24	Australian Scenes (Cartons)	1965	—	*£10.00*
50	Australian Sporting Celebrities	1932	£2.40	£120.00
X32	Australian Wild Flowers (Cartons)	1967	—	*£10.00*
50	Film Stars	1934	£1.80	£90.00
E16	Gemstones (Cartons)	1970	—	£7.50
50	Stars of British Films (B.D.V.)	1934	£1.60	£80.00
50	(De Reszke)	1934	£1.60	£80.00
50	(Greys)	1934	£1.60	£80.00
50	(No Brand)	1934	£1.75	£87.50
38	Test Cricketers (B.D.V.)	1932	£2.50	£95.00
38	(Greys)	1932	£2.50	£95.00
38	(No Brand)	1932	£2.60	£100.00
X32	The Barrier Reef (Cartons)	1968	—	£7.50
50	Victorian Footballers (B.D.V.)	1933	£2.00	£100.00
50	(Greys)	1933	£2.00	—
50	(No Brand)	1933	£2.00	—
75	Victorian Footballers	1933	£2.00	—
50	Victorian League & Association Footballers	1934	£2.25	—
100	Who's Who in Australian Sport	1933	£2.50	£250.00
SILK ISSUES				
M1	Allies Flags	1915	—	£8.00
G2	Allies Flags (Anon.)	1915	£8.00	—
G2	(B.D.V.)	1915	£8.00	—

GODFREY PHILLIPS LTD. — cont.

Qty		Date	Odds	Sets
M62	Arms of Countries & Territories	1912	£3.60	—
M32	Beauties-Modern Paintings	1910	£10.00	£320.00
P32	Beauties-Modern Paintings	1910	£40.00	—
M100	Birds	1921	£2.40	—
M12	Birds of the Tropics	1913	£10.00	£120.00
L12	Birds of the Tropics	1913	£12.50	—
P12	Birds of the Tropics	1913	£17.50	—
X24	British Admirals	1916	£5.00	£120.00
D50	British Butterflies & Moths	1922	£4.25	—
M108	British Naval Crests (Anon., Blue Nos.)	1915	£1.60	£173.00
M9	(Anon., Brown Nos.)	1915	£5.00	—
M108	(B.D.V.)	1915	£1.60	—
M23	Butterflies	1911	£8.75	£200.00
M47	Ceramic Art (70 x 43mm)	1925	£1.00	£47.00
M47	(70 x 48mm)	1925	80p	£38.00
L47	Ceramic Art	1925	£1.60	—
M65	Clan Tartans (68 x 44mm)	1922	£1.10	—
M65	(71 x 48mm) (B.D.V.)	1922	£1.00	£65.00
M49	(71 x 48mm) (Anon.)	1922	£1.00	£49.00
L56	Clan Tartans	1922	£2.50	—
P12	Clan Tartans	1922	£4.50	£54.00
M108	Colonial Army Badges	1913	£1.50	—
M17	County Cricket Badges (Anon.)	1921	£13.50	—
M17	(B.D.V.)	1921	£13.00	—
M108	Crests & Badges of the British Army			
	(Anon., Numbered)	1914	£1.10	£120.00
	(Anon., Unnumbered)	1914	£1.20	£130.00
	(B.D.V.)	1914	£1.10	£120.00
L108	Crests & Badges of the British Army (Anon.)	1914	£1.30	—
L108	(B.D.V.)	1914	£1.30	—
M143	Flags, Set 4-1 (Short)	1913	80p	—
M119	Flags, Set 4-2 (Short, Renumbered)	1913	90p	£107.00
M114	Flags, Set 4-3 (Short, Renumbered)	1913	90p	£100.00
L142	Flags, Set 4 (Long)	1913	£1.60	£227.50
M24	Flags, Set 5 (With Caption)	1913	80p	£19.00
M12	Flags, Set 5 (No Caption)	1913	£1.00	£12.00
P8	Flags, Set 5	1913	£12.50	—
M18	Flags, Set 6	1913	85p	£15.00
M20	Flags, Set 7	1913	85p	—
M50	Flags, 5th Series	1914	£1.60	£80.00
M120	Flags, 7th Series	1914	80p	£96.00
L120	Flags, 10th Series	1915	90p	£108.00
M120	Flags, 12th Series	1915	80p	£96.00
L65	Flags, 15th Series	1916	£1.10	£71.50
L64	Flags, 16th Series	1916	£1.10	£70.00
M120/132	Flags, 20th Series (B.D.V. Brown)	1917	85p	£100.00
M?48	(B.D.V. Orange)	1917	£2.00	—
M120/126	Flags, 25th Series	1917	80p	£96.00
L63	Flags, 25th Series	1917	£2.75	—
M112	Flags, 26th Series (in Brown)	1918	80p	—
M?38	(in Blue)	1918	£3.50	—
M70	Flags, 28th Series	1918	85p	£60.00
P22	Flags, Set 13	1914	£1.50	£27.00
G23	Flags, Set 13 (Anon.)	1914	£2.00	£46.00
G27	(B.D.V.)	1914	£1.75	£47.00

Qty		*Date*	*Odds*	*Sets*
M21	Football Colours (Anon.)	1914	£5.50	—
M86	(B.D.V.)	1920	£4.75	—
P78	Football Colours	1920	£4.50	—
M126	G.P. Territorial Badges	1913	£1.50	£190.00
L25	Great War Leaders (Sepia)	1915	£4.40	£110.00
M3	Great War Leaders & Celebrities (Anon.)	1916	£6.00	£18.00
M4	(B.D.V.)	1916	£6.00	£24.00
L3	Great War Leaders & Celebrities (Anon.)	1916	£6.00	£18.00
L2	(B.D.V.)	1916	£6.00	£12.00
P4	Great War Leaders & Celebrities (Anon.)	1916	£5.50	£22.00
P18	(B.D.V.)	1916	£5.50	—
G29	Great War Leaders & Celebrities (Anon.)	1916	£5.00	—
G45	(B.D.V.)	1916	£5.00	£225.00
P1	Great War Leaders (B.D.V. in Blue)	1916	—	£8.50
M52	Great War Leaders & Warships	1914	£5.50	—
M25	Heraldic Series (69 x 43mm)	1924	£1.00	£25.00
M25	(68 x 47mm)	1924	£1.00	£25.00
L25	Heraldic Series	1924	£2.50	—
P12	Heraldic Series	1924	£4.50	£54.00
M26	House Flags	1915	£7.50	£195.00
M10	Irish Patriots	1919	£11.00	£110.00
X10	Irish Patriots	1919	£11.50	—
P10	Irish Patriots	1919	£16.50	—
M1	Irish Republican Stamp	1925	—	£1.50
M1	Let 'Em All Come	1920	—	£10.00
X?	Miniature Rugs	1924	*£4.50*	—
M54	Naval Badges of Rank & Military Headdress	1917	£5.00	£270.00
G1	Nelson's Signal at Trafalgar	1921	—	*£40.00*
G40	Old Masters, Set 1	1911	£27.50	£1100.00
P20	Old Masters, Set 2 (Anon.)	1912	£4.00	£80.00
P20	(B.D.V. at Top)	1912	£3.60	£72.00
P20	(B.D.V. at Bottom)	1912	£5.00	—
M85	Old Masters, Set 3 (Anon.)	1912	£2.40	—
M40	(B.D.V.)	1912	£2.50	£100.00
M120	Old Masters, Set 4	1913	£1.80	—
M20	Old Masters, Set 5 (Anon., Unnumbered)	1922	£2.60	£52.00
M20	(Anon.,101-120)	1922	£1.60	£32.00
M60	(B.D.V. 1-60)	1922	£1.20	£72.00
M20	(B.D.V. 101-120)	1922	£1.60	£32.00
M50	Old Masters, Set 6	1924	£1.20	£60.00
M50	Old Masters, Set 7 (301-350)	1916	£2.00	£100.00
M50	Orders of Chivalry (Anon.)	1920	£2.20	£110.00
M24	Orders of Chivalry (B.D.V., 1-24)	1914	£1.60	£37.50
M24	(GP401-424)	1914	£1.80	£44.00
M25	Pilot & Signal Flags (Anon.)	1921	£2.50	£62.50
M25	(B.D.V.)	1921	£1.60	£40.00
L72	Regimental Colours	1914	£3.75	—
M50	Regimental Colours, Series 12	1918	£1.80	£90.00
M120	Regimental Colours & Crests (B.D.V.)	1915	£1.30	—
M120	(Anon.)	1915	£1.30	—
M40	(Anon., With Vignettes)	1915	£1.00	—
G120	Regimental Colours & Crests (Anon.)	1915	£5.25	—
G120	(B.D.V.)	1915	£4.75	—

GODFREY PHILLIPS LTD. — cont.

Qty		Date	Odds	Sets
M10	Religious Pictures	1911	£17.50	—
X10	Religious Pictures	1911	£20.00	—
P10	Religious Pictures	1911	£25.00	—
M75	Town & City Arms	1918	£1.80	£170.00
L75	Town & City Arms	1918	£2.25	—
M25	Victoria Cross Heroes I	1915	£10.00	—
M25	Victoria Cross Heroes II (With Flags)	1915	£11.00	—
M90	War Pictures	1915	£5.00	£450.00

JOHN PLAYER & SONS

44 Page Reference Book — £3.50

Qty		Date	Odds	Sets
25	Actors & Actresses	1898	£22.00	£550.00
50	Actresses	1897	£20.00	£1000.00
6/7	Advertisement Cards (Navy Cut Back)	1894	£250.00	—
4/5	(Testimonial Back)	1894	£250.00	—
1	Advertisement Card – Sailor	1929	—	£4.00
L1	Advertisement Card – Sailor	1929	—	*£17.50*
L1	Advertisement Card – Wants List	1936	—	£1.00
P6	Advertisement Postcards	1906	£80.00	—
50	Aeroplanes (Eire)	1935	£1.25	£62.50
50	Aeroplanes (Civil)	1935	80p	£40.00
50	Aircraft of the Royal Air Force	1938	90p	£45.00
X10	Allied Cavalry	1914	£8.00	£80.00
L24	A Nature Calendar	1930	£2.80	£67.00
50	Animals of the Countryside	1939	20p	£10.00
50	Ditto (Eire)	1939	85p	£42.50
L25	Aquarium Studies	1932	£1.60	£40.00
L25	Architectural Beauties	1927	£2.00	£50.00
50	Arms & Armour (Blue Back)	1909	£2.20	£110.00
50	Army Corps & Divisional Signs (1-50, 2 Printings)	1924	25p	£12.50
100	Army Corps & Divisional Signs 2nd (51-150)	1925	25p	£25.00
25	Army Life	1910	£1.70	£42.50
X12	Artillery in Action	1917	£4.00	£48.00
50	A Sectional Map of Ireland	1932	£2.30	£115.00
50	Association Cup Winners	1930	£1.60	£80.00
50	Aviary and Cage Birds	1933	80p	£40.00
50	Ditto (Transfers)	1933	30p	£15.00
L25	Aviary & Cage Birds	1935	£3.20	£80.00
50	Badges & Flags of British Regiments			
	(Green Back)	1903	£1.80	£90.00
	(Brown Back, Numbered)	1904	£1.80	£90.00
	(Brown Back, Unnumbered)	1904	£2.20	£110.00
50	Birds & Their Young	1937	20p	£9.00
50	(Eire) (Adhesive)	1937	85p	£42.50
50	(Eire) (Non-Adhesive)	1937	85p	£42.50
25	(Non-Adhesive)	Unissued	30p	£7.50
25	2nd (Non-Adhesive)	Unissued	20p	£4.00

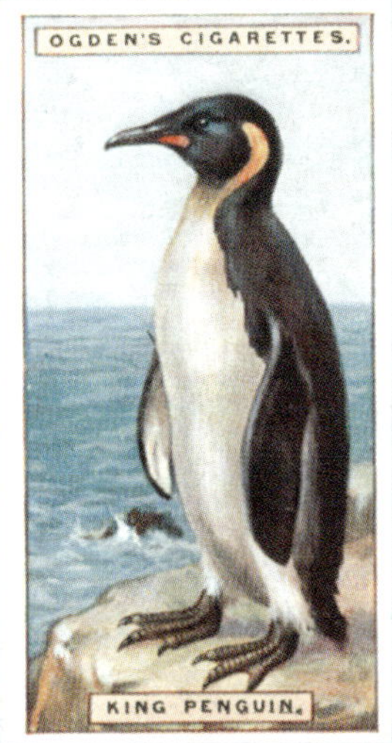

Foreign Birds
Ogdens

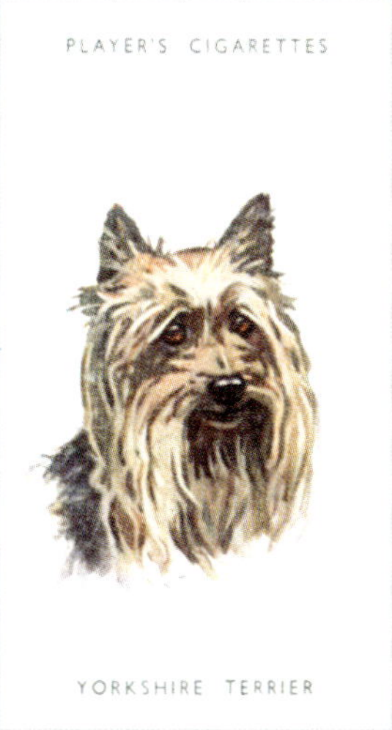

Dogs' Heads by Biegel
Player

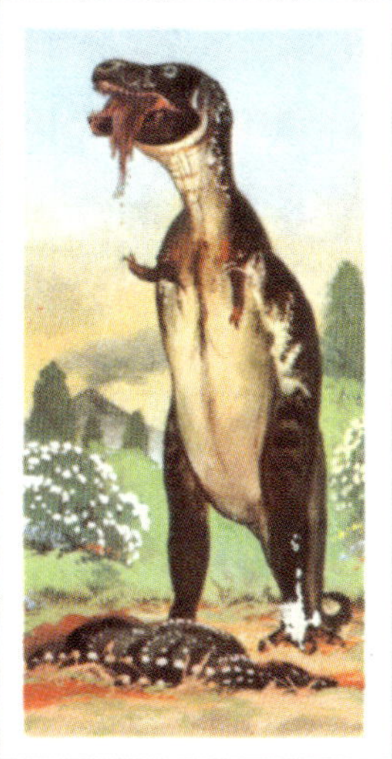

Prehistoric Animals
Brooke Bond

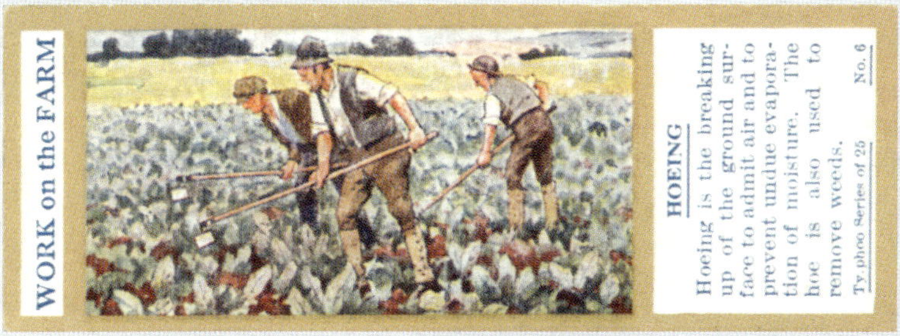

Work on the Farm
Typhoo

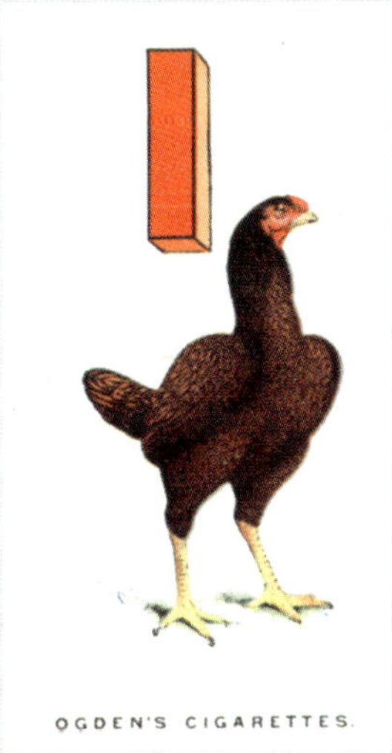

Poultry Alphabet
Ogdens. Also I.T.C. (Canada)

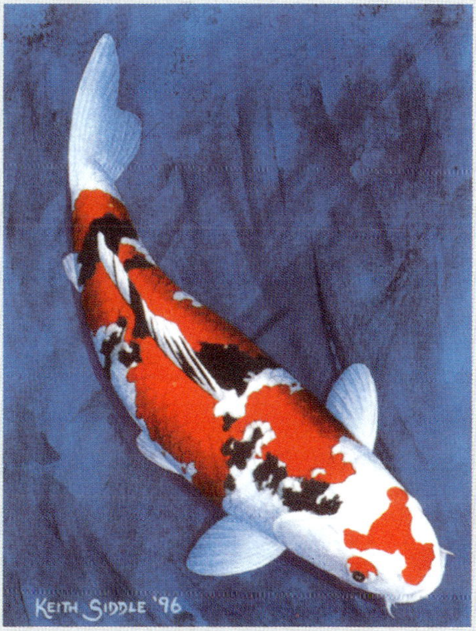

Nishikigoi – M.P. Cards

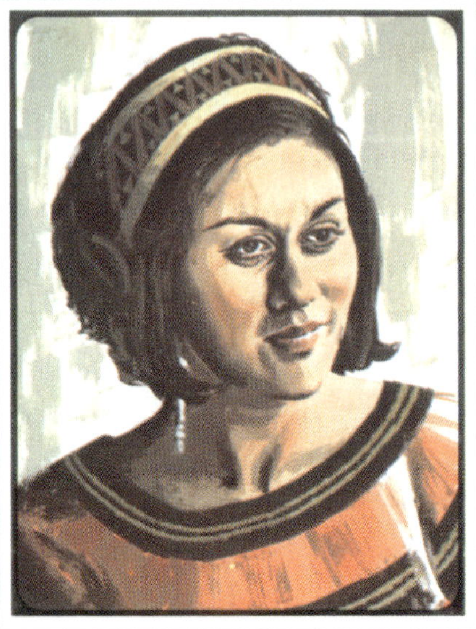

Famous New Zealanders
Sanitarium

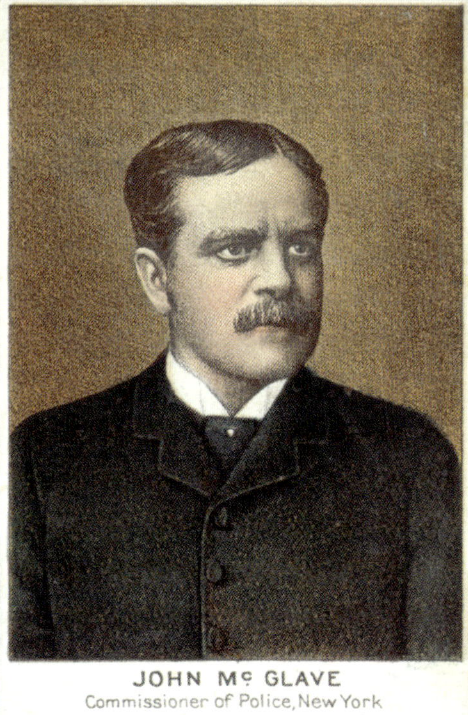

Police Inspectors & Captains
Buchner

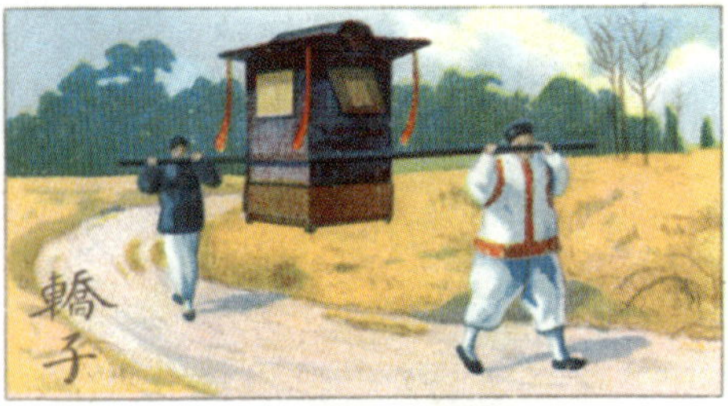

Chinese Transport
African Tobacco, Wills (Ruby Queen)

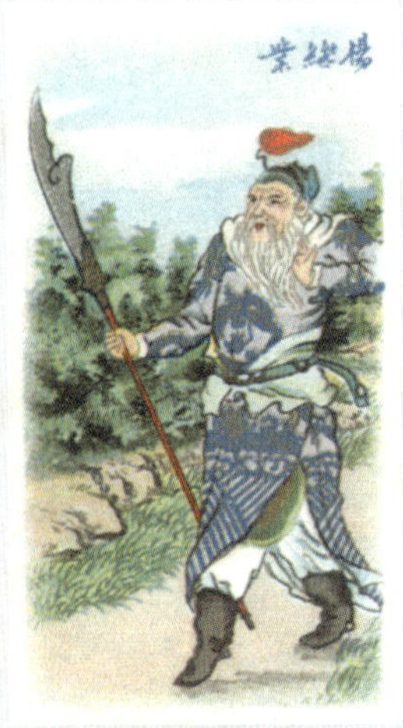

China's Ancient Warriors
Ogdens (Ruler), Wills (Scissors)

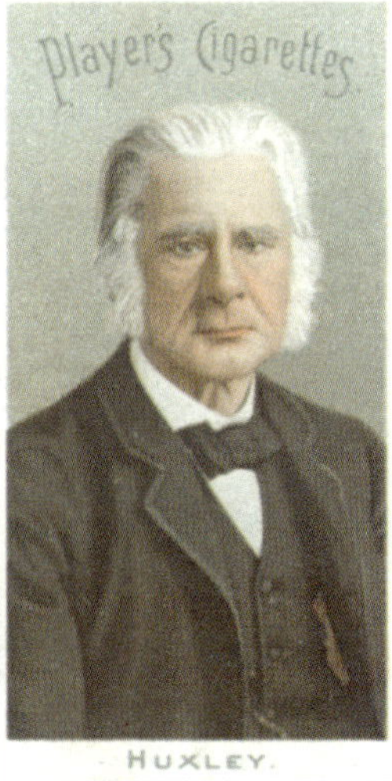

Famous Authors & Poets
Player

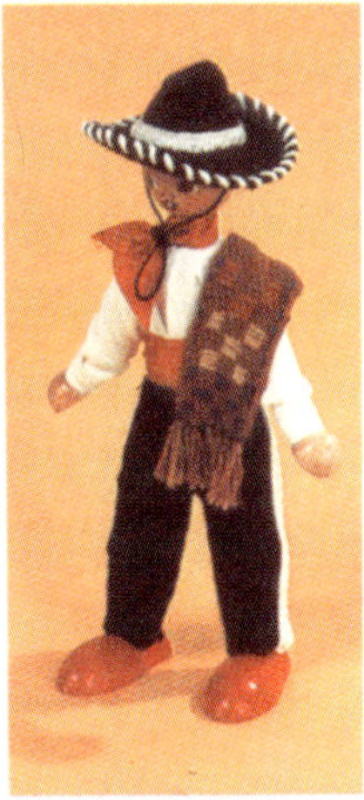

Wide World/People of Other Lands
Goodies

JOHN PLAYER & SONS — cont.

Qty		Date	Odds	Sets
K1	Bookmark (Calendar Back)	1902	—	*£110.00*
PF10	Bookmarks (Authors)	1900	£60.00	£600.00
25	Boxing (Eire)	1934	£6.00	£150.00
50	Boy Scout & Girl Guide	1933	35p	£17.50
50	Ditto (Transfers)	1933	25p	£12.50
L25	British Butterflies	1934	£3.80	£95.00
50	British Empire Series	1904	£1.20	£60.00
25	British Live Stock	1915	£2.00	£50.00
X25	British Live Stock (Blue Back)	1923	£2.20	£55.00
X25	(Brown Back)	1916	£2.80	£70.00
L25	British Naval Craft	1939	80p	£20.00
X20	British Pedigree Stock	1925	£2.65	£53.00
L25	British Regalia	1937	£1.00	£25.00
50	Butterflies	1932	£1.00	£50.00
50	Ditto (Transfers)	1932	30p	£15.00
50	Butterflies & Moths	1904	£1.60	£80.00
25	Bygone Beauties	1914	£1.20	£30.00
X10	Bygone Beauties	1916	£4.25	£42.50
G?30	Cabinet Size Pictures			
	(Brown Front, Printed Back)	1899	*£75.00*	—
	(Brown Front, Plain Back)	1899	*£75.00*	—
	(Green Front, Printed Back)	1899	£75.00	—
	(Green Front, Plain Back)	1899	£75.00	—
20	Castles Abbeys etc. (No Border)	1895	£25.00	£500.00
20	(White Border)	1895	£22.50	£450.00
L24	Cats	1936	£6.50	£156.00
50	Celebrated Bridges	1903	£2.40	£120.00
50	Celebrated Gateways	1909	£1.30	£65.00
25	Ceremonial and Court Dress	1911	£1.60	£40.00
L25	Championship Golf Courses	1936	£7.50	£187.50
25	Characters from Dickens, A Series (1-25)	1912	£2.00	£50.00
25	Characters from Dickens, 2nd Series (26-50)	1912	£2.00	£50.00
50	Characters from Dickens (Re-issue)	1923	£1.30	£65.00
X10	Characters from Dickens	1914	£5.00	£50.00
L25	Characters from Fiction	1933	£3.00	£75.00
25	Characters from Thackeray	1913	£1.20	£30.00
50	Cities of the World	1900	£3.50	£175.00
L20	Clocks – Old & New	1928	£4.50	£90.00
25	Colonial & Indian Army Badges	1917	£1.10	£27.50
50	Coronation Series – Ceremonial Dress	1937	20p	£10.00
25	Counties and Their Industries (Numbered)	1914	£1.70	£42.50
25	(Unnumbered)	1914	£1.70	£42.50
50	Countries Arms & Flags (Thick Card)	1905	80p	£40.00
50	(Thin Card)	1912	£1.00	£50.00
50	Country Seats and Arms (1-50)	1909	70p	£35.00
50	Country Seats and Arms, 2nd (51-100)	1910	65p	£32.50
50	Country Seats and Arms, 3rd (101-150)	1910	65p	£32.50
L25	Country Sports	1930	£5.20	£130.00
50	Cricketers 1930	1930	£1.25	£62.50
50	Cricketers 1934	1934	£1.00	£50.00
50	Cricketers 1938	1938	80p	£40.00
50	Cricketers, Caricatures by "RIP"	1926	£1.60	£80.00

Qty		Date	Odds	Sets
25	Cries of London, A Series	1913	£1.80	£45.00
X10	Cries of London, A Series	1912	£4.20	£42.00
X10	Cries of London, 2nd Series	1914	£3.25	£32.50
25	Cries of London, 2nd Series (Blue Back)	1916	80p	£20.00
25	(Black Back)	1916	£3.50	—
50	Curious Beaks	1929	75p	£37.50
50	Cycling	1939	80p	£40.00
50	(Eire) (Adhesive)	1939	£1.40	—
50	(Eire) (Non-Adhesive)	1939	£1.30	£65.00
50	Dandies	1932	30p	£15.00
L25	Dandies	1932	£1.80	£45.00
50	Decorations & Medals	Unissued	£1.80	£90.00
50	Derby and Grand National Winners	1933	£1.60	£80.00
50	(Transfers)	1933	40p	£20.00
50	Dogs (Scenic Background)	1925	80p	£40.00
X12	Dogs (Scenic Background)	1924	£2.50	£30.00
50	Dogs, by Wardle (Full Length)	1931	65p	£32.50
50	(Transfers)	1931	30p	£15.00
L25	Dogs, by Wardle (Full Length)	1933	£2.20	£55.00
50	Dogs, by Wardle (Heads)	1929	80p	£40.00
L20	Dogs, by Wardle, A Series (Heads)	1926	£2.40	£48.00
L20	Dogs, by Wardle, 2nd Series (Heads)	1928	£2.40	£48.00
25	Dogs, by Wardle, A Series (Eire) (Heads)	1927	£1.80	£45.00
25	Dogs, by Wardle 2nd Series (Eire) (Heads)	1929	£1.80	£45.00
50	Dogs' Heads by Biegel	Unissued	80p	£40.00
L25	Dogs (Heads)	Unissued	£1.30	£32.50
50	Dogs' Heads (Silver Background, Eire)	1940	£2.70	£135.00
50	Drum Banners & Cap Badges (2 Printings)	1924	75p	£37.50
25	Egyptian Kings & Queens and Classical Deities	1912	£1.60	£40.00
X10	Egyptian Sketches	1915	£3.50	£35.00
25	England's Military Heroes (Narrow)	1898	£27.50	£685.00
25	(Wide)	1898	£37.50	£935.00
25	(Narrow, Plain Back)	1898	£27.50	£685.00
25	(Wide, Plain Back)	1898	£37.50	—
25	England's Naval Heroes			
	(Non-Descriptive, Narrow)	1897	£22.00	£550.00
	(Non-Descriptive, Wide)	1897	£35.00	£875.00
25	England's Naval Heroes			
	(Descriptive, Narrow)	1898	£22.00	£550.00
	(Descriptive, Wide)	1898	£35.00	£875.00
25	Everyday Phrases (by Tom Browne)	1900	£13.00	£325.00
L25	Fables of Aesop	1927	£2.20	£55.00
20	Famous Authors & Poets (Narrow)	1900	£17.50	£350.00
20	(Wide)	1900	£25.00	£500.00
L25	Famous Beauties	1937	£1.60	£40.00
50	Famous Irish-Bred Horses	1936	£3.00	£150.00
50	Famous Irish Greyhounds	1935	£5.00	£250.00
X10	Famous Paintings	1913	£3.25	£32.50
50	Film Stars	1934	95p	£47.50
50	Film Stars, Second Series	1934	75p	£37.50
50	Ditto (Eire)	1934	£1.60	£80.00
50	Film Stars, Third Series	1938	65p	£32.50
L25	Film Stars	1934	£2.60	£65.00
L25	Ditto (Eire)	1934	£6.00	£150.00

Qty		Date	Odds	Sets
50	Fire-Fighting Appliances	1930	£1.40	£70.00
50	Fishes of the World	1903	£1.70	£85.00
50	Flags of the League of Nations	1928	40p	£20.00
50	Football Caricatures by "MAC"	1927	£1.20	£60.00
50	Footballers, Caricatures by "RIP"	1926	£1.20	£60.00
50	Footballers 1928	1928	£1.50	£75.00
25	Footballers 1928-9, 2nd Series	1929	£1.40	£35.00
50	Fresh-Water Fishes (Pink Back)	1933	£1.10	£55.00
50	(White Back)	1934	£1.30	£65.00
L25	Fresh-Water Fishes	1935	£2.40	£60.00
L25	Ditto (Eire, Non-Adhesive)	1935	£5.00	£125.00
25	From Plantation to Smoker	1926	25p	£6.25
50	Gallery of Beauty Series	1896	£20.00	£1000.00
5	Alternative Subjects	1896	£50.00	—
50	Game Birds and Wild Fowl	1927	£1.30	£65.00
L25	Game Birds & Wild Fowl	1928	£4.00	£100.00
25	Gems of British Scenery	1917	60p	£15.00
50	Gilbert and Sullivan, A Series	1925	£1.00	£50.00
X25	Gilbert & Sullivan, A Series	1926	£3.00	£75.00
50	Gilbert and Sullivan, 2nd Series	1927	£1.00	£50.00
L25	Gilbert & Sullivan, 2nd Series	1928	£3.20	£80.00
L25	Golf	1939	£7.50	£187.50
25	Hidden Beauties	1929	20p	£5.00
25	Highland Clans	1907	£3.20	£80.00
50	Hints on Association Football	1934	45p	£22.50
X10	Historic Ships	1910	£4.00	£40.00
50	History of Naval Dress	1930	£1.00	£50.00
L25	History of Naval Dress	1929	£2.00	£50.00
50	International Air Liners	1936	40p	£20.00
50	Ditto (Eire)	1936	90p	—
25	Irish Place Names, A Series	1927	£2.00	£50.00
25	Irish Place Names, 2nd Series	1929	£2.00	£50.00
1	Joker Cards (Eire)	1935	—	£3.00
M5	Jubilee Issue	1960	£1.20	£6.00
50	Kings & Queens of England	1935	£1.30	£65.00
L50	Kings & Queens of England	1935	£2.50	£125.00
50	Life on Board a Man of War – 1805 &1905	1905	£1.80	£90.00
25	Live Stock	1925	£3.00	£75.00
50	Military Head-Dress	1931	90p	£45.00
50	Military Series	1900	£17.00	£850.00
50	Military Uniforms of the British Empire Overseas	1938	75p	£37.50
25	Miniatures	1923	40p	£10.00
50	Modern Naval Craft	1939	45p	£22.50
50	Ditto (Eire)	1939	80p	£40.00
50	Motor Cars, A Series	1936	£1.20	£60.00
50	Motor Cars, A Series (Eire)	1936	£2.00	£100.00
50	Motor Cars, Second Series	1937	90p	£45.00
L20	Mount Everest	1925	£2.25	£45.00
25	Napoleon	1916	£1.50	£37.50
50	National Flags and Arms	1936	40p	£20.00
50	Ditto (Eire)	1936	75p	£37.50
50	Natural History	1924	25p	£12.50
X12	Natural History	1924	£1.00	£12.00
X12	Natural History, 2nd Series	1924	£1.00	£12.00

JOHN PLAYER & SONS — cont.

Qty		Date	Odds	Sets
50	Nature Series	1909	£1.10	£55.00
X10	Nature Series (Birds)	1908	£8.50	£85.00
X10	Nature Series (Mammals)	1913	£4.00	£40.00
50	Old England's Defenders	1898	£16.00	£800.00
L25	Old Hunting Prints	1938	£2.40	£70.00
L25	Old Naval Prints	1936	£2.30	£57.50
X25	Old Sporting Prints	1924	£2.75	£69.00
L25	Picturesque Bridges	1929	£2.50	£62.50
L25	Picturesque Cottages	1929	£2.50	£62.50
L25	Picturesque London	1931	£3.20	£80.00
25	Players Past & Present	1916	80p	£20.00
25	Polar Exploration, A Series	1915	£1.50	£37.50
25	Polar Exploration, 2nd Series	1916	£1.20	£30.00
L25	Portals of the Past	1930	£2.00	£50.00
50	Poultry	1931	£1.50	£75.00
50	Ditto (Transfers)	1931	30p	£15.00
25	Products of the World	1908	60p	£15.00
50	Products of the World (Different)	1928	20p	£10.00
25	Racehorses	1926	£5.00	£125.00
40	Racing Caricatures	1925	70p	£28.00
L25	Racing Yachts	1938	£3.20	£80.00
50	R.A.F. Badges (No Motto)	1937	60p	£30.00
50	(With Motto)	1937	60p	£30.00
50	Regimental Colours & Cap Badges (Regulars)	1907	£1.00	£50.00
50	Regimental Colours & Cap Badges (Territorials, Blue Back)	1910	£1.00	£50.00
	(Territorials, Brown Back)	1910	£1.00	£50.00
50	Regimental Standards and Cap Badges	1930	65p	£32.50
50	Regimental Uniforms (Blue Back)	1912	£1.70	£85.00
50	(Brown Back)	1914	£1.70	£85.00
X10	Regimental Uniforms (Different)	1914	£7.00	£70.00
50	Regimental Uniforms, 2nd Series (51-100)	1913	£1.00	£50.00
50	Riders of the World	1905	£1.50	£75.00
P30	Rulers & Views	1902	£80.00	—
50	Sea Fishes	1935	30p	£15.00
50	Ditto (Eire)	1935	80p	—
50	Screen Celebrities (Eire)	1938	£1.60	£80.00
25	Shakespearean Series	1917	80p	£20.00
L20	Ship-Models	1926	£2.40	£48.00
50	Shipping	Unissued	—	£65.00
25	Ships' Figure-Heads (2 Printings)	1912	£1.80	£45.00
L25	Ships' Figure-Heads	1931	£1.70	£42.50
L8	Snap Cards	1930	£6.25	£50.00
50	Speedway Riders	1937	£1.50	£75.00
S150	Stereoscopic Series	1904	£75.00	—
50	Straight Line Caricatures	1926	45p	£22.50
25	Struggle for Existence (2 Printings)	1923	20p	£5.00
50	Tennis	1936	80p	£40.00
116	The Corsair Game (Eire)	1965	85p	—
L25	The Nation's Shrines	1929	£2.00	£50.00
X1	The Royal Family	1937	—	£2.00
P6	The Royal Family	1901	£40.00	£240.00
25	Those Pearls of Heaven	1916	80p	£20.00

Qty		Date	Odds	Sets
66	Transvaal Series	1902	£4.50	—
L25	Treasures of Britain	1931	£1.60	£40.00
25	Treasures of Ireland	1930	£1.60	£40.00
L25	Types of Horses	1939	£3.40	£85.00
50	Uniforms of the Territorial Army	1939	75p	£37.50
50	Useful Plants & Fruits	1902	£1.60	£80.00
25	Victoria Cross	1914	£1.80	£45.00
90	War Decorations & Medals	1927	60p	£54.00
50	Wild Animals' Heads	1931	60p	£30.00
25	Ditto (Transfers)	1931	£1.30	—
50	Wild Animals' Heads (Transfers, Series of 50)	1927	40p	£20.00
L25	Wild Animals (Heads), A Series	1932	£1.60	£40.00
L25	Wild Animals (Heads), 2nd Series	1932	£1.60	£40.00
45	Wild Animals of the World (Narrow) (No Ltd)	1901	£4.60	—
45	(Narrow) (With Ltd)	1901	£4.60	—
45	(Narrow) ("Branch")	1901	£6.30	—
50	Wild Animals of the World (Wide) (No Ltd)	1901	£2.40	£120.00
50	(Wide) (With Ltd)	1901	£2.30	£115.00
50	(Wide) ("Branch")	1901	£4.25	—
50	Wild Birds	1932	40p	£20.00
50	Ditto (Transfers)	1932	30p	£15.00
L25	Wild Birds	1934	£2.60	£65.00
L25	Wildfowl	1937	£2.80	£70.00
50	Wonders of the Deep	1904	£1.50	£75.00
25	Wonders of the World (Blue Back)	1916	60p	£15.00
25	(Grey Back, Eire)	1926	£1.20	£30.00
X10	Wooden Walls	1908	£5.00	£50.00
25	Wrestling & Ju-Jitsu (Blue Back)	1913	£1.60	£40.00
25	(Grey Back, Eire)	1925	£1.30	£32.50
26	Your Initials (Transfers)	1932	50p	£13.00
L25	Zoo Babies	1938	50p	£12.50

OVERSEAS ISSUES

Qty		Date	Odds	Sets
50	Aeroplane Series	1926	£1.80	£90.00
50	Aircraft of the Royal Air Force	1938	£1.20	£60.00
50	Animals of the Countryside	1939	50p	£25.00
50	Arms & Armour (Grey Back)	1926	£2.70	£135.00
F50	Beauties	1925	£1.50	£75.00
MF50	Beauties (Coloured)	1925	£1.60	£80.00
F50	Beauties, 2nd Series	1925	£1.50	£75.00
50	Birds & Their Young	1937	50p	£25.00
52	Birds of Brilliant Plumage	1927	£3.00	—
25	"Bonzo" Dogs	1923	£4.40	£110.00
50	Boy Scouts	1924	£2.20	£110.00
L25	British Live Stock	1924	£6.50	£162.50
50	Butterflies (Girls)	1928	£5.00	£250.00
50	Coronation Series – Ceremonial Dress	1937	70p	£35.00
50	Cricketers 1938	1938	£1.50	£75.00
50	Cycling	1939	£1.30	£65.00
25	Dogs (Heads)	1927	£1.20	£30.00
32	Drum Horses	1911	£6.50	—
L25	Famous Beauties	1937	£2.00	£50.00
50	Film Stars, Third Series	1938	£1.30	—
25	Flag Girls of All Nations	1908	£6.00	—

JOHN PLAYER & SONS — cont.

Qty		Date	Odds	Sets
L25	Golf	1939	£6.50	£162.50
50	Household Hints	1928	80p	£40.00
50	International Air Liners	1936	80p	£40.00
50	Lawn Tennis	1928	£2.80	£140.00
50	Leaders of Men	1925	£1.70	£85.00
50	Military Uniforms of the British Empire Overseas			
	(Adhesive)	1938	£1.20	£60.00
	(Non-Adhesive)	1938	£1.25	£62.50
50	Modern Naval Craft	1939	80p	£40.00
50	Motor Cars, A Series	1936	£1.60	£80.00
50	Motor Cars, Second Series	1937	£1.60	£80.00
50	National Flags and Arms	1936	60p	£30.00
L25	Old Hunting Prints	1938	£3.20	£80.00
M15/22	Old Masters (Package Issue)	1966	£1.00	£15.00
P2	Old Masters (Package Issue)	1966	£2.50	£5.00
L25	Old Naval Prints	1936	£3.20	£80.00
48	Pictures of the East	1931	£2.00	£100.00
25	Picturesque People of the Empire	1938	£2.00	£50.00
M53	Playing Cards	1929	£1.25	—
50	Pugilists in Action	1928	£3.20	£160.00
L25	Racing Yachts	1938	£4.00	—
50	R.A.F. Badges	1937	90p	£45.00
50	Railway Working	1927	£1.60	£80.00
50	Sea Fishes	1935	60p	£30.00
50	Ships Flags & Cap Badges	1930	£1.60	£80.00
50	Signalling Series	1926	£1.20	£60.00
F50	The Royal Family at Home and Abroad	1927	£2.00	—
L25	Types of Horses	1939	£4.40	£110.00
25	Whaling	1930	£2.50	£62.50
L25	Zoo Babies	1937	£1.60	£40.00

MODERN ISSUES (DONCELLA)

Qty		Date	Odds	Sets
T32	Britain's Endangered Wildlife	1984	30p	£9.50
T30	Britain's Nocturnal Wildlife	1987	40p	£12.00
T30	Britain's Wild Flowers	1986	40p	£12.00
T32	British Butterflies	1984	35p	£11.50
T30	British Mammals	1983	40p	£12.00
T32	Country Houses and Castles	1981	20p	£4.50
T24	Golden Age of Flying	1977	25p	£6.00
T1	Golden Age of Flying Completion Offer	1978	—	£3.25
T24	Golden Age of Motoring	1975	25p	£6.00
T24	Golden Age of Motoring Completion Offer	1976	£3.25	£78.00
T24	Golden Age of Sail	1978	25p	£6.00
T1	Golden Age of Sail Completion Offer	1979	—	£3.00
T24	Golden Age of Steam	1976	25p	£6.00
T1	Golden Age of Steam Completion Offer	1977	—	£3.50
T24	History of the V.C.	1980	75p	£18.00
T1	History of the V.C. Completion Offer	1980	—	£3.75
T24	Napoleonic Uniforms	1980	25p	£6.00
T1	Napoleonic Uniforms Completion Offer	1980	—	£3.25
T30	The Living Ocean	1985	40p	£12.00

MODERN ISSUES (GRANDEE)

Qty		Date	Odds	Sets
T30	African Wildlife	1990	40p	£12.00

JOHN PLAYER & SONS — cont.

Qty		Date	Odds	Sets
T32	Britain's Endangered Wildlife	1984	25p	£8.00
T30	Britain's Nocturnal Wildlife	1987	25p	£7.50
T30	Britain's Wayside Wildlife	1988	25p	£7.50
T30	Britain's Wild Flowers	1986	25p	£7.50
T32	British Birds	1980	40p	£13.00
T32	British Butterflies	1983	40p	£13.00
T30	British Mammals (Imperial Tobacco Ltd.)	1982	20p	£6.00
T30	(Imperial Group plc.)	1983	20p	£6.00
T28	Famous M.G. Marques	1981	85p	£24.00
T7	Limericks	1977	£8.00	—
T30	The Living Ocean	1985	25p	£7.50
T25	Top Dogs	1979	£1.00	£25.00
T6	World of Gardening	1976	£8.00	£48.00

MODERN ISSUES (TOM THUMB)

Qty		Date	Odds	Sets
L30	Britain's Maritime History	1989	40p	£12.00
L32	Exploration of Space	1982	20p	£6.25
L30	History of Britain's Railways	1987	25p	£7.50
L30	History of British Aviation	1988	60p	£18.00
L30	History of Motor Racing (Imperial Tobacco Ltd.)	1986	£1.55	£46.50
L30	(Imperial Group plc.)	1986	60p	£18.00
L32	Myths & Legends	1981	80p	£26.00
L32	Wonders of the Ancient World	1984	40p	£13.00
L30	Wonders of the Modern World	1985	30p	£9.00

MODERN ISSUES (OTHER)

Qty		Date	Odds	Sets
44	Black Jack	1984	£1.25	—
M44	Black Jack	1984	50p	—
T44	Black Jack	1984	50p	—
T8	Panama Puzzles	1976	£6.00	—
T?	Player Clues	1987	50p	—
T?63	Player Games (Green)	1983	*50p*	—
T?29	Player Games (Yellow)	1983	*75p*	—
T?62	Player Games (Orange)	1984	*50p*	—
T?106	Player Games (Silver)	1984	50p	—
T?	Player Games (Yellow)	1984	*75p*	—
T?127	Player Quiz (Green)	1985	65p	—
T?	Player Quiz (Blue)	1986	65p	—
T?	Player Quiz (Red)	1986	*65p*	—
T6	Play Ladbroke Spot-Ball	1975	£6.00	—
T6	Play Panama Spot Six	1977	£6.00	—
T4	Recordbreakers	1976	*£5.00*	—
T50	Super Cars (35 x 90mm)	1987	65p	—
T50	(47 x 90mm)	1987	65p	—
60	Super Deal	1984	£1.25	—
M60	Super Deal	1984	65p	—
T60	Super Deal (35 x 90mm)	1984	£1.25	—
T60	(47 x 90mm)	1984	65p	—
T108	Super Year 88 (35 x 90mm)	1988	£1.25	—
T108	(47 x 90mm)	1988	65p	—
152	World Tour	1986	£1.25	—
M153	World Tour	1986	65p	—
T152	World Tour (35 x 90mm)	1986	£1.25	—
T152	(47 x 90mm)	1986	65p	—

JAMES PLAYFAIR & CO.

Qty		*Date*	*Odds*	*Sets*
25	How To Keep Fit	1912	£30.00	£750.00

PREMIER TOBACCO MFRS. LTD.

48	Eminent Stage & Screen Personalities	1936	£1.60	£80.00
K52	Miniature Playing Cards	1935	*£6.50*	—
50	Stage & Screen Personalities (Brown)	1936	£1.80	—
100	(Grey)	1936	£1.30	£130.00

PRITCHARD & BURTON

51	Actors & Actresses "FROGA" (Blue Back)	1899	£17.00	—
51	(Grey Back)	1899	*£40.00*	—
15	Beauties "PAC"	1899	£50.00	£750.00
20	Boer War Cartoons	1900	£85.00	—
30	Flags & Flags with Soldiers (Draped)	1902	£15.00	£450.00
15	(Different Back)	1902	£20.00	—
15	Flags & Flags with Soldiers (Undraped)	1902	£20.00	—
25	Holiday Resorts & Views	1902	£16.00	£400.00
40	Home & Colonial Regiments	1901	£45.00	—
25	Royalty Series	1902	£20.00	£500.00
25	South African Series	1901	£18.00	£450.00
25	Star Girls	1900	£125.00	—

G. PRUDHOE

30	Army Pictures, Cartoons, etc	1916	*£90.00*	—

Q.V. CIGARS

M?10	Barnum & Bailey's Circus Performers	1900	*£150.00*	—

JAS. QUINTON LTD.

26	Actresses "FROGA"	1899	£125.00	—

RAY & CO. LTD.

K7	Flags of the Allies (Shaped)	1916	£60.00	—
25	War Series (1-25)	1915	£12.00	—
75	War Series (26-100)	1915	£9.00	—
24	War Series (101-124)	1916	£20.00	—

RAYMOND REVUEBAR

MF25	Striptease Artistes (2 Printings)	1960	£12.50	—

RECORD CIGARETTE & TOBACCO CO.

Qty		*Date*	*Odds*	*Sets*
X36	The Talkie Cigarette Card (Record Cigarette Co.) ..	1934	£32.50	—
X36	(Record Tobacco Co.) ..	1934	£35.00	—

REDFORD & CO.

20	Actresses "BLARM"	1900	£70.00	—
25	Armies of the World	1901	£50.00	—
25	Beauties "GRACC"	1899	*£90.00*	—
30	Colonial Troops	1902	£45.00	—
24	Nautical Expressions	1900	*£65.00*	—
40	Naval & Military Phrases	1904	£50.00	—
25	Picture Series	1906	£65.00	—
25	Sports & Pastimes	1906	*£75.00*	—
50	Stage Artistes of the Day	1908	£15.00	£750.00

RELIANCE TOBACCO MFG. CO.

24	British Birds	1934	£4.25	—
35	Famous Stars	1934	£4.25	£150.00

A.S. RICHARDSON

M12	Manikin Cards (2 Printings)	1915	£75.00	—

RICHMOND CAVENDISH CO. LTD.

26	Actresses "FROGA"	1900	£25.00	£650.00
28	Actresses "PILPI I"	1902	£13.00	£360.00
F50	Actresses "PILPI II"	1903	£8.00	£400.00
?179	Actresses, Gravure (Back Top-Bottom)	1904	£6.00	—
50	Actresses, Gravure (Back Bottom-Top)	1904	£6.00	£300.00
14	Beauties "AMBS" (12 Backs)	1899	£42.50	—
52	Beauties P/C Inset	1897	£45.00	—
28	Chinese Actors & Actresses	1923	£3.50	£98.00
F50	Cinema Stars	1927	£3.25	—
40	Medals	1900	£18.00	£720.00
20	Music Hall Artistes	1901	£40.00	£800.00
12	Pretty Girl Series "RASH"	1899	£37.50	£450.00
20	Yachts (Black Back)	1900	£57.50	—
20	(White Back)	1900	£60.00	—

RITMEESTER CIGARS (Cigar Bands)

24	Austrian Cavalry Serie D	1976	£1.00	£24.00
X28	Austrian Cavalry Serie D	1976	75p	£21.00
24	English Cavalry Serie A	1976	80p	£20.00
X28	English Cavalry Serie A	1976	£1.25	£35.00

RITMEESTER CIGARS (Cigar Bands) — cont.

Qty		Date	Odds	Sets
24	French Cavalry Serie B	1976	£1.00	£24.00
X28	French Cavalry Serie B	1976	75p	£21.00
24	German Cavalry Serie C	1976	£1.00	£24.00
X28	German Cavalry Serie C	1976	60p	£16.00
24	Military Bandsmen Serie K	1978	—	£20.00

ROBERTS & SONS

Qty		Date	Odds	Sets
26	Actresses "FROGA"	1899	*£55.00*	—
25	Armies of the World (Plain Back)	1900	£42.50	—
25	(Printed Back)	1900	£45.00	—
M50	Beautiful Women	1898	*£160.00*	—
50	Beauties "CHOAB" (Black Back)	1900	£65.00	—
50	(Blue Back)	1900	*£70.00*	—
50	Colonial Troops	1902	£37.50	£1875.00
M28	Dominoes	1905	£55.00	—
K52	Miniature Playing Cards (Blue)	1905	*£50.00*	—
K52	(Pink)	1905	*£50.00*	—
K52	(Yellow)	1905	*£50.00*	—
24	Nautical Expressions (Navy Cut Cigarettes)	1902	£55.00	—
24	(No Brand)	1902	*£60.00*	—
70	Stories Without Words	1904	£50.00	—
25	Types of British & Colonial Troops	1900	£45.00	—

ROBINSON & BARNSDALE LTD.

Qty		Date	Odds	Sets
25	Actresses, Colin Campbell	1898	£125.00	—
?28	Actresses, Cupola	1898	*£150.00*	—
1	Advertisement Card, Colin Campbell	1897	—	£115.00
?13	Beauties, Collotype (Black Back, "NANA")	1895	*£135.00*	—
?13	(Red Back, "NANA")	1895	*£135.00*	—
?13	(Our Golden Beauties)	1895	*£135.00*	—
M?20	Beauties, Highest Honors ("Viginia")	1895	*£200.00*	—
M?20	("Virginia" Label)	1895	*£200.00*	—

E. ROBINSON & SONS LTD.

Qty		Date	Odds	Sets
10	Beauties (10 Brands)	1897	£55.00	—
?50	Derbyshire and the Peak	1903	*£100.00*	—
25	Egyptian Studies	1914	£22.00	—
25	King Lud Problems	1934	£17.50	—
6	Medals & Decorations	1902	*£135.00*	—
40	Nature Studies	1914	£18.00	—
25	Regimental Mascots	1916	£60.00	—
25	Wild Flowers	1915	£17.00	—

ROMAN STAR CIGARS

Qty		Date	Odds	Sets
26	Actresses "FROGA"	1899	*£115.00*	—
25	Beauties "BOCCA"	1899	*£115.00*	—

ROTHMANS LTD.

Qty		Date	Odds	Sets
40	Beauties of the Cinema	1939	£1.25	£50.00
L24	Beauties of the Cinema (Circular, Matt)	1939	£3.75	£90.00
L24	(Varnished)	1939	£3.75	£90.00
P25	Canterbury Bankstown District Rugby League Football Club (New Zealand)	1980	*£4.00*	—
24	Cinema Stars	1925	£1.25	£30.00
L25	Cinema Stars	1925	£1.00	£24.00
P30	Country Living Cards	1974	—	£11.00
28	Dominoes	1986	*£1.50*	—
L50	International Football Stars	1984	30p	£15.00
?40	Know Africa	1970	£2.25	—
?80	Know Your Language	1970	£2.25	—
36	Landmarks in Empire History	1936	£1.00	£36.00
?	Lucky Charms (Metal)	1930	£3.50	—
50	Modern Inventions	1935	£1.00	£50.00
LF54	New Zealand	1933	75p	£40.00
24	Prominent Screen Favourites	1934	90p	£21.50
F50	Punch Jokes	1935	60p	£30.00
5	Rare and Historic Banknotes	1970	£3.50	£17.50
L8	Wiggle-Woggle Picture Cards	1933	*£15.00*	—

WM. RUDDELL LTD.

Qty		Date	Odds	Sets
?	Couplet Cards	1924	*£10.00*	—
25	Grand Opera Series	1924	£7.00	£175.00
25	Rod & Gun	1924	£6.00	£150.00
50	Songs That Will Live For Ever	1924	£3.25	£162.50

I. RUTTER & CO.

Qty		Date	Odds	Sets
15	Actresses (Printed Back)	1900	£52.50	—
15	(Rubber Stamped Back)	1900	*£65.00*	—
15	(Plain Back)	1900	£22.00	—
1	Advertisement Card	1899	—	*£325.00*
7	Boer War Celebrities (Printed Back)	1901	£50.00	£350.00
7	(Plain Back)	1901	£22.50	—
54	Comic Phrases	1905	£16.00	£860.00
20	Cricketers Series	1902	£250.00	—
30	Flags & Flags with Soldiers	1901	£24.00	£720.00
24	Girls, Flags & Arms of Countries	1900	£35.00	£840.00
25	Proverbs (Green Seal)	1904	£40.00	—
25	(Red Seal)	1904	£40.00	—
25	Shadowgraphs	1903	£35.00	—

S.D.V. TOBACCO CO. LTD.

Qty		Date	Odds	Sets
16	British Royal Family	1901	*£175.00*	—

SACCONE & SPEED

Qty		Date	Odds	Sets
F55	Beauties	1912	*£7.00*	—
F55	(Red Overprint)	1912	£5.00	—

ST. PETERSBURG CIGARETTE CO. LTD.

Qty		Date	Odds	Sets
?	Footballers	1900	*£250.00*	—

SALMON & GLUCKSTEIN LTD.

Qty		Date	Odds	Sets
X1	Advertisement Card (Snake Charmer, 10 Different)	1897	—	£400.00
15	Billiard Terms (Large Numerals)	1905	£55.00	—
15	(Small Numerals)	1905	£55.00	£825.00
12	British Queens	1902	£42.50	£510.00
X30	Castles, Abbeys & Houses (Brown Back)	1906	£16.00	£480.00
X30	(Red Back)	1906	£22.50	—
32	Characters from Dickens	1903	£25.00	—
25	Coronation Series,1911	1911	£9.00	£225.00
L25	Famous Pictures (Brown)	1912	£9.00	£225.00
L25	Famous Pictures (Green, Different)	1912	£7.00	£175.00
6	Her Most Gracious Majesty Queen Victoria	1897	£50.00	£300.00
40	Heroes of the Transvaal War	1901	£10.00	£600.00
25	Magical Series	1923	£5.50	£137.50
30	Music Hall Stage Characters	1902	£50.00	£1500.00
25	Occupations	1898	*£350.00*	—
20	Owners & Jockeys Series	1900	£65.00	—
L50	Pottery Types (Silk, Numbered Front & Back)	1916	£3.50	£175.00
L50	(Silk, Numbered Backs Only)	1916	£3.50	£175.00
6	Pretty Girl Series "RASH"	1900	£60.00	£360.00
22	Shakespearian Series (Frame on Back)	1902	£22.50	£500.00
22	(No Frame on Back)	1902	£32.50	—
25	Star Girls (Brown Back)	1899	£110.00	—
25	(Red Back)	1899	£110.00	—
50	The Great White City	1908	£11.00	£550.00
48	The Post in Various Countries	1900	£22.00	£1050.00
25	Traditions of the Army & Navy (Large No.)	1917	£11.00	£275.00
25	(Small No.)	1917	£13.00	£325.00
25	Wireless Explained	1923	£5.00	£125.00

W. SANDORIDES & CO. LTD.

Qty		Date	Odds	Sets
25	Aquarium Studies From The London Zoo			
	(Large Numerals)	1925	£3.20	£80.00
	(Small Numerals)	1925	£3.00	£75.00
L25	Aquarium Studies from The London Zoo	1925	£3.40	£85.00
25	Cinema Celebrities	1924	£2.60	£65.00
X25	Cinema Celebrities	1924	£4.00	—
25	Cinema Stars (With Firm's Name)	1924	*£5.50*	—
25	(Big Gun)	1924	*£7.00*	—
25	(Lucana)	1924	*£5.50*	—
X25	Cinema Stars (Big Gun)	1924	£2.40	£60.00
X25	(Lucana 66)	1924	*£6.50*	—
X25	(Sandorides)	1924	£2.60	£65.00
50	Famous Racecourses	1926	£2.70	£135.00
L50	Famous Racecourses	1926	£3.70	£185.00
50	Famous Racehorses (With Firm's Name)	1923	£2.70	£135.00
50	(Big Gun Label)	1923	*£10.00*	—
12	London Views (4 Types)	1936	£4.00	£50.00
25	Sports & Pastimes	1924	*£11.00*	—

SANSOM'S CIGAR STORES

Qty		Date	Odds	Sets
?	London Views	1905	*£175.00*	—

NICOLAS SARONY & CO.

Qty		Date	Odds	Sets
25	A Day On The Airway	1928	90p	£22.50
L25	A Day On The Airway	1928	£1.00	£25.00
50	Around The Mediterranean	1926	90p	£45.00
L50	Around The Mediterranean	1926	£1.00	£50.00
?	Boer War Scenes	1901	*£200.00*	—
M100	Celebrities and Their Autographs (2 Printings)	1923	60p	£60.00
L100	Celebrities and Their Autographs (2 Printings)	1923	65p	£65.00
50	Cinema Stars	1933	£1.20	£60.00
P38	Cinema Stars	1930	£8.50	—
P42	Cinema Stars, Second Series	1930	£5.00	—
P50	Cinema Stars, Third Series	1930	£5.00	—
P42	Cinema Stars, Fourth Series	1930	£5.00	—
P25	Cinema Stars, Fifth Series	1930	£5.00	£125.00
25	Cinema Studies	1929	£1.00	£25.00
F54	Life at Whipsnade Zoo	1934	50p	£27.00
50	Links with the Past	1925	25p	£12.50
25	(Australia)	1926	60p	—
25	(New Zealand)	1926	60p	£15.00
L50	Links with the Past	1925	25p	£12.50
L25	(Australia)	1926	60p	—
L25	(New Zealand)	1926	50p	£12.50
L25	(Presentation Issue)	1926	£1.60	—
25	Museum Series	1927	30p	£7.50
25	(New Zealand)	1927	60p	£15.00
L25	Museum Series	1927	30p	£7.50
L25	(Australia)	1927	60p	—
L25	(New Zealand)	1927	60p	—
L25	(Presentation Issue)	1927	70p	£17.50
F36	National Types of Beauty	1928	30p	£11.00
MF36	National Types of Beauty	1928	30p	£11.00
15	Origin of Games	1923	£3.50	£52.50
L15	Origin of Games	1923	£4.00	£60.00
50	Saronicks	1929	30p	£15.00
M50	Saronicks	1929	30p	£15.00
50	Ships of All Ages	1929	70p	£35.00
M50	Ships of All Ages	1929	70p	£35.00
25	Tennis Strokes	1923	£2.80	£70.00

T. S. SAUNT

Qty		Date	Odds	Sets
30	Army Pictures, Cartoons, etc	1916	*£95.00*	—

SCOTTISH C.W.S. LTD.

Qty		Date	Odds	Sets
25	Burns (Large Numeral)	1924	£1.40	£35.00
25	(Small Numeral)	1924	£2.20	£55.00
25	(Plain Back)	1924	*£6.00*	—
20	Dogs	1925	£10.00	—

SCOTTISH C.W.S. LTD. — cont.

Qty		Date	Odds	Sets
25	Dwellings of All Nations (Large Numeral)	1924	£2.00	£50.00
25	(Small Numeral)	1924	£3.50	£87.50
25	(Plain Back)	1924	*£6.00*	—
L25	Famous Pictures	1924	£7.00	—
L25	Famous Pictures – Glasgow Gallery			
	(Adhesive)	1927	£1.20	£30.00
	(Non-Adhesive)	1927	£2.20	£55.00
L25	Famous Pictures – London Galleries			
	(Adhesive)	1927	£1.20	£30.00
	(Non-Adhesive)	1927	£2.20	£55.00
50	Feathered Favourites (Adhesive)	1926	£1.40	£70.00
	(Non-Adhesive, Grey Border)	1926	£2.00	£100.00
	(Non-Adhesive, White Border)	1926	£1.80	£90.00
25	Racial Types	1925	£8.00	£200.00
50	Triumphs of Engineering (Brown Border)	1926	£2.00	£100.00
50	(White Border)	1926	£2.00	—
50	Wireless	1924	£3.30	£165.00

SELBY'S TOBACCO STORES

M12	Manikin Cards	1915	*£75.00*	—

SHARPE & SNOWDEN

?	Views of England	1905	*£135.00*	—
?25	Views of London	1905	*£125.00*	—

W. J. SHEPHERD

25	Beauties "FECKSA"	1901	£80.00	—

SHORT'S

L?13	House Views (Numbered)	1924	*£60.00*	—
L9	House Views (Unnumbered)	1924	£35.00	—

SIMONETS LTD. (Channel Isles)

MF36	Beautiful Women	1928	£4.50	£160.00
F24	Cinema Scene Series	1926	£6.00	—
F27	Famous Actors and Actresses	1929	£4.50	—
50	Local Footballers	1925	£4.00	£200.00
25	Picture Series	1925	£3.60	£90.00
F27	Sporting Celebrities	1929	£7.50	—
LF50	Views of Jersey (Plain Back)	1926	£1.80	—

JOHN SINCLAIR LTD.

M?69	Actresses	1902	£65.00	—
F48	Birds (Numbered)	1924	£2.00	£96.00
F48	("Specimen Cigarette Card")	1924	£6.00	—

JOHN SINCLAIR LTD. — cont.

Qty		Date	Odds	Sets
LF50	Birds	1924	£4.75	—
50	British Sea Dogs	1928	£4.50	£225.00
F54	Champion Dogs, A Series	1938	80p	£44.00
LF52	Champion Dogs, A Series	1938	80p	£42.00
F54	Champion Dogs, 2nd Series	1939	£2.60	£140.00
LF52	Champion Dogs, 2nd Series	1939	£3.00	£156.00
F50	English & Scottish Football Stars	1935	£1.40	£70.00
F54	Film Stars (Series of 54 Real Photos)	1934	£1.75	£94.50
F54	Film Stars (Series of Real Photos)	1937	£1.50	£81.00
F54	Film Stars (55-108)	1937	£1.20	£65.00
M12	Flags (Numbered, Silk, 25-36)	1914	£13.50	—
M24	Flags (Unnumbered, Silk) (Blue Caption)	1914	£8.00	—
M24	(Bright Green)	1914	£6.50	—
M24	Flags (Unnumbered, Silk) (Olive Green)	1914	£6.50	—
M24	(Red Caption)	1914	£8.00	—
M25	Flags (Unnumbered, Silk) (Grey Caption)	1914	£10.00	—
M50	Flags, Fourth Series (Silk)	1914	£6.00	—
M50	Flags, Fifth Series (Silk)	1914	£6.00	—
D50	Flags, Sixth Series (Silk)	1914	£7.00	—
G10	Flags, Seventh Series (Silk)	1914	*£50.00*	—
F96	Flowers & Plants (Numbered)	1924	£2.00	£192.00
F96	("Specimen Cigarette Card")	1924	£6.00	—
51	Football Favourites (51-101)	1908	£90.00	—
4	North Country Celebrities	1904	£65.00	£260.00
F55	Northern Gems	1902	£55.00	—
50	Picture Puzzles & Riddles Series	1916	£22.00	—
F54	Radio Favourites	1935	£1.50	£81.00
L50	Regimental Badges (Silk)	1915	£5.00	—
D24	Regimental Colours (Silk) (38-61)	1914	£12.50	—
K53	Rubicon Cards (Miniature Playing Cards)	1933	£5.00	—
K53	(Red Overprint)	1933	£6.50	—
P1	The Allies Flags (No. 37, Silk)	1915	—	£34.00
50	Trick Series	1916	£23.00	—
50	Well Known Footballers – N.E.Counties	1938	£1.25	£62.50
50	Well Known Footballers – Scottish	1938	£1.20	£60.00
50	Worlds Coinage	1914	£16.50	£825.00

ROBERT SINCLAIR TOBACCO CO. LTD.

Qty		Date	Odds	Sets
X4	Battleships & Crests (Silk)	1915	£50.00	—
10	Billiards, First Set	1928	£7.50	£75.00
15	Billiards, Second Set	1928	£8.00	£120.00
3	Billiards, Third Set	1928	£15.00	—
28	Dominoes	1902	*£50.00*	—
M10	Flags (Silk)	1915	£25.00	—
?5	Footballers (Black & White on Card)	1900	*£225.00*	—
?2	Footballers (Mauve on Paper)	1900	*£250.00*	—
P6	Great War Area (Silk)	1915	£40.00	—
M10	Great War Heroes (Silk)	1915	£35.00	—
12	Policemen of the World	1899	£135.00	—
X1	Red Cross Nurse (Silk)	1915	—	£50.00
M5	Regimental Badges (Silk)	1915	£27.50	—
12	The Smiler Series	1924	£6.25	—
L12	The Smiler Series	1924	£11.00	—

J. SINFIELD

Qty		Date	Odds	Sets
24	Beauties "HUMPS"	1899	*£200.00*	—

SINGLETON & COLE LTD.

Qty		Date	Odds	Sets
50	Atlantic Liners	1910	£17.00	£850.00
25	Bonzo Series	1928	£6.50	£162.50
50	Celebrities-Boer War Period	1901	£17.00	£850.00
110	Crests & Badges of the British Army (Silk)	1915	£4.00	—
35	Famous Boxers (Numbered)	1930	£12.00	—
35	(Unnumbered)	1930	*£30.00*	—
25	Famous Film Stars	1930	£8.50	—
35	Famous Officers	1915	£13.00	£675.00
35	(Subtitled Hero Series)	1915	*£150.00*	—
50	Footballers	1905	£90.00	—
40	Kings & Queens	1902	£17.50	£700.00
M12	Manikin Cards	1915	*£75.00*	—
25	Maxims of Success (Orange Border)	1906	£25.00	£625.00
25	(Yellow Border)	1906	*£125.00*	—
10	Orient Line (Anonymous, 5 Ports on Back)	1904	£40.00	£400.00
10	(Anonymous,11 Ports on Back)	1904	£45.00	—
8	Orient Pacific Line (Anonymous)	1904	*£60.00*	—
8	Orient Royal Mail Line (Firm's Name)	1904	£40.00	£320.00
25	The Wallace-Jones Keep Fit System	1910	£22.00	£550.00

F. & J. SMITH

36 Page Illustrated Reference Book — £3.50

Qty		Date	Odds	Sets
24	Advertisement Cards	1897	£175.00	£4200.00
50	A Tour Round the World (Postcard Back)	1904	£40.00	£2000.00
50	(Script Back)	1904	£20.00	£1000.00
50	A Tour Round the World (Descriptive, Multi-Backed)	1906	£8.50	£425.00
50	Battlefields of Great Britain (15 Backs)	1913	£12.00	£600.00
25	Boer War Series (Black & White)	1901	£60.00	—
50	Boer War Series (Coloured)	1901	£24.00	£1200.00
50	Champions of Sport (Blue Back)	1902	£75.00	—
50	Champions of Sport (Red Multi-Backed)	1902	£65.00	—
25	Cinema Stars (8 Brands)	1920	£8.00	£200.00
50	Cricketers (1-50)	1912	£13.00	£650.00
20	Cricketers, 2nd Series (51-70)	1912	£27.50	£550.00
50	Derby Winners	1913	£12.00	£600.00
50	Famous Explorers	1911	£12.00	£600.00
50	Football Club Records	1917	£13.00	£650.00
50	Football Club Records (Different)	1922	£13.00	£650.00
120	Footballers (Brown Back)	1906	£30.00	—
100	Footballers (Blue Back, No Series Title)	1908	£10.00	£1000.00
150	Footballers (Titled, Dark Blue Backs)	1912	£10.00	£1500.00
150	(Titled, Light Blue Backs)	1912	£11.00	—
50	Fowls, Pigeons & Dogs	1908	£8.50	£425.00
25	Holiday Resorts	1925	£7.00	£175.00
50	Medals (Numbered, Smith Multi-Backed)	1902	£8.50	£425.00
50	(Numbered, Imperial Tobacco Co., Multi-Backed)	1903	£32.00	—
50	(Numbered, Imperial Tobacco Company, Multi-Backed)	1906	£9.00	£450.00
20	(Unnumbered)	1905	£13.00	£260.00

LITERATURE

Although there have been tens of thousands of card sets issued, there are comparatively few books about the hobby. Foremost among the works of reference are those published by the Cartophilic Society. These include a number of books on individual firms, such as Ogden and Wills. Most important however are the five volumes of the "World Tobacco Index" and the four of the "British Trade Index". Each of these builds on the previous volumes, and records new issues, old series that have recently been discovered, and additional subjects to those sets that had been only partially seen. Because it is published annually, our catalogue is often more advanced in its information, and we always welcome news about additions and amendments, which will always be passed on to the Society's research Editor.

A number of dedicated collectors have made their own contributions by compiling lists of a more specialised nature, and we have indeed published many of these ourselves. Among works recently available are three volumes dealing with errors and varieties, two on cricket and one on tennis, a work on tobacco football cards, and one each on all known golf and boxing cards and a comprehensive list of British silk issues.

There are only three general works now available. These are the well written "Cigarette Card Collecting", the well illustrated "collecting Cigarette and Trade Cards", and the one we should like to think is a combination of both these features, "The Story of Cigarette Cards". Details of all books that we stock are given in the first few pages of the catalogue.

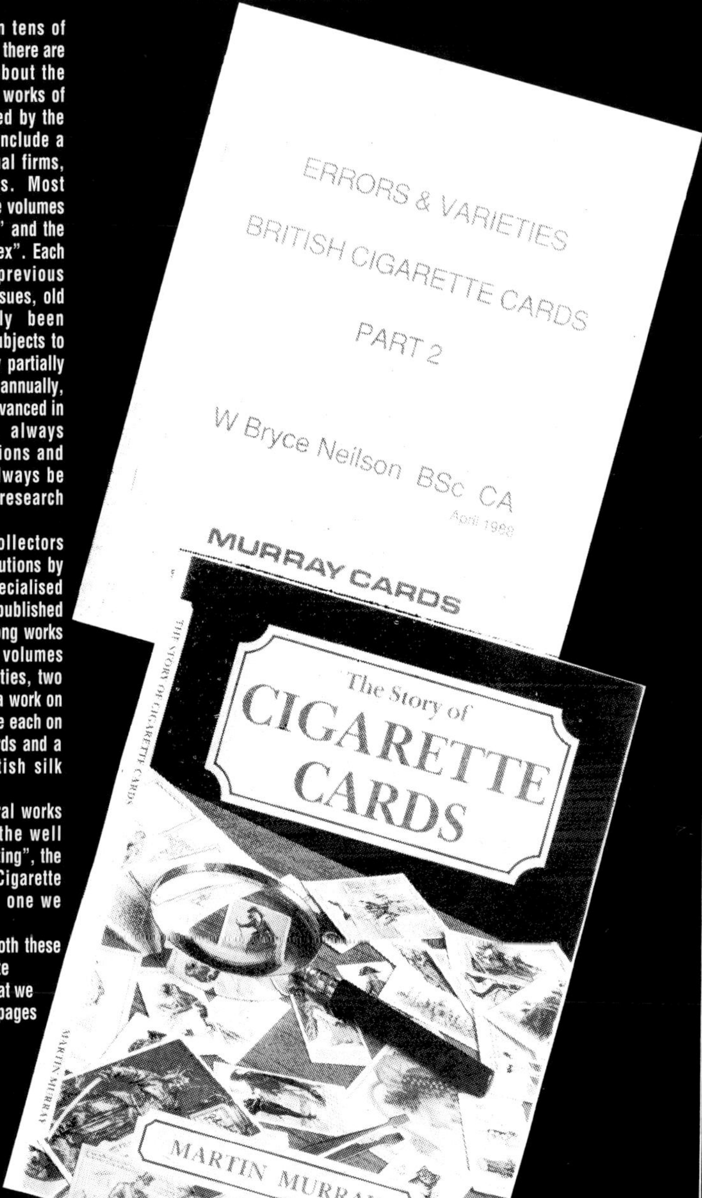

BRAND ISSUES

A brand issue is a card which bears the name of the cigarette with which it was inserted, but not the name of the issuing firm. This does not normally present a problem to compilers of catalogues and other lists, since most brand names have been registered, so that they cannot be used by a competitor—just as "Nostalgia" is a registered brand name for plastic albums!

Whenever possible we have listed brand issues under the name of the firm. This often enables us to bring together alternative printings of the same set, such as Hill Aviation and Decorations & Medals, each of which was issued either with the Hill name at the base or just advertising Gold Flake Honeydew. Similarly, under B. Morris there will be found four printings of Beauties CHOAB, 2 of which do not mention the firm's name.

One difficulty that occurs is that one Company may take over another, and inherit brand names. Hence Honest Long Cut was used by Duke and then the American Tobacco Co., which also took over brands such as Kinney's Sweet Caporal and Lorillard's Red Cross.

The most difficult problem however concerns groups of Companies which may use the same brand name under a different firm in different countries. Thus the Phillips Group used "Greys" as a U.K.T.C. brand in Britain, but as a Phillips brand in Australia. Similarly, Flag Cigarettes was used by Wills in Asia and U.T.C. in South Africa.

In the Catalogue on Pages 18-20 there appears an Index of brands with the name of the issuing firm (or firms), and the catalogue section in which they are listed. Names will only appear in the index when the firm's name does NOT appear AS WELL AS the brand on the card. When the issuer of the brand is not known, such as Field Favorite Cigarettes, the brand will not appear in the Index, and the set will be listed in the normal alphabetic order in the catalogue.

In a similar way to cigarette cards, there may also be brand issues of chocolates, periodicals etc. These have their own index at the beginning of section 3 of the Catalogue.

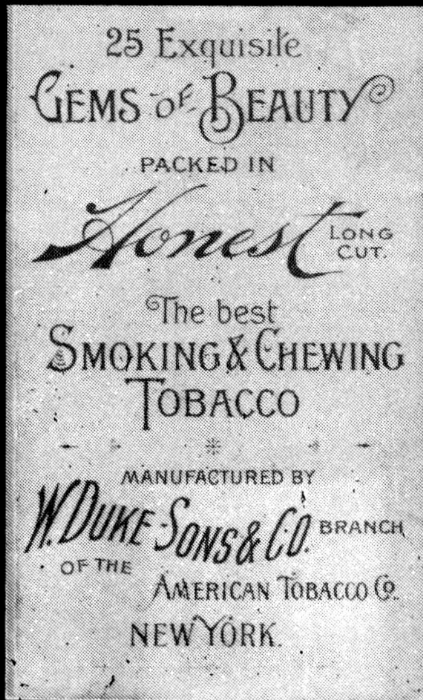

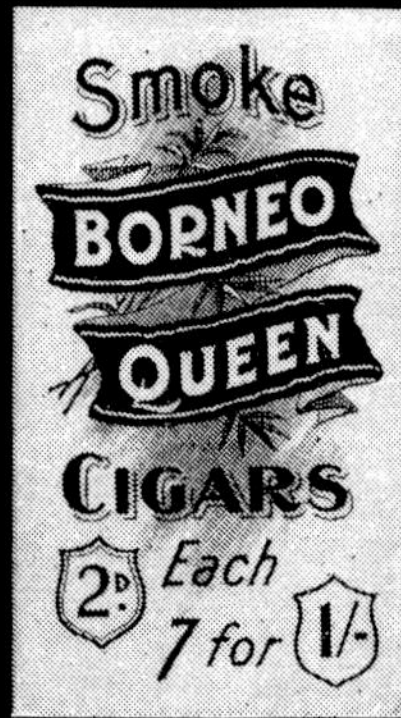

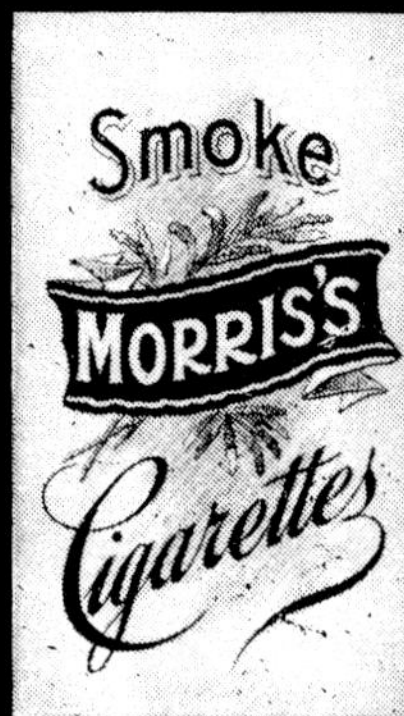

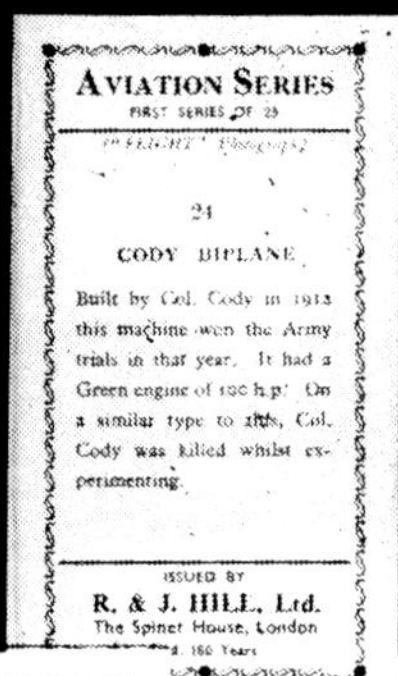

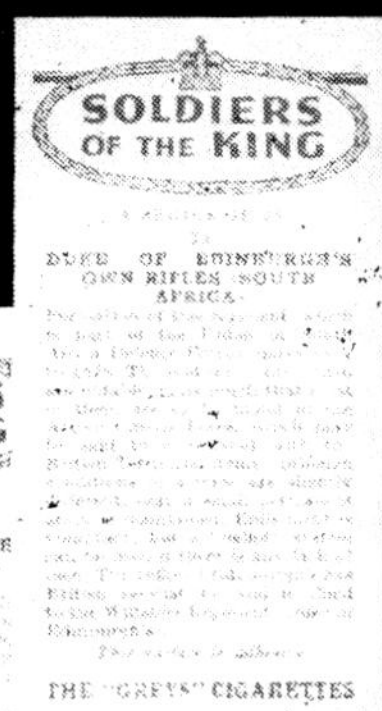

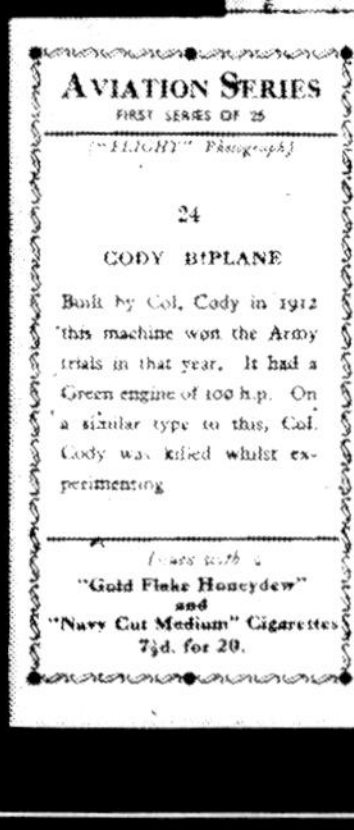

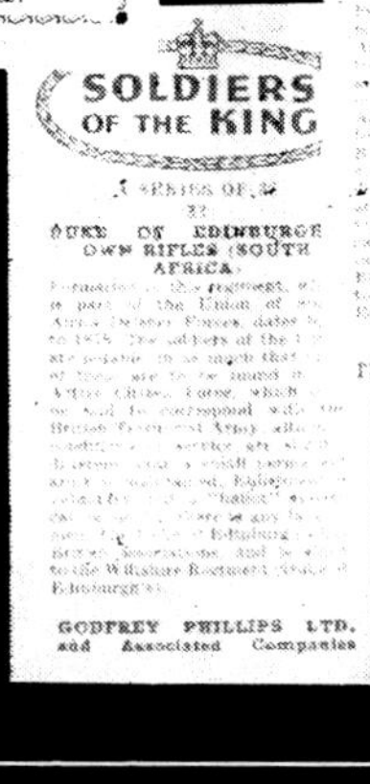

F. & J. SMITH — cont.

Qty		Date	Odds	Sets
G1	Medal Album (Printed)	1902	—	£135.00
50	Nations of the World	1923	£5.50	£275.00
50	Naval Dress & Badges			
	(Descriptive, Multi-Backed)	1911	£8.50	£425.00
	(Non-Descriptive, Multi-Backed)	1914	£8.50	£425.00
50	Phil May Sketches (Brown, 4 Brands)	1924	£5.00	£250.00
50	(Grey, Multi-Backed)	1908	£8.00	£400.00
25	Prominent Rugby Players	1924	£10.00	£250.00
40	Races of Mankind (No Title, Multi-Backed)	1900	£60.00	—
40	(Titled, Multi-Backed)	1900	£45.00	—
25	Shadowgraphs (7 Brands)	1915	£5.50	£137.50
25	War Incidents, A Series	1914	£5.50	£137.50
25	War Incidents, 2nd Series	1915	£5.50	£137.50

F. L. SMITH LTD. (ALBANY CIGARETTES)

L?20	Advertising Inserts	1957	£4.50	—

SNELL & CO.

25	Boer War Celebrities "STEW"	1901	*£130.00*	—

SOROKO

6	Jubilee Series	1935	*£30.00*	—
L6	Jubilee Series	1935	*£30.00*	—

S. E. SOUTHGATE & SON

25	Types of British & Colonial Troops	1900	£110.00	—

SOUTH WALES TOB. MFG. CO. LTD.

30	Army Pictures, Cartoons, etc	1915	*£85.00*	—
100	Game of Numbers	1912	*£65.00*	—
25	Views of London	1912	£22.00	£550.00

T. SPALTON

30	Army Pictures, Cartoons, etc	1916	*£85.00*	—

SPIRO VALLERI & CO.

?15	Noted Footballers	1908	*£250.00*	—

G. STANDLEY

M12	Manikin Cards	1915	*£75.00*	—

A. & A. E. STAPLETON

M12	Manikin Cards	1915	*£75.00*	—

STAR OF THE WORLD

Qty		Date	Odds	Sets
20	Boer War Cartoons	1901	£85.00	—
?50	Boer War Celebrities "JASAS"	1901	*£110.00*	—
30	Colonial Troops	1901	£65.00	—

H. STEVENS & CO.

Qty		Date	Odds	Sets
20	Dogs	1923	£9.00	£180.00
25	Zoo Series	1926	£5.50	—

A. STEVENSON

Qty		Date	Odds	Sets
50	War Portraits	1916	*£75.00*	—

ALBERT STOCKWELL

Qty		Date	Odds	Sets
30	Army Pictures, Cartoons, etc	1916	*£90.00*	—

STRATHMORE TOBACCO CO. LTD.

Qty		Date	Odds	Sets
M25	British Aircraft	1938	£2.60	£65.00

SWEET ALVA CIGARETTES

Qty		Date	Odds	Sets
?50	Boer War Celebrities "JASAS"	1901	*£90.00*	—

T.S.S.

Qty		Date	Odds	Sets
24	Nautical Expressions	1900	£80.00	—

TADDY & CO.

32 Page Reference Book — £3.50

Qty		Date	Odds	Sets
72	Actresses, Collotype	1897	£90.00	—
25	Actresses with Flowers	1899	£80.00	£2000.00
37	Admirals & Generals – The War (2 Backs)	1914	£15.00	£850.00
25	Admirals & Generals – The War (S. Africa)	1914	£32.50	£812.50
25	Autographs	1912	£16.00	£400.00
20	Boer Leaders	1901	£18.00	£360.00
50	British Medals & Decorations, Series 2			
	(Steel Blue Back)	1912	£11.00	£550.00
	(Black Back)	1912	£32.50	—
50	British Medals & Ribbons	1912	£11.00	£550.00
20	Clowns & Circus Artistes	—	£650.00	—
30	Coronation Series	1902	£19.00	£570.00
238	County Cricketers	1907	£40.00	—
50	Dogs	1900	£24.00	£1200.00
5	English Royalty	1897	£600.00	—
25	Famous Actors/Famous Actresses	1903	£16.00	£400.00
50	Famous Horses and Cattle	1912	£95.00	—
25	Famous Jockeys (No Frame)	1910	£28.00	£700.00
25	(With Frame)	1910	£24.00	£600.00
50	Footballers (New Zealand)	1906	£65.00	—
25	Heraldry Series	1911	£15.00	£375.00

TADDY & CO. — cont.

Qty		Date	Odds	Sets
25	Honours & Ribbons	1915	£17.00	£425.00
10	Klondyke Series	1900	£60.00	£600.00
60	Leading M.L.A.'s (South Africa)	1900	*£500.00*	—
25	Natives of the World	1899	£60.00	£1500.00
25	Orders of Chivalry	1911	£16.00	£400.00
25	Orders of Chivalry, Second Series	1912	£23.00	£575.00
595	Prominent Footballers (No Footnote)	1907	£12.00	—
400	Prominent Footballers (With Footnote)	1908	£12.00	—
383	Prominent Footballers (London Mixture)	1913	£32.00	—
20	Royalty, Actresses & Soldiers	1898	£180.00	—
25	Royalty Series	1903	£16.00	£400.00
25	Russo Japanese War (1-25)	1904	£16.00	£400.00
25	Russo Japanese War (26-50)	1904	£22.00	£550.00
15	South African Cricket Team, 1907	1907	£50.00	£750.00
26	South African Football Team, 1906-7	1906	£18.50	£500.00
25	Sports & Pastimes	1912	£17.00	£425.00
25	Territorial Regiments	1908	£18.00	£450.00
25	Thames Series	1903	£32.00	£800.00
20	Victoria Cross Heroes (1-20)	1901	£57.50	£1150.00
20	Victoria Cross Heroes (21-40)	1901	£55.00	£1100.00
20	V.C. Heroes – Boer War (41-60)	1902	£16.50	£330.00
20	V.C. Heroes – Boer War (61-80)	1902	£16.50	£330.00
20	V.C. Heroes – Boer War (81-100)	1902	£18.00	£360.00
25	Victoria Cross Heroes (101-125)	1904	£55.00	—
2	Wrestlers	1908	£275.00	—

TADDY & CO. (RE-REGISTERED)

(No Connection with Original Company)

Qty		Date	Odds	Sets
8	Advertisement Cards	1980	50p	£4.00
26	Motor Cars (Clown Cigarettes)	1980	—	£8.00
26	(Myrtle Grove Cigarettes)	1980	—	£12.00
26	Railway Locomotives (Clown Cigarettes)	1980	—	£12.00
26	(Myrtle Grove Cigarettes)	1980	—	£6.00

W. & M. TAYLOR

Qty		Date	Odds	Sets
8	The European War Series (Bendigo Cigarettes)	1915	*£40.00*	—
8	(Tipperary)	1915	*£40.00*	—
25	War Series (Bendigo Cigarettes)	1915	£20.00	£500.00
25	(Tipperary Cigarettes)	1915	£13.00	£325.00

TAYLOR WOOD

Qty		Date	Odds	Sets
18	Motor Cycle Series	1914	£75.00	—

TEOFANI & CO. LTD.

Qty		Date	Odds	Sets
25	Aquarium Studies From The London Zoo	1925	£11.00	—
50	Cinema Celebrities (Broadway Novelties)	1926	£4.00	—
50	(Anonymous)	1926	£3.50	—
25	Cinema Stars (Blue Band Cigarettes)	1924	*£6.50*	—
25	("Favourites" Printed)	1924	*£6.50*	—
25	("Favourites" Stamped)	1924	*£6.50*	—
25	(Three Star Cigarettes)	1924	*£6.50*	—
25	(Three Star Magnums)	1924	*£6.50*	—

TEOFANI & CO. LTD. — cont.

Qty		Date	Odds	Sets
X25	Cinema Stars	1924	*£6.50*	—
25	Famous Boxers	1925	£7.50	—
F32	Famous British Ships and Officers	1934	£2.80	£90.00
L50	Famous Racecourses (Favourite Cigarettes)	1926	£16.00	—
50	Famous Racehorses	1923	£10.00	—
12	Film Actors & Actresses (Plain Back)	1936	65p	£8.00
20	Great Inventors	1924	£4.50	£90.00
20	Head-Dress of All Nations (Plain Back)	1926	£12.00	£240.00
LF50	Icelandic Girls	1929	£5.50	—
LF50	Icelandic Stage Scenes & Artistes	1929	*£10.00*	—
12	London Views (Plain Back)	1936	50p	£6.00
12	(8 Different Printed Backs)	1936	£4.00	£50.00
48	Modern Movie Stars & Cinema Celebrities	1934	£1.00	£48.00
50	Natives in Costume (Plain Back)	1926	£13.00	—
24	Past & Present "A" – The Army (No Frame)	1938	£1.75	£42.00
24	(With Frame Line on Back)	1938	£2.00	£48.00
24	Past & Present "B" – Weapons of War	1938	£1.25	£30.00
4	Past & Present "C" – Transport	1939	£4.50	£18.00
50	Public Schools & Colleges	1923	£3.00	£150.00
50	Ships and their Flags	1925	£2.70	£135.00
25	Sports & Pastimes (Plain Back)	1924	£4.50	£125.00
25	(Printed Back)	1924	£12.50	—
22	Teofani Gems	1925	£2.00	£44.00
28	Teofani Gems	1925	80p	—
36	Teofani Gems	1925	£2.00	£72.00
48	Transport Then & Now	1939	50p	£24.00
50	Views of London	1925	£2.00	—
F36	Views of the British Empire	1927	£1.00	£36.00
24	Well-Known Racehorses	1923	£6.00	—
50	World's Smokers (Plain Back)	1926	£13.00	£650.00
50	Zoological Studies	1924	£3.50	—
L50	Zoological Studies	1924	*£6.25*	—

TETLEY & SONS

Qty		Date	Odds	Sets
1	The Allies	1915	*£250.00*	—
50	War Portraits	1916	£65.00	—
25	Worlds Coinage	1914	£55.00	—

THEMANS & CO.

Qty		Date	Odds	Sets
?10	Anecdotes & Riddles	1913	*£200.00*	—
55	Dominoes	1913	*£80.00*	—
18	Motor Cycle Series	1914	£70.00	—
50	War Portraits	1915	£45.00	—
14	War Posters	1916	£160.00	—

SILK ISSUES (MAINLY ANONYMOUS)

Qty		Date	Odds	Sets
M10	Crests of Warships (Series B4)	1914	£7.00	—
L2	Crests of Warships (Series C4)	1914	£10.00	—
M48	Film Stars (Series B6)	1914	£7.00	—
P14	Film Stars (Series D6)	1914	£7.00	—
M10	Flags (Series B1)	1914	£7.00	—

THEMANS & CO. — cont.

Qty		Date	Odds	Sets
M12	Flags (Series B2)	1914	£7.00	—
L4	Flags (Series C1)	1914	£10.00	—
L4	Flags (Series C2)	1914	£10.00	—
P1	Flags (Series D1)	1914	*£14.00*	—
P1	Flags (Series D2)	1914	*£14.00*	—
M12	Regimental Badges (Series B3)	1914	£7.00	—
L4	Regimental Badges (Series C3)	1914	£10.00	—
P1	Regimental Badges (Series D3)	1914	*£14.00*	—
M12	Views of Blackpool (Series B5)	1914	£20.00	—
P7	Views of Blackpool (Series D5)	1914	*£20.00*	—

THOMSON & PORTEOUS

Qty		Date	Odds	Sets
50	Arms of British Towns	1905	£13.00	£650.00
25	Boer War Celebrities "STEW"	1901	£50.00	—
25	Shadowgraphs	1902	£35.00	—
20	The European War Series	1915	£12.00	£240.00
41	V.C. Heroes (Firm's Name at Bottom)	1916	£12.00	£530.00
41	(Firm's Name at Top)	1916	£40.00	—

TOM NODDY

Qty		Date	Odds	Sets
P12	Children of the Year Series	1904	*£40.00*	—

TOPSY CIGARETTES

Qty		Date	Odds	Sets
F?11	Actresses	1896	*£185.00*	—

TURKISH MONOPOLY CIGARETTE CO. LTD.

Qty		Date	Odds	Sets
X?15	Boer War Scenes	1901	*£125.00*	—

UNITED KINGDOM TOBACCO CO. LTD.

Qty		Date	Odds	Sets
50	Aircraft	1938	£1.25	£62.50
P48	Beautiful Britain, A Series	1929	£1.50	£72.00
P48	Beautiful Britain, Second Series	1929	£1.50	£72.00
25	British Orders of Chivalry & Valour (2 Printings)	1936	£1.50	£37.50
24	Chinese Scenes	1933	75p	£18.00
32	Cinema Stars	1933	£1.60	£51.00
50	Cinema Stars (With Firm's Name)	1934	£1.40	£70.00
50	(Anonymous)	1934	£1.75	—
36	Officers Full Dress	1936	£1.75	£63.00
52	Soldiers (Metal)	1935	£12.50	—
36	Soldiers of the King	1937	£1.75	£63.00

UNITED SERVICES MFG. CO. LTD.

Qty		Date	Odds	Sets
50	Ancient Warriors	1938	£1.60	£80.00
25	Ancient Warriors	1957	£3.50	—
50	Bathing Belles	1939	50p	£25.00
100	Interesting Personalities	1935	£2.25	£225.00
50	Popular Footballers	1936	£3.80	£190.00

UNITED SERVICES MFG. CO. LTD. — cont.

Qty		*Date*	*Odds*	*Sets*
50	Popular Screen Stars	1937	£3.50	£175.00

UNITED TOBACCONISTS ASSOCIATION LTD.

Qty		Date	Odds	Sets
10	Actresses "MUTA"	1901	£125.00	—
12	Pretty Girl Series "RASH"	1900	*£135.00*	—

WALKERS TOBACCO CO. LTD. (W.T.C.)

Qty		Date	Odds	Sets
60	British Beauty Spots	1924	*£16.00*	—
28	Dominoes (Old Monk)	1908	*£60.00*	—
28	Dominoes (W.T.C.)	1924	£4.00	—
F30/32	Film Stars (Tatleys)	1936	£1.50	£45.00
F48	Film Stars (Walkers)	1935	£4.50	—

WALTERS TOBACCO CO. LTD.

Qty		Date	Odds	Sets
L6	Angling Information	1939	£1.50	—

E. T. WATERMAN

Qty		Date	Odds	Sets
30	Army Pictures, Cartoons, etc	1916	*£90.00*	—

WEBB & RASSELL

Qty		Date	Odds	Sets
50	War Portraits	1916	£70.00	—

HENRY WELFARE & CO.

Qty		Date	Odds	Sets
22	Prominent Politicians	1912	£70.00	—

WESTMINSTER TOBACCO CO. LTD.

Qty		Date	Odds	Sets
F36	Australia, First Series	1932	25p	£9.00
F36	Australia, 2nd Series (Plain Back)	1933	25p	£9.00
F48	British Royal and Ancient Buildings			
	(Unnumbered)	1925	75p	£36.00
	(Numbered)	1925	50p	£24.00
F48	British Royal and Ancient Buildings			
	Second Series	1926	25p	£12.00
F36	Canada, First Series	1926	50p	£18.00
F36	Canada, Second Series	1928	50p	£18.00
F48	Indian Empire, First Series	1925	25p	£12.00
F48	Indian Empire, Second Series	1926	25p	£12.00
F36	New Zealand, First Series	1928	25p	£9.00
F36	New Zealand, Second Series	1929	25p	£9.00
F36	South Africa, First Series	1928	50p	£18.00
F36	South Africa, Second Series	1928	50p	£18.00

OVERSEAS ISSUES

Qty		Date	Odds	Sets
L?200	Adamson's Oplevelser	1926	£16.50	—
MF50	Beauties	1924	£2.50	—

WESTMINSTER TOBACCO CO. LTD. — cont.

Qty		*Date*	*Odds*	*Sets*
MF100	Beautiful Women	1915	£2.25	—
M50	Birds, Beasts & Fishes	1923	£2.40	£120.00
100	British Beauties (Hand Coloured)	1915	£2.75	—
102	(Uncoloured)	1915	*£3.60*	—
F48	British Royal and Ancient Buildings	1925	80p	£38.00
50	Butterflies & Moths	1920	£2.30	£115.00
F36	Canada, First Series	1926	90p	£32.50
F36	Canada, Second Series	1928	90p	£32.50
30	Celebrated Actresses	1921	£5.00	£150.00
X25	Champion Dogs	1934	£3.60	£90.00
100	Cinema Artistes (Green Back)	1928	*£2.50*	—
50	Cinema Artistes (Grey Back)	1931	£2.40	—
48	Cinema Celebrities (C)	1935	*£2.75*	—
F50	Cinema Stars	1927	£2.40	—
MF50	Cinema Stars (Coloured)	1926	£2.75	—
MF50	(Uncoloured)	1930	£2.40	—
M27	Dancing Girls	1917	£5.00	£135.00
50	Do You Know?	1922	*£2.00*	—
24	Fairy Tales (Booklets)	1926	£5.00	—
M100	Famous Beauties (Blue Caption)	1916	£2.25	—
M100	Famous Beauties (Brown Caption)	1916	£2.00	£200.00
MF52	Film Favourites (Coloured)	1928	£3.50	—
MF52	(Uncoloured)	1928	£3.50	—
M50	Film Personalities	1931	*£3.50*	—
M50	Garden Flowers of the World	1917	£2.60	£130.00
L50	Garden Flowers of the World (Silk)	1913	£4.50	£225.00
F48	Indian Empire, First Series	1925	90p	£42.50
F48	Indian Empire, Second Series	1926	£1.00	—
MF50	Islenzkar Eimskipamyndir (Trawlers)	1931	£2.40	£120.00
MF50	Islenzkar Landslagsmyndir (Views)	1928	£2.00	£100.00
MF50	Islenzkar Landslagsmyndir Nr 2 (Views)	1929	£2.00	£100.00
40	Merrie England Studies	1914	£6.50	—
X24	Miniature Rugs	1924	£15.00	—
36	Modern Beauties	1938	*£3.00*	—
M?3	Monsterbeskyttet	1926	*£15.00*	—
MF52	Movie Stars	1925	£3.25	—
F36	New Zealand, First Series	1928	£1.00	—
F36	New Zealand, Second Series	1929	£1.00	—
53	Playing Cards (P.O.Box 78)	1934	£2.00	—
53	(Special Blend)	1934	£2.00	—
M55	Playing Cards (Blue Back)	1934	£1.75	—
M55	(Red Back)	1934	£1.75	—
F50	Popular Film Stars	1926	*£3.00*	—
50	Safety First	1936	£1.20	£60.00
L?200	Skjeggen's Oplevelser	1926	*£16.50*	—
F36	South Africa, First Series	1928	£1.00	—
F36	South Africa, Second Series	1928	£1.00	—
M49	South African Succulents	1937	20p	£10.00
M100	Stage & Cinema Stars (Black Caption)	1921	£2.30	—
M100	Stage & Cinema Stars (Grey Caption)	1921	£1.60	£160.00
MF50	Stars of Filmland (Firm in Brown)	1927	£2.75	—
MF50	(Firm in White)	1927	£3.25	—
50	Steamships of the World	1920	£6.50	£325.00
40	The Great War Celebrities	1914	£6.00	£240.00
50	The World of Tomorrow	1938	£1.00	£50.00

WESTMINSTER TOBACCO CO. LTD. — cont.

Qty		Date	Odds	Sets
M50	Uniforms of All Ages	1917	£9.00	£450.00
F50	Views of Malaya	1930	£6.00	£300.00
25	Wireless (Several Printings)	1923	£4.50	£112.50
M50	Women of Nations	1922	£3.80	£190.00

WHALE & COMPANY

?12	Conundrums	1900	£150.00	—

M. WHITE & CO.

20	Actresses "BLARM"	1900	£135.00	—

WHITFIELD'S

30	Army Pictures, Cartoons, etc.	1916	*£90.00*	—

WHITFORD & SONS

20	Inventors	1924	£42.50	—

WHOLESALE TOBACCO CO.

25	Armies of the World	1903	£65.00	—
40	Army Pictures (Home & Colonial Regiments)	1902	£85.00	—

P. WHYTE

30	Army Pictures, Cartoons, etc.	1916	*£90.00*	—

W. WILLIAMS & CO.

30	Aristocrats of the Turf, A Series	1924	£6.50	—
36	Aristocrats of the Turf, Second Series	1924	£13.50	—
25	Boer War Celebrities "STEW"	1901	*£65.00*	—
25	Boxing	1923	£8.00	—
50	Interesting Buildings	1912	£12.50	—
12	Views of Chester	1912	£27.50	£330.00
12	Views of Chester (As it Was), 2nd Series	1913	£27.50	£330.00

W. D. & H. O. WILLS LTD.

200 Page Illustrated Reference Book — £10.00

?9	Actresses (Typeset Back)	1895	*£750.00*	—
52	Actresses (Brown Back, P/C Inset)	1898	£14.00	£725.00
52	Actresses (Grey Back, P/C Inset)	1897	£15.00	£780.00
52	(Grey Back, No Inset)	1897	£16.00	£825.00
25	Actresses, Collotype (Wills', Brands Back)	1894	£75.00	—
25	(Wills', No Brands)	1894	£70.00	—
50	Actresses & Celebrities, Collotype			
	(Wills's, Four Brands on Back)	1894	£85.00	—
	(Wills's, Export Manufacturers Back)	1894	£85.00	—
1	Advertisement Card (Serving Maid)	1890	—	£600.00

Qty		*Date*	*Odds*	*Sets*
4	Advertisement Cards (Cigarette Packets)	1891	*£850.00*	—
11	Advertisement Cards (Tobacco Packings)	1891	£600.00	—
3	Advertisement Cards (Showcards, 7 brands)	1893	£250.00	—
6	Advertisement Cards (Showcards)	1893	£250.00	—
1	Advertisement Card – Three Castles	1965	—	£1.40
L1	Advertisement Card – Wants List	1935	—	60p
P4	Advertisement Postcards	1902	£100.00	—
50	Air Raid Precautions	1938	60p	£30.00
40	Ditto (Eire)	1938	90p	£36.00
50	Allied Army Leaders	1917	£1.60	£80.00
50	Alpine Flowers	1913	80p	£40.00
49	And When Did You Last See Your Father (Sect.)	1932	80p	£40.00
50	Animals & Birds (Descriptive)	1900	£18.00	£900.00
50	Animals & Birds in Fancy Costume	1896	£40.00	£2000.00
48	Animalloys (Sect.)	1934	25p	£12.00
L25	Animals and Their Furs	1929	£1.60	£40.00
50	Arms of Companies	1913	60p	£30.00
50	Arms of Foreign Cities (2 Printings)	1912	60p	£30.00
L42	Arms of Oxford & Cambridge Colleges	1922	£1.00	£42.00
L25	Arms of Public Schools, 1st Series	1933	£1.60	£40.00
L25	Arms of Public Schools, 2nd Series	1934	£1.60	£40.00
50	Arms of the Bishopric	1907	80p	£40.00
50	Arms of the British Empire	1910	60p	£30.00
L25	Arms of the British Empire, 1st Series	1933	£1.60	£40.00
L25	Arms of the British Empire, 2nd Series	1933	£1.60	£40.00
L25	Arms of Universities	1923	£1.40	£35.00
50	Association Footballers (Frame on Back)	1935	£1.20	£60.00
50	Association Footballers (No Frame on Back)	1939	£1.20	£60.00
50	(No Frame, Eire)	1939	£2.00	£100.00
L25	Auction Bridge	1926	£2.20	£55.00
50	Aviation	1910	£1.70	£85.00
?17	Beauties, Collotype (Firefly)	1894	*£95.00*	—
?17	(Wills Cigarettes)	1894	*£95.00*	—
?118	Beauties, Actresses & Children	1894	*£95.00*	—
K52	Beauties, Playing Card Inset	1896	£24.00	—
52	Beauties, Playing Card Inset	1897	£16.00	£830.00
10	Alternative Subjects	1897	£50.00	—
?50	Beauties (No Inset, Scroll Back)	1897	£135.00	—
?	(No Inset, Type Set Back)	1897	£180.00	—
?9	Beauties, Girl Studies	1895	*£750.00*	—
L25	Beautiful Homes	1930	£2.40	£60.00
48	Between Two Fires (Sect.)	1930	25p	£12.00
50	Billiards	1909	£1.70	£85.00
K9	Boer War Medallions (6 Brands)	1900	£75.00	—
50	Borough Arms (Scroll Back, Numbered)	1903	£9.00	£450.00
50	(Scroll Back, Unnumbered)	1903	85p	£42.50
50	(1-50 Descriptive)	1904	90p	£45.00
50	Second Edition (1-50)	1906	60p	£30.00
50	Borough Arms, Second Series (51-100)	1904	55p	£27.50
50	Second Edition (51-100)	1906	55p	£27.50
50	Borough Arms, 3rd Series (101-150 Red)	1905	60p	£30.00
50	(101-150 Grey)	1905	75p	£37.50
50	Second Edition (101-150)	1906	55p	£27.50
50	Borough Arms, Fourth Series (151-200)	1905	55p	£27.50
24	Britain's Part in the War	1917	80p	£20.00

Qty		Date	Odds	Sets
50	British Birds	1915	£1.00	£50.00
50	British Butterflies	1927	£1.00	£50.00
L25	British Castles	1925	£2.20	£55.00
1	British Commanders of the Transvaal War (Booklet)	1900	—	£75.00
L25	British School of Painting	1927	£1.20	£30.00
M48	British Sporting Personalities	1937	85p	£40.00
50	Builders of the Empire	1898	£6.00	£300.00
L40	Butterflies & Moths	1938	90p	£36.00
1	Calendar for 1911	1910	—	£11.00
1	Calendar 1912	1911	—	£6.00
L25	Cathedrals	1933	£2.80	£70.00
L25	Celebrated Pictures (2 Printings)	1916	£1.80	£45.00
L25	Celebrated Pictures, 2nd Series	1916	£2.00	£50.00
50	Celebrated Ships	1911	£1.00	£50.00
25	Cinema Stars, 1st Series	1928	£1.50	£37.50
25	Cinema Stars, 2nd Series	1928	£1.40	£35.00
50	Cinema Stars, 3rd Series	1931	£1.80	£90.00
P12	Cities of Britain	1929	£7.50	£90.00
25	Conundrums (No Album Clause)	1898	£7.00	£175.00
25	(With Album Clause)	1898	£6.00	£150.00
60	Coronation Series (Narrow Arrows)	1902	£5.50	£330.00
60	(Wide Arrows)	1902	£4.25	£255.00
50	Cricketers	1896	£60.00	£3000.00
25	Cricketer Series 1901 (Plain Background)	1901	£22.00	£550.00
50	(With Vignettes)	1901	£17.50	£875.00
25	Cricketers (WILLS'S)	1908	£7.00	£175.00
50	(WILLS's)	1908	£5.50	£275.00
50	Cricketers, 1928	1928	£1.70	£85.00
50	Cricketers, 2nd Series	1929	£1.80	£90.00
50	Dogs	1937	50p	£25.00
50	Ditto (Eire)	1937	£1.20	£60.00
L25	Dogs, A Series	1914	£3.00	£75.00
L25	Dogs, 2nd Series	1915	£3.00	£75.00
50	Double Meaning	1898	£8.00	£400.00
52	Ditto (P/C Inset)	1898	£8.50	£450.00
50	Do You Know, A Series	1922	30p	£15.00
50	Do You Know, 2nd Series	1924	30p	£15.00
50	Do You Know, 3rd Series	1926	30p	£15.00
50	Do You Know, 4th Series	1933	35p	£17.50
50	Engineering Wonders	1927	70p	£35.00
50	English Period Costumes	1929	90p	£45.00
L25	English Period Costumes	1927	£2.40	£60.00
L40	Famous British Authors	1937	£1.60	£64.00
L30	Famous British Liners, A Series	1934	£3.50	£105.00
L30	Famous British Liners, 2nd Series	1935	£3.00	£90.00
L25	Famous Golfers	1930	£16.00	£450.00
50	Famous Inventions	1915	90p	£45.00
50	First Aid (No Album Clause)	1913	£1.00	£50.00
50	(With Album Clause)	1913	£1.20	£60.00
50	Fish & Bait	1910	£1.80	£90.00
25	Flags of the Empire, A Series	1926	£1.00	£25.00
25	Flags of the Empire, 2nd Series	1929	90p	£22.50
50	Flower Culture in Pots	1925	40p	£20.00
L30	Flowering Shrubs	1934	90p	£27.00
50	Flowering Trees & Shrubs	1924	50p	£25.00

W. D. & H. O. WILLS LTD. — cont.

Qty		Date	Odds	Sets
66	Football Series	1902	£6.50	£425.00
50	Garden Flowers	1933	60p	£30.00
50	Garden Flowers by Sudell	1939	25p	£12.50
50	Ditto (Eire)	1939	40p	£20.00
L40	Garden Flowers – New Varieties, A Series	1938	70p	£28.00
L40	Garden Flowers – New Varieties, 2nd Series	1939	60p	£24.00
50	Garden Hints	1938	20p	£8.00
50	Ditto (Eire)	1938	30p	£15.00
50	Gardening Hints	1923	20p	£9.00
50	Garden Life	1914	40p	£20.00
50	Gems of Belgian Architecture	1915	55p	£27.50
50	Gems of French Architecture	1916	£1.20	£60.00
50	Gems of Italian Architecture (Coloured)	—	£90.00	—
F50	(Reproductions)	—	—	£35.00
50	Gems of Russian Architecture	1917	60p	£30.00
L25	Golfing	1924	£8.00	£200.00
X32	Happy Families	1939	£4.00	£128.00
L25	Heraldic Signs & Their Origin	1925	£1.80	£45.00
50	Historic Events	1912	£1.00	£50.00
F54	Homeland Events	1932	30p	£25.00
50	Household Hints (Title in White)	1927	30p	£15.00
50	Household Hints, 2nd Series	1930	50p	£25.00
50	Household Hints (Different)	1936	20p	£8.00
50	Ditto (Eire)	1936	30p	£15.00
50	Hurlers (Eire)	1927	£1.40	£70.00
2	Indian Series	1900	£225.00	—
P12	Industries of Britain	1930	£7.50	£90.00
25	Irish Beauty-Spots	1924	£4.00	£100.00
25	Irish Holiday Resorts	1924	£4.00	£100.00
50	Irish Industries ("Ask Your Retailer...")	1937	90p	£45.00
50	("This Surface...")	1937	£3.00	—
25	Irish Rugby Internationals	1926	£8.00	£200.00
50	Irish Sportsmen	1936	£3.20	£160.00
50	Japanese Series	1900	£33.00	£1650.00
50	Kings & Queens (Short Card, Brown Back)	1898	£9.00	£450.00
50	(Short Card, Grey Back)	1898	£4.50	£225.00
50/51	(Long, "Wills" at Base)	1902	£5.00	£250.00
50	(Long, "Wills" at Top)	1902	£11.50	—
L25	Lawn Tennis,1931	1931	£7.00	£175.00
50	Life in the Hedgerow	Unissued	50p	£25.00
50	Life in the Royal Navy	1939	20p	£10.00
50	Life in the Tree Tops	1925	40p	£20.00
50	Locomotives & Rolling Stock (No Clause)	1901	£6.50	£325.00
7	Additional Subjects	1902	£20.00	£140.00
50	Locomotives & Rolling Stock (With ITC Clause)	1902	£7.00	£350.00
50	Lucky Charms	1923	50p	£25.00
100	Maori Series (White Borders)	1900	£75.00	—
50	(Green Borders)	1900	£75.00	—
3	(Green Borders, Numbered Top Left)	1900	£135.00	—
4	(Green Borders, Unnumbered)	1900	£135.00	—
50	Medals	1906	£2.50	£125.00
50	Merchant Ships of the World	1924	£1.20	£60.00
50	Military Motors (Not Passed by Censor)	1916	£1.60	£80.00
50	(Passed by Censor)	1916	£1.60	£80.00

W. D. & H. O. WILLS LTD. — cont.

Qty		*Date*	*Odds*	*Sets*
53	Miniature Playing Cards			
	(Blue Back, Numbered, 4 Printings)	1931	40p	£20.00
	(Blue Back, Unnumbered)	1931	40p	£20.00
	(Blue Back, Red Overprint)	1931	40p	£20.00
	(3 Pink Backs)	1931	50p	£26.00
	(Eire, 7 Backs)	1931	£1.00	—
50	Mining	1916	£1.20	£60.00
L25	Modern Architecture	1931	£1.00	£25.00
L30	Modern British Sculpture	1928	£1.00	£30.00
48	Mother and Son (Sect.)	1931	25p	£12.00
50	Musical Celebrities	1912	£2.30	£115.00
50	Musical Celebrities, Second Series	1914	£3.00	£150.00
8	(Original Subjects)	1914	£200.00	—
25	National Costumes	1895	£165.00	—
?	National Types	1893	*£600.00*	—
50	Naval Dress & Badges	1909	£2.20	£110.00
50	Nelson Series	1905	£2.60	£130.00
50	Old English Garden Flowers	1910	£1.20	£60.00
50	Old English Garden Flowers, Second Series	1913	70p	£35.00
L25	Old Furniture, 1st Series	1923	£2.60	£65.00
L25	Old Furniture, 2nd Series	1924	£2.60	£65.00
L40	Old Inns, A Series	1936	£2.75	£110.00
L40	Old Inns, Second Series	1939	£1.60	£64.00
L25	Old London	1929	£3.00	£75.00
L30	Old Pottery & Porcelain	1934	£1.00	£30.00
L25	Old Silver	1924	£2.40	£60.00
L25	Old Sundials	1928	£2.60	£65.00
20	Our Gallant Grenadiers	1902	£27.50	£550.00
50	Our King & Queen	1937	20p	£9.00
50	Overseas Dominions (Australia)	1915	60p	£30.00
50	Overseas Dominions (Canada)	1914	50p	£25.00
50	Physical Culture	1914	85p	£42.50
25	Pond & Aquarium, 1st Series	Unissued	—	£6.00
25	Pond & Aquarium, 2nd Series	Unissued	—	£9.00
50	Portraits of European Royalty (1-50)	1908	£1.20	£60.00
50	Portraits of European Royalty (51-100)	1908	£1.50	£75.00
L25	Public Schools	1927	£2.40	£60.00
L25	Punch Cartoons, First Series	1916	£3.20	£80.00
L25	Punch Cartoons, Second Series	1917	£16.00	£400.00
L40	Racehorses & Jockeys, 1938	1939	£1.75	£70.00
50	Radio Celebrities, A Series	1934	70p	£35.00
50	Ditto (Eire)	1934	£1.40	—
50	Radio Celebrities, Second Series	1934	50p	£25.00
50	Ditto (Eire)	1934	£1.00	—
50	Railway Engines	1924	90p	£45.00
50	Railway Engines (Adhesive)	1936	80p	£40.00
50	Ditto (Eire)	1936	£1.40	—
50	Railway Equipment	1938	20p	£10.00
50	Railway Locomotives	1930	£1.40	£70.00
12	Recruiting Posters	1915	£7.50	£90.00
L25	Rigs of Ships	1929	£3.40	£85.00
50	Romance of the Heavens	1928	80p	£40.00
50	Roses, A Series (1-50)	1912	£1.00	£50.00

Qty		Date	Odds	Sets
50	Roses, Second Series (51-100)	1913	£1.00	£50.00
50	Roses (Different)	1926	80p	£40.00
L40	Roses (Different)	1936	£1.25	£50.00
M48	Round Europe	1936	20p	£10.00
50	Rugby Internationals	1929	£1.50	£75.00
50	Safety First	1934	90p	£45.00
50	Ditto (Eire)	1934	£1.50	—
50	School Arms	1906	60p	£30.00
50	Ditto (With" Series of 50")	1906	*£15.00*	—
50	Seaside Resorts (Mixed Backs)	1899	—	£400.00
	(Best Bird's Eye)	1899	£8.00	—
	(Capstan)	1899	£8.00	—
	(Gold Flake)	1899	£8.00	—
	(Three Castles)	1899	£8.00	—
	(Traveller)	1899	£8.00	—
	(Westward Ho)	1899	£8.00	—
40	Shannon Electric Power Scheme (Eire)	1931	£1.35	£54.00
25	Ships (Three Castles Back)	1895	£25.00	£625.00
25	(No "WILLS" on Front)	1895	£25.00	£625.00
50	(With "WILLS" on Front)	1896	£16.00	£800.00
100	(Brownish Card)	1897	£16.50	£1650.00
50	Ships' Badges	1925	70p	£35.00
50	Signalling Series	1911	£1.30	£65.00
50	Soldiers & Sailors (Blue Back)	1894	£37.50	£1875.00
50	(Grey Back)	1894	£40.00	£2000.00
100	Soldiers of the World (Ltd. Back)	1895	£6.25	£625.00
100/101	(No Ltd. on Back)	1895	£5.75	£575.00
52	(P/C Inset)	1896	£20.00	£1000.00
100	South African Personalities, Collotype (4 Different Printings)	1901	£90.00	—
50	Speed (Title in White)	1930	£1.30	£65.00
50	Speed (Different)	1938	25p	£12.50
50	(Eire)	1938	70p	£35.00
50	Sports of All Nations (Multi-Backed)	1901	£9.00	£450.00
50	Strange Craft	1931	£1.00	£50.00
48	The Boyhood of Raleigh (Sect.)	1931	25p	£12.00
P12	The British Empire	1929	£6.50	£78.00
50	The Coronation Series	1911	90p	£45.00
L40	The King's Art Treasures	1938	30p	£12.00
48	The Laughing Cavalior (Sect., 2 Backs)	1931	25p	£12.00
48	(Sect., Eire)	1931	£1.75	£84.00
50	The Life of H.M. King Edward VIII	Unissued	£16.00	—
50	The Reign of H.M. King George V	1935	50p	£25.00
50	The Sea-Shore	1938	20p	£10.00
50	Ditto (Eire)	1938	50p	£25.00
48	The Toast (Sect.)	1931	50p	£24.00
48	(Sect., Eire)	1931	£1.75	£84.00
25	The World's Dreadnoughts	1910	£2.50	£62.50
50	Time & Money in Different Countries	1908	£1.40	£70.00
50	Transvaal Series (Black Border)	1901	£8.00	—
66	(White Border)	1901	£1.50	£100.00
66	(Non Descriptive)	1902	£5.00	£330.00
L40	Trees	1937	£1.50	£60.00
L25	University Hoods & Gowns	1926	£2.40	£60.00
50	Vanity Fair Series (Unnumbered)	1902	£4.50	£225.00

Qty		Date	Odds	Sets
50	Vanity Fair, 1st Series	1902	£4.20	£210.00
50	Vanity Fair, 2nd Series	1902	£4.20	£210.00
50	Waterloo	Unissued	£90.00	—
50	Wild Animals of the World (Green Scroll Back)	1900	£4.00	£200.00
15	(Grey Descriptive Back)	1902	£26.00	£390.00
52	(P/C Inset)	1900	£10.00	£520.00
50	Wild Flowers (2 Printings)	1923	50p	£25.00
50	Wild Flowers, A Series (Adhesive)	1936	30p	£15.00
50	Ditto (Eire)	1936	60p	£30.00
50	Wild Flowers, 2nd Series	1937	20p	£9.00
50	Ditto (Eire)	1937	60p	£30.00
50	Wonders of the Past	1926	45p	£22.50
50	Wonders of the Sea	1928	40p	£20.00
MODERN ISSUES (CASTELLA)				
L30	Britain's Motoring History	1991	£1.20	£36.00
L30	Britain's Steam Railways	1998	£1.00	£30.00
X30	British Aviation	1994	£1.20	£36.00
P6	British Aviation	1994	40p	£2.50
L30	Classic Sports Cars	1996	—	—
X30	Donington Collection	1993	£1.20	£36.00
P6	Donington Collection	1993	—	£6.00
P6	History of Transport	1993	—	£4.50
X30	In Search of Steam	1992	£1.20	£36.00
X30	Soldiers of Waterloo	1995	£1.20	£36.00
L30	The Tank Story	1997	—	—
MODERN ISSUES (EMBASSY)				
56	Caribbean Treasure Cruise	1985	*£1.25*	—
M56	Caribbean Treasure Cruise	1985	65p	—
T48	Familiar Phrases	1986	£1.00	£48.00
L30	History of Britain's Railways	1987	£1.20	£36.00
L30	History of Motor Racing	1987	£1.50	—
T5	Pica Punchline	1984	£1.00	£5.00
L144	Punch Lines	1983	65p	—
T288	Punch Lines	1983	65p	—
T48	Ring the Changes	1985	85p	£41.00
56	Showhouse (33 x 60mm)	1988	*£1.25*	—
56	(35 x 80mm)	1988	50p	—
M56	Showhouse (47 x 68mm)	1988	*£1.25*	—
M56	(47 x 80mm)	1988	50p	£28.00
T56	Showhouse (47 x 90mm)	1988	*50p*	—
T10	Spot the Shot	1986	£2.00	£20.00
?	Wheel of Fortune	1985	£1.25	—
M?	Wheel of Fortune	1985	50p	—
56	Wonders of the World	1986	90p	—
M56	Wonders of the World	1986	65p	£36.50
T56	Wonders of the World	1986	50p	£28.00
M36	World of Firearms	1982	25p	£9.00
M36	World of Speed	1981	25p	£9.00
AUSTRALIAN ISSUES				
100	Actresses (Capstan)	1903	£2.50	£250.00
100	(Vice Regal)	1903	£2.50	—
1	Advertisement Card (Capstan)	1902	—	*£150.00*
60	Animals (Cut-Outs, Specialities)	1913	80p	£48.00
60	(Cut-Outs, Havelock)	1913	£1.60	—

Qty		*Date*	*Odds*	*Sets*
50	Arms & Armour (Capstan, "ALSO OBTAINABLE")	1910	£1.50	£75.00
50	(Capstan, No Extra Words)	1910	£1.50	£75.00
50	(Vice Regal)	1910	£1.50	£75.00
50	(Havelock)	1910	£2.75	—
50	Arms of the British Empire (Specialities)	1910	75p	£37.50
50	(Havelock)	1910	£1.60	—
M50	Arms of the British Empire (Silk)	1910	£2.50	£125.00
50	A Tour Round the World (Blue Caption)	1907	£2.40	£120.00
50	(Mauve Caption)	1907	£2.50	—
25	Australian & English Cricketers (Numbered)	1903	£13.00	£325.00
25	Australian & English Cricketers			
	(Blue Border, Capstan)	1909	£13.00	£325.00
	(Blue Border, Vice Regal)	1909	£13.00	£325.00
	(Red Border, Capstan)	1909	£13.00	£325.00
	(Red Border, Vice Regal)	1909	£13.00	£325.00
59	Australian & English Cricketers, Titled	1911	—	£650.00
50	Capstan, "SERIES OF 50"	1911	£11.00	—
50	Capstan, "SERIES OF "	1911	£11.00	—
9	51-59, Capstan, "SERIES OF 59"	1911	£12.00	—
50	Vice Regal, "SERIES OF 50"	1911	£11.00	—
50	Vice Regal, "SERIES OF "	1911	£11.00	—
9	51-59, Vice Regal, "SERIES OF 59"	1911	£12.00	—
50	Havelock	1911	£34.00	—
60	Australian & South African Cricketers	1910	—	£780.00
60	Light Background, Blue Border	1910	£13.00	—
60	Light Background, Red Border	1910	£13.00	—
24	Dark Background (Mixed Printing)	1910	—	£360.00
24	Dark Background, Blue Border, Capstan	1910	£15.00	—
24	Dark Background, Blue Border, Vice Regal	1910	£15.00	—
24	Dark Background, Red Border, Capstan	1910	£15.00	—
24	Dark Background, Red Border, Vice Regal	1910	£15.00	—
60	Light Background, Havelock	1910	£35.00	—
M50	Australian Butterflies (Silk)	1914	£2.60	£130.00
40/46	Australian Club Cricketers	1905	—	£640.00
40	Blue Back, With State	1905	£16.00	—
40	Blue Back, No State	1905	£16.00	—
40	Green Back	1905	£16.00	—
39/46	Blue Back, Brown Frame Line	1905	£20.00	—
MF100	Australian Scenic Series	1925	65p	£65.00
50	Australian Wild Flowers (Specialities)	1913	60p	£30.00
50	(Havelock)	1913	£1.40	—
1	Australia Day	1915	—	£12.50
75	Aviation (Black Back, Capstan)	1910	£1.60	£120.00
75	(Black Back, Vice Regal)	1910	£1.60	£120.00
75	(Black Back, Havelock)	1910	£2.50	—
75	(Green Back, Capstan)	1910	£1.75	—
75	(Green Back, Vice Regal)	1910	£1.75	—
75	(Green Back, Havelock)	1910	£3.00	—
85	(Capstan)	1910	£1.75	£150.00
85	(Vice Regal)	1910	£1.75	£150.00
50	Best Dogs of Their Breed (Specialities)	1914	£3.60	—
50	(Havelock)	1914	£5.50	—
M50	Birds and Animals of Australia (Silk)	1915	£3.00	£175.00
100	Birds of Australasia (Green, Capstan)	1912	£1.00	£100.00
100	(Green, Vice Regal)	1912	£1.00	£100.00
100	(Green, Havelock)	1912	£2.00	—
100	(Yellow Back)	1912	£1.00	£100.00
100	(Yellow, Havelock)	1912	£2.00	—

W. D. & H. O. WILLS LTD. — cont.

Qty		Date	Odds	Sets
50	Britain's Defenders (1-50)	1915	90p	£45.00
50	(Havelock)	1915	£2.00	£100.00
8	Britain's Defenders (51-58)	1915	£8.00	—
50	British Empire Series (Capstan)	1912	70p	£35.00
50	(Vice Regal)	1912	70p	£35.00
50	(Havelock)	1912	£1.60	£80.00
M68	Crests and Colours of Australian Universities, Colleges and Schools	1929	50p	£34.00
M50	Crests and Colours of Australian Universities, Colleges & Schools (Silk)	1916	£2.60	£130.00
M1	Crests and Colours of Australian Schools (Silk, Unnumbered)	1929	—	£24.00
50	Cricketer Series (Grey Scroll Back, No Frame)	1901	£90.00	—
25	Cricketer Series (Grey Scroll Back, Fancy Frame)	1902	£85.00	—
F63	Cricketers (Plain Back)	1926	£6.50	£415.00
F40/48	Cricket Season, 1928-29	1929	£2.50	£100.00
L20	Dogs, A Series (Three Castles & Vice Regal)	1927	£2.50	—
L20	(World Renowned, Album Clause)	1927	£2.50	—
L20	(World Renowned, No Album Clause)	1927	£2.50	—
L20	Dogs, 2nd Series	1928	£2.50	—
L25	English Period Costumes	1929	£1.60	£40.00
100	Famous Film Stars	1934	70p	£70.00
M100	Famous Film Stars	1933	£1.60	—
MF100	Famous Film Stars	1933	£2.40	—
M20	Fiestas (Cartons)	1968	65p	—
50	Fish of Australasia (Capstan)	1912	70p	£35.00
50	(Vice Regal)	1912	70p	£35.00
50	(Havelock)	1912	£1.30	—
50	Flag Girls of All Nations	1908	—	£80.00
50	Capstan, Small Captions	1908	£1.60	—
24	Capstan, Large Captions	1908	£2.75	—
50	Vice Regal, Small Captions	1908	£1.60	—
24	Vice Regal, Large Captions	1908	£2.75	—
8	Flags (Shaped, Metal, 4 Printings)	1915	£8.00	—
M13	Flags (Lace)	1916	£4.00	£52.00
28	Flags of the Allies (Silk, Capitals)	1915	£1.75	£49.00
23	(Silk, Small Letters)	1915	£2.00	£46.00
25	Flags of the Empire	1926	*£5.00*	—
28	Football Club Colours & Flags (Capstan)	1913	£3.00	£85.00
28	(Havelock)	1913	£5.00	—
200	Footballers 1933	1933	65p	£130.00
M200	Footballers 1933	1933	£1.20	—
?6	Footballers (Shaped)	1910	£65.00	—
?27	Football Pennants (Shaped, Capstan)	1905	*£32.50*	—
?27	(Shaped, Havelock)	1905	*£35.00*	—
50	Girls of All Nations (Capstan)	1908	£2.20	£110.00
50	(Vice Regal)	1908	£2.20	£110.00
X?	Havelock Comics	1904	*£65.00*	—
50	Historic Events (Specialities)	1913	85p	£42.50
50	(Havelock)	1913	£1.75	£87.50
L25	History of Naval Dress	1929	*£16.00*	—
50	Horses of Today (Capstan)	1906	£2.40	£120.00
50	(Vice Regal)	1906	£2.40	£120.00
50	(Havelock)	1906	£4.00	—
50	Interesting Buildings	1905	£1.80	£90.00
5	Islands of the Pacific	1917	*£150.00*	—
38	Kings & Queens of England (Silk)	1910	£4.50	£171.00

MULTI-BACKS

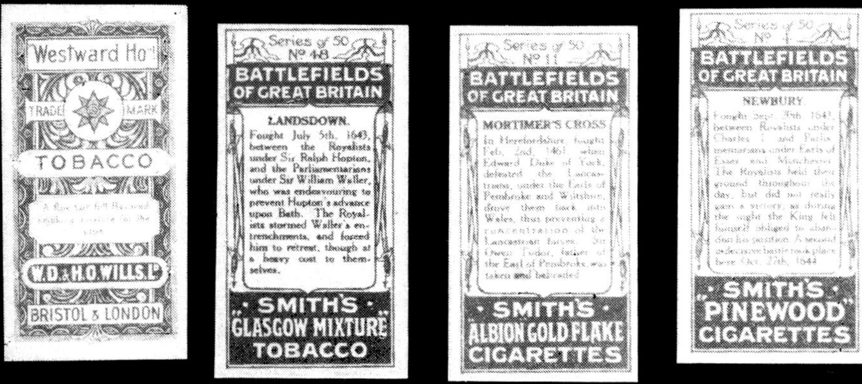

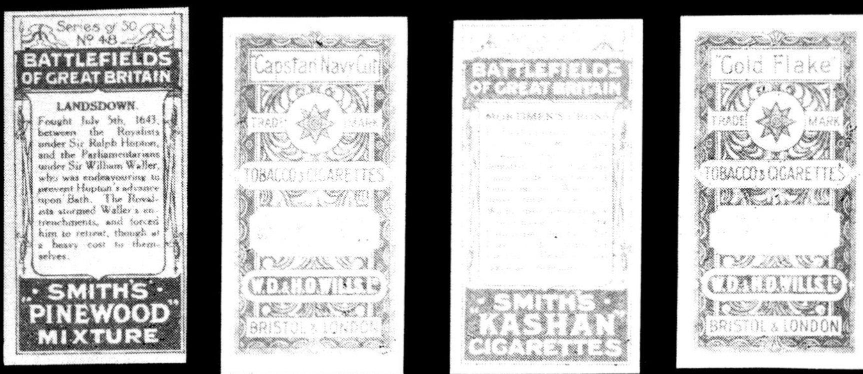

There are many instances in the enlarged catalogue when a set by one issuer is noted as occurring in more than one back. For example, each card in Wills Seaside Resorts can be found with six different brands advertised, while in the case of Smith Battlefields of Great Britain each number can have no less than 15 different advertisements!

In addition to these varieties there are also many series, particular among the earlier issues, where there are different backs, but not every front may be found with every back. These are known as multi-backs. A good example of this is the Wills set Sports of All Nations, which like Seaside Resorts also has six advertisements; however in this case each number only occurs with two different brands, and these run in distinct groups of numbers. The issues of Smith are also an excellent source of multi-backed series, with many series including Champions of Sport, Medals and Phil May Sketches featuring prominently. Indeed the Smith issues are so complicated that it has been necessary to publish a separate Reference Book detailing all the varieties known.

In the catalogue we now show when a series is multi-backed, but without indicating all the options available; this would have been too complicated, especially for a series such as Adkin Pretty Girl Series RASH, with its 50 different backs! Most type collectors would probably wish to obtain one of each of these multi-backs, and full information is normally to be found in the Cartophilic Society's Reference Books.

One additional term worth remembering is "vari-backed". This is used when there are different advertisements on the back, but where each front can be found with one back only.

IMPERIAL TOBACCO COMPANY

This huge Company was founded on 2nd November 1901 in order to combat the spreading influence in Britain of the American Tobacco Co. The founder members were headed by Wills, and included such well known card issuers as Player, Smith, Hignett and Lambert & Butler. During the next few years they were to acquire a number of other well known companies such as Churchman and Faulkner. However their most important acquisitions were probably those of Ogden at the conclusion of the Tobacco war, and Mardon Son & Hall, the printers who became responsible for the production of most of their cigarette cards.

The formation date is most important to cartophilists, because from that time onward the card issues of the constituent firms bore the message "Branch of the Imperial Tobacco Co. (of Great Britain and Northern Ireland) Ltd." in addition to the individual firm's name. Because, for example, there are two printings of Wills Locomotives and Faulkner Our Gallant Grenadiers, one with and one without the "I.T.C. clause" as it is popularly known, it is safe to say that each of these was issued around 1901-2; or that Vanity Fair came a little earlier and Borough Arms a little later.

Cards issued abroad (including the Channel Islands) which mentioned the I.T.C. member's names did NOT include the I.T.C. clause, since they were always issued by the British American Tobacco Co. which was partly owned by I.T.C.

A cartophilic consequence of the formation of the I.T.C. was the practice of issuing identical card series under several of the firm's, or indeed by B.A.T. Hence Garden Life was issued by Edwards Ringer & Bigg, Lambert & Butler and Wills; Angling by Faulkner, Mitchell and B.A.T.; Boy Scouts by Churchman, Ogden and I.T.C. (Canada). It is always likely that series issued by I.T.C. firms with the same series title will be the same basic set, such as Air Raid Precautions by Churchman, Hignett, Mitchell, Ogden and Wills.

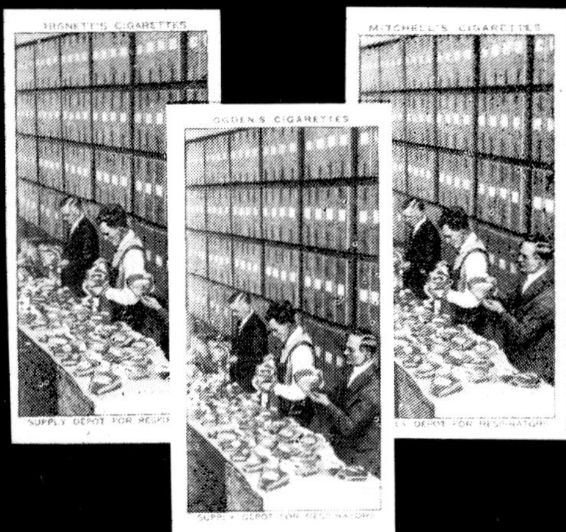

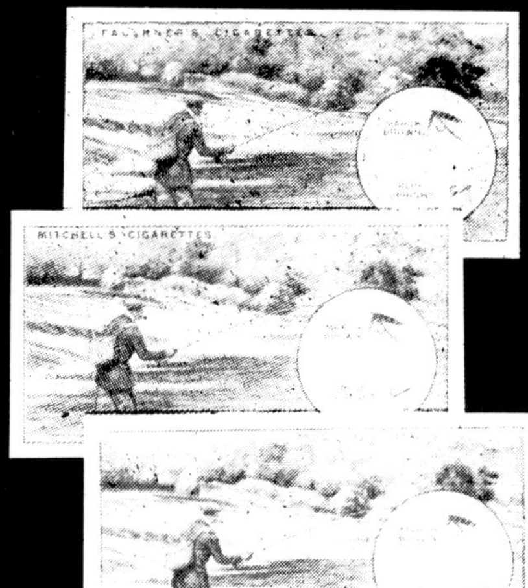

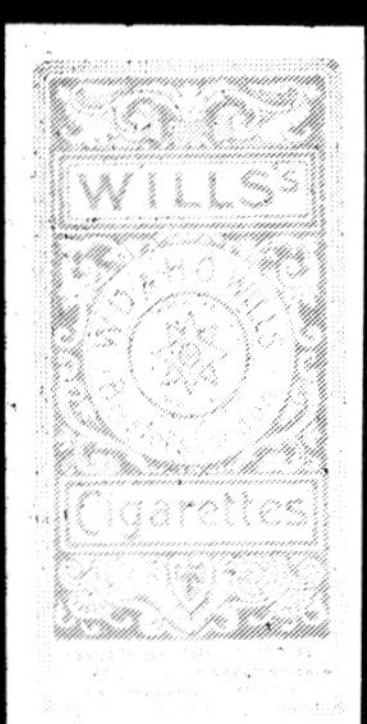

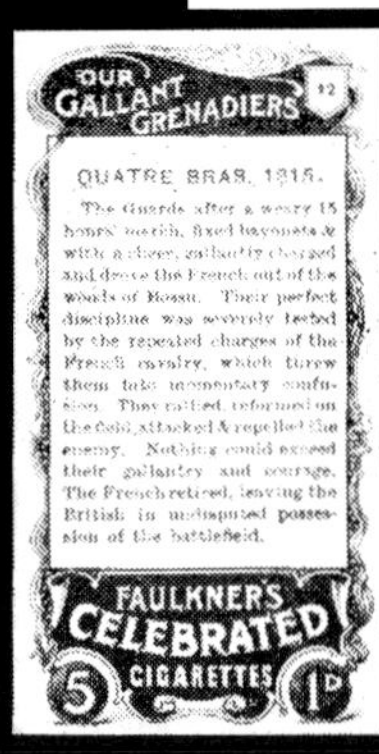

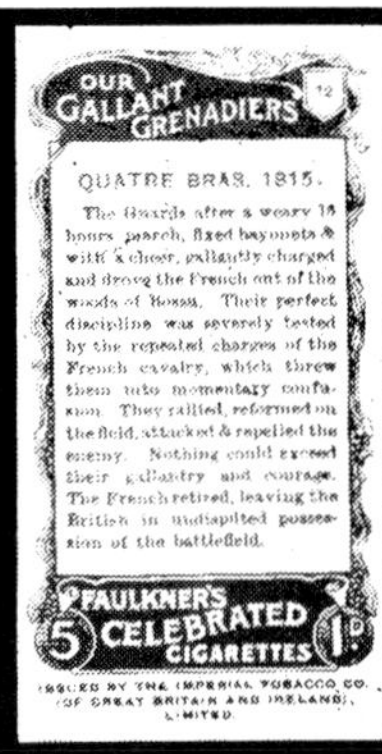

Qty		*Date*	*Odds*	*Sets*
45	Melbourne Cup Winners	1906	£6.00	—
40	Merrie England Studies	1916	£5.50	£220.00
50	Modern War Weapons (Specialities)	1915	£1.50	£75.00
50	(Havelock)	1915	£2.60	—
50	Past & Present Champions (Cigarettes)	1908	£4.50	—
50	(Tobacco)	1908	£4.50	£225.00
M50	Popular Flowers (Silk, Large Packets)	1913	£4.00	—
M50	(Silk, 1/- Packets)	1913	£3.60	£180.00
L70	Practical Wireless	1923	£5.75	—
50	Prominent Australian and English Cricketers (1-50)	1907	£11.00	£650.00
23	Prominent Australian and English Cricketers (51-73, Grey Captions)	1907	£15.00	£345.00
8	Prominent Australian and English Cricketers (66-73, Red Captions)	1907	£15.00	£120.00
10	Recruiting Posters (Anonymous Back)	1915	£6.50	£65.00
50	Riders of the World	1913	£1.40	£70.00
50	(Havelock)	1913	£2.75	—
50	Royal Mail (Capstan)	1913	£3.50	£175.00
50	(Vice Regal)	1913	£3.50	£175.00
50	(Anonymous Printed Back)	1913	£4.50	—
50	(Anonymous Plain Back)	1913	£5.00	—
50	(Havelock, 2 Printings)	1913	£4.50	—
50	Signalling Series (Capstan)	1912	£1.00	£50.00
50	(Vice Regal)	1912	£1.00	£50.00
50	(Havelock)	1912	£2.00	£100.00
39/40	Sketches in Black & White	1905	£2.20	£85.00
?39/40	(White on Black)	1905	*£65.00*	—
50	Soldiers of the World	1902	£6.50	£325.00
25	Sporting Terms (Capstan)	1905	£10.00	£250.00
25	(Vice Regal)	1905	£10.00	£250.00
50	Sports of the World	1917	£3.60	—
50	Stage & Music Hall Celebrities (Capstan)	1904	£2.80	£140.00
50	(Vice Regal)	1904	£2.80	—
50	(Havelock)	1904	£4.00	—
50	Stage & Music Hall Celebrities (Square)	1904	£3.00	—
L25	The Nation's Shrines	1928	£1.20	£30.00
25	The World's Dreadnoughts (Capstan)	1910	£1.80	£45.00
25	(Vice Regal)	1910	£1.80	£45.00
50	Time & Money in Different Countries			
	(Capstan)	1907	£1.20	£60.00
	(Vice Regal, Album Clause)	1907	£1.20	£60.00
	(Vice Regal, No Album Clause)	1907	£1.20	£60.00
	(Havelock)	1907	£2.40	£120.00
50	Types of the British Army			
	(Capstan, 2 Printings)	1912	£1.80	£90.00
	(Vice Regal, 2 Printings)	1912	£1.80	£90.00
50	Types of the Commonwealth Forces			
	(Capstan, 2 Printings)	1910	£2.00	£100.00
	(Vice Regal, 2 Printings)	1910	£2.00	£100.00
	(Havelock)	1910	£4.00	—
P1	Union Jack (Silk)	1915	—	£25.00
25	United States Warships (Capstan)	1911	£2.40	£60.00
25	(Vice Regal)	1911	£2.40	£60.00
25	(Havelock)	1911	£4.00	—

Qty		Date	Odds	Sets
25	Victoria Cross Heroes (Specialities)	1915	£2.00	£50.00
25	(Havelock)	1915	£3.60	£90.00
29	Victorian Football Pennants			
	(Capstan, Multi-Backed)	1910	£2.40	—
	(Vice-Regal, Multi-Backed)	1910	£2.40	—
	(Havelock, Multi-Backed)	1910	£4.00	—
FS165	Views of the World (Capstan)	1908	75p	—
FS165	(Vice Regal)	1908	75p	—
50	War Incidents, A Series (Specialities)	1915	£1.50	£75.00
50	(Havelock)	1915	£2.50	—
50	War Incidents, 2nd Series (Specialities)	1915	£2.00	£100.00
50	(Havelock)	1915	£3.00	—
L67	War Medals (Silk)	1916	£2.75	£185.00
50	War Pictures (Specialities)	1915	£1.00	£50.00
50	(Havelock)	1915	£2.00	£100.00
50	Wild Animals' Heads	1934	50p	£25.00
M25	Wild Animals (Heads)	1934	£1.20	£30.00
50	Wild Animals of the World	1906	£4.50	£225.00
LF50	Zoological Series	1922	£1.75	£87.50

BRAND ISSUES

(A) Autocar Cigarettes

Qty		Date	Odds	Sets
40	Chinese Trades	1905	£5.50	—

(B) Flag Cigarettes

Qty		Date	Odds	Sets
67	International Footballers, 1909-1910	1911	£7.50	—
50	Jiu-Jitsu	1911	£4.25	—
50	Types of the British Army	1912	£4.50	—

(C) Four Aces Cigarettes

Qty		Date	Odds	Sets
52	Birds of Brilliant Plumage (P/C Inset)	1924	£2.50	£130.00
75	Film Favourites	1928	£1.40	£105.00
25	Modes of Conveyance	1928	£1.60	£40.00
50	Stage & Film Stars (Numbered)	1926	£1.50	£75.00
50	(Unnumbered)	1926	£1.75	£87.50
F52	Stars of the Cinema	1926	£3.50	—

(D) Pirate Cigarettes

Qty		Date	Odds	Sets
G?	Advertisement Cards	1910	£65.00	—
?100	Baseball Series	1912	*£100.00*	—
52	Birds of Brilliant Plumage			
	(P/C Inset, Frame Line)	1916	£3.50	£180.00
	(P/C Inset, No Frame)	1916	£2.60	£135.00
100	China's Ancient Warriors (Multi-Backed)	1911	£2.00	£200.00
28	Chinese Actors & Actresses	1907	£2.75	£77.00
50	Chinese Beauties (Multi-Backed)	1909	£1.25	£62.50
50	Chinese Costumes	1928	£3.25	—
P25	Chinese Pagodas	1911	£34.00	—
50	Chinese Proverbs (Brown, 2 Backs)	1928	£1.20	£60.00
50	(Coloured, 4 Backs)	1915	£1.00	£50.00
33	Houses of Parliament	1914	£1.20	£40.00
50	Products of the World	1913	£1.10	£55.00

(E) Purple Mountain Cigarettes

Qty		Date	Odds	Sets
20	Flowers (Numbered)	1914	*£10.00*	—
100	Flowers (Unnumbered)	1915	*£8.00*	—

Qty		Date	Odds	Sets
25	Roses (Wills on Front)	1912	£5.50	£137.50
25	(Without Wills on Front)	1912	£5.00	£125.00
(F) Ruby Queen Cigarettes				
30	Birds & Animals (2 Backs)	1911	£2.00	£60.00
50	Birds of the East (Multi-Backs & Fronts)	1912	£1.20	£60.00
30	Chinese Children's Games (2 Backs)	1911	£1.75	—
50	Chinese Proverbs	1927	*£3.00*	—
50	Chinese Transport (3 Backs)	1914	£2.00	—
(G) Scissors Cigarettes				
50	Actresses (Black & White)	1904	£7.00	—
50	Actresses (Four Colour Surround)	1904	£6.00	—
30	Actresses (Green Surround)	1905	£3.00	£90.00
30	Actresses (Mauve Surround)	1916	£1.50	£45.00
30	(Orange Surround)	1916	£2.00	£60.00
30	Actresses (Purple Brown, Brown Back)	1908	£2.00	£60.00
30	(Purple Brown, Red Back)	1908	£1.60	£48.00
30	Actresses (Purple Brown, Long Card)	1909	£1.80	£54.00
25	Army Life	1914	£2.00	£50.00
30	Beauties (Green Surround)	1921	£4.25	—
52	Beauties (P/C Inset – Lattice Back)	1911	£2.60	£135.00
52	(P/C Inset – No Lattice Back)	1911	£4.50	—
52	(P/C Inset – No Packets)	1911	*£20.00*	—
32	Beauties (Picture Hats)	1914	£3.00	£96.00
40	Beauties (Brown Tint)	1913	£1.40	£56.00
30	Beauties & Children	1910	£2.30	£85.00
36	Boxers	1911	£7.00	£250.00
50	Britain's Defenders (Green Back)	1915	£1.50	£75.00
50	(Red Back & Front)	1915	£1.40	£70.00
50	Britain's Defenders (Blue Front)	1915	£1.30	£65.00
43	British Army Boxers Series	1913	£4.60	£200.00
25	Cinema Stars	1916	£2.20	£55.00
F50	Cinema Stars	1926	*£3.50*	—
27	Dancing Girls (27 Subjects)	1915	£2.25	£61.00
27/28	(28 Subjects)	1915	£2.25	£61.00
25	Derby Day Series	1914	£6.50	£162.50
25	Series A (No Series Title)	1914	£8.50	—
32	Drum Horses (Horizontal Back)	1909	£5.50	£176.00
32	(Vertical Back)	1909	£7.50	—
50	Famous Footballers	1914	£7.00	£350.00
25	Flag Girls of All Nations (Numbered)	1908	£8.00	£200.00
25	(Unnumbered)	1908	£10.00	—
50	Football Club Colours	1907	£6.00	£300.00
25	Governors-General of India	1912	£6.00	£150.00
30	Heroic Deeds	1913	£2.50	£75.00
50	Indian Regiments Series	1912	£6.00	£300.00
67	International Footballers, 1909-1910	1910	£7.00	—
50	Jiu-Jitsu	1910	£5.00	£250.00
53	Jockeys & Owners Colours (P/C Inset)	1914	£5.50	£290.00
25	Military Portraits	1917	£3.60	£90.00
50	Music Hall Celebrities	1911	£5.50	—
K52	Playing Cards	1906	*£10.00*	—
25	Puzzle Series (Green, United Service Backs)	1910	£5.00	£125.00
25	(Yellow, United Service Backs)	1910	£5.00	—
50	Regimental Colours & Cap Badges	1907	£1.25	£62.50

Qty		Date	Odds	Sets
33	Regimental Pets	1911	£5.00	£165.00
30	Sporting Girls	1913	£7.00	£210.00
50	Types of the British Army	1908	£4.50	£225.00
25	Victoria Cross Heroes	1915	£2.40	£60.00
50	War Incidents	1915	£1.70	£85.00
30	What It Means	1916	£1.00	£30.00
F50	"Zoo"	1927	£3.50	—
(H) United Service Cigarettes				
50	Arms & Armour	1910	£2.60	£130.00
32	Drum Horses	1909	£5.00	£160.00
25	Flag Girls of All Nations	1908	£2.40	£60.00
67	International Footballers, 1909-1910	1910	£7.00	—
	Puzzle Series-See Scissors Cigarettes			
50	Regimental Colours & Cap Badges (Blue Back)	1907	£1.20	£60.00
50	(Red Back)	1907	£1.25	£62.50
(I) Wild Woodbine Cigarettes				
50	British Army Uniforms	1909	£5.00	£250.00
CHANNEL ISLANDS ISSUES				
50	Air Raid Precautions	1938	70p	£35.00
50	Association Footballers	1935	£2.00	—
50	Dogs	1937	85p	£42.50
50	Garden Flowers by Sudell	1939	35p	£17.50
50	Garden Hints	1938	35p	£17.50
50	Household Hints	1936	35p	£17.50
50	Life in the Royal Navy	1939	35p	£17.50
50	Our King & Queen	1937	40p	£20.00
50	Railway Equipment	1938	40p	£20.00
50	Speed	1938	40p	£20.00
50	The Sea-Shore	1938	35p	£17.50
50	Wild Flowers, A Series	1936	45p	£22.50
50	Wild Flowers, 2nd Series	1937	35p	£17.50
NEW ZEALAND ISSUES				
F50	A Sporting Holiday in New Zealand	1928	60p	£30.00
LF50	A Sporting Holiday in New Zealand (Different)	1928	75p	£37.50
F50	Beautiful New Zealand	1928	20p	£10.00
50	Birds, Beasts and Fishes	1924	30p	£15.00
F48	British Royal and Ancient Buildings	1925	30p	£15.00
45	British Rugby Players	1930	£1.60	£72.00
50	Children of All Nations	1925	55p	£27.50
50	Coaches and Coaching Days	1925	£1.50	£75.00
50	Dogs	1926	70p	£35.00
P10	English Views and Buildings	1925	£10.00	—
F25	English Cricketers	1926	£2.20	£55.00
26	Etchings (Dogs)	1925	£1.60	£41.00
L26	Etchings (Dogs)	1925	£3.20	£83.00
P10	Famous Castles	1926	£8.50	£85.00
50	Famous Inventions	1926	65p	£32.50
L25	Heraldic Signs & Their Origin	1925	£1.40	£35.00
F50	Homeland Events	1927	40p	£30.00
50	Household Hints (Wills at Top Back)	1927	20p	£10.00
50	(Scroll at Top Back)	1927	£1.40	—
50	Lighthouses	1926	£1.40	£70.00
50	Merchant Ships of the World	1925	£1.00	£50.00
48	Motor Cars	1923	£1.60	£77.00
F50	Motor Cars	1926	£1.10	£55.00

Qty		Date	Odds	Sets
50	Motor Cycles	1926	£3.00	£150.00
50	New Zealand Birds	1925	50p	£25.00
F50	New Zealand – Early Scenes & Maori Life	1926	25p	£12.50
F50	New Zealand Footballers	1927	80p	£40.00
50	New Zealand Race Horses	1928	75p	£37.50
50	N.Z. Butterflies, Moths & Beetles	1925	60p	£30.00
25	Past & Present	1929	£1.00	£25.00
25	Picturesque People of the Empire	1928	80p	£20.00
25	Pirates & Highwaymen	1925	£1.00	£25.00
50	Products of the World	1929	20p	£10.00
50	Railway Engines	1925	80p	£40.00
50	Railway Working	1927	£2.00	—
50	Regimental Standards and Cap Badges	1928	50p	£25.00
50	Riders of the World	1926	75p	£37.50
50	Romance of the Heavens	1928	£1.30	—
50	Safety First	1935	70p	£35.00
F50	Ships and Shipping	1928	60p	£30.00
50	Ships' Badges	1925	70p	£35.00
P10	Splendours of New Zealand	1927	£8.50	£85.00
F50	The Royal Family at Home and Abroad	1927	50p	£25.00
F50	The Royal Navy	1929	£1.40	£70.00
F50	Units of the British Army and R.A.F.	1928	50p	£25.00
50	U.S.S. Co's. Steamers	1930	£2.50	£125.00
50	V.C.'s	1926	£1.40	£70.00
25	Village Models Series	1925	80p	£20.00
L25	Village Models Series	1925	*£5.00*	—
50	Warships	1926	£1.25	£62.50
25	Wonders of the World	1926	50p	£12.50
F50	"Zoo"	1926	20p	£10.00
OTHER OVERSEAS ISSUES				
50	Actors & Actresses "WALP" (Black)	1905	£3.00	—
50	(Flesh Tint)	1905	£2.20	£110.00
250	Actresses "ALWICS" (Black & Red Front)	1905	£1.30	£325.00
250	(All Red Front)	1905	£2.50	—
250	(All Black Front)	1905	£2.40	—
250	(No Address on Back)	1905	£3.00	—
25	Actresses, Tabs Type (101-125)	1902	£14.00	£350.00
50	Actresses, Four Colour Surround (Matt)	1904	£2.20	£110.00
50	(Varnished)	1904	£2.20	£110.00
50	Aeroplanes	1926	£2.75	—
50	Animals and Birds (With Series Title)	1912	£4.00	£200.00
50	(No Series Title)	1909	£4.00	£200.00
50	Arms of the British Empire	1911	80p	£40.00
50	Art Photogravures – Set 1	1912	50p	£25.00
M50	Art Photogravures – Set 1	1912	60p	£30.00
50	Art Photogravures – Set 2	1913	50p	£25.00
50	Aviation Series (Wills on Back)	1911	£3.25	—
50	(Anonymous Back, Album Clause)	1911	£2.80	£140.00
50	(Anonymous Back, No Clause)	1911	£2.80	£140.00
50	Beauties "LAWHA" (Red Tinted)	1905	£1.70	£85.00
40	Beauties (Brown Tint)	1913	£2.60	£104.00
52	Beauties (P/C Inset)	1911	£4.75	—
32	Beauties (Picture Hats)	1914	£5.25	£168.00
M72	Beauties	1923	£11.00	—
MF50	Beauties (Hand Coloured)	1925	£3.00	—
F25	Beauties	1925	£2.75	—

W. D. & H. O. WILLS LTD. — cont.

Qty		*Date*	*Odds*	*Sets*
F50	Beauties, 2nd Series	1925	£2.75	—
52	Birds of Brilliant Plumage (P/C Inset)	1914	£4.00	£208.00
36	Boxers	1911	£7.00	£250.00
50	Britain's Defenders	1915	£1.70	£85.00
101	British Beauties	1915	£1.75	£175.00
50	British Costumes from 100 BC to 1904	1905	*£50.00*	—
50	Chateaux	1925	£4.00	£200.00
50	Conundrums	1903	£9.00	£450.00
25	Derby Day Series A	1914	£7.00	—
32	Drum Horses	1909	£6.00	£192.00
26	Etchings (Gold Flake Cigarettes)	1925	£6.50	—
26	(Dutch Text, Frame on Back)	1925	£8.00	—
26	(Dutch Text, No Frame Line)	1925	£7.50	—
50	Famous Footballers	1914	£7.00	—
25	Flag Girls of All Nations	1908	£2.40	£60.00
126	Flags & Ensigns	1904	£1.25	£157.50
6	Flags of the Allies (Shaped)	1915	£11.50	£69.00
50	Girls of All Nations	1908	£2.40	—
32	Houses of Parliament	1912	£1.75	£56.00
50	Indian Regiments Series	1912	£7.50	—
24	Merveilles du Monde	1927	£5.50	—
M25	Miniatures (Metal)	1914	£50.00	—
F48	Movie Stars	1927	£2.75	—
50	National Flags and Arms	1936	£1.35	—
FS50	Nature Studies	1928	£1.30	—
25	Police of the World	1910	£8.00	£200.00
25	Products of the World	1913	£1.60	£40.00
50	Races of Mankind	1911	£11.00	£550.00
100	Royalty, Notabilities & Events, 1900-2	1902	£2.00	£200.00
27	Rulers of the World	1912	£7.00	£190.00
100	Russo Japanese Series (Black Front, 2 Printings)	1905	£1.50	£150.00
50	(Red Front)	1905	£6.50	—
LF48	Scenes from the Empire	1939	£1.75	£84.00
30	Semaphore Signalling	1910	£3.00	£90.00
36	Ships & Their Pennants	1913	£5.00	£180.00
75	Soldiers of the World	1903	£8.50	—
F52	Stars of the Cinema	1926	*£4.00*	—
25	The Evolution of the British Navy	1915	£2.60	£65.00
25	The World's Dreadnoughts	1910	£2.40	£60.00
50	Wild Animals of the World (Star,Circle & Leaves)	1906	£7.00	—

WILSON & CO.

50	War Portraits	1916	*£75.00*	—

W. WILSON

30	Army Pictures, Cartoons, etc	1916	*£85.00*	—

HENRI WINTERMANS (UK) LTD.

T30	Disappearing Rain Forest	1991	30p	£9.00
T30	Wonders of Nature	1993	30p	£9.00

A. & M. WIX

Qty		Date	Odds	Sets
D250	Cinema Cavalcade	1940	90p	£225.00
D250	Cinema Cavalcade, Volume II	1940	90p	£225.00
100	Film Favourites	1937	£1.80	—
100	Film Favourites, 2nd Series	1938	£1.80	—
100	Film Favourites, 3rd Series	1939	90p	£90.00
L?23	Maxims of Max (Package Issue)	1952	*£7.50*	—
X100	Men of Destiny	1934	£1.60	£160.00
D250	Speed – Through the Ages (English Text)	1938	40p	—
D250	(2 Languages)	1938	30p	£75.00
D250	This Age of Power & Wonder	1935	30p	£75.00

J. WIX & SONS LTD.

Qty		Date	Odds	Sets
F?	Animals	1928	*£35.00*	—
P80	Bridge Favours & Place Cards	1930	£12.00	—
P50	Bridge Hands	1930	*£14.00*	—
L48	British Empire Flags (Silk)	1934	80p	£38.50
L48	(Printed in U.S.A.)	1934	80p	£38.50
50	Builders of Empire	1937	30p	£15.00
42	Card Tricks	1938	£4.00	—
M42	Card Tricks	1938	£4.00	—
50	Coronation (Kensitas)	1937	25p	£12.50
50	(Wix)	1937	25p	£12.50
L50	Henry	1935	70p	£35.00
P25	Henry	1935	£2.50	£62.50
L50	Henry, 2nd Series (No Album Price)	1936	£1.75	—
L50	(With Album Price)	1936	80p	£40.00
P25	Henry, 2nd Series	1936	£2.80	£70.00
L50	Henry, 3rd Series	1936	70p	£35.00
L50	Henry, 4th Series	1936	70p	£35.00
L50	Henry, 5th Series	1937	70p	£35.00
L102	Jenkynisms, 1st Series (Yellow)	1932	75p	—
L50	Jenkynisms, 2nd Series(Yellow)	1932	75p	—
L25/30	Jenkynisms, 3rd Series (Yellow)	1932	75p	—
L1	Jenkynisms, 4th Series (Yellow)	1932	—	*£2.50*
8	Jenkynisms (Red Borders, Unnumbered)	1931	£3.00	—
?44	Jenkynisms (Red Borders, Numbered)	1931	£2.75	—
?30	Jenkynisms (Red Borders, Series B)	1931	*£3.50*	—
?19	Jenkynisms (Red Borders, Series C)	1931	*£3.50*	—
?34	Jenkynisms (Red Borders, Series D)	1931	*£3.50*	—
6	Jenkynisms (Red Borders, Vertical)	1931	£4.50	
M46	Jenkynisms (Red Borders, Unnumbered)	1931	*£3.50*	—
?M44	Jenkynisms (Red Borders, Numbered)	1931	£3.00	—
?M30	Jenkynisms (Red Borders, Series B)	1931	*£3.50*	—
?M19	Jenkynisms (Red Borders, Series C)	1931	*£3.50*	—
?M34	Jenkynisms (Red Borders, Series D)	1931	*£3.50*	—
M6	Jenkynisms (Red Borders, Vertical)	1931	*£4.50*	—
P96	Ken-Cards	1969	25p	£24.00
60	Kensitas Flowers (Silk, Plain Back)	1933	£2.80	£168.00
60	(Silk, 3 Printed Backs)	1933	£2.80	£168.00
L60	Kensitas Flowers (Silk, Plain Back)	1933	£4.40	£264.00
L60	(Silk, 3 Printed Backs)	1933	£4.40	£264.00
P30	Kensitas Flowers (Silk, Plain Backs)	1933	£40.00	—
P30	(Silk, 3 Printed Backs)	1933	£40.00	£1200.00
40	Kensitas Flowers, Second Series (Silk)	1934	£4.80	£344.00
L40	Kensitas Flowers, Second Series (Silk)	1934	£5.60	£438.00

J. WIX & SONS LTD. — cont.

Qty		Date	Odds	Sets
25	Love Scenes from Famous Films, 1st Series	1932	£2.60	£65.00
L25	Love Scenes from Famous Films, 1st Series	1932	£2.60	£65.00
P25	Love Scenes from Famous Films, 1st Series	1932	£4.50	—
19/25	Love Scenes from Famous Films, 2nd Series	1932	£2.50	£47.50
L19/25	Love Scenes from Famous Films, 2nd Series	1932	£3.00	—
P19/25	Love Scenes from Famous Films, 2nd Series	1932	*£7.00*	—
K53	Miniature Playing Cards (Blue Scroll)	1938	20p	£8.50
K53	(Red Scroll)	1938	20p	£9.00
K53	(Revenge)	1938	25p	£13.00
K53	(Victory)	1938	25p	£13.00
L60	National Flags (Silk)	1934	90p	£66.00
F24	Royal Tour in New Zealand	1928	£11.50	—
25	Scenes from Famous Films, Third Series	1932	£2.50	£62.50
P25	Scenes from Famous Films, Third Series	1932	*£6.50*	—

T. WOOD & SON

30	Army Pictures, Cartoons, etc	1916	*£85.00*	—

WOOD BROS.

28	Dominoes	1910	£60.00	—

JOHN J. WOODS

?25	Views of London	1905	*£130.00*	—

W. H. & J. WOODS LTD.

25	Aesop's Fables	1932	£1.60	£40.00
F50	Modern Motor Cars	1936	£4.50	£225.00
25	Romance of the Royal Mail	1931	£1.20	£30.00
25	Types of Volunteer & Yeomanry	1902	£25.00	—

J. & E. WOOLF

50	Beauties "KEWA"	1898	*£225.00*	—

M. H. WOOLLER

25	Beauties "BOCCA"	1899	*£225.00*	—

T.E. YEOMANS & SONS LTD.

M72	Beauties	1900	£150.00	—
50	War Portraits	1916	*£80.00*	—

JOHN YOUNG & SONS LTD.

12	Naval Skits	1904	£135.00	—
12	Russo Japanese Series	1904	£70.00	—

A. ZICALIOTTI

1	Milly-Totty Advertisement Card	1900	—	*£350.00*

Part 2

OVERSEAS TOBACCO MANUFACTURERS

AFRICAN TOBACCO MANUFACTURERS (S. Africa)

Qty		Date	Odds	Sets
L29	All Blacks South African Tour, 1928	1928	£12.50	—
60	Animals (2 Types)	1922	£3.25	—
MF48	British Aircraft	1926	£3.75	—
50	Chinese Transport	1923	£3.50	—
MF48	Cinema Artistes	1926	£3.25	£156.00
50	Cinema Stars "OMBI"	1923	£1.70	£85.00
50	Cinema Stars "OMBI", Second Series	1923	£1.80	£90.00
M50	Famous & Beautiful Women	1938	£2.00	—
L50	Famous & Beautiful Women	1938	£1.30	£65.00
33	Houses of Parliament	1923	£5.00	—
?60	Miniatures	1924	£5.50	—
MF48	National Costumes	1926	£2.70	£135.00
53	Playing Cards (MP)	1929	£1.75	—
53	(Scots)	1929	£1.60	—
MF48	Popular Dogs	1926	£4.00	£200.00
M100	Postage Stamps – Rarest Varieties	1930	£1.40	£140.00
M80	Prominent N.Z. & Australian Rugby Players & Springbok 1937 Touring Team	1937	£2.00	—
L80	Prominent N.Z. & Australian Rugby Players & Springbok 1937 Touring Team	1937	£1.80	£145.00
29	S. A. Rugby Football Team, 1912-1913	1912	£24.00	—
L30	Some Beautiful Roses (Silk)	1928	£8.00	£240.00
M132	S. A. Members of Legislative Assembly	1919	£24.00	—
25	The Arcadia Fair	1923	£8.00	—
25	The Race Course	1923	£9.00	—
M100	The World of Sport	1939	£2.50	—
L100	The World of Sport	1939	£2.25	—
L25	Types of British Birds (Silk)	1928	£7.50	£187.50
L20	Types of British Butterflies (Silk)	1928	£10.00	—
L25	Types of Railway Engines (Silk)	1928	£22.50	—
L25	Types of Sea Shells (Silk)	1928	£11.50	—

AGUERE (Belgium) (Imitation Cigar Bands)

Qty		Date	Odds	Sets
24	Military Head-Dress	1975	—	£5.00

M. V. ALBERT (France)

Qty		Date	Odds	Sets
12	Film Actors & Actresses	1936	£2.50	—

ALLEN TOBACCO CO. (U.S.A.)

Qty		Date	Odds	Sets
X250	Views & Art Studies (55 x 90mm)	1912	£3.00	—
X?120	Views & Art Studies (80 x 72mm)	1912	£4.00	—

ALLEN & GINTER (U.S.A.)

Qty		Date	Odds	Sets
50	American Editors	1887	£24.00	£1200.00
X50	American Editors	1887	£30.00	—
50	Arms of All Nations	1887	£17.00	£850.00
50	Birds of America	1888	£10.00	£500.00
X50	Birds of America	1890	£20.00	£1000.00
50	Birds of the Tropics	1889	£12.00	£600.00
X50	Birds of the Tropics	1889	£21.50	—
50	Celebrated American Indian Chiefs	1888	£25.00	£1250.00
50	City Flags	1888	£11.00	£550.00
50	Fans of the Period	1889	£20.00	£1000.00

ALLEN & GINTER (U.S.A.) — cont.

Qty		Date	Odds	Sets
50	Fish from American Waters	1889	£11.00	£550.00
X50	Fish from American Waters	1889	£22.00	—
48	Flags of All Nations	1887	£6.50	£315.00
50	Flags of All Nations, Second Series	1890	£8.00	£400.00
47	Flags of the States and Territories	1888	£9.00	£425.00
50	Fruits	1891	£16.50	£825.00
50	Game Birds	1889	£10.00	£500.00
X50	Game Birds	1889	£21.50	—
50	General Government and State Capitol Buildings of the United States	1889	£10.00	£500.00
50	Great Generals	1886	£26.00	£1300.00
50	Natives in Costume	1886	£23.00	£1150.00
50	Naval Flags	1887	£11.50	£575.00
50	Parasol Drill	1888	£18.00	£900.00
F?	Photographic Cards (Many Types)	1885	£2.50	—
F66	Photographic Cards (Girl Cyclists)	1885	£15.00	—
50	Pirates of the Spanish Main	1888	£24.00	£1200.00
50	Prize & Game Chickens	1892	£18.00	£900.00
50	Quadrupeds	1890	£12.50	£625.00
X50	Quadrupeds	1890	£22.50	—
50	Racing Colors of the World (No Border)	1888	£17.00	£850.00
50	(White Border)	1888	£16.00	£800.00
50	Song Birds of the World	1890	£10.50	£525.00
X50	Song Birds of the World	1890	£22.50	—
X50	The American Indian	1888	£32.50	—
50	The World's Beauties	1888	£16.50	£825.00
50	The World's Beauties, Second Series	1888	£17.00	£850.00
50	The World's Champions	1888	£20.00	—
50	The World's Champions, Second Series	1889	£24.00	—
X50	The World's Champions, Second Series	1889	£45.00	—
50	The World's Decorations	1890	£11.50	£575.00
X50	The World's Decorations	1890	£22.50	£1125.00
50	The World's Racers	1888	£20.00	—
50	Types of All Nations	1889	£16.50	£825.00
50	Wild Animals of the World	1888	£12.00	£600.00
50	World's Dudes	1889	£16.50	£825.00
50	World's Smokers	1888	£14.00	£700.00
50	World's Sovereigns	1889	£22.00	£1100.00

"SPECIAL ISSUES" (U.S.A. & BRITAIN)

Qty		Date	Odds	Sets
F?150	Actresses, Celebrities & Children, Gold Border	1887	£40.00	—
?25	Actresses, Collotype	1887	£62.50	—
50	Actresses (Group 4, Coloured)	1891	£8.00	—
20	Children, Gold Background, Set 1, (U.S.A.)	1887	£65.00	—
20	(Holborn Viaduct Address)	1887	£130.00	—
50	Children, Gold Background, Set 2, Plain Back	1887	£65.00	—
30	Children, Gold Background, Set 3	1887	£70.00	—
?	Sepia-Litho Series	1887	£50.00	—
9	Women Baseball Players (2 Types)	1887	£65.00	—
?	Woodburytype Series	1887	£62.50	—

PRINTED ALBUMS (EXCHANGED FOR COUPONS)

	Date	Odds	Sets
American Editors	1887	—	£150.00
Birds of America	1888	—	£70.00
Birds of the Tropics	1889	—	£85.00
Celebrated American Indian Chiefs	1888	—	*£250.00*

ALLEN & GINTER (U.S.A.) — cont.

Qty		Date	Odds	Sets
	City Flags	1888	—	£85.00
	Decorations of the Principal Orders	1890	—	£80.00
	Fish from American Waters	1889	—	£80.00
	Flags of All Nations	1890	—	£85.00
	Game Birds	1889	—	£80.00
	General Government and State Capitol Buildings of the United States	1889	—	£75.00
	George Washington	1889	—	£115.00
	Napoleon	1889	—	*£95.00*
	Our Navy	1889	—	£90.00
	Paris Exhibition 1889	1889	—	£90.00
	Quadrupeds	1890	—	*£100.00*
	Racing Colors of the World	1888	—	£150.00
	Song Birds of the World	1890	—	£80.00
	With the Poets in Smokeland	1890	—	£70.00
	World's Beauties, 1st Series	1888	—	*£115.00*
	World's Beauties, 2nd Series	1888	—	*£115.00*
	World's Champions, 1st Series	1888	—	*£400.00*
	World's Champions, 2nd Series	1889	—	*£375.00*
	World's Inventors	1888	—	£100.00
	World's Racers	1888	—	£150.00

AMERICAN CIGARETTE CO. (China)

Qty		Date	Odds	Sets
10	Admirals & Generals	1900	£42.50	£425.00
25	Beauties (Black Back)	1902	£16.50	—
?25	Beauties (Green Back)	1901	£16.00	—
53	Beauties, Playing Card Inset	1901	£42.50	—
?	Chinese Girls	1900	£65.00	—
50	Flowers	1902	£11.00	£550.00

AMERICAN EAGLE TOBACCO CO. (U.S.A.)

Qty		Date	Odds	Sets
?25	Actresses, Blue Frame (Double 5)	1886	£50.00	—
?20	Actresses, Brown Front	1886	£55.00	—
36	Flags of All Nations	1890	£25.00	—
36	Flags of States	1890	£25.00	—
50	Occupations for Women	1892	£42.50	—
F?	Photographic Cards	1886	£5.50	—
LF?	Photographic Cards	1886	£9.00	—
23	Presidents of the U.S	1890	£42.50	—

AMERICAN TOBACCO CO. (U.S.A.)

EARLY ISSUES

Qty		Date	Odds	Sets
F100	Actresses (Black Back)	1901	£2.50	—
F300	Actresses (Blue Back, 2 Types)	1901	£1.75	—
F?	Actresses (Richmond Straight Cut)	1902	£35.00	—
MF?	Actresses (Richmond Straight Cut)	1902	£26.50	—
44	Australian Parliament	1901	£3.25	£143.00
25	Battle Scenes	1901	£9.00	£225.00
177	Beauties (Typeset Back)	1901	£2.25	—
350	Beauties (Old Gold Back)	1901	£2.00	—
101	Beauties (Label Back) (2 Types)	1901	£3.00	—
?500	Beauties (Green Net Back)	1901	£2.00	—
?75	Beauties (Blue Net Back)	1901	£10.00	—
24	Beauties (Plain Back, Carton)	1901	£4.00	£100.00
25	Beauties, Black Background	1900	£8.00	£200.00
25	Beauties, Blue Frame Line	1900	£17.50	—

AMERICAN TOBACCO CO. (U.S.A.) — cont.

Qty		*Date*	*Odds*	*Sets*
25	Beauties, Curtain Background	1900	£7.00	£175.00
28	Beauties, Domino Girls (Blue Net Back)	1895	£17.00	£480.00
28	(Type Set Back)	1895	£16.00	£450.00
25	Beauties, Flower Girls	1900	£7.00	£175.00
25	Beauties, Flowers Inset (Green Back)	1900	£7.00	£175.00
25	(Yellow Back)	1900	£6.00	£150.00
25	Beauties, Fruit Girls	1903	*£30.00*	—
25	Beauties, International Code of Signals			
	1st Series, Green Back	1900	£7.75	—
	1st Series, Yellow Back	1900	£6.00	£150.00
25	Beauties, International Code of Signals			
	2nd Series, Green Back	1900	£7.00	£175.00
	2nd Series, Yellow Back	1900	£6.50	£162.50
50	Beauties, Marine & Universe Girls	1900	*£20.00*	—
25	Beauties, Numbered (Black Front)	1900	£16.00	—
25	(Mauve Front)	1900	£13.00	£325.00
25	Beauties, Orange Framelines	1900	£25.00	—
25	Beauties, Palette Girls (Plain Border)	1900	£7.50	£187.50
25	(Red Border)	1900	*£30.00*	—
F?	Beauties, Photographic	1894	*£12.50*	—
52	Beauties, Playing Card Inset, Set 1	1900	£8.00	—
52	Beauties, Playing Card Inset, Set 2	1900	£7.00	£365.00
	Beauties, Playing Card Superimposed			
52	("52 Subjects")	1900	£7.50	£400.00
53	("53 Subjects")	1900	£7.50	£400.00
25	Beauties, Star Girls (Green Net Back)	1900	£14.00	—
25	(Type Set Back)	1900	£13.00	—
25	Beauties, Star Series	1900	£12.00	—
25	Beauties, Stippled Background	1900	£8.00	£200.00
100	Beauties, Thick Border	1895	£24.00	—
25	Boer War, Series A (Numbered)	1901	£4.00	£100.00
25	(Unnumbered)	1901	£5.00	£125.00
25	(No Series Letter)	1901	£5.75	—
22	Boer War, Series B	1901	£6.00	£132.00
L47	Boer War Celebrities (Kimball)	1901	£25.00	—
L10	Boer War Celebrities "RUTAN"	1901	£27.50	£275.00
50	Butterflies	1895	£17.50	—
32	Celebrities	1900	£5.00	£160.00
25	Chinese Girls	1900	£9.00	—
1	Columbian & Other Postage Stamps	1895	—	£8.00
25	Comic Scenes	1901	£7.50	£187.50
50	Congress of Beauties, World's Fair	1893	£18.00	—
25	Constellation Girls	1894	£23.00	—
25	Dancers	1895	£10.00	—
50	Dancing Women	1895	£15.00	—
50	Fancy Bathers	1895	£15.00	—
25	Fish from American Waters (Green Net)	1900	£6.00	£150.00
50	(Back Listed)	1895	£9.00	—
28	Flags, Dominoes Superimposed (Carton)	1900	£4.50	£125.00
50	Flags of All Nations	1895	£8.00	—
50	Heroes of the Spanish American War (Carton)	1900	£6.00	—
?50	Japanese Girls	1900	£40.00	—
50	Jokes	1906	*£16.00*	—
25	Military Uniforms, A	1894	£12.50	—
25	Military Uniforms, B	1896	£11.00	£275.00

Qty		Date	Odds	Sets
27	Military Uniforms, C (Green Net Back)	1900	£5.00	£135.00
27	(Typeset Back)	1900	£6.50	£175.00
25	Military Uniforms, D	1900	£11.00	£275.00
50	Musical Instruments	1895	£12.00	—
50	National Flags & Arms (Green Net Back)	1895	£8.00	—
50	(Type Set Back)	1895	£8.00	—
25	National Flags & Flower-Girls	1900	£17.50	—
25	Old Ships, 1st Series	1900	£3.50	£87.50
25	Old Ships, 2nd Series	1900	£6.00	£150.00
50	Savage & Semi Barbarous Chiefs & Rulers	1895	£18.00	—
25	Songs A (2 Types)	1900	£9.00	£225.00
25	Songs B	1900	£10.00	£250.00
25	Songs C, 1st Group	1900	£6.00	£150.00
25	Songs C, 2nd Group	1900	£9.00	—
25	Songs D	1900	£6.00	£150.00
27	Songs E	1900	£9.00	£245.00
25	Songs F	1900	£8.50	£212.50
25	Songs G	1900	£7.50	£187.50
25	Songs H	1900	£14.00	£350.00
25	Songs I	1900	£20.00	—
F150	Views	1901	£2.00	—
LATER ISSUES				
L50	Actors	1907	£5.50	—
L50	Actresses "Between The Acts"	1902	£8.00	—
G25	Actresses "Turkish Trophies" (Premiums)	1902	£13.00	£325.00
M85	Actress Series	1904	£5.50	—
L80	Animals	1912	£1.75	£140.00
L25	Arctic Scenes	1916	£3.00	£75.00
53	Art Reproductions	1904	£4.50	—
21	Art Series (Grand Duke)	1902	£12.50	—
P10	Artistic Pictures	1910	£8.50	—
18	Ask Dad	1905	£11.00	—
L50	Assorted Standard Bearers of Different Countries	1910	£4.50	—
M25	Auto-Drivers	1910	£12.50	—
M50	Automobile Series	1908	£11.50	£575.00
L50	Baseball Folders	1907	£17.50	—
M121	Baseball Series (T204)	1907	*£30.00*	—
208	Baseball Series (T205, Gold Border)	1907	£13.50	—
522	Baseball Series (T206, White Border)	1907	£13.00	—
200	Baseball Series (T207, Brown Background)	1911	*£16.00*	—
?578	Baseball Series (T210, Red Borders)	1907	*£16.00*	—
75	Baseball Series (T211, Southern Assocation)	1907	*£17.50*	—
376	Baseball Series (T212, "Obak")	1907	*£17.50*	—
180	Baseball Series (T213, "Coupon")	1907	*£20.00*	—
?90	Baseball Series (T214, Victory Tobacco)	1907	*£50.00*	—
159	Baseball Series (T215, Red Cross)	1907	*£20.00*	—
L76	Baseball Triple Folders	1907	*£30.00*	—
50	Bird Series (Gold Border)	1912	£1.80	£90.00
50	Bird Series (White Border)	1912	£1.80	£90.00
30	Bird Series (Fancy Gold Frame)	1911	£2.25	£67.50
M361	Birthday Horoscopes	1910	£1.75	—
P80	Bridge Favors & Place Cards	1930	£5.00	—
P100	Bridge Game Hands	1930	£7.50	—

Qty		*Date*	*Odds*	*Sets*
M24	British Buildings	1939	£2.25	£54.00
M42	British Sovereigns	1939	£2.25	£95.00
M50	Butterfly Series	1908	£3.25	—
L153	Champion Athlete & Prizefighter Series	1910	£4.75	—
X50	Champion Athlete & Prizefighter Series (Prizefighters Only)	1910	£9.00	—
L50	Champion Pugilists	1910	£16.50	—
X100	Champion Women Swimmers	1906	£6.25	—
M150	College Series	1914	£2.00	£300.00
G25	College Series (Premiums)	1904	£26.00	—
M50	Costumes and Scenery for All Countries of the World	1912	£3.00	£150.00
X49	Cowboy Series	1914	£5.25	£257.50
M?50	Cross Stitch	1906	£8.00	—
L?17	Embarrassing/Emotional Moments	1906	*£13.00*	—
M50	Emblem Series	1908	£2.60	£130.00
L100	Fable Series	1913	£2.25	£225.00
PF?53	Famous Baseball Players, American Athletic Champions & Photoplay Stars	1910	*£30.00*	—
100	Fish Series	1909	£2.00	£200.00
200	Flags of All Nations Series	1909	£1.30	£260.00
L100	Flags of All Nations Series (Red Cross)	1904	*£8.00*	—
50	Foreign Stamp, Series A	1906	£4.75	—
L505	Fortune Series	1907	£1.75	—
G12	Hamilton King Girls (1-12, Sketches)	1902	£16.00	—
G12	Hamilton King Girls (13-24, Girls)	1902	£13.00	£156.00
G12	Hamilton King Girls (25-36, Bathing Girls)	1902	£13.00	£156.00
G25	Hamilton King Girls (37-61, Period Gowns)	1902	£12.00	£300.00
G25	Hamilton King Girls (62-86, Flag Girls)	1902	£12.00	£300.00
G25	Hamilton King Girls (1-25)	1913	£14.00	—
L?3	Helmar Girls	1902	*£35.00*	—
M79	Henry	1937	£2.00	£160.00
X50	Heroes of History	1912	£5.00	£250.00
M50	Historic Homes	1913	£3.20	£160.00
X24/25	Historical Events Series	1911	£5.00	£120.00
M15	Home Art Gallery Pictures	1915	£4.00	£60.00
M25	Hudson-Fulton Series	1908	£5.00	£125.00
45	Imitation Cigar Bands	1909	£2.50	—
L50	Indian Life in the "60's"	1914	£5.25	£262.50
L221	Jig Saw Puzzle Pictures	1910	£5.50	—
L50	Light House Series	1912	£4.00	£200.00
X50	Men of History, 2nd Series	1912	£5.00	£250.00
M100	Military Series (White Border)	1908	£3.7j5	£375.00
50	Military Series (Gold Border)	1908	£4.50	£225.00
50	Military Series (Recruit)	1908	£4.00	£200.00
50	Movie Stars	1915	£4.00	—
L100	Movie Stars	1915	£3.50	—
M25	Moving Pictures (Flip Books)	1910	*£15.00*	—
M33	Moving Picture Stars Series	1915	*£15.00*	—
X50	Murad Post Card Series	1905	£6.50	—
100	Mutt & Jeff Series (Black & White)	1908	£4.00	—
?183	Mutt & Jeff Series (Coloured)	1908	£4.25	—
F16	National League & American League Teams	1910	*£22.50*	—
G126	Prominent Baseball Players & Athletes (Premium)	1911	*£25.00*	—
50	Pugilistic Subjects	1908	*£15.00*	—
X18	Puzzle Picture Series	1904	*£12.50*	—

Qty		Date	Odds	Sets
L200	Riddle Series	1907	£2.25	—
X?60	Royal Bengal Souvenir Cards	1906	£5.50	—
M150	Seals of the United States & Coats of Arms of All Countries of the World	1912	£1.50	£225.00
L25	Series of Champions	1912	£20.00	—
X50	Sights & Scenes of the World	1912	£3.00	£150.00
X50	Silhouettes	1908	£6.00	—
L25	Song Bird Series	1905	*£8.00*	—
50	Sports Champions	1910	*£16.00*	—
45	Stage Stars (Transfers)	1910	*£6.00*	—
M25	State Girl Series	1910	£5.00	—
L50	Theatres Old and New Series	1912	£5.50	—
L?100	The World's Best Short Stories	1910	£11.50	—
L25	The World's Greatest Explorers	1914	£3.50	£87.50
L50	Toast Series (Sultan)	1910	*£6.00*	—
M550	Toast Series (Mogul)	1910	£1.50	—
L25	Toasts	1910	*£9.00*	—
50	Types of Nations Series	1912	£2.20	£110.00
M25	Up To Date Baseball Comics	1908	*£12.50*	—
L26	Up To Date Comics	1908	£6.50	—
250	Up To The Minute War Pictures	1916	£1.40	—
F?500	World Scenes & Portraits	1910	£1.80	—
X50	World's Champion Athletes	1909	£8.50	—

SILK ISSUES

Qty		Date	Odds	Sets
M111	Actresses	1910	£3.25	—
X2	Actresses	1910	*£50.00*	—
L15	Animals	1910	£6.00	—
P250	Athlete and College Seal	1910	£5.50	—
G250	Athlete and College Seal	1910	£6.50	—
M25	Automobile Pennants	1910	*£45.00*	—
M?100	Baseball – Actress Series	1910	£5.50	—
M125	Baseball Players	1910	*£15.00*	—
G25	Baseball Players	1910	*£24.00*	—
M25	Bathing Beach Girls	1910	£8.00	£200.00
G6	Bathing Girls	1910	£12.50	£75.00
T50	Birds, Set 1	1910	£4.50	—
M26	Birds, Set 2	1910	£4.50	—
L26	Birds, Set 2	1910	£4.75	—
M30	Birds, Set 3	1910	£4.50	—
L20	Birds in Flight	1910	£5.50	£110.00
L25	Breeds of Dogs	1910	£9.00	£225.00
L10	Breeds of Fowls	1910	£9.00	£90.00
P6	Butterflies	1910	£12.00	£72.00
L25	Butterflies & Moths, Set 1	1910	£4.50	—
L50	Butterflies & Moths, Set 2	1910	£3.50	—
L25	Butterflies & Moths, Set 3	1910	£3.50	—
M77	City Seals	1910	£3.50	—
G50	College Flag, Seal, Song, Yell	1910	£7.50	—
T44	College Pennants	1910	*£5.00*	—
M144	College Seals	1910	£2.00	—
G?13	College Yells	1910	*£12.50*	—
L10	Comics	1910	£8.00	—
M25	Domestic Animals' Heads	1910	£6.00	£150.00
G6	Domestic Animals' Heads	1910	£12.50	£75.00

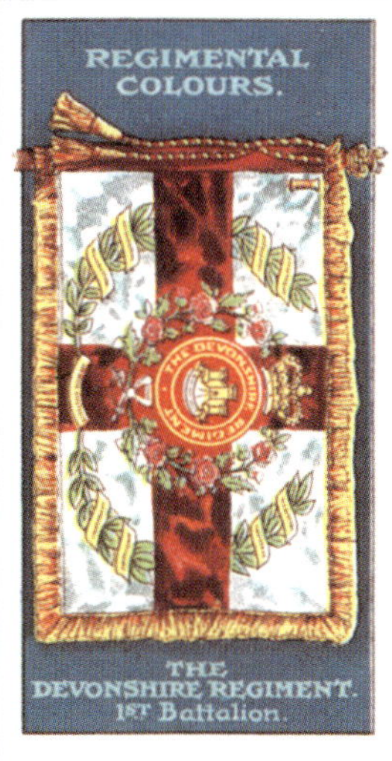

Regimental Colours & Standards
Gallaher. Also reprint

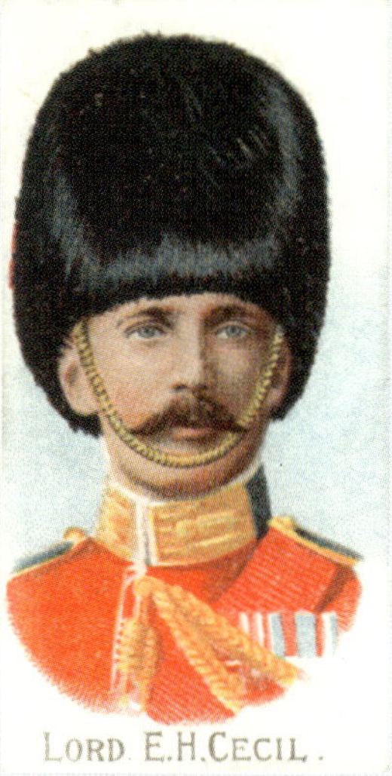

Celebrities, Coloured
Cohen Weenen

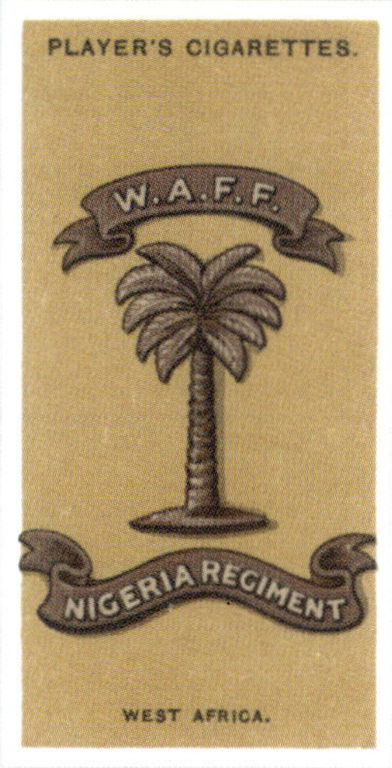

Colonial & Indian Army Badges
Player

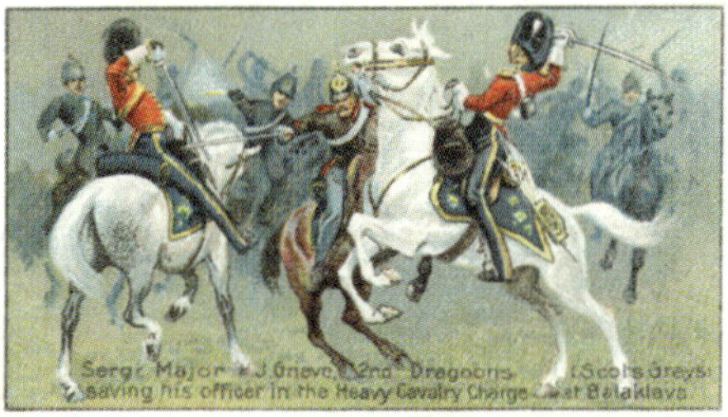

Heroic Deeds
B.A.T., Wills (Scissors)

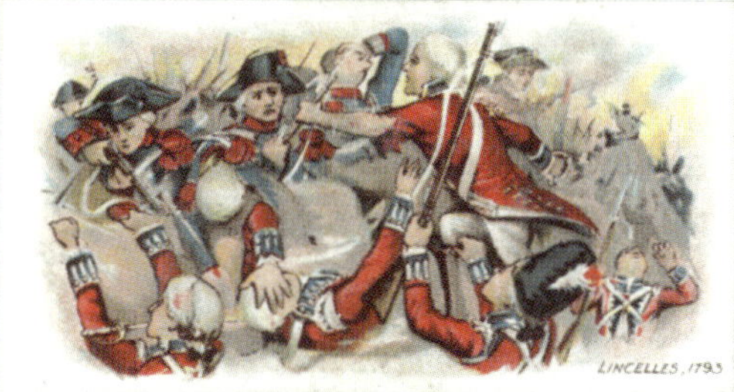

Our Gallant Grenadiers
Faulkner, Wills

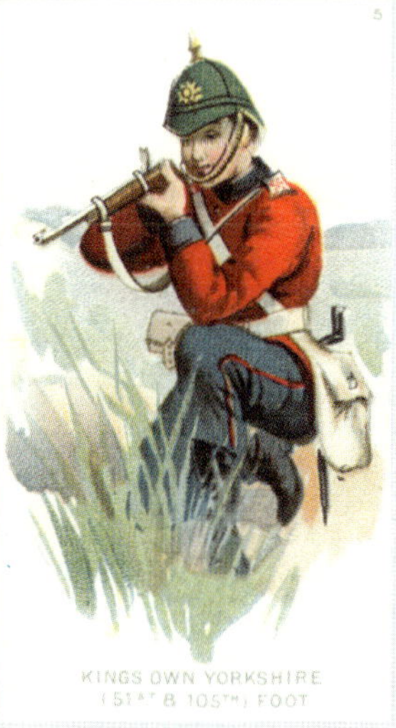

Military Uniforms
American Tobacco Co.

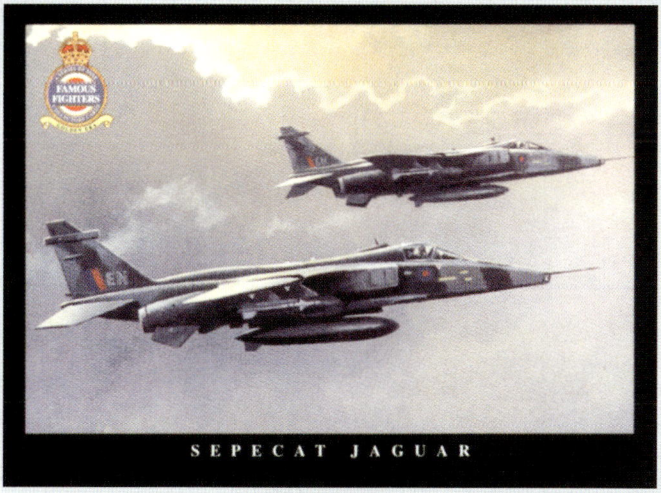

Famous Fighters
Golden Era

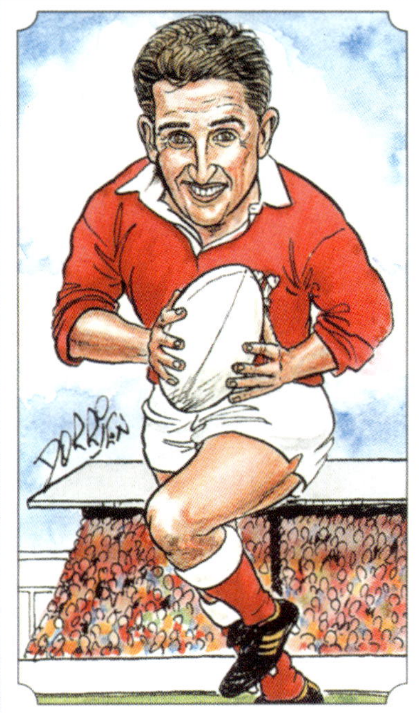

World Cup Heroes – Wales on Sunday

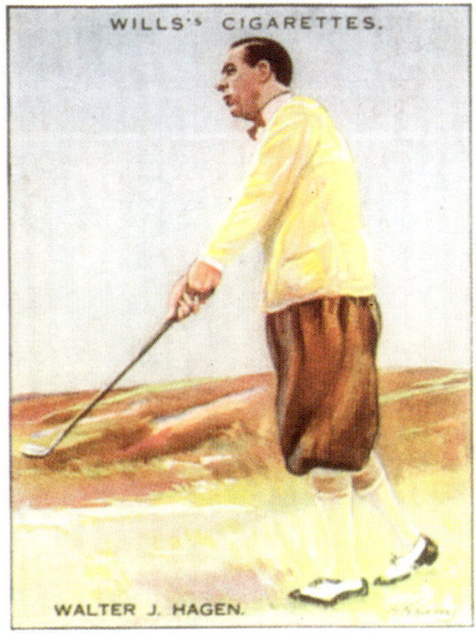

Famous Golfers – Wills. Also reprint

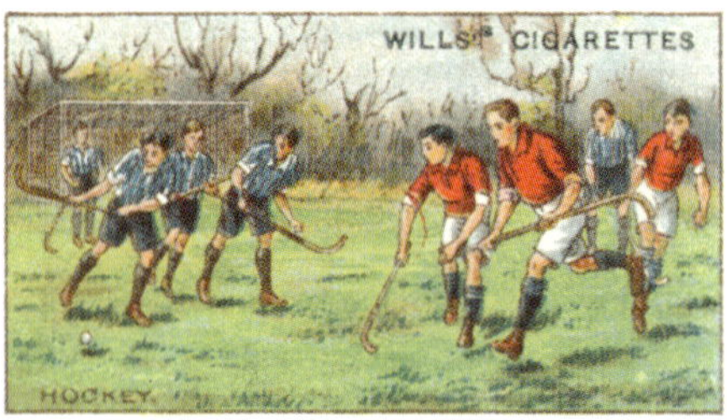

Sports of the World – Wills (Australian). Also B.A.T.

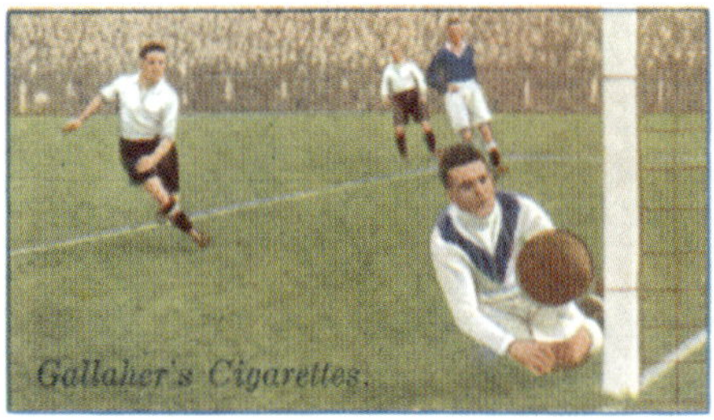

Footballers – Gallaher

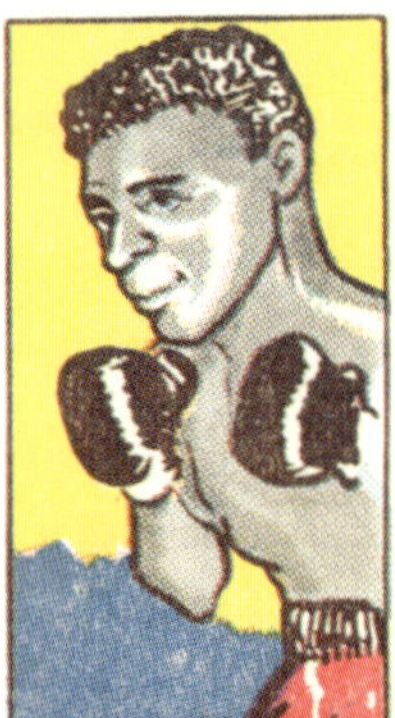

International Sporting Stars – Clevedon

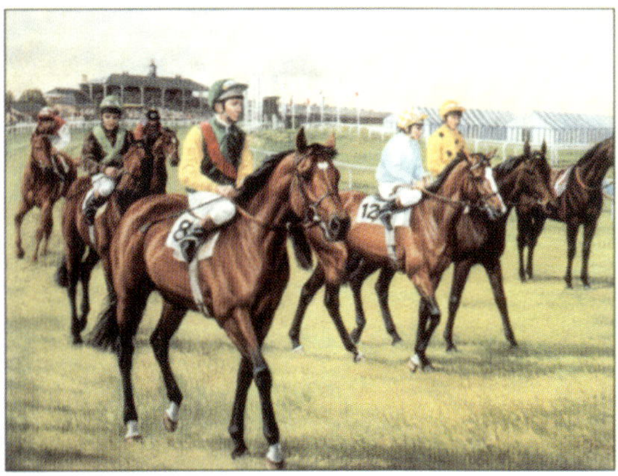

Racehorses & Jockeys – Field Galleries

AMERICAN TOBACCO CO. (U.S.A.) — cont.

Qty		Date	Odds	Sets
M50	Emblem Series	1910	£4.00	—
L15	Famous Queens	1910	£8.00	£120.00
L11	Feminine Types	1910	£7.50	£82.50
D322	Flags & Arms (Woven)	1910	£2.00	—
P24	Flag Girls of All Nations	1910	£7.50	£180.00
G24	Flag Girls of All Nations	1910	£9.00	—
X50	Flowers, Set 1	1910	£5.00	—
M25	Flowers, Set 2	1910	£4.25	—
L50	Flowers, Set 2	1910	£5.25	—
L54	Flowers, Set 3	1910	£5.00	—
M?	Foreign Postage Stamps	1910	*£25.00*	—
L10	Fruits	1910	£5.50	£55.00
G5	Generals	1910	*£65.00*	—
M10	Girls (Portrait in Circle)	1910	*£20.00*	—
L10	Girls (Portrait in Circle)	1910	£35.00	—
G10	Girls (Portrait in Circle)	1910	*£45.00*	—
G?50	Hatbands	1910	£11.00	—
M50	Indian Portraits	1910	£6.50	£325.00
G6	Indian Portraits	1910	£17.50	—
L25	Indian Portraits & Scenes	1910	£7.50	—
P10	Indian Portraits & Scenes	1910	£13.00	—
G12	King Girls	1910	£10.00	£120.00
G20	Kink Series	1910	*£40.00*	—
M51	Military & Lodge Medals	1910	£3.50	£175.00
L?7	Miniature National Flags	1910	*£20.00*	—
L10	Mottoes & Quotations	1910	£6.25	£62.50
L25	National Arms (Silko)	1910	£3.00	£75.00
M42	National Arms (Woven)	1910	£3.00	£126.00
L154	National Flags	1910	£1.60	—
T?	National Flags	1910	*£5.00*	—
G?150	National Flags (Many Styles)	1910	£2.75	—
L25	National Flags & Arms	1910	£2.25	—
X40	National Flags & Arms	1910	£2.25	—
P53	National Flags & Arms (Many Styles)	1910	£2.50	—
X27	National Flag, Song & Flower	1910	£4.50	—
P21	National Flag, Song & Flower	1910	£5.00	—
G17	National Flag, Song & Flower	1910	£6.00	—
E5	National Flag, Song & Flower	1910	*£7.00*	—
M50	Orders & Military Medals	1910	£5.50	—
M24	Presidents of U.S.	1910	£7.00	—
P24	Ruler with National Arms	1910	£11.00	—
P10	Rulers of the Balkans & Italy	1910	£12.50	£125.00
L120	Silk National Flags	1910	£1.50	—
M36	State Flags	1910	£3.50	—
M?11	State Flowers (80 x 45mm)	1910	*£7.25*	—
M25	State Flowers (Different, 80 x 47mm)	1910	£5.50	—
L25	State Girl & Flower	1910	£6.00	—
M50	State Maps & Maps of Territories	1910	£6.00	—
M48	State Seals	1910	£3.25	—
X?75	Twelfth Night Miscellany	1910	£8.00	—
M25	Women of Ancient Egypt	1910	£9.00	£225.00
L10	Zira Girls	1910	£8.00	£80.00

BLANKET ISSUES

Qty		Date	Odds	Sets
P?	Animal Pelts	1908	£7.50	—

AMERICAN TOBACCO CO. (U.S.A.) — cont.

Qty		Date	Odds	Sets
G90	Baseball Players	1908	*£17.50*	—
P?	Butterflies	1908	£5.00	—
G?	Butterflies	1908	£5.00	—
P135	College Athlete, Pennant, Seals	1908	£6.00	—
G10	College Pennants	1908	*£6.00*	—
G53	College Seals	1908	£3.00	—
X?	Conventional Rug Designs	1908	£3.50	—
P?	Conventional Rug Designs	1908	£4.00	—
G?	Conventional Rug Designs	1908	£5.00	—
X5	Domestic Pets	1908	£6.50	—
P?	Miniature Indian Blankets	1908	£7.50	—
G?	Miniature Indian Blankets	1908	£7.50	—
E6	National Arms	1908	£5.00	—
P45	National Flags	1908	£3.00	—
G71	National Flags	1908	£3.00	—
E31	National Flags	1908	£3.50	—
G?	National Flags and Arms	1908	£4.00	—
X9	Nursery Rhymes	1908	*£8.00*	—
X13	Soldiers	1908	£12.50	—

LEATHER ISSUES

Qty		Date	Odds	Sets
M15	Breeds of Dogs	1908	£7.00	—
X97	College Building, Shield, etc.	1908	£3.00	—
P19	College Buildings	1908	£3.25	—
M14	College Fraternity Seals	1908	*£6.50*	—
M166	College Pennants	1908	£1.30	—
M117	(Shaped)	1908	£1.75	—
X23	College Pennant, Yell, Emblem	1908	£3.75	—
M147	College Seals	1908	£1.25	—
M139	(Shaped)	1908	£1.75	—
M53	(Card Suit Shaped)	1908	£2.75	—
M20	Comic Designs	1908	£3.50	—
M24	Flowers	1908	£4.00	—
M10	Girls	1908	£5.50	—
M26	Girls (Alphabet Background)	1908	£6.50	—
M95	Mottoes & Quotations	1908	£2.75	—
M97	Movie Film Personalities	1908	£8.00	—
M22	National Flags	1908	*£3.25*	—
M48	Nursery Rhymes Illustrated	1908	£4.50	—
M56	State Seals	1908	£1.25	—
M18	(Pennant Shaped)	1908	£1.75	—

CELLULOID BUTTONS & PINS

Qty		Date	Odds	Sets
K245	Actresses	1901	£2.75	—
K152	Baseball Players	1901	*£12.00*	—
K8	Boer War Leaders	1901	£65.00	—
K362	Comic Pictures	1901	£3.25	—
K425	Comic Sayings	1901	£3.00	—
K14	Cricketers	1901	£125.00	—
K125	Flags	1901	£2.25	—
K48	Girls' Heads	1901	*£6.00*	—
K25	Jockeys	1901	*£17.50*	—
K48	State Arms	1901	£2.50	£120.00
K187	Yellow Kid Designs	1901	*£7.50*	—

A.T.C. OF NEW SOUTH WALES (Australia)

Qty		*Date*	*Odds*	*Sets*
25	Beauties, Group 1	1902	£9.00	£225.00
25	Beauties, Group 2	1902	£10.00	£250.00

A.T.C. OF VICTORIA LTD. (Australia)

100	Beauties	1902	£10.00	—

ANONYMOUS ISSUES (Cigar Bands)

48	Famous Buildings and Monuments	1976	—	£10.00
48	Great Inventions	1975	—	£7.00

THE ASHEVILLE TOBACCO WORKS CO. U.S.A.

?39	Actresses "ASVERI"	1890	£42.50	—

ATLAM CIGARETTE FACTORY (Malta)

150	Beauties	1924	*£4.00*	—
M65	Beauties	1924	£2.50	—
M519	Celebrities	1924	£1.00	£500.00
L50	Views of Malta	1924	*£5.00*	—
M128	Views of the World	1924	*£4.00*	—

BANNER TOBACCO CO. (U.S.A.)

X?25	Actors & Actresses	1890	£50.00	—
X25	Beauties	1890	£25.00	—

AUG. BECK & CO. (U.S.A.)

24	Actors & Actresses	1885	*£50.00*	—
?51	Beauties-Burdick 488	1888	£50.00	—
25	National Dances	1889	*£50.00*	—
F?	Photographic Cards	1886	£6.00	—
?34	Picture Cards	1893	£50.00	—
24	Presidents of the U.S.A.	1890	£50.00	—
?10	State Seals	1887	*£60.00*	—

DE BEER & CO. (Australia)

20	Admirals & Warships of the U.S.A.	1908	£40.00	—
?14	Caricatures of Cyclists	1908	*£60.00*	—

BOOKER TOBACCO CO. (U.S.A.)

35	Indian Series	1906	£32.50	£1150.00
?20	U.S. Battleships	1906	£32.50	—

NICOLA BOSIOS (Malta)

?83	Opera Singers	1920	£32.50	—

BRITISH AMERICAN TOBACCO CO. LTD. (B.A.T.)

336 Page Illustrated Tobacco War & B.A.T. Book — £12.50

Qty		Date	Odds	Sets
(1) SERIES WITH FIRM'S NAME				
30	Actrices	1905	*£5.50*	—
48	A Famous Picture Series, The Toast (Sect.)	1931	*£2.50*	—
MF50	Beauties	1925	£1.75	—
MF40	Beauties	1925	£1.75	—
25	Beauties, Art Series	1903	£10.00	—
25	Beauties, Black Background	1903	£8.50	—
25	Beauties, Blossom Girls	1903	£35.00	—
25	Beauties, Flower Girls	1903	£6.50	£162.50
25	Beauties, Fruit Girls	1903	£11.00	£275.00
25	Beauties, Girls in Costumes	1903	£10.00	£250.00
20	Beauties, Group 1	1903	£7.25	£145.00
25	Beauties, Lantern Girls	1903	£6.50	£162.50
50	Beauties, Marine & Universe Girls	1903	£8.50	£425.00
25	Beauties, Numbered	1903	£16.00	—
25	Beauties, Palette Girls (Plain Border)	1903	£8.00	£200.00
25	(Red Border)	1903	£11.50	—
53	Beauties, Playing Card Superimposed	1903	£6.50	£345.00
24	Beauties, Smoke Girls	1903	£13.00	£312.00
25	Beauties, Star Girls	1903	£13.00	—
25	Beauties, Stippled Background	1903	£6.50	£162.50
25	Beauties, Water Girls	1903	£6.50	£162.50
32	Beauties of Old China	1933	£2.50	—
M50	Birds, Beasts & Fishes	1934	£1.70	—
50	Buildings	1905	£8.00	—
25	Chinese Girls "A"	1904	£8.00	—
25	Chinese Girls "B" (Silver Borders)	1904	£8.50	—
25	Chinese Girls "C" (Sky Background)	1904	£8.50	£212.50
25	Chinese Girls "D"	1904	£8.00	—
25	Chinese Girls "E"	1904	£8.50	—
25	Chinese Girls "F1"	1904	£8.00	£200.00
25	Chinese Girls "F2"	1904	£8.00	£200.00
50	Chinese Girls "F3"	1904	£8.50	—
40	Chinese Trades	1904	£5.50	£220.00
50	Danish Athletes	1905	£10.00	£500.00
28	Dominoes	1905	£5.50	—
48	Fairy Tales	1928	*£3.00*	—
25	New York Views	1908	£8.50	—
53	Playing Cards	1908	£8.50	—
M50	Wild Animals	1930	£1.35	—
(2) SERIES WITH BRAND NAMES				
(A)	**Albert Cigarettes (Belgium Etc.)**			
L50	Aeroplanes (Civils)	1935	*£4.00*	—
50	Artistes de Cinéma (1-50)	1932	*£2.00*	—
50	Artistes de Cinéma (51-100)	1933	£1.75	—
50	Artistes de Cinéma (101-150)	1934	*£2.00*	—
MF72	Beauties	1928	£2.75	—
M75	Belles Vues de Belgique	1928	£2.40	£180.00
M50	Birds, Beasts & Fishes	1934	£3.00	—
M50	Butterflies (Girls)	1926	£4.50	—
M50	Cinema Stars, Set 1 (Brown)	1927	£2.25	—
M100	Cinema Stars, Set 2	1928	£2.00	—
M208	Cinema Stars, Set 3 (Unnumbered)	1928	£2.00	—

BRITISH AMERICAN TOBACCO CO. LTD. (B.A.T.) — cont.

Qty		Date	Odds	Sets
M100	Circus Scenes	1930	*£2.50*	—
M100	Famous Beauties	1916	*£3.00*	—
M100	La Faune Congolaise	1934	£1.25	—
M50	L'Afrique Equatoriale de L'Est à L'Ouest	1932	£2.40	—
M50	Les Grands Paquebots du Monde	1924	£5.00	—
M50	Merveilles du Monde	1927	£3.00	—
M50	Women of Nations	1922	£3.50	—
(B)	**Atlas Cigarettes (China)**			
50	Buildings	1907	*£5.00*	—
25	Chinese Beauties	1912	£2.25	—
50	Chinese Trades, Set 4	1912	£2.25	—
85	Chinese Trades, Set 6	1912	£2.40	—
(C)	**Battle Ax Cigarettes**			
M100	Famous Beauties	1916	£3.75	—
M50	Women of Nations	1922	£4.25	—
(D)	**Cameo Cigarettes (Australia)**			
50	Horses of To-Day	1906	*£8.00*	—
(E)	**Copain Cigarettes (Belgium)**			
52	Birds of Brilliant Plumage (P/C Inset)	1927	£5.00	—
(F)	**Domino Cigarettes (Mauritius)**			
25	Animaux et Reptiles	1961	—	£2.50
25	Coursaires et Boucaniers	1961	—	£2.50
25	Figures Historiques, Une Serie	1961	—	£2.50
25	Figures Historiques, Seconde Serie	1961	—	£12.50
25	Fleurs de Culture	1961	—	£2.50
25	Les Oiseaux et L'Art Japonais	1961	—	£16.00
25	Les Produits du Monde	1961	—	£2.50
50	Voitures Antiques	1961	—	£55.00
(G)	**Eagle Bird Cigarettes (China & Siam)**			
50	Animals & Birds	1909	£1.80	£90.00
50	Aviation Series	1912	£2.75	—
25	Birds of the East	1912	£1.75	—
25	China's Famous Warriors	1911	£2.50	—
25	Chinese Beauties, 1st Series (2 Types)	1908	£2.50	—
25	Chinese Beauties, 2nd Series (2 Types)	1909	£1.65	—
50	Chinese Trades	1908	£1.60	—
25	Cock Fighting	1911	£5.00	—
60	Flags & Pennons	1926	£1.20	£72.00
50	Romance of the Heavens	1929	£1.50	£75.00
50	Siamese Alphabet (2 Types)	1922	£1.20	£60.00
50	Siamese Dreams & Their Meaning	1923	£1.00	£50.00
50	Siamese Horoscopes	1916	£1.00	£50.00
50	Siamese Play – Inao	1916	£1.30	—
50	Siamese Play – Khun Chang Khun Phaen 1	1917	£1.20	£60.00
50	Siamese Play – Khun Chang Khun Phaen 2	1917	£1.20	£60.00
36	Siamese Play – Phra Aphai, 1st	1918	£1.25	£45.00
36	Siamese Play – Phra Aphai, 2nd	1919	£1.25	£45.00
150	Siamese Play – Ramakien I	1913	£1.00	—
50	Siamese Play – Ramakien II	1914	£1.30	—
50	Siamese Uniforms	1915	£1.70	£85.00
50	Views of Bangkok	1928	£2.00	—
50	Views of Siam (2 Types)	1928	£2.00	—
30	War Weapons	1914	£1.65	£50.00

BRITISH AMERICAN TOBACCO CO. LTD. (B.A.T.) — cont.

Qty		Date	Odds	Sets
(H)	**Gold Dollar Cigarettes (Germany)**			
M270	Auf Deutscher Scholle	1934	£1.50	—
M270	Der Weltkrieg (1914)	1933	£1.50	—
M270	Deutsche Kolonien	1931	£1.50	—
M270	Die Deutsche Wehrmacht	1935	£1.50	—
?50	Do You Know?	1928	£4.50	—
M100	Filmbilder	1935	£1.00	£100.00
M100	In Prarie Und Urwald	1930	£1.00	£100.00
100	Wild-West	1932	£1.30	—
(I)	**Kong Beng Cigarettes (China)**			
50	Animals	1912	£4.50	—
(J)	**Mascot Cigarettes (Germany)**			
100	Cinema Stars	1931	£2.60	—
M208	Cinema Stars	1924	£2.20	—
(K)	**Motor Cigarettes (Denmark)**			
50	Aviation Series (3 Printings)	1911	£7.50	—
50	Butterflies & Moths	1911	*£4.00*	—
50	Flag Girls of All Nations	1908	£7.00	—
50	Girls of All Nations	1908	£7.50	—
(L)	**Old Judge Cigarettes (Australia)**			
50	Horses of To Day	1906	*£8.00*	—
FS270	Views of the World	1908	*£7.00*	—
(M)	**Pedro Cigarettes (India)**			
50	Actors & Actresses	1906	*£3.00*	—
37	Nautch Girls (Red Border, 3 Types)	1905	£2.00	—
40	(Coloured)	1905	£2.00	—
52	(P/C Inset)	1905	£2.25	—
(N)	**Pinhead Cigarettes (China)**			
50	Chinese Modern Beauties	1912	£1.50	—
33	Chinese Heroes, Set 1	1912	£1.75	—
50	Chinese Heroes, Set 2	1913	£1.75	—
50	Chinese Trades, Set III (2 Types)	1908	£1.50	—
50	Chinese Trades, Set IV	1909	£1.50	—
50	Chinese Trades, Set V	1910	£1.50	—
50	Types of the British Army	1909	*£3.00*	—
(O)	**Railway Cigarettes (India)**			
37	Nautch Girl Series (2 Types)	1907	£2.00	£74.00
(P)	**Shantung Cigarettes (China)**			
50	Chinese Curios	1928	£5.00	—
(Q)	**Sunflower Cigarettes (China)**			
50	Chinese Trades	1906	£4.50	—
(R)	**Teal Cigarettes (Siam)**			
30	Chinese Beauties	1917	*£3.25*	—
50	Cinema Stars (Blue Back)	1930	£1.50	£75.00
50	(Red Back)	1930	£1.50	£75.00
30	Fish Series	1916	£1.75	£52.50
L15	Fish Series (Double Cards)	1916	£4.00	—
50	War Incidents	1916	£1.80	£90.00
(S)	**Tiger Cigarettes (India)**			
52	Nautch Girl Series (P/C Inset, 4 Types)	1911	£1.60	—
(T)	**Vanity Fair Cigarettes (Australia)**			
50	Horses of To Day	1906	*£8.00*	—

Qty		Date	Odds	Sets
(3) SERIES WITH PRINTED BACK, NO MAKER'S NAME OR BRAND				
(See also Imperial Tobacco Co. (Canada), United Tobacco Co.)				
250	Actresses "ALWICS" (Design Back)	1906	£2.50	—
50	Aeroplanes (Gilt Border)	1926	£1.80	£90.00
50	Aeroplanes of Today	1936	80p	£40.00
25	Angling	1930	£3.50	£82.50
25	Animaux Préhistoriques	1925	*£4.00*	—
L25	Arabic Proverbs (Silk)	1913	£11.50	—
50	Arms & Armour	1910	£3.50	—
L50	Arms of the British Empire (Silk, Blue Back)	1911	£2.50	£125.00
L50	(Silk, Brown Back)	1911	£4.00	—
25	Army Life	1908	£5.00	—
50	Art Photogravures	1912	85p	—
L50	Australian Wild Flowers (Silk)	1913	£3.00	£150.00
22	Automobielen	1923	*£6.00*	—
75	Aviation	1910	£2.75	—
50	Aviation Series	1911	£2.75	—
50	Beauties, Red Tinted (Design Back)	1906	£2.00	—
52	Beauties, Tobacco Leaf Back (P/C Inset)	1908	£2.50	£130.00
52	(No Inset)	1908	£3.50	—
F50	Beauties	1925	£1.30	—
MF50	Beauties (Hand Coloured)	1925	£1.50	—
F50	Beauties, 2nd Series	1926	£1.50	—
F50	Beauties, 3rd Series	1926	£1.30	£65.00
F50	Beauties of Great Britain	1930	60p	£30.00
F50	Beautiful England	1928	40p	£20.00
M?28	Belgian Footballers	1913	£6.50	—
50	Best Dogs of Their Breed	1913	£3.50	£175.00
L50	Best Dogs of Their Breed (Silk)	1913	£5.50	£275.00
50	Billiards	1929	£1.30	£65.00
50	Birds, Beasts and Fishes	1937	50p	£25.00
M50	Birds, Beasts & Fishes	1937	£1.10	£55.00
24	Birds of England	1924	£2.00	£50.00
50	Boy Scouts	1930	£1.70	£85.00
50	Britain's Defenders (Blue Front)	1914	£1.60	—
50	Britain's Defenders (Mauve Front)	1914	£1.30	£65.00
50	British Butterflies	1930	90p	£45.00
50	British Empire Series	1913	£2.25	—
25	British Trees & Their Uses	1930	£1.60	£40.00
50	British Warships and Admirals	1915	£2.50	£125.00
50	Butterflies & Moths	1911	£1.75	£87.50
50	Butterflies (Girls)	1928	£4.50	£225.00
M50	Butterflies (Girls)	1928	£5.00	£250.00
M50	Celebrities of Film and Stage (2 Types)	1930	£1.25	—
LF48	Channel Islands, Past & Present (2 Types)	1939	25p	£12.50
40	Characters from the Works of Dickens	1919	—	£44.00
38/40	Characters from the Works of Dickens	1919	60p	£24.00
50	Cinema Artistes (Black & White 1-50)	1928	£1.20	£60.00
50	Cinema Artistes (Black & White 101-150)	1930	£1.20	£60.00
60	Cinema Artistes, Set 1 (Brown, 2 Types)	1929	£1.20	—
50	Cinema Artistes, Set 2 (Brown, 2 Types)	1931	£1.20	£60.00
M48	Cinema Artistes, Set 3	1932	£1.40	—
48	Cinema Celebrities (C)	1935	80p	£40.00
L48	Cinema Celebrities (C)	1935	£1.00	£48.00
L56	Cinema Celebrities (D)	1937	£2.40	—

BRITISH AMERICAN TOBACCO CO. LTD. (B.A.T.) — cont.

Qty		*Date*	*Odds*	*Sets*
50	Cinema Favourites	1929	£2.00	£100.00
50	Cinema Stars, Set 2 (1-50)	1928	90p	—
50	Cinema Stars, Set 3 (51-100)	1930	£1.00	—
50	Cinema Stars, Set 4 (101-150)	1932	90p	—
100	Cinema Stars (Coloured)	1931	£1.50	—
F50	Cinema Stars, Set 1	1924	£1.00	£50.00
F50	Cinema Stars, Set 2	1924	85p	£42.50
F50	Cinema Stars, Set 3	1925	£1.00	£50.00
MF52	Cinema Stars, Set 4	1925	£1.40	£73.00
MF52	Cinema Stars, Set 5	1926	£1.40	£73.00
MF52	Cinema Stars, Set 6	1927	£1.50	—
LF48	Cinema Stars, Set 7	1927	£2.00	—
F50	Cinema Stars, Set 8	1928	£1.00	£50.00
F50	Cinema Stars, Set 9 (51-100)	1929	£1.00	—
F50	Cinema Stars, Set 10 (101-150)	1930	£1.00	—
F50	Cinema Stars, Set 11 (151-200)	1931	£1.00	—
110	Crests & Badges of the British Army (Silk)	1915	£2.50	—
M108	Crests & Badges of the British Army (Silk)	1915	£2.00	—
M50	Crests and Colours of Australian Universities, Colleges & Schools (Silk)	1916	£2.25	—
25	Derby Day Series A	1914	£7.50	—
50	Do You Know?	1930	30p	£15.00
50	Do You Know?, 2nd Series	1931	30p	£15.00
25	Dracones Posthistorici	1931	£5.50	—
?28	Dutch Footballers	1913	£6.50	—
25	Dutch Scenes	1928	£2.00	£50.00
50	Engineering Wonders (2 Types)	1929	40p	£20.00
40	English Costumes of Ten Centuries	1919	£1.25	£50.00
F25	English Cricketers	1926	£2.50	£62.50
26	Etchings (of Dogs)	1926	£2.00	£52.00
F50	Famous Bridges	1935	60p	£30.00
50	Famous Footballers, Set 1	1923	£2.50	£125.00
50	Famous Footballers, Set 2	1924	£2.50	£125.00
50	Famous Footballers, Set 3	1925	£2.50	£125.00
25	Famous Racehorses	1926	£2.40	£60.00
25	Famous Railway Trains	1929	£1.80	£45.00
50	Favourite Flowers	1923	60p	£30.00
50	Film and Stage Favourites	1926	£1.40	£70.00
75	Film Favourites	1928	£1.20	£90.00
50	Flags of the Empire	1928	70p	£35.00
50	Foreign Birds	1930	60p	£30.00
50	Game Birds and Wild Fowl	1929	£1.30	£65.00
LF45	Grace and Beauty (1-45)	1938	30p	£13.50
LF45	Grace and Beauty (46-90)	1939	20p	£9.00
LF48	Guernsey, Alderney & Sark	1937	25p	£12.00
LF48	Guernsey, Alderney & Sark (Second Series)	1938	25p	£12.00
L80	Guernsey Footballers, Priaulx League	1938	35p	£28.00
F52	Here There & Everywhere	1929	25p	£12.50
25	Hints & Tips for Motorists	1929	£2.20	—
48	Hints on Association Football (Chinese)	1934	20p	£7.00
F50	Homeland Events	1928	50p	£35.00
50	Horses of To Day	1906	£4.25	—
32	Houses of Parliament (Red Back)	1912	£1.60	£50.00
32	(Brown Back with Verse)	1912	*£8.00*	—
50	Indian Chiefs	1930	£7.00	£350.00

BRITISH AMERICAN TOBACCO CO. LTD. (B.A.T.) — cont.

Qty		*Date*	*Odds*	*Sets*
50	Indian Regiments Series	1912	£7.50	—
50	International Air Liners	1937	65p	£32.50
25	Java Scenes	1929	*£7.50*	—
LF48	Jersey Then & Now	1935	50p	£24.00
LF48	Jersey Then & Now, Second Series	1937	25p	£12.00
50	Jiu-Jitsu Series	1911	£2.50	£75.00
?96	Joueurs de Football Belges	1923	£6.00	—
50	Keep Fit	1939	80p	£40.00
M54	La Belgique Monumentale & Pittoresque	1926	£2.75	—
50	Leaders of Men	1929	£2.20	—
50	Life in the Tree Tops	1931	40p	£20.00
50	Lighthouses	1926	£1.20	£60.00
40	London Ceremonials	1929	£1.25	£50.00
F50	London Zoo	1927	60p	£30.00
50	Lucky Charms	1930	£1.40	£70.00
25	Marvels of the Universe Series	1925	£2.20	£55.00
45	Melbourne Cup Winners	1906	£4.60	£207.00
50	Merchant Ships of the World	1925	£3.50	—
25	Merchant Ships of the World	1925	£3.00	£75.00
25	Military Portraits	1917	£2.40	£60.00
LF36	Modern Beauties	1939	£1.25	£45.00
XF36	Modern Beauties	1936	£1.00	£36.00
36	Modern Beauties, First Series	1938	75p	£27.00
MF54	Modern Beauties	1937	85p	£45.00
36	Modern Beauties, Second Series	1938	50p	£18.00
MF54	Modern Beauties, Second Series	1938	85p	£45.00
XF36	Modern Beauties, Second Series	1936	70p	£25.00
MF36	Modern Beauties, Third Series	1938	£1.25	£45.00
XF36	Modern Beauties, Third Series	1937	75p	£27.00
MF36	Modern Beauties, Fourth Series	1939	85p	£31.00
XF36	Modern Beauties, Fourth Series	1937	£1.25	£45.00
XF36	Modern Beauties, Fifth Series	1938	85p	£30.00
XF36	Modern Beauties, Sixth Series	1938	75p	£27.00
XF36	Modern Beauties, Seventh Series	1938	£1.00	£36.00
LF36	Modern Beauties, Eighth Series	1939	£1.25	£45.00
LF36	Modern Beauties, Ninth Series	1939	£1.25	£45.00
50	Modern Warfare	1936	70p	£35.00
M48	Modern Wonders	1938	£1.60	—
25	Modes of Conveyance	1928	£1.60	£40.00
48	Motor Cars (Coloured)	1926	£3.00	£144.00
36	Motor Cars (Brown)	1929	£4.00	—
50	Motor Cycles	1927	£3.00	£150.00
FS50	Native Life in Many Lands (Stereo)	1932	75p	—
F50	Natural and Man Made Wonders of World	1937	50p	£25.00
FS50	Nature Studies	1928	50p	£25.00
50	Naval Portraits	1917	£2.00	£100.00
32	Nederlandsche Leger (Dutch Army)	1923	£4.00	£130.00
25	Notabilities	1917	£2.20	£55.00
25	Past & Present	1929	£1.60	£40.00
FS48	Pictures of the East	1930	£1.25	£60.00
M48	Picturesque China	1925	£1.00	£50.00
M53	Playing Cards	1940	20p	£6.00
36	Popular Stage, Cinema & Society Celebrities	1928	£2.50	—
25	Prehistoric Animals	1931	£2.40	£60.00
50	Prominent Australian and English Cricketers	1911	£32.50	—
25	Puzzle Series	1916	£4.00	£100.00

BRITISH AMERICAN TOBACCO CO. LTD. (B.A.T.) — cont.

Qty		Date	Odds	Sets
50	Railway Working	1927	£1.30	£65.00
33	Regimental Pets	1911	£5.00	—
50	Regimental Uniforms	1936	£1.25	£62.50
50	Romance of the Heavens (2 Types)	1929	60p	£30.00
FS50	Round the World in Pictures	1931	75p	£37.50
50	Royal Mail	1912	£3.00	—
27	Rulers of the World	1911	£6.00	—
40	Safety First	1931	75p	£30.00
25	Ships Flags & Cap Badges, A Series	1930	£2.00	£50.00
25	Ships Flags & Cap Badges, 2nd Series	1930	£2.00	£50.00
F50	Ships and Shipping	1928	70p	£35.00
50	Signalling Series	1913	£2.20	—
100	Soldiers of the World (Tobacco Leaf Back)	1902	£9.00	£900.00
50	Speed	1938	60p	£30.00
25	Sports & Games in Many Lands	1930	£3.50	£110.00
50	Stage & Film Stars	1926	£1.25	—
M50	Stars of Filmland	1927	£1.80	—
F50	The Royal Navy	1930	£1.60	—
F50	The World of Sport	1927	£1.70	£85.00
100	Transfers, Set 1	1930	£2.40	—
100	Transfers, Set 2	1930	£2.40	—
32	Transport of the World	1911	*£7.00*	—
20	Types of North American Indians	1930	£10.00	£200.00
F50	Types of the World	1936	60p	£30.00
F52	Ur Ollum Attum	1930	£3.00	—
FS270	Views of the World	1908	*£2.75*	—
48	Volaille, Pigeons & Chiens	1915	*£6.00*	—
50	War Incidents (Blue Black)	1915	£1.30	£65.00
50	War Incidents (Brown Back, Different)	1916	£1.40	£70.00
25	Warriors of All Nations (Gold Panel)	1937	£1.20	£30.00
50	Warships	1926	£2.50	—
25	Whaling	1930	£1.80	£45.00
F50	Who's Who in Sport (1926)	1927	£1.50	£150.00
50	Wild Animals of the World (Tobacco Leaf Back)	1903	£6.00	—
25	Wireless	1923	£3.00	—
50	Wonders of the Past	1930	65p	£32.50
50	Wonders of the Sea	1929	60p	£30.00
25	Wonders of the World	1928	60p	£15.00
40	World Famous Cinema Artistes	1933	£1.00	£40.00
L40	World Famous Cinema Artistes	1933	£1.10	£44.00
50	World's Products	1929	40p	£20.00
F50	Zoo	1935	50p	—
50	Zoological Studies	1928	40p	£20.00
M50	Zulu Chiefs (2 Types)	1932	£11.00	—
(4)	**SERIES WITH PLAIN BACKS**			
50	Actors & Actresses "WALP"	1906	£1.70	£85.00
50	Actresses "ALWICS"	1907	£1.75	—
50	Actresses, Four Colours Surround	1905	£1.70	£85.00
30	Actresses, Unicoloured (Light Brown)	1910	70p	£21.00
30	(Purple Brown)	1910	85p	£25.50
50	Animals & Birds	1912	£1.70	£85.00
60	Animals (Cut-Outs)	1912	£1.00	£60.00
50	Art Photogravures	1912	£1.25	—
50	Aviation Series	1911	£2.75	—
40	Beauties (Brown Tinted)	1913	£2.00	—

BRITISH AMERICAN TOBACCO CO. LTD. (B.A.T.) — cont.

Qty		Date	Odds	Sets
50	Beauties, Coloured Backgrounds	1911	£2.00	£100.00
50	Beauties, "LAWHA"	1906	£2.20	—
32	Beauties, Picture Hats I	1914	£2.50	£80.00
45	Beauties, Picture Hats II	1914	£2.50	£112.50
30	Beauties & Children	1912	*£3.75*	—
52	Birds of Brilliant Plumage (P/C Inset)	1914	£2.20	£115.00
30	Boy Scouts Signalling (English Caption)	1922	£2.20	£66.00
30	(Siamese Caption)	1922	£2.50	£75.00
50	Butterflies & Moths	1914	£1.40	£70.00
50	Cinema Artistes	1930	85p	—
50	Cinema Stars (1-50)	1927	85p	£42.50
50	Cinema Stars (51-100)	1928	£1.00	—
50	Cinema Stars (101-150)	1930	£1.00	—
100	Cinema Stars (201-300)	1932	85p	£85.00
50	Cinema Stars "BAMT"	1928	£1.00	£50.00
50	Cinema Stars "FLAG"	1929	£1.00	—
27	Dancing Girls	1913	£1.30	£35.00
32	Drum Horses	1910	£4.50	£144.00
50	English Period Costumes	1929	70p	£35.00
50	Flag Girls of All Nations	1908	£1.60	£80.00
165	Flags, Pennons & Signals	1907	65p	—
20	Flowers	1915	80p	£16.00
50	Girls of All Nations	1908	£1.75	£87.50
30	Heroic Deeds	1913	£1.75	£52.50
25	Hindoo Gods	1909	£6.00	—
32	Houses of Parliament	1914	£2.50	—
25	Indian Mogul Paintings	1909	£7.50	—
53	Jockeys & Owners Colours (P/C Inset)	1914	£2.40	£130.00
K36	Modern Beauties, 1st Series	1938	£2.50	—
36	Modern Beauties, 2nd Series	1939	£2.25	—
F48	Movie Stars	1928	£1.50	£72.00
F50	New Zealand, Early Scenes & Maori Life	1929	£1.25	—
50	Poultry & Pigeons	1926	£3.50	—
25	Products of the World	1914	85p	—
50	Royal Mail	1912	*£4.50*	—
36	Ships & Their Pennants	1913	£2.00	£72.00
75	Soldiers of the World	1904	£7.50	—
30	Sporting Girls	1913	£4.00	—
50	Sports of the World (Brown)	1917	£3.25	—
50	(Coloured)	1917	£3.00	£150.00
M50	Stars of Filmland	1927	£1.75	—
25	The Bonzo Series	1923	£3.20	£80.00
32	Transport of the World	1917	£1.15	£37.00
50	Types of the British Army (Numbered)	1908	£2.25	—
50	(Unnumbered)	1908	£2.00	—
F50	Types of the World	1936	*£1.75*	—
F50	Units of the British Army & R.A.F.	1930	*£1.75*	—
FS50	Views of the World	1908	£1.30	—
50	War Leaders and Scenes	1916	£4.50	—
M50	Women of Nations (Flag Girls)	1922	£2.50	—

BRITISH-AUSTRALASIAN TOBACCO CO. (Australia)

Qty		Date	Odds	Sets
?252	Flags of All Nations (2 Types)	1910	£5.50	—

BRITISH CIGARETTE CO. (China)

Qty		*Date*	*Odds*	*Sets*
25	Actresses and Beauties "FECKSA"	1900	£65.00	—
25	South African War Scenes	1900	£22.00	£550.00

BRITISH LEAF TOBACCO CO. (India)

?12	Actresses and Film Stars	1930	£7.50	—

BRITISH NEW GUINEA DEVELOPMENT CO.

50	Papuan Series 1	1910	£42.50	—

BROWN & WILLIAMSON TOBACCO CORPORATION (U.S.A.)

M50	Modern American Airplanes, Series A	1940	£3.50	£175.00
M50	Ditto (No Series Letter)	1940	£2.50	£125.00
M50	Modern Airplanes, Series B	1941	£2.50	£125.00
M50	Modern Airplanes, Series C	1942	£2.50	£125.00
50	Movie Stars	1940	£4.00	—

D. BUCHNER & CO. (U.S.A.)

M45	Actors	1888	£22.00	—
X?100	Actresses	1888	£22.00	—
X?60	American Scenes with a Policeman	1888	£37.50	—
M120	Baseball Players	1888	*£60.00*	—
X?10	Butterflies & Bugs	1888	£50.00	—
P200	Defenders & Offenders	1888	£32.50	—
M31	Jockeys	1888	£32.50	—
X51	Morning Glory Maidens	1888	£36.50	—
X31	Morning Glory Maidens & American Flowers	1888	*£60.00*	—
X25	Musical Instruments	1888	£42.50	—
X25	New York City Scenes	1888	£45.00	—
M101	Police Inspectors	1888	£20.00	—
X100	Police Inspectors & Captains	1888	£20.00	—
X12	Presidential Puzzle Cards	1888	*£60.00*	—
X25	Yacht Club Colors	1888	£40.00	—

BUKHSH ELLAHIE & CO.

53	Indian Girl, Playing Card Inset	1902	£20.00	—

CALCUTTA CIGARETTE CO. (India)

25	Actresses (Blue Front)	1906	£20.00	£500.00
25	(Brown Front)	1906	£25.00	—

A. G. CAMERON & CAMERON (U.S.A.)

?35	Actresses (Burdick 488)	1887	£55.00	—
24	Occupations for Women	1893	£42.50	—
F?	Photographic Cards	1893	£6.00	—
25	The New Discovery	1892	£26.00	£650.00

V. CAMILLERI (Malta)

MF104	Popes of Rome	1922	£1.60	£165.00

CAMLER TOBACCO COY. (Malta)

F250	Footballers	1926	*£5.00*	—
M96	Maltese Families Coats of Arms	1925	£1.10	£105.00

M. C. CARATHANASSIS & CO. (Turkey)

Qty		Date	Odds	Sets
48	The Post in Various Countries	1900	£27.50	—

CASTELANO BROS. LTD. (India)

Qty		Date	Odds	Sets
52	Beauties, Playing Card Inset	1899	£21.50	£1100.00

C. COLOMBOS (Malta)

Qty		Date	Odds	Sets
F?200	Actresses	1902	£2.75	—
MF?59	Actresses	1902	£13.00	—
59	Actresses (Coloured)	1900	£9.00	—
MF?57	Celebrities	1900	£16.00	—
F136	Dante's Divine Comedy	1914	£1.75	£240.00
MF72	Famous Oil Paintings, Serie A	1910	85p	£61.50
MF108	Famous Oil Paintings, Serie B	1911	85p	£92.00
MF240	Famous Oil Paintings, Serie C	1912	85p	£204.00
MF100	Famous Oil Paintings, Serie D	1913	85p	£85.00
XF?91	Famous Oil Paintings	1911	£5.50	—
MF100	Life of Napoleon Bonaparte	1914	£2.00	£200.00
MF70	Life of Nelson	1914	£2.25	£158.00
MF70	Life of Wellington	1914	£2.25	£158.00
MF100	National Types and Costumes	1908	£2.25	£225.00
F?30	Opera Singers	1899	£26.00	—
120	Paintings and Statues	1913	65p	£78.00
M112	Royalty and Celebrities	1908	£2.40	£270.00

COLONIAL TOBACCOS (PTY.) LTD. (South Africa)

Qty		Date	Odds	Sets
X150	World's Fairy Tales	1930	£3.50	—

CONDACHI BROTHERS & CO. (Malta)

Qty		Date	Odds	Sets
25	The Bride Retires	1905	£22.50	—

D. CONDACHI & SON (Malta)

Qty		Date	Odds	Sets
?15	Artistes & Beauties	1910	£17.50	—

CONGRESS CUT PLUG (U.S.A.)

Qty		Date	Odds	Sets
X12	Actresses	1890	£35.00	—

CONSOLIDATED CIGARETTE CO. (U.S.A.)

Qty		Date	Odds	Sets
25	Ladies of the White House	1893	£25.00	—
M14	Ladies of the White House	1898	£30.00	£420.00
M25	Turn Cards (72 x 41mm)	1894	£40.00	—
M25	(78 x 51mm)	1894	£45.00	—

A. G. COUSIS & CO. (Malta)

Qty		Date	Odds	Sets
254	Actors & Actresses	1924	75p	—
KF100	Actors & Actresses (Hand Coloured)	1906	£1.50	—
F100	Actors & Actresses (Hand Coloured)	1906	£1.50	—
F?	Actresses (Cairo Address)	1907	*£30.00*	—
KF100	Actresses Serie I	1907	£1.30	—
KF80	Actresses Serie II	1907	£1.30	—
F1900	Actresses Serie I to Serie XIX	1907	£1.50	—
KF?2281	Actresses (Unnumbered)	1905	75p	—
F?1300	Actresses (Unnumbered)	1905	85p	—

A. G. COUSIS & CO. (Malta) — cont.

Qty		Date	Odds	Sets
MF?221	Actresses (White Border)	1902	£7.00	—
KF100	Actresses, Partners & National Costumes (Cousis')	1906	£1.60	—
KF200	(Cousis's)	1906	£1.75	—
F100	Actresses, Partners & National Costumes	1906	£1.60	—
50	Beauties, Couples & Children (Red Back)	1923	£2.00	—
MF50	Beauties, Couples & Children, Collection No.1	1908	£2.60	—
MF50	Beauties, Couples & Children, Collection No.2	1908	£2.60	—
MF50	Beauties, Couples & Children, Collection No.3	1908	£2.60	—
F100	Bullfighters	1901	£5.50	—
F402	Celebrities (Numbered)	1906	£1.25	—
KF?2162	Celebrities (Unnumbered)	1905	75p	—
F?2162	Celebrities (Unnumbered)	1905	75p	—
XF?30	Celebrities & Warships (White Border)	1902	£8.50	—
MF72	Grand Masters of the Order of St. John	1909	£2.50	—
F100	National Costumes	1908	£1.75	—
MF60	Paris Exhibition, 1900	1900	£24.00	—
MF102	Paris Series	1902	£22.50	—
MF182	Popes of Rome (To A.D. 1241)	1904	£1.40	£255.00
MF81	Popes of Rome (Dubec, After A.D. 1241)	1904	£2.50	—
F100	Statues & Monuments (Numbered)	1905	£1.50	—
F100	(Unnumbered)	1905	£1.60	—
KF127	Views of Malta	1903	*£2.00*	—
F?100	Views of Malta (Numbered)	1903	85p	—
MF?127	Views of Malta (Numbered)	1903	85p	—
MF?65	(Unnumbered)	1903	85p	—
F?30	Views of the Mediterranean	1903	*£4.00*	—
MF?100	Views of the Mediterranean	1903	*£4.00*	—
F?559	Views of the World	1903	£1.00	—
MF?557	Views of the World	1903	£1.00	—
F99	Warships (White Border)	1910	£2.40	£240.00
KF850	Warships	1904	£1.00	—
MF850	Warships	1904	£1.25	—
MF?94	Warships & Liners (Dubec)	1904	£4.00	—
MF?25	Warships & Liners (Excelsior)	1904	£4.00	—
MF?50	Warships & Liners (Superior)	1904	£5.00	—

CRESCENT CIGAR FACTORY (U.S.A.)

T?12	Actresses	1886	£50.00	—

CROWN TOBACCO CO. (India)

X26	Actresses	1900	£42.00	—
E?25	Celebrities	1900	£40.00	—
96	National Types, Costumes & Flags	1900	£32.50	—
T96	National Types, Costumes & Flags	1900	£40.00	—
MF?	Photo Series	1900	£40.00	—

CHARLES C. DAVIS & CO. (U.S.A.)

?15	Actresses	1890	£45.00	—

DIAMOND INDIAN CIGARETTES

?25	Beauties	1924	£12.00	—

M. W. DIFFLEY (U.S.A.)

Qty		*Date*	*Odds*	*Sets*
36	Flags of All Nations	1890	£32.50	—

DIXSON (Australia)

Qty		*Date*	*Odds*	*Sets*
50	Australian M.P.s & Celebrities	1900	£12.00	—

DOMINION TOBACCO CO. (Canada)

Qty		*Date*	*Odds*	*Sets*
50	Photos (Actresses, "ALWICS")	1905	*£22.50*	—
100	Photos (Actresses, Plum Background)	1905	£22.50	—
50	The Smokers of the World	1904	£40.00	—

DOMINION TOBACCO CO. LTD. (New Zealand)

Qty		*Date*	*Odds*	*Sets*
50	Coaches and Coaching Days	1927	£2.00	£100.00
50	People and Places Famous in New Zealand History	1933	£1.60	£80.00
50	Products of the World	1929	80p	£40.00
50	U.S.S. Co's. Steamers	1928	£2.30	£115.00

DRUMMOND TOBACCO CO. (U.S.A.)

Qty		*Date*	*Odds*	*Sets*
?20	Actresses	1895	£50.00	—
?50	Bathing Girls	1895	£65.00	—
25	Beauties "CHOAB"	1897	£75.00	—
X?25	Girls	1896	*£50.00*	—

DUDGEON & ARNELL (Australia)

Qty		*Date*	*Odds*	*Sets*
M16	1934 Australian Test Team	1934	£5.50	£88.00
M55	Famous Ships	1933	£2.25	£125.00

W. DUKE & SONS LTD. (U.S.A.)

Qty		*Date*	*Odds*	*Sets*
50	Actors and Actresses, Series 1	1889	£12.50	£625.00
M50	Actors and Actresses, Series 1	1889	£32.50	—
50	Actors and Actresses, Series 2	1889	£12.50	£625.00
M50	Actors and Actresses, Series 2	1889	£32.50	—
X30	Actors and Actresses (As Above)	1889	£25.00	—
25	Actresses (Tobacco War – Overseas)	1900	£6.00	—
X25	Albums of American Stars	1886	£37.50	—
X25	Battle Scenes	1887	£26.00	£650.00
X25	Beauties, Black Border	1886	£22.00	£550.00
P25	Beauties, Folders	1886	£40.00	—
X25	Bicycle and Trick Riders	1891	£30.00	—
X25	Breeds of Horses	1892	£26.00	£650.00
X25	Bridges	1888	£21.00	£525.00
X25	Burlesque Scenes	1889	£24.00	—
50	Coins of All Nations	1889	£12.50	£625.00
X25	Comic Characters	1887	£22.00	£550.00
X25	Cowboy Scenes	1888	£28.00	£700.00
X50	Fairest Flowers in the World	1887	£21.50	—
F45	Famous Ships	1884	*£8.50*	—
50	Fancy Dress Ball Costumes	1887	£12.50	£625.00
M50	Fancy Dress Ball Costumes	1887	£32.50	—
X50	Fancy Dress Ball Costumes	1887	£22.00	—
50	Fishers and Fish	1888	£13.00	£650.00

W. DUKE & SONS LTD. (U.S.A.) — cont.

Qty		Date	Odds	Sets
X25	Fishes and Fishing	1888	£24.00	£600.00
X25	Flags and Costumes	1893	£24.00	£600.00
50	Floral Beauties & Language of Flowers	1892	£12.50	£625.00
X25	French Novelties	1891	£22.50	—
X25	Gems of Beauty (2 Types)	1884	£22.00	£550.00
50	Great Americans	1888	£17.00	£850.00
X16	Great Americans	1888	£27.50	—
25	Gymnastic Exercises (Duke in Blue)	1887	£26.50	—
25	(Duke in Brown)	1887	£22.00	£550.00
X25	Habitations of Man	1890	£22.00	£550.00
50	Histories of Generals (Booklets)	1889	£27.00	£1350.00
X50	Histories of Generals	1889	£30.00	—
50	Histories of Poor Boys & Other Famous People (Booklets)	1889	£22.00	£1200.00
50	Holidays	1890	£12.50	£625.00
X25	Honest Library (Booklets)	1896	£37.50	—
X25	Illustrated Songs	1893	£23.00	—
X25	Industries of the States	1889	£25.00	—
50	Jokes (2 Types)	1890	£13.00	£650.00
X25	Jokes	1890	£22.00	—
X25	Lighthouses (Die Cut)	1890	£24.00	£600.00
X25/26	Miniature Novelties	1891	£22.00	£550.00
50	Musical Instruments	1888	£17.00	£850.00
X25	Musical Instruments of the World	1888	£24.00	—
36	Ocean and River Steamers	1887	£22.00	£790.00
F?	Photographic Cards	1885	£1.25	—
MF?	Photographic Cards	1885	£2.50	—
XF?	Photographic Cards	1885	£2.40	—
53	Playing Cards (2 Types)	1888	£10.00	£530.00
50	Popular Songs and Dancers	1894	£17.50	—
50	Postage Stamps (3 Types)	1889	£13.00	£650.00
X25	Presidential Possibilities	1888	£24.00	£600.00
X15	Puzzles	1887	£35.00	—
51	Rulers, Coat of Arms, and Flag (Folders)	1888	£12.50	£630.00
X50	Rulers, Flags and Coats of Arms	1889	£21.00	—
50	Scenes of Perilous Occupations	1888	£17.00	£850.00
X25	Sea Captains	1887	£27.50	—
50	Shadows	1889	£13.00	£650.00
X25	Snapshots from "Puck"	1889	£22.00	£550.00
X25	Stars of the Stage (White Border)	1891	£22.00	£550.00
X25	Stars of the Stage, Second Series	1891	£23.00	£575.00
X25	Stars of the Stage, Third Series	1892	£22.00	£550.00
X25	Stars of the Stage, 4th Series (Die Cut)	1893	£24.00	£600.00
48	State Governors, Arms & Maps (Folders)	1888	£13.00	£624.00
X48	State Governors, Arms & Maps	1888	£22.50	—
X25	Talk of the Diamond	1893	£40.00	—
50	The Terrors of America & Their Doings	1889	£12.50	£625.00
M50	The Terrors of America & Their Doings	1889	£32.50	—
X50	The Terrors of America & Their Doings	1889	£22.00	—
50	Tinted Photos	1887	£17.00	—
50	Tinted Photos (Die-Cut)	1887	£13.00	—
X25	Transparencies	1888	£50.00	—
X24	Tricks with Cards	1887	£35.00	—
X25	Types of Vessels (Die Cut)	1889	£24.00	£600.00
50	Vehicles of the World	1888	£18.00	—
X50	Yacht Club Colors of the World	1890	£22.50	—

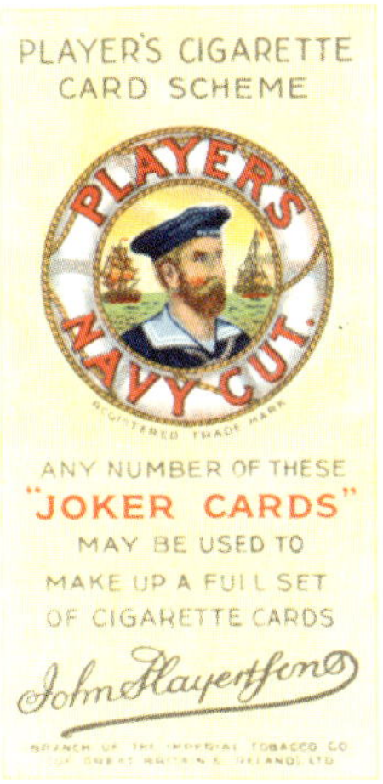

Joker Card – Player

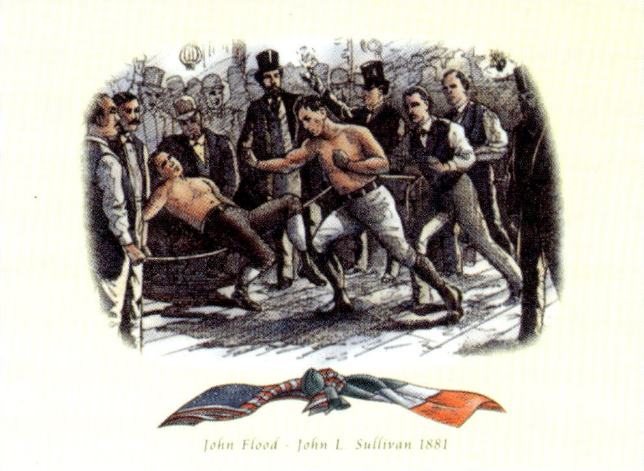

John L. Sullivan – Cradle to Grave – Sporting Profiles

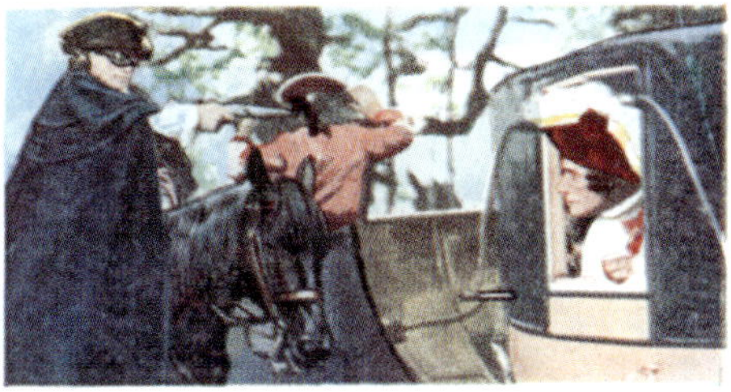

Scenes from the Films – A.B.C. (Cinemas)

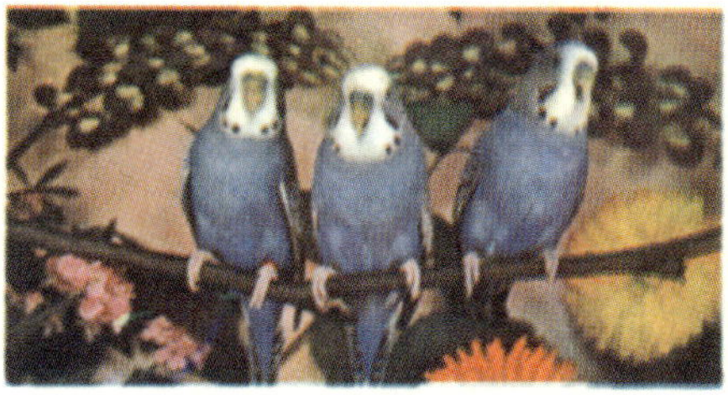

Budgerigars – Anonymous

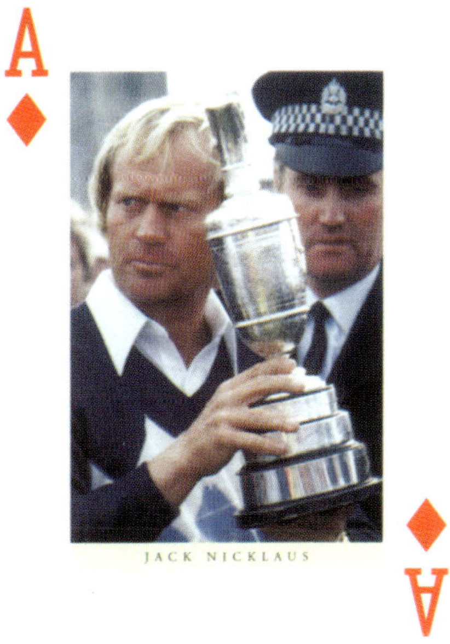

Masters of the Old Course – St. Andrews – Piatnik

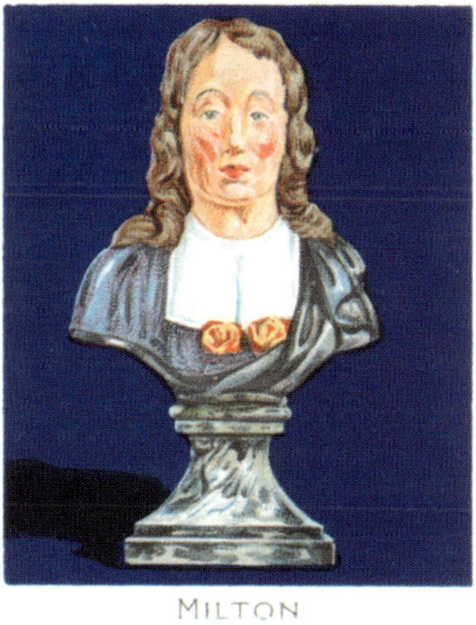

Old Staffordshire Figures – Carreras

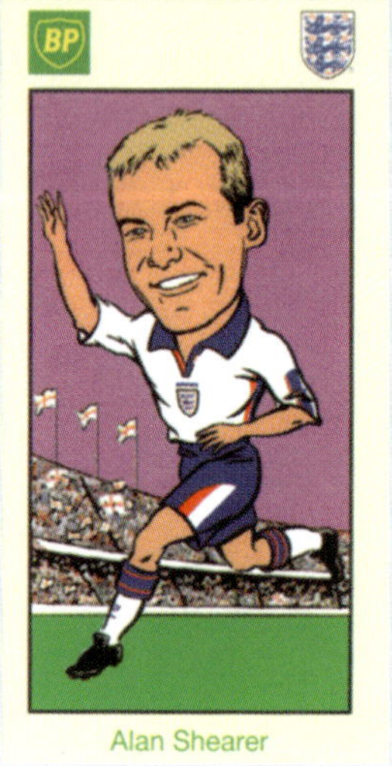

England '98 – B.P.

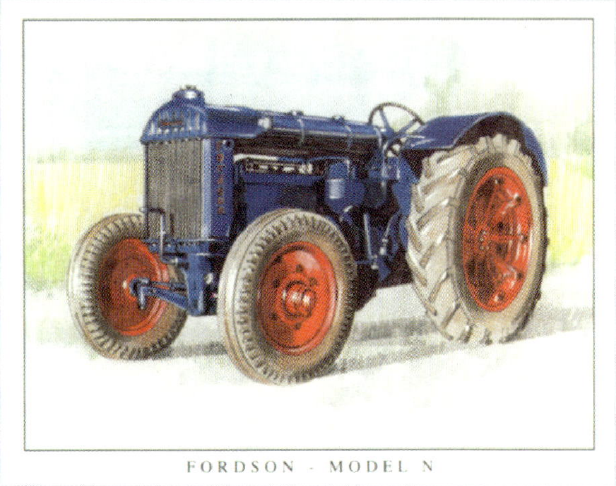

Classic Tractors – Golden Era

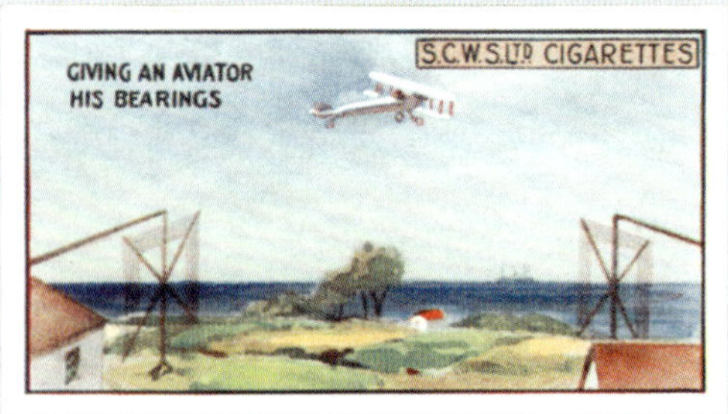

Wireless – Scottish C.W.S.

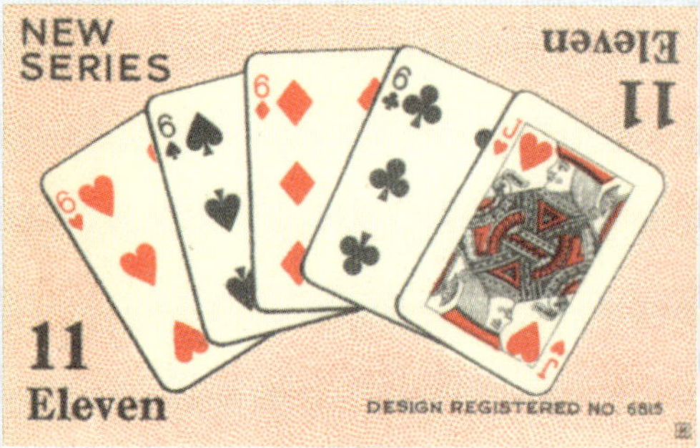

Poker Hands – Imperial Tobacco Co. of Canada

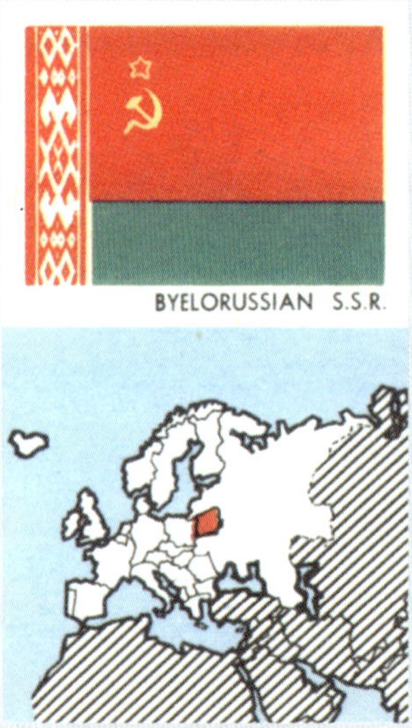

World Flag Series – Devlin

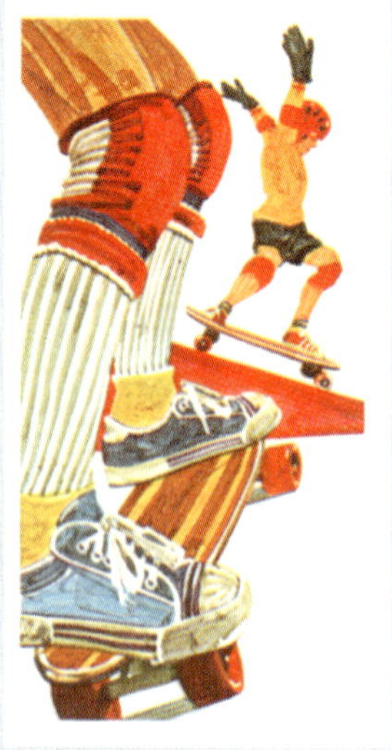

Skateboard Surfer – T. Wall & Sons

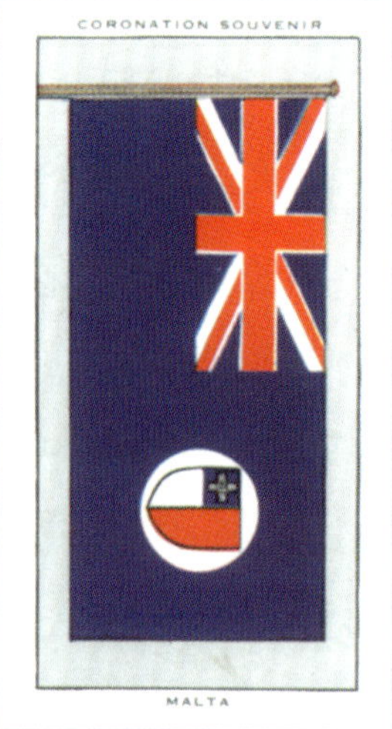

Coronation Series – Beaulah

W. DUKE & SONS LTD. (U.S.A.) — cont.

Qty		*Date*	*Odds*	*Sets*
50	Yacht Colors of the World	1890	£12.50	£625.00
M50	Yacht Colors of the World	1890	£32.50	—

PRINTED ALBUMS (EXCHANGED FOR COUPONS)

	Costumes of All Nations (3 Series)	1890	—	£110.00
	Governors, Coats of Arms & Maps	1889	—	£80.00
	Postage Stamp Album	1889	—	£120.00
	Shadows	1889	—	£120.00
	Sporting Girls	1888	—	*£250.00*
	The Heroes of the Civil War	1889	—	£350.00
	The Rulers, Flags, Coats of Arms	1889	—	£90.00
	The Terrors of America	1889	—	*£110.00*
	Yacht Colors of the World (3 Series)	1890	—	£120.00

DUNGEY, RALPH & CO. (Australia)

50	Australian Footballers	1906	*£24.00*	—
?	Racehorses (Black Back)	1906	*£50.00*	—
?56	Racehorses and Incidents	1906	*£24.00*	—

EAGLE CIGARETTES (Australia)

F50	Actresses & Sportsmen (Photographic)	1890	£70.00	—

EASTERN VIRGINIA CIGARETTE CO. (Asia)

60	Dutch East Indies Footballers	1926	£2.75	—

EGYPTIAN CIGARETTE COY. (Malta)

F120	Actresses	1906	£6.00	—
XF30	Actresses	1906	*£30.00*	—
264	Decorations & Medals	1908	£8.50	—
F100	Maltese Band Players	1910	£12.50	—

EGYPTIAN CIGARETTES MFG. CO. (China)

?50	Actresses ("MUREG")	1900	£40.00	—
25	Armies of the World	1900	£42.50	—
?	Beauties	1900	*£50.00*	—
30	Beauties, Nymphs	1900	£42.50	—
?30	Chinese & South African Series	1900	£55.00	—
25	National Flags & Flowers – Girls	1900	£45.00	—
30	Old Masters	1900	£40.00	—
?55	Russo-Japanese War Series	1904	£45.00	—
25	Types of British & Colonial Troops	1900	£40.00	—
25	Warships	1900	£35.00	—

H. ELLIS & CO. (U.S.A.)

25	Breeds of Dogs (5 Types)	1890	£36.00	—
25	Costumes of Women	1890	£50.00	—
25	Generals of the Late Civil War	1890	£62.50	—
F?	Photographic Cards	1887	£6.00	—

D. FANCIULLI & CO. (Malta)

50	Il Paradiso Perduto	1906	£6.50	—

LA FAVORITA (Canary Islands)

Qty		Date	Odds	Sets
M30/58	Flags & Soldiers (Silk)	1915	65p	£19.50

JOHN FINZER & BROS. (U.S.A.)

X10	Inventors & Inventions	1891	£32.50	£325.00

G.W. GAIL & AX (U.S.A.)

X25	Battle Scenes	1891	£27.50	—
X25	Bicycle and Trick Riders	1891	£32.50	—
X25	French Novelties	1891	£26.50	—
X25	Industries of the States	1891	£26.50	—
X25	Lighthouses (Die Cut)	1891	£25.00	—
X25	Navy Library	1890	£37.50	—
X25	Novelties (Die Cut)	1890	£26.50	—
XF?	Photographic Cards	1885	£2.30	—
X25	Stars of the Stage	1891	£25.00	—

GENERAL CIGAR CO. LTD. (Canada)

X36	Northern Birds	1977	£1.00	£40.00

GENESEE TOBACCO WORKS (U.S.A.)

?50	Actresses	1888	£40.00	—

ALEJANDRO GONZALEZ (Spain)

X8	Typical Portuguese Costumes	1962	—	£3.75

G. G. GOODE LTD. (Australia)

17	Prominent Cricketer Series	1924	£70.00	—

GOODWIN & CO. (U.S.A.)

50	Champions (2 Types)	1888	£27.50	—
50	Dogs of the World (3 Types)	1890	£17.00	£850.00
50	Flowers	1890	£17.00	£850.00
50	Games and Sports Series	1889	£24.00	£1200.00
50	Holidays	1889	£22.50	—
50	Occupations for Women	1887	£50.00	—
?25	Old Judge Cards	1886	£60.00	—
F?	Photographic Cards	1886	£2.25	—
50	Vehicles of the World	1888	£22.50	—
PRINTED ALBUMS (EXCHANGED FOR COUPONS)				
	Champions	1888	—	*£400.00*
	Floral Album	1890	—	*£125.00*
	Games & Sports	1889	—	*£250.00*

W. R. GRESH & SONS (U.S.A.)

X25	Actresses (Coloured)	1890	£40.00	—
X?	Actresses (Sepia)	1890	£30.00	—

L. O. GROTHE LTD. (Canada)

52	Bridge Hands (3 Types)	1927	£4.50	—

THOS. W. HALL (U.S.A)

Qty		Date	Odds	Sets
M153	Actors & Actresses (Dull Background)	1881	£7.00	—
M111	Actors & Actresses (Black Background)	1882	£8.00	—
M?297	Actors & Actresses (Fancy Corners)	1884	£16.00	—
M?158	Actors & Actresses (Sun's Rays)	1890	£12.00	—
M?52	Actresses (Tiled Wall)	1888	£16.50	—
M?12	Actresses (No Borders, Hall on Front)	1892	£27.50	—
M25	Actresses (No Borders, No Hall on Front)	1892	£22.00	£550.00
T20	Actresses ("Ours")	1885	£60.00	—
M12	Athletes	1881	£50.00	—
M8	Presidential Candidates & Actresses	1880	£60.00	—
M22	Presidents of the United States	1888	£26.50	—
25	Theatrical Types	1890	£28.00	£700.00

HARTLEY'S TOBACCO CO. (S. Africa)

53	Playing Cards (OK Cigarettes)	1929	£1.75	—
L19	South African English Cricket Tour 1929	1929	£62.50	—

HERNANDEZ (Brazil)

X24	Alphabet Cards	1960	—	£20.00

S. F. HESS & CO. (U.S.A.)

F?	Photographic Cards	1885	£7.50	—
55	Poker Puzzle Cards (2 Types)	1890	£40.00	—
25	Terms of Poker Illustrated	1890	£40.00	—

WM. G. HILLS (U.S.A.)

X25	Actresses	1888	£50.00	—

HILSON CO. (U.S.A.)

T25	Battleships & Signal Flags	1898	£22.00	£550.00
T25	National Types	1900	£21.00	£525.00

HOUDE & GROTHE (Canada)

L24	Wildfowl (Package Issue)	1953	£3.00	£72.00

T. S. H. HYPPO (Belgium) (Imitation Cigar Bands)

120	German Uniforms of the 19th Century	1975	—	£35.00

IMPERIAL CIGARETTE & TOBACCO CO. (Canada)

?24	Actresses	1900	£45.00	—

IMPERIAL TOBACCO CO. OF CANADA LTD. (Canada)

50	Actresses, Framed Border (Plain Back)	1910	£2.25	£112.50
L55/66	Aircraft Spotter Series (Packets)	1941	£1.50	£82.50
60	Animals (Millbank, 4 Types)	1916	70p	£42.00
L55	Animal with Flag (Silk)	1915	£2.80	£154.00
50	Arms of the British Empire	1911	£2.00	—

IMPERIAL TOBACCO CO. OF CANADA LTD. (Canada) — cont.

Qty		Date	Odds	Sets
50	Around the World Series (Numbered)	1912	£3.00	—
50	(Unnumbered)	1912	£4.50	—
50	Aviation Series	1910	£3.00	—
90	Baseball Series	1912	*£17.50*	—
30	Beauties – Art Series (Plain Back)	1911	£9.00	—
30	(Bouquet Cigarettes)	1902	*£42.50*	—
50	Beauties (Coloured, Black Border)	1912	£2.40	£120.00
25	Beauties – Girls in Costume	1904	*£42.50*	—
24	Beauties – Smoke Girls	1904	£42.50	—
M50	Birds, Beasts & Fishes (2 Types)	1923	£1.50	£75.00
30	Bird Series	1910	£1.80	£54.00
X100	Birds of Canada	1924	£2.50	—
X100	Birds of Canada (Western Canada)	1925	£4.50	—
50	Boy Scouts	1911	£4.20	£210.00
50	British Birds	1923	65p	£32.50
50	British Man of War Series (Plain Back)	1910	£8.00	£400.00
50	Buildings (Plain Back)	1902	£7.50	£375.00
L55	Butterflies (Silk)	1912	£4.00	—
50	Butterflies & Moths	1911	£1.75	—
L24	Canada's Corvettes, 1st Series	1943	£12.00	—
L24	Canada's Corvettes, 2nd Series	1944	*£12.00*	—
T50	Canadian Cities (Silk)	1914	£5.00	—
50	Canadian Historical Portraits	1913	£2.50	—
48	Canadian History Series (I.T.C. Name)	1926	£1.20	£60.00
50	(Anon.).	1926	£1.25	—
P50	Canadian History Series (Silk)	1914	£10.00	—
T121	Canadian Miscellany (Silk)	1912	£3.50	—
50	Children of All Nations	1924	75p	£37.50
23	Dogs Series	1924	£1.40	£32.00
50	Dogs, 2nd Series	1925	£1.20	£60.00
50	Famous English Actresses	1924	80p	£40.00
50	Film Favourites (4 Types)	1926	£2.75	—
50	Fish & Bait	1924	£1.30	£65.00
50	Fishes of the World	1924	£1.10	£55.00
50	Fish Series	1912	£2.00	—
L143	Flags (Silk)	1913	£2.00	—
50	Flower Culture in Pots	1925	50p	£25.00
50	Fowls,Pigeons & Dogs	1911	£2.75	—
30	Game Bird Series	1925	£1.20	£36.00
L55	Garden Flowers (Silk, Black Numerals)	1913	£2.30	£126.50
L50	(Silk, Red Numerals)	1913	£3.50	—
G5	Garden Flowers (Silk)	1913	£22.50	—
50	Gardening Hints	1923	40p	£20.00
L25	Heraldic Signs & Their Origin	1925	£1.00	£25.00
45	Hockey Players	1912	*£10.00*	—
36	Hockey Series (Coloured)	1911	*£10.00*	—
50	Hockey Series (Blue)	1910	*£12.00*	—
50	"How to do It" Series	1911	£2.25	£112.50
50	How To Play Golf	1925	£6.00	£300.00
50	Infantry Training (4 Types)	1915	£2.00	£100.00
100	Lacrosse Series, Set 1	1910	£4.00	£400.00
98	Lacrosse Series, Set 2	1911	£4.00	—
50	Lacrosse Series, Set 3	1912	£4.00	—
50	L'Histoire du Canada	1914	£1.10	—
M48	Mail Carriers and Stamps	1903	£22.50	—

IMPERIAL TOBACCO CO. OF CANADA LTD. (Canada) — cont.

Qty		Date	Odds	Sets
50	Merchant Ships of the World	1924	90p	£45.00
25	Military Portraits (2 Types)	1914	£2.00	£50.00
50	Modern War Weapons	1915	£3.25	£162.50
56	Motor Cars	1921	£1.60	£90.00
50	Movie Stars	1925	£1.40	—
50	Music Hall Artistes (Plain Back)	1911	£2.00	£100.00
50	Naval Portraits (2 Types)	1915	£2.20	£110.00
25	Notabilities (2 Types)	1915	£2.00	£50.00
L55	Orders & Military Medals (Silk)	1915	£2.30	£126.00
L50	Pictures of Canadian Life (2 Types)	1912	£5.25	—
53	Poker Hands (Many Types)	1924	£1.00	£53.00
25	Poultry Alphabet	1924	£2.00	£50.00
G6	Premium Silk – Flag Girls	1913	£32.50	—
G1	Premium Silk – George V	1915	—	£35.00
G1	Premium Silk – Motor Boat	1915	—	*£75.00*
G1	Premium Silk – Royal Arms	1914	—	£30.00
G1	Premium Silk – "Staunch and True"	1914	—	£40.00
G1	Premium Silk – Union Jack	1913	—	£20.00
G2	Premium Silk – Yachts	1915	*£50.00*	—
50	Prominent Men of Canada	1912	£2.65	—
50	Railway Engines (3 Types)	1924	80p	£40.00
L55	Regimental Uniforms of Canada (Silk)	1914	£3.25	£180.00
P25	Rulers with Flags (Silk)	1910	£12.00	£300.00
127	Smokers Golf Cards (2 Types)	1926	£4.50	—
50	The Reason Why	1924	80p	£40.00
25	The World's Dreadnoughts	1910	£2.50	—
50	Tricks & Puzzles Series	1911	£4.00	£200.00
50	Types of Nations	1910	£2.25	—
25	Victoria Cross Heroes (Blue Back)	1915	£2.40	£60.00
L45	Views of the World	1912	£5.00	—
L25	Wild Animals of Canada	1912	£10.00	—
M144	World War I Scenes & Portraits	1916	£1.60	£230.00
X49	Yacht Pennants & Views (Silk)	1915	£5.50	£270.00

IMPERIAL TOB. CO. OF INDIA LTD. (India)

Qty		Date	Odds	Sets
25	Indian Historical Views	1910	£1.60	£40.00
K52	Miniature Playing Cards	1933	80p	—
40	Nautch Girl Series (Pedro Cigarettes)	1908	£2.00	£80.00
40	(Railway Cigarettes)	1908	£2.00	£80.00
52	Nautch Girl Series (P/C Inset, Pedro)	1908	£1.75	£91.00
52	(P/C Inset, Railway)	1908	£1.75	£91.00
53	Playing Cards (3 Types)	1919	£1.50	—
1	Present Ticket	1917	—	£3.00

IMPERIAL TOBACCO CO. (NFLD) LTD. (Canada)

Qty		Date	Odds	Sets
M52	Playing Cards (2 Types)	1930	£7.00	—

JACK & JILL CIGARS (U.S.A.)

Qty		Date	Odds	Sets
T50	Actresses "JAKE"	1890	£45.00	—

JAMAICA TOBACCO CO.

Qty		Date	Odds	Sets
F?104	Miniature Post Card Series	1915	£6.00	—

BILL JONES (U.S.A.)

Qty		Date	Odds	Sets
X?25	Beauties	1885	£55.00	—

JUBILE (Belgium) (Imitation Cigar Bands)

Qty		Date	Odds	Sets
24	Ancient Military Uniforms	1975	—	£5.00
24	Inventions of Leonardo Da Vinci	1975	—	£6.00
24	Paintings of Manet	1975	—	£5.00
24	Riders of the World	1975	—	£7.50
24	Stained Glass Windows	1975	—	£5.00
12	U.S. War of Independence – Celebrities	1975	—	£4.00

DON JULIAN (Spain) (Imitation Cigar Bands)

Qty		Date	Odds	Sets
X28	European Stamps – Series 7	1978	—	£25.00
X28	European Stamps – Series 8	1978	—	£20.00

KENTUCKY TOBACCOS (PTY) LTD. (S. Africa)

Qty		Date	Odds	Sets
L120	The March of Mankind	1940	£1.40	—

KEY WEST FAVORS (U.S.A.)

Qty		Date	Odds	Sets
T50	Actresses "JAKE"	1890	*£45.00*	—

KHEDIVIAL COMPANY (U.S.A.)

Qty		Date	Odds	Sets
M10	Aeroplane Series No.103 (2 Types)	1912	£16.00	£160.00
M10	Prize Dog Series No.102 (2 Types)	1911	£16.50	£165.00
M25	Prize Fight Series No.101 (2 Types)	1910	£18.00	—
M25	Prize Fight Series No.102	1911	£21.50	—

WM. S. KIMBALL & CO. (U.S.A.)

Qty		Date	Odds	Sets
?33	Actresses, Collotype	1887	£55.00	—
72	Ancient Coins (2 Types)	1888	£26.00	—
48	Arms of Dominions	1888	£17.00	£820.00
50	Ballet Queens	1889	£17.00	£850.00
X20	Beautiful Bathers (2 Types)	1889	£25.00	—
52	Beauties, Playing Card Inset	1895	£17.50	—
50	Butterflies	1888	£18.00	—
50	Champions of Games and Sports (2 Types)	1888	£26.50	—
50	Dancing Girls of the World	1889	£16.00	£800.00
50	Dancing Women	1889	£16.00	£800.00
50	Fancy Bathers	1889	£17.00	£850.00
X25	French Novelties	1891	£32.50	—
X25	Gems of Beauty	1891	£32.50	—
50	Goddesses of the Greeks & Romans	1889	£19.00	£950.00
X25	Household Pets	1891	£25.00	£625.00
X15	National Flags	1887	£24.00	—
F?	Photographic Cards	1886	£3.75	—
XF?	Photographic Cards	1886	£5.00	—
X20	Pretty Athletes	1890	£26.00	—
50	Savage & Semi Barbarous Chiefs & Rulers	1890	£24.00	—
L?25	Wellstood Etchings	1887	*£65.00*	—

PRINTED ALBUMS (EXCHANGED FOR COUPONS)

	Date	Odds	Sets
Ancient Coins	1888	—	*£150.00*
Ballet Queens	1889	—	*£115.00*
Champions of Games & Sports	1888	—	*£250.00*

WM. S. KIMBALL & CO. (U.S.A.) — cont.

Qty		Date	Odds	Sets
	Dancing Girls of the World	1889	—	*£120.00*
	Dancing Women	1889	—	*£110.00*
	Fancy Bathers	1889	—	*£110.00*
	Goddesses of the Greeks & Romans	1889	—	*£125.00*
	Savage & Semi Barbarous Chiefs & Rulers	1890	—	£160.00

N. KIMURA & CO. (Japan)

Qty		Date	Odds	Sets
?50	Animals & Birds	1900	£15.00	—
?50	Japanese Uniforms	1900	£35.00	—
?50	Japanese Warships	1900	£25.00	—

KINNEY BROS. (U.S.A.)

Qty		Date	Odds	Sets
25	Actresses "Set 1"	1893	£7.00	£175.00
25	Actresses "Set 2"	1895	£10.00	£250.00
50	Actresses (Group 2)	1891	£5.00	—
50	Actresses (Group 3)	1892	£5.00	—
50	Actresses (Group 4, Coloured)	1893	£5.00	£250.00
150	Actresses (Group 4, Sepia, Plain Back)	1893	£2.00	—
25	Animals	1890	£16.00	£400.00
10	Butterflies of the World (White)	1888	£17.00	£170.00
50	Butterflies of the World (Gold)	1888	£13.00	£650.00
25	Famous Gems of the World	1889	£16.00	£400.00
25	Famous Running Horses (American)	1890	£18.00	£450.00
25	Famous Running Horses (English)	1889	£16.00	£400.00
F45	Famous Ships	1887	£8.50	—
25	Great American Trotters	1890	£20.00	£500.00
52	Harlequin Cards	1888	£16.00	£830.00
53	Harlequin Cards, Series 2	1889	£16.00	£850.00
L?4	Inaugural Types	1888	*£75.00*	—
X50	International Cards	1888	£32.50	—
K25	Jocular Oculars (2 Types)	1887	£35.00	—
25	Leaders	1889	£18.00	£450.00
50	Magic Changing Cards	1889	£20.00	—
50	Military Series A (Series 7)	1887	£4.50	£225.00
50	Military Series B (Series 8)	1887	£4.50	£225.00
30	Military Series C (Series 9)	1887	£4.50	£135.00
50	Military Series D (Coloured Background)	1887	£4.00	£200.00
50	Military Series E (1886)	1887	£4.00	£200.00
18	Military Series F (U.S. Continental)	1887	£4.50	£80.00
3	Military Series F (Vatican)	1887	£40.00	£120.00
5	Military Series F (Decorations)	1887	£37.50	£187.50
51	Military Series G (U.S. Army & Navy)	1887	£3.50	£180.00
85	Military Series H (U.S. State Types)	1887	£3.50	£295.00
60	Military Series I ("I.S.C." in 3 Lines)	1887	£7.50	—
50	Military Series J (England/N.G.S.N.Y.)	1887	£12.50	—
49/50	Military Series K (1853)	1887	£8.50	—
50	Military Series L (Foreign Types)	1887	£5.50	£275.00
15	Military Series M (French Army/Navy)	1887	£3.50	£52.50
5	Military Series M (State Seals)	1887	£27.50	—
50	National Dances (White Border)	1889	£12.50	£625.00
25	(No Border)	1889	£16.00	—
25	Naval Vessels of the World	1889	£18.00	£450.00
50	New Year 1890 Cards	1889	£17.00	£850.00
K25	Novelties (Circular, Thick Cards)	1888	£20.00	—

KINNEY BROS. (U.S.A.) — cont.

Qty		Date	Odds	Sets
K50	Novelties (Circular, Thin Cards)	1888	£9.00	£450.00
75	Novelties (Die Cut)	1888	£6.50	—
14	Novelties (Oval)	1888	£25.00	—
44	Novelties (Rectangular)	1888	£9.00	£400.00
F?	Photographic Cards	1886	£1.00	—
LF?	Photographic Cards	1886	£2.40	—
50	Surf Beauties	1889	£18.00	£900.00
1	Sweet Caporal Calendar	1890	—	£62.50
52	Transparent Playing Cards (3 Types)	1890	£12.50	£650.00
25	Types of Nationalities (Folders 4 Types)	1890	£22.50	£562.50

PRINTED ALBUMS (EXCHANGED FOR COUPONS)

		Date	Odds	Sets
	Butterflies	1889	—	£115.00
	Celebrated American & English Running Horses	1890	—	*£150.00*
	Leaders	1889	—	*£130.00*
	Liberty Album	1889	—	£95.00
	National Dances	1889	—	*£125.00*
	Natural History	1890	—	£90.00
	Reigning Beauties	1889	—	*£140.00*
	Singers & Opera Houses	1889	—	*£150.00*
	Surf Beauties	1889	—	*£135.00*

KRAMERS TOB. CO. (PTY) LTD. (S. Africa)

50	Badges of South African Rugby Football Clubs (Multi-Backed)	1933	£6.00	—

CIE. LAFERME (Germany)

25	Types of Smokers	1900	£25.00	—

THE LAKE ERIE TOBACCO CO. (U.S.A.)

X?48	State Governors	1888	£60.00	—

B. LEIDERSDORF & CO. (U.S.A.)

T25	Actresses	1895	£40.00	—

I. LEWIS & CO. (U.S.A.)

X?46	Girls and Men in Costumes	1906	£25.00	—

LEWIS & ALLEN CO. (U.S.A.)

X120	Views & Art Studies	1912	£5.00	—

LIGGETT & MYERS TOBACCO CO. (U.S.A)

26	Actresses	1890	£40.00	—

LONE JACK CIGARETTE CO. (U.S.A.)

25	Inventors and Inventions	1887	£47.50	—
50	Language of Flowers (3 Types)	1888	£22.50	—
F?	Photographic Cards	1886	£6.00	—

P. LORILLARD CO. (U.S.A.)

25	Actresses (Coloured)	1888	£20.00	£500.00
M25	Actresses (Irregular Gold Frame)	1889	£22.00	—

P. LORILLARD CO. (U.S.A.) — cont.

Qty		Date	Odds	Sets
M175	Actresses (Fancy Surrounds)	1889	£21.00	—
M75	Actresses (Plain Surround)	1890	£17.50	—
X25	Actresses (Burdick 263)	1889	£22.00	£550.00
X25	Actresses (Burdick 264-1)	1890	£22.00	£550.00
X25	Actresses (Burdick 264-2)	1890	£23.00	—
X25	Actresses (Burdick 264-3, Grey Border)	1890	£24.00	—
X25	Actresses in Opera Roles	1892	£32.50	—
T25	Ancient Mythology Burlesqued	1893	£21.00	£525.00
T50	Beautiful Women	1893	£20.00	£1000.00
X25	Boxing Positions & Boxers	1892	£65.00	—
M?20	Busts of Girls (Die Cut)	1886	£75.00	—
X25	Circus Scenes	1888	£55.00	—
X?15	Everyday Annoyances	1886	*£75.00*	—
25	National Flags	1888	£20.00	—
T52	Playing Card Inset Girls	1885	£25.00	—
X50	Prizefighters	1887	*£65.00*	—
X?17	Song Album	1887	*£50.00*	—
T25	Types of Flirtation	1892	£45.00	—
T25	Types of the Stage	1893	£21.00	£525.00

W. C. MACDONALD INC. (Canada)

Qty		Date	Odds	Sets
?350	Aeroplanes & Warships	1940	70p	—
53	Playing Cards (Many Printings)	1927	50p	—

B. & J. B. MACHADO (Jamaica)

Qty		Date	Odds	Sets
25	British Naval Series	1916	£16.00	—
F50	Popular Film Stars	1926	*£4.00*	—
F52	Stars of the Cinema	1926	*£4.00*	—
50	The Great War – Victoria Cross Heroes	1916	£14.00	—
F50	The Royal Family at Home and Abroad	1927	*£3.00*	—
F50	The World of Sport	1928	£5.00	—

MACLIN-ZIMMER (U.S.A.)

Qty		Date	Odds	Sets
X53	Playing Cards (Actresses)	1890	£20.00	£1000.00

MALTA CIGARETTE CO.

Qty		Date	Odds	Sets
135	Dante's Divine Comedy	1905	£11.00	—
M40	Maltese Families Arms & Letters	1905	£6.00	—
?43	Prominent People	1905	£12.00	—

H. MANDELBAUM (U.S.A.)

Qty		Date	Odds	Sets
20	Comic Types of People	1890	£45.00	—
36	Flags of Nations	1890	£32.50	—

MARBURG BROS. (U.S.A.)

Qty		Date	Odds	Sets
50	"National Costume" Cards (2 Types)	1887	£45.00	—
X100	Painting Reproductions	1890	£55.00	—
?X17	Presidents and Other Celebrities	1886	£60.00	—
50	Typical Ships	1887	£50.00	—

MASPERO FRERES LTD. (Palestine)

Qty		Date	Odds	Sets
50	Birds, Beasts & Fishes	1925	£3.25	—

S. MATTINNO & SONS (Malta)

Qty		*Date*	*Odds*	*Sets*
X36	Britain Prepared Series	1940	£3.00	—

P. H. MAYO & BROTHER (U.S.A.)

Qty		*Date*	*Odds*	*Sets*
M25	Actresses (Fancy Frame)	1890	£24.00	£600.00
?25	Actresses (Sepia)	1886	£50.00	—
M25	Actresses (Black Border)	1890	£22.50	—
L12	Actresses (Diagonal)	1888	£50.00	—
?50	Actresses (Burdick 488, 2 Types)	1888	£21.50	—
X25	Actresses	1887	£40.00	—
28	Baseball Game (Die Cut)	1890	*£45.00*	—
40	Baseball Players	1892	£65.00	—
35	College Football Stars	1892	*£45.00*	—
20	Costumes & Flowers	1892	£24.00	—
19	Costumes of Warriors & Soldiers	1892	£23.00	£440.00
25	Head Dresses of Various Nations	1890	£26.00	£650.00
?100	National Dances (Die Cut)	1890	*£40.00*	—
M25	National Flowers (Girl & Scene)	1891	£26.00	£650.00
20	Naval Uniforms	1892	£25.00	—
F?	Photographic Cards	1887	*£6.00*	—
24	Presidents of the U.S.	1888	*£32.50*	—
35	Prizefighters (2 Types)	1890	£35.00	—
20	Shakespeare Characters	1891	£25.00	£500.00
X12	The Seasons	1888	*£60.00*	—
X15	Wings of Birds of Plumage	1888	*£55.00*	—

M. MELACHRINO & CO. (MALTA)

Qty		*Date*	*Odds*	*Sets*
52	Peuples Exotiques "1 Série"	1925	80p	£42.00
52	Peuples Exotiques "2 Série"	1925	80p	£42.00
52	Peuples Exotiques "3 Série"	1925	80p	£42.00

MERCATOR (Belgium) (Imitation Cigar Bands)

Qty		*Date*	*Odds*	*Sets*
24	British Empire Military Head-Dress	1976	—	£15.00
24	European Military Head-Dress	1976	—	£15.00

MEXICAN PUFFS (U.S.A.)

Qty		*Date*	*Odds*	*Sets*
20	Actresses, Blue Border	1890	£50.00	—

MIFSUD & AZZOPARDI (Malta)

Qty		*Date*	*Odds*	*Sets*
KF59	First Maltese Parliament (2 Types)	1922	£6.00	—

MRS. G. B. MILLER & CO. (U.S.A.)

Qty		*Date*	*Odds*	*Sets*
X?	Actresses & Celebrities	1885	*£50.00*	—
X?	Alphabet Cards	1887	£45.00	—
22	Photographs of all the Presidents	1888	£50.00	—

L. MILLER & SONS (U.S.A.)

Qty		*Date*	*Odds*	*Sets*
49	Animals & Birds	1900	*£50.00*	—
X25	Battleships	1900	£24.00	£600.00

L. MILLER & SONS (U.S.A.) — cont.

Qty		Date	Odds	Sets
X100	Beauties "THIBS" (2 Types)	1900	£35.00	—
X25	Generals & Admirals (Spanish War)	1900	£25.00	—
X24	Presidents of the U.S.	1900	£21.00	£500.00
X50	Rulers of the World	1900	£18.00	£900.00

CHAS. J. MITCHELL (CANADA)

26	Actresses "FROGA" (Brown Back)	1900	£30.00	—
26	(Green Back)	1900	£25.00	—
26	Actresses "FROGA"(Playing Card Back)	1900	*£40.00*	—

MONARCH TOBACCO WORKS (U.S.A.)

X?4	American Indian Chiefs	1890	£65.00	—

MOORE & CALVI (U.S.A.)

X10	Actresses "RAEMA"	1887	£62.50	—
X53	Beauties, Playing Card Inset, Set 1	1886	£20.00	£1050.00
X53	Beauties, Playing Card Inset, Set 2	1890	£17.50	£925.00
X53	Beauties, Playing Card Inset, Set 3	1890	£17.50	£925.00

MURAI BROS. (Japan)

50	Actresses "ALWICS"	1910	£8.50	£425.00
?50	Actresses "MUREG"	1900	£36.00	—
50	Beauties	1902	£11.00	£550.00
24	Beauties "HUMPS"	1900	£24.00	—
100	Beauties, Thick Borders	1902	£25.00	—
50	Chinese Beauties (Stork Back)	1908	£4.00	£200.00
25	Chinese Beauties (Peacock Back)	1912	£2.60	£65.00
25	Chinese Beauties (Peacock, Different)	1912	£4.00	—
50	Chinese Children's Games (White Border)	1911	£2.00	£100.00
20	Chinese Children's Games (Coloured Border)	1911	£2.50	£50.00
M?	Chinese Girls (Various Series)	1905	£4.00	—
25	Chinese Pagodas	1911	£2.50	£62.50
30	Chinese Series	1910	£2.50	£75.00
50	Chinese Trades	1905	£25.00	—
26	Comic Phrases	1900	*£25.00*	—
50	Dancing Girls of the World	1900	£27.50	—
32	Flowers	1900	£22.50	—
25	Japanese Personalities	1900	£36.00	—
?50	Japanese Subjects – Symbol Inset	1900	£42.50	—
50	Wild Animals of the World	1900	£36.00	—
50	World's Distinguished Personages	1900	£22.00	—
50	World's Smokers	1900	£22.50	—

NATIONAL CIGARETTE & TOBACCO CO. (U.S.A.)

?12	Actresses	1886	£60.00	—
25	National Types (Sailor Girls)	1890	£22.00	£550.00
F?	Photographic Cards	1888	£4.00	—

NATIONAL CIGARETTE CO. (Australia)

13	English Cricket Team, 1897-8	1897	*£250.00*	—

NATIONAL TOBACCO WORKS (U.S.A.)

Qty		Date	Odds	Sets
GF?	Actresses, etc. (Newsboy)	1900	£13.00	—
G100	Actresses (Coloured)	1900	£24.00	—

OLD FASHION FINE CUT (U.S.A.)

TF?	Photographic Cards	1890	£6.00	—

OMEGA CIGARETTE FACTORY (Malta)

KF96	Cinema Stars	1936	£2.50	£240.00
F?36	Maltese Footballers	1928	*£11.00*	—
M?16	Maltese Politicians, Cartoons by 'Mike	1940	*£20.00*	—
M?4	World War II Leaders, Cartoons by Mike	1940	*£20.00*	—

OXFORD CIGARETTE CO. (Malta)

MF24	Egyptian Scenes (Anonymous)	1926	£7.50	—

PENINSULAR TOBACCO CO. LTD. (India)

50	Animals and Birds	1910	£1.50	—
52	Birds of Brilliant Plumage (P/C Inset)	1916	£2.50	—
25	Birds of the East, 1st Series	1912	£1.60	£40.00
25	Birds of the East, 2nd Series	1912	£1.60	£40.00
25	China's Famous Warriors (2 Types)	1912	£2.60	£65.00
25	Chinese Heroes	1913	£2.00	£50.00
50	Chinese Modern Beauties	1912	*£3.50*	—
50	Chinese Trades, Set 3	1912	*£2.50*	—
50	Chinese Trades, Set 5	1913	*£2.50*	—
30	Fish Series	1916	£1.85	£55.00
25	Hindoo Gods	1909	£2.00	—
37	Nautch Girl Series (3 Types)	1910	£4.50	—
25	Products of the World	1915	£1.50	£37.50

E. T. PILKINTON-CO. (U.S.A.)

X48	Fruits & Flowers	1890	£50.00	—

PIZZUTO (Malta)

50	Milton's "Paradise Lost"	1910	£7.50	—

THE PLANTERS STORES (India)

50	Actresses "FROGA"	1900	£27.50	—
25	Beauties "FECKSA"	1900	£32.50	—

POLICANSKY BROS. (South Africa)

M50	Birds, Beasts & Fishes (Nassa Cigarettes)	1924	£5.00	—
50	Regimental Uniforms (2 Types)	1937	£1.30	£65.00
50	South African Fauna (2 Types)	1925	£7.00	£350.00

RED MAN CHEWING TOBACCO (U.S.A.)

Qty		*Date*	*Odds*	*Sets*
X40	American Indian Chiefs	1952	£6.00	£240.00

LA REFORMA (Canary Islands)

Qty		*Date*	*Odds*	*Sets*
X8	Military Uniforms, Serie A-1 (Prussia)	1925	—	£15.00
X8	Military Uniforms, Serie A-3 (France)	1925	—	£15.00
D5	Military Uniforms, Serie A-4 (France)	1925	—	£10.00
D7	Military Uniforms, Serie A-5 (Spain)	1925	—	£15.00
X8	Military Uniforms, Serie A-6 (Prussia)	1925	—	£15.00
D6	Military Uniforms, Serie A-7 (Spain)	1925	—	£11.50
X6	Military Uniforms, Serie B-1 (Shaped)	1925	—	£11.50
X6	Military Uniforms, Serie B-2 (Shaped)	1925	—	£11.50

D. RITCHIE & CO. (Canada)

Qty		*Date*	*Odds*	*Sets*
30	Actresses "RITAN" (Printed Back)	1887	£27.00	—
30	(Plain Back)	1887	£25.00	—
?33	Actresses ("Our Production" Back)	1889	£40.00	—
?29	Actresses ("Derby" Front)	1889	£45.00	—
52	Beauties P/C Inset (Several Types)	1888	£22.50	—
36	Flags of All Nations	1888	£50.00	—
52	Playing Cards	1888	*£27.50*	—

D. E. ROSE & CO. (U.S.A.)

Qty		*Date*	*Odds*	*Sets*
G28	Imperial Cards	1890	£37.50	—

RUGGIER BROS. (Malta)

Qty		*Date*	*Odds*	*Sets*
M50	Story of the Knights of Malta	1924	£5.00	—

RUMI CIGARETTES (Germany)

Qty		*Date*	*Odds*	*Sets*
M56	Beauties (Franks)	1901	£32.50	—

JOHN SCERRI (Malta)

Qty		*Date*	*Odds*	*Sets*
147	Beauties & Children (Black & White)	1930	£1.00	—
180	Beauties & Children (Unicoloured)	1930	£14.00	—
?100	Beauties & Children (Large Numerals)	1930	£11.50	—
45	Beauties & Children (Coloured)	1930	£1.40	—
MF50	Beautiful Women	1931	£1.50	—
MF480	Cinema Artists	1931	£1.75	—
MF180	Cinema Stars	1931	£2.00	—
MF50	Famous London Buildings	1934	£2.75	£137.50
F60	Film Stars (First Serie)	1931	£1.80	—
F60	Film Stars (Second Serie)	1931	£1.80	—
52	Interesting Places of the World	1934	40p	£20.00
F25	International Footballers	1935	£10.00	—
401	Malta Views	1928	50p	—
MF51	Members of Parliament-Malta	1928	40p	£20.00
146	Prominent People	1930	£1.00	—
MF100	Scenes from Films	1932	£1.60	—
LF100	Talkie Stars	1932	£2.00	—
M100	World's Famous Buildings	1931	50p	£50.00

J. J. SCHUH TOBACCO CO. (Australia)

Qty		*Date*	*Odds*	*Sets*
60	Australian Footballers A (½ Length)	1920	£4.00	£240.00
40	Australian Footballers B (Rays)	1921	£4.25	£170.00
60	Australian Footballers C (Oval Frame)	1922	£7.50	—
60	Australian Jockeys	1921	£4.00	£240.00
F72	Cinema Stars (Black & White)	1924	£1.60	£115.00
60	Cinema Stars (Coloured)	1924	£1.60	£96.00
L12	Maxims of Success	1917	*£40.00*	—
F72	Official War Photographs (2 Types)	1918	£2.50	£180.00
F104	Portraits of our Leading Footballers	1920	£2.60	£270.00

G. SCLIVAGNOTI (Malta)

50	Actresses & Cinema Stars	1923	£2.00	£100.00
MF71	Grand Masters of the Order of Jerusalem	1898	£8.50	—
F102	Opera Singers	1898	£9.00	—
M100	Opera Singers	1898	£9.00	—
72	Scenes with Girls (Black & White)	1905	£32.50	—
M12	Scenes with Girls (Coloured)	1905	*£35.00*	—

SENATOR (Belgium) (Imitation Cigar Bands)

24	Decorations and Orders of Chivalry	1975	—	£5.00

SINSOCK & CO. (China)

?50	Chinese Beauties	1905	£12.50	—

SNIDERS & ABRAHAMS PTY. LTD. (Australia)

30	Actresses (Gold Background)	1905	£5.00	£150.00
14	(White Borders)	1905	£5.50	£77.00
20	Admirals & Warships of the U.S.A. (2 Types)	1908	£6.25	—
2	Advertisement Cards	1905	*£25.00*	—
60	Animals (Green, Descriptive Back)	1912	£3.00	—
60	Animals & Birds (2 Types)	1912	£2.25	£135.00
15	Australian Cricket Team	1905	£34.00	—
16	Australian Football – Incidents in Play	1906	£7.00	£112.00
72	Australian Footballers – Series A (Full Length)	1904	£8.00	—
76	Australian Footballers – Series B (½ Length)	1906	£6.00	—
76	Australian Footballers – Series C (½ Length)	1907	£5.75	—
56	Australian Footballers – Series D (Head/Shoulders)	1908	£5.00	£280.00
140	Australian Footballers – Series D (Head/Shoulders)	1909	£5.00	—
60	Australian Footballers – Series E (Head in Oval)	1910	£4.75	£285.00
60	Australian Footballers – Series F (Head in Rays)	1911	£5.50	—
60	Australian Footballers – Series G (With Pennant)	1912	£5.00	—
60	Australian Footballers – Series H (Head in Star) 2 Types	1913	£5.00	—
60	Australian Footballers – Series I (Head in Shield) 2 Types	1914	£5.00	—
56	Australian Footballers – Series J (½ - ¾ Length)	1910	£8.00	—
48	Australian Jockeys (Blue Back)	1907	£3.40	£165.00
60	Australian Jockeys (Brown Back)	1908	£3.75	£225.00
56	Australian Racehorses (Horizontal Back)	1906	£3.75	£210.00
56	Australian Racehorses (Vertical Back)	1907	£3.75	—
40	Australian Racing Scenes	1911	£3.75	£150.00
?133	Australian V.C.'s and Officers	1917	£5.00	—
?63	Belgian Views	1916	£2.50	—
12	Billiard Tricks	1908	£10.00	—
60	Butterflies & Moths (Captions in Capitals)	1914	£1.50	£90.00
60	(Captions in Mixed Letters)	1914	£1.50	£90.00

SNIDERS & ABRAHAMS PTY. LTD. (Australia) — cont.

Qty		Date	Odds	Sets
60	Cartoons & Caricatures (2 Types)	1907	£5.00	—
12	Coin Tricks	1908	£9.00	—
64	Crests of British Warships (2 Types)	1915	£4.50	£285.00
40	Cricketers in Action	1906	£40.00	—
12	Cricket Terms	1905	£25.00	—
32	Dickens Series	1909	£4.50	£144.00
16	Dogs (4 Types)	1910	£7.00	£112.00
90	European War Series	1916	£3.25	—
6	Flags (Shaped Metal)	1915	£3.25	—
6	Flags (Shaped Card)	1915	£3.50	—
60	Great War Leaders & Warships (3 Types)	1915	£3.00	£180.00
30	How to Keep Fit	1907	£4.50	£135.00
60	Jokes (3 Types)	1906	£3.50	£210.00
12	Match Puzzles	1908	£9.00	—
48	Medals & Decorations	1915	£4.50	—
M48	Melbourne Buildings	1914	£5.75	—
25	Natives of the World	1904	£12.50	£312.50
12	Naval Terms	1905	£6.00	£72.00
29	Oscar Asche, Lily Brayton & Lady Smokers	1911	£4.50	£130.00
40	Shakespeare Characters	1909	£4.50	£180.00
30	Signalling Series	1916	£5.50	—
?14	Statuary	1905	£7.50	—
60	Street Criers in London, 1707	1914	£6.50	—
32	Views of Victoria in 1857 (2 Types)	1906	£8.00	—
FS?250	Views of the World	1908	£2.50	—

SOUTH INDIAN TOBACCO MFG. CO.

Qty		Date	Odds	Sets
25	Actresses "ALWICS"	1905	£8.00	—
?25	Moslem Personalities	1905	£8.00	—

SPAULDING & MERRICK (U.S.A.)

Qty		Date	Odds	Sets
M25	Actresses	1888	£50.00	—
M24/25	Animals	1890	£20.00	£480.00

STAR TOBACCO CO. (India)

Qty		Date	Odds	Sets
?25	Beauties "STARA" (2 Types)	1898	£40.00	—
52	Beauties (P/C Inset) (3 Types)	1898	£22.00	—
52	Heroes of the Transvaal War (P/C Inset)	1901	*£50.00*	—
52	Indian Native Types (P/C Inset)	1898	£22.00	£1150.00

J. W. L. STUBBS (New Zealand)

Qty		Date	Odds	Sets
M?46	Barques and Sailing Boats	1926	*£24.00*	—
F?200	Photographic Cards	1926	£10.00	—

SUB ROSA CIGARETTES (U.S.A.)

Qty		Date	Odds	Sets
10	Actresses	1885	£50.00	—

SURBRUG CO. (U.S.A.)

Qty		Date	Odds	Sets
M10	Aeroplane Series No. 103	1912	£16.00	£160.00
M10	Prize Dog Series No. 102	1911	£17.50	£175.00
M25	Prize Fight Series No. 101 (2 Types)	1911	£20.00	£500.00

CIE. DE TABAC TERREBONNE (Canada)

Qty		Date	Odds	Sets
30	Bingo-Puzzle	1924	*£5.00*	—
30	Bingo-Puzzle, 2nd Series	1925	*£5.00*	—
30	Bingo-Puzzle, 3rd Series	1926	*£5.00*	—
30	Bingo-Puzzle, 4th Series	1927	£4.00	—
30	Bingo-Puzzle, 5th Series	1928	£4.00	—

THOMPSON, MOORE & CO. (U.S.A.)

Qty		Date	Odds	Sets
X10	Rope Knots	1888	£55.00	£550.00

TOBACCO PRODUCTS CORPORATION (Canada & U.S.A.)

Qty		Date	Odds	Sets
?48	Canadian Sports Champions	1917	*£10.00*	—
60	Do You Know?	1918	£5.00	—
60	Hockey Players	1918	*£16.50*	—
220	Movie Stars	1915	£2.00	—
120	Movie Stars (Portrait in Oval)	1915	£2.00	—
L?50	Movie Stars	1915	£3.00	—
L?100	Movie Stars, Series No.3	1916	£3.00	—
?180	Movie Stars, Series No.4	1916	*£3.00*	—
L100	Movie Stars, Series No.5	1916	£3.00	—
18	Ship Picture Letters	1915	*£7.50*	—

TUCKETT LTD. (Canada)

Qty		Date	Odds	Sets
M52	Aeroplane Series	1930	£3.50	—
M52	Aviation Series (3 Types)	1930	£3.50	—
25	Autograph Series (2 Types)	1913	£26.50	—
60	Badges (Regimental)	1917	£10.00	—
?50	Beauties & Scenes (2 Types)	1910	£6.25	—
25	Boy Scout Series	1914	*£17.50*	—
M8	British Gravures	1923	*£11.00*	—
L8	British Gravures	1923	*£11.00*	—
F100	British Views Plain Back	1912	£1.60	£160.00
F?250	British Views (3 Types)	1912	£1.75	—
F80	British Warships (2 Types)	1914	£8.00	—
F50	Canadian Scenes	1912	£1.50	—
?50	Card Trick Series	1928	£6.00	—
M48	Delivering Mail (Stamps)	1910	*£13.50*	—
?110	Girls and Warships	1924	*£10.00*	—
52	Playing Card Premium Certificates	1930	*£7.00*	—
M52	Tucketts Auction Bridge Series	1930	*£5.50*	—

TURCO-AMERICAN TOBACCO CO. (U.S.A.)

Qty		Date	Odds	Sets
M15	Foreign Views	1908	£12.50	—

TURKISH-MACEDONIAN TOBACCO CO. (Holland)

ANONYMOUS SILKS

Qty		Date	Odds	Sets
M?43	Animals, Birds and Butterflies	1926	£3.25	—
M18	Arms of Dutch Colonies	1926	£3.25	—
M21	Arms of Dutch & European Towns (White)	1926	£3.25	—
?32	Celebrities (White)	1926	£4.50	—
M20	Decorations and Medals	1926	£5.00	—
101	Dutch Celebrities	1934	£3.50	—
M86	Dutch Celebrities, Arms etc.	1926	£3.00	—
M12	Film Stars	1926	*£7.50*	—

LIEBIG

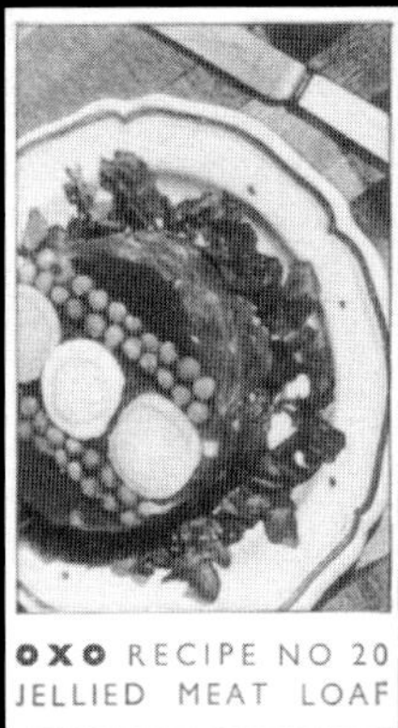

The Liebig Extract of Meat Co. Ltd. was formed in 1856 and was acquired by Brooke Bond in 1971. In Britain their product was renamed Oxo, which it is known as today. In a period of 100 years from 1872 the Company issued a large number of sets of cards, including postcards, menus, calendars, place cards and other novelty issues. The first series were issued in France, but eventually cards could be obtained all over Europe, in languages such as Danish, Czech, Spanish, and even Russian. Many series were printed in English, including the Oxo insert series, and issued in Britain and the U.S.A.

In all the company issued 2,000 different sets of cards. These covered an enormous variety of subjects, including the Trans-Siberian Railway, Shadowgraphs, Gulliver, Fans, Education in Ancient Greece, and the Left Bank of the River Po. There is even a set showing the life of Justus von Liebig, founder of the firm, and another showing how the cards themselves are prepared and printed.

Because of the size of the subject a separate catalogue is available (price £4.95) listing all the issues, and a small selection of series is listed on pages 247 and 248.

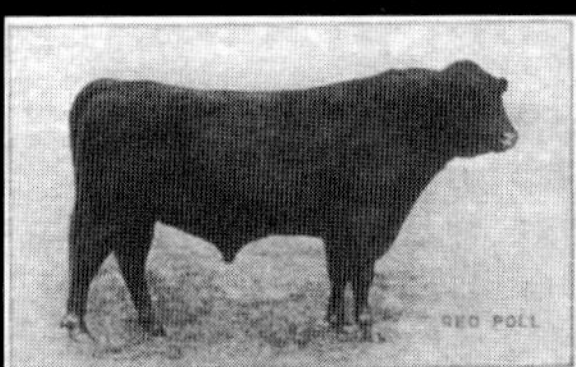

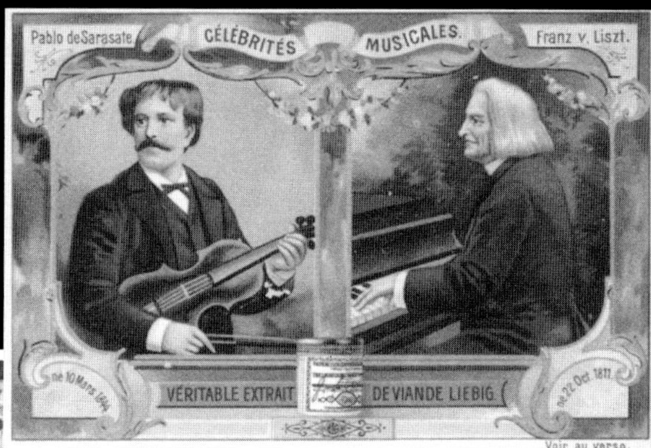

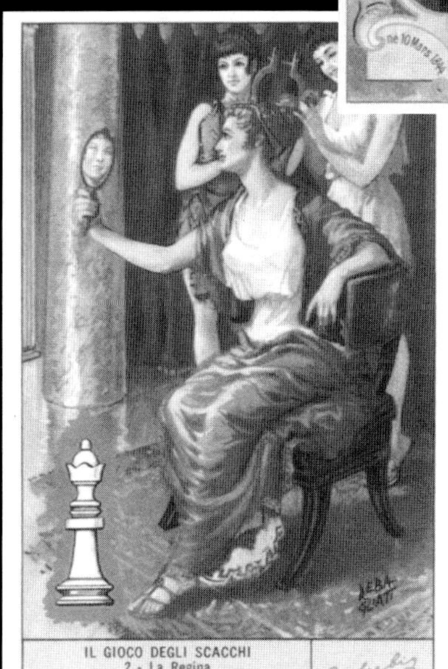

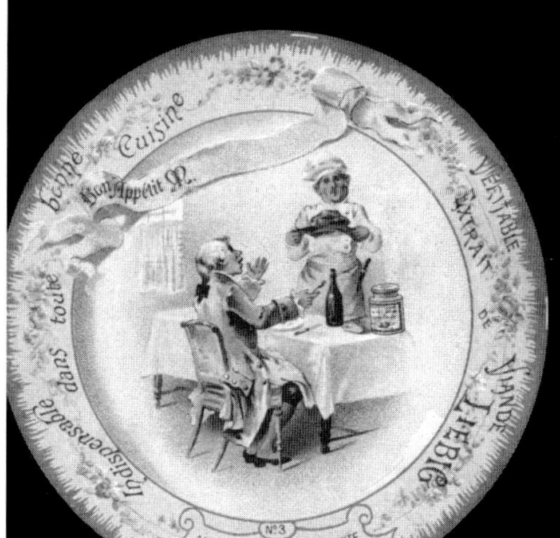

B.A.T. ISSUES

In 1902 at the conclusion of the "Tobacco War", the British American Tobacco Co. was incorporated in Britain for the purpose of marketing all I.T.C. and A.T.C. tobacco products in countries other than the U.S.A., Cuba, Great Britain and Ireland.

In many British Empire countries B.A.T. began to market under the name of a subsidiary Company. In Canada it was the Imperial Tobacco Co. of Canada, while in India the Imperial Tobacco Co. of India shared the stage with the Peninsular Tobacco Co. In South Africa the dominant name was United Tobacco Co. and in South America Cia Chilena and Cia Nobleza. In Australia the majority of issues bore the Wills name, either with Capstan or Vice-Regal, except that some also appeared as Havelock Cigarettes, with no issuer's name. Brands in New Zealand appeared under the names of Lambert & Butler, Player and Wills, as well as the local Dominion Tobacco Co; local arrangements were made with companies such as Ardath, as may be deduced from their issue in New Zealand of their versions of sets such as Churchman Eastern Proverbs, Player Tennis and Ogden Swimming Diving & Life Saving.

Card issues appeared with all the above firms' names, as well as some, particularly earlier issues such as the tobacco war Beauties, which have the B.A.T. name. There were also many in foreign languages such as Motor Cigarettes (Portugal), Albert (Belgium) and Gold Dollar (Germany), as well as a number in Chinese and Siamese characters. A large section of B.A.T.'s card output however appears with no clues as to the issuer, both with printed backs (often mentioning cigarettes) and with plain backs.

When the B.A.T. issue utilises the name of a British firm, such as Ogden or Wills, then in the Catalogue the cards will be found listed under that firm, often in a separate group. Anonymous series that were issued exclusively in Canada or South Africa are included in Part 2 under Imperial Tobacco Co. of Canada or United Tobacco Co. respectively. All other Anonymous sets known to have been produced by B.A.T. are listed under that firm in Part 2.

A more detailed explanation of the foundation and ramifications of B.A.T. may be found in the B.A.T. Reference Book, price £12.50.

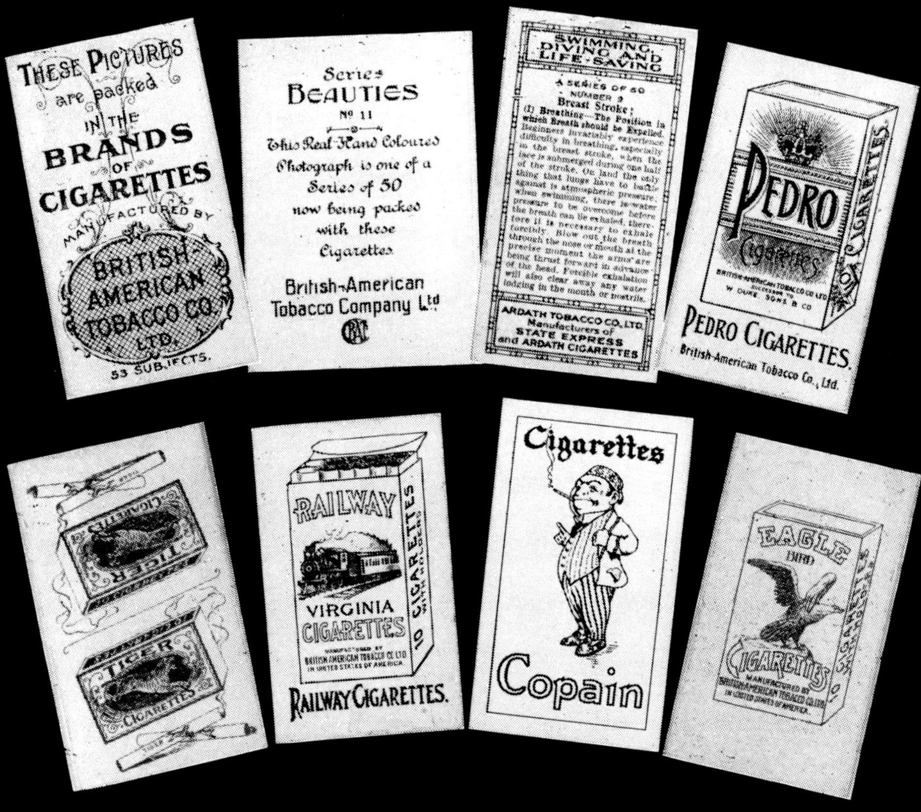

TURKISH-MACEDONIAN TOBACCO CO. (Holland) — cont.

Qty		Date	Odds	Sets
M249	Flags, Arms and Standards	1926	£1.60	£400.00
D166	Flags and Arms, Series 2	1926	£2.00	—
?31	Flowers	1926	£5.00	—
M34	Flowers	1926	£3.50	—
M20	Flowers (Europa/Afrika)	1926	£4.25	—
M89	Flower Series (A-E)	1926	£3.50	—
M3	Girls of Many Lands (Black Silk)	1926	£5.00	£15.00
M50	(White Silk)	1929	£3.50	£175.00
M54	Illustrated Initials	1926	£3.00	—
M12	Japanese Series	1926	£6.50	—
M?46	Javanese Figures	1926	£3.50	—
M34	National Costumes	1926	£3.25	£110.00
D62	National Flags (White Silk)	1926	£2.75	—
M141	National Flags (Paper Backs)	1926	£2.75	—
M16	Nature Calendar	1926	£4.00	—
M20	Ships of All Ages	1926	*£7.50*	—
?85	Sporting Figures (Series A-E)	1926	£5.00	—
25	Sporting Figures (CA1-25)	1926	£5.00	£125.00
X18	Town Arms of Holland	1926	£4.00	—
M26	World Celebrities	1926	£5.50	—
M56	Youth Series and Miscellaneous	1926	£3.00	—

U. S. TOBACCO CO. (U.S.A.)

Qty		Date	Odds	Sets
X25	Actresses	1890	£40.00	—

UNITED CIGAR STORES (U.S.A.)

Qty		Date	Odds	Sets
L25	The Aviators (2 Types)	1911	£18.00	£450.00

UNITED TOBACCO COMPANIES (SOUTH) LTD. (S. Africa)

Qty		Date	Odds	Sets
50	Aeroplanes of To-day (2 Types)	1936	£1.40	£70.00
50	African Fish	1937	£1.25	£62.50
48	All Sports Series	1926	*£20.00*	—
L48	All Sports Series	1926	*£20.00*	—
50	Animals & Birds (2 Types)	1923	£6.00	—
L24	Arms and Crests of Universities and Schools of South Africa	1930	£1.20	£30.00
FS50	Beauties of Great Britain	1930	£1.50	—
L52	Boy Scout, Girl Guide & Voortrekker Badges	1932	£1.60	£80.00
M50	British Aeroplanes	1933	£1.30	£65.00
L20	British Butterflies (Silk)	1924	£8.50	—
L30	British Roses (Silk)	1924	£9.00	—
L62	British Rugby Tour of South Africa	1938	£1.50	£93.00
50	Children of All Nations	1928	80p	£40.00
50	Cinema Stars (Flag Cigarettes)	1922	£1.80	£110.00
X?12	Conundrums	1910	*£40.00*	—
40	Cricketers & Their Autographs (Plain Back)	1922	£24.50	£960.00
60	Do You Know?	1930	50p	£30.00
50	Do You Know? 2nd Series	1930	50p	£25.00
50	Do You Know? 3rd Series	1931	50p	£25.00
30	Do You Know? (Different)	1933	60p	£18.00
50	Eminent Film Personalities	1930	£2.00	£100.00
50	English Period Costumes	1932	80p	£40.00
L50	Exercises for Men and Women	1932	90p	£45.00

UNITED TOBACCO COMPANIES (SOUTH) LTD. (S. Africa) — cont.

Qty		*Date*	*Odds*	*Sets*
96	Fairy Tales	1926	£1.40	£135.00
24	Fairy Tales (Folders)	1926	£7.50	£180.00
25	Famous Figures from S. A. History	1932	£1.80	£45.00
L100	Famous Works of Art	1939	20p	£20.00
L120	Farmyards of South Africa	1934	35p	£42.00
L65	Flags of All Nations (Silk)	1910	£2.50	—
25	Flowers of South Africa	1932	£1.60	£40.00
FS52	Here There and Everywhere	1930	75p	£37.50
L50	Household Hints	1926	£1.20	—
M50	Humour in Sport	1929	£2.50	—
25	Interesting Experiments	1930	£1.20	£30.00
L100	Medals and Decorations of the British Commonwealth of Nations	1941	85p	£85.00
50	Merchant Ships of the World	1925	£1.00	£50.00
30	Merrie England Studies – Female	1914	£7.00	£210.00
52	Miniature Playing Cards (Flag)	1938	£1.00	—
53	(Lifeboat)	1938	£1.75	—
53	(Lotus)	1938	*£1.75*	—
53	(Rugger)	1938	*£2.00*	—
50	Motor Cars	1928	£3.40	£170.00
FS48	Nature Studies	1930	75p	—
X28	1912-13 Springboks	1912	*£35.00*	—
X?12	Nursery Rhymes	1910	*£40.00*	—
M25	Old Masters (Silk)	1926	£8.00	—
L100	Our Land	1938	20p	£20.00
M150	Our South African Birds	1942	25p	£37.50
L150	Our South African Birds	1942	20p	£30.00
M100	Our South African Flora	1940	20p	£15.00
L100	Our South African Flora	1940	20p	£15.00
M100	Our South African National Parks	1941	20p	£15.00
L100	Our South African National Parks	1941	20p	£15.00
L200	Our South Africa – Past & Present	1938	20p	£30.00
X60	Ozaka's System of Self Defence	1911	*£40.00*	—
L24	Pastel Plates	1930	£1.10	£26.50
L88	Philosophical Sayings	1938	£1.00	£88.00
L50	Pictures of South Africa's War Effort	1940	20p	£10.00
FS48	Pictures of the East	1930	75p	£36.00
25	Picturesque People of the Empire	1929	£1.30	£32.50
L50	Pottery Types (Silk)	1926	£5.00	£250.00
M50	Pottery Types (Silk)	1926	£7.00	—
L50	Race Horses – South Africa (Set 1)	1929	£1.60	£80.00
L52	Race Horses – South Africa (Set 2), (2 Types)	1930	£1.60	£83.00
50	Riders of the World (Firm's Name)	1931	£1.00	£50.00
50	(C.T. Ltd.)	1931	£1.20	£60.00
L52	S. A. Flora (2 Types)	1935	30p	£16.00
M40	Ships of All Times	1931	£1.50	£60.00
10	Silhouettes of M.L.A.'s	1914	£26.00	—
25	South African Birds, A Series	1927	£1.20	£30.00
25	South African Birds, Second Series	1927	£1.20	£30.00
L52	South African Butterflies	1937	60p	£30.00
L52	South African Coats of Arms	1931	45p	£23.50
L17	South African Cricket Touring Team	1929	£20.00	—
L17	Ditto (Autographed)	1929	£16.00	£270.00
M100	South African Defence	1941	20p	£20.00
L50	South African Flowers (Silk)	1913	£3.50	£175.00

UNITED TOBACCO COMPANIES (SOUTH) LTD. (S. Africa) — cont.

Qty		*Date*	*Odds*	*Sets*
L50	South African Flowers (Second Series)	1913	£3.50	—
L50	South African Places of Interest	1934	20p	£10.00
L65	South African Rugby Football Clubs	1933	£1.20	£78.00
L52	Sports & Pastimes in South Africa	1936	£1.40	£70.00
L47	Springbok Rugby & Cricket Teams	1931	£2.50	£117.50
FS50	Stereoscopic Photographs	1928	80p	£40.00
FS50	Stereoscopic Photographs of South Africa	1929	80p	£40.00
25	"Studdy" Dogs (Bonzo)	1925	£4.00	—
M50	Tavern of the Seas	1939	40p	£20.00
50	The Story of Sand	1934	85p	£42.50
50	The World of Tomorrow	1938	80p	£40.00
?84	Transfers	1925	£5.00	—
L40	Views of South African Scenery	1918	£4.00	£160.00
L36	Views of South African Scenery, Second Series	1920	£4.00	£144.00
25	Warriors of All Nations (Swords at Base)	1937	£1.50	£37.50
25	What's This?	1929	£1.60	£40.00
50	Wild Animals of the World	1932	£1.20	£60.00
25	Wild Flowers of South Africa, A Series	1925	£1.00	£25.00
25	Wild Flowers of South Africa, Second Series	1926	£1.00	£25.00
M40	Wonders of the World	1931	85p	£34.00
M100	World-Famous Boxers	1939	£5.00	—

UNIVERSAL TOBACCO CO. (India)

F50	Actresses (Plain Back)	1900	£18.00	—
F50	(Printed Back)	1900	£21.00	—

UNIVERSAL TOBACCO CO. (PTY.) LTD. (S. Africa)

835	Flags of All Nations	1935	90p	—
M?368	Park Lane Fashions	1934	*£6.50*	—

S. W. VENABLE TOBACCO CO. (U.S.A.)

X?56	Actresses (Multi-Backed)	1888	£27.50	—
X12	Baseball & Seashore Scenes (7 Backs)	1888	£65.00	—

R. WHALEN & CO. (U.S.A.)

L25	Actresses	1890	£45.00	—

WYNEN ZIGARETTEN (Germany)

50	Tanzerinnen Aller Welt	1900	£35.00	—

GEO. F. YOUNG (U.S.A.)

X?76	Actresses	1889	£25.00	—
X12	Baseball & Seashore Scenes	1888	*£65.00*	—
X10	National Sports – Girls	1887	£60.00	—
X?	Photographic Cards	1886	£4.50	—

"NOSTALGIA" REPRINTS

An exciting concept for collectors. Reproductions of Classic card sets, all of which are almost impossible to obtain, at a price that everyone can afford.

These cards are of the highest quality, and the latest technology has been used to recreate as closely as possible the beauty of the originals. They have received universal acclaim in the cigarette card world, and are indeed becoming collector's items in their own right.

Because of the difficulty of distinguishing our reproductions from the originals each reprint has 'A Nostalgia Reprint' printed on the back of the card.

TITLES CURRENTLY AVAILABLE

Taddy County Cricketers

15 Derbyshire
15 Essex
16 Gloucestershire
15 Hampshire
15 Kent
15 Lancashire
14 Leicestershire
15 Middlesex
15 Northamptonshire
14 Nottinghamshire
15 Somersetshire (sic)
15 Surrey
15 Sussex
15 Warwickshire
14 Worcestershire
15 Yorkshire

ONLY £2.00 per County, or all 238 cards for £27.50

Taddy Prominent Footballers

15 Aston Villa
15 Chelsea
15 Everton
15 Leeds City
15 Liverpool
15 Manchester United
15 Middlesborough
15 Newcastle
15 Queen's Park Rangers
15 Sunderland
15 Tottenham Hotspur
15 West HamUnited
15 Woolwich Arsenal

ONLY £2.00 per Club

Allen & Ginter	50	American Indian Chiefs	**£7.50**
Allen & Ginter	50	Fruits	**£7.50**
Berlyn	25	Humorous Golfing Series	**£6.00**
Cope	50	Cope's Golfers	**£7.50**
Cope	50	Dickens Gallery	**£7.50**
Cope	50	Shakespeare Gallery	**£7.50**
Ellis	25	Generals of the Late Civil War	**£6.00**
Gabriel	20	Cricketers Series	**£3.50**
Jones Bros.	18	Spurs Footballers	**£2.00**
Kinney	25	Leaders	**£6.00**
Player	50	Military Series	**£7.50**
Taddy	20	Clowns and Circus Artistes	**£6.00**
Thomson	24	Motor Bike Cards	**£6.00**
Thomson	20	Motor Cycles	**£6.00**
U.S. Tobacco	28	Baseball Greats of the 1890's	**£6.00**
Wills	50	Cricketers 1896	**£7.50**
Wills	50	Cricketers Series 1901	**£15.00**

A specially designed frame, is available for Taddy Clowns priced at £30 (to include special mounting board, glass and set).

Part 3

NON-TOBACCO ISSUES

INDEX OF BRANDS (Non-Tobacco)

These may appear on cards without the manufacturer's name (see also Information opposite Page 129)

A-1 DAIRIES LTD. (Tea)

Qty		Date	Odds	Sets
25	Birds and their Eggs	1965	£1.00	—
25	Butterflies and Moths	1964	—	£2.00
25	The Story of Milk	1967	—	£2.50

A-1 DOLLISDALE TEA

Qty		Date	Odds	Sets
25	Do you know about Shipping & Trees?	1963	—	£2.00

A.B.C. (Cinemas)

Qty		Date	Odds	Sets
10	Animals	1952	£1.60	£16.00
10	An Adventure in Space	1950	£2.50	£25.00
10	Birds	1958	—	£5.00
10	Birds & Bird-Watching	1953	£2.50	—
10	British Athletes	1955	—	£6.00
20	British Soldiers (Black Back)	1949	35p	£7.00
20	(Brown Back)	1949	20p	£4.00
10	Colorstars	1962	—	£4.50
10	Colorstars (2nd Series)	1962	£2.75	—
10	Colorstars (3rd Series)	1962	£1.50	£15.00
10	Dogs	1957	—	£15.00
L16	Film Stars	1935	£4.00	—
10	Film Stars	1948	£2.00	—
10	Horses	1958	—	£7.00
10	Interesting Buildings	1956	—	£5.00
10	Journey by Land	1954	£2.25	—
10	Journey by Water	1954	£2.25	—
10	Journey to the Moon	1955	—	£10.00
10	Parliament Buildings	1957	—	£5.00
10	Railway Engines	1951	£2.75	£27.50
10	Scenes from the Films	1953	£3.00	£30.00
10	Sea Exploration	1957	—	£6.00
10	Sea Scenes	1958	—	£5.00
10	Sports on Land	1956	—	£6.00
12	Star Series	1936	£4.25	—
10	Travel of the Future	1956	—	£6.00
10	Water Sports	1956	—	£5.00

A. & B. C. GUM

40 Page Illustrated Reference Book — £3.50

Qty		Date	Odds	Sets
M120	All Sport Series	1954	£3.00	£400.00
P17	Banknotes	1971	£3.00	£51.00
X55	Batman (Pink Back, Fan Club Panel)	1966	£1.50	£82.50
X55	(Pink Back, No Panel)	1966	£1.00	£55.00
X55	Batman (Numbered on Front)	1966	£1.80	£99.00
X44	Batman (1A-44A)	1966	£2.25	£99.00
X44	Batman (1B-44B)	1966	£3.00	£132.00
X38	Batman (Black Back)	1966	£3.00	£114.00
X38	(Black Back, Dutch)	1966	£4.00	£152.00
M1	Batman Secret Decoder	1966	—	£12.50

Qty		Date	Odds	Sets
X73	Battle Cards	1966	£1.20	£90.00
X66	Battle of Britain	1970	£1.20	£80.00
X60	Bazooka Joe and his Gang	1968	£3.50	—
X60	Beatles (Black & White)	1964	£3.00	£180.00
X45	Beatles, 2nd Series	1965	£5.00	—
X40	Beatles (Coloured)	1965	£8.00	—
K120	Car Stamps	1971	£2.50	—
X21	Car Stamps Albums	1971	£5.00	£105.00
L?56	Christian Name Stickers	1967	£2.25	—
X15	Civil War Banknotes	1965	£3.00	£45.00
X88	Civil War News	1965	£2.00	£200.00
X43	Comic Book Foldees	1968	£1.30	£56.00
P24	Crazy Disguises	1970	£7.00	—
X48	Cricketers	1959	£1.25	£60.00
X48	Cricketers, 1961 Test Series 94 x 68mm	1961	£2.00	£95.00
X48	90 x 64mm	1961	£2.00	£95.00
X66	Elvis Presley Series	1956	£8.00	£528.00
X36	Exploits of William Tell	1960	£1.00	£36.00
M22	Famous Indian Chiefs	1968	£3.25	—
X54	Fantastic Twisters	1972	£4.00	—
M48	Film & TV Stars	1953	£2.75	£132.00
M48	Film & TV Stars, No.2 Series (49-96)	1953	£2.75	£132.00
M48	Film & TV Stars, No.3 Series (97-144)	1953	£2.75	£132.00
X48	Film Stars (Plain Back)	1954	£2.00	£120.00
X73	Flags (Cut-Outs)	1971	55p	£40.00
L80	Flags of the World	1960	80p	£64.00
X80	Flags of the World	1959	80p	£64.00
40	Flag Stickers	1966	£3.50	—
X46	Footballers (Planet, 1-46)	1958	£1.00	£46.00
X46	(Without "Planet", 1-46)	1958	£1.00	£46.00
X46	Footballers (Planet, 47-92)	1958	£3.00	£138.00
X46	(Without "Planet", 47-92)	1958	*£4.00*	—
X49	Footballers (Football Quiz, 1-49)	1959	£1.75	£86.00
X49	Footballers (Football Quiz, 50-98)	1959	£3.25	—
X42	Footballers (Black Back, 1-42)	1960	£1.30	£55.00
X42	Footballers (Black Back, 43-84)	1960	£2.00	£84.00
XF64	Footballers (Plain Back)	1961	£1.75	£112.00
XF44	Footballers (Plain Back, Scottish)	1961	£6.00	—
X82	Footballers (Bazooka)	1962	£3.00	£246.00
X55	Footballers (Make-a-Photo, 1-55)	1963	£2.00	£110.00
X55	Footballers (Make-a-Photo, 56-110)	1963	£2.00	£110.00
X81	Footballers (Make-a-Photo, Scottish)	1963	£5.25	—
X58	Footballers (Quiz, 1-58)	1964	£1.60	£93.00
X45	Footballers (Quiz, 59-103)	1964	£3.50	—
X46	Footballers (Quiz, 104-149)	1964	£5.00	—
X81	Footballers (Quiz, Scottish)	1964	£5.25	—
X55	Footballers (In Pairs, 1-110)	1966	£2.00	£110.00
X55	Footballers (In Pairs, 111-220)	1966	£3.50	—
X55	Footballers (In Pairs, Scottish)	1966	£4.00	—
X55	Footballers (Star Players)	1967	£1.50	£82.50
P12	Footballers	1967	£4.00	£48.00
X45	Footballers (Football Quiz, Scottish)	1968	£5.25	—
X54	Footballers (Yellow, 1-54)	1968	£2.00	£108.00

A. & B. C. GUM — cont.

Qty		Date	Odds	Sets
X47	Footballers (Yellow, 55-101)	1968	£1.20	£56.50
M20	Football Team Emblems	1968	£3.50	£70.00
E26	Football Team Pennants	1968	£4.25	—
X65	Footballers (Football Facts, 1-64)	1969	80p	£52.00
X54	Footballers (Football Facts, 65-117)	1969	70p	£38.00
X55	Footballers (Football Facts, 117-170)	1969	70p	£38.50
MF36	Footballers	1969	£1.50	£54.00
X42	Footballers (Football Facts, Scottish, 1-41)	1969	£3.50	—
X35	Footballers (Football Facts, Scottish, 42-75)	1969	£4.50	£157.50
MF15	Footballers (Scottish)	1969	£4.00	—
X85	Footballers (Orange Back, 1-85)	1970	80p	£68.00
X85	Footballers (Orange Back, 86-170)	1970	50p	£42.50
X85	Footballers (Orange Back, 171-255)	1970	£1.00	£85.00
72	Football Colour Transparencies	1970	£2.00	—
P14	Footballers, Pin-Ups	1970	£2.50	£35.00
X85	Footballers (Green Back, Scottish, 1-85)	1970	£1.00	£85.00
X86	Footballers (Green Back, Scottish, 86-171)	1970	£1.00	£86.00
P28	Footballers, Pin-Ups (Scottish)	1970	£4.25	—
X109	Footballers (Did You Know, 1-109)	1971	70p	£76.50
X110	Footballers (Did You Know, 110-219)	1971	60p	£66.00
X71	Footballers (Did You Know, 220-290)	1971	£1.00	—
X73	Footballers (Did You Know, Scottish, 1-73)	1971	15p	£8.50
X71	Footballers (Did You Know, Scottish, 74-144)	1971	£2.00	—
16/23	Football Club Crests	1971	50p	£8.00
16	Football Club Crests (Scottish)	1971	£1.50	£24.00
X109	Footballers (Orange/Red, 1-109)	1972	60p	£65.50
X110	Footballers (Orange/Red, 110-219)	1972	60p	£66.00
M22	Football Card Game	1972	50p	£11.00
M23	Footballers, Superstars	1972	£3.00	£69.00
X89	Footballers (Rub Coin, Scottish, 1-89)	1972	£2.00	£178.00
X89	Footballers (Orange/Red, Scottish, 90-179)	1972	£2.25	—
M32	Footballers (Autographed Photos)	1973	£1.50	£48.00
X131	Footballers (Blue Back, 1-131)	1973	70p	—
X130	Footballers (Blue Back, 132-263)	1973	£1.20	—
X90	Footballers (Red Back, Scottish, 1-90)	1973	£2.00	£180.00
X88	Footballers (Red Back, Scottish, 91-178)	1973	£1.75	£154.00
E16	Football Giant Team Posters	1973	£4.00	—
X132	Footballers (Red Back, Rub Coin)	1974	75p	£99.00
X132	Footballers (Green Back, Scottish, Rub Coin)	1974	50p	£66.00
X40	Fotostars	1961	90p	£36.00
X66	Funny Greetings	1961	75p	£50.00
X66	Funny Valentines	1961	£1.00	£66.00
X36	Golden Boys (Matt)	1958	£2.25	£80.00
XF40	(Glossy)	1958	£3.00	£120.00
L27	Grand Prix	1970	25p	£6.75
D200	Hip Patches	1968	*£1.50*	—
X55	Huck Finn	1968	£1.00	—
X60	Kung Fu	1974	£1.00	£60.00
X55	Land of the Giants	1969	£3.00	£165.00
X55	Lotsa Laffs	1970	50p	£27.50
X84	Love Initials	1970	40p	£33.50
X36	Magic	1967	£1.50	—
L1	Magic Circle Club Application	1969	—	£7.00
X74	Man on the Moon	1969	£1.20	—

A. & B. C. GUM — cont.

Qty		Date	Odds	Sets
X55	Mars Attacks	1965	£10.00	£550.00
X52	Mickey Takers	1970	£2.50	£130.00
M24	Military Emblem Stickers	1966	£3.00	—
X55	Monkees (Black & White)	1967	90p	£50.00
X55	Monkees (Coloured)	1967	£1.00	£55.00
X30	Monkees Hit Songs	1967	£1.50	£45.00
E16	Monster Tattoos	1970	£4.25	—
X49	Nutty Initial Stickers	1968	£2.50	—
E16	Olympic Posters	1972	£3.00	£48.00
X36	Olympics	1972	£2.00	£72.00
X50	Outer Limits	1966	£3.00	£150.00
X55	Partridge Family	1972	60p	£33.00
X120	Planes (88 x 64 mm)	1960	70p	£84.00
X120	Planes (94 x 67 mm)	1960	85p	—
X44	Planet of the Apes	1968	£2.00	£88.00
M96	Pop Stars Fab. Photo Stamps	1965	£3.00	£288.00
X33	Put-on Stickers	1969	£2.00	—
X48	Railway Quiz	1958	80p	£40.00
X72	Railway Quiz	1959	£1.00	£72.00
M24	Royal Portraits	1953	£2.00	£48.00
M34	Silly Stickers	1966	*£2.00*	—
X25	Sir Francis Drake	1961	£1.60	£40.00
X88	Space Cards	1958	£1.50	—
X44	Stacks of Stickers	1971	£1.75	£77.00
X55	Star Trek	1969	£5.00	£275.00
X66	Superman in the Jungle	1968	£1.50	£100.00
X16	Superman in the Jungle (Jig-Saw)	1968	£2.75	£44.00
X45	The Champions	1969	£2.40	£108.00
M1	The Champions Secret Decoder	1969	—	£15.00
X25	The Girl from U.N.C.L.E.	1965	£2.20	£55.00
X36	The High Chaparral	1969	£1.25	£45.00
X54	The Legend of Custer	1968	£1.00	£54.00
L55	The Man from U.N.C.L.E.	1965	80p	£44.00
X40	The Rolling Stones	1965	£6.00	£240.00
X50	Top Stars	1964	£2.40	£120.00
X40	Top Stars (Different)	1964	£2.25	£90.00
E16	T.V. Cartoon Tattoos	1972	£5.00	—
X56	TV Westerns	1959	£1.60	£90.00
X44	Ugly Stickers	1967	£1.25	£55.00
P88	Wacky Plaks	1962	£1.40	£125.00
E16	Walt Disney Characters Tattoos	1973	£6.50	—
E16	Wanted Posters	1968	£4.00	—
X70	Who-Z-At Star?	1958	£2.00	£140.00
X55	Winston Churchill Cards	1965	20p	£11.00
X37	World Cup Footballers	1970	£2.00	£74.00
30	World Cup Football Stickers	1966	£4.50	—
E16	World Cup Posters	1970	£3.25	—
X66	You'll Die Laughing (Creature Feature)	1974	£1.25	£82.50
X48	You'll Die Laughing (Purple Back)	1967	75p	£36.00

A.H.C. (Confectionery)

Qty		Date	Odds	Sets
25	Tropical Birds (Anon.)	1955	—	£7.50
25	Wonders of the Universe	1955	—	£3.50

A & P PUBLICATIONS

Qty		*Date*	*Odds*	*Sets*
24	British Classic Cars	1992	—	£4.00

ABBEY GRANGE HOTEL

15	Fighting Vessels	1986	—	£2.50

ACE (Commercial)

X33	Sporting Greats - Football	1988	—	£5.00
X33	Sporting Greats - Motor Racing	1988	—	£5.00
X33	Sporting Greats - Tennis	1988	—	£5.00

P. A. ADOLPH ("Subbuteo")

24	Famous Footballers, A Series	1954	—	£20.00
24	Famous Footballers, Second Series	1954	—	£20.00

A. W. ALLEN (Confectionery, Australia)

32	Bradman's Records	1931	£20.00	—
72	Butterflies & Moths	1920	£1.65	—
36	Cricketers (Brown Front)	1932	£9.00	£325.00
36	Cricketers (Brown Front, Different)	1933	£10.00	—
36	Cricketers (Flesh Tinted, Frame Back)	1934	£7.00	£250.00
36	Cricketers (Flesh Tinted, No Frame)	1936	£6.50	£234.00
36	Cricketers (Coloured)	1938	£6.50	£234.00
M24	Fliers	1926	£5.00	—
48	Footballers (Action)	1939	£2.00	—
144	Footballers (Striped Colours)	1933	£1.50	—
72	Footballers (Pennants)	1934	£1.50	—
49	Kings & Queens of England	1937	£1.30	£65.00
36	Medals	1938	£1.50	—
36	Soldiers of the Empire	1938	£1.60	—
36	Sports & Flags of Nations	1936	£2.40	£86.00
M24	Wrestlers	1926	£4.50	—

ALMA CONFECTIONERY

48	James Bond 007 Moonraker	1980	£2.75	—

JAMES ALMOND & SONS (Confectionery)

25	Sports and Pastimes	1925	£7.00	£200.00

AMABALINO PHOTOGRAPHIC (Commercial)

L30	Display Fireworks	1988	—	£6.50

AMALGAMATED PRESS LTD.

24	Aeroplanes (Plain Back)	1933	£2.75	—
32	Aeroplanes & Carriers	1932	£2.25	£72.00

AMALGAMATED PRESS LTD. — cont.

Qty		Date	Odds	Sets
M32	Australian & English Cricket Stars	1932	£8.00	£250.00
M12	Catchy Tricks and Teasers	1933	£3.00	£36.00
M16	England's Test Match Cricketers	1928	£8.00	£128.00
M22	English League (Div.1) Footer Captains	1926	£2.60	£57.50
M16	Exploits of the Great War	1929	£2.00	£32.00
16	Famous Aircraft	1927	£3.00	£48.00
M16	Famous Australian Cricketers	1928	£8.00	£128.00
16	Famous Film Stars	1927	£4.50	£72.00
M24	Famous Footer Internationals	1926	£3.00	£72.00
F8	Famous Screen Stars (Anon., Film Fun)	1930	£4.50	£36.00
M22	Famous Shipping Lines	1926	£4.50	£99.00
M32	Famous Test Match Cricketers	1926	£4.50	£144.00
24	Famous Trains & Engines	1932	£2.25	£54.00
16	Fighting Planes of the World	1934	£3.00	—
32	Football Fame Series	1936	£2.75	£88.00
M16	Great War Deeds	1927	£2.25	£36.00
M32	Great War Deeds (Different)	1928	£2.25	£72.00
M16	Heroic Deeds of the Great War	1927	£2.50	£40.00
32	Makes of Motor Cars and Index Marks	1923	£2.50	£80.00
32	Mechanical Wonders of 1935	1935	£2.00	£64.00
32	Modern Motor Cars	1926	£5.00	—
24	Motors (Plain Back)	1933	£3.25	—
24	Ships of the World (Champion)	1924	£2.00	£48.00
33	Ships of the World (Different, Anon.)	1935	£2.50	—
MF66	Sportsmen	1922	£1.00	£66.00
32	Sportsmen of the World	1934	£2.25	£72.00
M12	Sports "Queeriosities"	1933	£2.75	£33.00
X40	Test Match Favourites	1934	£6.50	£260.00
M24	The Great War 1914-1918	1928	£2.50	£60.00
M16	The Great War 1914-1918, New Series	1929	£2.25	£36.00
M16	The R.A.F. at War (Plain Back)	1940	£3.00	£48.00
M32	Thrilling Scenes from the Great War	1927	£2.25	£72.00
M16	Thrills of the Dirt Track	1929	£7.00	—
M16	Tip-Top Tricks & Teasers	1927	£2.75	£44.00
M14	V.C.'s & Their Deeds of Valour (Plain Back)	1939	£3.50	—
M24	Wonderful London	1926	£4.00	£96.00

AMANDA'S FLOWERS

Qty		Date	Odds	Sets
L12	Flower Children	1990	—	£4.00

AMARAN TEA

Qty		Date	Odds	Sets
25	Coins of the World	1964	—	£7.50
25	Dogs Heads	1965	—	£3.00
25	Do You Know	1969	—	£5.00
25	Flags and Emblems	1964	—	£3.00
25	Naval Battles	1971	—	£10.00
25	Old England	1969	—	£2.00
25	Science in the 20th Century	1966	—	£2.00
25	The Circus	1966	—	£7.00
25	Veteran Racing Cars	1965	—	£12.50

AMATEUR PHOTOGRAPHER (Periodical)

Qty		Date	Odds	Sets
P4	Advertising Postcards	1990	—	£1.50

THE ANGLERS MAIL (Periodical)

Qty		Date	Odds	Sets
E3	Terminal Tackle Tips	1976	—	£3.00

ANGLING TIMES (Magazine)

Qty		Date	Odds	Sets
X15	Baits	1980	—	£4.00
X24	Collect-A-Card (Floats)	1986	—	£4.50
M24	Collect-A-Card (Fish)	1988	—	£4.50
X15	Floats	1980	—	£4.00
X15	Sea Fish	1980	—	£4.00
X15	Species	1980	—	£4.00

ANGLO-AMERICAN CHEWING GUM LTD.

Qty		Date	Odds	Sets
L36	Kidnapped (Thriller Chewing Gum)	1935	£3.75	—
X66	The Horse	1966	25p	£16.50
40	Underwater Adventure	1966	—	£4.00
50	Zoo Stamps of the World	1966	80p	£40.00

ANGLO CONFECTIONERY LTD.

Qty		Date	Odds	Sets
X66	Captain Scarlet and The Mysterons	1968	£1.75	£115.00
L12	Football Hints (Folders)	1970	£1.00	£12.00
L84	Football Quiz	1969	70p	£60.00
X66	Joe 90	1968	£2.75	£180.00
L56	National Team Colours	1970	£2.50	£140.00
X84	Railway Trains & Crests	1974	50p	£42.00
X66	Space	1967	75p	£50.00
X66	Tarzan	1967	£1.00	£66.00
X66	The Beatles — Yellow Submarine	1968	£6.50	£430.00
X66	The Horse	1966	£1.75	—
L56	The New James Bond 007	1970	£5.00	—
L64	U F O	1971	£1.75	£112.00
M24	Vintage Cars Series	1970	£2.75	£66.00
L78	Walt Disney Characters	1971	£3.20	£250.00
L66	Wild West	1970	60p	£40.00
L48	World Cup 1970	1970	£1.20	£57.50

ANONYMOUS — TRADE ISSUES

Qty		Date	Odds	Sets
50	Animals of the World	1954	—	£3.00
29	Boy Scouts Signalling	1910	£5.00	—
25	Bridges of the World	1958	—	£2.00
25	British Uniforms of the 19th Century			
	(Black Back)	1957	—	£4.00
	(Blue Back)	1957	—	£2.00
20	Budgerigars	1950	50p	£10.00

ANONYMOUS — TRADE ISSUES — cont.

Qty		Date	Odds	Sets
25	Cacti	1961	—	£2.00
25	Careless Moments	1922	70p	£17.50
M56	Caricatures of Cricketers by Durling	1959	—	£18.00
M164	Caricatures of Cricketers	1959	—	£50.00
25	Castles of Britain	1962	—	£5.00
25	Children of All Nations	1958	—	£2.50
25	Cinema and Television Stars (Barbers Tea Reprint)	1993	—	£5.00
MF12	Cinema Stars	1929	£4.25	—
F6	Cinema Stars (Name in Black)	1930	£4.50	£27.00
F6	Cinema Stars (Name in White)	1930	£4.50	£27.00
25	Dogs	1958	—	£10.00
25	Do You Know?	1963	—	£2.00
25	Evolution of the Royal Navy	1957	—	£10.00
25	Family Pets	1964	—	£3.00
25	Flags & Emblems	1961	—	£3.00
25	Flowers	1971	—	£3.00
25	Football Clubs & Badges	1962	—	£3.00
40	Greats from the States (Golf)	1994	—	£8.00
25	Jockeys and Owners Colours	1963	—	£4.00
100	Miscellaneous Subjects (Gum)	1965	—	£10.00
25	Modern Aircraft	1958	—	£2.00
X12	Motor Cycles (Collectors Series)	1987	—	£2.50
25	Musical Instruments	1971	—	£2.50
25	Pigeons	1971	—	£4.00
25	Pond Life	1963	—	£2.00
M24	R.A.F. Badges	1985	—	£8.00
1	Soldier-Bugler	1965	—	£2.50
25	Sports of the Countries	1967	—	£7.50
25	The Circus	1966	—	£7.50
25	The Wild West	1960	—	£5.00
50	Train Spotters	1962	—	£5.00
1	Venice in London	1965	—	£1.00
SILK ISSUES				
M1	Field-Marshal Earl Kitchener	1915	—	£2.50
M4	Great War Incidents	1916	£11.50	£46.00
M1	King of Belgium	1915	—	£2.00
P1	King of Belgium	1915	—	£2.50
P1	Nurse Cavell with Dogs	1915	—	£3.00
M10	Review Titles Travestied	1915	£12.50	£125.00
M4	Warships	1915	£12.50	£50.00
BELGIAN ISSUES				
X90	Belgian Military Uniforms	1970	—	£20.00
X26	Cartouche (Film)	1960	—	£10.00
X100	Famous Men	1938	—	£12.00
X38	Sindbad The Sailor (Film)	1960	—	£15.00
U.S. ISSUES ("Strip Cards")				
10	Boy Scouts	1926	—	£20.00
10	Film Stars "A"	1926	—	£12.00
10	Film Stars "B"	1926	—	£12.00
10	Film Stars "C"	1926	—	£12.00
10	Film Stars "D"	1926	—	£15.00
T60	Pinocchio (Bread Issue)	1939	—	£40.00

ANONYMOUS — TRADE ISSUES — cont.

Qty		Date	Odds	Sets
10	Presidents "A"	1926	—	£17.50
10	Presidents "B"	1926	—	£17.50
10	Western Pioneers	1926	—	£17.50

SPANISH ISSUES

X40	Footballers (P/C Backs)	1930	£1.00	£40.00

APLIN & BARRETT (Cheese)

X25	Whipsnade	1937	£1.00	£25.00

ARBUCKLE COFFEE CO. (U.S.A.)

P50	Animals	1890	£4.50	£225.00
P50	Cooking Subjects	1889	£4.50	—
P100	General Subjects (Unnumbered)	1890	£6.50	—
P50	General Subjects (51-100)	1890	£6.00	—
P50	History of Sports & Pastimes of the World	1893	£7.00	£350.00
P50	History of United States & Territories	1892	£7.00	£350.00
P50	Illustrated Atlas of U.S.	1889	£7.50	£375.00
P100	Illustrated Jokes	1890	£6.00	—
P50	Principal Nations of the World	1889	£6.00	£300.00
P50	Views from a Trip Around the World	1891	£6.00	£300.00

ARDMONA (Tinned Fruit, Australia)

X50	International Cricket Series III	1980	—	£9.00

ARMITAGE BROS. LTD. (Pet Foods)

25	Animals of the Countryside	1964	—	£2.50
25	Country Life	1968	—	£2.50

ARMY CAREERS INFORMATION OFFICE

M24	British Regiments	1991	—	£7.50
M24	British Regiments, 2nd Series	1992	—	£7.50

ARROW CONFECTIONERY CO.

13	Conundrums	1904	£27.50	—
12	Shadowgraphs	1904	£27.50	—

ASKEY'S (Biscuits)

25	People & Places	1971	—	£2.50
25	Then and Now	1971	—	£2.50

AUSTIN MOTOR CO. LTD.

L13	Famous Austin Cars	1953	£10.00	—

AUSTRALIAN DAIRY CORPORATION

Qty		Date	Odds	Sets
X63	Kanga Cards (Cricket)	1985	—	£8.00
X54	Super Cricket Card Series 1982-3	1983	—	£8.00
X50	Super Cricket Card Series 1983-4	1984	—	£8.00

AUSTRALIAN LICORICE PTY. LTD.

?27	Australian Cricketers	1930	£10.00	—
24	Australian Cricketers	1931	£10.00	£240.00
24	English Cricketers (Blue Back)	1928	£10.00	£240.00
24	English Cricketers (Black Back)	1930	£10.00	—
18	English Cricketers ("18 in Set")	1932	£10.00	£180.00
12	South African Cricketers	1931	£10.00	£120.00

AUTOBRITE (Car Polish)

25	Vintage Cars	1965	60p	£15.00

AUTOMATIC MACHINE CO.

25	Modern Aircraft	1958	—	£6.00

AUTOMATIC MERCHANDISING CO.

X25	Adventure Twins and The Treasure Ship	1958	—	£20.00

AVON RUBBER CO. LTD.

30	Leading Riders of 1963	1963	£2.00	£60.00

B.B.B. PIPES

25	Pipe History	1926	£8.00	—

B.J.B. CARDS (Commercial, Canada)

L25	Famous Golfers of the 40's and 50's 1st Series	1992	—	£7.50

BP OIL UK

25	England '98 (Soccer)	1998	—	£6.50
1	Album for above	1998	—	£1.00

B.T. LTD. (Tea)

25	Aircraft	1961	—	£8.00
25	British Locomotives	1961	50p	—
25	Do You Know?	1967	40p	£10.00
25	Holiday Resorts	1963	—	£3.00
25	Modern Motor Cars	1962	—	£15.00
25	Occupations	1962	—	£5.00
25	Pirates and Buccaneers	1961	80p	£20.00
25	The West	1964	—	£5.00

SILKS

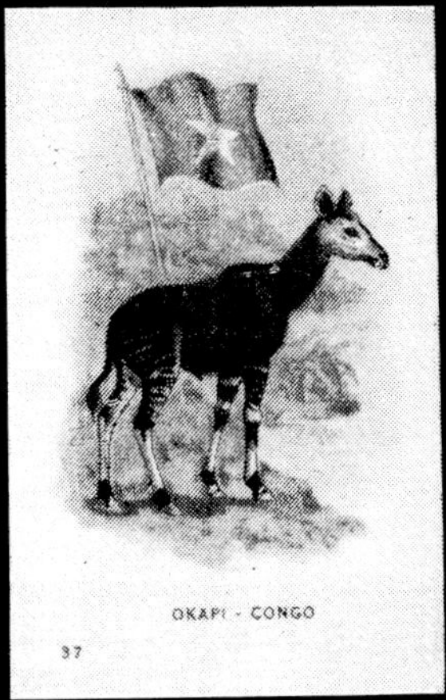

In the world of cigarette card collecting silks is the name given to all items woven in, or printed on, fabrics of all sorts, including satin, canvas, blanket and leather.

Many tobacco and a few other trade firms issued silks in the early part of this century. The best known of these are Godfrey Phillips in Britain, mainly with their B.D.V. brand, the American Tobacco Co. in the U.S.A. and the British American Tobacco Co. in the Commonwealth, usually under the names of their subsidiaries such as the I.T.C. (Canada) or United Tobacco Co. (South Africa). Among trade issues the majority were given away with magazines such as Happy Home and My Weekly. Noteworthy however are the series of cabinet size silks given with each Christmas number of 'The Gentlewoman' between 1890 and 1915.

In some cases the subjects on silks are repeats of card issues, such as 'Best Dogs of their Breed', but the majority are new subjects, and cover a very wide range of interests. These include Flags, Regimental Badges and Colours, County Cricket Badges, Famous Queens, Paintings, Red Indians, Great War Leaders, Dogs, Flowers and even Automobile Pennants. Manufacturers encouraged the smokers to use the satin issues to make cushion covers and the like — I.T.C. of Canada issued large centrepieces for this purpose, and Godfrey Phillips even issued a set of CARDS entitled 'Prizes for Needlework'.

Silks are often thought of as a specialised subject, but the general collector should consider some of these as an attractive addition to his album. We can supply an illustrated book listing all known British silks for £5.00 (post paid).

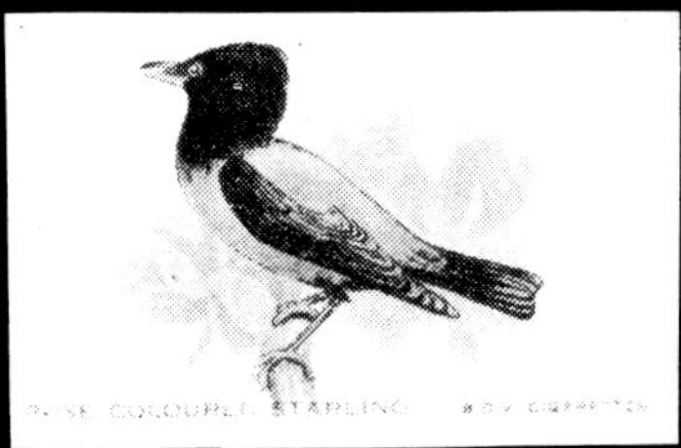

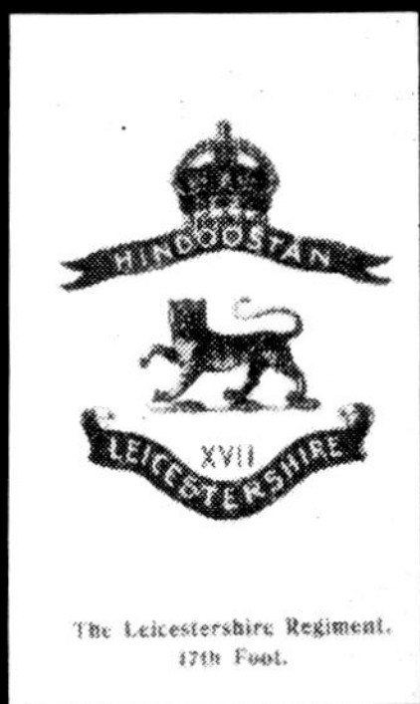

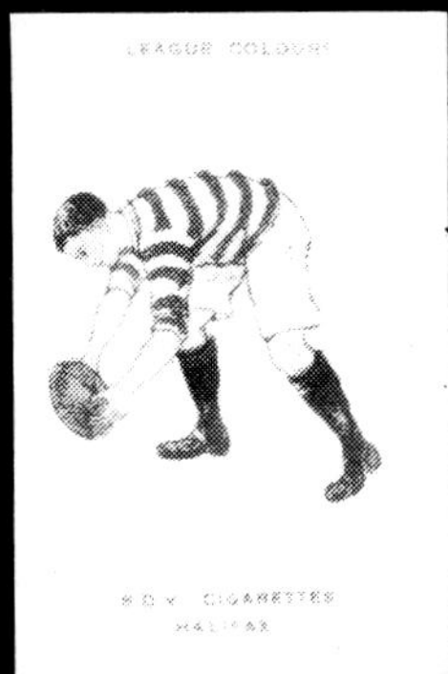

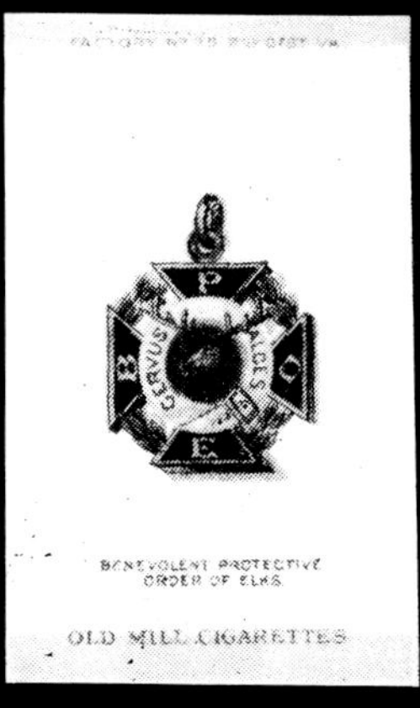

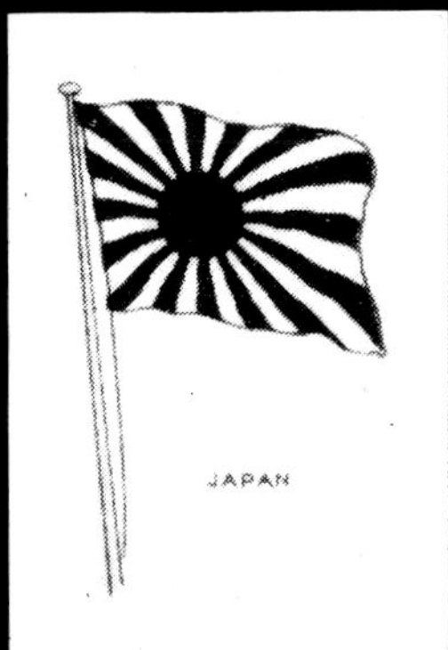

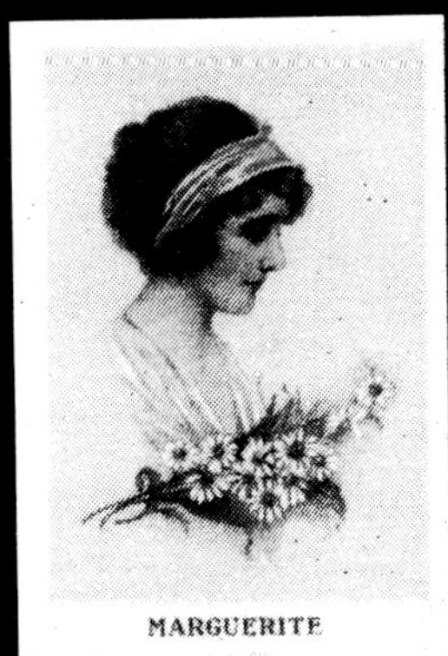

REPRINTS & FORGERIES

Tobacco Companies occasionally felt the need to reprint their own cards; the most notable example of this was Player after the Great War not having any new series prepared, and therefore re-issuing 'Cries of London 2nd Series, Miniatures, Players Past & Present and Characters from Dickens. However a new dimension was achieved by Brooke Bond, who have reprinted many of their earlier sets (with a different coloured back) SOLELY FOR SELLING TO COLLECTORS.

Several other commercial reprints appeared before Murray Cards (International) Ltd., began their "Nostalgia" reprints; these are carefully selected old series, which are very difficult to obtain in the original form, such as Wills 1896 Cricketers, Cope Golfers and Player Military Series. More recently Victoria Gallery and Imperial Publishing have printed under license from Imperial Tobacco Co. a number of their series, including two that were never actually issued! There have also been a number of reprints in North America, mainly of Baseball and Hockey cards, but also of the modern set, Mars Attacks. All these cards are clearly marked to show that they are reprints.

Early fears about the proliferation of reprints have proved to be unfounded. Their advantages are that on the one hand they have made available to a large number of collectors, cards that they would otherwise be unable to obtain or afford. In the other case they have fulfilled a demand for cards to be sold commercially in frames, and thereby relieved some of the pressure on supply of the originals, to the benefit of general collectors. In no case has the presence of reprints adversely affected the value of the originals.

One problem that has arisen, is the attempt by some dishonest people to remove all mention of the reprint and attempt to pass the cards off as originals. This has also happened in the case of Taddy Clowns and Wills Advertisement Cards, which have been cut from book illustrations and doctored. It therefore behoves the collector to be extremely careful when offered such rarities, or better still only to buy from a reputable dealer.

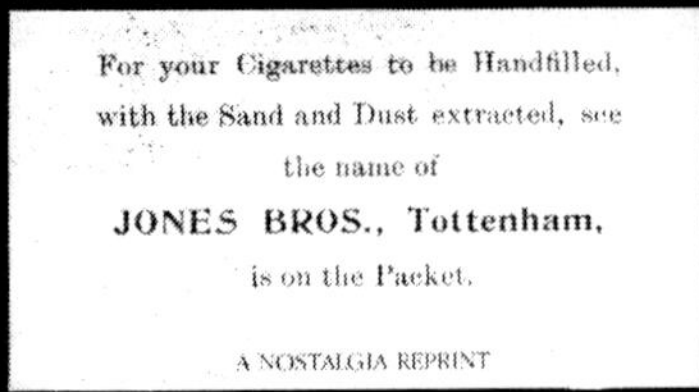

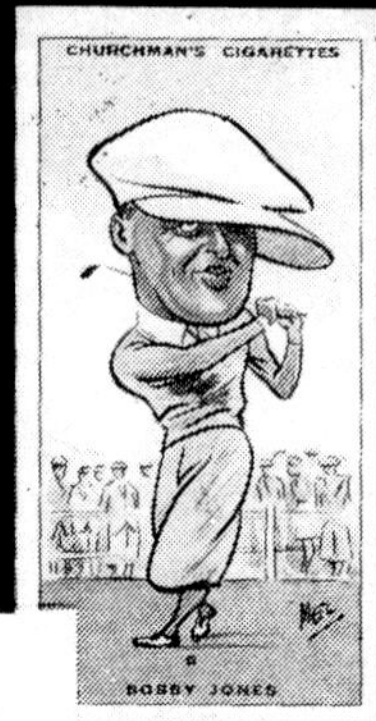

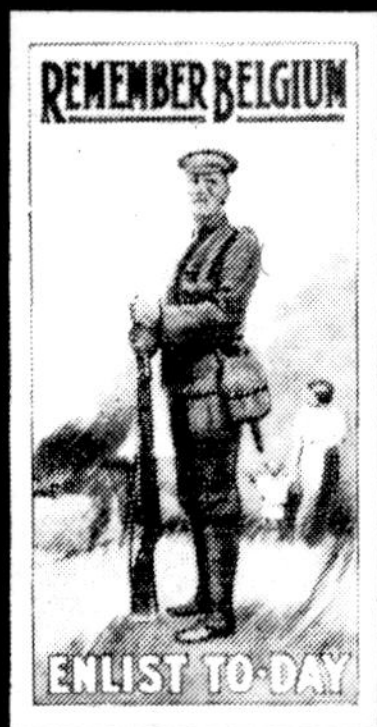

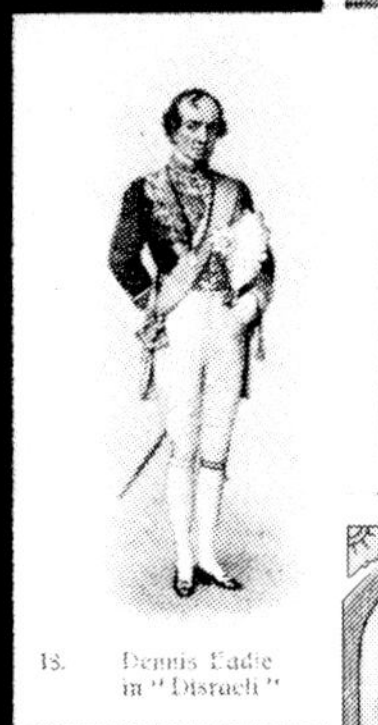

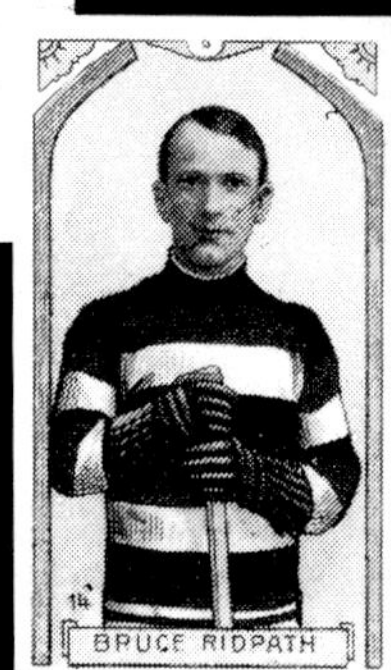

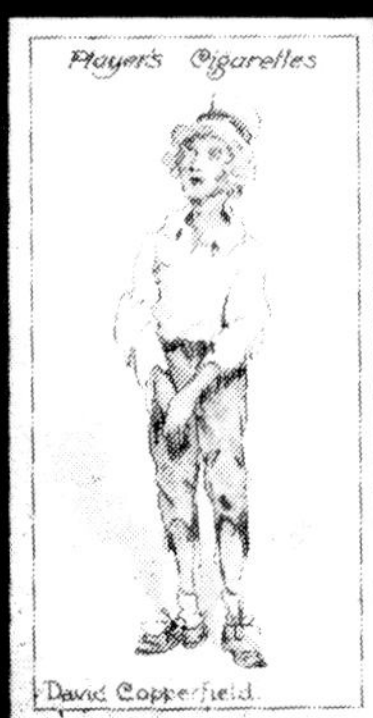

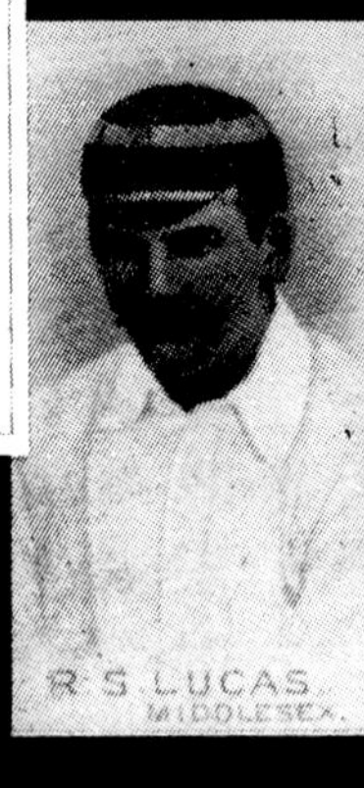

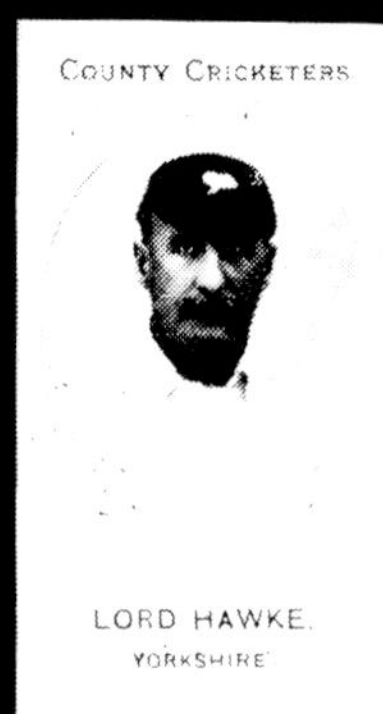

BADSHAH TEA CO.

Qty		Date	Odds	Sets
25	British Cavalry Uniforms of the 19th Century	1963	—	£7.50
25	Butterflies and Moths	1971	—	£2.00
25	Fish and Bait	1971	—	£3.00
25	Fruits of Trees and Shrubs	1965	—	£7.50
25	Garden Flowers	1963	—	£7.50
25	Naval Battles	1971	—	£7.50
25	People & Places	1970	—	£2.00
25	Regimental Uniforms of the Past	1971	—	£2.50
25	Romance of the Heavens	1968	£1.00	—
24	The Island of Ceylon	1955	£3.00	—
25	Wonders of the World (Series of 50)	1970	—	£7.50

BAILEY'S (Toffee)

25	War Series (Ships)	1916	£15.00	—

J. BAINES (Commercial)

L?200	Football Cards (Shaped)	1897	£7.50	—

BAKE-A-CAKE LTD.

56	Motor Cars	1952	£3.00	£168.00

BAKER, WARDELL & CO. (Tea)

25	Animals in the Service of Man	1964	£2.00	£50.00
36	Capital Tea Circus Act	1964	£3.25	£120.00
25	Do You Know? 1st Series	1962	£2.50	—
25	Do You Know? 2nd Series	1962	£2.50	—
25	Irish Patriots	1962	*£5.00*	—
25	The History of Flight 1st Series	1963	£6.00	—
25	The History of Flight 2nd Series	1963	£5.00	—
25	They Gave Their Names	1963	£2.00	£50.00
25	Transport Present and Future	1962	£4.00	—
25	World Butterflies	1964	£5.00	—

BARBERS TEA LTD.

1	Advertising Card — Cinema & T.V. Stars	1955	—	£3.50
1	Advertising Card — Dogs	1956	—	50p
1	Advertising Card — Railway Equipment	1958	—	£3.00
25	Aeroplanes	1956	—	£6.25
24	Cinema and Television Stars	1955	£1.50	£75.00
24	Dogs	1961	—	£2.00
5	Ferry to Hong Kong	1957	£10.00	—
25	Locomotives	1956	80p	£20.00
24	Railway Equipment	1958	—	£10.00

BARCLAYS BANK

X21	Sunderland A.F.C.	1990	—	£7.00

JOHN O. BARKER (IRELAND) LTD. (Gum)

Qty		*Date*	*Odds*	*Sets*
X24	Circus Scenes	1970	£1.50	£36.00
X24	Famous People	1970	—	£20.00
25	The Wild West	1970	£3.00	—

BARRATT & CO. LTD. (Confectionery)

Qty		*Date*	*Odds*	*Sets*
M30	Aircraft (Varnished)	1941	£3.50	£105.00
M30	Aircraft (Unvarnished, Different)	1943	£4.00	—
25	Animals in the Service of Man	1964	—	£2.00
16	Australian Cricketers, Action Series	1926	£12.00	—
15	Australian Test Players	1930	£17.50	—
45	Beauties — Picture Hats	1911	£15.00	—
25	Birds	1960	—	£6.00
50	Botany Quest	1966	£1.50	£75.00
25	British Butterflies	1965	£2.20	£55.00
25	Butterflies and Moths	1969	—	£2.00
25	Cage & Aviary Birds	1960	—	£6.00
50	Captain Scarlet and The Mysterons	1967	£1.80	£90.00
50	Cars of the World	1965	£1.20	£60.00
M122	Characters from Film Cartoons	1940	£7.00	—
K4	Coronation & Jubilee Medallions	1902	£22.50	—
25	Coronation, 1911	1911	£16.00	—
20	Cricket Team Folders	1933	£15.00	—
?260	Cricketers, Footballers & Football Teams	1925	£9.00	—
L60	Disneyland "True Life"	1956	£1.00	£60.00
L50	F.A. Cup Winners	1935	£10.00	—
25	Fairy Stories	1926	£2.60	£70.00
12	Famous British Constructions, Aircraft	1925	£16.50	—
25	Famous Cricketers (Numbered)	1931	£8.50	—
50	Famous Cricketers (Unnumbered)	1932	£8.50	—
X9	Famous Cricketers (Folders)	1932	£16.00	—
X34	Famous Cricketers (Folders)	1934	£12.00	—
M7	Famous Cricketers (Unnumbered)	1936	£12.00	—
M60	Famous Cricketers (Unnumbered)	1937	£8.00	—
M40	Famous Cricketers (Numbered)	1938	£8.00	—
35	Famous Film Stars	1961	£1.80	£63.00
M100	Famous Footballers (Unnumbered, Black)	1935	£6.00	—
M98	Famous Footballers (Unnumbered, Sepia)	1936	£6.00	—
M110	Famous Footballers (Numbered)	1937	£5.50	—
M20	Famous Footballers (Numbered)	1938	£6.00	—
M10	Famous Footballers (Numbered)	1939	£5.50	—
M79	Famous Footballers (Non-Descriptive)	1947	£5.50	—
M50	Famous Footballers, New Series	1950	£4.00	—
M50	Famous Footballers, New Series (Different)	1952	£3.50	—
M50	Famous Footballers Series, A.1	1953	£3.00	£150.00
M50	Famous Footballers Series, A.2	1954	£3.00	£150.00
M50	Famous Footballers Series, A.3	1955	£3.00	£150.00
60	Famous Footballers Series, A.4	1956	£2.00	£120.00
60	Famous Footballers Series, A.5	1957	£2.50	—
60	Famous Footballers Series, A.6	1958	£2.50	—
60	Famous Footballers Series, A.7	1959	£2.75	—
50	Famous Footballers Series, A.8	1960	£2.00	£100.00
50	Famous Footballers Series, A.9	1961	£2.00	£100.00
50	Famous Footballers Series, A.10	1962	£1.00	£50.00
50	Famous Footballers Series, A.11	1963	£2.00	£100.00
50	Famous Footballers Series, A.12	1964	£2.00	£100.00

BARRATT & CO. LTD. (Confectionery) — cont.

Qty		*Date*	*Odds*	*Sets*
50	Famous Footballers Series, A.13	1965	£2.00	£100.00
50	Famous Footballers Series, A.14	1966	£2.20	—
50	Famous Footballers Series, A.15	1967	30p	£15.00
50	Famous Sportsmen	1971	£1.00	—
M45	Fastest on Earth	1953	£1.20	£54.00
32	Felix Pictures	1930	£17.50	—
50	Film Stars (No Company Name)	1934	£7.00	—
48	Film Stars (With Company Name)	1936	£7.00	—
25	Fish and Bait	1962	—	£7.50
12	Football Action Caricatures	1928	£15.00	—
100	Football Stars	1930	*£15.00*	—
50	Football Stars	1974	£3.00	—
X157	Football Team Folders	1933	£12.50	—
M66	Football Teams — 1st Division	1930	£8.50	—
48	Giants in Sport	1959	£3.25	—
P12	Gold Rush (Packets)	1960	£5.50	—
25	Head-Dresses of the World	1962	—	£5.00
25	Historical Buildings	1960	—	£2.50
48	History of the Air (English Text)	1959	£1.00	£50.00
32	History of the Air (Bi-Lingual)	1959	£3.75	—
25	History of the Air (Different)	1960	—	£5.00
25	Interpol	1964	£2.50	£62.50
40	Knight Rider	1987	20p	£8.00
50	Leaders of Sport	1927	£9.00	—
45	Looney Tunes (Dominoes)	1995	—	*£5.00*
35	Magic Roundabout	1968	75p	—
25	Merchant Ships of the World (Black Back)	1962	—	£8.00
25	(Blue Back)	1962	—	£2.50
L40	Modern Aircraft	1957	£1.50	£60.00
M45	Modern British Aircraft	1959	£2.50	—
13	National Flags	1914	£16.00	—
64	Natural History (Plain Back)	1940	£5.25	—
M24	Naval Ships (Plain Back)	1939	£6.25	—
M6	Our King & Queen (Plain Back)	1940	£7.50	—
25	People & Places	1965	—	£2.00
25	Pirates and Buccaneers	1960	—	£4.00
P25	Pop Stars	1980	—	£8.50
12	Prominent London Buildings	1912	£15.00	—
30	Robin Hood	1961	£2.00	£60.00
36	Sailing into Space	1959	£2.25	£81.00
50	Soccer Stars	1973	£1.75	£87.50
50	Soldiers of the World	1966	30p	£15.00
16	South African Cricketers	1929	£16.50	—
25	Space Mysteries	1965	—	£5.00
L20	Speed Series	1930	£6.50	—
50	Tarzan	1967	—	£17.00
35	Test Cricketers, Series A	1956	£4.00	£140.00
48	Test Cricketers, Series B	1957	£6.00	£288.00
50	The Secret Service	1970	£1.00	£50.00
24	The Wild West	1961	—	£4.00
25	The Wild West (Different)	1963	—	£6.00
50	The Wild Wild West	1969	£1.20	£60.00
25	The Young Adventurer	1965	£2.00	£50.00
50	Thunderbirds	1967	£3.00	£150.00
50	Thunderbirds, Second Series	1968	80p	£40.00

BARRATT & CO. LTD. (Confectionery) — cont.

Qty		Date	Odds	Sets
50	Tom & Jerry	1970	—	£20.00
50	Trains	1970	—	£10.00
50	Trains of the World	1964	—	£12.50
35	T.V.'s Huckleberry Hound & Friends	1961	£1.40	£50.00
35	T.V.'s Sea Hunt	1961	£1.80	£63.00
35	T.V.'s Yogi Bear	1969	£3.50	—
35	T.V.'s Yogi Bear & Friends	1971	50p	£17.50
70	U F O	1971	60p	£42.00
1	Victory V Sign	1940	—	£8.50
M35	Walt Disney Characters	1956	£3.00	£105.00
50	Walt Disney Characters, 2nd Series	1957	£2.70	£135.00
36	Walt Disney's Robin Hood	1957	£1.50	£54.00
35	Walt Disney's True Life	1962	£1.20	£42.00
25	Warriors Through the Ages	1962	—	£4.00
25	WHAT Do You Know?	1964	—	£2.25
X72	Wild Life	1972	50p	£36.00
M50	Wild Animals by George Cansdale	1954	£1.40	£70.00
36	Wild West Series No.1	1959	£1.50	£54.00
25	Willum	1961	£5.00	—
50	Wisecracks	1970	—	£3.50
50	Wisecracks, 2nd Series	1970	30p	£15.00
50	Wisecracks, 3rd Series	1971	30p	£15.00
50	Wonders of the World	1962	—	£3.50
P6	World Beaters (World Cup Action)	1994	—	£5.00
P6	World Beaters (Worlds Greatest Players)	1994	—	£5.00
25	World Locomotives	1961	—	£7.00
50	Wunders Der Welt	1968	—	£5.00
50	Zoo Pets	1964	£1.00	£50.00

GEO. BASSETT & CO. LTD. (Confectionery)

Qty		Date	Odds	Sets
25	Motor Cars — Vintage & Modern	1968	£1.00	£25.00
25	Nursery Rhymes	1966	50p	£12.50
25	Popular Dogs	1967	—	£6.00
70	U F O	1974	—	£12.50
25	Victoria Cross Heroes in Action	1970	—	£6.50
BARRATT DIVISION				
50	Age of the Dinosaurs	1979	90p	£45.00
40	Ali Cat Magicards	1978	£1.20	—
50	Asterix in Europe	1977	25p	£12.50
50	Athletes of the World	1980	20p	£10.00
48	Bananaman	1986	—	£4.00
M20	Battle (Packets)	1985	£1.35	£27.00
50	Cricket, First Series	1978	£5.00	—
50	Cricket, Second Series	1979	£2.25	£112.50
48	Dandy — Beano Collection (Black Back)	1989	—	£7.50
48	Dandy — Beano Collection (Blue Back, different)	1990	—	£7.50
50	Disney — Health & Safety	1977	—	£25.00
50	Football Action	1977	£1.70	£85.00
50	Football Action	1978	£2.00	—
50	Football 1978-79	1979	£1.20	—
50	Football 1979-80	1980	30p	£15.00
50	Football 1980-81	1981	30p	£15.00
50	Football 1981-82	1982	£1.00	—
50	Football 1982-83	1983	80p	£40.00

GEO. BASSETT & CO. LTD. (Confectionery) — cont.

Qty		Date	Odds	Sets
50	Football 1983-84	1984	15p	£6.00
50	Football 1984-85	1985	30p	£15.00
48	Football 1985-86	1986	15p	£6.50
48	Football 1986-87	1987	40p	£20.00
48	Football 1987-88	1988	—	£7.50
48	Football 1988-89	1989	—	£10.00
48	Football 1989-90	1990	—	£10.00
48	Football 1990-91	1991	—	£10.00
50	Football Stars	1974	75p	—
50	Football Stars 1975-6	1975	£1.40	£70.00
M50	Guinness Book of Records	1990	—	£8.50
48	Hanna Barbera's Cartoon Capers	1984	75p	£36.00
24	Hologrems (Plain Backs)	1986	30p	£7.50
24	(Red Backs)	1986	—	£6.00
50	House of Horror	1982	75p	£37.50
50	Living Creatures of our World	1979	20p	£10.00
50	Play Cricket 1980	1980	30p	£15.00
25	Pop Stars	1974	—	£3.00
L5	Scratch and Match	1990	—	£3.75
35	Secret Island	1976	£1.00	—
40	Secret Island, Second Series	1976	—	£3.50
M20	Sky Fighters (Packets)	1986	80p	£16.00
49/50	Space 1999	1976	£1.00	£49.00
50	Super Heroes	1984	70p	£35.00
50	Survival on Star Colony 9	1979	40p	£20.00
40	Swim & Survive	1983	40p	£16.00
M20	The A Team	1986	—	£10.00
50	The Conquest of Space	1980	40p	£20.00
50	Tom & Jerry	1974	£2.00	—
50	World Cup Stars	1974	—	£5.00
40	World of the Vorgans	1978	£1.00	—
50	World Record Breakers	1983	80p	£40.00
49/50	Yogi's Gang	1976	70p	—

BATTLEAXE TOFFEE

Qty		Date	Odds	Sets
24	British and Empire Uniforms	1915	£22.00	—

BAYTCH BROS. (Commercial)

Qty		Date	Odds	Sets
64	Fighting Favourites	1951	£9.00	—

BEANO LTD. (Gum)

Qty		Date	Odds	Sets
1	Bang-O Spacesuit Coupon	1950	—	50p
25	Fascinating Hobbies	1950	£3.00	—
50	Modern Aircraft (Beano)	1951	£1.00	£50.00
50	(British Educational)	1951	—	£6.00
50	Ships of the Royal Navy	1955	40p	£20.00
50	The Conquest of Space	1956	—	£5.00
50	This Age of Speed No.1 (Aeroplanes)	1954	30p	£15.00
50	This Age of Speed No.2 (Buses & Trams)	1954	80p	£40.00
50	Wonders of Modern Transport (Aircraft)	1955	—	£25.00
25	Wonders of the Universe (Foto Gum)	1960	—	£2.00

BEATALL'S (Rubber Goods)

Qty		Date	Odds	Sets
F?24	Beauties	1924	£22.50	—

S. N. BEATTIE & CO. (Commercial)

Qty		Date	Odds	Sets
24	Safety Signs	1955	£2.50	—

J. J. BEAULAH (Canned Goods)

Qty		Date	Odds	Sets
1	Boston Stump	1953	—	60p
25	Coronation Series	1953	—	£32.50
24	Marvels of the World	1954	—	£2.00
24	Modern British Aircraft	1953	—	£5.00

T. W. BECKETT & CO. LTD. (South Africa)

Qty		Date	Odds	Sets
M50	Animals of South Africa, Series 3	1966	15p	£7.50
M50	Birds of South Africa, Series 1	1965	15p	£7.50
M50	Birds of South Africa, Series 2	1966	—	£7.50

THE BEEHIVE STORES

Qty		Date	Odds	Sets
25	British Uniforms of the 19th Century	1959	—	£12.50

BELLS SCOTCH WHISKY

Qty		Date	Odds	Sets
42	Other Famous Bells (Shaped)	1975	—	£20.00
40/42	Ditto	1975	40p	£16.00

J. BELLAMY & SONS LTD. (Confectionery)

Qty		Date	Odds	Sets
25	Vintage & Modern Trains of the World	1975	—	£6.00

BILLY BEMBO (Commercial)

Qty		Date	Odds	Sets
X54	Vanity Fair 1st Edition (Playing Cards)	1995	—	£7.50
X54	Vanity Fair 2nd Edition (Playing Cards)	1995	—	£7.50

BENSEL WORK FORCE LTD.

Qty		Date	Odds	Sets
20	Occupations	1991	—	£3.50

VAN DEN BERGHS LTD. (Margarine Etc.)

Qty		Date	Odds	Sets
P8	Birds	1974	—	£3.50
70	Countryside Cards	1975	60p	£42.00
X24	Pirates	1965	£2.40	£57.50
M12	Recipes from Round the World	1958	£2.25	£27.00
M12	Regional Recipes	1958	£2.25	£27.00
X24	This Modern World	1965	£1.60	£38.50

DE BEUKELAER (Biscuits)

Qty		Date	Odds	Sets
KF100	All Sports	1932	60p	£60.00
M125	Dumbo	1940	£1.20	£150.00
KF900	Film Stars (101-1000)	1932	85p	—

DE BEUKELAER (Biscuits) — cont.

Qty		Date	Odds	Sets
KF100	Film Stars (1001-1100)	1937	85p	£85.00
KF100	Film Stars (B1-100)	1935	£1.00	£100.00
K160	Film Stars (Gold Background)	1936	£1.20	—
132	Film Stars (Gold Background)	1938	£1.00	—
M125	Gulliver's Travels	1940	£1.20	£150.00
M125	Pinocchio Series	1940	£1.20	£150.00
M60	Sixty Glorious Years	1940	£1.25	—
M100	Snow White Series	1940	£1.40	—

J. BIBBY & SONS LTD. (Cooking Fat)

Qty		Date	Odds	Sets
L25	Don't You Believe It	1955	80p	£20.00
L25	Good Dogs	1955	£2.20	£55.00
L25	How What and Why	1955	80p	£20.00
L25	Isn't It Strange	1955	£1.00	£25.00
L25	They Gave It a Name	1955	£2.00	£50.00
L25	This Wonderful World	1955	£1.00	£25.00

BIRCHGREY LTD. (Sporting Promotions)

Qty		Date	Odds	Sets
L25	Panasonic European Open	1989	—	£15.00
L15	The Ryder Cup	1988	—	£15.00

ALFRED BIRD & SONS (Custard)

Qty		Date	Odds	Sets
K48	Happy Families	1938	£1.25	£60.00

BIRDS EYE FOODS LTD.

Qty		Date	Odds	Sets
X6	Birds Eye Book of Record Breakers	1970	£2.50	£15.00
T12	England's Football Team	1980	—	£40.00
30	Wonders of the Seven Seas	1978	—	£15.00

BIRKUM (Cheese, Denmark)

Qty		Date	Odds	Sets
25	Motor Cars	1956	80p	£20.00

BISHOPS STORTFORD DAIRY FARMERS (Tea)

Qty		Date	Odds	Sets
25	Dogs Heads	1967	—	£15.00
25	Freshwater Fish	1964	—	£15.00
25	Historical Buildings	1964	—	£6.00
25	History of Aviation	1964	—	£12.50
25	Passenger Liners	1965	—	£2.50
25	Pond Life	1966	—	£2.00
25	Science in the 20th Century	1966	—	£2.00
25	The Story of Milk	1966	—	£3.00

BLAKEY'S BOOT PROTECTORS LTD.

Qty		Date	Odds	Sets
72	War Series	1916	£5.00	—

BLUE BAND SERIES (Stamps)

Qty		Date	Odds	Sets
24	History of London's Transport, 1st Series			
	Black Front	1954	—	£10.00
	Blue Front	1954	—	£12.00
	Orange Front	1954	—	£10.00
24	History of London's Transport, 2nd Series	1955	£2.25	£54.00
16	See Britain by Coach	1954	—	£4.00

BLUE BIRD STOCKINGS

P12	Exciting Film Stars	1963	—	£15.00
24	Star Cards	1963	£6.00	—

BLUE CAP LTD. (Cheese)

K144	Flixies	1952	75p	£108.00
PACKAGE SERIES				
12	Animal Series D	1953	£1.50	—
8	Animal Series E	1953	£1.50	—
12	Farm Series A	1953	£1.50	£18.00
12	Farm Series B	1953	£1.50	£18.00
12	Farm Series C	1953	£1.50	£18.00
12	Sports Series D	1953	£2.00	£24.00
8	Sports Series E	1953	£2.50	—

E. H. BOOTH & CO. LTD. (Tea)

25	Badges & Uniforms of Famous British Regiments and Corps	1967	—	£2.00
25	Ships and Their Workings	1971	50p	—
24	The Island of Ceylon	1955	£3.25	£78.00

BOW BELLS (Periodical)

MF6	Handsome Men on the British Screen	1922	£6.00	£36.00

BOYS CINEMA (Periodical)

MF6	Cinema Stars (Anon.)	1931	£3.50	£21.00
MF6	Famous Film Heroes	1922	£3.50	£21.00
M24	Famous Heroes	1922	£3.00	£72.00
F7	Film Stars (Anon.)	1932	£3.00	£21.00
MF8	Film Stars (Brown Front)	1930	£3.75	£30.00
MF8	Film Stars (Black Front, Different)	1931	£3.75	£30.00

BOYS COMIC LIBRARY

4	Heroes of the Wild West	1910	£13.50	—

BOYS FRIEND (Periodical)

3	Famous Boxers Series	1911	£12.00	£36.00

BOYS FRIEND (Periodical) — cont.

Qty		Date	Odds	Sets
3	Famous Flags Series	1911	£7.00	£21.00
3	Famous Footballers Series	1911	£12.00	£36.00
3	Famous Regiments Series	1911	£7.50	£22.50
MF4	Footballers (½ Length)	1923	£4.50	£18.00
MF5	Footballers (2 per Card)	1922	£5.00	£25.00
MF15	Rising Boxing Stars	1922	£3.30	£50.00

BOYS MAGAZINE (Periodical)

Qty		Date	Odds	Sets
M8	Boxers	1922	£7.50	—
M8	Coloured Studies — Famous Internationals	1922	£4.50	£36.00
M10	Cricketers	1922	£9.00	£90.00
F10	Famous Cricketers Series	1929	£6.00	£70.00
F12	Famous Footballers Series	1929	£3.75	£45.00
MF10	Football Series	1922	£2.50	£25.00
X9	Football Teams	1925	£10.00	—
M30	Footballers (Picture 49 x 39mm)	1922	£4.00	£120.00
M64	Footballers & Sportsmen (Picture 56 x 35mm)	1922	£4.00	—
12	Zat Cards (Cricketers)	1930	£8.00	£96.00
M11	Zat Cards (Cricketers)	1930	£9.00	£100.00

BOYS REALM (Periodical)

Qty		Date	Odds	Sets
MF15	Famous Cricketers	1922	£3.00	£45.00
MF9	Famous Footballers	1922	£3.00	£27.00

C. & T. BRIDGEWATER LTD. (Biscuits)

Qty		Date	Odds	Sets
KF48	Coronation Series	1937	20p	£7.50
KF96	Film Stars, 1st (CE Over No.)	1932	20p	£20.00
KF96	Film Stars, 2nd (E Below No.)	1933	80p	—
KF96	Film Stars, 3rd (Black & White)	1934	80p	—
KF48	Film Stars, 4th	1935	50p	£24.00
KF48	Film Stars, 5th	1937	£1.50	£72.00
KF48	Film Stars, 6th (F Before No.)	1938	£1.50	£72.00
F48	Film Stars, 7th	1939	£1.50	£72.00
KF48	Film Stars, 8th	1940	75p	£36.00
KF48	Radio Stars 1st (Black & White)	1935	£1.50	£72.00
KF48	Radio Stars 2nd (Coloured)	1936	40p	£20.00

JOHN M. BRINDLEY (Printers)

Qty		Date	Odds	Sets
30	Australian Cricketers	1986	—	£12.00
12	Bob Hoare Cricket Characatures	1992	—	£2.50
20	Car Badges and Emblems	1987	—	£5.00
30	Cricketers, A Series	1985	—	£12.50
30	Cricketers, 2nd Series	1985	—	£15.00
X16	Cricketers, Howzat, 3rd Series	1985	—	£10.00
30	Cricketers, 4th Series	1986	—	£10.00
X20	Cricketers, 5th Series (Sketches)	1986	—	£10.00
30	Cricket, The Old School	1987	—	£10.00
18	Famous Operatic Roles	1992	—	£3.00
20	Golf	1987	—	£7.50
20	Horse Racing	1987	—	£4.50
20	Locos	1987	—	£3.00

JOHN M. BRINDLEY (Printers) — cont.

Qty		*Date*	*Odds*	*Sets*
30	London, Brighton & South Coast Railway	1986	—	£6.50
20	Military	1987	—	£3.00
16	Players of the Past (Soccer)	1992	—	£3.00
L6	World Boxers	1992	—	£2.50
L6	World Boxers Part 2 (7-12)	1993	—	£2.50

BRISTOL-MYERS CO. LTD. (Toothpaste)

50	Speed	1964	£3.50	£175.00

BRITISH AUTOMATIC CO. (Weight)

24	British Aircraft	1950	£1.25	£30.00
24	British Birds	1950	£1.25	£30.00
24	British Locomotives	1948	75p	£18.00
36	British Motor Cars	1954	£2.75	—
44	Coronation Information	1953	£1.00	—
32	Dogs, A Series	1953	30p	£10.00
32	Dogs (A Series, No "Weigh Daily", As 2nd)	1953	85p	£27.00
32	Dogs, Second Series	1953	80p	£25.00
24	Famous Trains of the World, A Series	1952	£1.50	£36.00
24	Famous Trains of the World, Second Series	1952	£1.50	£36.00
37	Fortunes, 1st Series	1950	£1.00	—
32	Fortunes, 2nd Series	1953	50p	£16.00
32	Fortunes, 3rd Series	1954	75p	£24.00
24	Fresh Water Fish	1950	£1.25	£30.00
24	History of Transport	1948	20p	£5.00
44	Jokes	1951	35p	£15.00
24	Olympic Games	1952	£3.00	—
37	Quotations	1951	75p	—
24	Racing & Sports Cars	1957	£2.25	£54.00
24	Space Travel	1955	£1.50	£36.00
24	Speed	1949	25p	£6.00
24	Sportsmen	1955	£2.25	£54.00
20	Twenty Questions	1952	£1.75	£35.00
24	Warships of the World	1954	£1.25	£30.00
1	Watch Your Weight	1950	—	75p

BRITISH GAS

X20	Leeds RLFC	1992	—	£4.00

C. BRITTON PUBLISHING (Commercial)

L24	Golf Courses of the British Isles, 1st Series	1993	—	£7.50

BROOKE BOND & CO. LTD. (Tea)

72 Page Illustrated Reference Book — £7.25

(Special albums available for most series — ask for quote)

50	Adventurers & Explorers	1973	15p	£4.00
50	African Wild Life	1962	25p	£12.50
25	A Journey Downstream	1990	15p	£2.50
L25	A Journey Downstream (Double Cards)	1990	50p	£12.50
50	Asian Wild Life	1962	20p	£10.00

BROOKE BOND & CO. LTD. (Tea) — cont.

Qty		*Date*	*Odds*	*Sets*
50	Bird Portraits (No Address)	1957	£1.50	£75.00
50	(With Address)	1957	60p	£30.00
20	British Birds	1954	£2.00	£40.00
50	British Butterflies	1963	20p	£10.00
50	British Costume	1967	15p	£5.00
50	British Wild Life (Brooke Bond Great Britain Ltd.)	1958	90p	£45.00
	(Brooke Bond Tea Ltd.)	1958	50p	£25.00
	(Brooke Bond & Co. Ltd.)	1958	£1.20	£60.00
50	Butterflies of the World	1964	15p	£7.50
12	Chimp Stickers	1986	50p	£6.00
M24	Creatures of Legend	1994	20p	£5.00
X12	Creatures of Legend (Double Cards)	1994	80p	£10.00
50	Discovering our Coast	1989	15p	£4.00
L25	Discovering our Coast (Double Cards)	1989	40p	£10.00
50	Famous People	1969	15p	£4.50
50	Features of the World	1984	15p	£4.00
L25	Features of the World (Double Cards)	1984	40p	£10.00
50	Flags and Emblems of the World	1967	15p	£5.00
X40	40 years of the chimps television advertising	1996	—	£8.00
50	Freshwater Fish	1960	40p	£20.00
M40	Going Wild	1994	15p	£5.00
X20	Going Wild	1994	—	£7.50
50	History of Aviation	1972	15p	£5.00
50	History of the Motor Car	1968	20p	£10.00
40	Incredible Creatures (Last Line Sheen Lane)	1985	20p	£8.00
	(Last Line Walton...)	1986	20p	£8.00
	(Last Line P.O. Box...)	1986	15p	£4.00
	(Thick Cards, Stickers)	1987	£2.75	—
	(Green Back, Irish)	1986	£1.00	£40.00
L20	Incredible Creatures (Double, Sheen)	1986	£1.20	£24.00
L20	(Double, Walton)	1986	£2.00	—
L20	(Double, P.O. Box)	1986	80p	£16.00
X20	International Soccer Stars	1998	*15p*	—
50	Inventors & Inventions	1975	15p	£4.00
40	Natural Neighbours	1992	15p	£6.00
L20	Natural Neighbours (Double Cards)	1992	40p	£8.00
40	Olympic Challenge 1992	1992	15p	£6.00
L20	Olympic Challenge 1992 (Double Cards)	1992	60p	£12.00
40	Olympic Greats	1979	25p	£10.00
50	Out Into Space ("Issued with...")	1956	£5.00	—
50	("Issued in...")	1958	60p	£30.00
40	Play Better Soccer	1976	15p	£3.50
40	Police File	1977	15p	£3.50
P10	Poly Filla Modelling Cards	1974	*£1.40*	—
50	Prehistoric Animals	1972	15p	£6.00
X45	Pyramid Power	1996	—	£10.00
50	Queen Elizabeth I — Queen Elizabeth II	1982	15p	£4.00
L25	Queen Elizabeth I — II (Double Cards)	1982	£1.20	—
40	Small Wonders	1981	15p	£3.50
12	Teenage Mutant Hero Turtles	1990	15p	£2.00
L6	Teenage Mutant Hero Turtles (Doubles)	1990	85p	£5.00
20	The Dinosaur Trail (Postcode BB11PG)	1993	15p	£3.00
20	(Postcode BB111PG)	1993	50p	£10.00
L10	The Dinosaur Trail (Doubles) (Postcode BB11PG)	1993	40p	£4.00
L10	(Doubles) (Postcode BB111PG)	1993	£1.00	£10.00

Qty		Date	Odds	Sets
12	The Language of Tea	1988	20p	£2.50
25	The Magical World of Disney	1989	20p	£4.00
L25	The Magical World of Disney (Doubles)	1989	60p	£15.00
50	The Race Into Space	1971	15p	£4.00
50	The Saga of Ships	1970	15p	£4.00
50	The Sea — Our Other World	1974	15p	£4.00
X50	The Secret Diary of Kevin Tipps	1995	20p	£10.00
50	Transport through the Ages	1966	15p	£5.00
50	Trees in Britain	1966	15p	£4.50
50	Tropical Birds	1961	16p	£8.00
40	Unexplained Mysteries of the World	1987	15p	£3.50
L20	Unexplained Mysteries (Double Cards)	1988	40p	£8.00
40	Vanishing Wildlife	1978	15p	£3.50
50	Wild Birds in Britain	1965	15p	£4.00
50	Wild Flowers, A Series	1955	£1.60	£80.00
50	Wild Flowers, Series 2 (With "issued by")	1959	25p	£12.50
50	(No "issued by")	1959	£1.75	£87.50
50	Wild Flowers, Series 3	1964	15p	£6.00
50	Wildlife in Danger	1963	15p	£4.50
50	Wonders of Wildlife	1976	15p	£4.00
40	Woodland Wildlife	1980	15p	£3.50
X50	Zena Skinner International Cookery	1974	*£2.25*	—
BLACK BACK REPRINTS				
50	African Wild Life	1973	—	£3.50
50	British Butterflies	1973	—	£3.50
50	British Costume	1973	—	£3.50
50	Discovering our Coast	1994	—	£7.50
50	Famous People	1973	—	£3.50
50	Flags and Emblems of the World	1973	—	£8.00
50	Freshwater Fish	1973	—	£10.00
50	History of the Motor Car	1974	—	£6.00
40	Olympic Greats	1988	—	*£12.00*
50	Queen Elizabeth I — Queen Elizabeth II	1987	—	£5.00
40	Small Wonders	1988	—	£3.50
50	The Race Into Space	1974	—	£3.50
50	The Saga of Ships	1973	—	£3.50
50	Transport through the Ages	1973	—	£12.50
50	Trees in Britain	1973	—	£3.50
50	Tropical Birds	1974	—	£3.50
40	Vanishing Wildlife	1988	—	£3.00
50	Wild Birds in Britain	1973	—	£4.50
50	Wild Flowers, Series 2	1973	—	£3.50
50	Wildlife in Danger	1973	—	£3.50
40	Woodland Wildlife	1988	—	£5.00
CARD GAMES BASED ON REGULAR SERIES				
L36	British Costume Snap Game	1974	—	£12.50
L36	Flags & Emblems Snap Game	1974	—	£12.50
L36	Motor History Snap Game	1974	—	£12.50
CANADIAN ISSUES				
48	African Animals	1964	—	£5.00
48	Animals and Their Young ("Products")	1972	—	£7.00
48	(Tea/Coffee)	1972	£6.00	—
48	Animals of North America			
	("Roland" Back) (2 Printings)	1960	80p	£40.00
	("Rolland" Back)	1960	80p	£40.00

BROOKE BOND & CO. LTD. (Tea) — cont.

Qty		Date	Odds	Sets
48	Birds of North America	1962	50p	£24.00
48	Butterflies of North America	1965	80p	£40.00
48	Canadian/American Songbirds	1966	£1.50	£72.00
48	Dinosaurs	1963	£1.75	£84.00
48	Exploring the Oceans	1971	—	£4.00
48	Indians of Canada	1974	—	£5.00
48	North American Wildlife in Danger	1970	—	£4.00
48	Songbirds of North America			
	(Red Rose/Blue Ribbon)	1959	£1.25	£60.00
	(Red Rose Only, "Albums Available")	1959	£2.50	£120.00
	(Red Rose Only, "Mount Your Collection")	1959	£2.75	—
48	The Arctic	1973	—	£4.50
48	The Space Age	1969	—	£4.00
48	Transportation Through the Ages (Top Line Black)	1967	25p	£12.00
48	(Top Line Red)	1967	£3.25	—
48	Trees of North America	1968	30p	£15.00
48	Tropical Birds (Top Line Black)	1964	75p	£36.00
48	(Top Line Red)	1964	£3.00	—
48	Wild Flowers of North America	1961	60p	£30.00
RHODESIAN ISSUES				
50	African Birds	1965	£1.80	£90.00
50	African Wild Life	1963	£2.50	—
50	Asian Wild Life	1963	£2.00	£100.00
50	Butterflies of the World	1966	£2.00	£100.00
50	Tropical Birds	1962	£2.00	£100.00
50	Wildlife in Danger	1964	£2.50	£125.00
SOUTH AFRICAN ISSUES				
50	Our Pets	1967	£2.50	—
50	Out Into Space	1966	£2.50	£125.00
50	Wild Van Afrika (Bilingual)	1965	£3.00	—
50	(One Language)	1965	£5.00	—
U.S.A. ISSUES				
48	Animals of North America (Black Back)	1960	£8.00	—
48	(Blue Back)	1960	£6.00	£300.00
48	Birds of North America	1962	£5.00	—
48	Butterflies of North America	1964	£3.50	£170.00
48	Canadian/American Songbirds	1966	£2.00	£96.00
48	Dinosaurs	1963	£5.25	—
48	Tropical Birds	1964	£2.80	£140.00
48	Wild Flowers of North America (Dark Blue)	1961	£3.50	£175.00
48	(Light Blue)	1961	£6.00	—

BROOK MOTORS

Qty		Date	Odds	Sets
G12	Motor Cycles (Cut from Calendars)	1975	—	£8.00
P12	Steam Engines	1973	—	£12.00
P12	Steam Engines (Different)	1970	—	£30.00
P12	The Traction Engine	1967	—	£24.00
P12	Veteran Cars	1961	—	£20.00

BROOKFIELD SWEETS (Ireland)

Qty		Date	Odds	Sets
50	Animals of the World	1956	£3.00	—
25	Aquarium Fish, 1st Series	1957	£3.00	—

BROOKFIELD SWEETS (Ireland) — cont.

Qty		Date	Odds	Sets
25	Aquarium Fish, 2nd Series	1957	£3.00	—
25	Motor Cars	1954	£3.00	—
50	The Conquest of Space	1956	£3.00	—

BROOKS DYE WORKS LTD.

P4	Interesting Shots of Old Bristol	1950	—	£4.00

DAVID BROWN (Tractors)

XF3	Is Your Slip Showing?	1954	£3.00	£9.00

BROWN & POLSON (Custard)

X25	Recipe Cards	1925	£4.00	—

BROWNE BROS. LTD. (Tea)

25	Birds	1964	—	£12.50
25	British Cavalry Uniforms of the 19th Century	1964	—	£10.00
25	Garden Flowers	1965	£1.00	—
25	History of the Railways, 1st Series	1964	—	£10.00
25	History of the Railways, 2nd Series	1964	—	£8.00
25	Passenger Liners	1966	£1.00	—
25	People & Places	1965	—	£2.00
24	The Island of Ceylon	1961	£3.50	—
25	Tropical Birds	1966	—	£2.50
25	Wonders of the Deep	1965	—	£2.50
25	Wonders of the World	1970	—	£5.00

BRYANT & MAY LTD. (Matches)

50	Kings & Queens of England (Player Reprint)	1991	—	£7.50
50	Life in the Hedgerow (Wills Reprint)	1991	—	£7.50
L12	The Thirties	1992	—	£8.00

BUCHANAN'S (JAM)

24	Birds and their Eggs	1924	£7.50	—

JOHNNY BUNNY (Medicines)

25	Football Clubs and Badges	1958	£1.50	—

BUNSEN CONFECTIONERY CO.

?100	Famous Figures Series	1925	£11.00	—

BURDALL & BURDALL (Gravy Salt)

30	Wild Animals	1924	£5.50	—

BURTON'S WAGON WHEELS (Biscuits)

Qty		*Date*	*Odds*	*Sets*
25	Indian Chiefs	1972	—	£8.00
L7	Pictures of the Wild West	1983	£5.00	—
25	The West	1972	—	£3.00
25	Wild West Action	1972	—	£4.00

BUTTAPAT DAIRIES

25	People of the World	1915	£15.00	—

BUTTERCUP BREAD CO. (Australia)

L24	Alan Border Tribute	1994	—	£7.50
L24	Border's Ashes Heroes	1993	—	£7.50
L24	1993-94 World Series All Stars	1993	—	£7.50

C. & G. CONFECTIONERY CO.

25	Box of Tricks, 1st Series	1965	£2.50	—
25	Box of Tricks, 2nd Series	1965	£2.50	£62.50

CBS IRONMONGERY LTD.

30	Glamorgan Cricketers	1984	—	£12.50

CADBURY BROS. LTD. (Chocolate)

12	Age of the Dinosaur	1971	75p	—
T12	Antarctic Series	1913	£25.00	—
X6	Bay City Rollers	1975	—	*£5.00*
L12	Birds in Springtime	1983	—	£3.00
6	Bournville Series B	1906	£17.00	£100.00
P3	Bournville Views (Script at Side)	1906	£2.50	£7.50
P6	Bournville Views (Block at Side)	1906	£3.50	£21.00
P6	Bournville Views (White Borders)	1906	£3.25	£19.50
P8	Bournville Views (Gravure)	1906	£3.50	—
6	Bournville Village Series	1906	£17.50	—
P25	British Birds (Reward Cards)	1910	£6.50	—
12	British Birds & Eggs	1910	£9.00	—
P12	British Birds & Their Eggs (Reward Cards)	1910	£7.00	£84.00
P32	British Butterflies & Moths (Reward Cards)	1910	£4.00	£128.00
6	British Colonies, Maps & Industries	1908	£15.00	£90.00
120	British Marvels	1932	£1.00	—
120	British Marvels, Album No. 2	1933	£1.00	—
12	British Trees Series (2 Printings)	1911	£5.50	£66.00
80	Cadbury's Picture Making	1936	£1.25	—
12	Cathedral Series	1913	£6.00	£72.00
6	Colonial Premiers Series	1908	£15.00	£90.00
12	Constellations Series	1912	£6.50	£78.00
24	Copyright (Inventors) Series	1914	£11.00	—
1	Coronation	1911	—	£24.00
48	Dangerous Animals	1970	40p	£20.00
6	Dog Series	1908	£30.00	—
P12	English Industries	1908	£27.50	—
25	Fairy Tales	1924	£2.40	£60.00

CADBURY BROS. LTD. (Chocolate) — cont.

Qty		Date	Odds	Sets
27	Famous Steamships	1923	£2.50	£67.50
12	Fish	1910	£10.00	—
P6	Fish & Bait Series	1909	£27.50	—
12	Flag Series	1912	£2.50	£30.00
P6	Flag Series (Joined Pairs)	1912	£5.00	£30.00
P12	Flag Series (Different)	1910	£20.00	—
X12	Flight (Birds)	1982	50p	£6.00
32	Happy Families	1950	£1.40	—
?X5	Knotty Problems	1910	£16.00	—
1	Largest Steamers in the World	1907	—	*£40.00*
6	Locomotive Series	1906	£25.00	—
12	Match Puzzles	1906	£30.00	—
6	Old Ballad Series	1906	£18.00	—
X6	Panama Series	1910	£24.00	—
X5	Pop Stars	1975	80p	£4.00
1	Poster Series	1910	—	£27.50
X8	Prehistoric Monsters	1975	—	£5.00
P1	Puzzle Card	1910	—	£17.50
P6	Rivers of the British Isles (Reward Cards)	1910	£13.00	£78.00
24	Shadow Series	1914	£12.00	—
6	Shipping Series (4 Sizes)	1910	£10.00	—
T6	Sports Series	1906	*£35.00*	—
24	Strange But True	1970	—	£2.00
25	Transport	1925	20p	£5.00
G1	The Magic Bournville Cocoa Tins	1910	—	£15.00
L6	Wildlife Stickers	1986	—	£2.00

CADET SWEETS

Qty		Date	Odds	Sets
25	Arms and Armour	1961	—	£2.00
50	Buccaneers	1957	—	£10.00
50	Buccaneers (Different)	1959	—	£15.00
25	Daktari	1969	—	£7.50
50	Doctor Who and The Daleks	1965	£2.00	£100.00
25	Dogs, 1st Series	1958	—	£15.00
25	Dogs, 2nd Series	1958	—	£15.00
25	Evolution of the Royal Navy	1959	—	£3.00
M22	Famous Explorers (Packets)	1960	£5.00	—
50	Fifty Years of Flying	1953	—	£35.00
50	Footballers	1956	—	£10.00
50	Footballers (Different) Large Wording	1959	—	£12.00
50	Small Wording	1959	—	£15.00
25	How?	1969	—	£10.00
50	Motor Cars	1954	—	£20.00
25	Prehistoric Animals	1961	—	£16.00
50	Railways of the World (Cadet)	1956	—	£7.50
50	(Paramount Laboratories)	1956	40p	£20.00
50	(Paramount Sweets)	1956	—	£12.50
50	Record Holders of the World	1956	—	£6.50
50	Stingray	1965	—	£30.00
48	The Adventures of Rin Tin Tin	1960	50p	£24.00
50	The Conquest of Space	1957	—	£6.50
25	Treasure Hunt	1964	—	£2.50
50	U.N.C.L.E. (Line Drawings)	1966	£2.00	£100.00

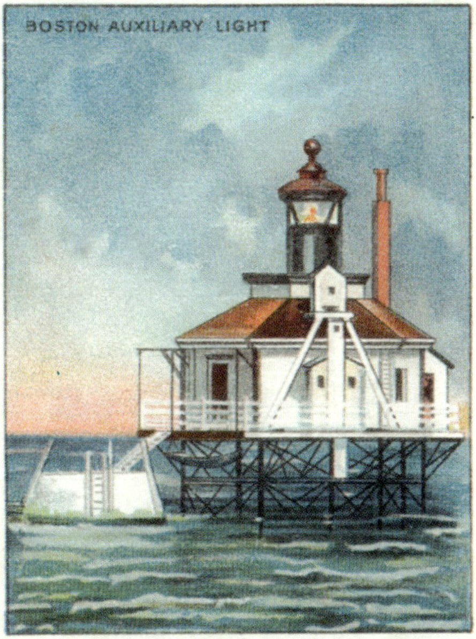

Light House Series – American Tobacco Co.

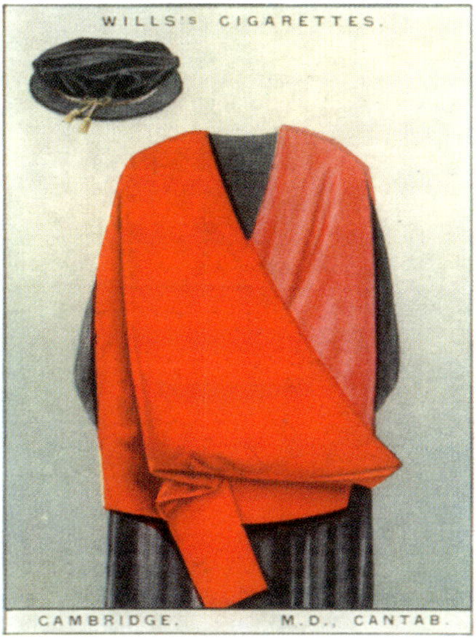

University Hoods & Gowns – Wills

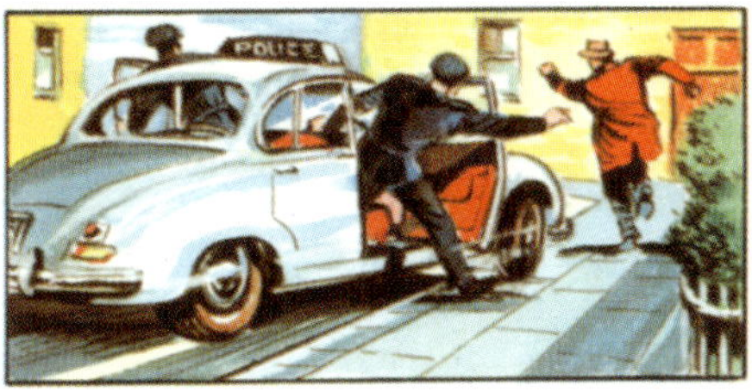

Z-Cars – Primrose

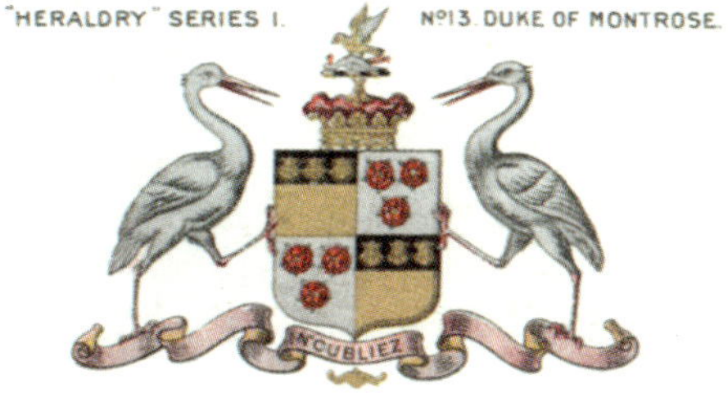

Heraldry Series – Taddy

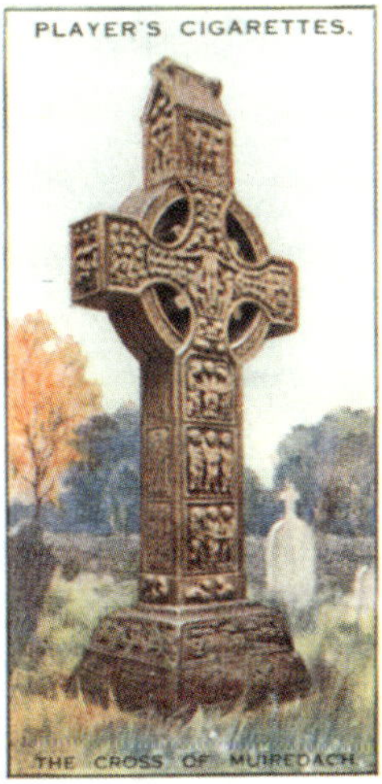

Treasures of Ireland – Player

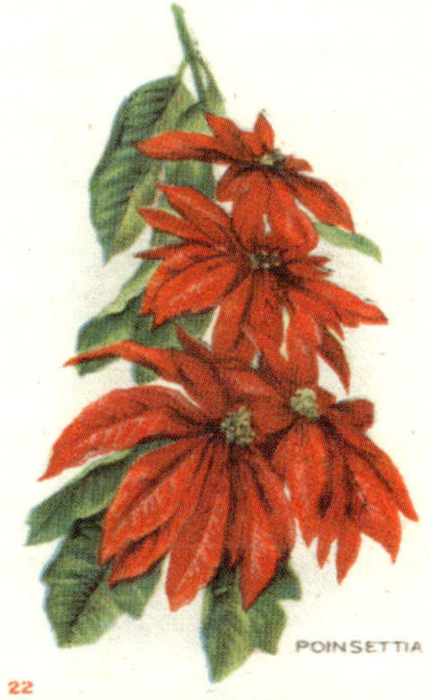

Garden Flowers of the World – Westminster

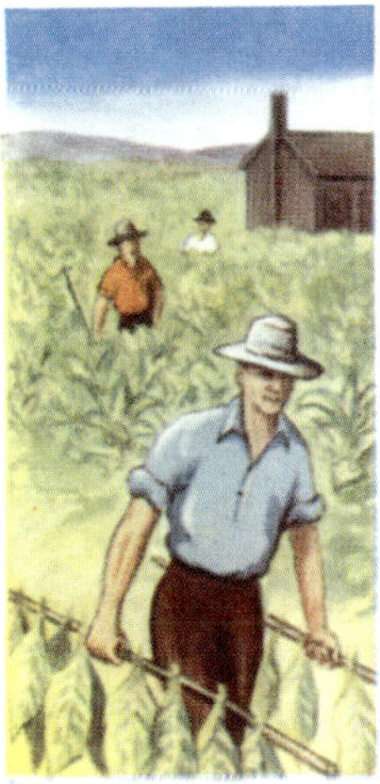

Products of the World – Edwards

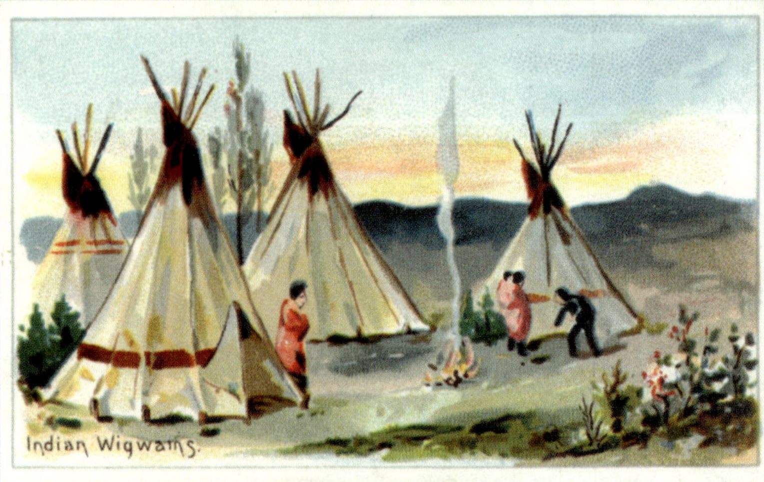

Habitations of Man
Duke

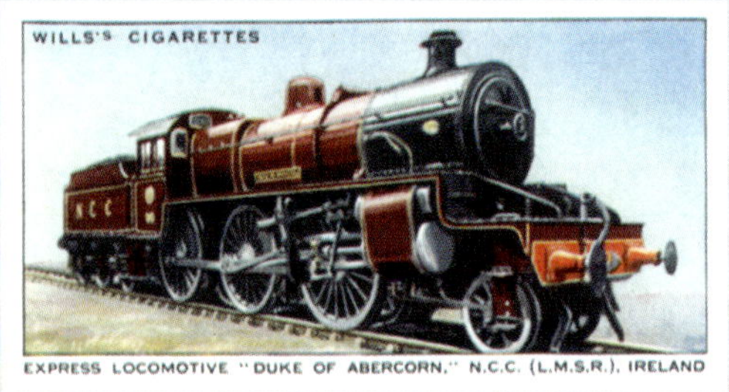

Railway Engines (1936)
Wills. Also reprint

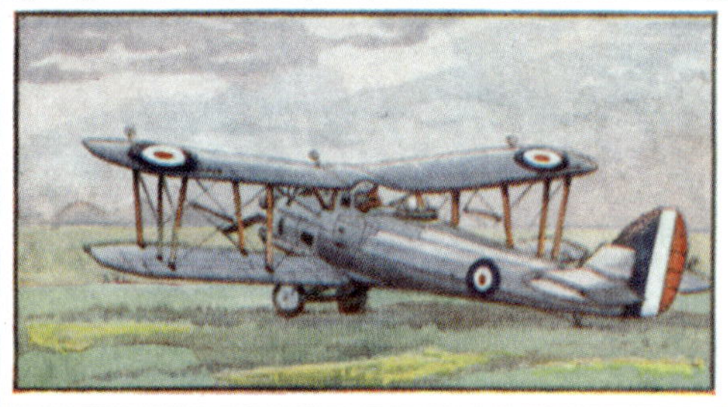

Types of Aeroplanes
Murray

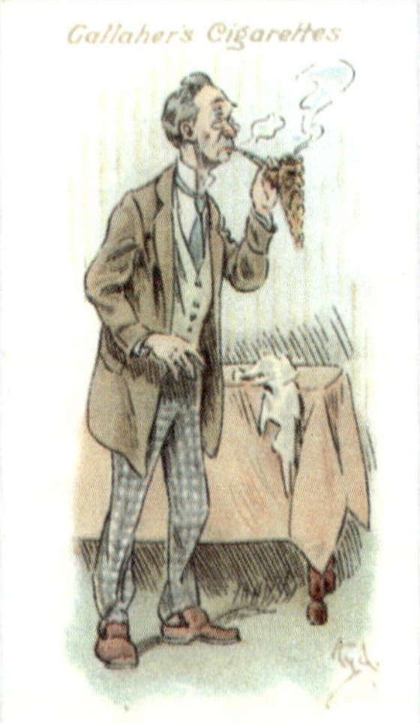

Votaries of the Weed
Gallaher

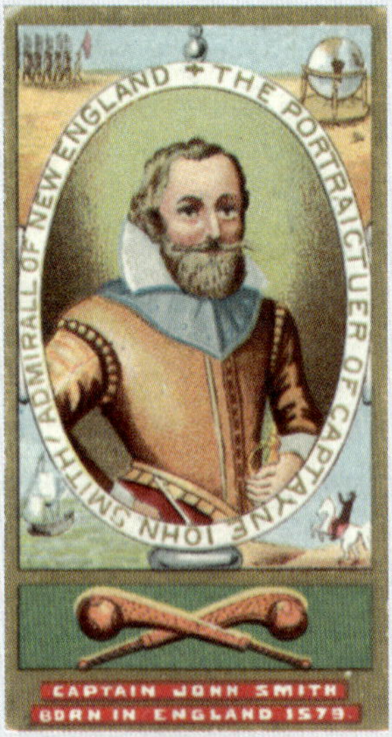

The New Discovery
Cameron & Cameron

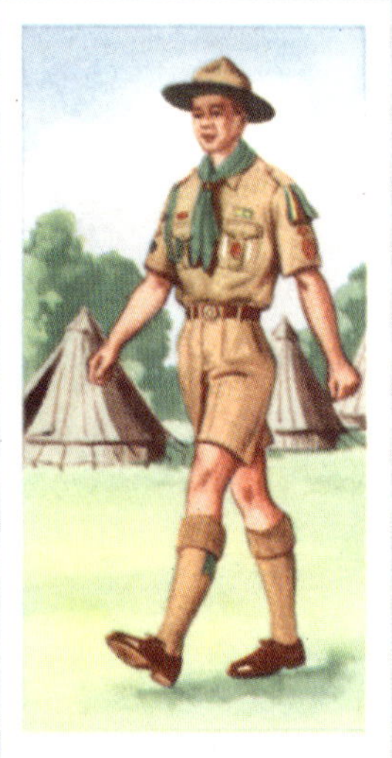

People in Uniform
Priory Tea

CADET SWEETS — cont.

Qty		Date	Odds	Sets
50	U.N.C.L.E. (Photos)	1966	—	£60.00
25	WHAT Do You Know?	1965	—	£12.50

A. J. CALEY & SON (Confectionery)

K24	Film Stars	1930	£7.00	£168.00
10	Passenger Liners	1939	£9.00	—
48	Wisequacks (Mickey Mouse Weekly)	1932	£7.00	—

CALTEX OIL (Australia)

P6	Stargazer (Haley's Comet)	1986	—	£1.50

F. C. CALVERT & CO. LTD. (Toothpaste)

25	Dan Dare Series	1954	£3.00	£75.00

CANDY GUM (Italy)

50	Autosprint I Serie (Printed Back)	1975	—	£6.00
50	(Plain Back)	1975	—	£7.50
30	Autosprint II Serie (Printed Back)	1975	—	£6.00
30	(Plain Back)	1975	—	£7.50

CANDY NOVELTY CO.

25	Animals of the Countryside	1964	£4.50	—
50	Animals of the World	1964	£3.50	—
M25/50	Dog Series — A1 Set	1953	—	£3.50
32	Motor Car Series	1953	£3.50	—
25	Ships Through the Ages, 2nd Series	1957	£4.00	—
32	Western Series	1953	£4.00	—

CANNINGS (Jam)

25	Types of British Soldiers	1914	£12.00	—

F. CAPERN (Bird Seed)

?10	British Birds	1925	£10.00	—
12	Cage Birds	1924	£10.00	—
P54	Cage Birds	1926	£2.25	—
24	Picture Aviary	1964	—	£15.00
1	Picture Aviary Introductory Card	1964	—	25p

CAPEZIO (Ballet Shoes, U.S.A.)

XF12	Famous Dancers Gallery	1950	—	£30.00

CARD INSERT LTD.

1	Famous Footballers	1953	—	£4.00

CARD PROMOTIONS (Commercial)

Qty		Date	Odds	Sets
25	Battleships & Crests (Hill Reprint)	1995	—	£6.00
P12	Big Events on the Turf (Boguslavsky Reprint)	1995	—	£7.50
50	British Sea Dogs (John Sinclair Reprint)	1997	—	£7.50
50	British Warriors (Cope Reprint)	1996	—	£7.50
25	Conan Doyle Characters (Boguslavsky Reprint)	1996	—	£6.00
75	Cricketers Series (Pattrieouex Reprint)	1997	—	£13.50
50	Famous Airmen & Airwomen (Carreras Reprint)	1996	—	£7.50
25	Famous Jockeys (Taddy Reprint)	1996	—	£6.00
25	Famous Running Horses (English) (Kinney Reprint)	1996	—	£6.00
50	Flowers to Grow (Lea Reprint)	1997	—	£7.50
75	Footballers (Carreras Reprint)	1997	—	£13.50
50	Lawn Tennis Celebrities (Lambert & Butler Reprint)	1997	—	£7.50
25/24	Motor Cars (Gallaher Reprint)	1995	—	£6.00
25	Parrot Series (C.W.S. Reprint)	1996	—	£6.00
50	Pirates of the Spanish Main (Allen & Ginter Reprint)	1996	—	£7.50
48	Poultry (C.W.S. Reprint)	1996	—	£7.50
25	Railway Engines (Godfrey Phillips Reprint)	1997	—	£6.00
50	Regimental Colours & Standards (Gallaher Reprint)	1995	—	£7.50
30	Regimental Nicknames (Hustler Reprint)	1997	—	£6.00
50/48	Signed Portraits of Famous Stars (Gallaher Reprint)	1997	—	£7.50
25	Territorial Regiments (Taddy Reprint)	1995	—	£6.00
25	Thames Series (Taddy Reprint)	1996	—	£6.00
25	Types of British Soldiers (Godfrey Phillips Reprint)	1997	—	£6.00
50	Types of the British Army (Gallaher Reprint)	1995	—	£7.50
50	Types of the British Army 51-100 (Gallaher Reprint)	1996	—	£7.50
25	Types of Volunteer & Yeomanry (Woods Reprint)	1996	—	£6.00
25	Uniforms (Cope Reprint)	1996	—	£6.00
20	Victoria Cross Heroes (1-20) (Taddy Reprint)	1996	—	£6.00
20	Victoria Cross Heroes (21-40) (Taddy Reprint)	1996	—	£6.00
20	Victoria Cross Heroes (41-60) (Taddy Reprint)	1997	—	£6.00
20	Victoria Cross Heroes (61-80) (Taddy Reprint)	1997	—	£6.00
20	Victoria Cross Heroes (81-100) (Taddy Reprint)	1997	—	£6.00
25	Victoria Cross Heroes (101-125) Taddy (Reprint)	1996	—	£6.00
25	Winners on the Turf (Boguslavsky Reprint)	1995	—	£6.00

CARDS TO COLLECT (Commercial)

Qty		Date	Odds	Sets
50	Deep Sea Diving	1996	—	£10.50

CARR'S BISCUITS

Qty		Date	Odds	Sets
M30	Animals of the World	1930	£7.50	—
G20	Cricketers	1967	£3.50	£70.00

CARSON'S CHOCOLATE

Qty		Date	Odds	Sets
72	Celebrities	1902	£12.00	—

CARTER'S LITTLE LIVER PILLS

Qty		Date	Odds	Sets
28	Dominoes	1911	£1.00	£28.00

F. C. CARTLEDGE (Razor Blades)

Qty		Date	Odds	Sets
X48	Epigrams "A"	1939	20p	£7.50
X64	Epigrams "B"	1939	20p	£10.00
X96	Epigrams "C"	1941	20p	£20.00
50	Famous Prize Fighters	1938	£2.40	£120.00

CARTOPHILIC SOCIETY

16	London Branch Personalities	1980	—	£5.00
20	London Branch Personalities, 2nd Series	1995	—	£4.00

CASH & CO. (Shoes)

20	War Series	1916	£11.50	—

CASSELLS (Periodical)

M6	British Engines	1923	£10.00	£60.00
M12	Butterflies & Moths Series	1923	£6.00	£72.00

CASTROL OIL

X18	Famous Riders	1955	£3.00	£54.00
X24	Racing Cars	1956	£2.25	£54.00

CAVE AUSTIN & CO. LTD. (Tea)

20	Inventors Series	1923	£9.00	—

CCC LTD.

L15	Arsenal Cup Winners 1992-1993	1993	—	£6.00
L20	Doctor Who	1993	—	£9.00
L1	Doctor Who Promotional Card	1993	—	50p
L6	Wild Cats	1994	—	£3.00

CECIL COURT COLLECTORS CENTRE

L25	Ashes Winning Captains	1993	—	£8.00
L20	Christopher Columbus	1992	—	£6.00
L1	Promotional Card	1992	—	50p
L20	Famous Film Directors	1992	—	£6.00
L1	Promotional Card (Hitchcock)	1992	—	50p

CEDE LTD.

25	Coins of the World	1956	—	£3.50

CENTRAL ELECTRICITY AUTHORITY

M10	Interesting Careers	1961	—	£2.00

CEREBOS (Salt)

100	Sea Shells	1925	£1.60	£160.00

CEYLON TEA CENTRE

Qty		Date	Odds	Sets
24	The Island of Ceylon	1955	—	£2.00

CHANNEL 4/CHEERLEADER PRODUCTIONS (TV)

Qty		Date	Odds	Sets
L20	All Time Great Quarterbacks	1989	—	£25.00

H. CHAPPEL & CO. (Confectionery)

Qty		Date	Odds	Sets
10	British Celebrities	1905	£25.00	—

CHARTER TEA & COFFEE CO. LTD.

Qty		Date	Odds	Sets
25	Prehistoric Animals, First Series	1962	—	*£15.00*
25	Prehistoric Animals, Second Series	1962	—	*£15.00*
25	Strange But True First, Series	1961	80p	£20.00
25	Strange But True, Second Series	1961	—	£12.50
25	Transport Through the Ages, First Series	1961	80p	£20.00
25	Transport Through the Ages, Second Series	1961	60p	£15.00

CHEF & BREWER

Qty		Date	Odds	Sets
L20	Historic Pub Signs	1984	—	£6.50

CHIVERS & SONS LTD. (Preserves)

Qty		Date	Odds	Sets
L125	Firm Favourites	1932	£2.00	—
K53	Miniature Playng Cards	1965	£1.00	—
P6	Studies of English Fruits, Series 1	1924	£5.50	£33.00
P6	Studies of English Fruits, Series 2	1924	£5.50	£33.00
24	Wild Wisdom	1964	£2.50	£60.00
48	Wild Wisdom in Africa	1964	£2.25	£108.00
48	Wild Wisdom, River and Marsh	1964	£2.25	£108.00
PACKAGE ISSUES				
L15	Children of Other Lands	1952	80p	£12.00
L15	Chivers British Birds	1951	80p	£12.00
L20	On Chivers Farms	1951	75p	£15.00

CHIX CONFECTIONERY CO. LTD.

Qty		Date	Odds	Sets
M12	Batman (Packets)	1990	—	£6.00
X50	Famous Footballers	1960	£3.25	—
X48	Famous Footballers, No.1 Series	1953	£2.75	£132.00
X48	Famous Footballers, No.2 Series	1956	£2.75	£132.00
X48	Famous Footballers, No.3 Series	1958	£3.25	£156.00
X50	Famous Last Words	1970	70p	£35.00
X24	Footballers (Portrait & Action) 1-24	1956	—	£15.00
X24	Footballers (Portrait & Action) 25-48	1956	—	£30.00
L50	Funny Old Folk	1970	—	£12.00
L50	Happy Howlers	1970	70p	£35.00
L50	Krazy Kreatures from Outer Space	1970	£1.25	£62.50
T36	Looney Tunes (Packets)	1990	—	£8.00
L6	Looney Tunes (Packets)	1990	—	£2.50
L50	Military Uniforms	1970	—	£17.50

CHIX CONFECTIONERY CO. LTD. — cont.

Qty		Date	Odds	Sets
L50	Moon Shot	1966	£1.60	£80.00
X50	Popeye	1960	£3.00	£150.00
X24	Scottish Footballers	1960	£6.00	£144.00
X50	Ships of the Seven Seas	1968	£1.60	£80.00
X50	Soldiers of the World	1962	80p	£40.00
X50	Sport through the Ages	1968	£2.75	£137.50
L6	The Joker (Batman Packets)	1989	—	£8.00
P52	The Real Ghostbusters (Package Slides)	1990	—	£25.00
96	T.V. and Radio Stars	1954	£1.75	—
X50	Wild Animals	1960	£1.30	£65.00

CHUMS (Periodical)

Qty		Date	Odds	Sets
MF23	Cricketers	1923	£5.00	£115.00
MF20	Football Teams	1922	£2.50	£50.00
F8	Football Teams New Series	1923	£3.00	£24.00
X10	Real Colour Photos (Footballers)	1922	£6.00	£60.00

CHURCH & DWIGHT (Baking Soda, U.S.A.)

Qty		Date	Odds	Sets
M60	Beautiful Birds, New Series	1896	£3.25	£195.00
60	Beautiful Birds, New Series (Miniature)	1896	£4.00	—
60	Beautiful Birds, New Series (Standard)	1896	£5.25	—
M60	Beautiful Birds of America	1894	£4.00	£240.00
60	Beautiful Birds of America	1894	£5.25	—
M60	Beautiful Flowers	1895	£3.00	£180.00
60	Beautiful Flowers	1895	£3.75	—
X10	Birds of Prey	1976	—	£10.00
M30	Champion Dog Series	1902	£7.00	—
30	Champion Dog Series	1902	£7.25	—
M30	Dairy Animals	1895	£8.00	—
30	Dairy Animals	1895	£8.00	—
M30	Fish Series	1900	£3.00	£90.00
30	Fish Series	1900	£4.25	—
M30	Game Bird Series	1904	£3.50	£105.00
30	Game Bird Series	1904	£4.25	—
M60	Interesting Animals	1897	£3.75	£225.00
60	Interesting Animals (Miniature)	1897	£5.00	—
60	Interesting Animals (Standard)	1897	£6.50	—
M30	Interesting Animals (Re-Issue)	1915	£5.00	—
30	Interesting Animals (Re-Issue)	1915	£7.50	—
M30	Mother Goose Series	1900	£5.00	£150.00
30	Mother Goose Series	1900	£6.25	—
M30	New Series of Birds	1908	£2.25	£67.50
30	New Series of Birds	1908	£3.25	—
M30	New Series of Dogs	1910	£7.00	—
30	New Series of Dogs	1910	£7.50	—
M30	Useful Birds of America	1915	£2.50	£75.00
30	Useful Birds of America	1915	£3.00	—
M30	Useful Birds of America, 2nd Series	1918	£2.25	£67.50
30	Useful Birds of America, 2nd Series	1918	£3.00	—
M30	Useful Birds of America, 3rd Series	1922	£2.25	£67.50
30	Useful Birds of America, 3rd Series	1922	£2.25	£67.50
M30	Useful Birds of America, Series 4	1924	£2.50	£75.00
30	Useful Birds of America, Series 4	1924	£2.25	£67.50

CHURCH & DWIGHT (Baking Soda, U.S.A.) — cont.

Qty		*Date*	*Odds*	*Sets*
M15	Useful Birds of America, Series 5	1924	£2.00	£30.00
M15	Useful Birds of America, Series 6	1924	£2.00	£30.00
M15	Useful Birds of America, Series 7	1924	£2.00	£30.00
M15	Useful Birds of America, Series 8	1924	£1.80	£27.00
M15	Useful Birds of America, Series 9	1926	40p	£6.00
M15	Useful Birds of America, Series 10	1926	50p	£7.50

CIBA PHARMACEUTICAL PRODUCTS (U.S.A.)

P12	Medicine Men	1960	—	£16.50

CLARNICO (Confectionery)

30	Colonial Troops (Many Backs)	1900	£25.00	—
25	Great War Leaders	1915	£16.50	—
29	Wolf Cubs Signalling	1910	£24.00	—

CLASSIC GAMES INC. (U.S.A.)

X100	Deathwatch 2,000	1993	—	£13.00

THE CLASSIC MOTOR CYCLE

16	Motor Races 1931 (Ogden Reprints)	1989	—	£2.50

CLEVEDON CONFECTIONERY LTD.

50	British Aircraft	1958	£2.25	—
25	British Orders of Chivalry & Valour	1960	£3.25	—
50	British Ships	1959	£2.65	—
M50	British Trains and Engines	1958	£5.00	—
25	Dan Dare	1961	£5.00	£125.00
40	Did You Know?	1963	£3.00	—
40	Famous Cricketers	1959	£8.50	—
25	Famous Cricketers (Different)	1962	£8.00	—
50	Famous Football Clubs	1964	£2.00	£100.00
50	Famous Footballers	1961	£3.50	—
50	Famous International Aircraft	1963	£1.40	£70.00
M50	Famous Screen Stars	1959	£3.25	—
40	Film Stars	1958	£2.75	—
50	Football Club Managers	1959	£5.50	—
50	Hints on Association Football	1961	£2.40	—
50	Hints on Road Safety	1962	£2.25	—
50	International Sporting Stars	1960	£2.00	—
M50	Regimental Badges	1959	£3.00	—
X25	Sporting Memories	1962	£6.00	—
50	The Story of the Olympics	1961	£1.80	£90.00
50	Trains of the World	1962	£1.75	—
M60	Wagon Train	1963	£3.75	—

CLEVELAND (Petrol)

P20	Golden Goals	1970	—	£16.00

CLIFFORD (Commercial)

Qty		*Date*	*Odds*	*Sets*
50	Footballers	1950	£10.00	—

CLOVER DAIRIES LTD.

Qty		*Date*	*Odds*	*Sets*
25	Animals and Reptiles	1970	—	£2.00
25	British Rail	1973	—	£2.00
25	People & Places	1972	—	£2.00
25	Prehistoric Animals	1965	—	£2.25
25	Science in the 20th Century	1971	—	£2.00
25	Ships and Their Workings	1971	—	£2.00
25	The Story of Milk	1970	—	£2.50
25	Transport through the Ages	1971	—	£2.00

COCA COLA (Drinks)

Qty		*Date*	*Odds*	*Sets*
M100	Our Flower Paradise (S. Africa)	1960	—	£35.00
X96	The World of Nature (U.S.A.)	1960	—	£40.00

COFTON COLLECTIONS (Shop)

Qty		*Date*	*Odds*	*Sets*
25	Dogs, 1st Series	1988	—	£4.50
25	Dogs, 2nd Series	1988	—	£4.50
25	Dogs, 3rd Series	1988	—	£4.50
L25	Nursery Rhymes	1992	—	£7.50
L20	Worcestershire County Cricket Club	1989	—	£6.50

CECIL COLEMAN LTD. (Confectionery)

Qty		*Date*	*Odds*	*Sets*
24	Film Stars	1935	£6.50	—

COLGATE-PALMOLIVE (Toiletries)

Qty		*Date*	*Odds*	*Sets*
D24	Famous Sporting Trophies	1979	—	£7.00
P4	Royal Britain	1951	£1.75	£7.00

COLINVILLE LTD. (Gum)

Qty		*Date*	*Odds*	*Sets*
M56	Look'n See	1958	£4.25	—
X25	Prairie Pioneers	1959	£3.00	£75.00
L28	Space Fantasy, 1st Series (1-28)	1959	£3.75	£105.00
L28	Space Fantasy, 2nd Series (29-56)	1959	£4.50	—

COLLECT-A-CARD CORPORATION (U.S.A.)

Qty		*Date*	*Odds*	*Sets*
X100	Harley-Davidson Series 2	1992	—	£20.00
X100	Harley-Davidson Series 3	1993	—	£20.00
X109	Vette Set (Corvette Cars, including Hologram)	1991	—	£22.00

COLLECTABLES OF SPALDING (Shop)

Qty		*Date*	*Odds*	*Sets*
25	British Cavalry Uniforms	1987	—	£4.50

COLLECTABLES OF SPALDING (Shop) — cont.

Qty		Date	Odds	Sets
25	Military Maids	1987	—	£4.50
25	Warriors through the Ages	1987	—	£4.50

COLLECTOR & HOBBYIST (Periodical)

Qty		Date	Odds	Sets
25	Fascinating Hobbies	1950	—	£2.00

COLLECTORS' CORNER

Qty		Date	Odds	Sets
L20	Halifax As It Was	1989	—	£4.50

COLLECTORS FARE

Qty		Date	Odds	Sets
16	Reading F.C. Simod Cup Winners	1990	—	£2.25
X16	Reading F.C. Simod Cup Winners	1990	—	£2.50

COLLECTORS SHOP

Qty		Date	Odds	Sets
25	Bandsmen of the British Army	1960	—	£10.00
3	Bonus Cards	1961	*£1.00*	—
2	Bonus Cards 1961-62	1961	—	£2.50

COLMAN'S MUSTARD

Qty		Date	Odds	Sets
X8	Boer War Celebrities	1900	£20.00	—

COLT 45 (Drink)

Qty		Date	Odds	Sets
X5/6	Advertising Slogans (Silk)	1976	£3.50	—
P4	American Scenes (Beer Mats)	1975	—	£3.00

COMET SWEETS ("C.S.")

Qty		Date	Odds	Sets
25	A. & M. Denis on Safari, 1st Series	1961	—	£2.50
25	A. & M. Denis on Safari, 2nd Series	1961	—	£2.50
50	Footballers and Club Colours	1963	50p	£25.00
25	Modern Wonders (Black Back)	1961	—	£2.50
25	(Blue Back)	1961	—	*£15.00*
25	Olympic Achievements, 1st Series	1960	—	£12.50
25	Olympic Achievements, 2nd Series	1960	—	£12.50
M22	Olympic Achievements (Package)	1960	£6.00	—
25	Record Holders of the World	1962	—	£5.00
25	Ships through the Ages, 1st Series	1963	60p	—
25	Ships through the Ages, 2nd Series	1963	60p	—

COMIC LIFE (Periodical)

Qty		Date	Odds	Sets
MF4	Sports Champions	1922	£5.00	£20.00

COMMODEX (Gum)

Qty		Date	Odds	Sets
L88	Operation Moon	1969	£1.50	£132.00
L120	Super Cars	1970	£1.30	£156.00

COMMONWEALTH SHOE & LEATHER CO. (U.S.A.)

Qty		Date	Odds	Sets
M12	Makes of Planes	1930	£3.25	£39.00

COMO CONFECTIONERY PRODUCTS LTD.

Qty		Date	Odds	Sets
M52	Adventures of Fireball XL5	1965	£7.50	—
L25	History of the Wild West, Series No.1	1963	£2.75	—
L25	History of the Wild West, Series No.2	1963	—	£10.00
50	Lenny's Adventures	1961	£1.20	£60.00
50	Noddy and His Playmates	1962	—	£15.00
M25	Noddy's Adventures	1958	£5.00	—
L25	Noddy's Adventures, 1st Series	1958	£2.00	£50.00
L25	Noddy's Adventures, 2nd Series	1958	£2.25	—
25	Noddy's Budgie & Feathered Friends, 1st Series	1964	£1.50	—
25	Noddy's Budgie & Feathered Friends, 2nd Series	1964	£1.50	—
M25	Noddy's Friends Abroad	1959	£5.00	—
L50	Noddy's Friends Abroad	1959	£1.30	£65.00
M25	Noddy's Nursery Rhyme Friends	1959	£5.00	—
L50	Noddy's Nursery Rhyme Friends	1959	£1.30	£65.00
L50	Sooty's Adventures	1960	£1.30	£65.00
L50	Sooty's New Adventures, Second Series	1961	£1.00	—
50	Sooty's Latest Adventures, 3rd Series	1963	£1.50	—
25	Speed, 1st Series	1962	£1.60	£40.00
25	Speed, 2nd Series	1962	—	£6.00
25	Supercar, 1st Series	1962	£3.50	—
25	Supercar, 2nd Series	1962	£2.50	£62.50
25	Top Secret, 1st Series	1965	£1.80	£45.00
25	Top Secret, 2nd Series	1965	£1.50	£37.50
L26	XL5, 1st Series	1965	£10.00	£260.00
L26	XL5, 2nd Series	1966	£10.00	—

COMPTON'S GRAVY SALT

Qty		Date	Odds	Sets
22	Footballers, Serie A (Black)	1924	£10.00	—
22	Footballers, Serie A (Coloured)	1924	£10.00	—
22	Footballers, Serie B (Black)	1924	£7.00	—
22	Footballers, Serie B (Coloured)	1924	£10.00	—
22	Footballers, Serie C	1924	£10.00	—
22	Footballers, Serie D	1924	£10.00	—

COOPER & CO. LTD. (Tea)

Qty		Date	Odds	Sets
50	Do You Know?	1962	—	£5.00
25	Inventions & Discoveries, 1st Series	1962	—	£30.00
25	Inventions & Discoveries, 2nd Series	1962	—	£30.00
25	Mysteries & Wonders of the World, 1st Series	1961	—	£15.00
25	Mysteries & Wonders of the World, 2nd Series	1961	—	£7.50
25	Prehistoric Animals, First Series	1962	—	£27.50
25	Prehistoric Animals, Second Series	1962	—	£27.50
25	Strange But True, First Series	1961	—	£3.00
25	Strange But True, Second Series	1961	—	£4.00
24	The Island of Ceylon	1955	£2.50	—
25	Transport through the Ages, 1st Series	1961	—	£7.50
25	Transport through the Ages, 2nd Series	1961	40p	£10.00

CO-OPERATIVE SOCIETIES (Shops)

Qty		Date	Odds	Sets
D306	Espana '82. Complete with Album	1982	—	£18.00
	Special Poster for above (only if ordered at the same time)	1982	—	£1.00
M48	World Cup Teams & Players, Complete with Poster	1982	—	£6.00

CORNERSTONE COMMUNICATIONS INC. (Commercial U.S.A.)

Qty		Date	Odds	Sets
X110	Doctor Who	1994	—	£20.00
X110	Doctor Who Series 2	1995	—	£17.50
X110	Doctor Who Series 3	1996	—	£15.00
X90	Doctor Who Series 4	1996	—	£15.00
X81	The Avengers	1992	—	£30.00
X99	The Avengers in Colour Series 2	1993	—	£20.00
X86	The Avengers Return Series 3	1995	—	£20.00

COUNTY PRINT SERVICES (Commercial)

Qty		Date	Odds	Sets
M25	Australian Test Cricketers	1993	—	£10.00
X48	County Cricket Teams 1900-1914	1992	—	£9.00
20	Cricket Pavilions	1991	—	£10.00
X24	Cricket Teams 1884-1900	1990	—	£7.00
12	Cricket Terms (Faulkner Reprint)	1991	—	£10.00
50	Cricketers 1890	1989	—	£8.00
50	Cricketers 1896	1989	—	£8.00
50	Cricketers 1900	1990	—	£8.00
50	Cricketers 1906	1992	—	£8.00
20	Cricketers (Murray Reprint)	1991	—	£7.50
25	Cricketers (Reeves Ltd. Reprint)	1993	—	£8.00
M25	Cricket's Golden-Age	1991	—	£9.00
X12	Cricket's Pace Partners	1995	—	£8.00
X12	Cricket's Spin Twins	1995	—	£8.00
L25	Derbyshire Test Cricketers	1994	—	£10.00
L25	Essex Test Cricketers	1993	—	£10.00
M27	Famous Cricket Crests	1992	—	£12.50
M25	Famous Cricket Ties	1992	—	£9.00
X12	First Knock (Cricket's Opening Pairs)	1994	—	£9.00
L25	Glamorgan Test Cricketers	1993	—	£10.00
L25	Gloucestershire Test Cricketers	1994	—	£10.00
L25	Hampshire Test Cricketers	1995	—	£10.00
L25	Kent Test Cricketers	1993	—	£10.00
L25	Lancashire Test Cricketers	1993	—	£10.00
L25	Leicestershire Test Cricketers	1995	—	£10.00
L25	Middlesex Test Cricketers	1994	—	£10.00
50	1912 Triangular Tournament	1992	—	£8.00
M24	1920's Test Cricketers	1994	—	£10.00
M24	1920's Test Cricketers, 2nd Series	1995	—	£10.00
25	1950's England Cricket Characters	1995	—	£12.00
M50	1960's Test Cricketers	1992	—	£12.50
25	1995 England Cricket Characters	1995	—	£10.00
L25	Northamptonshire Test Cricketers	1993	—	£10.00
L25	Nottinghamshire Test Cricketers	1994	—	£10.00
L25	Somerset Test Cricketers	1994	—	£10.00
15	South African Cricket Team 1907 (Taddy Reprint)	1993	—	£6.00

COUNTY PRINT SERVICES (Commercial) — cont.

Qty		Date	Odds	Sets
M15	South African Cricket Team 1965	1994	—	£6.00
L25	Surrey Test Cricketers	1994	—	£10.00
L25	Sussex Test Cricketers	1994	—	£10.00
14	The England Cricket Team 1903-1904	1991	—	£4.00
15	The England Cricket Team 1907-1908	1992	—	£10.00
17	The England Cricket Team 1932-33	1995	—	£6.00
16	The England Cricket Team 1990-91	1990	—	£6.00
16	The South African Cricket Team 1894	1990	—	£6.00
M15	The South African Cricket Team 1965	1994	—	£6.00
M30	Vic Lewis Cricket Club 1952-1992	1992	—	£6.00
L25	Warwickshire Test Cricketers	1994	—	£10.00
L25	Worcestershire Test Cricketers	1995	—	£10.00
L25	Yorkshire Test Cricketers	1993	—	£10.00

COW & GATE (Baby Food)

X24	Advertisement Cards	1928	£1.50	£36.00
X48	Happy Families	1928	75p	£36.00

COWANS (Confectionery, Canada)

24	Dog Pictures	1930	£5.25	£126.00
24	Horse Pictures	1930	£5.00	£120.00
24	Learn to Swim	1929	£5.50	—
24	Noted Cats	1930	£5.25	£126.00

CREATIVE MARKETING ASSOCIATES (Commercial)

X81	Hammer Horror Series 1	1995	—	£24.95
X82	Hammer Horror Series 2	1996	—	£14.95
X90	Laurel & Hardy	1997	—	£11.95

CRESCENT CONFECTIONERY CO.

100	Sportsmen	1928	£15.00	—

CROMWELL STORES

25	Do You Know?	1963	—	£6.00
25	Racing Colours	1963	—	£8.00

CROSBIE (Preserves)

K54	Miniature Playing Cards	1938	80p	—

JOSEPH CROSFIELD & SONS LTD. (Soap)

36	Film Stars	1924	£7.00	—

CRYSELCO ELECTRIC LAMPS

X25	Beautiful Waterways	1939	80p	£20.00
X25	Buildings of Beauty	1938	80p	£20.00
X12	Interesting Events of Sixty Years Ago	1955	—	*£25.00*

D. CUMMINGS & SON (Commercial)

Qty		Date	Odds	Sets
64	Famous Fighters	1949	£3.00	£192.00

D & V (Commercial)

Qty		Date	Odds	Sets
25	Famous Boxers (Hudden Reprint)	1992	—	£5.00
35	Famous Boxers (Singleton & Cole Reprint)	1992	—	£6.00

DAILY HERALD (Newspaper)

Qty		Date	Odds	Sets
32	Cricketers	1954	£3.00	£96.00
32	Footballers	1954	£2.00	£64.00
32	Turf Personalities	1955	£1.00	£32.00

DAILY ICE CREAM CO.

Qty		Date	Odds	Sets
24	Modern British Locomotives	1954	£2.00	£48.00

DAILY MAIL (Newspaper)

Qty		Date	Odds	Sets
P176	War Photographs	1916	£1.75	—

DAILY MIRROR (Newspaper)

Qty		Date	Odds	Sets
M72	Chart Toppers	1989	—	£4.50
M100	Star Soccer Sides	1972	30p	£30.00

DAILY SKETCH (Newspaper)

Qty		Date	Odds	Sets
40	World Cup Souvenir	1970	£1.50	£60.00

THE DAILY TELEGRAPH (Newspaper)

Qty		Date	Odds	Sets
26	England Rugby World Cup 1995	1995	—	£5.00
26	Ireland Rugby World Cup 1995	1995	—	£5.00
26	Scotland Rugby World Cup 1995	1995	—	£5.00
26	Wales Rugby World Cup 1995	1995	—	£5.00

DAINTY NOVELS

Qty		Date	Odds	Sets
10	World's Famous Liners	1912	£11.00	—

DANDY GUM

Qty		Date	Odds	Sets
M200	Animal Fables (Black Back)	1971	25p	£50.00
M200	(Red Back)	1971	35p	—
X42	Batman Stickers (Australian)	1989	—	£10.00
M200	Birds (F1-200)	1968	—	£60.00
K50	Bird Series (Transfers)	1950	£1.40	—
M160	Cars and Bikes	1977	60p	£96.00
M97	Film & Entertainment Stars (Serie G)	1968	60p	£60.00
M116	Flag Parade	1965	—	£24.00
M160	Flag Parade	1978	—	£36.00
M55	Football World Cup (Playing Card Inset)	1986	—	£15.00
M72	Motor Cars	1966	75p	£54.00
M53	Our Modern Army (Playing Card Inset)	1958	—	£40.00
M43/53	Ditto	1958	20p	£8.50

DANDY GUM — cont.

Qty		Date	Odds	Sets
M53	Pin Ups (Playing Card Inset)	1956	£1.65	£88.00
M53	Pin Ups (Playing Card Inset, Different)	1978	—	*£16.00*
M70	Pop Stars (Serie P)	1977	35p	£25.00
M100	Soldier Parade	1970	30p	£30.00
M200	Struggle for the Universe	1970	*25p*	*£50.00*
M72	Veteran & Vintage Cars (V1-72)	1966	£1.00	£72.00
K48	Wiggle Waggle Pictures	1969	£2.25	£108.00
M100	Wild Animals (H1-100)	1969	—	£20.00
M200	Wonderful World (Y1-200)	1978	—	£35.00

DART FLIPCARDS INC. (Canada)

Qty		Date	Odds	Sets
X90	Pepsi Cola Premium Trading Cards	1996	—	£15.00
X100	Pepsi Cola Trading Cards	1994	—	£13.00
X72	The Frighteners	1996	—	£15.00
X90	The Munsters Collection	1996	—	£15.00

LIAM DEVLIN & SONS (Confectionery)

Qty		Date	Odds	Sets
M36	Coaching Gaelic Football	1960	*£7.50*	—
48	Corgi Toys	1971	—	£60.00
50	Do You Know?	1964	—	£4.00
M50	Famous Footballers (New Series)	1952	£10.00	—
M50	Famous Footballers, Series A.1	1953	£10.00	—
M50	Famous Footballers, Series A.2	1954	£10.00	—
50	Famous Footballers, Series A.3	1955	£10.00	—
M54	Famous Speedway Stars	1960	*£10.00*	—
M45	Fastest on Earth	1953	£3.25	—
36	Flags of the Nations	1960	£2.75	—
48	Gaelic Sportstars	1960	£6.00	—
48	Irish Fishing	1962	50p	£24.00
L36	Irish Theatre and Showland Stars	1965	£4.00	£144.00
50	Modern Transport	1966	—	£7.50
48	Our Dogs	1963	£5.00	—
48	Right or Wrong?	1963	£4.00	—
M35	Walt Disney Characters	1956	*£4.50*	—
M48	Wild Animals by George Cansdale	1954	£3.50	—
48	Wild Wisdom	1970	£2.50	—
50	Wonders of the World	1972	—	£4.00
100	World Flag Series	1970	£5.00	—

DIAMOND COLLECTION (Commercial)

Qty		Date	Odds	Sets
L20	Rock N Roll	1997	—	£7.50

DICKSON ORDE & CO. (Confectionery)

Qty		Date	Odds	Sets
50	Footballers	1960	—	£7.50
25	Ships through the Ages	1961	£2.75	—
25	Sports of the Countries	1962	—	£6.50

DINKIE PRODUCTS LTD. (Hair Grips)

Qty		Date	Odds	Sets
L24	Films (Plain Backs)	1952	£2.50	£60.00

DINKIE PRODUCTS LTD. (Hair Grips) — cont.

Qty		Date	Odds	Sets
L20	Gone with the Wind, Fifth Series	1948	£5.00	£100.00
X20	M.G.M. Films, Third Series	1948	—	£35.00
L24	M.G.M. Films, Ninth Series	1950	£3.75	—
L24	M.G.M. Films, Tenth Series	1951	£4.25	—
L24	M.G.M. Stars, Seventh Series	1949	£2.75	—
L24	Paramount Pictures, Eighth Series	1950	£2.75	—
X24	Stars & Starlets, First Series	1947	£1.65	£40.00
X20	Stars & Starlets, Second Series	1947	—	£35.00
L24	United Artists Releases, Eleventh Series	1951	£4.25	—
L24	Warner Bros. Artists, Fourth Series	1948	£2.50	—
L24	Warner Bros. Films, Sixth Series	1949	£2.50	—

DIRECT ACCESS (Commercial)

L8	British Sporting Stars	1992	—	£6.50

DIRECT TEA SUPPLY CO.

25	British Uniforms of the 19th Century	1958	—	£16.50

F. M. DOBSON (Confectionery)

X144	Flags of the World	1980	20p	—
100	Newcastle & Sunderland's 100 Greatest Footballers	1982	—	£6.50
2	Error Cards	1982	—	£1.00

PETER DOMINIC (Vintner)

P17	Cricket Badges	1990	—	£16.00

A. & J. DONALDSON (Commercial)

64	Golden Series (Soccer)	1955	£9.00	—
?500	Sports Favourites	1953	£6.00	—

DONRUSS (Gum, U.S.A.)

X59	B.M.X. Card Series	1984	—	£15.00
X66	Disneyland	1965	—	£60.00
X66	Elvis	1978	—	£35.00
X66	Magnum P.I.	1983	—	£17.50
X66	1980 P.G.A. Tour	1981	—	£50.00
X66	1981 P.G.A. Tour	1982	—	£60.00
X66	Sgt. Pepper's Lonely Hearts Club Band	1978	—	£15.00
X74	Tron	1983	—	£5.00

DORMY COLLECTION (Commercial)

25	Golf — The Modern Era	1994	—	£8.00

DOUBLE DIAMOND (Beer)

Qty		Date	Odds	Sets
P5	Puzzle Pictures (Beer Mats)	1976	—	£2.50

DRYFOOD LTD. (Confectionery)

Qty		Date	Odds	Sets
50	Animals of the World	1956	—	£4.00
K50	Zoo Animals	1955	—	£4.00

DUCHESS OF DEVONSHIRE DAIRY CO. LTD.

Qty		Date	Odds	Sets
L25	Devon Beauty-Spots	1936	£4.00	£100.00

DUNHILLS (Confectionery)

Qty		Date	Odds	Sets
25	Ships and Their Workings	1962	—	£6.00

DUNKIN (Confectionery, Spain)

Qty		Date	Odds	Sets
X88	Martial Arts	1976	65p	£57.50
M50	Motor Cycles of the World	1976	£1.70	£85.00

DUNNS (Chocolate)

Qty		Date	Odds	Sets
60	Animals	1924	£5.75	—
48	British Birds & Their Eggs	1924	£3.50	—

DUOCARDS (U.S.A.)

Qty		Date	Odds	Sets
X90	Gone With The Wind	1996	—	£10.00

DUTTON'S BEER

Qty		Date	Odds	Sets
12	Team of Sporting Heroes	1981	—	£2.40

THE EAGLE (Periodical)

Qty		Date	Odds	Sets
16	Wallet of Soccer Stars	1965	—	£24.00

EAST KENT NATIONAL BUS CO.

Qty		Date	Odds	Sets
X8	British Airways Holidays	1984	—	£1.50

J. EDMONDSON & CO. (Confectionery)

Qty		Date	Odds	Sets
26	Actresses "FROGA"	1901	£45.00	—
4	Aeroplane Models	1939	£12.50	—
?40	Art Picture Series	1914	£12.00	—
15	Birds & Their Eggs	1924	£8.50	—
?20	Boy Scout Proficiency Badges	1924	£24.00	—
25	British Army Series	1914	£18.00	—

J. EDMONDSON & CO. (Confectionery) — cont.

Qty		Date	Odds	Sets
20	British Ships	1925	£2.25	£45.00
20	Dogs	1924	£6.00	£120.00
20	Famous Castles	1925	£5.00	£100.00
30	Flags & Flags With Soldiers	1905	£13.50	—
40	Flags of All Nations	1923	£6.50	—
24	Pictures from the Fairy Stories	1930	£4.50	—
24	Popular Sports	1930	£8.50	—
25	Sports & Pastimes Series	1916	£12.00	—
12	Throwing Shadows on the Wall	1937	£3.25	£40.00
25	War Series	1916	£12.00	—
12	Woodbine Village	1936	£3.00	£36.00
26	Zoo Alphabet	1935	£5.50	—

EDWARDS & SONS (Confectionery)

27	Popular Dogs	1954	£3.00	£81.00
12	Products of the World	1957	—	£1.50
25	Transport Present and Future (Descriptive)	1956	—	£2.00
25	(Non-Descriptive)	1955	—	£2.50
25	Wonders of the Universe	1956	—	£2.00

ELECTROLUX (Leisure Appliances)

P16	Weekend Tours	1990	—	£5.75

ELKES BISCUITS LTD.

25	Do You Know?	1964	—	£2.25

ELY BREWERY CO. LTD.

M24	Royal Portraits	1953	£1.80	£45.00

EMAP LTD. (Magazines)

X14/15	World Class Winners (Sport)	1997	—	£10.00

EMERALD COLLECTABLES (Commercial)

M72	Birds and Their Eggs	1996	—	£12.75

EMPIRE MARKETING BOARD

12	Empire Shopping	1926	£2.50	£30.00

H.E. EMPSON & SONS LTD. (Tea)

25	Birds	1962	—	£10.00
25	British Cavalry Uniforms of the 19th Century	1963	—	£10.00
25	Garden Flowers	1966	£1.00	£25.00
25	History of the Railways, 1st Series	1966	£1.20	£30.00
25	History of the Railways, 2nd Series	1966	£1.20	£30.00

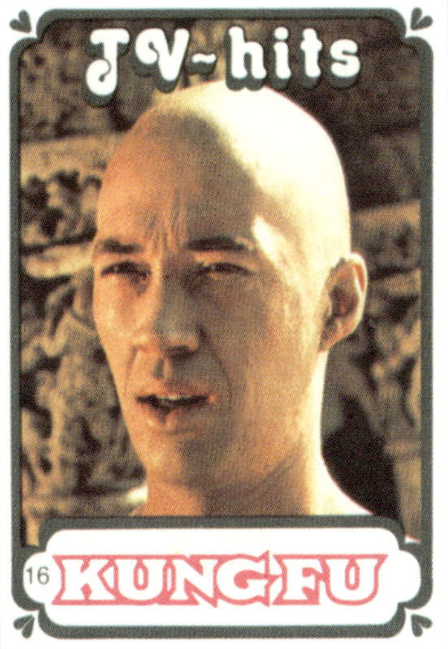

T.V. hits – Monty Gum

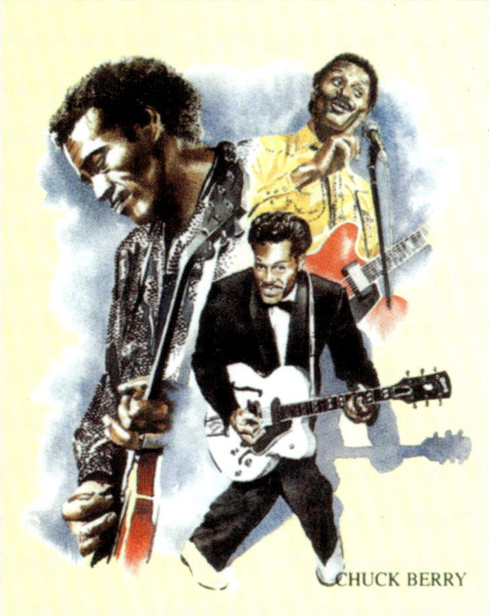

Rock N Roll – Diamond Collection

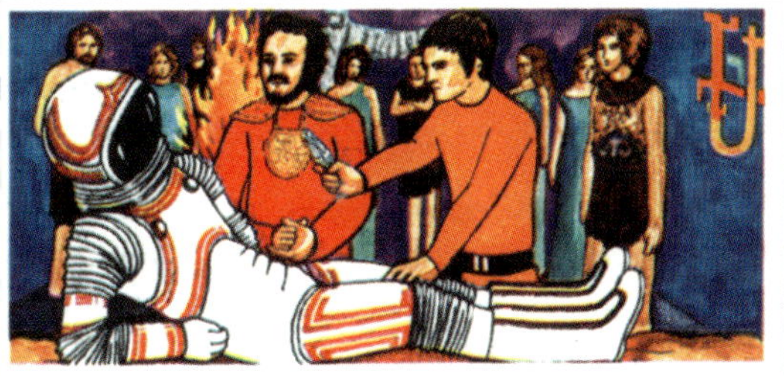

Space 1999 – Lyons Maid

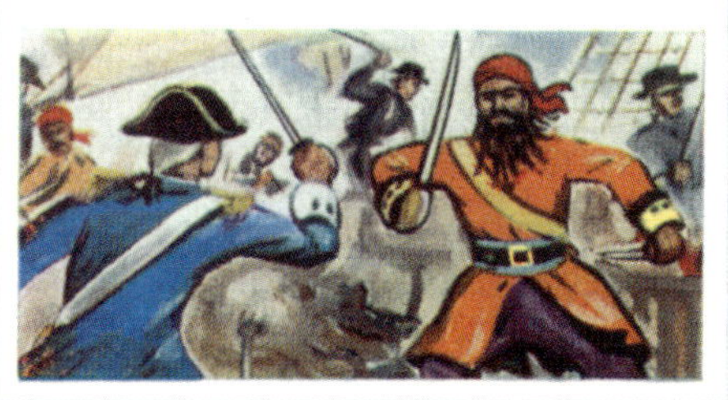

Buccaneers – Cadet Sweets

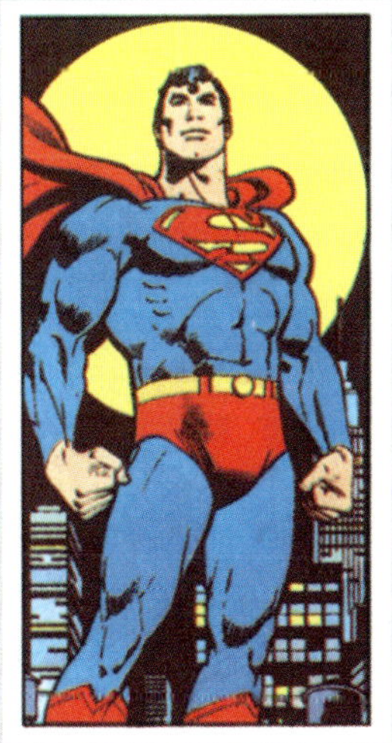

Super Heroes – Bassett

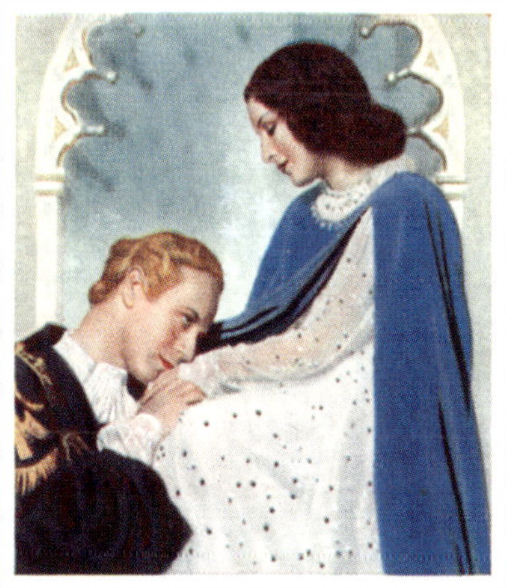

Famous Love Scenes – Godfrey Phillips

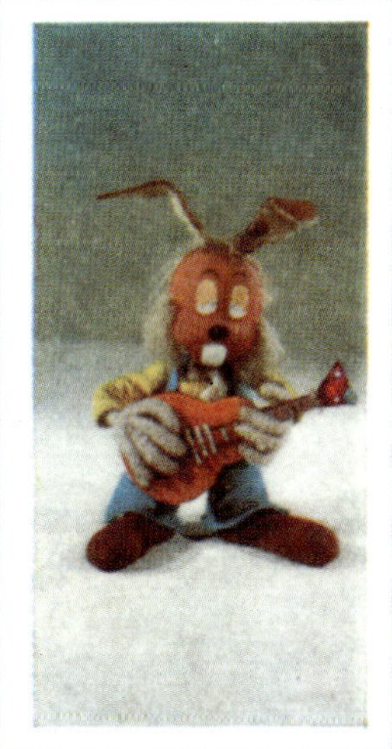

Magic Roundabout – Barratt

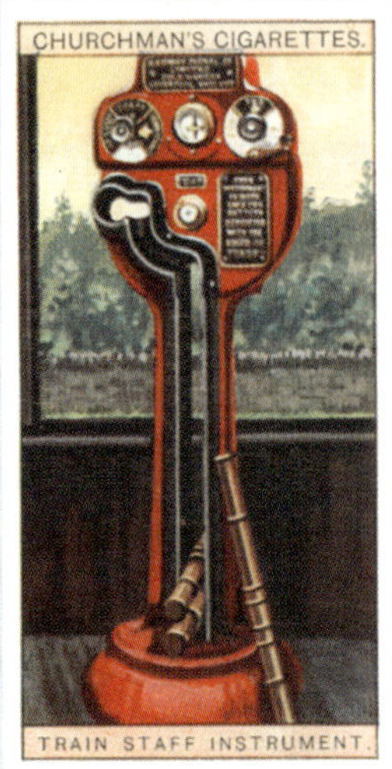

Railway Working
Churchman. Also B.A.T.

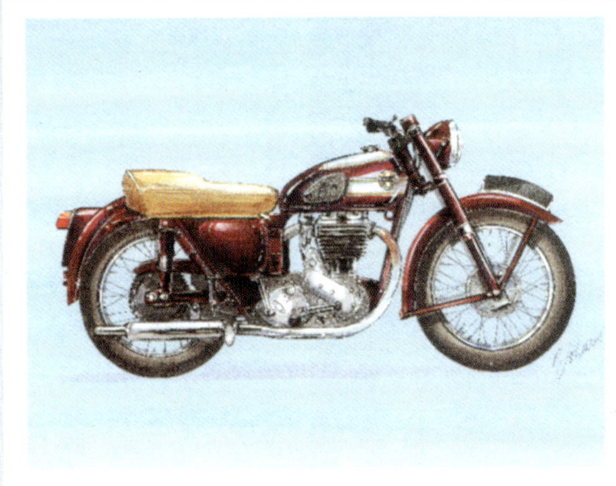

Some of Britain's Finest Bikes
Newmarket Hardware

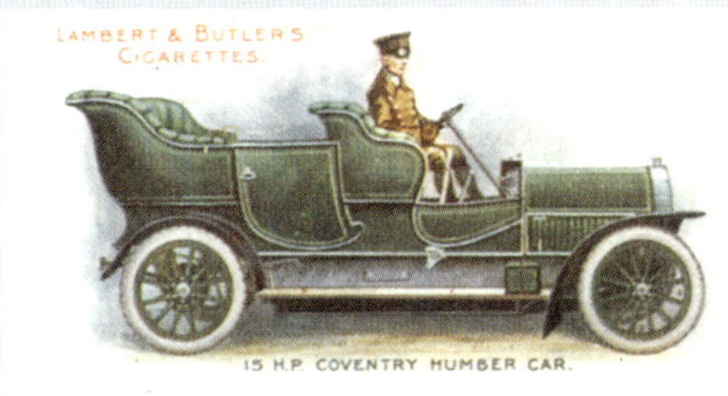

Motors
Lambert & Butler. Also reprint

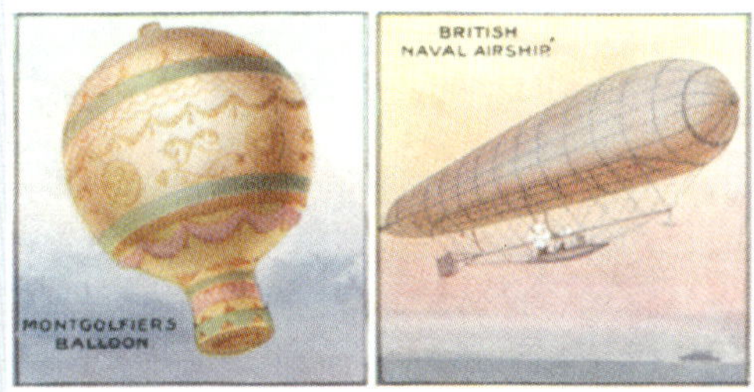

The Old & The New
Rowntree

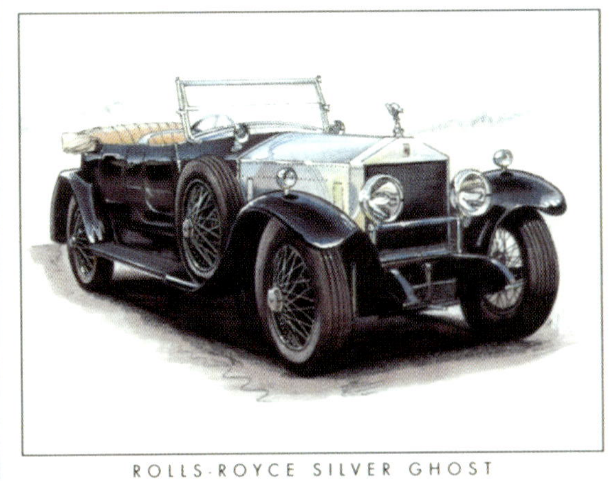

Classic Rolls Royce Models
Golden Era

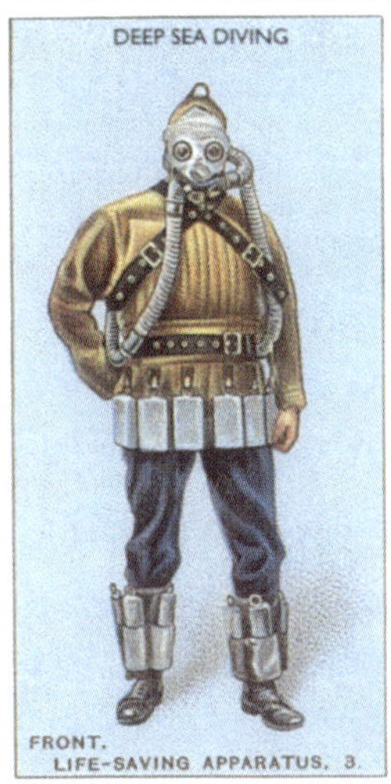

Deep Sea Diving
Cards to Collect

H.E. EMPSON & SONS LTD. (Tea) — cont.

Qty		Date	Odds	Sets
25	Passenger Liners	1964	£1.00	£25.00
24	The Island of Ceylon	1955	£3.50	—
25	Tropical Birds	1966	50p	£12.50
25	Wonders of the Deep	1965	—	£2.50

ENGLISH & SCOTTISH C.W.S. (Shops)

Qty		Date	Odds	Sets
50	British Sport Series	1904	£27.50	—
25	Humorous Peeps into History (1-25)	1927	£2.75	£70.00
25	Humorous Peeps into History (26-50)	1928	£4.00	—
25	In Victoria's Days	1930	£2.50	£62.50
X12	The Rose of the Orient, Film Series	1925	50p	£6.00
X12	The Rose of the Orient, 2nd Film Series	1925	50p	£6.00
X12	The Story of Tea (Blue Back)	1925	75p	£9.00
X12	The Story of Tea (Brown Back, Different)	1925	65p	£7.80

ENSIGN FISHING TACKLE

Qty		Date	Odds	Sets
L6	Birds of Prey	1996	—	£2.50
L20	Freshwater Fish	1995	—	£7.50
L6	Game Birds	1995	—	£2.50
L6	Garden Birds	1996	—	£2.50
L6	Owls	1996	—	£2.50
L25	Salmon Flies	1994	—	£7.50
L6	The Art of Angling, A Series	1996	—	£2.50
L6	The Art of Angling, 2nd Series	1996	—	£2.50

EPOL (South Africa)

Qty		Date	Odds	Sets
M30	Dogs	1974	65p	£20.00

JOHN E. ESSLEMONT LTD. (Tea)

Qty		Date	Odds	Sets
25	Before our Time	1966	—	£5.00
25	Into Space	1966	30p	£7.50
24	The Island of Ceylon	1961	£4.00	—

ESSO PETROLEUM CO.

Qty		Date	Odds	Sets
P20	Olympics	1972	£1.75	£35.00
M16	Squelchers (Football)	1970	£1.25	£20.00

ESTA MEDICAL LABORATORIES INC. (U.S.A.)

Qty		Date	Odds	Sets
E6	Curiosa of Conception	1960	—	£8.50

EVERSHED & SON LTD. (Soap)

Qty		Date	Odds	Sets
25	Sports and Pastimes	1914	£12.00	—

EVERY GIRL'S PAPER

Qty		Date	Odds	Sets
MF17	Film Stars	1924	£3.00	£51.00

EWBANKS LTD. (Confectionery)

Qty		*Date*	*Odds*	*Sets*
25	Animals of the Farmyard	1960	—	£2.50
25	British Uniforms	1956	—	£4.00
25	Miniature Cars & Scooters	1960	—	£6.00
50	Ports and Resorts of the World	1960	—	£4.00
25	Ships Around Britain	1961	—	£2.00
25	Sports and Games	1958	—	£4.00
25	Transport through the Ages (Black Back)	1957	—	£2.00
25	(Blue Back)	1957	—	£10.00

EXPRESS WEEKLY (Periodical)

25	The Wild West (No Overprint)	1958	—	£5.00
25	(Red Overprint)	1958	—	£2.75

EXTRAS

24	Prehistoric Monsters and the Present	1979	£1.75	—

F1 SPORTSCARD MARKETING INC. (Canada)

X200	Formula 1 Racing Cards	1992	—	£20.00

F.A.I. INSURANCE GROUP (Australia)

X24	Australian Cricket Team 1989/90	1989	—	£7.50

FACCHINO'S CHOCOLATE WAFERS

100	Cinema Stars	1936	60p	£60.00
50	How or Why!	1937	50p	£25.00
50	People of All Lands	1937	£1.75	—
50	Pioneers	1937	£1.40	£70.00

FAITH PRESS (Commercial)

10	Boy Scouts (LCC)	1928	£5.00	£50.00

FAMILY STAR (Periodical)

MF4	Film Stars (Pairs)	1956	£5.00	£20.00
K52	Fortune Telling Cards	1952	50p	—

FARM-TO-DOOR SUPPLIES (LUTON) LTD.

25	Castles of Great Britain	1965	£3.25	—
25	Cathedrals of Great Britain	1964	£3.25	—

FARROWS (Sauces)

50	Animals in the Zoo	1925	£5.50	£275.00

FASHODA (Commercial)

Qty		Date	Odds	Sets
50	Motor Races 1931 (Ogdens Reprint)	1993	—	£7.50
50	Poultry (Player Reprint)	1993	—	£7.50

FAULDER'S CHOCOLATES

10	Ancient v. Modern Sports	1924	£4.00	—
10	Birds and Nests	1924	£4.00	—
10	Fruits	1924	£4.00	—
10	Game	1924	£4.00	—

FAX-PAX (Commercial)

X36	ABC and Numbers	1987	—	£3.50
X36	Animal Spelling	1988	—	£3.50
X50	Butterflies of the British Isles	1996	—	£3.50
X40	Castles	1990	—	£3.50
X40	Cathedrals & Minsters	1989	—	£3.50
X39	Dinosaurs	1993	—	£4.00
X36	Fables	1987	—	£3.50
X40	Famous Golfers	1993	—	£5.00
X42	First Ladies of the United States	1997	—	£3.50
X36	Football Greats	1989	—	£6.00
X36	Football Stars	1989	—	£5.00
X40	Historic Houses	1990	—	£3.50
X36	Kings & Queens	1988	—	£3.50
X36	London	1987	—	£3.50
X36	Nursery Rhymes	1987	—	£3.50
X41	Presidents of the United States	1991	—	£4.00
X40	Ringlords	1991	—	£4.00
X40	Scotland's Heritage	1990	—	£3.50
X38	Tennis	1987	—	£8.50
X40	The American West	1993	—	£3.50
X50	Wild Flowers	1996	—	£3.50
X40	World of Sport	1993	—	£3.50

ALEX FERGUSON (Confectionery)

41	V.C. Heroes	1916	£15.00	—

THE FESTIVAL OF 1000 BIKES COMMITTEE

L24	The Vintage Motor Cycle Club	1993	—	£6.00

FIELD GALLERIES

L7	Racehorses & Jockeys, A Series	1997	—	£3.00
L7	Racehorses & Jockeys, 2nd Series	1997	—	£3.00

FILM PICTORIAL (Periodical)

P2	Film Stars (Silk)	1923	£27.50	£55.00

JOHN FILSHILL LTD. (Confectionery)

Qty		Date	Odds	Sets
24	Birds & Their Eggs	1924	£5.00	£120.00
25	Footballers	1924	£12.00	£300.00
25	Types of British Soldiers	1914	£20.00	—

FINDUS (Frozen Foods)

20	All About Pirates	1967	—	£6.00

FINE FARE TEA

25	Inventions & Discoveries, 1st Series	1965	50p	£12.50
25	Inventions & Discoveries, 2nd Series	1965	50p	£12.50
12	Your Fortune in a Tea-Cup	1966	—	£2.75

FISH MARKETING BOARD

18	Eat More Fish	1930	£2.50	—

FITCHETT'S LTD. (Soap)

27	Advertisement Series	1910	£17.50	—

FIZZY FRUIT (Confectionery)

25	Buses and Trams	1959	—	£20.00

FLEER GUM INC. (U.S.A.)

X72	Here's Bo!	1980	—	£5.00
E12	Here's Bo! Posters	1980	—	£3.00

FLEETWAY PUBLICATIONS LTD.

P1	Billy Fury (June)	1960	—	60p
P28	Football Teams 58/59	1959	£2.00	£56.00
P28	Football Teams 59/60	1960	£2.00	£56.00
P2	Pop Stars (Roxy)	1961	—	£1.50
50	Star Footballers of 1963	1963	90p	£45.00

FLORENCE CARDS (Commercial)

24	Luton Corporation Tramways	1983	—	£1.75
T20	Tramway Scenes	1985	—	£1.75

FORD MOTOR CO. LTD.

M50	Major Farming	1955	£5.50	—

FOSTER CLARK PRODUCTS (Malta)

50	The Sea — Our Other World	1974	—	£10.00

FOSTER'S LAGER

Qty		Date	Odds	Sets
P4	How To Order Your Foster's (Beermats)	1988	—	£1.50

FRAMEABILITY (Commercial)

Qty		Date	Odds	Sets
L17	Fire Engines	1996	—	£5.00
L17	Fire Engines 2nd Series	1998	—	£6.00

A. C. W. FRANCIS (Confectionery, Grenada)

Qty		Date	Odds	Sets
25	Football Clubs and Badges	1967	—	£16.00
25	Pond Life	1967	—	£7.50
25	Sports of the Countries	1967	—	£15.00

LES FRERES (Shop)

Qty		Date	Odds	Sets
25	Aircraft of World War II	1964	—	£17.50

J. S. FRY & SONS LTD. (Confectionery)

Qty		Date	Odds	Sets
3	Advertisement Cards	1910	£22.50	—
50	Ancient Sundials	1924	£2.50	£125.00
50	Birds & Poultry	1912	£2.25	£112.50
24	Birds and Their Eggs	1912	£3.00	£72.00
15	China & Porcelain	1907	£12.00	£180.00
P2	Coronation Postcards	1911	£8.00	—
25	Days of Nelson	1906	£10.00	£250.00
25	Days of Wellington	1906	£10.00	£250.00
25	Empire Industries	1924	£6.00	—
50	Exercises for Men & Women	1926	£4.00	—
48	Film Stars	1934	£2.25	—
50	Fowls, Pigeons & Dogs	1908	£3.50	£175.00
P12	Fun Cards	1972	—	£2.00
25	Match Tricks	1921	*£25.00*	—
15	National Flags	1908	£5.50	£82.50
50	Nursery Rhymes	1917	£3.00	£150.00
50	Phil May Sketches	1905	£3.00	£150.00
25	Red Indians	1927	£6.00	—
25	Rule Britannia	1915	£5.00	£125.00
50	Scout Series	1912	£5.00	£250.00
48	Screen Stars	1928	£2.50	£120.00
120	This Wonderful World	1935	£1.25	—
50	Time & Money in Different Countries	1908	£2.50	£125.00
50	Tricks and Puzzles (Black Back)	1924	£3.00	£150.00
50	Tricks & Puzzles (Blue Back)	1918	£3.00	£150.00
L1	Vinello Advertisement Card	1922	—	£25.00
6	War Leaders (Campaign Packets)	1915	£25.00	—
25	With Captain Scott at the South Pole	1913	£9.00	£225.00

CANADIAN ISSUES

Qty		Date	Odds	Sets
50	Children's Nursery Rhymes	1912	*£9.00*	—
25	Hunting Series	1912	*£12.50*	—
25	Radio Series	1912	£7.00	—
50	Scout Series — Second Series	1913	£9.00	—
50	Treasure Island Map	1912	£5.25	—

FUTERA (Commercial)

Qty		Date	Odds	Sets
X90	Arsenal Football Club – Fans Selection	1997	—	£17.00
X99	Liverpool Football Club	1998	—	£25.00
X100	Manchester United	1997	—	£22.50
X99	Manchester United	1998	—	£25.00
X90	Manchester United – Fans Selection	1997	—	£17.00

G. B. & T. W. (Commercial)

L20	Golfing Greats	1989	—	£8.50

GALBRAITH'S STORES LTD.

25	Animals in the Service of Man	1960	£3.50	—

GAMEPLAN LEISURE LTD. (Commercial)

L25	Open Champions (Golf)	1995	—	£7.50

GARDEN NEWS

T6	Flowers	1988	—	£4.00
T6	Vegetables	1988	—	£4.00

GATEAUX (Ireland)

22	Irish World Cup Squad (Soccer)	1990	£4.50	£100.00

GAUMONT CHOCOLATE BAR

KF50	Film Stars	1936	£2.50	—

GAYCON PRODUCTS LTD. (Confectionery)

25	Adventures of Pinky & Perky, 1st Series	1961	£2.00	—
25	Adventures of Pinky & Perky, 2nd Series	1961	£2.00	—
50	British Birds and Their Eggs	1961	—	£5.00
25	British Butterflies	1962	—	£15.00
25	Do You Know?, 1st Series	1964	£1.40	£35.00
25	Do You Know?, 2nd Series	1964	£1.40	£35.00
50	Flags of All Nations	1963	£1.50	£75.00
25	History of the Blue Lamp, 1st Series	1962	—	£9.00
25	History of the Blue Lamp, 2nd Series	1962	—	£9.00
30	Kings and Queens	1961	—	£3.00
25	Modern Motor Cars	1959	£3.25	—
25	Modern Motor Cars of the World, 1st Series	1962	£3.00	£75.00
25	Modern Motor Cars of the World, 2nd Series	1962	£3.25	—
25	Red Indians, 1st Series	1960	—	£7.50
25	Red Indians, 2nd Series	1960	—	£7.50
25	Top Secret, 1st Series	1963	£1.60	£40.00
25	Top Secret, 2nd Series	1963	£1.75	—

GEES FOOD PRODUCTS

30	Kings and Queens	1961	—	£12.00
16	See Britain by Coach	1959	—	£2.00

GEM LIBRARY (Periodical)

Qty		Date	Odds	Sets
MF4	Footballers — Autographed Action Series	1923	£3.50	£14.00
MF6	Footballers — Autographed Real Action Photo Series	1922	£3.00	£18.00
MF15	Footballers — Special Action Photo	1922	£3.00	£45.00
L16	Marvels of the Future	1929	£2.40	£38.50

GENERAL FOODS (S.A.) (PTY) LTD. (South Africa)

X50	Animals and Birds	1973	20p	£10.00

ALFRED GERBER (Cheese)

M143	Glorious Switzerland	1952	90p	—

GIRLS CINEMA (Periodical)

F6	Film Stars (Autographed)	1929	£5.00	£30.00

GIRLS FRIEND (Periodical)

M6	Actresses (Silk)	1913	£9.00	£54.00

GIRLS MIRROR (Periodical)

MF10	Actors & Actresses	1922	£3.00	£30.00

GIRLS WEEKLY

12	Flower Fortune Cards	1912	£12.00	—

GLENGETTIE TEA

25	Animals of the World	1964	—	£2.50
25	Birds and Their Eggs	1970	—	£5.00
25	British Locomotives	1959	—	£3.00
25	Do You Know?	1970	—	£2.00
25	Historical Scenes	1968	—	£2.00
25	History of the Railways, 1st Series	1974	—	£2.00
25	History of the Railways, 2nd Series	1974	—	£2.00
25	International Air-Liners	1963	—	£2.50
25	Medals of the World (Black Back)	1959	—	£2.00
25	(Blue Back)	1959	—	£10.00
25	Modern Transport (Black Back)	1963	—	£12.00
25	(Blue Back)	1963	—	£12.00
25	Naval Battles	1971	—	£2.00
25	Rare British Birds	1967	—	£4.00
25	Sovereigns, Consorts & Rulers of G.B., 1st	1970	—	£12.50
25	Sovereigns, Consorts & Rulers of G.B., 2nd	1970	—	£12.50
25	The British Army 1815 (Black Back)	1976	—	£2.50
25	(Blue Back)	1976	—	£2.00
25	Trains of the World	1966	—	£4.00
25	Veteran and Vintage Cars	1966	—	£15.00
25	Wild Flowers	1961	—	£5.00

GLENTONS LTD. (Shop)

Qty		Date	Odds	Sets
24	World's Most Beautiful Butterflies	1910	£5.00	—

J. GODDARD & SONS LTD. (Metal Polish)

Qty		Date	Odds	Sets
L4	Cleaning a Silver Teapot	1928	£2.75	—
L3	Four Generations	1923	£1.25	£3.75
L12	London Views	1925	£1.50	£18.00
L12	Old Silver	1924	£1.20	£14.00
L9	Old Silver at the Victoria & Albert Museum	1933	£1.60	£15.00
L12	Ports of the World	1928	£2.00	£24.00
L12	Present Day Silverware	1937	£1.40	£16.50
L4	Silverware with Flowers I	1928	£1.75	£7.00
L8	Silverware with Flowers II	1933	£2.00	£16.00
L2	Use & Cleaning of Silverware I	1926	75p	£1.50
L6	Use & Cleaning of Silverware II	1937	£3.50	£21.00
L8	Views of Leicester	1934	£4.00	£32.00
L12	Views of Old Leicester	1928	£4.25	£51.00

GOLD ENTERTAINMENT INC. (U.S.A.)

Qty		Date	Odds	Sets
X5	Babe Ruth Series (Holograms)	1992	—	£10.00

GOLDEN ERA (Commercial)

Qty		Date	Odds	Sets
T25	Aircraft of the First World War	1993	—	£7.50
L7	A.J.S.	1995	—	£2.50
L7	Alfa Romeo	1998	—	£2.50
L7	Antique Dolls	1996	—	£2.50
L7	Ariel	1995	—	£2.50
L10	Austin	1996	—	£3.75
L7	Aston Martin	1993	—	£2.50
L7	Austin Healey: The Big Healeys 1953-68	1995	—	£2.50
T25	British Motor Cycles of the Fifties	1993	—	£7.50
L7	BSA Motor Cycles	1993	—	£2.50
L26	Cat Portraits	1995	—	£7.50
L25	Cats	1993	—	£7.50
L10	Classic American Motor Cycles	1998	—	£3.75
L26	Classic British Motor Cars	1992	—	£7.50
T25	Classic British Motor Cycles of the 1950s & 1960s	1993	—	£7.50
L7	Classic Lotus	1995	—	£2.50
L7	Classic Lotus — 2nd Series	1997	—	£2.50
L7	Classic MG	1992	—	£2.50
L7	Classic MG —2nd Series	1993	—	£2.50
L7	Classic MG Sports Cars	1996	—	£2.50
L7	Classic Morgan Sports Cars	1997	—	£2.50
L13	Classic Porsche	1996	—	£4.50
L7	Classic Rolls Royce Models	1997	—	£2.50
L7	Classic Rover	1995	—	£2.50
L10	Classic Tractors	1998	—	£3.75
L7	Classic TVR	1997	—	£2.50
L13	Classic V.W.	1993	—	£4.50
L7	Cobra	1996	—	£2.50

GOLDEN ERA (Commercial) — cont.

Qty		Date	Odds	Sets
X10	Corvette	1994	—	£4.50
L7	Dolls	1996	—	£2.50
X10	Famous Bombers	1997	—	£4.50
X10	Famous Fighters	1997	—	£4.50
L10	Famous TT Riders	1998	—	£3.75
L6	Ford Executive	1994	—	£2.50
L10	Ford in the Sixties	1996	—	£3.75
L10	Formula 1	1996	—	£3.75
L10	Grand Prix Greats	1996	—	£3.75
L26	Grand Prix: The Early Years	1992	—	£7.50
L7	Jaguar Classics	1992	—	£2.50
L7	Jaguar Classics, 2nd Series	1993	—	£2.50
L7	Jaguar Classics, 3rd Series	1997	—	£2.50
L7	Lancia	1998	—	£2.50
L7	Land Rover Series I	1996	—	£2.50
L7	Land Rover Series II	1996	—	£2.50
L7	Land Rover Series III	1996	—	£2.50
L10	London's Buses of the Post-War Years	1997	—	£3.75
L10	London's Buses of the Pre-War Years	1997	—	£3.75
L7	Mansell (Motor Racing Victories)	1994	—	£3.00
L7	Matchless	1995	—	£2.50
L7	Mercedes SL	1994	—	£2.50
P4	Mini Cooper	1994	—	£2.25
P4	Monte Carlo Minis	1994	—	£2.25
L9	Morris Minor	1993	—	£3.75
P4	Morris Minor Van	1994	—	£2.25
L9	Morris Minor – Fifty Years	1998	—	£3.75
L10	Motorcycling Greats	1997	—	£3.75
X10	Mustang	1994	—	£4.50
L7	Norton Motor Cycles	1993	—	£2.50
L7	Norton Motor Cycles, 2nd Series	1998	—	£2.50
L7	Old Teddy Bears	1995	—	£2.50
P4	Police Vehicles	1994	—	£2.25
L7	Range Rover	1996	—	£2.50
L7	Spitfire (Triumph)	1994	—	£2.50
L7	Sporting Ford	1992	—	£2.50
L7	Teddies	1997	—	£2.50
L7	Teddy Bears (Antique)	1994	—	£2.50
L7	The Classic Bentley	1997	—	£2.50
L7	The Classic Ferrari Collection	1993	—	£2.50
L7	The E - Type Collection	1993	—	£2.50
L10	The Ford Capri	1995	—	£3.75
L10	The Mini Legend	1995	—	£3.75
L7	The World Famous Mini Cooper	1994	—	£2.50
L10	Thirty Five Years of the Mini	1993	—	£3.75
L7	TR Collection	1992	—	£2.50
L7	Triumph Motor Cycles	1993	—	£2.50
L7	Triumph Motor Cycles, 2nd Series	1998	—	£2.50
L7	Triumph Stag 1970–1977	1995	—	£2.50
L7	Velocette Motor Cycles	1993	—	£2.50
L7	Vincent	1995	—	£2.50

GOLDEN FLEECE (Australia)

X36	Pedigree Dogs	1972	—	£17.50

GOLDEN GRAIN TEA

Qty		Date	Odds	Sets
25	Birds	1970	—	£15.00
25	British Cavalry Uniforms of the 19th Century	1964	—	£5.00
25	Garden Flowers	1971	—	£2.50
25	Passenger Liners	1970	—	£2.50

GOLDEN WONDER (Potato Crisps)

Qty		Date	Odds	Sets
24	Soccer All Stars	1978	50p	£12.00
14	Space Cards (Round Corners)	1979	—	£2.00
14	(Square Corners)	1979	—	£3.00
24	Sporting All Stars	1979	—	£2.50
24	TV All Stars	1979	—	£2.00
36	World Cup Soccer All Stars	1978	25p	£9.00

GOLF GIFTS LTD. (Commercial)

Qty		Date	Odds	Sets
M24	Ryder Cup '89	1991	—	£12.50

GOODIES LTD. (Confectionery)

Qty		Date	Odds	Sets
50	Doctor Who and The Daleks	1965	£7.00	—
25	Flags and Emblems	1961	—	£3.25
25	Indian Tribes	1975	£2.00	—
25	Mini Monsters	1975	£1.30	£32.50
24	Olympics	1972	£2.00	£50.00
25	Pirates	1976	£1.40	£35.00
25	Prehistoric Animals	1969	£2.40	—
25	Robbers & Thieves	1976	£1.40	£35.00
25	The Monkees, First Series	1967	80p	£20.00
25	The Monkees, Second Series	1968	£3.00	—
25	Vanishing Animals	1977	£1.50	£37.50
25	Weapons through the Ages	1974	£1.30	£32.50
25	Wicked Monarchs	1973	£1.20	£30.00
25	Wide World/People of Other Lands	1968	£1.20	£30.00
25	Wild Life	1977	£1.20	£30.00
25	World Cup	1974	£2.00	£50.00

D. W. GOODWIN & CO. (Flour)

Qty		Date	Odds	Sets
36	Careers for Boys & Girls	1930	£7.00	—
24	Extra Rhymes, Second Series	1930	£11.00	—
36	Flags of All Nations	1930	£5.00	—
36	Jokes Series	1930	£9.00	—
36	Optical Illusions	1930	£10.00	—
X60	Recipe Cards (Vertical Back, 1-60)	1930	£1.75	—
X60	Recipe Cards (Horizontal Back, 301-360)	1930	£1.75	—
36	Ships Series	1930	£8.25	—
25	Wireless	1930	£12.50	—
36	World Interest Series	1930	£6.50	—
24	World's Most Beautiful Birds	1930	*£8.00*	—
24	World's Most Beautiful Fishes	1930	£8.00	—

WILLIAM GOSSAGE & SONS LTD. (Soap)

Qty		Date	Odds	Sets
48	British Birds & Their Eggs	1924	£2.00	£96.00
48	Butterflies & Moths	1924	£1.25	£60.00

GOWERS & BURGONS (Tea)

Qty		*Date*	*Odds*	*Sets*
25	British Birds and Their Nests	1970	—	£6.50
25	Family Pets	1964	—	£2.00
25	People & Places	1970	—	£2.00
25	Prehistoric Animals	1969	80p	£20.00
25	Sailing Ships through the Ages	1971	80p	£20.00
25	The Circus	1964	—	*£25.00*
25	Veteran and Vintage Cars	1965	£1.00	£25.00
25	Veteran Racing Cars	1964	£1.00	£25.00

GRAFFITI INC. (U.S.A.)

X90	Goldeneye	1995	—	£17.50

GRAIN PRODUCTS (New Zealand)

L20	Fire Engines	1988	—	£10.00
P10	Vintage & Veteran Cars	1985	—	£5.00

GRANGER'S

12	Dr. Mabuse Series	1926	£8.00	£96.00

GRANOSE FOODS LTD.

M48	Adventures of Billy the Buck	1956	—	£3.50
L16	Air Transport	1957	—	£2.00
L16	Animal Life	1957	—	£2.00
25	Animals in the Service of Man	1965	*£2.50*	—
L16	Aquatic & Reptile Life	1957	—	£2.00
M48	King of the Air	1956	35p	—
M48	Life Story of Blower the Whale	1956	50p	—
M48	Lone Leo the Cougar	1955	40p	—
L20	150 Years of British Locomotives	1981	—	£15.00
L16	Our Winged Friends	1957	30p	—
L16	Plant Life	1957	*75p*	—
M48	Silver Mane the Timber Wolf	1955	—	£4.00
L16	Space Travel	1957	—	£5.00
M48	Tippytail the Grizzly Bear	1956	—	£3.00
L16	Water Transport	1957	—	£2.00
L16	World Wide Visits	1957	—	£2.00

WILLIAM GRANT & SONS LTD. (Distillers)

25	Clan Tartans	1993	—	£6.50

GREGG (Jelly, New Zealand)

M48	Aquatic Birds	1974	25p	—
M40	Introduced and Other Birds	1967	30p	£12.00
M40	Land Birds of New Zealand	1974	—	£12.00
M40	Native Birds of New Zealand	1971	30p	£12.00
M35	Rare and Endangered Birds	1974	—	£12.50
M40	Remarkable Birds of the World	1974	30p	—
M35	Unusual Birds of the World	1974	—	£10.00

H.B. ICE CREAM LTD. (Ireland)

Qty		Date	Odds	Sets
24	Did You Know	1968	£2.50	—

NICHOLAS HALL & SONS (Tea)

Qty		Date	Odds	Sets
25	War Series	1917	£16.50	—

HALPINS (Tea)

Qty		Date	Odds	Sets
25	Aircraft of the World	1958	—	£2.00
L20	Aircraft of the World (Double Cards)	1958	85p	£17.00
25	Nature Studies	1958	—	£4.00

HAMPSHIRE CRICKET CLUB

Qty		Date	Odds	Sets
24	Sunday League Era	1987	—	£6.00

HAPPY HOME (Periodical)

Qty		Date	Odds	Sets
M32	Child Studies (Silk)	1912	£12.50	—
M9	Flags (Silk)	1914	£6.50	£58.50
M9	Our Lucky Flowers (Silk)	1912	£11.50	—
K14	The Happy Home Silk Button (Silk)	1914	£6.00	£84.00
M12	Women on War Work (Silk)	1914	£6.50	£78.00

HARBOUR REPROGRAPHICS

Qty		Date	Odds	Sets
30	Cricket, Surrey v Yorkshire	1988	—	£9.00

HARDEN BROS. & LINDSAY LTD. (Tea)

Qty		Date	Odds	Sets
50	Animals of the World	1960	—	£15.00
50	British Birds and Their Eggs	1960	—	£17.50
50	National Pets	1961	—	£4.00

HARRISON (Pomade)

Qty		Date	Odds	Sets
25	Beauties	1902	£22.00	£550.00

JOHN HAWKINS & SONS LTD. (Cotton)

Qty		Date	Odds	Sets
LF30	The Story of Cotton	1925	£5.00	£150.00

HEINZ (Foods)

Qty		Date	Odds	Sets
E1	Australian Cricket Team	1964	—	£4.00

S. HENDERSON & SONS LTD. (Biscuits)

Qty		Date	Odds	Sets
T132	General Interest Series	1908	£10.00	£1300.00

HERALD ALARMS

Qty		Date	Odds	Sets
10	Feudal Lords	1986	—	£15.00
X10	Feudal Lords	1986	—	£7.50

HERON PETROL

K16	Holidays	1960	£1.20	—

HERTFORDSHIRE POLICE FORCE

X12	Postage Stamps	1985	—	£5.00

HIGSONS (Brewery)

X26	Famous Old Higsonians	1987	£1.00	—

JOHN HINDHAUGH & CO. (Bread)

25	Railway Engines	1913	£27.50	—

HITCHMAN'S DAIRIES LTD.

25	Aircraft of World War II (Black Back)	1966	—	£8.50
25	(Blue Back)	1966	—	£16.50
25	Animals of the World	1964	—	£10.00
25	British Birds and their Nests	1970	—	£20.00
25	British Railways	1971	—	£3.50
25	Buses and Trams	1966	—	£2.00
25	Merchant Ships of the World	1970	—	£10.00
25	Modern Wonders	1962	—	£7.50
25	Naval Battles	1971	—	£3.50
25	People & Places	1971	—	£4.00
25	Regimental Uniforms of the Past	1973	—	£2.00
25	Science in the 20th Century	1966	—	£4.00
25	The Story of Milk	1965	—	£12.50
25	Trains of the World	1970	—	£20.00

HOADLEY'S CHOCOLATES (Australia)

50	British Empire Kings & Queens	1940	£1.40	£70.00
?33	Cricketers (Black Front)	1928	£11.50	—
36	Cricketers (Brown Front)	1933	£8.00	£288.00
50	Early Australian Series	1938	£1.40	£70.00
50	Empire Games and Test Teams	1932	£7.00	£350.00
40	Test Cricketers	1936	£10.00	£400.00
M36	Test Cricketers (Different)	1938	£11.50	—
50	The Birth of a Nation	1938	£1.40	£70.00
50	Victorian Footballers (Heads,1-50)	1938	£1.80	£90.00
50	Victorian Footballers (51-100)	1938	£1.80	£90.00
50	Victorian Footballers (Action)	1938	£2.00	£100.00
50	Wild West Series	1938	£1.40	£70.00

HOBBYPRESS GUIDES (Books)

Qty		Date	Odds	Sets
X6	Horse Racing Series	1984	—	£2.00
20	Preserved Railway Locomotives	1983	—	£2.50
20	Preserved Steam Railways, 1st Series	1983	—	£2.00
20	Preserved Steam Railways, 2nd Series	1984	—	£2.00
X12	Railway Engines	1984	—	£9.00
X6	Railway Engines, 2nd Series	1984	—	£9.00
20	The World's Great Cricketers	1984	—	£4.00

THOMAS HOLLOWAY LTD. (Pharmaceutics)

Qty		Date	Odds	Sets
X39	Natural History Series (Animals' Heads)	1900	£6.00	£240.00
X39	Natural History Series (Birds)	1900	£6.00	£240.00
X60	Natural History Series (Full Length)	1900	£5.50	£330.00
X50	Pictorial History of the Sports and Pastimes of All Nations	1900	£8.50	£425.00

HOME & COLONIAL STORES LTD.

Qty		Date	Odds	Sets
26	Advertising Alphabet	1914	£5.00	£130.00
M100	Flag Pictures	1916	£3.25	—
M40	War Heroes	1916	£4.50	£180.00
M40	War Pictures	1916	£4.00	£160.00
100	War Pictures (Different)	1916	£3.00	£300.00

HOME COUNTIES DAIRIES TEA

Qty		Date	Odds	Sets
25	Country Life	1964	—	£3.50
25	International Air-Liners	1965	—	£2.00
25	The Story of Milk	1965	—	£5.00

HOME MIRROR (Periodical)

Qty		Date	Odds	Sets
M4	Cinema Star Pictures (Silk)	1919	£12.00	—

HOME WEEKLY (Periodical)

Qty		Date	Odds	Sets
12	Little Charlie Cards	1920	£17.50	—

GEORGE W. HORNER & CO. (Confectionery)

Qty		Date	Odds	Sets
P24	Wireless Cards	1926	£12.50	—

HORNIMAN (Tea)

Qty		Date	Odds	Sets
P10	Boating Ways	1910	£16.00	—
P12	British Birds & Eggs	1910	£14.00	—
48	Dogs	1961	—	£4.00
P10	Naval Heroes	1910	£16.00	£160.00
48	Pets	1960	—	£4.50
48	Wild Animals	1958	—	£4.00

HORSLEY'S STORES

Qty		*Date*	*Odds*	*Sets*
25	British Uniforms of the 19th Century	1968	—	£8.00
25	Castles of Britain	1968	80p	—
25	Family Pets	1968	—	£8.00

VAN HOUTEN (Chocolate)

P12	How Nature Protects the Weak	1908	£8.00	£96.00

HUDDERSFIELD TOWN F.C.

M37	Huddersfield Town Players & Officials	1935	£8.00	—

HUGHES BISCUITS

20	War Series	1915	£11.50	—

HULL CITY FOOTBALL CLUB

X20	Footballers	1950	£6.00	£120.00

HUNT CROPP & SONS (Vedast)

15	Characters from Dickens	1912	£9.00	£135.00

HUNTLEY & PALMER (Biscuits)

63 Page Illustrated Reference Book — £10.00

P12	Animals	1900	£6.50	£78.00
P12	Aviation	1900	£45.00	—
P12	Biscuits in Various Countries	1900	£5.00	£60.00
P6	Biscuits with Travellers	1900	£6.00	£36.00
P12	Children of Nations I (Gold Border)	1900	£5.50	£66.00
P12	Children of Nations II (White Border)	1900	£5.00	£60.00
P12	Children at Leisure & Play	1900	£6.00	£72.00
P12	Harvests of the World	1900	£12.50	—
P12	Hunting	1900	£6.50	£78.00
P8	Inventors	1900	£16.00	—
X12	Rhondes Enfantines	1900	£17.50	—
P12	Scenes with Biscuits	1900	£5.00	£60.00
X8	Shakespearian Series	1900	£5.50	£44.00
P12	Soldiers of Various Countries	1900	£10.00	£120.00
P12	Sports (Semi-Circular Background)	1900	£12.00	£144.00
P12	Sports (Plain Background)	1900	£12.00	£144.00
P12	The Seasons	1900	£11.00	—
P12	Travelling During the 19th Century	1900	£16.00	—
P12	Views of Italy & The French Riviera	1900	£8.00	£96.00
P12	Warships of Nations	1900	£10.00	£120.00
P8	Watteau	1900	£6.00	£48.00
P8	Wonders of the World	1900	£15.00	—

HUSTLER SOAP

20	Animals, First Series	1925	90p	£18.00
20	Animals, Second Series	1925	90p	£18.00

HUSTLER SOAP — cont.

Qty		Date	Odds	Sets
20	Animals, Third Series	1925	90p	£18.00
30	Regimental Nicknames	1924	£2.00	£60.00

R. HYDE & CO. LTD. (Bird Seed)

Qty		Date	Odds	Sets
80	British Birds	1928	£1.25	£100.00
80	Cage Birds	1930	£1.00	£80.00
80	Canary Culture	1930	£1.00	£96.00
M10	Cartoons	1908	£10.00	—
M24	Modern Wonders	1924	£10.00	£240.00

I.P.C. MAGAZINES LTD.

Qty		Date	Odds	Sets
M25	Lindy's Cards of Fortune	1975	—	£5.00
M160	My Favourite Soccer Stars (Blue Back)	1970	50p	£80.00
M160	My Favourite Soccer Stars (Red Back)	1971	50p	£80.00

IDEAL ALBUMS LTD.

Qty		Date	Odds	Sets
L25	Boxing Greats	1991	—	£7.50
L2	Promotional Cards	1991	—	60p

IMPEL MARKETING INC. (U.S.A.)

Qty		Date	Odds	Sets
X120	Star Trek: The Next Generation 1991/92	1992	—	£15.00

IMPERIAL PUBLISHING LTD. (Commercial)

Officially authorised reprints of Imperial Tobacco Co. series

Qty		Date	Odds	Sets
50	A.F.C. Nicknames (Ogdens)	1996	—	£7.50
50	Aircraft of the R.A.F. (Player)	1990	—	£7.50
L20	American Golfers (Original)	1990	—	£8.50
25	Angling (Mitchell)	1993	—	£6.00
25	Aviation (Lambert & Butler)	1997	—	£6.00
15	Billiard Terms (Salmon & Gluckstein)	1997	—	£5.00
L24	Cats (Player)	1997	—	£7.50
25	Characters from Dickens, 2nd Series (Player)	1990	—	£6.00
50	Cricket Caricatures by "RIP" (Player)	1993	—	£7.50
50	Cricketers 1934 (Player)	1993	—	£7.50
25	Dance Band Leaders (Lambert & Butler)	1992	—	£6.00
50	Dog's Heads (Player, Eire)	1994	—	£7.50
50	Firefighting Appliances (Player)	1991	—	£7.50
54	Frisky (with 2 instructions) (Churchman)	1994	—	£7.50
50	Gilbert & Sullivan, 2nd Series (Player)	1990	—	£7.50
25	Highland Clans	1997	—	£6.00
25	Hints & Tips for Motorists (Lambert & Butler)	1994	—	£6.00
50	Horsemanship (Lambert & Butler)	1994	—	£7.50
50	Kings & Queens of England (Player)	1990	—	£7.50
50	Landmarks in Railway Progress (Churchman)	1994	—	£7.50
25	London Characters (Lambert & Butler)	1992	—	£6.00
50	Military Aircraft (Wills)	1991	—	£8.50
50	Military Motors(Wills)	1994	—	£7.50
50	Modern Railways (Ogdens)	1995	—	£7.50
50	Motor Cars 1st & 2nd (Lambert & Butler)	1989	—	£7.50
25	Motor Cars 1934 (Lambert & Butler)	1992	—	£6.00

COUNTRIES OF ISSUE

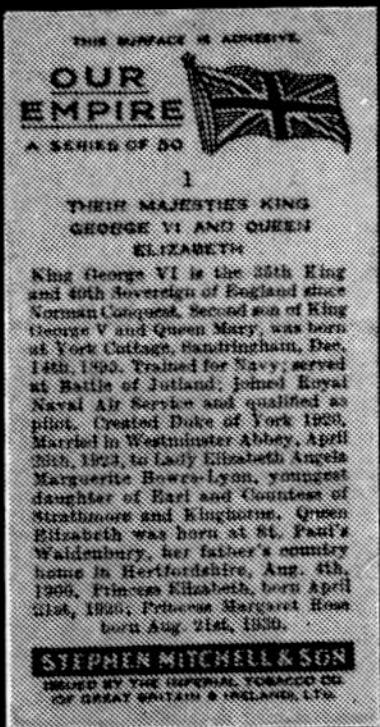

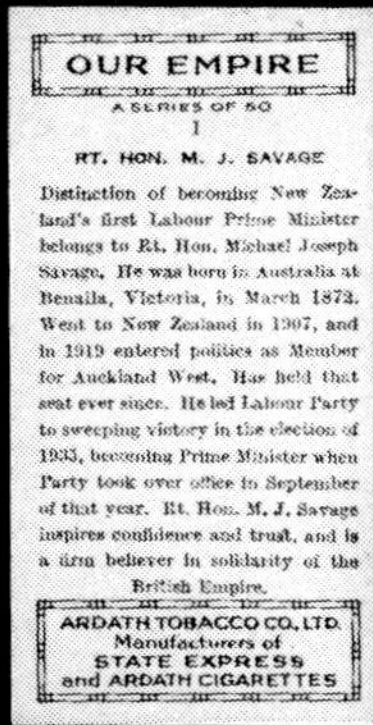

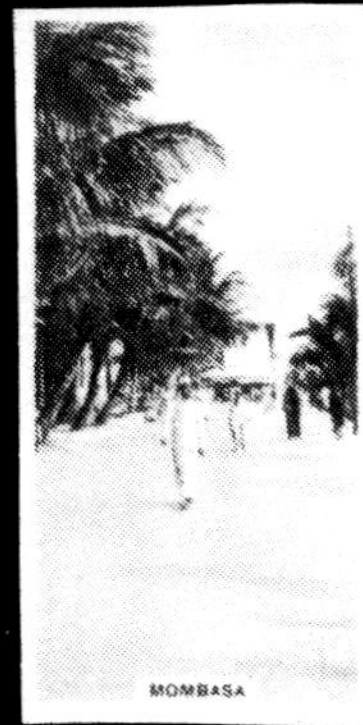

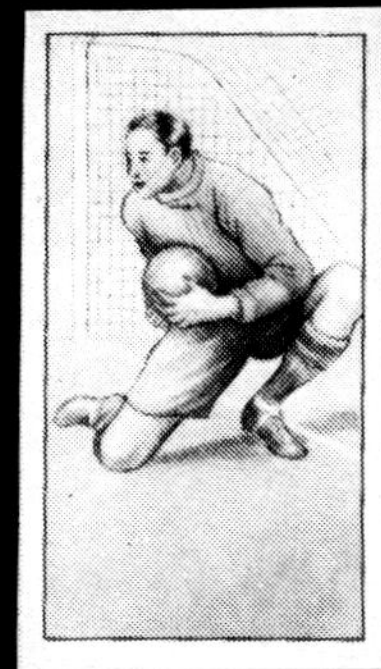

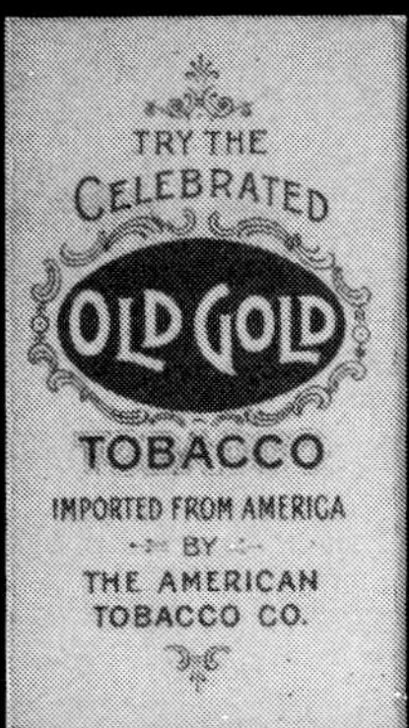

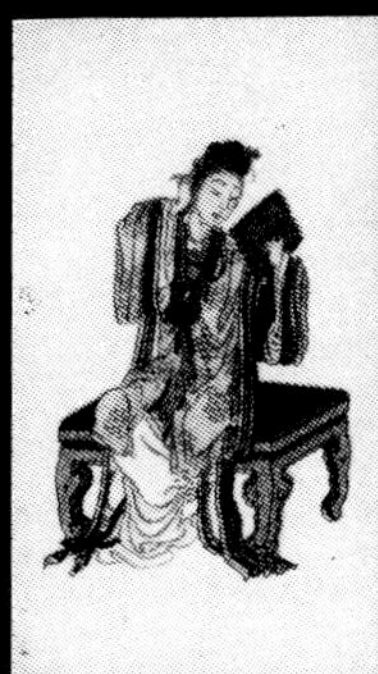

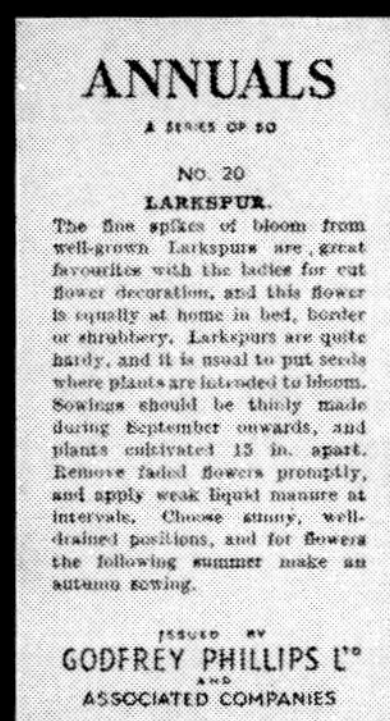

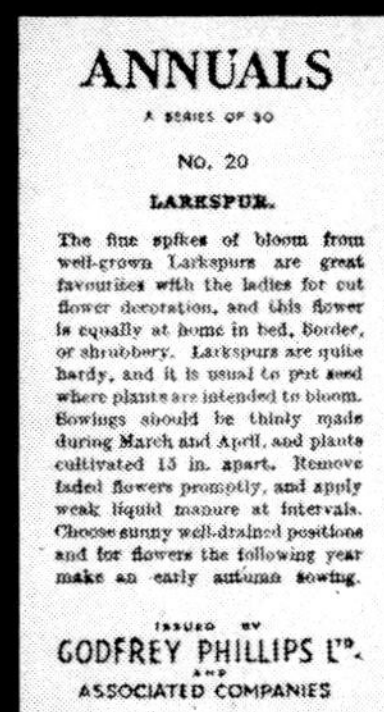

Nowadays one is accustomed to reading of multi-national corporations. Surprisingly many of the larger cigarette card issuers were such almost a century ago. Duke issued cards in South Africa, Goodwin in Australia, Allen & Ginter in Britain and the Canadian firm Ritchie in Germany, Australia, India and England. The American Tobacco Co. issued many cards in Britain with its Old Gold brand, and eventually through its purchase of Ogden, which precipitated the Tobacco War. British firms flourished in their expected spheres of influence, the British Empire, with many issues in Malta, India and Australia. In some cases a series was prepared specifically for one country, but often a set would be issued in several areas.

Sometimes the series had to be adapted to suit the requirements of the country in which it was to be issued. The text of the New Zealand version of Godfrey Phillips Annuals was amended to show different dates for "planting out", while Ardath changed just one card of the Mitchell Our Empire set to include the current New Zealand Prime Minister. In the case of the Player Hints on Association Football the fronts were redrawn to show Oriental features for the B.A.T. Chinese set.

The criterion in this catalogue for determining whether series should be shown in Part 1 or Part 2 is generally based on the main location of the issuer rather than the area of issue. So all American based Companies will be found in Part 2. Ritchie, which issued cards in Britain, is essentially a Canadian firm, so is also in Part 2. Firms such as International Tobacco Co. and A. & M. Wix, which were based in England, but most of whose issues were abroad, are nevertheless shown in Part 1. One major exception is British American Tobacco Co., which was incorporated in Britain, but all of whose cigarettes were sold abroad, and is therefore shown in Part 2. The decision has in several cases been marginal, and entirely subjective, so when in doubt consult BOTH sections!

MODERN CARDS

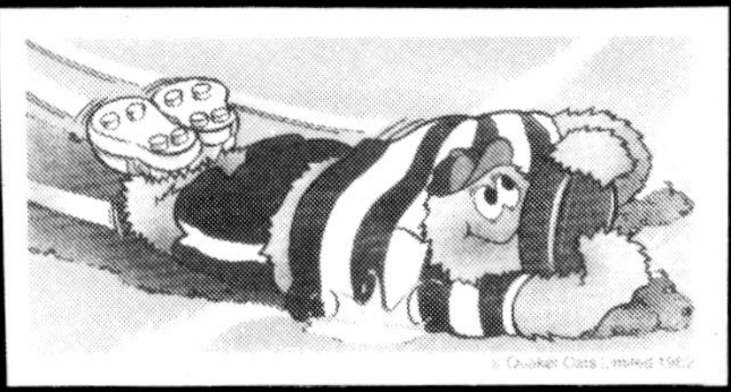

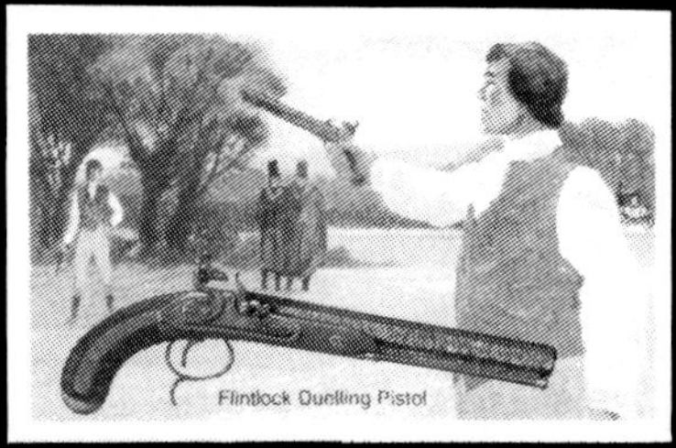

The last few years have seen but a trickle of cigarette cards, albeit in cigar packets such as Doncella and Tom Thumb. For the most part however collectors have had to be satisfied with trade cards for their new acquisitions.

The most significant of these has been Brooke Bond, which has been issuing cards continuously since 1954 (British Birds) and has now issued over 40 different sets, usually with special albums, in Britain, North America, and Africa. One would like to think that the success of the Company, which incidentally also owns Liebig, owes as much to the quality and appeal of the cards as to the tea itself. Its rivals failed to sustain any competition in card issues, although many, such as Lyons, Horniman and Lipton, made some attempts.

Confectionery is another prolific area for card collectors, chiefly with sweet cigarettes (now discreetly called "Candy Sticks") and bubble gum. Barratt/Bassett is the premier issuer of the former, and A. & B. C./Topps of the latter, although the competition in these items is intense. Many other firms appear in these pages such as Dandy, Monty, Primrose & Somportex, and often collectors try to obtain the box or wrapper in addition to the set of cards.

Cereal products are also a fruitful source for the cartophilist. Kellogg, Nabisco and Welgar regularly include among their free incentive inserts collectable series of cards, often in novel form such as transfers or cut-outs.

The last rewarding area for cards is that of periodicals. A new feature of these has been the appearance of Panini, with free inserts in magazines and newspapers, followed by the opportunity to complete the very long sets by purchasing packets of cards. Often these sets are of footballers, and Panini invests some of its profits (with further advertising) in sponsoring family enclosures at soccer grounds.

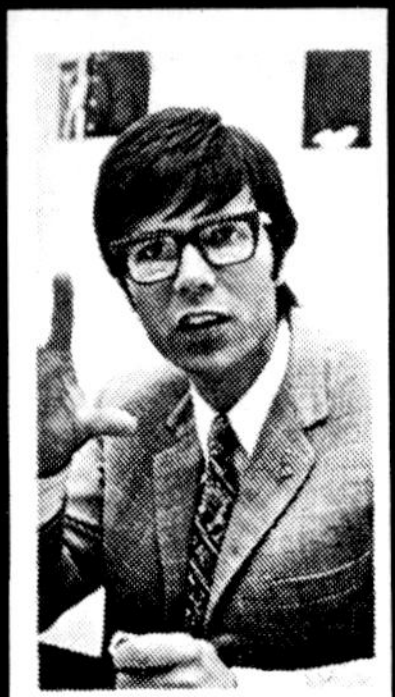

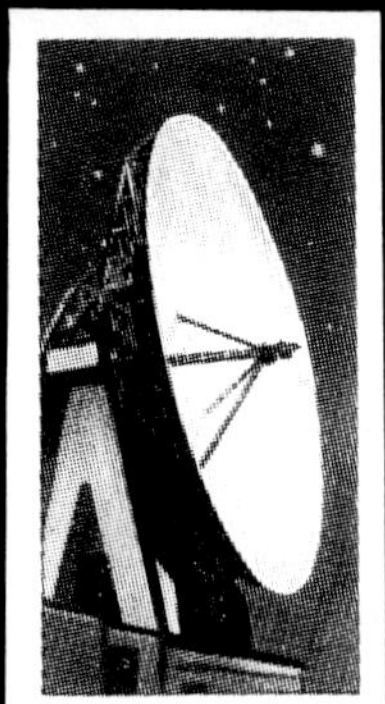

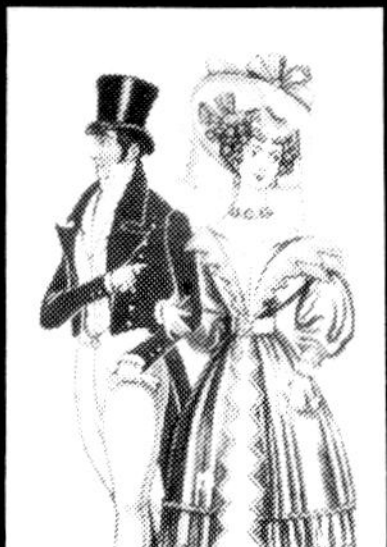

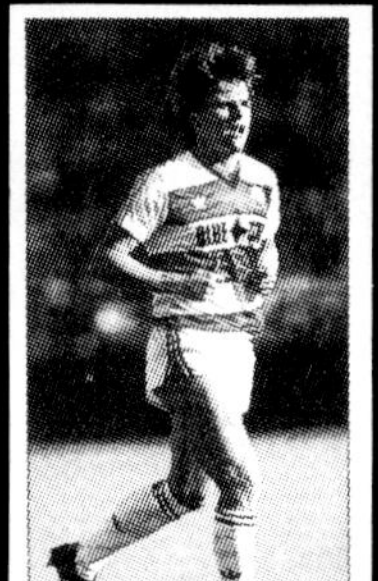

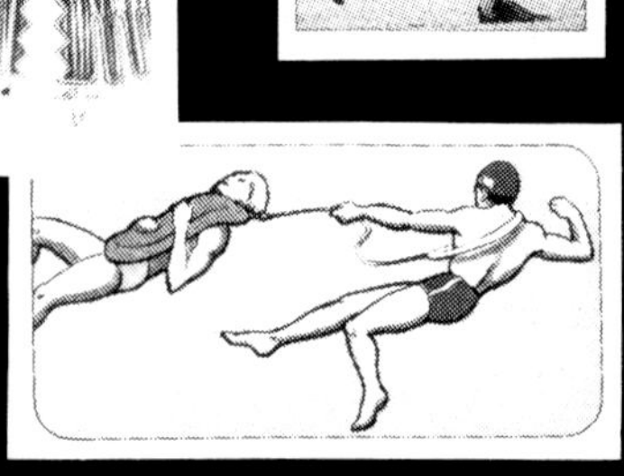

IMPERIAL PUBLISHING LTD. (Commercial) — cont.

Qty		Date	Odds	Sets
50	Motor Cars, A Series (Player)	1990	—	£7.50
50	Motor Cycles (Lambert & Butler)	1990	—	£7.50
L20	Native North Americans (Original)	1995	—	£7.50
50	Naval Dress & Badges (Wills)	1997	—	£7.50
25	Old English Garden Flowers, Second Series (Wills)	1994	—	£6.00
L25	Old Hunting Prints (Player)	1997	—	£7.50
L6	Old Inns (Wills)	1990	—	£2.50
L25	Old Naval Prints (Player)	1997	—	£7.50
L48	Olympic Champions	1996	—	£10.00
L25	Picturesque London (Player)	1997	—	£7.50
25	Poultry (1-25, with Ogdens on Front)	1998	—	£6.00
50	Prominent Golfers (Churchman)	1993	—	£7.50
25	Prominent Racehorses (Faulkner)	1993	—	£6.00
25	Prominent Rugby Players (Smith)	1992	—	£8.00
L40	Puppies (Wills)	1990	—	£12.50
50	Railway Engines, 1924 (Wills)	1996	—	£7.50
50	Railway Engines, 1936 (Wills)	1993	—	£7.50
50	Railway Equipment (Wills)	1993	—	£7.50
50	Railway Locomotives (Wills)	1993	—	£7.50
25	Regimental Crests & Collar Badges (Mitchell)	1993	—	£6.00
50	Regimental Standards and Cap Badges (Player)	1993	—	£7.50
50	Regimental Uniforms, 2nd Series (51-100) (Player)	1995	—	£7.50
50	Roses, A Series (Wills)	1994	—	£7.50
50	Rugby Internationals (Wills)	1996	—	£7.50
L18	Snooker Celebrities (Original)	1993	—	£8.50
50	Soldiers of the King (Ogdens)	1993	—	£7.50
L24	The History of the Olympic Games	1996	—	£6.00
M48	The R.A.F. at Work (Churchman)	1995	—	£14.00
25	The World's Dreadnoughts (Wills)	1994	—	£6.00
L24	Treasures of Britain (Player)	1995	—	£7.50
L25	Types of Horses (Player)	1998	—	£7.50
50	Types of the British Army (Wills)	1995	—	£7.50
50	Uniforms of the Territorial Army (Player)	1990	—	£7.50
50	War Incidents, 2nd Series (Wills)	1995	—	£7.50
50	Waterloo (Wills)	1990	—	£10.00
L25	Wild Birds (Player)	1997	—	£7.50
25	Winter Sports (Lambert & Butler)	1998	—	£6.00
50	World's Locomotives (Lambert & Butler)	1989	—	£7.50

INDIA & CEYLON TEA CO. LTD.

Qty		Date	Odds	Sets
24	The Island of Ceylon	1996	£3.50	—

IN LINE (Commercial, U.S.A.)

Qty		Date	Odds	Sets
X6	Classic Motorcycles (Prototype Set)	1992	—	£3.00
X57	Classic Motorcycles Series 1 (including Hologram)	1993	—	£10.00

INKWORKS (Commercial, U.S.A.)

Qty		Date	Odds	Sets
X90	The Adventures of Pinocchio	1996	—	£12.00
X90	The Phantom	1966	—	£14.00

INTREPID T.C. INTERNATIONAL (Commercial, Australia)

Qty		Date	Odds	Sets
X100	ATP Tennis Tour	1996	—	£12.00

JOHN IRWIN SONS & CO. LTD. (Tea)

Qty		Date	Odds	Sets
12	Characters from Dickens Works	1912	£16.00	—
6	Characters from Shakespeare	1912	£15.00	£90.00
8	The European War Series	1916	£12.50	£100.00

JACOB & CO. (Biscuits)

D24	Banknotes that made History (with Album)	1975	—	£2.00
D32	Famous Picture Cards from History (with Album)	1978	—	£2.00
E16	Jacob's Club Circus	1970	£2.00	£32.00
M16	Nursery Rhyme Competition	1969	85p	£13.50
M30	School of Dinosaurs	1994	25p	£7.50
25	Vehicles of All Ages	1924	£2.40	£60.00
25	Zoo Series (Brown Back)	1924	£1.30	£32.50
25	(Green Back)	1924	90p	£22.50

M. V. JASINSKI (Commercial, U.S.A.)

X36	Flash Gordon	1990	—	£12.50
X36	Flash Gordon Conquers the Universe	1992	—	£7.50
X36	Flash Gordon's Trip to Mars	1991	—	£7.50

JESK (Confectionery)

25	Buses and Trams	1959	—	£12.50

JIBCO (Tea)

28	Dominoes	1956	£3.00	—
K53	Miniature Playing Cards	1956	£3.00	—
K50	Puzzle Cards	1955	£3.50	—
K25	Screen Stars	1955	£3.50	—
K25	Screen Stars, 2nd Edition	1956	90p	£22.50

JIFFI (Condoms)

M64	Kama Sutra	1989	—	£40.00

JONDER PROMOTIONS (Commercial)

X55	Doctor Who Playing Cards	1996	—	£7.50

R. L. JONES & CO. LTD. (Drink)

24	Jet Aircraft of the World	1956	—	£3.00

JUBBLY (Drink)

50	Adventurous Lives	1967	—	£4.00

JUNIOR PASTIMES (Commercial)

51/52	Popular English Players	1951	£2.25	£115.00
52	Popular Players (Footballers)	1951	£3.00	—

JUNIOR PASTIMES (Commercial) — cont.

Qty		*Date*	*Odds*	*Sets*
51/52	Popular Railway Engines	1951	£2.00	£100.00
L77/80	Star Pix	1951	£1.20	£90.00

JUST SEVENTEEN (Magazine)

T17	Posters	1986	—	£2.00

K. P. NUTS & CRISPS

12	Sports Adventure Series	1978	—	£10.00
20	Wonderful World of Nature	1983	60p	£12.00

KANE PRODUCTS LTD. (Confectionery)

36	ATV Stars (Packets)	1957	£2.00	—
50	British Birds and Their Eggs	1960	—	£25.00
25	Cricket Clubs & Badges	1957	—	£2.50
L50	Disc Stars	1960	£1.50	£75.00
X50	Disc Stars	1960	£1.20	£60.00
50	Dogs	1955	£1.80	£90.00
X72	Film Stars (Plain Back)	1955	£1.25	£90.00
50	Flags of All Nations	1959	—	£8.50
25	Football Clubs & Colours	1956	—	£2.50
50	Historical Characters	1957	—	£4.50
25	International Football Stars	1957	—	£8.00
30	Kings and Queens	1959	—	£7.00
X30	Kings & Queens	1959	—	£6.00
25	Modern Motor Cars	1959	—	£15.00
50	Modern Racing Cars	1954	25p	£12.50
25	National Pets Club, Part I	1958	—	£5.00
25	National Pets Club, Part II	1958	£2.00	£50.00
25	1956 Cricketers, 1st Series	1956	60p	£15.00
25	1956 Cricketers, 2nd Series	1956	60p	£15.00
25	Red Indians, 1st Series	1957	—	£17.50
25	Red Indians, 2nd Series	1957	—	£17.50
25	Roy Rogers Colour Series	1958	£1.60	£40.00
25	Roy Rogers Series	1957	£2.80	£70.00
50	Space Adventure	1955	—	£27.50
50	20th Century Events	1955	£1.25	£62.50
K50	Wild Animals	1954	—	£4.00

KARDOMAH (Tea)

K?500	General Interest (Various Series)	1900	£2.50	—

KAYO CARDS LTD. (U.S.A.)

X10	Heavyweight Holograms	1992	—	£15.00

M. & S. KEECH

15	Australian Cricket Team 1905	1986	—	£3.00
15	English Cricketers 1902	1987	—	£3.00

KEEPSAKE COLLECTIBLES (Commercial, U.S.A.)

Qty		*Date*	*Odds*	*Sets*
X72	The Blue And The Gray	1997	—	£17.50
X93	The Civil War (includes 3 Banknotes)	1996	—	£17.50
X72	Wild West	1996	—	£10.00

KEILLER (Confectionery)

Qty		Date	Odds	Sets
KF?	Actresses & Views	1905	£7.00	—
F?	Actresses & Views	1905	£7.00	—
LF18	Film Favourites	1926	£8.00	—
25	Scottish Heritage	1976	—	£6.50

KELLOGG LTD. (Cereals)

Qty		Date	Odds	Sets
16	A History of British Military Aircraft	1963	50p	£8.00
16	Animals (3D)	1971	£2.50	£40.00
12	Famous Firsts	1963	15p	£1.50
L20	Gardens to Visit	1988	—	£5.00
12	International Soccer Stars	1963	75p	£9.00
M8	International Soccer Tips	1970	£3.00	—
40	Motor Cars (Black and White)	1949	£2.50	£100.00
40	(Coloured)	1949	£3.00	£120.00
X56	Playing Cards	1986	—	£4.00
8	Prehistoric Monsters and the Present	1985	60p	£5.00
16	Ships of the British Navy	1962	50p	£8.00
M6	Space (Surprise Gifts)	1989	—	£1.50
P4	Sticky Pix	1988	—	£3.25
12	The Story of the Bicycle	1964	£2.75	£33.00
	The Story of the Locomotive, A Series			
16	(English Issue)	1963	75p	£12.00
12	(Irish Issue)	1963	£4.00	£48.00
16	The Story of the Locomotive, Series 2	1963	50p	£8.00
16	(Without Series 2)	1963	£2.50	£40.00
K8	Tony Racing Stickers	1988	—	£2.00
16	Veteran Motor Cars	1962	50p	£8.00
CANADIAN ISSUES				
M150	General Interest, 1st Set	1940	£1.10	£165.00
M150	General Interest, 2nd Set	1940	£1.25	—
M150	General Interest, 3rd Set	1940	£1.25	—

KENT COUNTY CONSTABULARY

Qty		Date	Odds	Sets
X30	Olympic Athletes	1988	£1.20	£36.00

KENT COUNTY CRICKET CLUB

Qty		Date	Odds	Sets
51	Cricketers of Kent	1986	—	£7.50

KERRANG (Magazine)

Qty		Date	Odds	Sets
X52	Rock Stars (Playing Card Inset)	1994	—	£8.50

KIDDYS FAVOURITES LTD. (Commercial)

Qty		*Date*	*Odds*	*Sets*
52	New Popular Film Stars	1950	£2.50	—
50	Popular Boxers	1950	£1.60	£105.00
51/52	Popular Cricketers	1948	£3.00	£153.00
65	Popular Film Stars	1950	£2.00	—
51/52	Popular Footballers	1948	£2.25	£114.00
51/52	Popular Olympics	1948	£2.00	£102.00
52	Popular Players (Hearts on Front)	1950	£3.00	—
51/52	Popular Players (Shamrocks on Front)	1950	£2.00	£102.00
52	Popular Speedway Riders	1950	£2.50	—

KINGS OF YORK (Laundry)

25	Flags of All Nations (Silk)	1954	£1.80	£45.00
30	Kings & Queens of England	1954	—	£2.00

KINGS LAUNDRIES LTD. (Walthamstow, E. London)

25	Famous Railway Engines	1953	£3.50	—
25	Modern British Warplanes	1953	£2.60	£65.00
25	Modern Motor Cycles	1953	£3.00	£75.00
25	Radio & Television Stars	1953	£2.60	£65.00

KING'S SPECIALITIES (Food Products)

26	Alphabet Rhymes	1915	£11.00	—
25	"Dont's" or Lessons in Etiquette	1915	£8.00	—
25	Great War Celebrities	1915	£8.00	—
25	Heroes of Famous Books	1915	£7.00	—
25	King's "Discoveries"	1915	£7.00	—
25	King's "Servants"	1915	£7.00	—
25	Proverbs	1915	£8.00	—
37	Unrecorded History	1915	£7.00	—
100	War Pictures	1915	£9.00	—
25	Where King's Supplies Grow	1915	£7.00	—

KITCHEN SINK PRESS (Commercial, U.S.A.)

X90	The Crow	1996	—	£15.00

KLENE (Confectionery)

L144	Animals of the World	1954	80p	£115.00
L144	Birds of the World	1954	75p	£108.00
L292	Film Stars	1954	£1.40	—
L50	Footballers	1935	£20.00	—
L48	Natural History Sketches	1954	£2.75	—
L72	Popeye	1954	£3.50	—
L50	Shirley Temple Cards (1-50)	1935	£5.50	—
L20	Shirley Temple Cards (81-100, Coloured)	1935	£5.50	—
L60	Shirley Temple Cards (101-160)			
	(Black Title)	1935	£5.50	—
	(Blue Title, Different)	1935	£5.50	—
L50	Shirley Temple Cards (161-210)	1935	£5.50	—

KNOCKOUT (Periodical)

Qty		Date	Odds	Sets
20	Super Planes of Today	1956	—	£4.00

KNORR (Cheese)

Qty		Date	Odds	Sets
T6	Great Trains of Europe	1983	£3.25	—

KRAFT CHEESE

Qty		Date	Odds	Sets
12	Historic Military Uniforms	1971	—	£2.50

KYDD'S JAMS

Qty		Date	Odds	Sets
20	Fruits and Recipes	1912	£6.50	—

LACEY'S CHEWING GUM

Qty		Date	Odds	Sets
50	Footballers	1923	£15.00	—
?50	Uniforms	1923	£15.00	—

F. LAMBERT & SONS LTD. (Tea)

Qty		Date	Odds	Sets
25	Before our Time	1961	—	£2.00
25	Birds and Their Eggs	1962	—	£10.00
25	Butterflies and Moths	1960	—	£2.00
25	Cacti	1962	—	£2.00
25	Car Registration Numbers, A Series	1959	—	£5.00
25	Car Registration Numbers, Second Series	1960	—	£12.00
25	Football Clubs and Badges	1958	—	£2.00
25	Game Birds and Wild Fowl	1964	—	£7.50
25	Historic East Anglia	1961	—	£2.00
25	Interesting Hobbies	1965	—	£10.00
25	Passenger Liners	1965	—	£10.00
25	Past & Present	1964	—	£2.00
25	People & Places	1966	—	*£5.00*
25	Pond Life	1964	—	£7.50
25	Sports and Games	1964	—	£2.25

LANCASHIRE CONSTABULARY

Qty		Date	Odds	Sets
24	Cop-a-Cards	1987	—	£7.50
D11	Cop-a-Cards, Series 3	1989	—	£2.00
X12	Motor Cars	1987	—	£5.00

LANCASTER REPRINTS (Canada)

Qty		Date	Odds	Sets
36	Hockey Series (I.T.C. Canada)	1987	—	£12.00
X9	The Seven Ages of Golf	1995	—	£4.50

HERBERT LAND (Cycles)

Qty		Date	Odds	Sets
30	Army Pictures, Cartoons, etc	1915	£25.00	—

LEAF BRANDS INC. (Confectionery)

Qty		*Date*	*Odds*	*Sets*
X50	Cliff Richard	1960	£2.00	—
X50	Do You Know?	1961	15p	£5.00
X90	Famous Artistes	1960	£1.25	—
X50	Famous Discoveries and Adventures	1962	£1.25	£62.50
X50	Footballers	1961	£1.25	£62.50
X40	The Flag Game	1960	30p	£15.00
X50	Totem Pole Talking Signs	1962	50p	£25.00

LEGENDS WALL OF FAME (London)

L20	British Rock Legends	1992	—	£8.00

LENG PAPERS

X36	Illustrated Songs	1915	£3.00	—

LEVER BROS. (Soap)

20	British Birds and Their Nests	1961	—	£2.00
F150	Celebrities	1900	£3.50	—
L39	Celebrities	1901	£6.00	£234.00
P24	The Life of Queen Victoria (Series 3)	1902	£8.00	—

LEWIS'S LTD. (Store)

FX25	Real Photos of Wild Animals	1930	£7.00	—

LIEBIG EXTRACT OF MEAT CO. (see also Oxo)

This firm issued nearly 2,000 different sets throughout Europe between 1872 and 1974. Because inclusion of all these in this volume would be impracticable we have produced a separate catalogue of Liebig cards. See separate announcement for details. Some recent issues are included below as a sample of the scope of these series.

6	Birds' Feathers and their Uses	1928	—	£5.00
6	Birds of Paradise	1943	—	£12.50
6	Bizarre Rocks	1931	—	£4.50
6	Buddha	1930	—	£12.50
6	Chateaux of the Loire	1933	—	£7.00
6	Crustaceans	1938	—	£4.50
6	Dangerous Occupations I	1928	—	£5.00
6	Famous Chemists	1929	—	£5.50
6	Glacier Formation and Mountain Flowers	1927	—	£6.00
6	Hindu Temples	1930	—	£4.50
6	Horsemen	1939	—	£6.50
6	In a Steel Works	1938	—	£4.00
6	Italian Gardens	1930	—	£5.00
6	Jupiter	1932	—	£5.00
6	Land Insects which Develop in Water	1937	—	£7.50
6	Life among Bees	1933	—	£6.50
6	Life in the Alps	1933	—	£6.00
6	Loading and Unloading Ships	1932	—	£5.00
6	Marriage through the Ages	1938	—	£9.00
6	Masks Around the World	1949	—	£10.00
6	Molluscs and Oysters	1941	—	£5.00
6	Old Belgian Bridges	1941	—	£9.00
6	Old Houses that have become Museums	1939	—	£6.00

LIEBIG EXTRACT OF MEAT CO. (see also Oxo) — cont.

Qty		Date	Odds	Sets
6	Orpheus	1931	—	£5.00
18	Peoples of the Belgian Congo	1955	—	£10.00
6	Perseus	1927	—	£8.50
6	Picturesque Abruzzo	1949	—	£12.50
6	Pre-Columbian Mexican Culture	1950	—	£8.50
6	Preparation of an Illustrated Paper	1934	—	£4.50
6	Processions and Pilgrimages in Belgium	1936	—	£5.50
6	Scenes from Venetian History	1931	—	£4.50
6	Sensitive Plants	1928	—	£5.50
6	Slugs and Snails	1940	—	£9.00
6	Stages in the History of the U.S.A.	1938	—	£7.50
6	Strange Feminine Hairstyles	1936	—	£5.50
6	The Apple as a Symbol	1929	—	£4.00
6	The Cheese Industry	1947	—	£12.50
6	The History of Italy XX	1960	—	£10.00
6	The History of Our Provinces – Limbourg	1951	—	£4.00
6	The Holy Year and Its Origin III	1949	—	£8.00
6	The Inhabitants of Tierra Del Fuego	1929	—	£5.00
6	The Legend of St. Nicholas	1928	—	£17.50
6	The Life and Works of Giotto	1967	—	£7.50
6	The Linen Industry in Belgium	1939	—	£6.00
6	The Mahabharata	1931	—	£8.50
6	Theseus	1928	—	£7.50
6	Tobacco	1939	—	£9.50
6	Turandot (Opera by Puccini)	1939	—	£15.00
6	Unusual Outdoor Occupations	1928	—	£6.50
6	White Coal (Hydro-Electricity)	1933	—	£4.50

LIFEGUARD PRODUCTS (Soap)

25	British Butterflies	1955	—	£2.00

LIME ROCK CO. INC. (Commercial, U.S.A.)

X110	Dream Machines (Cars)	1991	—	£15.00

JOSEPH LINGFORD & SON (Baking Powder)

36	British War Leaders	1949	£1.25	£45.00

LIPTON LTD. (Tea)

Qty		Date	Odds	Sets
48	Animals and Their Young (Canadian)	1991	—	£16.00
60	Flags of the World	1967	—	£8.00
50	The Conquest of Space	1962	—	£5.00

LITTLE CHEF (Restaurants)

M8	Disney Characters	1990	—	£6.50

LOCAL AUTHORITIES (School Meals)

5	British Sports Personalities	1997	—	£1.50

LONGLEAT HOUSE

25	Longleat House	1967	—	£2.00

LOT-O-FUN (Periodical)

MF4	Sports Champions	1922	£4.50	£18.00

G. F. LOVELL & CO. (Confectionery)

36	British Royalty Series	1910	£25.00	—
36	Football Series	1910	£35.00	—
25	Photos of Football Stars	1926	£12.50	—

J. LYONS & CO. LTD. (Ice Cream & Tea)

40	All Systems Go	1968	£1.00	£40.00
48	Australia	1959	15p	£4.00
M20	Banknotes	1974	—	£6.50
M12	Beautiful Butterflies	1974	—	£3.00
25	Birds and Their Eggs	1962	—	£6.50
40	British Wildlife	1970	85p	£34.00
L16	Catweazle Magic Cards	1971	—	£5.00
M20	County Badge Collection	1974	—	£2.00
X12	Did You Know?	1983	40p	£5.00
40	European Adventure	1969	£1.00	—
40	Famous Aircraft	1965	30p	£12.00
40	Famous Cars	1966	£1.25	£50.00
40	Famous Locomotives	1964	£1.60	£64.00
48	Famous People	1966	50p	£24.00
D12	Farmyard Stencils	1977	—	£6.50
M14	Flowers (Cut-Out)	1976	—	£22.50
32	HMS 1902-1962 (Descriptive)	1962	15p	£2.00
32	(Non-Descriptive)	1962	—	£2.00
X12	Horses in the Service of Man	1984	—	£3.00
L35	Illustrated Map of the British Isles	1959	60p	£21.00
40	International Footballers	1972	£2.25	£90.00
40	Into the Unknown	1969	£1.00	£40.00
15	Jubilee	1977	£1.00	£15.00
X10	Junior Champs	1983	—	£2.00
M24	Kings of the Road	1977	*£1.00*	—
P6	150th Anniversary of Postage Stamps	1990	—	£1.75

J. LYONS & CO. LTD. (Ice Cream & Tea) — cont.

Qty		Date	Odds	Sets
50	100 Years of Motoring	1964	90p	£45.00
40	On Safari	1970	75p	£30.00
40	Pop Scene	1971	£1.30	£52.00
40	Pop Stars	1970	£1.75	—
L10	Pop Stars (Shaped)	1975	—	£3.50
K48	Quick Puzzle Cards	1955	75p	—
40	Soccer Stars	1971	£2.25	£90.00
40	Space Age Britain	1968	£1.00	£40.00
40	Space Exploration	1963	£1.00	£40.00
25	Space 1999	1976	£2.00	£50.00
25	Star Trek	1979	£3.50	£87.50
50	Train Spotters	1962	40p	£20.00
K100	Tricks & Puzzles	1926	£2.00	—
40	Views of London	1967	80p	£32.00
48	What Do You Know?	1957	15p	£3.00
24	Wings Across the World (Descriptive Back)	1962	15p	£2.00
24	(Non-Descriptive)	1961	—	£4.00
24	Wings of Speed (Descriptive Back)	1961	15p	£2.00
24	(Non-Descriptive)	1961	25p	£6.00

M.P. CARDS (Commercial)

Qty		Date	Odds	Sets
L14	Nishikigoi (Koi Carp)	1997	—	£10.00
L12	Samurai Warriors	1996	—	£10.00
L12	The Geisha Collection	1997	—	£10.00
L6	The Staffordshire Bull Terrier	1995	—	£2.50

M.P.L. LTD. (Records)

Qty		Date	Odds	Sets
M5	Wings — Back to the Egg	1981	—	£10.00

MACFISHERIES (Shops)

Qty		Date	Odds	Sets
L12	Gallery Pictures	1924	80p	£10.00
L14	Japanese Colour Prints	1924	£1.00	£14.00
L12	Poster Pointers	1925	90p	£11.00
L12	Sporting Prints	1923	£3.00	£36.00

MACGIRR & CO. (Tea)

Qty		Date	Odds	Sets
24	Birds & Their Eggs	1912	£6.50	—

JOHN MACKINTOSH & SONS (Confectionery)

Qty		Date	Odds	Sets
15	Camping & Hiking Hints	1932	£11.50	—

MACROBERTSON (Confectionery, Australia)

Qty		Date	Odds	Sets
24	Flags of All Nations	1916	£5.00	—
24	Naval & Military Decorations	1916	£6.50	—
24	Sons/Allies of the Empire	1916	£7.00	—
50	Sports of the World	1916	£2.80	£140.00

Wm. McEWAN & CO. LTD. (Brewers)

Qty		Date	Odds	Sets
25	Old Glasgow	1929	£8.50	—

McVITIE & PRICE (Food)

Qty		Date	Odds	Sets
8	The European War Series	1916	£12.50	£100.00

McVITIE'S (Biscuits)

Qty		Date	Odds	Sets
M10	Superstars	1976	—	£13.50

MADISON CONFECTIONERY PRODUCTIONS LTD.

Qty		Date	Odds	Sets
X16/32	Christmas Greeting Cards	1957	£1.25	—
X48	Disc Jockey, 1st Series	1957	£1.60	£75.00
X48	Disc Jockey, 2nd Series	1958	£1.20	£60.00
X50	Recording Stars	1958	£1.00	£50.00

THE MAGNET LIBRARY (Periodical)

Qty		Date	Odds	Sets
MF15	Footballers	1922	£3.00	£45.00
MF6	Football Teams	1922	£3.50	£21.00
MF4	Football Teams	1923	£3.50	£14.00

MANCHESTER EVENING NEWS (Newspaper)

Qty		Date	Odds	Sets
L30	Footballers	1976	£1.25	—

MANCHESTER UNITED FOOTBALL CLUB

Qty		Date	Odds	Sets
X26	Manchester United Footballers	1991	—	£12.50

MAPLE LEAF GUM

Qty		Date	Odds	Sets
K90	Motor Car & Motor Cycle Badges (Metal)	1960	90p	—
K75	National Flags (Metal)	1960	60p	—

R. MARCANTONIO LTD. (Ice Lollies)

Qty		Date	Odds	Sets
50	Interesting Animals	1953	—	£4.00

A. T. MARKS (Commercial)

Qty		Date	Odds	Sets
11	1892 Gloucestershire (Cricketers)	1990	—	£1.75
11	1892 Middlesex	1990	—	£1.75
11	1892 Surrey	1990	—	£2.75
11	1892 Sussex	1990	—	£2.75
12	1903 Middlesex	1990	—	£1.75
12	1903 Yorkshire	1990	—	£1.75
11	1912 Northamptonshire	1990	—	£2.75

MARLOW CIVIL ENGINEERING LTD.

Qty		Date	Odds	Sets
25	Famous Clowns	1990	—	£30.00

MARS CONFECTIONS LTD.

Qty		Date	Odds	Sets
25	Ceremonies of the Coronation			
	(Brown Back, Blue Caption)	1937	80p	£20.00
	(Brown Back, Brown Caption)	1937	£1.40	£35.00
	(Blue Back)	1937	£3.75	—
50	Famous Aeroplanes, Pilots & Airports	1938	£1.20	£60.00

MARS CONFECTIONS LTD. — cont.

Qty		*Date*	*Odds*	*Sets*
50	Famous Escapes	1937	85p	£42.50
50	Famous Film Stars	1939	£1.10	£55.00
25	Wonders of the Queen Mary	1936	£1.00	£25.00

JAMES MARSHALL (GLASGOW) LTD. (Food)

30	Colonial Troops	1900	£30.00	—
1	Marshall's Products Illustrated	1926	—	£4.00
40	Recipes	1926	£4.00	—

MASTER VENDING CO. LTD. (Gum)

X25	A Bombshell for the Sheriff	1959	70p	£17.50
X50	Cardmaster Football Tips	1958	80p	£40.00
X16	Cricketer Series — New Zealand 1958	1958	80p	£12.50
X50	Did You Know? (Football)	1959	40p	£20.00
X100	Jet Aircraft of the World	1958	80p	£80.00
X100	Ditto (German Text)	1958	£1.00	—
X25	Taxing the Sheriff	1959	50p	£12.50
X36	Tommy Steele	1958	£2.50	£90.00

J. JOHN MASTERS & CO. (Matches)

X12	Food from Britain	1987	—	£1.50

MATCH (Periodical)

X31	F.A. Cup Fact File	1986	—	£6.50

MATCHBOX INTERNATIONAL LTD. (Toys)

75	Matchbox Model Vehicles	1985	40p	£30.00

MAXILIN MARKETING CO.

25	Motor Cars	1951	—	£4.00

MAYNARDS LTD. (Confectionery)

12	Billy Bunter Series	1926	£22.50	—
?20	Football Clubs	1933	£15.00	—
18	Girl Guide Series	1921	£13.50	—
50	Girls of All Nations	1921	£4.00	£200.00
12	Strange Insects	1935	£4.00	£50.00
8	The European War Series	1916	£16.00	£128.00
12	Wonders of the Deep	1935	£5.00	£60.00
12	World's Wonder Series (Numbered)	1930	£4.50	£54.00
10	World's Wonder Series (Unnumbered)	1930	£5.00	£50.00

MAYPOLE (Grocers)

25	War Series	1915	£6.00	£150.00

MAZAWATTEE (Tea)

X39	Kings and Queens	1902	£3.50	£140.00

MEADOW DAIRY CO.

50	War Series	1915	£6.00	£300.00

J. F. MEARBECK (Printer)

30	Army Pictures, Cartoons, etc	1915	£25.00	—

MELLINS FOOD

K2	Diamond Jubilee Coins	1897	£8.50	£17.00

MELOX (Dog Food)

L50	Famous Breeds of Dogs	1937	£4.80	£240.00
M32	Happy Families (Dogs)	1935	£6.50	£208.00

MERLIN TRADING CARDS (Commercial)

X161	F.A. Premier League	1996	—	£15.00
X161	Premier Gold	1997	—	£16.00
X156	Premier Gold 98	1997	—	£25.00
X120	Premier League	1994	—	£12.00
X125	Star Wars Trilogy	1997	—	£11.50
X160	The Rugby Football League	1991	—	£10.00

MERRYSWEETS LTD.

Qty		*Date*	*Odds*	*Sets*
X48	Telegum TV Stars	1958	60p	£30.00
X48	Tracepiks	1960	£5.00	—
X48	World Racing Cars	1959	£1.75	£84.00

GEOFFREY MICHAEL PUBLISHERS LTD.

40	Modern Motor Cars	1949	£1.00	£40.00
F48	Mystery Cards — Modern Motor Cars	1953	£4.50	—

MICKEY MOUSE AND FRIENDS (Periodical)

K48	Disney Stickers (With Album)	1990	—	£7.00

MIDLAND CARTOPHILIC BRANCH

L24	Silhouettes of Veteran & Vintage Cars	1991	—	£6.00

MIDLAND COUNTIES (Ice Cream)

12	Action Soldiers (with Cadbury)	1976	—	£3.50
M20	Banknotes	1974	—	£12.50
D12	Farmyard Stencils	1977	—	£2.50
M24	Kings of the Road	1977	—	£6.50
X10	Steam Power	1978	—	£4.00

MILK MARKETING BOARD

Qty		*Date*	*Odds*	*Sets*
P10	Milk Recipe Cards	1979	—	£2.50
25	Prehistoric Animals	1963	—	£3.50

MILLERS (Tea)

Qty		Date	Odds	Sets
25	Animals & Reptiles	1962	—	£2.00

ROBERT R. MIRANDA (Confectionery)

Qty		Date	Odds	Sets
50	150 Years of Locomotives	1956	—	£6.00
50	100 Years of Motoring	1955	—	£4.50
25	Ships through the Ages	1957	—	£7.50
50	Strange Creatures	1961	—	£4.00

MISTER SOFTEE LTD. (Ice Cream)

Qty		Date	Odds	Sets
12	Action Soldiers (with Cadbury)	1976	—	£6.00
M12	Beautiful Butterflies	1977	35p	£4.00
M20	County Badge Collection	1976	15p	£2.50
L12	Did You Know?	1976	35p	£4.00
25	Do You Know?	1961	£3.00	—
D12	Farmyard Stencils	1977	—	£4.00
M24	1st Division Football League Badges	1972	—	£6.00
M24	Kings of the Road	1977	25p	£6.00
E1	Map of the British Isles	1976	—	£1.50
15	Moon Mission	1962	75p	—
M24	Pop Discs	1972	75p	£18.00
P24	Pop Parade	1969	—	£16.00
M10	Pop Stars (Shaped)	1975	80p	£8.00
X1	Secret Code Computer	1977	—	60p
D20	Sports Cups (Shaped)	1975	—	£7.50
M20	Stamp in a Million	1976	40p	£8.00
P12	Star Cards (Numbered, With Address)	1966	£1.00	£12.00
P12	Star Cards (Numbered, No Address)	1967	75p	£9.00
P24	Star Cards (Unnumbered)	1968	£1.00	£24.00
X24	Star Discs	1970	75p	£18.00
X10	Steam Power	1978	—	£3.00
M4	Super Human Heroes	1979	—	£3.00
P12	Top 10	1964	—	£4.50
P12	Top Ten (Address N.7.)	1965	£1.00	£12.00
P12	(Address W.6.)	1966	£4.00	—
20	Top 20	1963	75p	£15.00
25	T.V. Personalities	1962	£2.00	—
P12	Your World	1963	—	£2.50

MITCHAM FOODS LTD.

Qty		Date	Odds	Sets
25	Aircraft of Today	1955	—	£3.00
25	Aquarium Fish, 1st Series	1957	—	£22.50
25	Aquarium Fish, 2nd Series	1957	—	£3.00
50	Butterflies and Moths	1959	£1.00	£50.00
25	Footballers	1956	£1.00	—
50	Mars Adventure	1958	£4.00	—
25	Motor Racing	1960	80p	£20.00

MIZZ MAGAZINE

Qty		Date	Odds	Sets
P4	The Seasons	1986	—	£1.50

MOBIL OIL CO. LTD.

Qty		Date	Odds	Sets
M30	Football Club Badges (Silk)	1983	£2.00	£60.00
X36	The Story of Grand Prix Motor Racing	1971	—	£10.00
25	Veteran and Vintage Cars	1962	£1.25	—
24	Vintage Cars	1966	—	£3.50

MODERN WEEKLY (Periodical)

Qty		Date	Odds	Sets
P3	Film Couples (Silk)	1928	£25.00	£75.00

MOFFAT B. & G. LTD. (Confectionery)

Qty		Date	Odds	Sets
D102	Money That Made History	1981	—	£7.00

MOFFAT BROS. (Confectionery)

Qty		Date	Odds	Sets
L100	Cinema Artistes	1914	£9.00	—

THE MOLASSINE CO. (Dog Food)

Qty		Date	Odds	Sets
50	Dogs (Full Length)	1963	80p	£40.00
50	Dogs (Heads)	1964	£1.50	£75.00
25	Dogs at Work	1970	—	£2.50
12	Dogs of All Countries	1925	£9.00	—
50	Puppies	1967	£1.50	£75.00

MONTAGUE MOTOR MUSEUM

Qty		Date	Odds	Sets
M24	Veteran & Vintage Cars	1965	£3.50	£84.00

MONTY GUM

Qty		Date	Odds	Sets
M54	Bay City Rollers	1978	—	£27.00
M98	Bruce Lee	1980	—	£17.50
L72	Daily Fables, 1st Series	1968	—	£17.50
X50	Elvis	1978	£1.50	—
M72	Flag Parade	1972	—	£9.00
M100	Flags of All Nations	1980	—	£4.00
X56	Footballers (P/C Inset)	1970	£2.00	—
M54	Hitmakers (P/C Inset)	1978	50p	—
L72	International Football Teams	1970	75p	£54.00
M72	Kojak	1975	50p	£36.00
M54	Kojak (P/C Inset, Black Back)	1976	—	£20.00
M56	Kojak (P/C Inset, Red Back)	1976	—	£20.00
X56	Motor Cars (P/C Inset)	1956	£1.10	£61.50
M50	Pop Star Pictures	1980	60p	£30.00
M64	Space Alpha 1999	1976	50p	£32.00
M72	Starsky and Hutch	1978	40p	—
M100	The Cops, 1st Series	1976	25p	—
M124	The High Chaparral	1970	—	£30.00
M100	T.V. Hits	1975	—	£12.50

MOORE'S TOFFEE

Qty		Date	Odds	Sets
T48	The Post in Many Lands	1900	£20.00	—

MORNING FOODS LTD.

Qty		Date	Odds	Sets
1	Advertisement Card	1953	—	*£3.00*
F25	British Planes (Numbered)	1978	£3.50	—
F25	(Unnumbered)	1953	—	£15.00
F50	British Trains	1952	£4.50	—
25	British Uniforms	1954	—	£4.00
50	Modern Cars	1954	30p	£15.00
50	Our England	1955	—	£4.00
25	Test Cricketers	1953	£1.00	—
12	The Cunard Line (Black Back)	1957	—	£3.00
12	(Blue Back)	1957	—	£4.00
25	World Locomotives (Black Back)	1954	—	£2.50
25	(Blue Back)	1954	—	£15.00

E. D. L. MOSELEY (Confectionery)

Qty		Date	Odds	Sets
M25	Historical Buildings	1954	—	£2.00

MOTOR CYCLE NEWS

Qty		Date	Odds	Sets
24	'Best of British' Collection (With Folder)	1988	—	£2.00
L6	Motorcycle Classics	1995	—	£2.50

V. MUHLENEN & CO. (Cheese)

Qty		Date	Odds	Sets
M6	Swiss Views, Series III	1955	—	£7.50
M6	Swiss Views, Series IV	1955	—	£7.50

MURCO PETROLEUM

Qty		Date	Odds	Sets
P28	English Counties	1986	—	£3.50
M50	World's Airlines	1978	—	£4.50

C. R. S. MURRAY & CO. LTD. (Chocolates)

Qty		Date	Odds	Sets
1	The Caramel Chief	1930	—	£16.00

MUSEUM OF BRITISH MILITARY UNIFORMS

Qty		Date	Odds	Sets
25	British Cavalry Uniforms	1987	—	£5.00
25	Military Maids	1987	—	£5.00
25	Warriors through the Ages	1987	—	£5.00

MUSICAL COLLECTABLES (Commercial)

Qty		Date	Odds	Sets
26	The Gilbert & Sullivan Collection 1st Series (Player Reprint)	1994	—	£6.00
26	The Gilbert & Sullivan Collection 2nd Series (Player Reprint)	1994	—	£6.00

THEMATIC COLLECTING

Many people come into the hobby not because of an interest in cards themselves, but as an extension of an already existing interest. For there cannot be one subject that is not covered by at least one set of cards, in every case with an illustration and often with informative text.

One of the most popular themes to be collected is sport, and particularly cricket, golf and soccer. The value to the enthusiast can be shown by series such as Taddy County Cricketers and Prominent Footballers which depicted almost every first class player of the time, and the series of 2,462 different Footballers issued in the 1920's by Godfrey Phillips with their Pinnace Cigarettes. In the U.S.A. Baseball is the main cartophilic interest, while in Canada it is hockey. Other games sought by collectors are tennis, billiards, chess and archery.

Militaria, shipping and cinema are other themes that were issued in large numbers and have many devotees. Subjects such as aviation, opera, motoring, music hall and railways are also extensively covered, as are modern subjects such as space exploration and television. The significance of most of these is that they are contemporary records, and one can trace the development of the subject through a period of nearly a century.

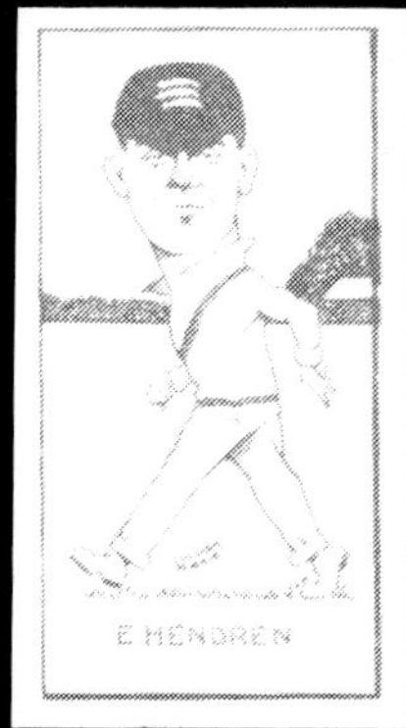

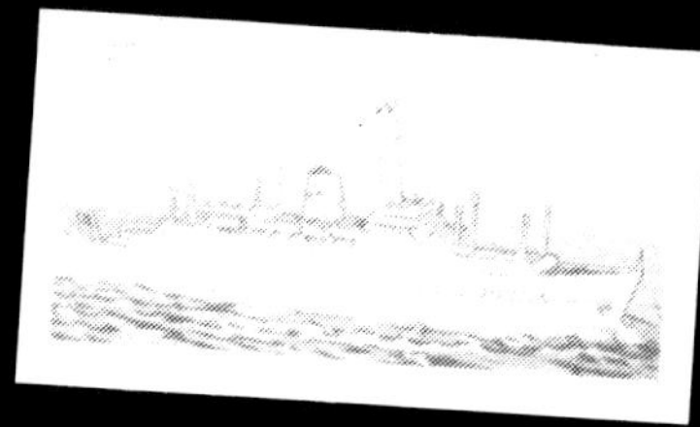

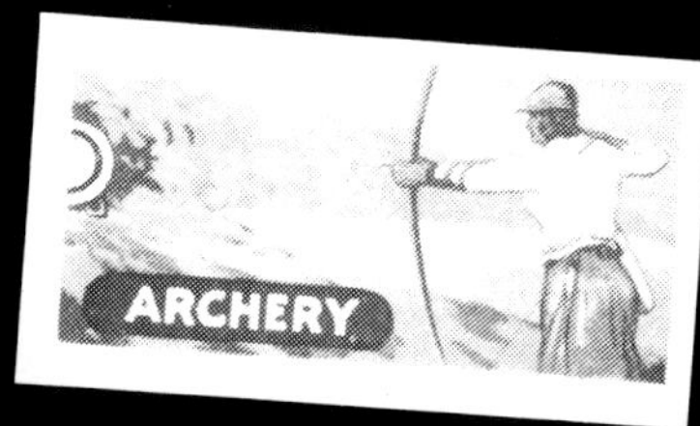

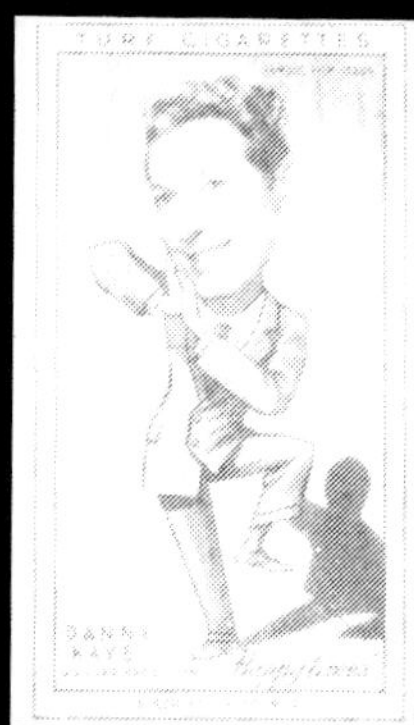

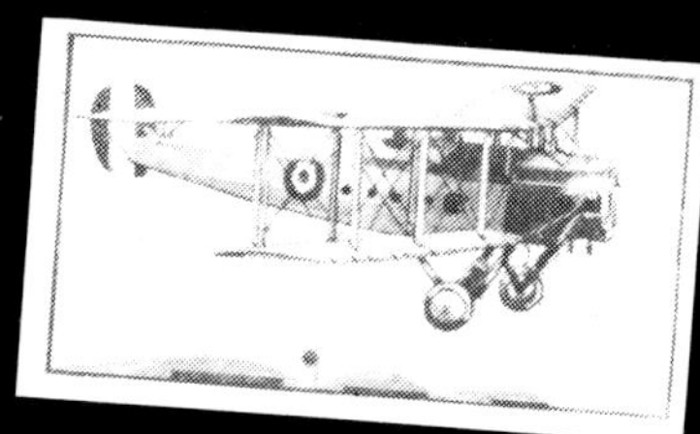

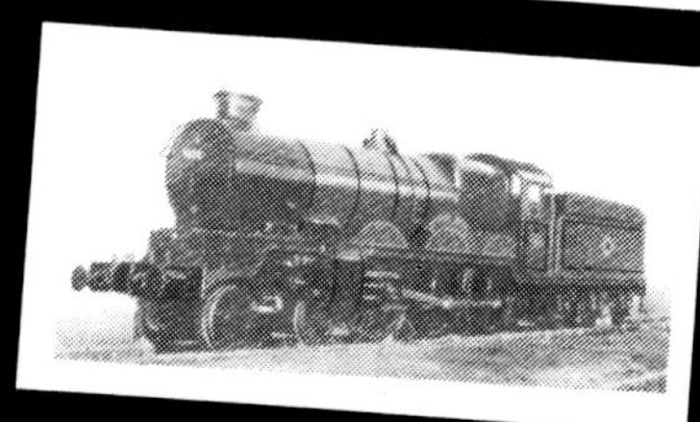

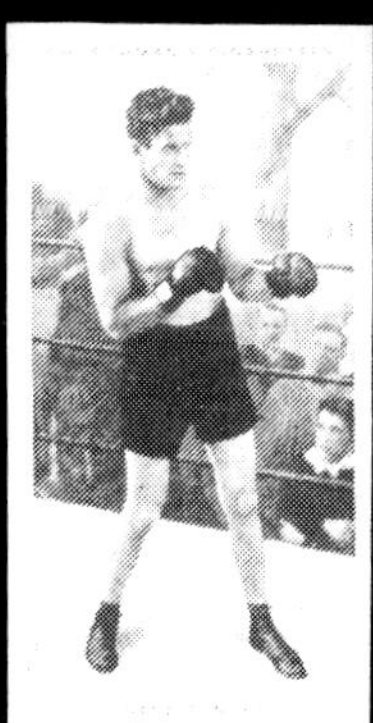

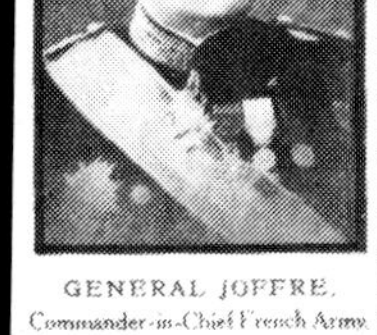

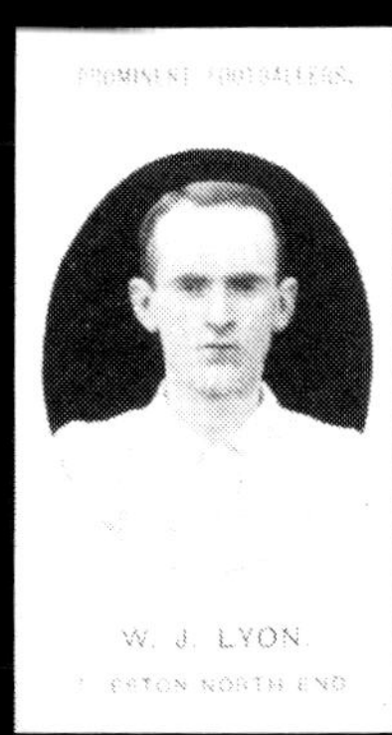

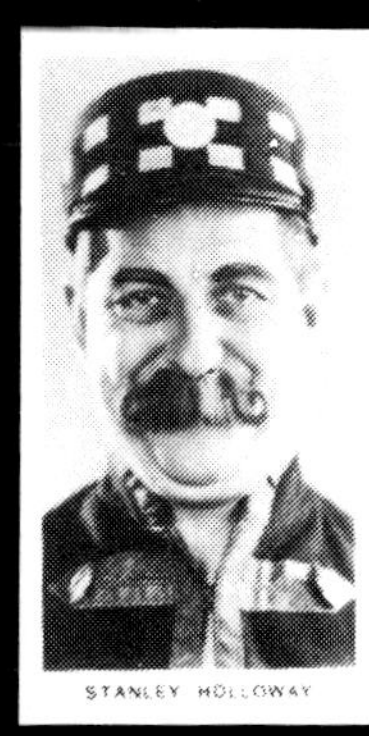

In view of the enormous number of cards that have been produced, most of which have detailed descriptions, it is hardly surprising that mistakes occur occasionally. In some cases these were brought to light at an early stage, and a corrected card was also issued, but sometimes the error remained undetected until many years after the set appeared.

Some of the mistakes can best be described as 'Howlers', and among the best known are Carreras Figures of Fiction showing Uncle Tom with white feet, Pattreiouex Coastwise giving the date of the Battle of Trafalgar as 1812 and Player Sea Fishes with three versions of the Monk (or Angel) Fish, one of which states that it is inedible, while another describes its flesh as 'quite wholesome'. Gallaher, in its Great War Series, showed a Tommy with his rifle sloped on the wrong shoulder, and Carreras Britains Defence No. 47 can be found with the picture upside down. Most of these have been illustrated elsewhere, so we have shown here a different selection, with no comments other than – find the mistake for yourself.

Varieties occur as the result of deliberate changes by the issuer. Common examples of this are the updating of army ranks and decorations, new sports statistics, and changes of rank or title caused by a death. The most fruitful series for a study of varieties are probably in the series of Guinea Gold cards and also Wills Transvaal series, where over 250 different cards can be collected within the 66 numbers of the series.

Three books including all known British varieties are listed on page 12.

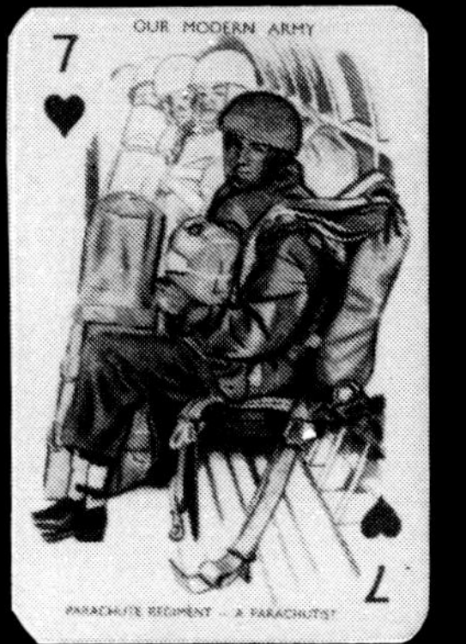

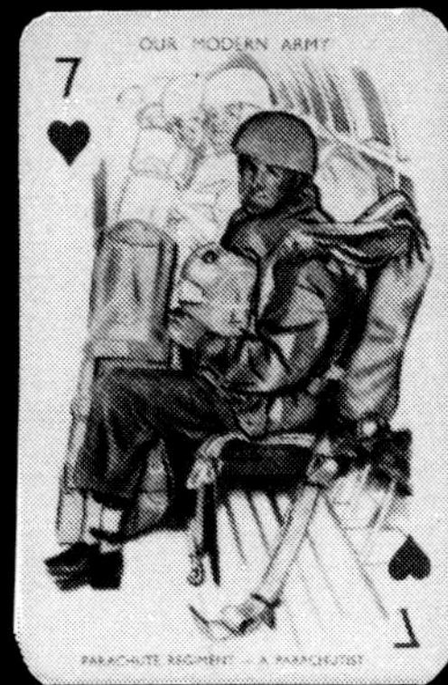

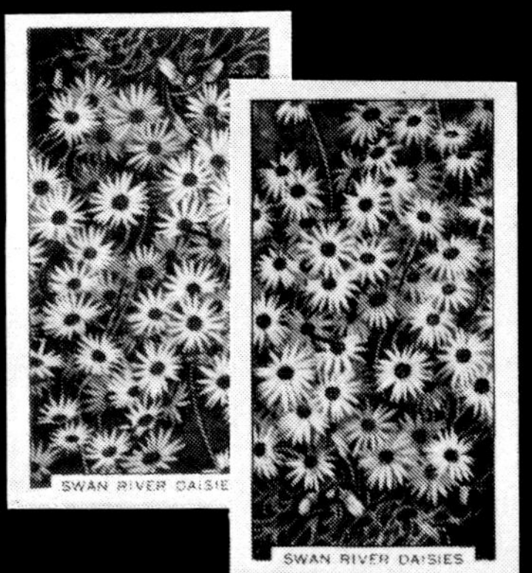

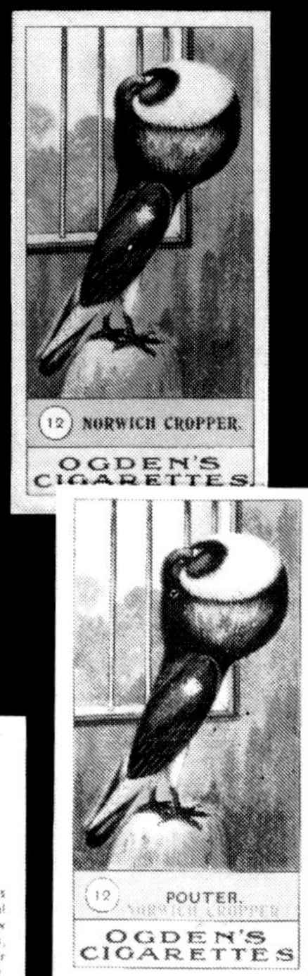

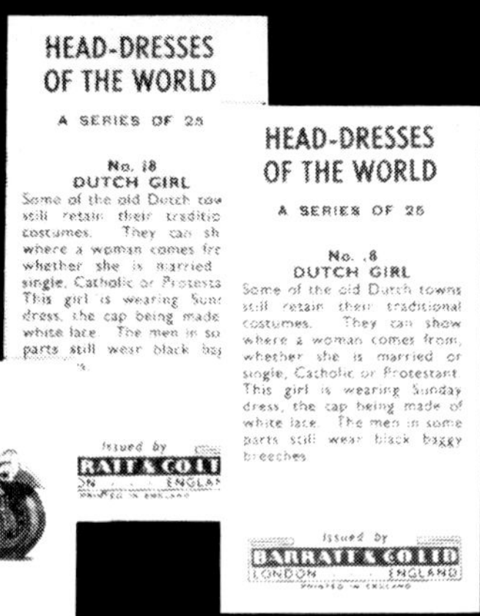

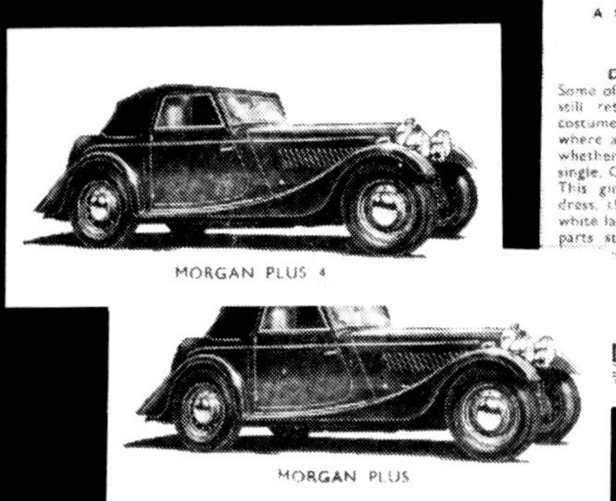

MUSGRAVE BROS. LTD. (Tea)

Qty		Date	Odds	Sets
25	Birds	1961	—	£7.50
20	British Birds	1960	£6.00	£120.00
50	British Wild Life	1962	£6.00	£300.00
50	Butterflies of the World	1964	£5.00	£250.00
25	Into Space	1961	—	£4.00
25	Modern Motor Cars	1962	40p	£10.00
25	Pond Life	1963	—	£6.00
25	Products of the World	1961	—	£2.00
50	Transport through the Ages	1966	£3.00	£150.00
25	Tropical Birds	1964	—	£2.50
25	Wild Flowers	1961	—	£7.50

MYERS & METREVELI (Gum)

Qty		Date	Odds	Sets
KF48	Film Stars	1953	£2.50	—
X48	Film Stars & Biographies	1953	£4.00	—
X60	Hollywood Peep Show	1953	£2.75	£165.00
L50	Spot the Planes	1953	£3.25	—

MY WEEKLY (Periodical)

Qty		Date	Odds	Sets
M9	Battle Series (Silk)	1916	£6.00	£54.00
M12	Floral Beauties (Silk)	1914	£5.25	£63.00
M15	Language of Flowers (Silk)	1914	£6.25	—
M54	Lucky Emblems (Silk)	1912	£8.00	—
M6	Lucky Flowers (Silk)	1913	£11.00	—
M12	Our Soldier Boys (Silk)	1915	£5.75	£69.00
M14	Soldiers of the King (Silk)	1914	£5.50	£77.00
M6	Sweet Kiss Series (Silk)	1913	£7.00	—
M6	War Heroes (Silk)	1916	£6.00	£36.00

NABISCO FOODS LTD.

Qty		Date	Odds	Sets
M5	Aces in Action	1980	£3.00	£15.00
M24	Action Shots of Olympic Sports	1980	£1.50	£36.00
X4	Adventure Books	1970	£2.50	£10.00
12	British Soldiers	1971	—	£1.25
P20	Champions of Sport	1961	£2.00	£40.00
P6	Eagle Eye Games	1979	—	£2.00
P8	England's Soccer Stars Tactic Cards	1980	£2.50	£20.00
12	E.T.	1983	—	£6.00
L24	Footballers	1970	£1.50	£36.00
G12	Freshwater Fishes of Britain	1974	—	£4.00
L10	History of Aviation	1970	£1.80	£18.00
D4	Johan Cruyff Demonstrates	1980	£4.00	£16.00
P10	Kevin Keegan's Keep Fit with the Stars	1978	—	£12.00
P10	Motor Show	1960	£2.25	£22.50
P6	Play 'n Score	1989	—	£6.50
L6	World Super Stars & Sporting Trophies	1980	£3.00	—
AUSTRALIAN ISSUES				
32	Leading Cricketers (Crispies etc.)	1948	£3.00	£96.00
M66	Popular Pets	1962	—	£12.00
L24	United Nations in Action	1968	—	£9.00

EDWARD NASSAR & CO. LTD. (Coffee, Gold Coast)

Qty		Date	Odds	Sets
25	Transport, Present & Future	1955	—	£2.50

NATIONAL SPASTICS SOCIETY

Qty		Date	Odds	Sets
24	Famous County Cricketers (Booklet)	1958	—	£35.00
24	Famous Footballers	1959	—	£16.00

NEEDLER'S (Confectionery)

Qty		Date	Odds	Sets
12	Military Series	1916	£18.00	—

PHILIP NEILL COLLECTABLES (Commercial)

Qty		Date	Odds	Sets
20	Red Legends (Manchester United)	1998	—	£5.50
L18	Super Reds	1998	—	£7.50

NEILSON'S (Confectionery)

Qty		Date	Odds	Sets
50	Interesting Animals	1954	—	£4.00

NELSON LEE LIBRARY (Periodical)

Qty		Date	Odds	Sets
MF15	Footballers	1922	£3.00	£45.00
MF6	Modern British Locomotives	1922	£6.00	£36.00

NESTLE LTD. (Chocolate)

Qty		Date	Odds	Sets
L12	Animal Bars (Wrappers)	1970	—	£1.50
24	Animals of the World	1962	—	£12.00
P12	British Birds (Reward Cards)	1900	£10.00	—
49	Happy Families	1935	90p	£50.00
144	Pictorial World Atlas	1934	£2.00	—
100	Stars of the Silver Screen	1936	£1.20	£120.00
50	Stars of the Silver Screen, Volume II	1937	£1.80	—
136	This England	1936	70p	£95.00
T24	Wild Animals, Serie II	1910	£6.00	—
156	Wonders of the World, Volume I	1932	60p	—
144	Wonders of the World, Volume II	1933	60p	—

NEW ENGLAND CONFECTIONERY CO. (U.S.A.)

Qty		Date	Odds	Sets
M12	Real Airplane Pictures	1929	£3.00	£36.00

NEW HOLLAND MACHINE CO.

Qty		Date	Odds	Sets
P12	Traction Engines	1960	£4.00	£48.00

NEWMARKET HARDWARE

Qty		Date	Odds	Sets
L24	Some of Britain's Finest Bikes	1993	—	£6.00

NEWS CHRONICLE (Newspaper)

Qty		Date	Odds	Sets
L10	Everton F.C.	1955	—	£12.00
L13	Swinton R.F.C.	1955	—	£13.00
L12	The Story of Stirling Moss	1955	£4.00	—

NEWTON, CHAMBERS & CO. (Toilet Rolls)

P18	More Rhyme Time (19-36)	1934	£3.00	£54.00
P18	Nursery Rhyme Pictures (1-18)	1934	£3.00	£54.00

NEW ZEALAND MEAT PRODUCERS BOARD

X25	Scenes of New Zealand Lamb	1930	£2.50	£62.50

90 MINUTES (Magazine)

X56	Footballers (Playing Card Inset)	1993	—	£16.50

NORTHERN CO-OPERATIVE SOCIETY LTD. (Tea)

25	Birds	1963	90p	£22.50
25	History of the Railways, 1st Series	1964	—	£7.50
25	History of the Railways, 2nd Series	1964	—	£10.00
25	Passenger Liners	1963	—	£3.00
25	Then and Now	1963	—	£4.50
25	Tropical Birds	1962	—	£10.00
25	Weapons of World War II	1962	—	£10.00
25	Wonders of the Deep	1965	—	£2.00

NORTH WEST TOURIST BOARD

T40	Stockport	1995	—	£5.00
T40	Wigan	1992	—	£5.00

NOSTALGIA REPRINTS

28	Baseball Greats of 1890 (USA Tobacco)	1991	—	£6.00
2	Baseball Stars (Ruth, Sisler)	1992	—	50p
50	Celebrated American Indian Chiefs (Allen & Ginter)	1989	—	£7.50
20	Clowns and Circus Artistes (Taddy)	1991	—	£6.00
50	Cope's Golfers	1984	—	£7.50
238	County Cricketers (Taddy)	1987	—	£27.50
15	Derbyshire	1987	—	£2.00
15	Essex	1987	—	£2.00
16	Gloucestershire	1987	—	£2.00
15	Hampshire	1987	—	£2.00
15	Kent	1987	—	£2.00
15	Lancashire	1987	—	£2.00
14	Leicestershire	1987	—	£2.00
15	Middlesex	1987	—	£2.00
15	Northamptonshire	1987	—	£2.00
14	Nottinghamshire	1987	—	£2.00
15	Somersetshire	1987	—	£2.00
15	Surrey	1987	—	£2.00
15	Sussex	1987	—	£2.00

NOSTALGIA REPRINTS — cont.

Qty		Date	Odds	Sets
15	Warwickshire	1987	—	£2.00
14	Worcestershire	1987	—	£2.00
15	Yorkshire	1987	—	£2.00
50	Cricketers 1896 (Wills)	1983	—	£7.50
50	Cricketer Series 1901 (Wills)	1984	—	£15.00
20	Cricketers Series 1902 (Gabriel)	1992	—	£3.50
50	Dickens Gallery (Cope)	1989	—	£7.50
50	Fruits (Allen & Ginter)	1989	—	£7.50
25	Generals of the Late Civil War (Ellis)	1991	—	£6.00
25	Humorous Golfing Series (Berlyn)	1989	—	£6.00
25	Leaders (Kinney)	1990	—	£6.00
50	Military Series (Player)	1984	—	£7.50
24	Motor Bike Cards (Thomson)	1993	—	£6.00
20	Motor Cycles (Thomson)	1993	—	£6.00
	Prominent Footballers (Taddy, 1907)			
15	Aston Villa	1992	—	£2.00
15	Chelsea	1998	—	£2.00
15	Everton	1998	—	£2.00
15	Leeds City	1992	—	£2.00
15	Liverpool	1992	—	£2.00
15	Manchester United	1992	—	£2.00
15	Middlesborough	1998	—	£2.00
15	Newcastle United	1992	—	£2.00
15	Queen's Park Rangers	1992	—	£2.00
15	Sunderland	1998	—	£2.00
15	Tottenham Hotspur	1998	—	£2.00
15	West Ham United	1998	—	£2.00
15	Woolwich Arsenal	1992	—	£2.00
4	Promotional Cards	1992	—	75p
50	Shakespeare Gallery (Cope)	1989	—	£7.50
18	Spurs Footballers (Jones)	1987	—	£2.00

NUGGET POLISH CO.

X30	Allied Series	1910	£12.00	—
50	Flags of All Nations	1925	£4.25	—
X40	Mail Carriers and Stamps	1910	£12.00	£480.00

NUMBER ONE (Periodical)

P5	Get Fit and Have Fun	1991	—	£1.00

NUNBETTA (Grocer)

25	Motor Cars	1955	£7.00	£175.00

O.V.S. TEA COMPANY

K25	Modern Engineering	1955	—	£4.00

O'CARROLL KENT LTD. (Confectionery)

50	Railway Engines	1955	£3.50	£175.00

TONY L. OLIVER (Commercial)

Qty		*Date*	*Odds*	*Sets*
25	Aircraft of World War II	1964	£2.60	£65.00
50	German Orders & Decorations	1963	60p	£30.00
50	German Uniforms	1971	—	£8.50
M25	Vehicles of the German Wehrmacht	1965	—	£25.00

O-PEE-CHEE CO. LTD. (Gum, Canada)

X99	Dick Tracy	1990	—	£10.00
X75	Wrestlers, 2nd Series	1988	—	£10.00

ORBIT ADVERTISING (Commercial)

28	Great Rugby Sides (N.Z. Tourists 1905)	1987	—	£2.50
16	New Zealand Cricketers 1958	1988	—	£5.00

OVALTINE BISCUITS

25	Do You Know?	1965	—	£8.00

OWBRIDGE'S (Pharmaceutics)

32	Happy Families	1914	£5.00	—

OXO LTD. (Meat Extract)

K47	Advertisement Series	1926	£4.50	—
K20	British Cattle	1934	£2.80	£56.00
15	Bull Series	1937	£2.40	£36.00
K24	Feats of Endurance	1934	£2.25	£54.00
K20	Furs and Their Story	1932	£2.25	£45.00
K36	Lifeboats and Their History	1935	£2.50	£90.00
K30	Mystery Painting Pictures	1928	£2.50	£75.00
P6	Oxo Cattle Studies	1930	£27.50	—
25	Oxo Recipes	1936	£2.20	£55.00

P. M. R. ASSOCIATES LTD. (Commercial)

25	England, The World Cup, Spain '82	1982	—	£2.00

PACIFIC TRADING CARDS INC. (Commercial, U.S.A.)

X110	I Love Lucy	1991	—	£12.00
X110	The Wizard of Oz	1990	—	£12.00

H. J. PACKER & CO. LTD. (Confectionery)

K30	Footballers	1924	£25.00	—
50	Humorous Drawings	1936	£3.00	£150.00

PAGE WOODCOCK WIND PILLS

Qty		*Date*	*Odds*	*Sets*
20	Humorous Sketches by Tom Browne	1902	£20.00	—

PALMER MANN & CO. LTD. (Salt)

24	Famous Cricketers	1950	*£12.00*	—
24	Famous Footballers	1950	*£10.00*	—
12	Famous Jets	1950	£8.00	—
12	Famous Lighthouses	1950	£8.00	—

PALS (Periodical)

MF27	Australian Sportsmen	1923	£7.00	£190.00
M8	Famous Footballers	1922	£6.00	£48.00
MF12	Football Series	1922	£3.00	£36.00

PANINI (Commercial, with Albums)

M240	A Team	1983	—	£17.50
M240	Auto 2000	1988	—	£17.50
X44	England Soccer Stars (No Album)	1996	—	£12.00
M204	Superman (Italian)	1979	—	£17.50
M400	Tarzan	1985	—	£17.50
X190	The Royal Family	1988	—	£17.50

JAMES PASCALL LTD. (Confectionery)

48	Boy Scout Series	1912	£8.00	—
24	British Birds	1925	£2.50	£60.00
30	Devon Ferns	1927	£1.60	£48.00
30	Devon Flowers	1927	£1.60	£48.00
24	Devon Worthies	1927	£2.00	£48.00
18	Dogs	1924	£3.00	£54.00
10	Felix the Film Cat	1928	£17.50	—
30	Flags & Flags with Soldiers	1905	£11.00	—
30	Glorious Devon	1929	£1.60	£48.00
36	Glorious Devon, 2nd Series (Black Back)	1929	£1.60	£57.50
36	(Green Back)	1929	£1.60	£57.50
36	(Non-Descriptive)	1929	£4.50	—
2	King George V & Queen Mary	1910	£25.00	—
44	Military Series	1912	£14.00	—
20	Pascall's Specialities	1926	£13.00	—
12	Royal Naval Cadet Series	1912	£14.00	—
?	Rulers of the World	1916	*£25.00*	—
65	Town and Other Arms	1914	£10.00	—
50	Tricks and Puzzles	1926	£6.00	—
?13	War Portraits	1915	*£16.50*	—

J. PATERSON AND SON LTD. (Biscuits)

M48	Balloons	1960	£1.75	£84.00

PATRICK (Garages)

Qty		Date	Odds	Sets
T24	The Patrick Collection (Cars)	1986	—	£12.00
P24	The Patrick Collection (With Coupons)	1986	—	£15.00

GEORGE PAYNE (Tea)

Qty		Date	Odds	Sets
25	American Indian Tribes	1962	—	*£15.00*
25	British Railways	1962	—	£2.50
12	Characters from Dickens' Works (Numbered)	1912	£12.50	—
6	(Unnumbered)	1912	£14.00	—
25	Dogs Heads	1963	—	£7.50
25	Science in the 20th Century	1963	—	£2.50

PEEK FREAN & CO. (Biscuits)

76 Page Illustrated Reference Book — £13.50

Qty		Date	Odds	Sets
X12	English Scenes	1884	£8.00	£96.00
X4	Shakespeare Scenes	1884	£14.00	£56.00
X4	Views Abroad	1883	£12.00	£48.00

PENGUIN BISCUITS

Qty		Date	Odds	Sets
E6	Farm Animal Series (Pairs)	1968	£2.00	£12.00
E6	(Singles)	1968	£2.00	—
E10	Home Hints	1974	£1.75	—
E12	Lake Nakuru Wildlife	1973	£2.00	—
E10	Making the Most of Your Countryside	1975	£1.75	£17.50
E10	Pastimes	1972	£1.60	£16.00
E12	Playday	1973	£1.60	£20.00
E5	Zoo Animal Series (Pairs)	1969	£2.00	£10.00

PENNY MAGAZINE

Qty		Date	Odds	Sets
MF12	Film Stars	1931	£3.50	£42.00

PERFETTI (Gum)

Qty		Date	Odds	Sets
40	Famous Trains	1983	£1.75	£70.00

PETERKIN (Foods)

Qty		Date	Odds	Sets
M8	English Sporting Dogs	1930	£12.00	£96.00

PETPRO LTD.

Qty		Date	Odds	Sets
35	Grand Prix Racing Cars	1962	—	£7.00

PHILADELPHIA CHEWING GUM CORP. (U.S.A.)

Qty		Date	Odds	Sets
X88	War Bulletin	1965	£1.25	£110.00

PHILLIPS (Tea)

Qty		Date	Odds	Sets
25	Army Badges Past and Present	1964	—	£2.00
25	British Birds and Their Nests	1966	—	£30.00
25	British Rail	1965	—	£7.50

PHOTO ANSWERS (Periodical)

Qty		Date	Odds	Sets
X12	Holiday Fax	1990	—	£2.00

FERD, PIATNIK & SONS (Austria)

Qty		Date	Odds	Sets
X55	Elvis Playing Cards	1997	—	£6.00
X55	Hollywood Movie Stars Playing Cards No. 1190	1997	—	£6.00
X55	Hollywood Movie Stars Playing Cards No. 1191	1997	—	£6.00
X55	Masters of the Old Course – St. Andrews – Open Champions	1998	—	£6.00

STEVE PILKINGTON (Engineering)

Qty		Date	Odds	Sets
X18	Central Lancashire Cricket League Clubs and Pavilions	1997	—	£7.00

PLANET LTD. (Gum)

Qty		Date	Odds	Sets
X50	Racing Cars of the World	1965	£2.25	£112.50

PLANTERS NUT & CHOCOLATE CO. (U.S.A.)

Qty		Date	Odds	Sets
M25	Hunted Animals	1933	£2.80	£70.00

PLUCK (Periodical)

Qty		Date	Odds	Sets
MF27	Famous Football Teams	1922	£2.50	£68.00

POLAR PRODUCTS LTD. (Ice Cream, Barbados)

Qty		Date	Odds	Sets
25	International Air-Liners	1970	—	£10.00
25	Modern Motor Cars	1970	—	£15.00
25	Tropical Birds	1970	—	£10.00
25	Wonders of the Deep	1970	—	£8.00

H. POPPLETON & SONS (Confectionery)

Qty		Date	Odds	Sets
50	Cricketers Series	1926	£22.50	—
16	Film Stars	1928	£7.00	—
?20	War Series	1916	£20.00	—
?12	Wembley Empire Exhibition Series	1924	£25.00	—

THE POPULAR (Periodical)

Qty		Date	Odds	Sets
G26	Railway Locomotives	1922	£5.00	£130.00

POPULAR MOTORING (Periodical)

Qty		Date	Odds	Sets
X4	P.M. Car Starter	1972	—	£2.00

POSTER STAMP ASSOCIATION

Qty		Date	Odds	Sets
25	Modern Transport	1957	—	£2.25

PRESCOTT (Confectionery)

Qty		Date	Odds	Sets
L36	Speed Kings	1966	50p	£18.00

PRESCOTT-PICKUP & CO. (Commercial)

Qty		Date	Odds	Sets
P60	Papal Visit	1982	—	£8.00
50	Railway Locomotives	1980	—	£6.00
P70	Royal Family — Birth of a Prince	1982	—	£15.00

PRESTON DAIRIES (Tea)

Qty		Date	Odds	Sets
25	Country Life	1966	—	£2.00

PRICES PATENT CANDLE CO. LTD.

Qty		Date	Odds	Sets
P12	Famous Battles	1910	£10.00	£120.00

W. R. PRIDDY (Antiques)

Qty		Date	Odds	Sets
80	Famous Boxers	1992	—	£7.50

PRIMROSE CONFECTIONERY CO. LTD.

Qty		Date	Odds	Sets
24	Action Man	1976	£1.75	£42.00
50	Amos Burke — Secret Agent	1970	—	£40.00
50	Andy Pandy	1960	—	£20.00
50	Bugs Bunny	1964	—	*£25.00*
50	Burke's Law	1967	£2.50	—
25	Captain Kid	1975	—	£90.00
50	Chitty Chitty Bang Bang	1971	—	£20.00
50	Cowboy	1960	—	£6.50
25	Cup Tie Quiz	1973	—	£2.50
25	Dads Army	1973	—	£3.50
50	Famous Footballers F.B.S.I.	1961	—	£13.50
25	Football Funnies	1974	—	£6.00
25	Happy Howlers	1975	—	£2.00
50	Joe 90	1969	£1.20	£60.00
50	Krazy Kreatures from Outer Space	1970	—	£6.00
50	Laramie	1964	£1.20	£60.00
50	Laurel & Hardy	1968	£1.80	£90.00
M22	Mounties (Package Issue)	1960	£5.50	£121.00
50	Popeye	1960	£5.00	£250.00
50	Popeye, 2nd Series	1961	£3.00	£150.00
50	Popeye, 3rd Series	1962	—	£10.00
50	Popeye, 4th Series	1963	—	£10.00
50	Queen Elizabeth 2	1969	50p	£25.00
50	Quick Draw McGraw	1964	£1.25	—
50	Space Patrol	1970	—	£10.00
50	Space Race	1969	—	£3.50
12	Star Trek	1971	—	£5.00

PRIMROSE CONFECTIONERY CO. LTD. — cont.

Qty		Date	Odds	Sets
50	Superman	1968	—	£14.00
50	The Flintstones	1963	—	£20.00
50	Yellow Submarine	1968	£2.50	—
50	Z-Cars	1968	25p	£12.50

PRINCE EDWARD THEATRE

XF?4	Josephine Baker Cards	1930	£20.00	—

MICHAEL PRIOR (Commercial)

25	Racing Colours	1987	—	£3.50

S. PRIOR (Bookshop)

25	Do You Know?	1964	—	£15.00

PRIORY TEA CO. LTD.

50	Aircraft	1961	—	£16.50
50	Birds	1962	40p	£20.00
24	Bridges	1960	—	£2.50
24	Cars	1958	£3.00	—
50	Cars (Different)	1964	65p	£32.50
50	Cycles & Motorcycles	1963	£1.50	£75.00
24	Dogs	1957	—	£2.00
24	Flowering Trees	1959	—	£2.00
24	Men at Work	1959	—	£2.00
24	Out and About	1957	—	£3.00
24	People in Uniform	1956	£1.50	£36.00
24	Pets	1957	—	£3.00
50	Wild Flowers	1963	50p	£25.00

PRO SET INC. (Commercial, U.S.A.)

X100	Bill & Ted's Movie Cards	1991	—	£5.00
X100	Footballers and Fixture Lists	1991	—	£6.00
X100	Guinness Book of Records	1992	—	£5.50
X100	P.G.A. Tour Cards	1990	—	£13.50
X100	Thunderbirds	1992	15p	£8.00

PROPERT SHOE POLISH

25	British Uniforms	1955	—	£3.00

PUKKA TEA CO. LTD.

50	Aquarium Fish	1961	—	£40.00

PYREX LTD. (Glassware)

P16	Guide to Simple Cooking	1976	—	£2.50

QUAKER OATS

Qty		Date	Odds	Sets
X12	Armour through the Ages	1968	£1.00	£12.00
M4	Famous Puffers	1983	£4.50	£18.00
M54	Historic Arms of Merrie England	1938	80p	—
X8	Historic Ships	1967	£3.50	£28.00
M6	Honey Monster's Circus Friends	1985	£2.00	—
15	Honey Monster's Crazy Games Cards	1985	£1.20	—
M16	Jeremy's Animal Kingdom	1980	£1.25	£20.00
X4	Minibooks	1969	£2.25	£9.00
12	Monsters of the Deep	1984	£1.10	£13.00
M6	Nature Trek	1976	35p	£2.00
X12	Prehistoric Animals	1967	£3.75	—
L8	Return to Oz	1985	£1.50	£12.00
X12	Space Cards	1968	£4.00	—
X12	Vintage Engines	1967	£3.75	£45.00
PACKAGE ISSUES				
12	British Customs	1961	60p	£7.50
L36	British Landmarks	1961	60p	—
12	Characters in Literature	1961	£1.00	—
12	Exploration & Adventure	1974	75p	£9.00
12	Famous Explorers	1961	75p	£9.00
12	Famous Inventors	1961	75p	£9.00
12	Famous Ships	1961	£1.00	—
12	Famous Women	1961	75p	—
12	Fascinating Costumes	1961	50p	£6.00
12	Great Feats of Building	1961	50p	£6.00
L36	Great Moments of Sport	1961	£1.75	—
12	History of Flight	1961	85p	£10.00
12	Homes and Houses	1961	75p	£9.00
L36	Household Hints	1961	60p	—
12	National Maritime Museum	1974	£1.00	—
12	National Motor Museum	1974	£1.40	£17.00
12	On the Seashore	1961	50p	£6.00
L36	Phiz-Quiz	1961	85p	—
L36	Railways of the World	1961	£1.75	—
12	Royal Air Force Museum	1974	£1.25	—
12	Science & Invention	1974	75p	£9.00
L36	The Story of Fashion	1961	60p	—
12	The Wild West	1961	75p	£9.00
12	Weapons & Armour	1961	85p	£10.00

QUEEN ELIZABETH LAUNDRY

45	Beauties	1912	£13.50	—

QUEENS OF YORK (Laundry)

30	Kings & Queens of England	1955	—	£25.00

QUORN SPECIALITIES LTD. (Foods)

25	Fish and Game	1963	£3.50	—

R. K. CONFECTIONERY CO. LTD.

32	Felix Pictures	1930	£25.00	—

RADIO FUN (Periodical)

Qty		Date	Odds	Sets
20	British Sports Stars	1956	—	£3.00

RADIO REVIEW (Periodical)

Qty		Date	Odds	Sets
L36	Broadcasting Stars	1936	£3.00	£108.00
E20	Broadcasting Stars	1936	£3.50	£70.00

RALEIGH BICYCLES

Qty		Date	Odds	Sets
L48	Raleigh the All-Steel Bicycle	1957	£1.50	£72.00

REDDINGS TEA CO.

Qty		Date	Odds	Sets
25	Castles of Great Britain	1965	£1.20	£30.00
25	Cathedrals of Great Britain	1964	£1.20	£30.00
25	Heraldry of Famous Places	1966	£1.20	£30.00
48	Ships of the World	1964	—	£6.50
25	Strange Customs of the World	1970	—	£2.50
48	Warriors of the World	1962	£1.50	£72.00

REDDISH MAID CONFECTIONERY

Qty		Date	Odds	Sets
50	Famous International Aircraft	1963	£2.50	£125.00
25	Famous International Athletes	1964	*£4.00*	—
25	International Footballers of Today	1965	£4.25	—

RED HEART (Pet Food)

Qty		Date	Odds	Sets
P6	Cats	1954	—	£27.00
P6	Dogs, First Series	1953	—	£27.00
P6	Dogs, Second Series	1953	—	£27.00
P6	Dogs, Third Series	1954	—	£27.00

RED LETTER (Periodical)

Qty		Date	Odds	Sets
P29	Charlie Chaplin Cards	1920	£11.00	£300.00
P?100	Fortune Cards (Playing Card Backs)	1932	£2.75	—
M4	Luck-Bringers (Silk)	1924	£15.00	£80.00
X98	Midget Message Cards	1920	£2.00	—
M100	The Handy Cooking Cards	1926	£1.00	—

REEVES LTD. (Confectionery)

Qty		Date	Odds	Sets
25	Cricketers	1912	£24.00	£600.00

REFLECTIONS OF A BYGONE AGE (Fairs)

Qty		Date	Odds	Sets
12	Nottingham Heritage Cards	1996	—	£2.00
6	Railways Around Nottingham	1996	—	£1.00
12	Visitors to Nottingham Card Fair	1993	—	£2.00

REGENT OIL

Qty		Date	Odds	Sets
T25	Do You Know?	1965	—	£2.00

RICHARDS COLLECTION (Commercial)

Qty		Date	Odds	Sets
25	Soccer Stars of Yesteryear, Second Series	1997	—	£8.75
25	Soccer Stars of Yesteryear, Third Series	1997	—	£8.75
25	Soccer Stars of Yesteryear, Fourth Series	1998	—	£4.75

ESTEVE RIERA S.A. (Chocolate, Spain)

Qty		Date	Odds	Sets
X24	Costumes Through the Ages	1923	—	£30.00

RIDGWAY'S TEA

Qty		Date	Odds	Sets
X20	Journey to the Moon (Package Issue)	1958	£5.50	—

RINGTONS LTD. (Tea)

Qty		Date	Odds	Sets
25	Aircraft of World War II	1962	£1.00	—
25	British Cavalry Uniforms of the 19th Century	1971	£1.00	—
25	Do You Know?	1964	—	£2.50
25	Fruits of Trees and Shrubs	1964	—	£2.00
25	Head-Dresses of the World	1973	—	£2.00
25	Historical Scenes	1964	—	£3.50
25	Old England	1964	—	£2.00
25	People & Places	1964	—	£2.50
25	Regimental Uniforms of the Past	1966	—	£5.00
25	Sailing Ships through the Ages	1967	—	£3.00
25	Ships of the Royal Navy	1961	—	£3.00
25	Sovereigns, Consorts & Rulers, First Series	1961	—	£6.50
25	Sovereigns, Consorts & Rulers, Second Series	1961	—	£6.50
25	The West	1968	—	£3.00
25	Then & Now	1970	—	£20.00
25	Trains of the World	1970	—	£2.00

RISCA TRAVEL AGENCY

Qty		Date	Odds	Sets
25	Holiday Resorts	1957	—	£20.00

D. ROBBINS & CO. (Bread, U.S.A.)

Qty		Date	Odds	Sets
P24	Frontiers of Freedom	1942	—	£40.00
P24	Good Neighbors of the Americas	1942	—	£40.00
P24	Modern Wonders of the World	1942	—	£40.00
P24	Our Friend — The Dog	1942	£3.50	—
P23/24	Story of Transportation	1942	—	£30.00

ROBERTSON LTD. (Preserves)

Qty		Date	Odds	Sets
1	Advertisement Gollywog	1962	—	£1.50
6	British Medals	1914	£20.00	—
L6	British Medals (Circular)	1914	£30.00	—
10	Musical Gollywogs (Shaped)	1962	£3.00	£30.00
10	Sporting Gollywogs (Shaped)	1962	£3.25	£32.50

ROBERTSON & WOODCOCK (Confectionery)

Qty		Date	Odds	Sets
50	British Aircraft Series	1933	£1.80	£90.00

CHRIS ROBINSON ARTWORKSHOP (Commercial)

X16	The Pilgrims F.A.Cup Squad 1983-84	1984	—	£5.00

ROBINSON'S BARLEY WATER

X30	Sporting Records (with Folder)	1983	—	£3.25

ROBINSON BROS. & MASTERS (Tea)

25	Tea from the Garden to the Home	1930	£7.00	£175.00

ROB ROY CARDS (Commercial)

L20	Manchester United Series 1	1995	—	£8.00

ROCHE & CO. LTD. (Matches)

K49/50	Famous Footballers	1927	£6.00	—

THE ROCKET (Periodical)

MF11	Famous Knock-Outs	1923	£8.00	£88.00

RODEO BUBBLE GUM

M42	Western Stars	1953	£3.00	—

ROLLS ROYCE (Cars)

X25	Bentley Cars	1986	—	£35.00
X25	Bentley Cars, Second Edition	1987	—	£30.00
X25	Rolls Royce Cars	1986	—	*£35.00*
X25	Rolls Royce Cars, Second Edition	1987	—	*£35.00*

ROSSI'S (Ice Cream)

M48	Flag Cards	1975	15p	£5.00
25	The History of Flight, 1st Series	1963	60p	£15.00
25	The History of Flight, 2nd Series	1963	50p	£12.50
25	World's Fastest Aircraft	1964	—	£15.00

ROWNTREE & CO. (Confectionery)

K12	British Birds (Packet Issue)	1955	—	£12.00
25	Celebrities	1905	£21.00	—
X8	Circus Cut-Outs	1960	£5.00	—
M20	Merry Monarchs	1978	—	£4.00
M18	Prehistoric Animals	1978	—	£5.00

ROWNTREE & CO. (Confectionery) — cont.

Qty		*Date*	*Odds*	*Sets*
L6	Punch & Judy Show	1976	£1.60	£10.00
X42	Railway Engines (Caramac)	1976	—	£12.00
L2	Smartie Models	1976	—	£3.00
M10	Texan Tall Tales of the West	1977	£1.50	—
48	The Old & The New	1934	£3.75	£187.50
120	Treasure Trove Pictures	1932	£1.50	—
24	York Views	1924	£9.00	—

ROYAL ARMY MEDICAL CORPS HISTORICAL MUSEUM

T16	Centenary Year RAMC Victoria Crosses	1998	—	£5.00

ROYAL LEAMINGTON SPA CORPORATION

25	Royal Leamington Spa	1975	—	£2.00

ROYAL NATIONAL LIFEBOAT INSTITUTION

M16	Lifeboats	1979	—	£3.00

ROYAL SOCIETY FOR THE PREVENTION OF ACCIDENTS

24	Modern British Cars	1954	£1.50	£36.00
22	Modern British Motor-Cycles	1953	£3.00	£66.00
25	New Traffic Signs	1958	—	£5.50
24	Veteran Cars, First Series	1955	£1.40	£33.50
24	Veteran Cars, Second Series	1957	£1.10	£26.50

RUBY (Periodical)

T10	Famous Beauties of the Day	1923	£5.50	—
T6	Famous Film Stars	1923	£7.50	—

RUGBY FOOTBALL UNION

50	English Internationals 1980-1991	1991	—	£12.50

S & B PRODUCTS (Commercial)

64	Torry Gillick's Internationals	1948	£7.00	—

SAGION STUFFING

28	Dominoes without the Dot	1939	25p	£7.00

J. SAINSBURY LTD. (Groceries)

M12	British Birds	1924	£6.00	£72.00
M12	Foreign Birds	1924	£6.00	£72.00

SANDERS BROS. (CUSTARD)

Qty		Date	Odds	Sets
25	Birds, Fowls, Pigeons & Rabbits	1925	£5.00	£125.00
20	Dogs	1926	£3.50	£70.00
25	Recipes	1924	£3.60	£90.00

SANITARIUM HEALTH FOOD CO. (Oceania)

Qty		Date	Odds	Sets
X12	Alpine Flora of New Zealand	1975	—	£2.50
X12	Alpine Sports	1986	—	£3.00
X12	Amazing Animals of the World	1985	—	£2.50
X12	Animals of New Zealand	1974	—	£4.50
L30	Another Look at New Zealand	1971	—	£3.00
L30	Antarctic Adventure	1972	—	£5.00
X25	Australian Bird Life	1963	—	£2.50
X12	Ball Sports	1989	—	£4.00
L20	Big Rigs	1983	—	£3.00
L20	Big Rigs at Work	1986	—	£3.00
L20	Big Rigs 3	1992	—	£2.50
X12	Bush Birds of New Zealand	1981	—	£3.00
L20	Cars of the Seventies	1976	—	£5.00
X12	Clocks through the Ages	1990	—	£4.00
L20	Conservation — Caring for Our Land	1974	—	£2.50
X12	Curious Conveyances	1984	—	£3.00
L20	Discover Indonesia	1977	—	£3.00
L20	Discover Science with the DSIR	1989	—	£2.50
X12	Discovering New Zealand's Reptile World	1983	—	£2.50
L20	Exotic Cars	1987	—	£5.00
L20	Exploring our Solar System	1982	—	£3.00
L24	Famous New Zealanders	1971	—	£4.00
L20	Farewell to Steam	1981	—	£5.00
L30	Fascinating Orient	1974	—	£2.50
X12	Focus on New Zealand, Series 1	1979	—	£2.50
X12	Focus on New Zealand, Series 2	1982	—	£2.50
X12	Historic Buildings	1982	—	£3.00
X12	Historic Buildings 2nd Series	1984	—	£3.00
L20	History of Road Transport — New Zealand	1979	—	£5.00
X12	Horse Breeds	1990	—	£4.00
X12	Jet Aircraft	1974	—	£5.00
L20	Kiwis Going for Gold	1992	—	£3.00
L20	Living in Space	1992	—	£2.50
L20	Looking at Canada	1978	—	£2.50
L20	Mammals of the Sea	1985	—	£2.50
X12	Man Made Wonders of the World	1987	—	£2.50
X12	Mountaineering	1987	—	£3.00
X25	National Costumes of the Old World	1966	—	£4.50
L25	National Costumes of the Old World (Different)	1968	—	£4.50
X12	New Zealand Disasters	1991	—	£2.50
X12	New Zealand Inventions and Discoveries	1991	—	£2.50
X12	New Zealand Lakes, Series 1	1977	—	£2.50
X12	New Zealand Lakes, Series 2	1978	—	£3.00
L30	New Zealand National Parks	1973	—	£5.00
L20	New Zealand Reef Fish	1984	—	£2.50
L20	New Zealand Summer Sports	1984	—	£3.00
L30	New Zealand To-Day	1974	—	£4.00
L20	New Zealand's Booming Industries	1975	—	£2.00
L20	New Zealanders in Antarctica	1987	—	£4.00

SANITARIUM HEALTH FOOD CO. (Oceania) — cont.

Qty		Date	Odds	Sets
L20	New Zealanders on Top of the World	1991	—	£2.50
L20	'1990 – Look at How We've Grown'	1990	—	£2.50
L20	N.Z. Energy Resources	1976	—	£3.00
L20	N.Z. Rod and Custom Cars	1979	—	£5.00
X12	N.Z. Waterfalls	1981	—	£3.00
X12	N.Z.R. Steam Engines	1976	—	£7.00
X12	Ocean Racers	1986	—	£3.00
L20	100 Years of New Zealand National Parks	1987	—	£2.50
L20	Our Asian Neighbours	1972	—	£2.50
X12	Our Fascinating Fungi	1980	—	£3.00
L20	Our Golden Fleece	1981	—	£2.50
L20	Our South Pacific Island Neighbours	1974	—	£4.00
L20	Our Weather	1980	—	£2.50
X12	Power Boats in New Zealand	1990	—	£3.50
L20	Saving The World's Endangered Wildlife	1991	—	£2.50
X12	Shipping in our Coastal Waters	1988	—	£2.50
X25	Snow Holiday	1966	—	£3.00
X12	Spanning New Zealand (Bridges)	1992	—	£2.50
L20	Spectacular Sports	1974	—	£4.50
L20	Super Cars	1972	—	£5.00
X12	Surf Live-Saving	1986	—	£3.00
X20	The Bradman Collection	1995	—	£10.00
L20	The Many-Stranded Web of Nature	1983	—	£2.50
L60	The Maori Way of Life	1969	—	£6.00
L20	The 1990 Commonwealth Games	1989	—	£4.00
L20	The Story of New Zealand Aviation	1977	—	£5.00
L20	The Story of New Zealand in Stamps	1977	—	£5.00
L20	The Wild South	1986	—	£2.50
M20	This World of Speed	1968	—	£3.25
L20	Timeless Japan	1974	—	£3.00
L20	Timeless Japan (Different)	1975	—	£3.00
M20	Traditional Uniforms of the World	1969	—	£4.00
L20	Treasury of Maori Life	1980	—	£2.50
X12	Veteran Cars	1971	—	£5.00
L20	Vintage Cars	1973	—	£6.50
X12	Wild Flowers of N.Z.	1979	—	£3.00
TS16	Wild Life of the World	1964	—	£3.50
X12	Windsports	1989	—	£3.00
L20	Wonderful Ways of Nature	1978	—	£2.50
X12	Wonderful Wool	1988	—	£2.50
L20	'World's Greatest Fun Parks'	1990	—	£4.00
L20	Your Journey through Disneyland	1988	—	£6.00

SAVOY PRODUCTS LTD. (Foods)

Qty		Date	Odds	Sets
M56	Aerial Navigation	1926	£1.80	£100.00
M56	Aerial Navigation, Series B	1927	£1.50	£85.00
M56	Aerial Navigation, Series C	1928	£1.50	£85.00
M56	Famous British Boats	1928	£1.40	£80.00

SCANLEN'S (Gum, Australia)

Qty		Date	Odds	Sets
M172	Cricket Series No.2 (Including Album)	1983	—	£30.00
X84	Cricket World Series	1990	—	£12.50

SCANLEN'S (Gum, Australia) — cont.

Qty		Date	Odds	Sets
X84	International Cricketers	1989	—	£15.00
X90	World Series Cricket	1982	—	£15.00

THE SCHOOL FRIEND (Periodical)

L6	Famous Film Stars	1927	£9.00	£54.00
X10	Popular Girls of Cliff House School	1922	£10.00	£100.00
XF6	Popular Pictures	1923	£3.00	£18.00

THE SCHOOLGIRL (Periodical)

MF16	Zoological Studies	1923	£2.50	£40.00

SCHOOLGIRLS OWN (Periodical)

12	Characters from Cliff House School	1932	£4.00	£48.00
F7	Film Stars (Anon.)	1929	£4.00	£28.00
12	Film Stars (Anon., Brown)	1932	£3.50	£42.00
12	The Royal Family (Anon., Brown)	1932	£3.25	£39.00

THE SCHOOLGIRLS' WEEKLY (Periodical)

F12	Famous Film Stars (Anon.)	1929	£4.50	—
XF1	HRH The Duke of York	1922	—	£5.00
XF4	Popular Pictures	1922	£3.50	£14.00

SCOTTISH DAILY EXPRESS

X24	Scotcards (Soccer)	1972	£4.00	—

THE SCOUT (Periodical)

L9	Birds' Eggs	1925	£5.00	£45.00
M12	Railway Engines	1924	£5.50	£66.00

SCRAPBOOK MINICARDS

27	Pendon Museum (Model Railway etc.)	1978	—	£2.00

SCREEN STORIES (Periodical)

F8	Film Stars (Anon.)	1930	£4.50	—

SECRETS (Periodical)

K52	Film Stars (Miniature Playing Cards)	1935	90p	—

SELF SERVICE LAUNDRETTES

50	150 Years of Locomotives	1955	£3.50	—

SELLOTAPE PRODUCTS LTD. (Adhesive Tape)

Qty		*Date*	*Odds*	*Sets*
35	Great Homes and Castles	1974	—	£10.00

A. J. SEWARD & CO. LTD. (Perfumes)

40	Stars of the Screen	1939	£10.00	—

SEYMOUR MEAD & CO. LTD. (Tea)

24	The Island of Ceylon	1964	—	£2.00

SHARMAN (Newspapers)

T24	Golden Age of Flying	1979	—	£12.00
T24	Golden Age of Motoring	1979	—	£12.00
T24	Golden Age of Steam	1979	—	£12.00

EDWARD SHARP & SONS (Confectionery)

20	Captain Scarlet	1970	£5.00	£100.00
25	Hey Presto!	1970	—	£2.50
K53	Miniature Playing Cards	1924	£2.25	—
100	Prize Dogs	1924	£4.00	—

TONY SHELDON COLLECTIBLES PROMOTIONS

20	Olden Goldies (Cricketers)	1998	—	£8.00
X18	Out of the Blue Into the Red (The Labour Cabinet)	1997	—	£6.75
20	The Don – 90th Birthday Celebration	1998	—	£9.75

SHELL (Oil)

M16	Animals (3-D)	1975	£1.00	£16.00
14	Bateman Series	1930	£6.00	£84.00
P20	Great Britons	1972	£1.25	£25.00
K20	Historic Cars (Medals) including Mount	1970	—	£18.00
K16	Man in Flight (Medals) including Mount	1970	£1.00	£16.00
M12	Olympic Greats (with Album)	1992	—	£2.00
M16	Wonders of the World (3-D)	1976	50p	£8.00
AUSTRALIAN ISSUES				
M60	Beetle Series (301-360)	1962	25p	£15.00
M60	Birds (121-180)	1960	40p	£24.00
M60	Butterflies and Moths (181-240)	1960	30p	£18.00
M60	Citizenship Series	1965	—	£11.00
M60	Discover Australia with Shell	1959	—	£27.50
M60	Meteorology Series (361-420)	1963	—	£12.00
M60	Pets (481-540)	1964	—	£20.00
M60	Shells, Fish and Coral (61-120)	1959	—	£18.50
M60	Transportation Series (241-300)	1961	—	£20.00

SHELL (Oil) — cont.

Qty		Date	Odds	Sets
NEW ZEALAND ISSUES				
M48	Aircraft of the World	1970	—	£7.50
M60	Cars of the World	1970	—	£15.00
M48	Racing Cars of the World	1970	50p	£24.00
40	Vintage Cars (Transfers)	1970	30p	£12.00
L40	World of Cricket	1992	—	£8.00
P20	World of Cricket (Doubles)	1992	—	£12.00

SHELLEY'S ICE CREAM

25	Essex-County Champions	1984	25p	£6.25

SHEPHERDS DAIRIES LTD.

100	War Series	1915	£6.50	—

SHERIDAN COLLECTIBLES (Commercial)

X12	Bobby Jones and St. Andrews	1995	—	£6.50
X1	Bobby Jones and St. Andrews, Promotional Card.	1995	—	50p
L7	Railway Posters – Golf	1996	—	£2.50
X1	St. Andrews, Advertisement Card	1995	—	50p
X12	The Bobby Jones Story	1993	—	£6.50
L6	The Golf Adventures of Par Bear	1994	—	£3.00
X25	The Players of the Ryder Cup '93	1994	—	£10.00
X12	The Tom Morris Story	1994	—	£6.50
X2	The Tom Morris Story, Substitute Cards	1995	—	£1.00
L7	"Underground Art" Football & Wembley	1996	—	£2.50
L7	"Underground Art" Rugby	1996	—	£2.50
L7	"Underground Art" Wimbledon	1996	—	£2.50
L7	"Underground Art" Windsor	1996	—	£2.50
L12	Winners of the Ryder Cup '95	1996	—	£6.50

SHERMAN'S POOLS LTD.

P8	Famous Film Stars	1940	55p	£4.40
P37	Famous Teams	1938	£3.00	£111.00
P2/37	Ditto (Aston Villa & Blackpool)	1938	—	£1.00
P38	Searchlight on Famous Players	1937	£3.50	—

W. SHIPTON LTD. (Commercial)

75	Trojan Gen-Cards	1959	80p	£60.00

SHUREY'S PUBLICATIONS LTD.

P?750	Views (Various Printings)	1906	80p	—

SIDELINES (Commercial)

L23	19th Century Cricket Teams	1988	—	£3.00

SILVER KING & CO. (Theatrical)

Qty		Date	Odds	Sets
1	Advertisement Card	1905	—	£10.00

SINGER SEWING MACHINE CO.

Qty		Date	Odds	Sets
52	Beauties (Playing Card Inset)	1898	£10.00	£520.00
P36	Costumes of All Nations	1892	£7.50	£270.00
P18	Costumes of All Nations (Different)	1894	£12.00	£220.00

SKETCHLEY CLEANERS

Qty		Date	Odds	Sets
25	A Nature Series	1960	—	£5.00
25	Communications	1960	—	£8.00
25	Tropical Birds	1960	—	£10.00

SKYBOX INTERNATIONAL (Commercial, U.S.A.)

Qty		Date	Odds	Sets
X60	Babylon 5	1996	—	£15.00
X100	Spider-Man Premium '96	1996	—	£15.00
P60	Star Trek: First Contact (Widevision)	1996	—	£18.00
X90	Star Trek: Master Series	1993	—	£12.50
X96	Star Trek: TNG: The Episodes – Season 2	1995	—	£18.00
X108	Star Trek: TNG: The Episodes – Season 3	1995	—	£18.00
X108	Star Trek: TNG: The Episodes – Season 4	1995	—	£18.00
X108	Star Trek: TNG: The Episodes – Season 5	1996	—	£12.00
X100	Star Trek: Voyager Season Two	1996	—	£25.00

SLADE & BULLOCK LTD. (Confectionery)

Qty		Date	Odds	Sets
25	Cricket Series	1924	*£50.00*	—
25	Football Terms	1924	£15.00	—
25	Modern Inventions	1925	£9.00	—
20	Now & Then Series	1925	£11.00	—
25	Nursery Rhymes	1925	£13.00	—
25	Science & Skill Series	1925	£11.00	—
25	Simple Toys & How to Make Them	1925	£12.00	—

P. SLUIS (Bird Food)

Qty		Date	Odds	Sets
X30	Tropical Birds	1962	—	£10.00

SMART NOVELS (Periodical)

Qty		Date	Odds	Sets
MF12	Stage Artistes & Entertainers	1924	£4.00	£48.00

JOHN SMITH (Brewers)

Qty		Date	Odds	Sets
P5	Limericks (Beer Mats)	1976	—	£2.50

SNAP CARDS (Gum)

Qty		Date	Odds	Sets
L50	ATV Stars, Series No. 1	1959	£1.20	£60.00

SNAP CARDS (Gum) — cont.

Qty		Date	Odds	Sets
L48	ATV Stars, Series No. 2	1960	£1.00	£48.00
L50	Associated-Rediffusion Stars	1960	£1.40	£70.00
L50	Dotto Celebrities	1959	90p	£45.00

H. A. SNOW (Films)

12	Hunting Big Game in Africa	1923	£5.00	£60.00

SOCCER BUBBLE GUM

M48	Soccer Teams, No.1 Series	1956	£1.25	£60.00
M48	Soccer Teams, No.2 Series	1958	£2.25	£108.00

SODASTREAM (Confectionery)

25	Historical Buildings	1957	—	£2.00

SOLDIER MAGAZINE

M24	The British Army - 1993	1993	—	£4.50

SOMPORTEX LTD. (Gum Vending)

X72	Adventures of Sexton Blake	1968	£1.00	£72.00
L60	Famous T.V. Wrestlers	1966	£1.75	£105.00
L60	Film Scene Series, James Bond 007	1966	£3.50	£210.00
L72	John Drake Danger Man	1966	£2.25	£162.00
L50	The Exciting World of James Bond 007	1965	£3.50	—
L72	The Saint	1967	£3.50	—
L71/72	Thunderball	1967	£1.25	£89.00
L72	Ditto	1967	—	£110.00
X73	Thunderbirds (Coloured)	1967	£3.50	£255.00
L72	Thunderbirds (Black & White)	1967	£3.50	£252.00
X72	Thunderbirds (Black & White)	1967	£2.25	£162.00
X36	Weirdies	1968	85p	£30.00
26	You Only Live Twice (Film Strips)	1969	£8.00	—

SONNY BOY (Confectionery)

50	Railway Engines	1960	—	£8.00

SOUTH AFRICAN EGGS

L6	Oeufs Travel Collection	1988	—	£2.75

SOUTH WALES CONSTABULARY

X36	British Stamps	1983	—	£8.50
L36	Castles and Historic Places in Wales	1988	—	£10.00
X36	Merthyr Tydfil Borough Council	1987	—	£10.00
X37	Payphones Past and Present	1987	—	£25.00
X36	Ryhmney Valley District Council	1986	—	£7.50
M32	Sport-A-Card	1991	—	£12.00
X35	The '82 Squad (Rugby)	1982	80p	£42.00

SPAR GROCERS

Qty		Date	Odds	Sets
X30	Disney on Parade	1972	£2.50	—

SPILLERS NEPHEWS (Biscuits)

Qty		Date	Odds	Sets
25	Conundrum Series	1910	£17.50	—
40	Views of South Wales & District	1910	£16.50	—

SPORT AND ADVENTURE (Periodical)

Qty		Date	Odds	Sets
M46	Famous Footballers	1922	£2.50	£115.00

SPORTING PROFILES (Commercial)

Qty		Date	Odds	Sets
L40	Henry Cooper: A Career History	1977	—	£10.95
L23	Heroes of the Prize Ring	1993	—	£6.00
X11	John L. Sullivan Cradle to Grave	1997	—	£5.00
L50	The Greatest (Muhammad Ali)	1993	—	£12.00

SPORT IN PRINT (Commercial)

Qty		Date	Odds	Sets
M64	Nottinghamshire Cricketers	1989	—	£12.50

SPORT PHOTOS (Commercial)

Qty		Date	Odds	Sets
96	"Smashers" (Soccer)	1950	£7.00	—

SPORTS TIME, INC. (Commercial, U.S.A.)

Qty		Date	Odds	Sets
X100	Baywatch	1995	—	£10.00
X100	Marilyn Monroe (1-100)	1993	—	£15.00
X100	Marilyn Monroe (101-200)	1995	—	£12.50

SPRATTS PATENT LTD. (Pet Food)

Qty		Date	Odds	Sets
K100	British Bird Series (Numbered)	1935	£3.25	—
K50	(Unnumbered)	1935	£2.25	£112.50
42	British Birds	1926	£3.50	£147.50
36	Champion Dogs	1926	£10.00	—
K20	Fish	1935	£10.00	—
K100	Poultry Series	1935	£8.00	—
12	Prize Dogs	1910	£30.00	—
12	Prize Poultry	1910	£27.50	—
25	The Bonzo Series	1924	£5.00	£125.00

STAR JUNIOR CLUB

Qty		Date	Odds	Sets
10	Animals	1960	£1.00	£10.00
10	Sports & Games (Numbered)	1960	£1.60	£16.00
5	Sports & Games (Unnumbered)	1960	£2.00	£10.00

STATE OF THE ARTS (Commercial)

Qty		Date	Odds	Sets
L6	Sex, Drugs & Rock'N'Roll	1994	—	£4.50

STAVELEY'S (Shop)

Qty		Date	Odds	Sets
24	World's Most Beautiful Birds	1924	£5.00	—

STEAM RAILWAY (Magazine)

Qty		Date	Odds	Sets
16	Railway Cigarette Cards	1988	—	£4.00

STOKES & DALTON (Cereals)

Qty		Date	Odds	Sets
M20	The Crimson Cobra	1950	£1.75	£35.00

STOLL (Films)

Qty		Date	Odds	Sets
25	Stars of To-Day	1930	£6.25	—
25	The Mystery of Dr. Fu-Manchu	1930	£8.50	—

STOLLWERCK (Chocolate)

Qty		Date	Odds	Sets
T144	Animal World	1902	£1.10	£160.00
F?100	Views of the World	1915	£4.00	—

THE SUN (Newspaper)

Qty		Date	Odds	Sets
M134	Football Swap Cards	1970	40p	£53.50
M52	Gallery of Football Action	1975	£1.60	£83.00
M6	How to Play Football	1975	£2.50	£15.00
M54	Page 3 Playing Cards	1979	—	£7.50
40	Pocket Book of Soccer Stickers (With Folders)	1989	—	£3.00
160	Royal Album Stickers (& Album)	1989	—	£5.00
P50	3D Gallery of Football Stars	1972	£2.00	—

SUNBLEST (Bread, Australia)

Qty		Date	Odds	Sets
M24	Sports Action Series	1975	—	£7.50
M25	Sunblest Explorer Cards	1975	—	£4.00

SUNBLEST TEA

Qty		Date	Odds	Sets
25	Inventions & Discoveries, 1st Series	1960	—	£7.50
25	Inventions & Discoveries, 2nd Series	1960	—	£10.00
25	Prehistoric Animals, 1st Series	1960	—	£7.50
25	Prehistoric Animals, 2nd Series	1960	—	£6.00

SUNDAY EMPIRE NEWS

Qty		Date	Odds	Sets
48	Famous Footballers of Today (Durling)	1953	£3.00	£144.00

SUNDAY STORIES (Periodical)

Qty		Date	Odds	Sets
M5	Flags (Silk)	1916	£12.00	—
M6	The King & His Soldiers (Silk)	1916	£12.50	£75.00

THE SUNDAY TIMES (Newspaper)

Qty		*Date*	*Odds*	*Sets*
X100	Great Cars of the World (With Album)	1989	—	£6.00
40	Seaside Project (& Wallchart)	1989	—	£3.00
40	200 Years of Cricket (& Wallchart)	1989	—	£5.00
40	Young Persons Guide to the Orchestra (& Wallchart).	1989	—	£3.00

SWEETACRE (Confectionery, Australia)

48	Aircraft of the World	1932	£2.50	£120.00
36	Cricketers (Minties)	1926	£9.00	£325.00
24	Cricketers (Caricatures)	1938	*£17.50*	—
48	Favourite Dogs	1932	£3.25	—
32	Prominent Cricketers (33-64)	1932	£3.25	£104.00
48	Sports Champions	1930	£3.00	£300.00
48	Steamships of the World	1932	£2.50	£125.00
32	Test Records (1-32)	1932	£3.25	£104.00
48	This World of Ours	1932	£3.00	—

SWEETULE PRODUCTS (Confectionery)

18	Aircraft (Packet)	1954	£4.50	£80.00
25	A Nature Series	1960	—	£2.50
25	Animals of the Countryside	1959	—	£2.50
25	Archie Andrews Jokes	1957	£6.00	—
25	Birds and Their Eggs	1954	—	£2.00
25	Birds and Their Eggs (Black Back)	1959	—	£5.00
25	(Blue Back)	1959	—	£5.00
25	Birds & Their Haunts	1958	£3.25	—
52	Birds, Fish & Flowers (P/C Inset)	1961	—	£13.50
25	Birds of the British Commonwealth (Black Back)	1954	—	£2.00
25	(Blue Back)	1954	—	£2.50
M12	Coronation Series 1953 (Packet)	1953	£6.00	—
25	Do You Know?	1963	—	£3.00
25	Family Crests	1961	—	£2.25
25	Famous Sports Records	1957	—	£11.00
25	Football Club Nicknames	1959	—	£6.50
K18	Historical Cars & Cycles	1957	—	£9.00
18	Home Pets (Packet)	1954	£6.00	—
25	International Footballers (Packet)	1962	£5.50	£137.50
25	Junior Service Quiz	1959	—	£2.50
18	Landmarks of Flying (Packet)	1961	£4.50	£81.00
50	Modern Aircraft	1954	—	£6.00
25	Modern Transport	1955	—	£2.00
18	Motor Cars (Packet)	1952	£7.50	—
50	Motorcycles Old and New	1963	—	£70.00
30	National Flags & Costumes	1962	—	£15.00
25	Naval Battles	1959	—	£3.00
25	Products of the World	1958	—	£2.00
24	Racing Cars of the World (Packet)	1960	£7.00	—
18	Railway Engines — Past & Present (Packet)	1953	£6.00	£108.00
25	Sports Quiz	1958	—	£3.50
1	Stamp Card (Real Stamp Attached)	1962	—	35p
25	Stamp Cards	1961	—	£3.50
25	The Wild West (Black Back)	1960	—	£10.00
25	(Blue Back)	1960	—	£2.00
X30	Trains of the World	1960	—	£40.00

SWEETULE PRODUCTS (Confectionery) — cont.

Qty		*Date*	*Odds*	*Sets*
25	Treasure Island	1957	—	£6.00
25	Tropical Birds	1954	—	£3.50
25	Vintage Cars	1964	—	£7.50
25	Weapons of Defence	1959	—	£2.50
25	Wild Animals	1958	—	£2.50
25	Wild Flowers	1961	—	£2.00
25	Wonders of the World	1956	—	£2.00

SWETTENHAM (Tea)

25	Aircraft of the World	1959	—	£10.00
25	Animals of the Countryside	1959	—	£2.00
25	Birds and Their Eggs	1958	—	£2.00
25	British Coins and Costumes	1958	—	£3.50
25	Butterflies and Moths	1958	—	£2.00
25	Evolution of the Royal Navy	1957	—	£2.00
25	Into Space	1959	—	£2.25
24	The Island of Ceylon (Conqueror Tea)	1964	£3.00	—
25	Wild Animals	1958	—	£5.00

W. SWORD & CO. (Biscuits)

25	British Empire at Work	1925	£10.00	—
20	Dogs	1926	£11.00	—
20	Inventors & Their Inventions	1926	*£10.00*	—
25	Safety First	1927	*£10.00*	—
25	Sports & Pastimes Series	1926	*£10.00*	—
25	Vehicles of All Ages	1924	*£10.00*	—
25	Zoo Series (Brown)	1928	£8.00	£200.00
25	Zoo Series (Coloured, Different)	1928	£10.00	—

TEACHER'S WHISKY

L12	Scottish Clans & Castles (Circular)	1955	£2.00	—

TEAMS LTD. (Commercial)

40	40 Years of Cards (Brooke Bond)	1994	—	£4.00

TEASDALE & CO. (Confectionery)

50	Cinema Stars (Anon.)	1935	£4.50	—
25	Great War Series	1916	£16.50	—

TESCO STORES

P6	Nature Trail Stickers	1989	—	£1.25

TETLEY TEA

48	British Birds	1970	£2.00	£96.00

TEXACO PETROL

Qty		*Date*	*Odds*	*Sets*
12	Texaco Trophy Cricket Cards	1984	30p	£3.50

D. C. THOMSON & CO. LTD. (Periodical)

Qty		Date	Odds	Sets
L30	Adventure Pictures	1929	£2.25	£67.50
M16	Badges of the Fighting Fliers	1939	£2.25	£36.00
P26	Battles for the Flag	1939	£4.00	—
K80	Boys of All Nations	1936	90p	—
20	British Birds and Eggs	1930	£2.25	£45.00
F11	British Team of Footballers	1923	£2.50	£27.50
L20	Canvas Masterpieces (Silk)	1925	£8.50	—
16	Catch-My-Pal Cards	1939	£1.25	£20.00
X12	Coloured Photos of Star Footballers	1927	£4.25	—
64	County Cricketers	1955	£2.00	£128.00
16	Cricket Crests	1934	£7.50	£120.00
KF8	Cricketers	1923	£2.50	£20.00
X24	Cricketers	1924	£7.25	£174.00
P16	Cup-Tie Stars of All Nations	1962	£2.50	£40.00
12	Dandy Dogs	1928	£3.50	—
K28	Dominoes — School Caricatures	1936	£2.00	£56.00
20	Easy Scientific Experiments	1930	£2.00	—
MF18	Famous British Footballers (English)	1923	£2.25	£40.00
K80	Famous Feats	1937	£1.00	—
24	Famous Fights	1935	£1.60	—
25	Famous Footballers	1955	£1.40	£35.00
24	Famous Footballers (Different)	1956	£1.35	£32.50
20	Famous Liners	1930	£2.75	£55.00
L32	Famous Ships	1931	£3.50	£112.00
P12	Famous Teams in Football History	1961	£3.50	£42.00
P16	Famous Teams in Football History, 2nd Series	1962	£3.50	£56.00
16	Flags of All Nations	1934	£2.00	£32.00
K80	Flags of the Sea	1937	85p	—
KF137	Footballers	1923	80p	—
F18	Footballers	1923	£1.75	£31.50
X8	Footballers	1933	£5.00	£40.00
K52	Footballers — Hunt the Cup Cards	1934	£2.00	—
24	Footballers — Motor Cars (Double-Sided)	1929	£6.25	£150.00
MF22	Footballers — Signed Real Photos	1923	£1.65	£36.50
F40	Football Photos	1925	£4.25	—
48	Football Stars	1957	£1.50	£72.00
44	Football Stars of 1959	1959	£2.00	£88.00
K60/64	Football Team Cards	1934	90p	£54.00
64	Football Tips & Tricks	1955	75p	£48.00
L32	Football Towns and Their Crests	1931	£3.75	£120.00
T12	Great Captains	1972	£3.25	£39.00
12	Guns in Action	1938	£1.50	£18.00
M8	Hidden Treasure Clue Cards	1930	£11.50	—
P16	International Cup Teams	1964	£2.50	£40.00
6	Ju-Jitsu Cards	1925	£4.00	£24.00
24	Motor Bike Cards	1926	£5.00	£120.00
20	Motor Cycles	1930	£5.50	—
K100	Motor Cars	1934	90p	—
11	Mystic Menagerie	1925	£5.00	£55.00
36	1930 Speedway Stars	1930	£5.75	£210.00
K80	Punishment Cards	1936	£1.00	—

D. C. THOMSON & CO. LTD. (Periodical) — cont.

Qty		Date	Odds	Sets
12	Queer Animals	1928	£2.25	£27.00
16	Queer Birds	1934	£2.00	£32.00
K80	Secrets of Cricket	1936	£1.75	—
36	Spadgers Monster Collection of Spoofs	1936	£2.25	—
48	Speed	1937	80p	£40.00
12	Speedsters of the Wilds	1928	£2.25	£27.00
48	Stars of Sport and Entertainment	1960	£1.25	£60.00
8/12	Star Footballers (Metal)	1932	£10.00	—
P22	Star Teams of 1961	1961	£2.50	£55.00
P16	The Great Stars of Football	1968	£2.25	£36.00
20	The Wireless Telephone	1930	£2.00	£40.00
32	The World's Best Cricketers (Green)	1932	£2.00	£64.00
36	The World's Best Cricketers (Mauve)	1930	£5.00	£180.00
72	The World's Best Cricketers	1958	£1.75	£126.00
X12	The World's Biggest	1937	£5.50	£66.00
32	This Seasons Latest Motor Cars (Metal)	1926	£12.50	—
K24	This Year's Motor Car Crests (Metal)	1926	£12.50	—
24	This Year's Top-Form Footballers	1924	£2.00	£48.00
P12	Top Cup Teams (Hornet)	1966	£3.50	£42.00
10	Vanguard Photo Gallery	1923	£10.00	—
96	VP Flips	1925	£1.00	—
24	Warrior Cards (Sectional Back)	1929	£2.00	£48.00
K28	Warrior Cards (Domino Back)	1936	£1.50	£42.00
K80	Warrior Cards	1937	90p	—
20	Why?	1930	£1.75	—
K28	Wild West Dominoes	1936	£1.75	£50.00
20	Wonders of the Rail	1930	£3.50	£70.00
20	Wonders of the World	1930	£1.75	£35.00
64	World Cup Footballers	1958	£2.00	£128.00
M72	World Cup Stars	1971	£2.00	£144.00

THURMER & SYMES (Biscuits)

Qty		Date	Odds	Sets
M96	Ocean Giants	1954	£2.00	—

TIMARU MILLING CO. (Cereals, New Zealand)

Qty		Date	Odds	Sets
36	Focus on Fame	1948	—	£12.00
37	Peace & Progress	1947	—	£12.00
36	Victory Album Cards	1946	—	£17.50

TIMES CONFECTIONERY CO. LTD.

Qty		Date	Odds	Sets
MF24	Roy Rogers — In Old Amarillo (Plain Back)	1955	—	£8.00
M24	(Printed Back)	1955	—	£12.50
MF24	Roy Rogers — South Of Caliente (Plain Back)	1955	—	£8.00
M24	(Printed Back)	1955	—	£12.50

TIMPERLEY CARD COLLECTORS (Club)

Qty		Date	Odds	Sets
10	Timperley Types	1980	—	£7.50
10	Timperley Types, Second Series	1981	—	£4.50
10	Timperley Types, Third Series	1981	—	£4.50
10	Timperley Types, Fourth Series	1982	—	£4.00

TIMPERLEY CARD COLLECTORS (Club) — cont.

Qty		*Date*	*Odds*	*Sets*
10	Timperley Types, Fifth Series	1982	—	£4.00
10	Timperley Types, Sixth Series	1983	—	£4.00
10	Timperley Types, Seventh Series	1983	—	£4.00
10	Timperley Types, Eighth Series	1985	—	£4.00
10	Timperley Types, Nineth Series	1987	—	£4.00
10	Timperley Types, Tenth Series	1989	—	£4.00
10	Timperley Types, Eleventh Series	1990	—	£4.00
10	Timperley Types, Twelfth Series	1991	—	£4.00
10	Timperley Types, Thirteenth Series	1991	—	£4.00

TIP TOP (Ice Cream, New Zealand)

Qty		Date	Odds	Sets
M10	Galactic Bar	1977	—	£10.00

TIP TOP SALES COMPANY (Malta)

Qty		Date	Odds	Sets
M25	European Football Action, Series A	1932	£8.00	£200.00

TIT-BITS (Periodical)

Qty		Date	Odds	Sets
K54	Pin-Ups (P/C Inset)	1976	—	£5.00
TF17	Star Cover Girls	1953	£4.00	—
T12	Tit-Bits Clubs	1977	—	£15.00

CHOCOLAT TOBLER LTD.

Qty		Date	Odds	Sets
50	Famous Footballers	1939	£7.50	—
T186	General Interest Series	1900	£1.10	£205.00

TOBY (Periodical)

Qty		Date	Odds	Sets
24	Dogs (Anon.)	1926	£3.60	£86.50
24	Dogs, 2nd Series (25-48, Anon.)	1926	£3.75	—
24	Sights of London (Anon.)	1926	£3.00	£72.00
24	Toby's Bird Series	1926	*£3.00*	—
24	Toby's Ship Series	1926	£3.25	£78.00
24	Toby's Travel Series	1926	£3.00	£72.00

TODAY (Newspaper)

Qty		Date	Odds	Sets
X14	Around Britain	1991	—	£2.00

TOMMY GUNN (Toys)

Qty		Date	Odds	Sets
50	Medals (Plain Back)	1971	—	£4.00

TOM THUMB (New Zealand)

Qty		Date	Odds	Sets
M24	Supercars	1980	—	£10.00

TONIBELL (Ice Cream)

Qty		Date	Odds	Sets
12	Action Soldiers (with Cadbury)	1976	—	£2.50
M20	Banknotes	1974	15p	£3.00
M12	Beautiful Butterflies	1974	15p	£2.00
M20	County Badge Collection	1974	15p	£3.00
25	Did You Know?	1963	—	£2.50
L12	Did You Know? (Different)	1975	50p	—
X12	England's Soccer Stars	1970	£2.50	£30.00
D19	Famous Sports Trophies	1976	—	£7.00
D12	Farmyard Stencils	1977	—	£4.00
M24	1st Division Football League Club Badges	1972	£1.25	£30.00
X12	Horses in the Service of Man	1984	75p	£9.00
25	Inventions that Changed the World	1963	—	£2.50
X10	Junior Champs	1983	50p	£5.00
M24	Kings of the Road	1977	75p	—
L24	Pop Star Cameos	1975	—	£6.50
K36	Team of All Time	1971	£1.50	£54.00
25	The World's Passenger Liners	1963	—	£2.50
25	This Changing World (With Line)	1963	—	£5.00
25	(Without Line)	1963	—	£6.00
25	Wonders of the Heavens	1963	—	£7.50

TOP FLIGHT (Confectionery)

Qty		Date	Odds	Sets
25	Top Flight Stars (Sport)	1960	—	£60.00

TOPICAL TIMES (Periodical)

Qty		Date	Odds	Sets
E8	Cricketers	1938	£12.50	£100.00
M6	Football Teams (Metal)	1924	£12.00	—
MF6	Football Teams	1924	£4.50	£27.00
MF10	Footballers (Pairs)	1924	£3.00	—
E12	Footballers, Panel Portraits	1932	£4.00	£48.00
E24	Footballers, Panel Portraits	1933	£3.50	—
E14	Footballers, Panel Portraits	1934	£3.00	£42.00
E14	Footballers, Panel Portraits	1935	£3.00	£42.00
E16	Footballers, Panel Portraits (Coloured)	1936	£3.50	£56.00
E14	Footballers, Panel Portraits	1938	£3.00	£42.00
E16	Footballers, Panel Portraits	1939	£3.00	£48.00
E8	Footballers, Special Issue (Coloured)	1934	£5.00	£40.00
E8	Footballers, Triple Portraits	1937	£5.00	£40.00
L24	Great Players	1938	£2.50	£60.00
P24	Miniature Panel Portraits	1937	£2.50	£60.00
P24	Stars of To-Day	1938	£2.50	£60.00

TOP NOTE SLIDES

Qty		Date	Odds	Sets
P9	Pop Singers	1952	£4.50	—

TOPPS CHEWING GUM INC.

Qty		Date	Odds	Sets
L80	A.L.F.	1988	—	£12.50
L88	American Baseball Stars	1988	—	£17.50
L88	American Baseball Stars	1989	—	£17.50

TOPPS CHEWING GUM INC. — cont.

Qty		Date	Odds	Sets
X99	Autos of 1977	1977	£1.25	—
X98	Batman Returns (with Stickers)	1993	—	£3.00
X132	Battlestar Galactica	1979	20p	£26.00
X66	Bay City Rollers	1978	30p	£20.00
X49	Comic Book Heroes	1975	£1.50	£75.00
X99	Dick Tracy	1990	—	£10.00
P18	England World Cup Supersquad	1990	—	£9.00
X220	Footballers (Red Back)	1975	60p	—
X88	Footballers (Scottish, Blue Back)	1975	£1.00	—
X330	Footballers (Blue Back)	1976	40p	£132.00
X132	Footballers (Scottish, Red Back)	1976	£1.00	—
X330	Footballers (Red Back)	1977	50p	£165.00
X132	Footballers (Scottish, Yellow Back)	1977	60p	£80.00
X396	Footballers (Orange Back)	1978	20p	£80.00
X132	Footballers (Scottish, Green Back)	1978	50p	£66.00
X396	Footballers (Pale Blue Back)	1979	40p	—
X132	Footballers (Scottish, Red Back)	1979	50p	£66.00
X66	Footballers (Pink Back)	1980	£1.00	—
X65	Footballers (Blue Back)	1981	60p	£39.00
X200	Footballers Stadium Club	1992	—	£10.00
X10/14	Footballers Stadium Club Promotion Cards	1992	—	£1.50
E18	Football Posters	1980	75p	£13.50
X21	Funny Puzzles	1978	£1.25	—
L41	Garbage Pail Kids, 1st Series A	1986	—	£10.00
L41	Garbage Pail Kids, 1st Series B	1986	—	£10.00
L42	Garbage Pail Kids, 2nd Series A	1986	—	£10.00
L42	Garbage Pail Kids, 2nd Series B	1986	—	£12.50
L55	Garbage Pail Kids, 3rd Series A	1987	—	£10.00
L70	Garbage Pail Kids, 3rd Series B	1987	—	£12.50
L48	Garbage Pail Kids, 4th Series A	1987	—	£10.00
L76	Garbage Pail Kids, 4th Series B	1987	—	£12.50
L60	Garbage Pail Kids, 5th Series A	1988	—	£10.00
L70	Garbage Pail Kids, 5th Series B	1988	—	£10.00
L44	Garbage Pail Kids, 6th Series A	1988	—	£10.00
L88	Garbage Pail Kids, 6th Series B	1988	—	£12.50
X77	Home Alone 2 (with Stickers)	1993	—	£3.00
X44	Home and Away	1987	—	£5.00
X110	Hook (with Stickers)	1991	—	£8.50
X99	Jurassic Park (with Stickers)	1993	—	£10.00
X49	Marvel Super Heroes	1980	£1.00	£49.00
X48	Monster In My Pocket	1991	—	£4.00
X66	Planet of the Apes	1974	£1.25	—
M75	Pro-Cycling	1988	—	£7.50
X72	Railway Quiz (See A. & B. C.)	1959	—	—
L264	Saint & Greavsie	1988	—	£20.00
X50	Shocking Laffs	1977	£1.00	—
X66	Spitting Image	1990	—	£10.00
X88	Star Trek, The Motion Picture	1980	£1.25	—
X66	Star Wars (1-66)	1978	£1.00	—
X66	Star Wars (1A-66A)	1978	£1.75	—
X66	Superman The Movie, 1st Series (1-66)	1979	30p	£20.00
X66	Superman The Movie, 2nd Series (67-132)	1979	25p	£16.50
X77	Teenage Mutant Hero Turtles (T.V.)	1990	—	£7.50
X143	Teenage Mutant Ninja Turtles (Film)	1990	—	£6.00
M44	Terminator 2	1991	20p	—
X88	The Black Hole	1980	30p	£27.00

TOPPS CHEWING GUM INC. — cont.

Qty		Date	Odds	Sets
X99	The Flintstones (with Stickers)	1994	—	£6.00
X110	The Simpsons (with Stickers)	1990	—	£6.50
X66	The Very Best of Stingray, Thunderbirds and Captain Scarlet	1993	—	£6.00
X30	Wacky Packages	1982	—	£7.50
X66	Wacky Wrestling	1993	—	£3.00
X42	Wanted Posters	1978	50p	£21.00
X66	World Championship Wrestling	1992	—	£3.00

U.S. ISSUES

Qty		Date	Odds	Sets
X154	Batman — The Movie (with Stickers)	1989	—	£20.00
X88	Buck Rogers in the 25th Century	1979	20p	£18.00
X77	Close Encounters	1982	—	£15.00
X36	Donkey Kong	1982	—	£5.00
P72	Dragonhearts (Widevision)	1996	—	£12.00
X66	Funny Valentines	1960	—	£40.00
X99	Ghostbusters II (with Stickers)	1989	—	£17.50
X99	Greatest Olympics	1983	—	£10.50
X88	Gremlins 2	1990	—	£9.00
X59	Jaws 2	1978	—	£12.50
X99	Jurassic Park (with Stickers)	1993	—	£15.00
X33	Michael Jackson, 1st Stickers	1984	—	£5.00
X55	Mysteries of India	1967	—	£32.00
X66	Rambo	1985	—	£12.00
X22	Rambo (Stickers)	1985	—	£4.50
X99	Rocky II	1981	—	£10.00
X22	Rocky II (Stickers)	1981	—	£5.00
X66	Rocky IV	1986	—	£7.00
X11	Rocky IV (Stickers)	1986	—	£4.00
G12	Smurf Tattoos	1983	—	£17.50
X90	Star Wars Finest	1996	—	£39.00
X66	Star Wars Series 3 (Yellow)	1977	—	£35.00
X66	Star Wars Series 4 (Green)	1977	—	£35.00
X66	Star Wars Series 5 (Orange)	1977	—	£35.00
X90	Star Wars: Shadows of the Empire	1996	—	£16.00
P72	Star Wars Trilogy (Widevision)	1997	—	£17.50
X88	Superman II	1981	—	£15.00
X99	Superman III	1983	—	£10.00
X143	Teenage Mutant Ninja Turtles (Film)	1990	—	£10.00
X99	Teenage Mutant Ninja Turtles (T.V.)	1989	—	£7.50
X66	The 'A' Team	1983	—	£7.50
P144	The Empire Strikes Back (Widevision)	1995	—	£23.00
X86	The Goonies	1987	—	£12.00
X72	The X Files Season One	1995	—	£14.00
X72	The X Files Season Two	1996	—	£12.00
X72	The X Files Season Three	1996	—	£12.00
P72	The X Files Showcase (Widevision)	1997	—	£15.00
X55	Weird Wheels	1980	—	£7.50

JOHN TORDOFF & SON LTD. (Tea)

Qty		Date	Odds	Sets
25	Safety First	1926	£7.50	—
25	The Growth and Manufacture of Tea	1926	£7.50	—

TOTAL PETROL

Qty		Date	Odds	Sets
X25	Return to Oz	1985	—	£3.50

TOWER TEA

Qty		Date	Odds	Sets
24	Illustrated Sayings	1910	£20.00	—

TREBOR BASSETT LTD. (Confectionery)

Qty		Date	Odds	Sets
48	Football 1991-2	1991	—	£10.00
48	Football 1992-3	1992	—	£6.00
48	Football 1995-6	1995	—	£7.50
P20	Jurassic Park (Slides)	1993	—	£8.00
48	Premier Players	1995	—	£6.00
48	Sonic the Hedgehog	1991	—	£6.00
48	World Beaters (Soccer)	1994	—	£6.00

TREBOR/SHARP (Confectionery)

Qty		Date	Odds	Sets
25	Famous Pets	1972	—	£3.00
M48	Space Series	1964	£2.00	—
M48	V.C. Heroes	1964	£2.00	—

TRENOUTHS (Shop)

Qty		Date	Odds	Sets
24	World's Most Beautiful Butterflies	1924	£5.00	—

TRIO BARS (Confectionery)

Qty		Date	Odds	Sets
M6	Roland Rat Superstar	1990	—	£4.00

TRUCARDS (Commercial)

Qty		Date	Odds	Sets
M30	Animals	1972	—	£2.50
M30	Battle of Britain	1972	—	£4.00
M30	Flowers	1972	—	£3.00
M30	History of Aircraft	1972	—	£3.00
M30	Sport	1972	—	£3.00
M30	Veteran & Vintage Cars	1972	—	£3.00
M30	World War I	1972	—	£3.00
M30	World War II	1972	—	£2.00

TUCKETT'S (Confectionery)

Qty		Date	Odds	Sets
25	Photos of Cricketers	1925	£25.00	—
50	Photos of Film Stars	1939	£5.50	—
25	Photos of Football Stars	1925	£15.00	—

W. & E. TURNER (Shoes)

Qty		Date	Odds	Sets
20	War Pictures	1915	£12.00	£240.00

TWININGS TEA

Qty		Date	Odds	Sets
30	Rare Stamps	1960	50p	£15.00
30	Rare Stamps, 2nd Series	1960	—	£4.00
30	2nd Series (Red Overprint)	1961	—	£2.50

TYPHOO TEA LTD.

36 Page Illustrated Reference Book — £3.50

Qty		Date	Odds	Sets
25	Aesop's Fables	1924	£2.40	£60.00
25	Ancient & Annual Customs	1922	£1.40	£35.00
T25	Animal Friends of Man	1927	£3.60	£90.00
T25	Animal Offence & Defence	1926	£1.40	£35.00
T25	A Tale of Two Cities	1931	£2.60	£65.00
24	British Birds & Their Eggs	1914	£8.00	—
T25	British Birds and Their Eggs	1936	£1.30	£32.50
29/30	British Empire at Work	1925	£1.00	£30.00
30	British Empire at Work Continuation Card	1925	£6.00	—
1	British Empire at Work Last Chance Card	1925	—	£7.00
25	Calendar 1934 (Dogs)	1933	£20.00	—
25	Calendar 1936	1935	£10.00	—
T1	Calendar 1937	1936	—	£8.00
T25	Characters from Shakespeare	1937	£1.00	£25.00
25	Common Objects Highly Magnified	1925	£1.00	£25.00
25	Conundrums	1915	£13.50	—
24	Do You Know	1962	—	£2.00
T25	Famous Voyages	1934	£1.20	£30.00
M20	Flags & Arms of Countries	1916	£11.00	£220.00
24	Great Achievements	1962	—	£17.50
T25	Historic Buildings	1936	£1.10	£27.50
T25	Homes of Famous Men	1934	60p	£15.00
T25	Horses	1935	£1.00	£25.00
T25	Important Industries of the British Empire	1939	50p	£12.50
T25	Interesting Events in British History	1938	50p	£12.50
T25	John Halifax, Gentleman	1932	£2.00	£50.00
T25	Lorna Doone	1930	£2.80	£70.00
10	Nursery Rhymes	1914	£18.00	—
24	Our Empire's Defenders	1916	£22.00	£525.00
48	Puzzle Pictures	1913	£24.00	—
T30	Robin Hood & His Merry Men	1928	£5.50	£165.00
M12	The Amazing World of Doctor Who	1976	£1.75	£21.00
T30	The Story of David Copperfield	1929	£2.20	£66.00
T25	The Swiss Family Robinson	1935	£1.50	£37.50
24	Travel through the Ages	1962	—	£2.00
T25	Trees of the Countryside	1938	60p	£15.00
T25	Whilst We Sleep	1928	£1.60	£40.00
24	Wild Flowers	1961	—	£2.00
T25	Wild Flowers in their Families	1936	90p	£22.50
T25	Wild Flowers in their Families, 2nd Series	1937	90p	£22.50
T25	Wonder Cities of the World	1933	£1.20	£30.00
M24	Wonderful World of Disney	1975	£2.25	£54.00
T25	Work on the Farm	1933	£1.30	£32.50
25	Zoo Series	1932	70p	£17.50
PACKAGE ISSUES				
20	By Pond & Stream	1955	30p	£6.00
20	Common British Birds	1955	30p	£6.00
20	Costumes of the World	1955	40p	£8.00

TYPHOO TEA LTD. — cont.

Qty		Date	Odds	Sets
24	Do You Know	1962	30p	£7.50
20	Famous Bridges	1955	30p	£6.00
20	Famous Buildings	1955	20p	£4.00
24	Famous Football Clubs	1962	£1.00	£24.00
24	Famous Football Clubs, 2nd Series	1963	£1.00	£24.00
35	Football Club Plaques	1973	£3.00	—
24	Football Stars, New Series	1973	£2.00	£48.00
24	Great Voyages of Discovery	1962	40p	£10.00
24	International Football Stars	1967	£1.75	£42.00
24	International Football Stars, 2nd Series	1969	£2.25	—
24	100 Years of Great British Achievements	1972	50p	£12.00
20	Pets	1955	25p	£5.00
20	Some Countryside Animals	1955	25p	£5.00
20	Some Popular Breeds of Dogs	1955	65p	£13.00
20	Some World Wonders	1955	30p	£6.00
24	Travel through the Ages	1962	25p	£6.00
20	Types of Ships	1955	30p	£6.00
20	Wild Animals	1955	20p	£4.00
24	Wild Flowers	1961	50p	£12.00
PREMIUM ISSUES				
E24	Famous Football Clubs	1964	£8.50	—
E24	Famous Football Clubs, 2nd Series	1965	£6.50	£156.00
E24	Football Stars	1973	£6.50	£156.00
G24	Great Voyages of Discovery	1967	*£3.00*	—
E24	International Football Stars, 1st Series	1967	£6.00	£144.00
E24	International Football Stars, 2nd Series	1969	£6.00	£144.00
G24	100 Years of British Achievements	1972	—	£17.50

TYSON & CO. (Soap)

Qty		Date	Odds	Sets
28	Semaphore Signals	1912	£13.00	£365.00

UNION JACK (Periodical)

Qty		Date	Odds	Sets
MF6	Monarchs of the Ring	1923	£8.00	£48.00
M8	Police of All Nations	1922	£5.00	£40.00

UNITED AUTOMOBILE SERVICES

Qty		Date	Odds	Sets
25	Castles (Series No. 1)	1925	£5.50	—
25	Churches (Series No. 2)	1925	£5.50	—
25	Places of Interest (Series No. 4)	1925	£5.50	—
25	"United" (Series No. 3)	1925	£5.50	—

UNITED CONFECTIONERY CO.

Qty		Date	Odds	Sets
50	Wild Animals of the World	1905	£8.50	—

UNITED DAIRIES

Qty		Date	Odds	Sets
25	Aquarium Fish	1962	—	£5.00
25	Birds and Their Eggs	1961	—	£10.00
25	British Uniforms of the 19th Century	1962	—	£10.00
25	The Story of Milk	1966	—	£7.50
25	The West	1963	—	£12.50

UNIVERSAL AUTOMATICS LTD.

Qty		Date	Odds	Sets
X30	Trains of the World	1958	—	£16.50

UNIVERSAL CIGARETTE CARD CO. LTD.

Qty		Date	Odds	Sets
15	Australian Cricket Team 1905	1986	—	£3.00
13	Car Registration Numbers (Irish)	1987	—	£4.00
15	English Cricketers 1902	1987	—	£3.00
25	Military Maids	1987	—	£4.50
25	People of the World	1987	—	£3.50

UNUSUALLY FUNNY FACTORY LTD. (Gum)

Qty		Date	Odds	Sets
M40	Prehistorigum	1990	—	£6.50
M40	Team — Spirits	1990	—	£6.50

VAUXHALL MOTORS LIMITED

Qty		Date	Odds	Sets
L25	Vauxhall Motor Sport Series	1993	—	£7.50
L25	Vauxhall's 90th Anniversary Series	1993	—	£7.50

VENORLANDUS (Commercial)

Qty		Date	Odds	Sets
M48	World of Sport — Our Heroes	1980	—	£17.50

VERKADE'S FABRIEKEN N.V. (Biscuits, Holland)

Qty		Date	Odds	Sets
T120	Cactussen	1931	—	£13.00
T140	De Bloemen en Haar Vrienden	1933	—	£14.00
T140	De Boerderij	1935	—	£26.50
T138	Hans de Torenkraai	1936	—	£14.00
T132	Kamerplanten	1928	—	£26.50
T126	Mijn Aquarium	1925	—	£26.50
T126	Vetplanten	1926	—	£16.50

VICTORIA GALLERY (Commercial)

Officially Authorised Reprints of Imperial Tobacco Co. Series

Qty		Date	Odds	Sets
P4	Advertisement Postcards (Wills)	1988	—	£5.00
50	Aeroplanes (Civil) (Player)	1990	—	£7.50
50	Aviary & Cage Birds (Player)	1989	—	£7.50
L25	Aviary & Cage Birds (Player)	1987	—	£7.50
50	Boxing Personalities (Churchman)	1990	—	£7.50
25	Characters from Dickens (Player)	1990	—	£6.00
25	Cinema Stars (Smith)	1988	—	£6.00
50	Derby and Grand National Winners (Player)	1988	—	£7.50
L25	Dogs (Wills)	1987	—	£7.50
25	England's Naval Heroes (Player)	1988	—	£10.00
L25	Famous Golfers (Wills)	1987	—	£7.50
50	Film Stars, Third Series (Player)	1989	—	£7.50
50	Fish & Bait (Wills)	1990	—	£7.50
L25	Game Birds & Wild Fowl (Player)	1987	—	£7.50

VICTORIA GALLERY (Commercial) — cont.

Qty		Date	Odds	Sets
L25	Golf (Player)	1986	—	£7.50
50	Jockeys, 1930 (Ogdens)	1990	—	£7.50
L25	Lawn Tennis, 1931 (Wills)	1988	—	£7.50
50	Motor Cycles (B.A.T.)	1991	—	£7.50
25	Motors (Lambert & Butler 1908)	1992	—	£6.00
58	Musical Celebrities, Second Series (Wills)	1988	—	£8.50
25	Napoleon (Player)	1989	—	£6.00
L12	Prominent Golfers (Churchman)	1989	—	£5.00
50	Racing Greyhounds (Churchman)	1989	—	£7.50
L25	Racing Yachts (Player)	1987	—	£7.50
12	Recruiting Posters (Wills)	1988	—	£3.00
L25	Rigs of Ships (Wills)	1987	—	£7.50
	Original Issues			
L6	A Gathering of Spirits	1994	—	£2.50
L20	American Civil War Leaders	1992	—	£6.00
L20	Boxing Champions	1991	—	£10.00
L21	Boxing Champions, Second Series	1992	—	£6.00
L6	British Birds of Prey	1994	—	£2.50
L6	British Birds of Prey (Different)	1996	—	£2.50
L20	Caricatures of the British Army	1994	—	£6.00
L20	Caricatures of the British Army II	1994	—	£6.00
L6	Classic Motor Cycles (Harley Davidson)	1993	—	£2.50
L20	Endangered Wild Animals	1991	—	£6.00
L25	Hollywood Moviemen	1993	—	£7.50
L2	Promotional Cards	1993	—	60p
L20	Legends of Hollywood	1991	—	£6.00
L1	Promotional Card (John Wayne)	1991	—	50p
L25	Olympic Greats	1992	—	£7.50
L20	Partners (Cinema)	1992	—	£6.00
L20	Snooker Celebrities	1988	—	£6.00
L10	Spirit of A Nation	1991	—	£5.00
L25	The Ryder Cup, 1991	1991	—	£15.00
L12	The Twelve Days of Christmas	1992	—	£6.00
L20	Uniforms of the American Civil War	1992	—	£6.00
L24	Uniforms of the War of Independence	1993	—	£8.00
L48	Wild West	1993	—	£15.00

CHOCOLAT DE VILLARS

Qty		Date	Odds	Sets
24	British Birds and Their Eggs	1926	£2.25	£54.00

VOMO AUTOMATICS

Qty		Date	Odds	Sets
X50	Flags of the World	1965	65p	£32.50

JONATHAN WALES LTD.

Qty		Date	Odds	Sets
25	The History of Flight, 1st Series	1963	£6.50	—
25	The History of Flight, 2nd Series	1963	£6.50	—

WALES ON SUNDAY (Newspaper)

Qty		Date	Odds	Sets
T36	World Cup Heroes (Rugby)	1995	—	£15.00

WALKER, HARRISON & GARTHWAITES LTD.

Qty		Date	Odds	Sets
M15	Dogs	1902	£20.00	—

T. WALL & SONS (Ice Cream)

Qty		Date	Odds	Sets
24	Do You Know	1965	—	£3.00
36	Dr. Who Adventure	1966	£2.40	£86.50
20	Incredible Hulk Records	1979	£2.00	£40.00
48	Moon Fleet	1967	—	£6.50
M6	Prehistoric Animals (Magicards)	1971	—	£2.00
P6	Sea Creatures	1971	—	£2.25
20	Skateboard Surfer	1978	—	£5.00
20	Time Travel with Starship 4	1984	£2.50	—

WALTERS PALM TOFFEE

Qty		Date	Odds	Sets
50	Some Cap Badges of Territorial Regiments	1938	60p	£30.00

WAND CONFECTIONERY LTD.

Qty		Date	Odds	Sets
X10	Chubby Checker — How to do the Twist	1964	*£6.00*	—
25	Commemoration Stamp Series	1963	£2.20	£55.00
X35	Pop D.J.'s	1964	£2.40	£84.00
25	They Gave Their Names	1963	—	£10.00
23/25	Ditto	1963	—	£2.00

WARNOCK & CO. (Tea)

Qty		Date	Odds	Sets
24	The Island of Ceylon	1955	£2.75	£66.00

WARWICK DISTRICT COUNCIL

Qty		Date	Odds	Sets
30	England's Historic Heartland	1980	—	£2.00

WATFORD BISCUIT CO.

Qty		Date	Odds	Sets
KF48	Cinema Stars	1952	£1.50	—

WEBCOSA & CO.

Qty		Date	Odds	Sets
X20	Trail Town	1963	£1.50	£30.00
M48	Victoria Cross Heroes	1964	£2.00	—

WEEKLY WELCOME (Periodical)

Qty		Date	Odds	Sets
12	Lest We Forget Cards	1916	£8.50	—

WEETABIX LTD. (Cereals)

Qty		Date	Odds	Sets
XS25	Animal Cards	1960	50p	—
T28	Asterix — His Friends & Foes	1976	£1.75	£49.00
T18	Batman and Wonderwoman	1979	£2.50	£45.00

WEETABIX LTD. (Cereals) — cont.

Qty		Date	Odds	Sets
XS25	British Birds Cards	1962	£1.80	£45.00
XS25	British Cars	1963	£2.70	£67.50
L25	Conquest of Space, Series A	1959	£1.20	£30.00
L25	Conquest of Space, Series B	1959	£1.20	£30.00
L4	Double Jigsaw	1991	—	£2.00
T24	Dr Who (Coloured Background)	1977	£3.50	£84.00
T24	Dr Who (White Background)	1975	£3.50	£84.00
T18	Flash Gordon	1981	£1.80	£32.50
T18	Huckleberry Hound	1977	£2.50	£45.00
T18	Mickey Mouse's Playmates	1978	£2.50	£45.00
XS25	Our Pets Cards	1961	40p	£10.00
T18	Robin Hood	1980	£1.60	£29.00
T18	Star Trek	1979	£3.00	£54.00
T18	Superman	1978	£2.25	£40.00
L25	The Western Story	1959	40p	£10.00
XS25	Thrill Cards	1960	£1.75	£44.00
P5	Weeta-Card	1989	—	£6.00
XS25	Working Dog Cards	1961	—	£6.00
T18	World of Sport	1986	£3.00	—

JAMES O. WELCH (Confectionery, U.S.A.)

50	Comics	1950	—	£150.00

WELSH RUGBY UNION

50	Great Welsh Rugby Players	1981	—	£4.00

JOHN WEST FOODS LTD.

M8	Famous Sea Adventurers	1972	—	£2.00

WEST LONDON SYNAGOGUE

50	Jewish Life in Many Lands	1961	—	£20.00
50	Jewish Symbols and Ceremonies	1961	—	£30.00
25/50	Ditto	1961	—	£2.00

WESTCO (Confectionery)

F60	Westco Autocards	1954	£5.50	—

WEST MIDLANDS COLLECTORS CENTRE

24	Busby Babes	1990	—	£3.50
30	England Captains	1997	—	£5.00
24	Golden Wolves	1989	—	£3.00
24	Vintage Spurs	1993	—	£4.00

WEST MIDLANDS POLICE

X24	Cop Card-Toons	1989	—	£6.50
X36	Pictorial History — Walsall & District	1986	—	£20.00

WEST MIDLANDS POLICE — cont.

Qty		Date	Odds	Sets
X8	Play Safe — Stay Safe (With Album)	1992	—	£1.50
X24	The Old Bill Collection (With Album)	1990	—	£6.00

WESTON BISCUIT CO. LTD. (Australia)

Qty		Date	Odds	Sets
L24	Veteran & Vintage Cars, 1st Series	1961	—	£39.00
L24	Veteran & Vintage Cars, 2nd Series	1962	—	£7.50

WEST RIDING COUNTY COUNCIL

Qty		Date	Odds	Sets
20	Health Cards	1924	£5.00	£100.00

WHAT CAMERA? (Magazine)

Qty		Date	Odds	Sets
P12	Photocards	1989	—	£3.00

WHITBREAD & CO. LTD. (Brewers)

Qty		Date	Odds	Sets
M1	Duke Without a Head	1958	—	£5.50
M50	Inn Signs, 1st Series (Metal)	1951	£2.40	£120.00
M50	Inn Signs, 2nd Series (Metal)	1951	£2.40	£120.00
M50	Inn Signs, 3rd Series (Metal)	1952	£3.50	£175.00
M50	(Card)	1952	£2.60	£130.00
M50	Inn Signs, 4th Series	1952	£2.60	£130.00
M50	Inn Signs, 5th Series	1953	£3.00	£150.00
M25	Inn Signs, Bournemouth	1973	£3.00	£75.00
M25	Inn Signs, Devon & Somerset	1973	£1.60	£40.00
M25	Inn Signs, Isle of Wight	1974	£3.00	—
M25	Inn Signs, Kent	1973	£3.50	—
M15	Inn Signs, London	1973	£2.00	£45.00
M10	Inn Signs, London (Different)	1974	£3.00	—
M25	Inn Signs, Marlow	1973	£2.60	£65.00
M25	Inn Signs, Portsmouth	1973	£3.20	£80.00
M4	Inn Signs, Special Issue	1955	£3.50	£14.00
M25	Inn Signs, Stratford-upon-Avon	1974	£2.80	£70.00
M25	Inn Signs, West Pennine	1973	£3.00	—
M25	Maritime Inn Signs	1974	30p	£7.50
M1	The Britannia Inn (Plain Back)	1958	—	£24.00
M1	(Printed Back)	1958	—	£45.00
M1	The Railway	1958	—	£6.00
M1	The Startled Saint	1958	—	£30.00

WHITE FISH AUTHORITY

Qty		Date	Odds	Sets
25	The Fish We Eat	1954	—	£2.00

WHITEHAVEN LIBRARY

Qty		Date	Odds	Sets
M6	The Port of Whitehaven	1978	—	£3.00

WHITEHEAD (Lollies)

Qty		Date	Odds	Sets
X25	Kings & Queens	1980	—	£2.00

WIGAN POLICE

Qty		Date	Odds	Sets
X24	Riversiders	1991	—	£7.50

WIKO (Germany)

Qty		Date	Odds	Sets
50	Soldaten Der Welt	1969	—	£16.50

WILBUR-SUCHARD CHOCOLATE CO. (U.S.A.)

Qty		Date	Odds	Sets
35/36	Flags	1960	£1.75	

WILCOCKS & WILCOCKS LTD. (Tea)

Qty		Date	Odds	Sets
25	Birds	1965	£1.20	—
25	British Cavalry Uniforms of the 19th Century	1963	—	£8.00
25	Garden Flowers	1964	—	£6.00
25	Passenger Liners	1967	—	£12.50
25	People & Places	1966	—	£3.00
24	The Island of Ceylon	1955	£4.00	—
25	Tropical Birds	1965	—	£8.00
25	Wonders of the Deep	1965	—	£3.00
25	Wonders of the World	1971	—	£5.00

A.S. WILKIN LTD. (Confectionery)

Qty		Date	Odds	Sets
25	Into Space	1960	—	£5.00

W.R. WILKINSON & CO. (Confectionery)

Qty		Date	Odds	Sets
M25	Popular Footballers	1956	£12.50	—

WIMPY (Restaurants)

Qty		Date	Odds	Sets
M20	Super Heroes Super Villains	1979	80p	£16.00

WOMAN'S FRIEND (Periodical)

Qty		Date	Odds	Sets
K52	Fortune Telling Cards	1925	£2.00	—

1

WOMAN'S OWN (Periodical)

Qty		Date	Odds	Sets
F8	Film Stars	1955	£5.50	—

E. WOODHEAD & SONS (Tea)

Qty		Date	Odds	Sets
25	Types of British Soldiers	1916	£18.00	£450.00

WOOLWORTH (Stores)

Qty		Date	Odds	Sets
M24	Fascinating Facts	1989	—	£4.00

WRIGHTS BISCUITS LTD.

Qty		Date	Odds	Sets
24	Marvels of the World	1954	—	£2.00
24	Mischief goes to Mars (Mischief Club)	1954	—	£5.00
24	(Wright at Side)	1954	—	£3.00
24	(Wright at Base)	1954	50p	£12.00

YOUNG BRITAIN (Periodical)

MF15	Favourite Cricketers Series (In Pairs)	1922	£5.00	£75.00

CENTRAL LONDON BRANCH

For the convenience of our customers why not visit our branch in Central London? Less than 100 yards from Trafalgar Square, it is in an ideal location for visitors to London. It is three minutes walk from Charing Cross Main Line Station, and just around the corner from Charing Cross and Leicester Square underground stations (Bakerloo, Jubilee, Northern and Victoria Lines).

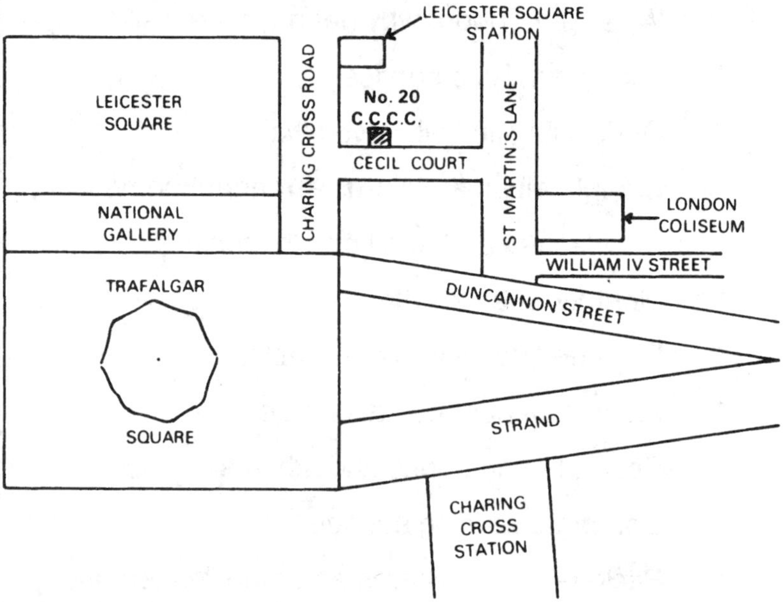

Cecil Court Collectors Centre is open from 10.30 a.m. to 5.30 p.m. Monday to Saturday. As well as cigarette cards you may purchase banknotes, coins, share certificates, telephone cards and stamps all under one roof.

Since we cannot split our stocks of the scarcer and more elusive cards the items available at Cecil Court will be restricted to those shown below. We can however arrange for any specific items not covered by this list to be made available for collection at the Collectors Centre provided that we have at least 72 hours warning. All correspondence and telephone calls should still be made to our Head Office at 51 Watford Way, Hendon Central (0181 202-5688).

Available at Cecil Court Collectors Centre

* A large selection of complete sets only.
* Liebig sets, albums and frames.
* Framed sets and framing kits.
* Nostalgia and Hendon albums without postal charges.
* Catalogues, books and other accessories.
* New issues hot off the press, including American Trading cards.

CECIL COURT COLLECTORS CENTRE
20 Cecil Court, Charing Cross Road, London WC2

NOTES

NOTES

NOTES

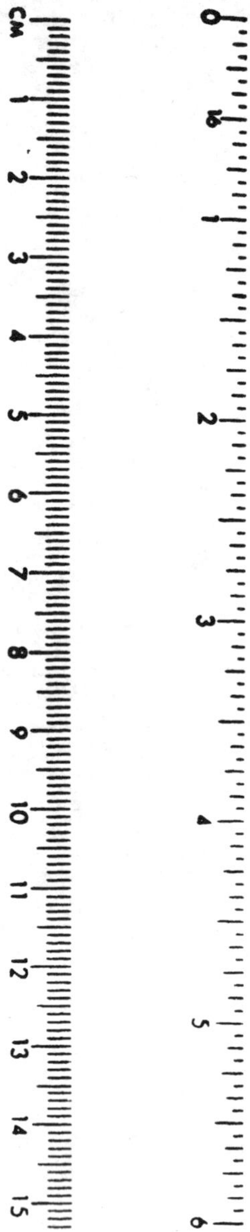

PRINTED BY STOATE & BISHOP (PRINTERS) LTD. (01242) 236741